ESSENTIALS OF ECONOMICS

FOURTH EDITION

Damodar N. Gujarati

Professor Emeritus of Economics, United States Military Academy, West Point

Dawn C. Porter

University of Southern California

Boston   Burr Ridge, IL   Dubuque, IA   Madison, WI   New York   San Francisco   St. Louis
Bangkok   Bogotá   Caracas   Kuala Lumpur   Lisbon   London   Madrid   Mexico City
Milan   Montreal   New Delhi   Santiago   Seoul   Singapore   Sydney   Taipei   Toronto

The McGraw·Hill Companies

ESSENTIALS OF ECONOMETRICS
FOURTH EDITION
International Edition 2010

09 08 07
15 14 13
CTP MPM

When ordering this title, use ISBN 978-007-127607-8 or MHID 007-127607-6

Printed in Singapore

www.mhhe.com

For Joan Gujarati, Diane Gujarati-Chesnut,
Charles Chesnut, and my grandchildren,
"Tommy" and Laura Chesnut.
DNG

For Judy, Lee, Brett, Bryan, Amy, and Autumn Porter.
But especially for my adoring father, Terry.
DCP

ABOUT THE AUTHORS

DAMODAR N. GUJARATI

After teaching for more than 25 years at the City University of New York and 17 years in the Department of Social Sciences, U.S. Military Academy at West Point, New York, Dr. Gujarati is currently Professor Emeritus of economics at the Academy. Dr. Gujarati received his M.Com. degree from the University of Bombay in 1960, his M.B.A. degree from the University of Chicago in 1963, and his Ph.D. degree from the University of Chicago in 1965. Dr. Gujarati has published extensively in recognized national and international journals, such as the *Review of Economics and Statistics,* the *Economic Journal,* the *Journal of Financial and Quantitative Analysis,* and the *Journal of Business.* Dr. Gujarati was a member of the board of editors of the *Journal of Quantitative Economics,* the official journal of the Indian Econometric Society. Dr. Gujarati is also the author of *Pensions and the New York City Fiscal Crisis* (the American Enterprise Institute, 1978), *Government and Business* (McGraw-Hill, 1984), and *Basic Econometrics* (McGraw-Hill, 5th ed., 2009). Dr. Gujarati's books on econometrics have been translated into several languages.

Dr. Gujarati was a Visiting Professor at the University of Sheffield, U.K. (1970–1971), a Visiting Fulbright Professor to India (1981–1982), a Visiting Professor in the School of Management of the National University of Singapore 1985–1986), and a Visiting Professor of Econometrics, University of New South Wales, Australia (summer of 1988). Dr. Gujarati has lectured extensively on micro- and macroeconomic topics in countries such as Australia, China, Bangladesh, Germany, India, Israel, Mauritius, and the Republic of South Korea.

DAWN C. PORTER

Dawn Porter has been an assistant professor in the Information and Operations Management Department at the Marshall School of Business of the University of Southern California since the fall of 2006. She currently teaches undergraduate, M.B.A., and graduate elective statistics courses in the business school. Prior to joining the faculty at USC, from 2001–2006, Dawn was an assistant professor at the McDonough School of Business at Georgetown University and also served as a Visiting Professor in the Psychology Department at the Graduate School of Arts and Sciences at NYU. At NYU she taught a number of advanced statistical methods courses and was also an instructor at the Stern School of Business. Her Ph.D. is from the Stern School in Statistics, and her undergraduate degree is in mathematics from Cornell University.

Dawn's areas of research interest include categorical analysis, agreement measures, multivariate modeling, and applications to the field of psychology. Her current research examines online auction models from a statistical perspective. She has presented her research at the Joint Statistical Meetings, the Decision Sciences Institute meetings, the International Conference on Information Systems, several universities including the London School of Economics and NYU, and various e-commerce and statistics seminar series. Dawn is also a co-author on *Essentials of Business Statistics,* 2nd edition and *Basic Econometrics,* 5th edition, both from McGraw-Hill.

Outside academics, Dawn has been employed as a statistical consultant for KPMG, Inc. She also has worked as a statistical consultant for many other major companies, including Ginnie Mae, Inc.; Toys R Us Corporation; IBM; Cosmaire, Inc; and New York University (NYU) Medical Center.

CONTENTS

PREFACE

OBJECTIVE OF THE BOOK

As in the previous editions, the primary objective of the fourth edition of *Essentials of Econometrics* is to provide a user-friendly introduction to econometric theory and techniques. The intended audience is undergraduate economics majors, undergraduate business administration majors, MBA students, and others in social and behavioral sciences where econometrics techniques, especially the techniques of linear regression analysis, are used. The book is designed to help students *understand* econometric techniques through extensive examples, careful explanations, and a wide variety of problem material. In each of the previous editions, I have tried to incorporate major developments in the field in an intuitive and informative way without resorting to matrix algebra, calculus, or statistics beyond the introductory level. The fourth edition continues that tradition.

Although I am in the eighth decade of my life, I have not lost my love for econometrics and I strive to keep up with the major developments in the field. To assist me in this endeavor, I am now happy to have Dr. Dawn Porter, Assistant Professor of Statistics at the Marshall School of Business at the University of Southern California in Los Angeles, as my co-author. Both of us have been deeply involved in bringing the fourth edition of *Essentials of Econometrics* to fruition.

MAJOR FEATURES OF THE FOURTH EDITION

Before discussing the specific changes in the various chapters, the following features of the new edition are worth noting:

1. In order to streamline topics and jump right into information about linear regression techniques, we have moved the background statistics material (formerly Chapters 2 through 5) to the appendix. This allows for easy reference to more introductory material for those who need it, without disturbing the main content of the text.
2. Practically all the data used in the illustrative examples have been updated from the previous edition.
3. Several new examples have been added.

4. In several chapters, we have included extended concluding examples that illustrate the various points made in the text.
5. Concrete computer printouts of several examples are included in the book. Most of these results are based on **EViews** (version 6), **STATA** (version 10), and **MINITAB** (version 15).
6. Several new diagrams and graphs are included in various chapters.
7. Several new data-based exercises are included throughout the book.
8. Small-sized data are included in the book, but large sample data are posted on the book's Web site, thereby minimizing the size of the text. The Web site also contains all the data used in the book.

SPECIFIC CHANGES

Some of the chapter-specific changes in the fourth edition are as follows:

Chapter 1: A revised and expanded list of Web sites for economic data has been included.

Chapters 2 and 3: An interesting new data example concerning the relationship between family income and student performance on the S.A.T. is utilized to introduce the two-variable regression model.

Chapter 4: We have included a brief explanation of nonstochastic versus stochastic predictors. An additional example regarding educational expenditures among several countries that adds to the explanation of regression hypothesis testing.

Chapter 5: The math S.A.T. example is revisited to illustrate various functional forms. Section 5.10 has been added to handle the topic of regression on standardized variables. Also, several new data exercises have been included.

Chapter 6: An example concerning acceptance rates among top business schools has been added to help illustrate the usefulness of dummy variable regression models. Several new data exercises also have been added.

Chapter 8: Again, we have added several new, updated data exercises dealing with the issue of multicollinearity.

Chapter 9: To illustrate the concept of heteroscedasticity, a new example relating wages to education levels and years of experience has been included, as well as more real data exercises.

Chapter 10: A new section concerning the Newey-West standard error correction method using a data example has been added. Also, a new appendix has been included at the end of the chapter to cover the Breusch-Godfrey test of autocorrelation.

Chapter 12: An expanded treatment of logistic regression has been included in this chapter with new examples to illustrate the results.

Appendixes A–D: As noted above, the material in these appendixes was formerly contained in Chapters 2–5 of the main text. By placing them in the back of the book, they can more easily serve as reference sections to the main text. Data examples have been updated, and new exercises have been added.

Besides these specific changes, errors and misprints in the previous editions have been corrected. Also, our discussion of several topics in the various chapters has been streamlined.

MATHEMATICAL REQUIREMENTS

In presenting the various topics, we have used very little matrix algebra or calculus. *We firmly believe that econometrics can be taught to the beginner in an intuitive manner, without a heavy dose of matrix algebra or calculus.* Also, we have not given any proofs unless they are easily understood. We do not feel that the nonspecialist needs to be burdened with detailed proofs. Of course, the instructor can supply the necessary proofs as the situation demands. Some of the proofs are available in our *Basic Econometrics* (McGraw-Hill, 5th ed., 2009).

SUPPLEMENTS AID THE PROBLEM SOLVING APPROACH

The comprehensive Web site for the fourth edition contains the following supplementary material to assist both instructors and students:

- Data from the text, as well as additional large set data referenced in the book.
- A *Solutions Manual* providing answers to all of the questions and problems throughout the text is provided for the instructors to use as they wish.
- A digital image library containing all of the graphs and tables from the book.

For more information, please visit the Online Learning Center at **www.mhhe .com/gujaratiess4e.**

COMPUTERS AND ECONOMETRICS

It cannot be overemphasized that what has made econometrics accessible to the beginner is the availability of several user-friendly computer statistical packages. The illustrative problems in this book are solved using statistical software packages, such as EViews, Excel, MINITAB, and STATA. Student versions of some of these packages are readily available. The data posted on the Web site is in Excel format and can also be read easily by many standard statistical packages such as LIMDEP, RATS, SAS, and SPSS.

In Appendix E we show the outputs of EViews, Excel, MINITAB, and STATA, using a common data set. Each of these software packages has some unique features although some of the statistical routines are quite similar.

IN CLOSING

To sum up, in writing *Essentials of Econometrics*, our primary objective has been to introduce the wonderful world of econometrics to the beginner in a relaxed but informative style. We hope the knowledge gained from this book will prove to be of lasting value in the reader's future academic or professional career and that the reader's knowledge learned in this book can be further widened by reading some advanced and specialized books in econometrics. Some of these books can be found in the selected bibliography given at the end of the book.

ACKNOWLEDGMENTS

Our foremost thanks are to the following reviewers who made very valuable suggestions to improve the quality of the book.

Michael Allison	*University of Missouri, St. Louis*
Giles Bootheway	*Saint Bonaventure University*
Bruce Brown	*California State Polytechnic University, Pomona*
Kristin Butcher	*Wellesley College*
Juan Cabrera	*Queens College*
Tom Chen	*Saint John's University*
Joanne Doyle	*James Madison University*
Barry Falk	*Iowa State University*
Eric Furstenberg	*University of Virginia, Charlottesville*
Steffen Habermalz	*Northwestern University*
Susan He	*Washington State University, Pullman*
Jerome Heavey	*Lafayette College*
George Jakubson	*Cornell University*
Elia Kacapyr	*Ithaca College*
Janet Kohlhase	*University of Houston*
Maria Kozhevnikova	*Queens College*
John Krieg	*Western Washington University*
William Latham	*University of Delaware*
Jinman Lee	*University of Illinois, Chicago*
Stephen LeRoy	*University of California, Santa Barbara*
Dandan Liu	*Bowling Green State University*
Fabio Milani	*University of California, Irvine*
Hillar Neumann	*Northern State University*
Jennifer Rice	*Eastern Michigan University*
Steven Stageberg	*University of Mary Washington*
Joseph Sulock	*University of North Carolina, Asheville*
Mark Tendall	*Stanford University*
Christopher Warburton	*John Jay College*
Tiemen Woutersen	*Johns Hopkins University*

We are very grateful to Douglas Reiner, our publisher at McGraw-Hill, for helping us through this edition of the book. We are also grateful to Noelle Fox, editorial coordinator at McGraw-Hill, for working with us through all of our setbacks. We also need to acknowledge the project management provided by Manjot Singh Dodi, and the great copy editing by Ann Sass, especially since this type of textbook incorporates so many technical formulas and symbols.

Damodar N. Gujarati
United States Military Academy, West Point

Dawn C. Porter
University of Southern California, Los Angeles

CHAPTER 1

THE NATURE
AND SCOPE
OF ECONOMETRICS

Research in economics, finance, management, marketing, and related disciplines is becoming increasingly quantitative. Beginning students in these fields are encouraged, if not required, to take a course or two in econometrics—a field of study that has become quite popular. This chapter gives the beginner an overview of what econometrics is all about.

1.1 WHAT IS ECONOMETRICS?

Simply stated, **econometrics** means economic measurement. Although quantitative measurement of economic concepts such as the gross domestic product (GDP), unemployment, inflation, imports, and exports is very important, the scope of econometrics is much broader, as can be seen from the following definitions:

> **Econometrics** may be defined as the social science in which the tools of economic theory, mathematics, and statistical inference are applied to the analysis of economic phenomena.[1]

> **Econometrics,** the result of a certain outlook on the role of economics, consists of the application of mathematical statistics to economic data to lend empirical support to the models constructed by mathematical economics and to obtain numerical results.[2]

---

[1]Arthur S. Goldberger, *Econometric Theory*, Wiley, New York, 1964, p. 1.
[2]P. A. Samuelson, T. C. Koopmans, and J. R. N. Stone, "Report of the Evaluative Committee for *Econometrica*," *Econometrica*, vol. 22, no. 2, April 1954, pp. 141–146.

1.2 WHY STUDY ECONOMETRICS?

As the preceding definitions suggest, econometrics makes use of economic theory, mathematical economics, economic statistics (i.e., economic data), and mathematical statistics. Yet, it is a subject that deserves to be studied in its own right for the following reasons.

Economic theory makes statements or hypotheses that are mostly qualitative in nature. For example, microeconomic theory states that, other things remaining the same (the famous *ceteris paribus* clause of economics), an increase in the price of a commodity is expected to decrease the quantity demanded of that commodity. Thus, economic theory postulates a negative or inverse relationship between the price and quantity demanded of a commodity—this is the widely known law of downward-sloping demand or simply *the law of demand*. But the theory itself does not provide any numerical measure of the strength of the relationship between the two; that is, it does not tell by how much the quantity demanded will go up or down as a result of a certain change in the price of the commodity. It is the econometrician's job to provide such numerical estimates. Econometrics gives empirical (i.e., based on observation or experiment) content to most economic theory. If we find in a study or experiment that when the price of a unit increases by a dollar the quantity demanded goes down by, say, 100 units, we have not only confirmed the law of demand, but in the process we have also provided a numerical estimate of the relationship between the two variables—price and quantity.

The main concern of **mathematical economics** is to express economic theory in mathematical form or equations (or models) without regard to measurability or empirical verification of the theory. Econometrics, as noted earlier, is primarily interested in the empirical verification of economic theory. As we will show shortly, the econometrician often uses mathematical models proposed by the mathematical economist but puts these models in forms that lend themselves to empirical testing.

Economic statistics is mainly concerned with collecting, processing, and presenting economic data in the form of charts, diagrams, and tables. This is the economic statistician's job. He or she collects data on the GDP, employment, unemployment, prices, etc. These data constitute the raw data for econometric work. But the economic statistician does not go any further because he or she is not primarily concerned with using the collected data to test economic theories.

Although *mathematical statistics* provides many of the tools employed in the trade, the econometrician often needs special methods because of the unique nature of most economic data, namely, that the data are not usually generated as the result of a controlled experiment. The econometrician, like the meteorologist, generally depends on data that cannot be controlled directly. Thus, data on consumption, income, investments, savings, prices, etc., which are collected by public and private agencies, are nonexperimental in nature. The econometrician takes these data as given. This creates special problems not normally dealt with in mathematical statistics. Moreover, such data are likely to contain errors of measurement, of either omission or commission, and the econometrician may be called upon to develop special methods of analysis to deal with such errors of measurement.

For students majoring in economics and business there is a pragmatic reason for studying econometrics. After graduation, in their employment, they may be called upon to forecast sales, interest rates, and money supply or to estimate demand and supply functions or price elasticities for products. Quite often, economists appear as expert witnesses before federal and state regulatory agencies on behalf of their clients or the public at large. Thus, an economist appearing before a state regulatory commission that controls prices of gas and electricity may be required to assess the impact of a proposed price increase on the quantity demanded of electricity before the commission will approve the price increase. In situations like this the economist may need to develop a demand function for electricity for this purpose. Such a demand function may enable the economist to estimate the price elasticity of demand, that is, the percentage change in the quantity demanded for a percentage change in the price. Knowledge of econometrics is very helpful in estimating such demand functions.

It is fair to say that econometrics has become an integral part of training in economics and business.

1.3 THE METHODOLOGY OF ECONOMETRICS

How does one actually do an econometric study? Broadly speaking, econometric analysis proceeds along the following lines.

1. Creating a statement of theory or hypothesis.
2. Collecting data.
3. Specifying the mathematical model of theory.
4. Specifying the statistical, or econometric, model of theory.
5. Estimating the parameters of the chosen econometric model.
6. Checking for model adequacy: Model specification testing.
7. Testing the hypothesis derived from the model.
8. Using the model for prediction or forecasting.

To illustrate the methodology, consider this question: Do economic conditions affect people's decisions to enter the labor force, that is, their willingness to work? As a measure of economic conditions, suppose we use the unemployment rate (UNR), and as a measure of labor force participation we use the labor force participation rate (LFPR). Data on UNR and LFPR are regularly published by the government. So to answer the question we proceed as follows.

Creating a Statement of Theory or Hypothesis

The starting point is to find out what economic theory has to say on the subject you want to study. In labor economics, there are two rival hypotheses about the effect of economic conditions on people's willingness to work. The **discouraged-worker hypothesis (effect)** states that when economic conditions worsen, as reflected in a higher unemployment rate, many unemployed workers give up hope of finding a job and drop out of the labor force. On the other hand, the **added-worker hypothesis (effect)** maintains that when economic conditions worsen, many secondary workers who are not currently in the labor market (e.g., mothers with children) may decide to join the labor force if the main breadwinner in the family loses his or her job. Even if the jobs these secondary workers get are low paying, the earnings will make up some of the loss in income suffered by the primary breadwinner.

Whether, on balance, the labor force participation rate will increase or decrease will depend on the relative strengths of the added-worker and discouraged-worker effects. If the added-worker effect dominates, LFPR will increase even when the unemployment rate is high. Contrarily, if the discouraged-worker effect dominates, LFPR will decrease. How do we find this out? This now becomes our empirical question.

Collecting Data

For empirical purposes, therefore, we need quantitative information on the two variables. There are three types of data that are generally available for empirical analysis.

1. Time series.
2. Cross-sectional.
3. Pooled (a combination of time series and cross-sectional).

Times series data are collected over a period of time, such as the data on GDP, employment, unemployment, money supply, or government deficits. Such data may be collected at regular intervals—daily (e.g., stock prices), weekly (e.g., money supply), monthly (e.g., the unemployment rate), quarterly (e.g., GDP), or annually (e.g., government budget). These data may be **quantitative** in nature (e.g., prices, income, money supply) or **qualitative** (e.g., male or female, employed or unemployed, married or unmarried, white or black). As we will show, qualitative variables, also called *dummy* or *categorical* variables, can be every bit as important as quantitative variables.

Cross-sectional data are data on one or more variables collected at one point in time, such as the census of population conducted by the U.S. Census Bureau every 10 years (the most recent was on April 1, 2000); the surveys of consumer expenditures conducted by the University of Michigan; and the opinion polls such as those conducted by Gallup, Harris, and other polling organizations.

In **pooled data** we have elements of both time series and cross-sectional data. For example, if we collect data on the unemployment rate for 10 countries for a period of 20 years, the data will constitute an example of pooled data—data on the unemployment rate for each country for the 20-year period will form time series data, whereas data on the unemployment rate for the 10 countries for any single year will be cross-sectional data. In pooled data we will have 200 observations—20 annual observations for each of the 10 countries.

There is a special type of pooled data, **panel data,** also called **longitudinal** or **micropanel data,** in which the same cross-sectional unit, say, a family or firm, is surveyed over time. For example, the U.S. Department of Commerce conducts a census of housing at periodic intervals. At each periodic survey the same household (or the people living at the same address) is interviewed to find out if there has been any change in the housing and financial conditions of that household since the last survey. The panel data that result from repeatedly interviewing the same household at periodic intervals provide very useful information on the dynamics of household behavior.

Sources of Data   A word is in order regarding data sources. The success of any econometric study hinges on the quality, as well as the quantity, of data. Fortunately, the Internet has opened up a veritable wealth of data. In Appendix 1A we give addresses of several Web sites that have all kinds of microeconomic and macroeconomic data. Students should be familiar with such sources of data, as well as how to access or download them. Of course, these data are continually updated so the reader may find the latest available data.

For our analysis, we obtained the time series data shown in Table 1-1. This table gives data on the civilian labor force participation rate (CLFPR) and the civilian unemployment rate (CUNR), defined as the number of civilians unemployed as a percentage of the civilian labor force, for the United States for the period 1980–2007.[3]

Unlike physical sciences, most data collected in economics (e.g., GDP, money supply, Dow Jones index, car sales) are nonexperimental in that the data-collecting agency (e.g., government) may not have any direct control over the data. Thus, the data on labor force participation and unemployment are based on the information provided to the government by participants in the labor market. In a sense, the government is a passive collector of these data and may not be aware of the added- or discouraged-worker hypotheses, or any other hypothesis, for that matter. Therefore, the collected data may be the result of several factors affecting the labor force participation decision made by the individual person. That is, the same data may be compatible with more than one theory.

Specifying the Mathematical Model of Labor Force Participation

To see how *CLFPR* behaves in relation to *CUNR,* the first thing we should do is plot the data for these variables in a **scatter diagram,** or **scattergram,** as shown in Figure 1-1.

The scattergram shows that *CLFPR* and *CUNR* are inversely related, perhaps suggesting that, on balance, the discouraged-worker effect is stronger than the added-worker effect.[4] As a *first approximation,* we can draw a straight line

---

[3]We consider here only the aggregate CLFPR and CUNR, but data are available by age, sex, and ethnic composition.

[4]On this, see Shelly Lundberg, "The Added Worker Effect," *Journal of Labor Economics,* vol. 3, January 1985, pp. 11–37.

TABLE 1-1 U.S. CIVILIAN LABOR FORCE PARTICIPATION RATE (CLFPR), CIVILIAN UNEMPLOYMENT RATE (CUNR), AND REAL AVERAGE HOURLY EARNINGS (AHE82)* FOR THE YEARS 1980–2007

Year	CLFPR (%)	CUNR (%)	AHE82 ($)
1980	63.8	7.1	8.00
1981	63.9	7.6	7.89
1982	64.0	9.7	7.87
1983	64.0	9.6	7.96
1984	64.4	7.5	7.96
1985	64.8	7.2	7.92
1986	65.3	7.0	7.97
1987	65.6	6.2	7.87
1988	65.9	5.5	7.82
1989	66.5	5.3	7.75
1990	66.5	5.6	7.66
1991	66.2	6.8	7.59
1992	66.4	7.5	7.55
1993	66.3	6.9	7.54
1994	66.6	6.1	7.54
1995	66.6	5.6	7.54
1996	66.8	5.4	7.57
1997	67.1	4.9	7.69
1998	67.1	4.5	7.89
1999	67.1	4.2	8.01
2000	67.1	4.0	8.04
2001	66.8	4.7	8.12
2002	66.6	5.8	8.25
2003	66.2	6.0	8.28
2004	66.0	5.5	8.24
2005	66.0	5.1	8.18
2006	66.2	4.6	8.24
2007	66.0	4.6	8.32

*AHE82 represents average hourly earnings in 1982 dollars.
Source: Economic Report of the President, 2008, CLFPR from Table B-40, CUNR from Table B-43, and AHE82 from Table B-47.

through the scatter points and write the relationship between *CLFPR* and *CUNR* by the following simple mathematical model:

$$CLFPR = B_1 + B_2 \, CUNR \tag{1.1}$$

Equation (1.1) states that *CLFPR* is *linearly* related to *CUNR*. B_1 and B_2 are known as the **parameters** of the linear function.[5] B_1 is also known as the **intercept;** it

[5]Broadly speaking, a parameter is an unknown quantity that may vary over a certain set of values. In statistics a probability distribution function (PDF) of a random variable is often characterized by its parameters, such as its mean and variance. This topic is discussed in greater detail in Appendixes A and B.

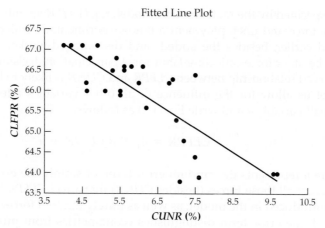

FIGURE 1-1 Regression plot for civilian labor force participation rate (%) and civilian unemployment rate (%)

gives the value of *CLFPR* when *CUNR* is zero.[6] B_2 is known as the **slope.** The *slope measures the rate of change in CLFPR for a unit change in CUNR,* or more generally, the rate of change in the value of the variable on the left-hand side of the equation for a unit change in the value of the variable on the right-hand side. The slope coefficient B_2 can be positive (if the added-worker effect dominates the discouraged-worker effect) or negative (if the discouraged-worker effect dominates the added-worker effect). Figure 1-1 suggests that in the present case it is negative.

Specifying the Statistical, or Econometric, Model of Labor Force Participation

The purely mathematical model of the relationship between *CLFPR* and *CUNR* given in Eq. (1.1), although of prime interest to the mathematical economist, is of limited appeal to the econometrician, for such a model assumes an *exact,* or *deterministic, relationship* between the two variables; that is, for a given *CUNR,* there is a unique value of *CLFPR.* In reality, one rarely finds such neat relationships between economic variables. Most often, the relationships are *inexact,* or *statistical,* in nature.

This is seen clearly from the scattergram given in Figure 1-1. Although the two variables are inversely related, the relationship between them is not perfectly or exactly linear, for if we draw a straight line through the 28 data points, not all the data points will lie exactly on that straight line. Recall that to draw a straight line we need only two points.[7] Why don't the 28 data points lie exactly on the straight

---

[6]In Chapter 2 we give a more precise interpretation of the intercept in the context of regression analysis.

[7]We even tried to fit a parabola to the scatter points given in Fig. 1-1, but the results were not materially different from the linear specification.

line specified by the mathematical model, Eq. (1.1)? Remember that our data on labor force and unemployment are nonexperimentally collected. Therefore, as noted earlier, besides the added- and discouraged-worker hypotheses, there may be other forces affecting labor force participation decisions. As a result, the observed relationship between *CLFPR* and *CUNR* is likely to be imprecise.

Let us allow for the influence of all other variables affecting *CLFPR* in a catchall variable *u* and write Eq. (1.2) as follows:

$$CLFPR = B_1 + B_2CUNR + u \tag{1.2}$$

where *u* represents the **random error term,** or simply the **error term.**[8] We let *u* represent all those forces (besides *CUNR*) that affect *CLFPR* but are not explicitly introduced in the model, as well as purely random forces. As we will see in Part II, the error term distinguishes econometrics from purely mathematical economics.

Equation (1.2) is an example of a *statistical,* or *empirical* or *econometric, model.* More precisely, it is an example of what is known as a **linear regression model,** which is a prime subject of this book. In such a model, the variable appearing on the left-hand side of the equation is called the **dependent variable,** and the variable on the right-hand side is called the **independent,** or **explanatory, variable.** In linear regression analysis our primary objective is to explain the behavior of one variable (the dependent variable) in relation to the behavior of one or more other variables (the explanatory variables), allowing for the fact that the relationship between them is inexact.

Notice that the econometric model, Eq. (1.2), is derived from the mathematical model, Eq. (1.1), which shows that mathematical economics and econometrics are mutually complementary disciplines. This is clearly reflected in the definition of econometrics given at the outset.

Before proceeding further, a warning regarding **causation** is in order. In the regression model, Eq. (1.2), we have stated that *CLFPR* is the dependent variable and *CUNR* is the independent, or explanatory, variable. Does that mean that the two variables are *causally* related; that is, is *CUNR* the cause and *CLFPR* the effect? In other words, does regression imply causation? Not necessarily. As Kendall and Stuart note, "A statistical relationship, however strong and however suggestive, can never establish causal connection: our ideas of causation must come from outside statistics, ultimately from some theory or other."[9] In our example, it is up to economic theory (e.g., the discouraged-worker hypothesis) to establish the cause-and-effect relationship, if any, between the dependent and explanatory variables. If causality cannot be established, it is better to call the relationship, Eq. (1.2), a *predictive relationship:* Given *CUNR*, can we predict *CLFPR*?

---

[8]In statistical lingo, the random error term is known as the *stochastic error* term.
[9]M. G. Kendall and A. Stuart, *The Advanced Theory of Statistics,* Charles Griffin Publishers, New York, 1961, vol. 2, Chap. 26, p. 279.

Estimating the Parameters of the Chosen Econometric Model

Given the data on *CLFPR* and *CUNR,* such as that in Table 1-1, how do we esti-mate the parameters of the model, Eq. (1.2), namely, B_1 and B_2? That is, how do we find the numerical values (i.e., **estimates**) of these **parameters?** This will be the focus of our attention in Part II, where we develop the appropriate methods of computation, especially the method of *ordinary least squares (OLS).* Using OLS and the data given in Table 1-1, we obtained the following results:

$$\widehat{CLFPR} = 69.4620 - 0.5814 CUNR \qquad\qquad (1.3)$$

Note that we have put the symbol $\wedge$ on *CLFPR* (read as "CLFPR hat") to remind us that Eq. (1.3) is an *estimate* of Eq. (1.2). The estimated regression line is shown in Figure 1-1, along with the actual data points.

As Eq. (1.3) shows, the estimated value of B_1 is ≈ 69.5 and that of B_2 is ≈ -0.58, where the symbol $\approx$ means approximately. Thus, if the unemployment rate goes up by one unit (i.e., one percentage point), *ceteris paribus, CLFPR* is ex-pected to decrease *on the average* by about 0.58 percentage points; that is, as eco-nomic conditions worsen, on average, there is a net decrease in the labor force participation rate of about 0.58 percentage points, perhaps suggesting that the discouraged-worker effect dominates. We say "on the average" because the presence of the error term *u,* as noted earlier, is likely to make the relationship somewhat imprecise. This is vividly seen in Figure 1-1 where the points not on the estimated regression line are the actual participation rates and the (vertical) distance between them and the points on the regression line are the estimated *u*'s. As we will see in Chapter 2, the estimated *u*'s are called *residuals.* In short, the estimated regression line, Eq. (1.3), gives the relationship between *average CLFPR* and *CUNR;* that is, on average how *CLFPR* responds to a unit change in *CUNR.* The value of about 69.5 suggests that the average value of *CLFPR* will be about 69.5 percent if the *CUNR* is zero; that is, about 69.5 percent of the civil-ian working-age population will participate in the labor force if there is full employment (i.e., zero unemployment).[10]

Checking for Model Adequacy: Model Specification Testing

How adequate is our model, Eq. (1.3)? It is true that a person will take into account labor market conditions as measured by, say, the unemployment rate before entering the labor market. For example, in 1982 (a recession year) the civilian un-employment rate was about 9.7 percent. Compared to that, in 2001 it was only 4.7 percent. A person is more likely to be discouraged from entering the labor mar-ket when the unemployment rate is more than 9 percent than when it is 5 percent. But there are other factors that also enter into labor force participation decisions. For example, hourly wages, or earnings, prevailing in the labor market also will

---

[10]This is, however, a mechanical interpretation of the intercept. We will see in Chapter 2 how to interpret the intercept term meaningfully in a given context.

be an important decision variable. In the short run at least, a higher wage may attract more workers to the labor market, other things remaining the same (*ceteris paribus*). To see its importance, in Table 1-1 we have also given data on real average hourly earnings (AHE82), where real earnings are measured in 1982 dollars. To take into account the influence of AHE82, we now consider the following model:

$$CLFPR = B_1 + B_2 CUNR + B_3 AHE82 + u \qquad (1.4)$$

Equation (1.4) is an example of a *multiple linear regression model,* in contrast to Eq. (1.2), which is an example of a *simple (two-variable* or *bivariate) linear regression model.* In the two-variable model there is a single explanatory variable, whereas in a multiple regression there are several, or multiple, explanatory variables. Notice that in the multiple regression, Eq. (1.4), we also have included the error term, u, for no matter how many explanatory variables one introduces in the model, one cannot fully explain the behavior of the dependent variable. How many variables one introduces in the multiple regression is a decision that the researcher will have to make in a given situation. Of course, the underlying economic theory will often tell what these variables might be. However, keep in mind the warning given earlier that regression does not mean causation; the relevant theory must determine whether one or more explanatory variables are causally related to the dependent variable.

How do we estimate the parameters of the multiple regression, Eq. (1.4)? We cover this topic in Chapter 4, after we discuss the two-variable model in Chapters 2 and 3. We consider the two-variable case first because it is the building block of the multiple regression model. As we shall see in Chapter 4, the multiple regression model is in many ways a straightforward extension of the two-variable model.

For our illustrative example, the empirical counterpart of Eq. (1.4) is as follows (these results are based on OLS):

$$\widehat{CLFPR} = 81.2267 - 0.6384 CUNR - 1.4449 AHE82 \qquad (1.5)$$

These results are interesting because both the slope coefficients are negative. The negative coefficient of *CUNR* suggests that, *ceteris paribus* (i.e., holding the influence of *AHE82* constant), a one-percentage-point increase in the unemployment rate leads, on average, to about a 0.64-percentage-point decrease in *CLFPR*, perhaps once again supporting the discouraged-worker hypothesis. On the other hand, holding the influence of *CUNR* constant, an increase in real average hourly earnings of one dollar, on average, leads to about a 1.44 percentage-point decline in *CLFPR*.[11] Does the negative coefficient for *AHE82* make economic sense? Would one not expect a positive coefficient—the higher the hourly

---

[11]As we will discuss in Chapter 4, the coefficients of CUNR and AHE82 given in Eq. (1.5) are known as *partial regression coefficients*. In that chapter we will discuss the precise meaning of partial regression coefficients.

earnings, the higher the attraction of the labor market? However, one could justify the negative coefficient by recalling the twin concepts of microeconomics, namely, the *income effect* and the *substitution effect*.[12]

Which model do we choose, Eq. (1.3) or Eq. (1.5)? Since Eq. (1.5) *encompasses* Eq. (1.3) and since it adds an additional dimension (earnings) to the analysis, we may choose Eq. (1.5). After all, Eq. (1.2) was based implicitly on the assumption that variables other than the unemployment rate were held constant. But where do we stop? For example, labor force participation may also depend on family wealth, number of children under age 6 (this is especially critical for married women thinking of joining the labor market), availability of day-care centers for young children, religious beliefs, availability of welfare benefits, unemployment insurance, and so on. Even if data on these variables are available, we may not want to introduce them all in the model because the purpose of developing an econometric model is not to capture total reality, but just its salient features. If we decide to include every conceivable variable in the regression model, the model will be so unwieldy that it will be of little practical use. The model ultimately chosen should be a reasonably good replica of the underlying reality. In Chapter 7, we will discuss this question further and find out how one can go about developing a model.

Testing the Hypothesis Derived from the Model

Having finally settled on a model, we may want to perform **hypothesis testing.** That is, we may want to find out whether the estimated model makes economic sense and whether the results obtained conform with the underlying economic theory. For example, the discouraged-worker hypothesis postulates a negative relationship between labor force participation and the unemployment rate. Is this hypothesis borne out by our results? Our statistical results seem to be in conformity with this hypothesis because the estimated coefficient of *CUNR* is negative.

However, hypothesis testing can be complicated. In our illustrative example, suppose someone told us that in a prior study the coefficient of *CUNR* was found to be about –1. Are our results in agreement? If we rely on the model, Eq. (1.3), we might get one answer; but if we rely on Eq. (1.5), we might get another answer. How do we resolve this question? Although we will develop the necessary tools to answer such questions, we should keep in mind that the answer to a particular hypothesis may depend on the model we finally choose.

The point worth remembering is that in regression analysis we may be interested not only in estimating the parameters of the regression model but also in testing certain hypotheses suggested by economic theory and/or prior empirical experience.

---

[12]Consult any standard textbook on microeconomics. One intuitive justification of this result is as follows. Suppose both spouses are in the labor force and the earnings of one spouse rise substantially. This may prompt the other spouse to withdraw from the labor force without substantially affecting the family income.

Using the Model for Prediction or Forecasting

Having gone through this multistage procedure, you can legitimately ask the question: What do we do with the estimated model, such as Eq. (1.5)? Quite naturally, we would like to use it for **prediction,** or **forecasting.** For instance, suppose we have 2008 data on the *CUNR* and *AHE82*. Assume these values are 6.0 and 10, respectively. If we put these values in Eq. (1.5), we obtain 62.9473 percent as the predicted value of *CLFPR* for 2008. That is, if the unemployment rate in 2008 were 6.0 percent and the real hourly earnings were $10, the civilian labor force participation rate for 2008 would be about 63 percent. Of course, when data on *CLFPR* for 2008 actually become available, we can compare the predicted value with the actual value. The discrepancy between the two will represent the *prediction error.* Naturally, we would like to keep the prediction error as small as possible. Whether this is always possible is a question that we will answer in Chapters 2 and 3.

Let us now summarize the steps involved in econometric analysis.

Step	Example
1. Statement of theory	The added-/discouraged-worker hypothesis
2. Collection of data	Table 1-1
3. Mathematical model of theory:	$CLFPR = B_1 + B_2CUNR$
4. Econometric model of theory:	$CLFPR = B_1 + B_2CUNR + u$
5. Parameter estimation:	$CLFPR = 69.462 - 0.5814CUNR$
6. Model adequacy check:	$CLFPR = 81.3 - 0.638CUNR - 1.445AHE82$
7. Hypothesis test:	$B_2 < 0$ or $B_2 > 0$
8. Prediction:	What is *CLFPR*, given values of *CUNR* and *AHE82*?

Although we examined econometric methodology using an example from labor economics, we should point out that a similar procedure can be employed to analyze quantitative relationships between variables in any field of knowledge. As a matter of fact, regression analysis has been used in politics, international relations, psychology, sociology, meteorology, and many other disciplines.

1.4 THE ROAD AHEAD

Now that we have provided a glimpse of the nature and scope of econometrics, let us see what lies ahead. The book is divided into four parts.

Appendixes A, B, C, and D review the basics of probability and statistics for the benefit of those readers whose knowledge of statistics has become rusty. The reader should have some previous background in introductory statistics.

Part I introduces the reader to the bread-and-butter tool of econometrics, namely, the *classical linear regression model* (CLRM). A thorough understanding of CLRM is a must in order to follow research in the general areas of economics and business.

Part II considers the practical aspects of regression analysis and discusses a variety of problems that the practitioner will have to tackle when one or more assumptions of the CLRM do not hold.

Part III discusses two comparatively advanced topics—simultaneous equation regression models and time series econometrics.

This book keeps the needs of the beginner in mind. The discussion of most topics is straightforward and unencumbered with mathematical proofs, derivations, etc.[13] We firmly believe that the apparently forbidding subject of econometrics can be taught to beginners in such a way that they can see the value of the subject without getting bogged down in mathematical and statistical minutiae. The student should keep in mind that an introductory econometrics course is just like the introductory statistics course he or she has already taken. As in statistics, econometrics is primarily about estimation and hypothesis testing. What is different, and generally much more interesting and useful, is that the parameters being estimated or tested are not just means and variances, but relationships between variables, which is what much of economics and other social sciences is all about.

A final word: The availability of comparatively inexpensive computer software packages has now made econometrics readily accessible to beginners. In this book we will largely use four software packages: EViews, Excel, STATA, and MINITAB. These packages are readily available and widely used. Once students get used to using such packages, they will soon realize that learning econometrics is really great fun, and they will have a better appreciation of the much maligned "dismal" science of economics.

KEY TERMS AND CONCEPTS

The key terms and concepts introduced in this chapter are

Econometrics

Mathematical economics

Discouraged-worker hypothesis
 (effect)

Added-worker hypothesis (effect)

Time series data
  a) quantitative
  b) qualitative

Cross-sectional data

Pooled data

Panel (or longitudinal or micropanel
 data)

Scatter diagram (scattergram)
  a) parameters
  b) intercept
  c) slope

Random error term (error term)

Linear regression model:
  dependent variable
  independent (or explanatory)
  variable

Causation

Parameter estimates

Hypothesis testing

Prediction (forecasting)

---

[13]Some of the proofs and derivations are presented in our *Basic Econometrics*, 5th ed., McGraw-Hill, New York, 2009.

QUESTIONS

1.1. Suppose a local government decides to increase the tax rate on residential properties under its jurisdiction. What will be the effect of this on the prices of residential houses? Follow the eight-step procedure discussed in the text to answer this question.

1.2. How do you perceive the role of econometrics in decision making in business and economics?

1.3. Suppose you are an economic adviser to the Chairman of the Federal Reserve Board (the Fed), and he asks you whether it is advisable to increase the money supply to bolster the economy. What factors would you take into account in your advice? How would you use econometrics in your advice?

1.4. To reduce the dependence on foreign oil supplies, the government is thinking of increasing the federal taxes on gasoline. Suppose the Ford Motor Company has hired you to assess the impact of the tax increase on the demand for its cars. How would you go about advising the company?

1.5. Suppose the president of the United States is thinking of imposing tariffs on imported steel to protect the interests of the domestic steel industry. As an economic adviser to the president, what would be your recommendations? How would you set up an econometric study to assess the consequences of imposing the tariff?

PROBLEMS

1.6. Table 1-2 gives data on the Consumer Price Index (CPI), S&P 500 stock index, and three-month Treasury bill rate for the United States for the years 1980–2007.
  a. Plot these data with time on the horizontal axis and the three variables on the vertical axis. If you prefer, you may use a separate figure for each variable.
  b. What relationships do you expect to find between the CPI and the S&P index and between the CPI and the three-month Treasury bill rate? Why?
  c. For each variable, "eyeball" a regression line from the scattergram.

TABLE 1-2 CONSUMER PRICE INDEX (CPI, 1982–1984 = 100), STANDARD AND POOR'S COMPOSITE INDEX (S&P 500, 1941–1943 = 100), AND THREE-MONTH TREASURY BILL RATE (3-m T BILL, %)

Year	CPI	S&P 500	3-m T bill	Year	CPI	S&P 500	3-m T bill
1980	82.4	118.78	12.00	1994	148.2	460.42	4.29
1981	90.9	128.05	14.00	1995	152.4	541.72	5.51
1982	96.5	119.71	11.00	1996	156.9	670.50	5.02
1983	99.6	160.41	8.63	1997	160.5	873.43	5.07
1984	103.9	160.46	9.58	1998	163.0	1,085.50	4.81
1985	107.6	186.84	7.48	1999	166.6	1,327.33	4.66
1986	109.6	236.34	5.98	2000	172.2	1,427.22	5.85
1987	113.6	286.83	5.82	2001	177.1	1,194.18	3.45
1988	118.3	265.79	6.69	2002	179.9	993.94	1.62
1989	124.0	322.84	8.12	2003	184.0	965.23	1.02
1990	130.7	334.59	7.51	2004	188.9	1,130.65	1.38
1991	136.2	376.18	5.42	2005	195.3	1,207.23	3.16
1992	140.3	415.74	3.45	2006	201.6	1,310.46	4.73
1993	144.5	451.41	3.02	2007	207.3	1,477.19	4.41

Source: Economic Report of the President, 2008, Tables B-60, B-95, B-96, and B-74, respectively.

TABLE 1-3 U.K. POUND / $ EXCHANGE RATE BETWEEN U.K. POUND
AND U.S. DOLLAR AND THE CPI IN THE UNITED STATES
AND THE U.K., 1985–2007

Period	£ / $	CPI U.S.	CPI U.K.
1985	1.2974	107.6	111.1
1986	1.4677	109.6	114.9
1987	1.6398	113.6	119.7
1988	1.7813	118.3	125.6
1989	1.6382	124.0	135.4
1990	1.7841	130.7	148.2
1991	1.7674	136.2	156.9
1992	1.7663	140.3	162.7
1993	1.5016	144.5	165.3
1994	1.5319	148.2	169.3
1995	1.5785	152.4	175.2
1996	1.5607	156.9	179.4
1997	1.6376	160.5	185.1
1998	1.6573	163.0	191.4
1999	1.6172	166.6	194.3
2000	1.5156	172.2	200.1
2001	1.4396	177.1	203.6
2002	1.5025	179.9	207.0
2003	1.6347	184.0	213.0
2004	1.8330	188.9	219.4
2005	1.8204	195.3	225.6
2006	1.8434	201.6	232.8
2007	2.0020	207.3	242.7

Source: Economic Report of the President, 2008. U.K. Pound/ $
from Table B-110; CPI (1982–1984 = 100) from Table B-108.

1.7. Table 1-3 gives you data on the exchange rate between the U.K. pound and the
U.S. dollar (number of U.K. pounds per U.S. dollar) as well as the consumer
price indexes in the two countries for the period 1985–2007.
   a. Plot the exchange rate (ER) and the two consumer price indexes against time,
   measured in years.
   b. Divide the U.S. CPI by the U.K. CPI and call it the relative price ratio (RPR).
   c. Plot ER against RPR.
   d. Visually sketch a regression line through the scatterpoints.
1.8. Table 1-4 on the textbook Web site contains data on 1247 cars from 2008.[14] Is
there a strong relationship between a car's MPG (miles per gallon) and the
number of cylinders it has?
   a. Create a scatterplot of the combined MPG for the vehicles based on the number of cylinders.
   b. Sketch a straight line that seems to fit the data.
   c. What type of relationship is indicated by the plot?

[14]Data were collected from the United States Department of Energy Web site at **http://www.
fueleconomy.gov/**.

APPENDIX 1A: Economic Data on the World Wide Web[15]

Economic Statistics Briefing Room: An excellent source of data on output, income, employment, unemployment, earnings, production and business activity, prices and money, credits and security markets, and international statistics.
http://www.whitehouse.gov/fsbr/esbr.htm

Federal Reserve System Beige Book: Gives a summary of current economic conditions by the Federal Reserve District. There are 12 Federal Reserve Districts.
www.federalreserve.gov/FOMC/BeigeBook/2008

National Bureau of Economic Research (NBER) Home Page: This highly regarded private economic research institute has extensive data on asset prices, labor, productivity, money supply, business cycle indicators, etc. NBER has many links to other Web sites.
http://www.nber.org

Panel Study: Provides data on longitudinal survey of representative sample of U.S. individuals and families. These data have been collected annually since 1968.
http://www.umich.edu/~psid

The Federal Web Locator: Provides information on almost every sector of the federal government; has international links.
www.lib.auburn.edu/madd/docs/fedloc.html

WebEC:WWW Resources in Economics: A most comprehensive library of economic facts and figures.
www.helsinki.fi/WebEc

American Stock Exchange: Information on some 700 companies listed on the second largest stock market.
http://www.amex.com/

Bureau of Economic Analysis (BEA) Home Page: This agency of the U.S. Department of Commerce, which publishes the *Survey of Current Business,* is an excellent source of data on all kinds of economic activities.
www.bea.gov

Business Cycle Indicators: You will find data on about 256 economic time series.
http://www.globalexposure.com/bci.html

CIA Publication: You will find the *World Fact Book* (annual).
www.cia.gov/library/publications

Energy Information Administration (Department of Energy [DOE]): Economic information and data on each fuel category.
http://www.eia.doe.gov/

FRED Database: Federal Reserve Bank of St. Louis publishes historical economic and social data, which include interest rates, monetary and business indicators, exchange rates, etc.
http://www.stls.frb.org/fred/

---

[15]It should be noted that this list is by no means exhaustive. The sources listed here are updated continually. The best way to get information on the Internet is to search using a key word (e.g., unemployment rate). Don't be surprised if you get a plethora of information on the topic you search.

International Trade Administration: Offers many Web links to trade statistics, cross-country programs, etc.
http://www.ita.doc.gov/

STAT-USA Databases: The National Trade Data Bank provides the most comprehensive source of international trade data and export promotion information. It also contains extensive data on demographic, political, and socioeconomic conditions for several countries.
http://www.stat-usa.gov/

Bureau of Labor Statistics: The home page contains data related to various aspects of employment, unemployment, and earnings and provides links to other statistical Web sites.
http://stats.bls.gov

U.S. Census Bureau Home Page: Prime source of social, demographic, and economic data on income, employment, income distribution, and poverty.
http://www.census.gov/

General Social Survey: Annual personal interview survey data on U.S. households that began in 1972. More than 35,000 have responded to some 2500 different questions covering a variety of data.
www.norc.org/GCS+Website

Institute for Research on Poverty: Data collected by nonpartisan and nonprofit university-based research center on a variety of questions relating to poverty and social inequality.
http://www.ssc.wisc.edu/irp/

Social Security Administration: The official Web site of the Social Security Administration with a variety of data.
http://www.ssa.gov

Federal Deposit Insurance Corporation, Bank Data and Statistics:
http://www.fdic.gov/bank/statistical/

Federal Reserve Board, Economic Research and Data:
http://www.federalreserve.gov/econresdata

U.S. Census Bureau, Home Page:
http://www.census.gov

U.S. Department of Energy, Energy Information Administration:
www.eia.doe.gov/overview_hd.html

U.S. Department of Health and Human Services, National Center for Health Statistics:
http://www.cdc.gov/nchs

U.S. Department of Housing and Urban Development, Data Sets:
http://www.huduser.org/datasets/pdrdatas.html

U.S. Department of Labor, Bureau of Labor Statistics:
http://www.bls.gov

U.S. Department of Transportation, TranStats:
http://www.transtats.bts.gov

U.S. Department of the Treasury, Internal Revenue Service, Tax Statistics:
http://www.irs.gov/taxstats

Rockefeller Institute of Government, State and Local Fiscal Data:
www.rockinst.org/research/sl_finance
American Economic Association, Resources for Economists:
http://www.rfe.org
American Statistical Association, Business and Economic Statistics:
www.amstat.org/publications/jbes
American Statistical Association, Statistics in Sports:
http://www.amstat.org/sections/sis/
European Central Bank, Statistics:
http://www.ecb.int/stats
World Bank, Data and Statistics:
http://www.worldbank.org/data
International Monetary Fund, Statistical Topics:
http://www.imf.org/external/np/sta/
Penn World Tables:
http://pwt.econ.upenn.edu
Current Population Survey:
http://www.bls.census.gov/cps/
Consumer Expenditure Survey:
http://www.bls.gov/cex/
Survey of Consumer Finances:
http://www.federalreserve.gov/pubs/oss/
City and County Data Book:
http://www.census.gov/statab/www/ccdb.html
Panel Study of Income Dynamics:
http://psidonline.isr.umich.edu
National Longitudinal Surveys:
http://www.bls.gov/nls/
National Association of Home Builders, Economic and Housing Data:
http://www.nahb.org/page.aspx/category/sectionID=113
National Science Foundation, Division of Science Resources Statistics:
http://www.nsf.gov/sbe/srs/
Economic Report of the President:
http://www.gpoaccess.gov/eop/
Various Economic Data Sets:
http://www.economy.com/freelunch/
The Economist Market Indicators:
http://www.economist.com/markets/indicators
Statistical Resources on the Military:
http://www.lib.umich.edu/govdocs/stmil.html
World Economic Indicators:
http://devdata.worldbank.org/
Economic Time Series Data:
http://www.economagic.com/

THE LINEAR
REGRESSION MODEL

The objective of Part I, which consists of five chapters, is to introduce you to the "bread-and-butter" tool of econometrics, namely, the linear regression model.

Chapter 2 discusses the basic ideas of linear regression in terms of the simplest possible linear regression model, in particular, the two-variable model. We make an important distinction between the population regression model and the sample regression model and estimate the former from the latter. This estimation is done using the method of least squares, one of the popular methods of estimation.

Chapter 3 considers hypothesis testing. As in any hypothesis testing in statistics, we try to find out whether the estimated values of the parameters of the regression model are compatible with the hypothesized values of the parameters. We do this hypothesis testing in the context of the classical linear regression model (CLRM). We discuss why the CLRM is used and point out that the CLRM is a useful starting point. In Part II we will reexamine the assumptions of the CLRM to see what happens to the CLRM if one or more of its assumptions are not fulfilled.

Chapter 4 extends the idea of the two-variable linear regression model developed in the previous two chapters to multiple regression models, that is, models having more than one explanatory variable. Although in many ways the multiple regression model is an extension of the two-variable model, there are differences when it comes to interpreting the coefficients of the model and in the hypothesis-testing procedure.

The linear regression model, whether two-variable or multivariable, only requires that the parameters of the model be linear; the variables entering the model need not themselves be linear. **Chapter 5** considers a variety of models that are linear in the parameters (or can be made so) but are not necessarily linear in the variables. With several illustrative examples, we point out how and where such models can be used.

Often the explanatory variables entering into a regression model are qualitative in nature, such as sex, race, and religion. **Chapter 6** shows how such variables can be measured and how they enrich the linear regression model by taking into account the influence of variables that otherwise cannot be quantified.

Part I makes an effort to "wed" practice to theory. The availability of user-friendly regression packages allows you to estimate a regression model without knowing much theory, but remember the adage that "a little knowledge is a dangerous thing." So even though theory may be boring, it is absolutely essential in understanding and interpreting regression results. Besides, by omitting all mathematical derivations, we have made the theory "less boring."

CHAPTER 2

BASIC IDEAS OF LINEAR REGRESSION: THE TWO-VARIABLE MODEL

In Chapter 1 we noted that in developing a model of an economic phenomenon (e.g., the law of demand) econometricians make heavy use of a statistical technique known as **regression analysis.** The purpose of this chapter and Chapter 3 is to introduce the basics of regression analysis in terms of the simplest possible linear regression model, namely, the two-variable model. Subsequent chapters will consider various modifications and extensions of the two-variable model.

2.1 THE MEANING OF REGRESSION

As noted in Chapter 1, **regression analysis** is concerned with the study of the relationship between one variable called the **explained,** or **dependent, variable** and one or more other variables called **independent,** or **explanatory, variables.**

Thus, we may be interested in studying the relationship between the quantity demanded of a commodity in terms of the price of that commodity, income of the consumer, and prices of other commodities competing with this commodity. Or, we may be interested in finding out how sales of a product (e.g., automobiles) are related to advertising expenditure incurred on that product. Or, we may be interested in finding out how defense expenditures vary in relation to the gross domestic product (GDP). In all these examples there may be some underlying theory that specifies why we would expect one variable to be dependent or related to one or more other variables. In the first example, the *law of demand* provides the rationale for the dependence of the quantity demanded of a product on its own price and several other variables previously mentioned.

For notational uniformity, from here on we will let Y represent the dependent variable and X the independent, or explanatory, variable. If there is more than one explanatory variable, we will show the various X's by the appropriate sub-scripts (X_1, X_2, X_3, etc.).

It is very important to bear in mind the warning given in Chapter 1 that, although regression analysis deals with the relationship between a dependent variable and one or more independent variables, *it does not necessarily imply causation;* that is, it does not necessarily mean that the independent variables are the *cause* and the dependent variable is the *effect*. If causality between the two exists, it must be justified on the basis of some (economic) theory. As noted ear-lier, the law of demand suggests that if all other variables are held constant, the quantity demanded of a commodity is (inversely) dependent on its own price. Here microeconomic theory suggests that the price may be the causal force and the quantity demanded the effect. *Always keep in mind that regression does not nec-essarily imply causation. Causality must be justified, or inferred, from the theory that underlies the phenomenon that is tested empirically.*

Regression analysis may have one of the following objectives:

1. To estimate the *mean*, or *average*, value of the dependent variable, given the values of the independent variables.
2. To test hypotheses about the nature of the dependence—hypotheses sug-gested by the underlying economic theory. For example, in the demand function mentioned previously, we may want to test the hypothesis that the price elasticity of demand is, say, –1.0; that is, the demand curve has unitary price elasticity. If the price of the commodity goes up by 1 per-cent, the quantity demanded on the average goes down by 1 percent, assuming all other factors affecting demand are held constant.
3. To predict, or forecast, the mean value of the dependent variable, given the value(s) of the independent variable(s) beyond the sample range. Thus, in the S.A.T. example discussed in Appendix C, we may wish to predict the average score on the critical reasoning part of the S.A.T. for a group of students who know their scores on the math part of the test (see Table 2-15).
4. One or more of the preceding objectives combined.

2.2   THE POPULATION REGRESSION FUNCTION (PRF): A HYPOTHETICAL EXAMPLE

To illustrate what all this means, we will consider a concrete example. In the last two years of high school, most American teenagers take the S.A.T. college en-trance examination. The test consists of three sections: critical reasoning (formerly called the verbal section), mathematics, and an essay portion, each scored on a scale of 0 to 800. Since the essay portion is more difficult to score, we will focus pri-marily on the mathematics section. Suppose we are interested in finding out whether a student's family income is related to how well students score on the mathematics section of the test. Let Y represent the math S.A.T. score and X rep-resent annual family income. The income variable has been broken into 10 classes:

TABLE 2-1   MATHEMATICS S.A.T. SCORES IN RELATION TO ANNUAL FAMILY INCOME

Math S.A.T. Scores

Student	\$5,000	\$15,000	\$25,000	\$35,000	\$45,000	\$55,000	\$65,000	\$75,000	\$90,000	\$150,000
					Family Income					
1	460	480	460	520	500	450	560	530	560	570
2	470	510	450	510	470	540	480	540	500	560
3	460	450	530	440	450	460	530	540	470	540
4	420	420	430	540	530	480	520	500	570	550
5	440	430	520	490	550	530	510	480	580	560
6	500	450	490	460	510	480	550	580	480	510
7	420	510	440	460	530	510	480	560	530	520
8	410	500	480	520	440	540	500	490	520	520
9	450	480	510	490	510	510	520	560	540	590
10	490	520	470	450	470	550	470	500	550	600
Mean	452	475	478	488	496	505	512	528	530	552

(<\$10,000), (\$10,000–\$20,000), (\$20,000–\$30,000), . . . , (\$80,000–\$100,000), and (>\$100,000). For simplicity, we have used the midpoints of each of the classes, estimating the last class midpoint at \$150,000, for the analysis. Assume that a hypothetical *population* of 100 high school students is reported in Table 2-1.

Table 2.1 can be interpreted as follows: For an annual family income of \$5,000, one student scored a 460 on the math section of the S.A.T. Nine other students had similar family incomes, and their scores, together with the first student, averaged to 452. For a family income of \$15,000, one student scored a 480 on the section, and the average of 10 students in that income bracket was 475. The remaining columns are similar.

A **scattergram** of these data is shown in Figure 2-1. For this graph, the horizontal axis represents annual family income and the vertical axis represents the students' math S.A.T. scores. For each income level, there are several S.A.T. scores; in fact, in this instance there are 10 recorded scores.[1] The points connected with the line are the mean values for each income level. It seems as though there is a general, overall upward trend in the math scores; higher income levels tend to be associated with higher math scores. This is especially evident with the connected open circles, representing the average scores per income level. These connected circles are formally called the **conditional mean** or **conditional expected values** (see Appendix B for details). Since we have assumed the data represent the population of score values, the line connecting the conditional means is called the **population regression line (PRL)**. *The PRL gives the average, or mean, value of the dependent variable (math S.A.T. scores in this*

---

[1]For simplicity, we are assuming there are 10 scores for each income level. In reality, there may be a very large number of scores for each X (income) value, and each income level need not have the same number of observations.

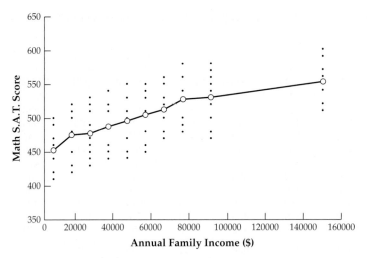

FIGURE 2-1   Annual family income ($) and math S.A.T. score

example) corresponding to each value of the independent variable (here, annual family income) in the population as a whole. Thus, corresponding to an annual income of $25,000, the *average* math S.A.T. score is 478, whereas corresponding to an annual income of $45,000, the *average* math S.A.T. score is 496. In short, the PRL tells us how the mean, or average, value of Y (or any dependent variable) is related to each value of X (or any independent variable) in the whole population.

Since the PRL in Figure 2-1 is approximately linear, we can express it mathematically in the following functional form:

$$E(Y \mid X_i) = B_1 + B_2 X_i \qquad (2.1)$$

which is the mathematical equation of a straight line. In Equation (2.1), $E(Y \mid X_i)$ means the mean, or expected value, of Y corresponding to, or *conditional* upon, a given value of X. The subscript i refers to the ith subpopulation. Thus, in Table 2-1, $E(Y \mid X_i = 5000)$ is 452, which is the mean, or expected, value of Y in the first subpopulation (i.e., corresponding to X = $5000).

The last row of Table 2-1 gives the conditional mean values of Y. It is very important to note that $E(Y \mid X_i)$ is a function of X_i (linear in the present example). This means that the dependence of Y on X, technically called the *regression of Y on X,* can be defined simply as the mean of the distribution of Y values (as in Table 2-1), which has the given X. In other words, *the population regression line (PRL) is a line that passes through the conditional means of Y.* The mathematical form in which the PRL is expressed, such as Eq. (2.1), is called the **population regression function (PRF)**, as it represents the regression line in the population as a whole. In the present instance the PRF is linear. (The more technical meaning of linearity is discussed in Section 2.6.)

In Eq. (2.1), B_1 and B_2 are called the **parameters,** also known as the **regression coefficients.** B_1 is also known as the **intercept** (coefficient) and B_2 as the **slope** (coefficient). *The slope coefficient measures the rate of change in the (conditional) mean value of Y per unit change in X.* If, for example, the slope coefficient (B_2) were 0.001, it would suggest that if annual family income were to increase by a dollar, the (conditional) mean value of Y would increase by 0.001 points. Because of the scale of the variables, it is easier to interpret the results for a one-thousand-dollar increase in annual family income; for each one-thousand-dollar increase in annual family income, we would expect to see a 1 point increase in the (conditional) mean value of the math S.A.T. score. B_1 is the (conditional) mean value of Y if X is zero; it gives the average value of the math S.A.T. score if the annual family income were zero. We will have more to say about this interpretation of the intercept later in the chapter.

How do we go about finding the estimates, or numerical values, of the intercept and slope coefficients? We explore this in Section 2.8.

Before moving on, a word about terminology is in order. Since in regression analysis, as noted in Chapter 1, we are concerned with examining the behavior of the dependent variable *conditional upon the given values of the independent variable(s), our approach to regression analysis can be termed* **conditional regression analysis.**[2] As a result, there is no need to use the adjective "conditional" all the time. Therefore, *in the future expressions like E (Y | X_i) will be simply written as E (Y),* *with the explicit understanding that the latter in fact stands for the former.* Of course, where there is cause for confusion, we will use the more extended notation.

2.3   STATISTICAL OR STOCHASTIC SPECIFICATION OF THE POPULATION REGRESSION FUNCTION

As we just discussed, the PRF gives the average value of the dependent variable corresponding to each value of the independent variable. Let us take another look at Table 2-1. We know, for example, that corresponding to $X = \$75{,}000$, the average Y is 528 points. But if we pick one student at *random* from the 10 students corresponding to this income, we know that the math S.A.T. score for that student will not necessarily be equal to the mean value of 528. To be concrete, take the last student in this group. His or her math S.A.T. score is 500, which is below the mean value. By the same token, if you take the first student in that group, his or her score is 530, which is above the average value.

How do you explain the score of an individual student in relation to income? The best we can do is to say that any individual's math S.A.T. score is equal to

---

[2]The fact that our analysis is conditional on X does not mean that X causes Y. It is just that we want to see the behavior of Y in relation to an X variable that is of interest to the analyst. For example, when the Federal Reserve Bank (the Fed) changes the Federal funds rate, it is interested in finding out how the economy responds. During the economic crisis of 2008 in the United States, the Fed reduced the Federal Funds rate several times to resuscitate the ailing economy. One of the key determinants of the demand for housing is the mortgage interest rate. It is therefore of great interest to prospective homeowners to track the mortgage interest rates. When the Fed reduces the Federal Funds rate, all other interest rates follow suit.

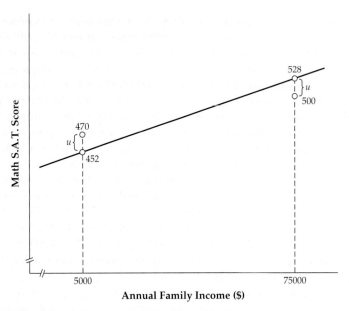

FIGURE 2-2 Math S.A.T. scores in relation to family income

the average for that group plus or minus some quantity. Let us express this mathematically as

$$Y_i = B_1 + B_2X_i + u_i \qquad (2.2)$$

where u is known as the **stochastic, or random, error term,** or simply the **error term.**[3] We have already encountered this term in Chapter 1. The error term is a *random variable* (r.v.), for its value cannot be controlled or known a priori. As we know from Appendix A, an r.v. is usually characterized by its probability distribution (e.g., the normal or the t distribution).

How do we interpret Equation (2.2)? We can say that a student's math S.A.T. score, say, the ith individual, corresponding to a specific family income can be expressed as the sum of two components. The first component is $(B_1 + B_2X_i)$, which is simply the mean, or average, math score in the ith subpopulation; that is, the point on the PRL corresponding to the family income. This component may be called the *systematic*, or *deterministic*, component. The second component is u_i, which may be called the *nonsystematic*, or random, component (i.e., determined by factors other than income). The error term u_i is also known as the **noise component.**

To see this clearly, consider Figure 2-2, which is based on the data of Table 2-1.

As this figure shows, at annual family income = $5000, one student scores 470 on the test, whereas the average math score at this income level is 452. Thus, this

---

[3]The word *stochastic* comes from the Greek word *stokhos* meaning a "bull's eye." The outcome of throwing darts onto a dart board is a stochastic process, that is, a process fraught with misses. In statistics, the word implies the presence of a random variable—a variable whose outcome is determined by a chance experiment.

student's score exceeds the systematic component (i.e., the mean for the group) by 18 points. So his or her u component is +18 units. On the other hand, at income = \$75,000, a randomly chosen second student scores 500 on the math test, whereas the average score for this group is 528. This person's math score is less than the systematic component by 28 points; his or her u component is thus −28.

Eq. (2.2) is called the **stochastic (or statistical) PRF**, whereas Eq. (2.1) is called the **deterministic, or nonstochastic, PRF**. The latter represents the means of the various Y values corresponding to the specified income levels, whereas the former tells us how individual math S.A.T. scores vary around their mean values due to the presence of the stochastic error term, u.

What is the nature of the u term?

2.4 THE NATURE OF THE STOCHASTIC ERROR TERM

1. The error term may represent the influence of those variables that are not explicitly included in the model. For example in our math S.A.T. scenario it may very well represent influences, such as a person's wealth, the area where he or she lives, high school GPA, or math courses taken in school.
2. Even if we included all the relevant variables determining the math test score, some intrinsic randomness in the math score is bound to occur that cannot be explained no matter how hard we try. Human behavior, after all, is not totally predictable or rational. Thus, u may reflect this inherent randomness in human behavior.
3. u may also represent errors of measurement. For example, the data on annual family income may be rounded or the data on math scores may be suspect because in some communities few students plan to attend college and therefore don't take the test.
4. The *principle of Ockham's razor*—that descriptions be kept as simple as possible until proved inadequate—would suggest that we keep our regression model as simple as possible. Therefore, even if we know what other variables might affect Y, their combined influence on Y may be so small and nonsystematic that you can incorporate it in the random term, u. Remember that a model is a simplification of reality. If we truly want to build reality into a model it may be too unwieldy to be of any practical use. In model building, therefore, some abstraction from reality is inevitable. By the way, William Ockham (1285–1349) was an English philosopher who maintained that a complicated explanation should not be accepted without good reason and wrote *"Frustra fit per plura, quod fieri potest per pauciora*—It is vain to do with more what can be done with less."

It is for one or more of these reasons that an individual student's math S.A.T. score will deviate from his or her group average (i.e., the systematic component). And as we will soon discover, this error term plays an extremely crucial role in regression analysis.

2.5   THE SAMPLE REGRESSION FUNCTION (SRF)

How do we estimate the PRF of Eq. (2.1), that is, obtain the values of B_1 and B_2? If we have the data from Table 2-1, the whole population, this would be a relatively straightforward task. All we have to do is to find the conditional means of Y corresponding to each X and then join these means. Unfortunately, in practice, we rarely have the entire population at our disposal. Often we have only a *sample* from this population. (Recall from Chapter 1 and Appendix A our discussion regarding the population and the sample.) Our task here is to estimate the PRF on the basis of the sample information. How do we accomplish this?

Pretend that you have never seen Table 2-1 but only had the data given in Table 2-2, which presumably represent a randomly selected sample of Y values corresponding to the X values shown in Table 2-1.

Unlike Table 2-1, we now have only one Y value corresponding to each X. The important question that we now face is: From the sample data of Table 2-2, can we estimate the average S.A.T. math score in the population as a whole corresponding to each X? In other words, can we estimate the PRF from the sample data? As you can well surmise, we may not be able to estimate the PRF accurately because of *sampling fluctuations*, or *sampling error*, a topic we discuss in Appendix C. To see this clearly, suppose another random sample, which is shown in Table 2-3, is drawn from the population of Table 2-1. If we plot the data of Tables 2-2 and 2-3, we obtain the scattergram shown in Figure 2-3.

Through the scatter points we have drawn visually two straight lines that fit the scatter points reasonably well. We will call these lines the **sample regression lines (SRLs).** Which of the two SRLs represents the true PRL? If we avoid the temptation of looking at Figure 2-1, which represents the PRL, there is no way we can be sure that either of the SRLs shown in Figure 2-3 represents the true PRL. For if we had yet another sample, we would obtain a third SRL. Supposedly, each SRL represents the PRL, but because of sampling variation, each is at best an approximation of the true PRL. In general, we would get K different SRLs for K different samples, and all these SRLs are not likely to be the same.

TABLE 2-2   A RANDOM SAMPLE FROM TABLE 2-1

Y	X
410	5000
420	15000
440	25000
490	35000
530	45000
530	55000
550	65000
540	75000
570	90000
590	150000

TABLE 2-3   A RANDOM SAMPLE FROM TABLE 2-1

Y	X
420	5000
520	15000
470	25000
450	35000
470	45000
550	55000
470	65000
500	75000
550	90000
600	150000

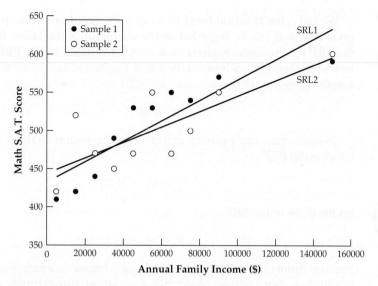

FIGURE 2-3   Sample regression lines based on two independent samples

Now analogous to the PRF that underlies the PRL, we can develop the concept of the **sample regression function (SRF)** to represent the SRL. The sample counterpart of Eq. (2.1) may be written as

$$\hat{Y}_i = b_1 + b_2 X_i \tag{2.3}$$

where ^ is read as "hat" or "cap," and

where $\hat{Y}_i$ = estimator of $E(Y \mid X_i)$, the estimator of the population conditional mean
  b_1 = estimator of B_1
  b_2 = estimator of B_2

As noted in Appendix D, an **estimator,** or a **sample statistic,** is a rule or a formula that suggests how we can estimate the population parameter at hand. A particular numerical value obtained by the estimator in an application, as we know, is an **estimate.** (See Appendix D for the discussion on point and interval estimators.)

If we look at the scattergram in Figure 2-3, we observe that not all the sample data lie exactly on the respective sample regression lines. Therefore, just as we developed the stochastic PRF of Eq. (2.2), we need to develop the stochastic version of Eq. (2.3), which we write as

$$Y_i = b_1 + b_2 X_i + e_i \tag{2.4}$$

where e_i = the estimator of u_i.

We call e_i the **residual term,** or simply the **residual.** Conceptually, it is analogous to u_i and can be regarded as the estimator of the latter. It is introduced in the SRF for the same reasons as u_i was introduced in the PRF. *Simply stated, e_i represents the difference between the actual Y values and their estimated values from the sample regression. That is,*

$$e_i = Y_i - \hat{Y}_i \tag{2.5}$$

To summarize, our primary objective in regression analysis is to estimate the (stochastic) PRF

$$Y_i = B_1 + B_2 X_i + u_i$$

on the basis of the SRF

$$Y_i = b_1 + b_2 X_i + e_i$$

because more often than not our analysis is based on a single sample from some population. But because of sampling variation, our estimate of the PRF based on the SRF is only approximate. This approximation is shown in Figure 2-4. *Keep in mind that we actually do not observe B_1, B_2, and u. What we observe are their proxies, b_1, b_2, and e, once we have a specific sample.*

For a given X_i, shown in this figure, we have one (sample) observation, Y_i. In terms of the SRF, the observed Y_i can be expressed as

$$Y_i = \hat{Y}_i + e_i \tag{2.6}$$

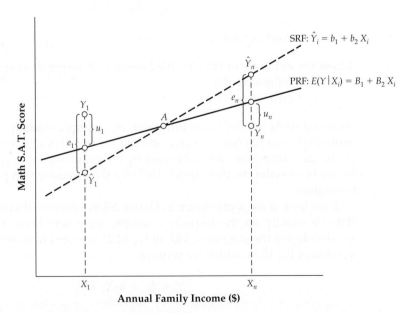

FIGURE 2-4   The population and sample regression lines

and in terms of the PRF it can be expressed as

$$Y_i = E(Y \mid X_i) + u_i \tag{2.7}$$

Obviously, in Figure 2-4, $\hat{Y}_1$ underestimates the true mean value $E(Y \mid X_1)$ for the X_1 shown therein. By the same token, for any Y to the right of point A in Figure 2-4 (e.g., $\hat{Y}_n$), the SRF will *overestimate* the true PRF. But you can readily see that such over- and underestimation is inevitable due to sampling fluctuations.

The important question now is: Granted that the SRF is only an approximation of the PRF, can we find a method or a procedure that will make this approximation as close as possible? In other words, how should we construct the SRF so that b_1 is as close as possible to B_1 and b_2 is as close as possible to B_2, because generally we do not have the entire population at our disposal? As we will show in Section 2.8, we can indeed find a "best-fitting" SRF that will mirror the PRF as faithfully as possible. *It is fascinating to consider that this can be done even though we never actually determine the PRF itself.*

2.6 THE SPECIAL MEANING OF THE TERM "LINEAR" REGRESSION

Since in this text we are concerned primarily with "linear" models like Eq. (2.1), it is essential to know what the term *linear* really means, for it can be interpreted in two different ways.

Linearity in the Variables

The first and perhaps the more "natural" meaning of linearity is that the conditional mean value of the dependent variable is a linear function of the independent variable(s) as in Eq. (2.1) or Eq. (2.2) or in the sample counterparts, Eqs. (2.3) and (2.4).[4] In this interpretation, the following functions are not linear:

$$E(Y) = B_1 + B_2 X_i^2 \tag{2.8}$$

$$E(Y) = B_1 + B_2 \frac{1}{X_i} \tag{2.9}$$

because in Equation (2.8) X appears with a power of 2, and in Eq. (2.9) it appears in the inverse form. For regression models linear in the explanatory variable(s), the rate of change in the dependent variable remains constant for a unit change in the explanatory variable; that is, the slope remains constant. But for a regression

---

[4]A function $Y = f(X)$ is said to be linear in X if (1) X appears with a power of 1 only; that is, terms such as X^2 and $\sqrt{X}$ are excluded; and (2) X is not multiplied or divided by another variable (e.g., $X \cdot Z$ and X/Z, where Z is another variable).

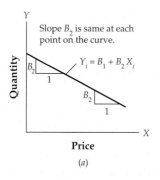
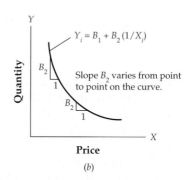

FIGURE 2-5 (a) Linear demand curve; (b) nonlinear demand curve

model nonlinear in the explanatory variables the slope does not remain constant. This can be seen more clearly in Figure 2-5.

As Figure 2-5 shows, for the regression (2.1), the slope—the rate of change in $E(Y)$—the mean of Y, remains the same, namely, B_2 no matter at what value of X we measure the change. But for regression, say, Eq. (2.8), the rate of change in the mean value of Y varies from point to point on the regression line; it is actually a curve here.[5]

Linearity in the Parameters

The second interpretation of linearity is that the conditional mean of the dependent variable is a linear function of the parameters, the B's; it may or may not be linear in the variables. Analogous to a linear-in-variable function, a function is said to be linear in the parameter, say, B_2, if B_2 appears with a power of 1 only. On this definition, models (2.8) and (2.9) are both linear models because B_1 and B_2 enter the models linearly. It does not matter that the variable X enters nonlinearly in both models. However, a model of the type

$$E(Y) = B_1 + B_2^2 X_i \qquad (2.10)$$

is nonlinear in the parameter model since B_2 enters with a power of 2.

In this book we are primarily concerned with models that are linear in the parameters. *Therefore, from now on the term* **linear regression** *will mean a regression that is linear in the parameters, the B's (i.e., the parameters are raised to the power of 1 only); it may or may not be linear in the explanatory variables.*[6]

---

[5]Those who know calculus will recognize that in the linear model the slope, that is, the derivative of Y with respect to X, is constant, equal to B_2, but in the nonlinear model Eq. (2.8) it is equal to $-B_2(1/X_i^2)$, which obviously will depend on the value of X at which the slope is measured, and is therefore not constant.

[6]This is not to suggest that nonlinear (in-the-parameters) models like Eq. (2.10) cannot be estimated or that they are not used in practice. As a matter of fact, in advanced courses in econometrics such models are studied in depth.

2.7   TWO-VARIABLE VERSUS MULTIPLE LINEAR REGRESSION

So far in this chapter we have considered only the **two-variable,** or **simple, regression** models in which the dependent variable is a function of just one explanatory variable. This was done just to introduce the fundamental ideas of regression analysis. But the concept of regression can be extended easily to the case where the dependent variable is a function of more than one explanatory variable. For instance, if the math S.A.T. score is a function of income (X_2), number of math classes taken (X_3), and age of the student (X_4), we can write the extended math S.A.T. function as

$$E(Y) = B_1 + B_2X_{2i} + B_3X_{3i} + B_4X_{4i} \qquad (2.11)$$

[*Note:* $E(Y) = E(Y \mid X_{2i}, X_{3i}, X_{4i})$.]

Equation (2.11) is an example of a **multiple linear regression,** a regression in which more than one independent, or explanatory, variable is used to explain the behavior of the dependent variable. Model (2.11) states that the (conditional) mean value of the math S.A.T. score is a linear function of income, number of math classes taken, and age of the student. The score function of a student (i.e., the stochastic PRF) can be expressed as

$$Y_i = B_1 + B_2X_{2i} + B_3X_{3i} + B_4X_{4i} + u_i$$
$$= E(Y) + u_i \qquad (2.12)$$

which shows that the individual math S.A.T. score will differ from the group mean by the factor u, which is the stochastic error term. As noted earlier, even in a multiple regression we introduce the error term because we cannot take into account all the forces that might affect the dependent variable.

Notice that both Eqs. (2.11) and (2.12) are linear in the parameters and are therefore *linear regression models.* The explanatory variables themselves do not need to enter the model linearly, although in the present example they do.

2.8   ESTIMATION OF PARAMETERS: THE METHOD OF ORDINARY LEAST SQUARES

As noted in Section 2.5, we estimate the population regression function (PRF) on the basis of the sample regression function (SRF), since in practice we only have a sample (or two) from a given population. How then do we estimate the PRF? And how do we find out whether the estimated PRF (i.e., the SRF) is a "good" estimate of the true PRF? We will answer the first question in this chapter and take up the second question—of the "goodness" of the estimated PRF—in Chapter 3.

To introduce the fundamental ideas of estimation of the PRF, we consider the simplest possible linear regression model, namely, the two-variable linear regression in which we study the relationship of the dependent variable Y to a single explanatory variable X. In Chapter 4 we extend the analysis to the multiple regression, where we will study the relationship of the dependent variable Y to more than one explanatory variable.

The Method of Ordinary Least Squares

Although there are several methods of obtaining the SRF as an estimator of the true PRF, in regression analysis the method that is used most frequently is that of *least squares (LS)*, more popularly known as the **method of ordinary least squares (OLS)**.[7] We will use the terms LS and OLS methods interchangeably. To explain this method, we first explain the **least squares principle.**

The Least Squares Principle   Recall our two-variable PRF, Eq. (2.2):

$$Y_i = B_1 + B_2X_i + u_i$$

Since the PRF is not directly observable (Why?), we estimate it from the SRF

$$Y_i = b_1 + b_2X_1 + e_i$$

which we can write as

$$e_i = \text{actual } Y_i - \text{predicted } Y_i$$

$$= Y_i - \hat{Y}_i$$

$$= Y_i - b_1 - b_2X_i \text{ [using Eq. (2.3)]}$$

which shows that the residuals are simply the differences between the actual and estimated Y values, the latter obtained from the SRF, Eq. (2.3). This can be seen more vividly in Figure 2-4.

Now the best way to estimate the PRF is to choose b_1 and b_2, the estimators of B_1 and B_2, in such a way that the residuals e_i are as small as possible. The method of **ordinary least squares (OLS)** states that b_1 and b_2 should be chosen in such a way that the **residual sum of squares (RSS),** $\sum e_i^2$, is as small as possible.[8]

Algebraically, the least squares principle states

$$Minimize \sum e_i^2 = \sum (Y_i - \hat{Y})^2$$

$$= \sum (Y_i - b_1 - b_2X_i)^2 \qquad \textbf{(2.13)}$$

[7]Despite the name, there is nothing ordinary about this method. As we will show, this method has several desirable statistical properties. It is called OLS because there is another method, called the *generalized least squares* (GLS) method, of which OLS is a special case.

[8]Note that the smaller the e_i is, the smaller their sum of squares will be. The reason for considering the squares of e_i and not the e_i themselves is that this procedure avoids the problem of the sign of the residuals. Note that e_i can be positive as well as negative.

As you can observe from Eq. (2.13), once the sample values of Y and X are given, RSS is a function of the estimators b_1 and b_2. Choosing different values of b_1 and b_2 will yield different e's and hence different values of RSS. To see this, just rotate the SRF shown in Figure 2-4 any way you like. For each rotation, you will get a different intercept (i.e., b_1) and a different slope (i.e., b_2). We want to choose the values of these estimators that will give the smallest possible RSS.

How do we actually determine these values? This is now simply a matter of arithmetic and involves the technique of differential calculus. Without going into detail, it can be shown that the values of b_1 and b_2 that actually minimize the RSS given in Eq. (2.13) are obtained by solving the following two simultaneous equations. (The details are given in Appendix 2A at the end of this chapter.)

$$\sum Y_i = nb_1 + b_2 \sum X_i \qquad (2.14)$$

$$\sum Y_i X_i = b_1 \sum X_i + b_2 \sum X_i^2 \qquad (2.15)$$

where n is the sample size. These simultaneous equations are known as the (least squares) **normal equations.**

In Equations (2.14) and (2.15) the unknowns are the b's and the knowns are the quantities involving sums, squared sums, and the sum of the cross-products of the variables Y and X, which can be easily obtained from the sample at hand. Now solving these two equations simultaneously (using any high school algebra trick you know), we obtain the following solutions for b_1 and b_2.

$$b_1 = \overline{Y} - b_2 \overline{X} \qquad (2.16)$$

which is the estimator of the population intercept, B_1. The sample intercept is thus the sample mean value of Y minus the estimated slope times the sample mean value of X.

$$\begin{aligned} b_2 &= \frac{\sum x_i y_i}{\sum x_i^2} \\ &= \frac{\sum (X_i - \overline{X})(Y_i - \overline{Y})}{\sum (X_i - \overline{X})^2} \\ &= \frac{\sum X_i Y_i - n\overline{X}\,\overline{Y}}{\sum X_i^2 - n\overline{X}^2} \end{aligned} \qquad (2.17)$$

which is the estimator of the population slope coefficient B_2. Note that

$$x_i = (X_i - \overline{X}) \quad \text{and} \quad y_i = (Y_i - \overline{Y})$$

that is, *the small letters denote deviations from the sample mean values, a convention that we will adopt in this book.* As you can see from the formula for b_2, it is simpler to write the estimator using the deviation form. *Expressing the values of a variable from its mean value does not change the ranking of the values, since we are subtracting the same constant from each value.* Note that b_1 and b_2 are solely expressed in terms of quantities that can be readily computed from the sample at hand. Of course, these days the computer will do all the calculations for you.

The estimators given in Equations (2.16) and (2.17) are known as **OLS estimators,** since they are obtained by the method of OLS.

Before proceeding further, we should note a few interesting features of the OLS estimators given in Eqs. (2.16) and (2.17):

1. The SRF obtained by the method of OLS passes through the sample mean values of X and Y, which is evident from Eq. (2.16), for it can be written as

$$\overline{Y} = b_1 + b_2\overline{X} \tag{2.18}$$

2. The mean value of the residuals, $\bar{e}(=\Sigma e_i/n)$ is always zero, which provides a check on the arithmetical accuracy of the calculations (see Table 2-4).
3. The sum of the product of the residuals e and the values of the explanatory variable X is zero; that is, these two variables are uncorrelated (on the definition of correlation, see Appendix B). Symbolically,

$$\sum e_i X_i = 0 \tag{2.19}$$

This provides yet another check on the least squares calculations.
4. The sum of the product of the residuals e_i and the estimated $Y_i(=\hat{Y}_i)$ is zero; that is, $\Sigma e_i \hat{Y}_i$ is zero (see Question 2.25).

2.9 PUTTING IT ALL TOGETHER

Let us use the sample data given in Table 2-2 to compute the values of b_1 and b_2. The necessary computations involved in implementing formulas (2.16) and (2.17) are laid out in Table 2-4. Keep in mind that the data given in Table 2-2 are a random sample from the population given in Table 2-1.

From the computations shown in Table 2-4, we obtain the following sample math S.A.T. score regression:

$$\hat{Y}_i = 432.4138 + 0.0013X_i \tag{2.20}$$

where Y represents math S.A.T. score and X represents annual family income. *Note that we have put a cap on Y to remind us that it is an estimator of the true population mean corresponding to the given level of X (recall Eq. 2.3).* The estimated regression line is shown in Figure 2-6.

TABLE 2-4   RAW DATA (FROM TABLE 2-2) FOR MATH S.A.T. SCORES

Y_i	X_i	$\sum Y_i X_i$	X_i^2	x_i	y_i	x_i^2	y_i^2	$\sum y_i x_i$	$\hat{Y}_i$	e_i	e_i^2	$\sum e_i x_i$
410	5000	2050000	25000000	−51000	−97	2601000000	9409	4947000	439.073	−29.0733	845.255	1482737.069
420	15000	6300000	225000000	−41000	−87	1681000000	7569	3567000	452.392	−32.3922	1049.257	1328081.897
440	25000	11000000	625000000	−31000	−67	961000000	4489	2077000	465.711	−25.7112	661.066	797047.4138
490	35000	17150000	1225000000	−21000	−17	441000000	289	357000	479.030	10.9698	120.337	−230366.3793
530	45000	23850000	2025000000	−11000	23	121000000	529	−253000	492.349	37.6509	1417.587	−414159.4828
530	55000	29150000	3025000000	−1000	23	1000000	529	−23000	505.668	24.3319	592.0412	−24331.89655
550	65000	35750000	4225000000	9000	43	81000000	1849	387000	518.987	31.0129	961.8019	279116.3793
540	75000	40500000	5625000000	19000	33	361000000	1089	627000	532.306	7.69397	59.1971	146185.3448
570	90000	51300000	8100000000	34000	63	1156000000	3969	2142000	552.284	17.7155	313.8396	602327.5862
590	150000	88500000	22500000000	94000	83	8836000000	6889	7802000	632.198	−42.1982	1780.694	−3966637.931
5070	560000	305550000	47600000000	0	0	16240000000	36610	21630000	5070	0	7801.0776	0

Note: $x_i = (X_i - \bar{X})$; $y_i = (Y_i - \bar{Y})$; $\bar{X} = 56000$; $\bar{Y} = 507$.

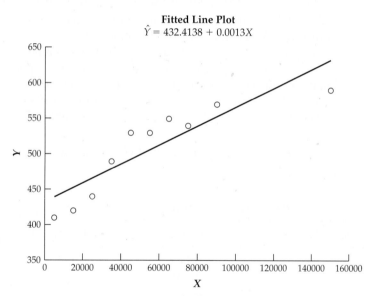

Fitted Line Plot
$$\hat{Y} = 432.4138 + 0.0013X$$

FIGURE 2-6   Regression line based on data from Table 2-4

Interpretation of the Estimated Math S.A.T. Score Function

The interpretation of the estimated math S.A.T. score function is as follows: The slope coefficient of 0.0013 means that, other things remaining the same, if annual family income goes up by a dollar, the *mean* or *average* math S.A.T. score goes up by about 0.0013 points. The intercept value of 432.4138 means that if family income is zero, the mean math score will be about 432.4138. Very often such an interpretation has no economic meaning. For example, we have no data where an annual family income is zero. *As we will see throughout the book, often the intercept has no particular economic meaning.* In general you have to use common sense in interpreting the intercept term, for very often the sample range of the X values (family income in our example) may not include zero as one of the observed values. *Perhaps it is best to interpret the intercept term as the mean or average effect on Y of all the variables omitted from the regression model.*

2.10 SOME ILLUSTRATIVE EXAMPLES

Now that we have discussed the OLS method and learned how to estimate a PRF, let us provide some concrete applications of regression analysis.

Example 2.1. Years of Schooling and Average Hourly Earnings

Based on a sample of 528 observations, Table 2-5 gives data on average hourly wage $Y(\$)$ and years of schooling (X).

Suppose we want to find out how Y behaves in relation to X. From human capital theories of labor economics, we would expect average wage to increase with years of schooling. That is, we expect a positive relationship between the two variables; it would be bad news if such were not the case.

The regression results based on the data in Table 2-5 are as follows:

$$\hat{Y}_i = -0.0144 + 0.7241X_i \qquad \textbf{(2.21)}$$

TABLE 2-5   AVERAGE HOURLY WAGE BY EDUCATION

Years of schooling	Average hourly wage ($)	Number of people
6	4.4567	3
7	5.7700	5
8	5.9787	15
9	7.3317	12
10	7.3182	17
11	6.5844	27
12	7.8182	218
13	7.8351	37
14	11.0223	56
15	10.6738	13
16	10.8361	70
17	13.6150	24
18	13.5310	31

Source: Arthur S. Goldberger, *Introductory Econometrics*, Harvard University Press, Cambridge, Mass., 1998, Table 1.1, p. 5 (adapted).

As these results show, there is a positive association between education and earnings, which accords with prior expectations. For every additional year of schooling, the mean wage rate goes up by about 72 cents per hour.[9] The negative intercept in the present instance has no particular economic meaning.

Example 2.2. Okun's Law

Based on the U.S. data for 1947 to 1960, the late Arthur Okun of the Brookings Institution and a former chairman of the President's Council of Economic Advisers obtained the following regression, known as Okun's law:

$$Y_t = -0.4(X_t - 2.5) \tag{2.22}$$

where Y_t = change in the unemployment rate, percentage points
  X_t = percent growth rate in real output, as measured by real GDP
  2.5 = the long-term, or trend, rate of growth of output historically observed in the United States

In this regression the intercept is zero and the slope coefficient is −0.4. Okun's law says that for every percentage point of growth in real GDP above 2.5 percent, the unemployment rate declines by 0.4 percentage points.

Okun's law has been used to predict the required growth in real GDP to reduce the unemployment rate by a given percentage point. Thus, a growth rate of 5 percent in real GDP will reduce the unemployment rate by 1 percentage point, or a growth rate of 7.5 percent is required to reduce the unemployment rate by 2 percentage points. In Problem 2.17, which gives comparatively more recent data, you are asked to find out if Okun's law still holds.

This example shows how sometimes a simple (i.e., two-variable) regression model can be used for policy purposes.

Example 2.3. Stock Prices and Interest Rates

Stock prices and interest rates are key economic indicators. Investors in stock markets, individual or institutional, watch very carefully the movements in the interest rates. Since interest rates represent the cost of borrowing money, they have a vast effect on investment and hence on the profitability of a company. Macroeconomic theory would suggest an inverse relationship between stock prices and interest rates.

As a measure of stock prices, let us use the S&P 500 composite index ($1941–1943 = 10$), and as a measure of interest rates, let us use the three-month

---

[9]Since the data in Table 2-5 refer to the mean wage for the various categories, the slope coefficient here should strictly be interpreted as the average increase in the mean hourly earnings.

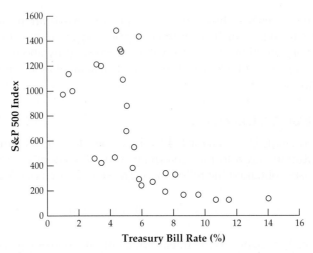

FIGURE 2-7   S&P 500 composite index and three-month Treasury bill rate, 1980–2007

Treasury bill rate (%). Table 2-6, found on the textbook's Web site, gives data on these variables for the period 1980–2007.

Plotting these data, we obtain the scattergram as shown in Figure 2-7. The scattergram clearly shows that there is an inverse relationship between the two variables, as per theory. But the relationship between the two is not linear (i.e., straight line); it more closely resembles Figure 2-5(*b*). Therefore, let us maintain that the true relationship is:

$$Y_t = B_1 + B_2(1/X_i) + u_i \tag{2.23}$$

Note that Eq. (2.23) is a linear regression model, as the parameters in the model are linear. It is, however, nonlinear in the variable X. If you let $Z = 1/X$, then the model is linear in the parameters as well as the variables Y and Z.

Using the EViews statistical package, we estimate Eq. (2.23) by OLS, giving the following results:

$$\hat{Y}_t = 404.4067 + 996.866(1/X_t) \tag{2.24}$$

How do we interpret these results? The value of the intercept has no practical economic meaning. The interpretation of the coefficient of $(1/X)$ is rather tricky. Literally interpreted, it suggests that if the reciprocal of the three-month Treasury bill rate goes up by one unit, the average value of the S&P 500 index will go up by about 997 units. This is, however, not a very enlightening interpretation. If you want to measure the rate of change of (mean) Y with respect to X (i.e., the derivative of Y with respect to X), then as footnote 5 shows, this rate of change is given by $-B_2(1/X_i^2)$, which depends on the value taken by X. Suppose $X = 2$. Knowing that the estimated B_2 is 996.866, we find the rate of change at this X value as -249.22 (approx). That is, starting with a Treasury bill rate of about 2 percent, if that rate goes up by one percentage point, on average, the S&P 500 index will decline by about 249 units. Of course, an increase in the Treasury bill rate from 2 percent to 3 percent is a substantial increase.

Interestingly, if you had disregarded Figure 2-5 and had simply fitted the straight line regression to the data in Table 2-6, (found on the textbook's Web site), you would obtain the following regression:

$$\hat{Y}_t = 1229.3414 - 99.4014X_t \qquad \textbf{(2.25)}$$

Here the interpretation of the intercept term is that if the Treasury bill rate were zero, the average value of the S&P index would be about 1229. Again, this may not have any concrete economic meaning. The slope coefficient here suggests that if the Treasury bill rate were to increase by one unit, say, one percentage point, the average value of the S&P index would go down by about 99 units.

Regressions (2.24) and (2.25) bring out the practical problems in choosing an appropriate model for empirical analysis. Which is a better model? How do we know? What tests do we use to choose between the two models? We will provide answers to these questions as we progress through the book (see Chapter 5). *A question to ponder*: In Eq. (2.24) the sign of the slope coefficient is positive, whereas in Eq. (2.25) it is negative. Are these findings conflicting?

Example 2.4. Median Home Price and Mortgage Interest Rate in the United States, 1980–2007

Over the past several years there has been a surge in home prices across the United States. It is believed that this surge is due to sharply falling mortgage interest rates. To see the impact of mortgage interest rates on home prices, Table 2-7 (found on the textbook's Web site) gives data on median home prices (1000 $) and 30-year fixed rate mortgage (%) in the United States for the period 1980–2007.

These data are plotted in Figure 2-8.

As a first approximation, if you fit a straight line regression model, you will obtain the following results, where Y = median home price (1000 $) and X = 30-year fixed rate mortgage (%):

$$\hat{Y}_t = 329.0041 - 17.3694X_t \qquad \textbf{(2.26)}$$

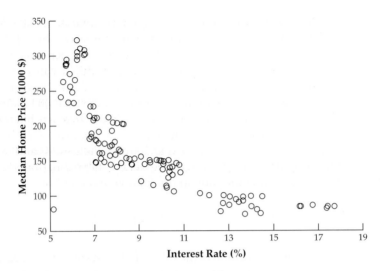

FIGURE 2-8   Median home prices and interest rates, 1980–2007

These results show that if the mortgage interest rate goes up by 1 percentage point,[10] on average, the median home price goes down by about 17.4 units or about $17,400. (*Note*: Y is measured in thousands of dollars.) Literally interpreted, the intercept coefficient of about 329 would suggest that if the mortgage interest rate were zero, the median home price on average would be about $329,000, an interpretation that may stretch our credulity.

It seems that falling interest rates do have a substantial impact on home prices. *A question*: If we had taken median family income into account, would this conclusion still stand?

Example 2.5. Antique Clocks and Their Prices

The Triberg Clock Company of Schonachbach, Germany, holds an annual antique clock auction. Data on about 32 clocks (the age of the clock, the number of bidders, and the price of the winning bid in marks) are given in Table 2-14 in Problem 2.19. Note that this auction took place about 25 years ago.

If we believe that the price of the winning bid depends on the age of the clock—the older the clock, the higher the price, *ceteris paribus*—we would expect a positive relationship between the two. Similarly, the higher the number of bidders, the higher the auction price because a large number of bidders for a particular clock would suggest that that clock is more valuable, and hence we would expect a positive relationship between the two variables.

---

[10]Note that there is a difference between a 1 percentage point increase and a 1 percent increase. For example, if the current interest rate is 6 percent but then goes to 7 percent, this represents a 1 percentage point increase; the percentage increase is, however, $\left(\frac{7-6}{6}\right) \times 100 = 16.6\%$.

Using the data given in Table 2-14, we obtained the following OLS regressions:

$$\text{Price} = -191.6662 + 10.4856\,\text{Age} \tag{2.27}$$

$$\text{Price} = 807.9501 + 54.5724\,\text{Bidders} \tag{2.28}$$

As these results show, the auction price is positively related to the age of the clock, as well as to the number of bidders present at the auction.

In Chapter 4 on multiple regression we will see what happens when we regress price on age and number of bidders together, rather than individually, as in the preceding two regressions.

The regression results presented in the preceding examples can be obtained easily by applying the OLS formulas Eq. (2.16) and Eq. (2.17) to the data presented in the various tables. Of course, this would be very tedious and very time-consuming to do manually. Fortunately, there are several statistical software packages that can estimate regressions in practically no time. In this book we will use the EViews and MINITAB software packages to estimate several regression models because these packages are comprehensive, easy to use, and readily available. (Excel can also do simple and multiple regressions.) *Throughout this book, we will reproduce the computer output obtained from these packages.* But keep in mind that there are other software packages that can estimate all kinds of regression models. Some of these packages are LIMDEP, MICROFIT, PC-GIVE, RATS, SAS, SHAZAM, SPSS, and STATA.

2.11   SUMMARY

In this chapter we introduced some fundamental ideas of regression analysis. Starting with the key concept of the population regression function (PRF), we developed the concept of linear PRF. This book is primarily concerned with linear PRFs, that is, regressions that are *linear in the parameters* regardless of whether or not they are linear in the variables. We then introduced the idea of the stochastic PRF and discussed in detail the nature and role of the stochastic error term u. PRF is, of course, a theoretical or idealized construct because, in practice, all we have is a sample(s) from some population. This necessitated the discussion of the sample regression function (SRF).

We then considered the question of how we actually go about obtaining the SRF. Here we discussed the popular method of ordinary least squares (OLS) and presented the appropriate formulas to estimate the parameters of the PRF. We illustrated the OLS method with a fully worked-out numerical example as well as with several practical examples.

Our next task is to find out how good the SRF obtained by OLS is as an estimator of the true PRF. We undertake this important task in Chapter 3.

KEY TERMS AND CONCEPTS

The key terms and concepts introduced in this chapter are

Regression analysis
  a) explained, or dependent, variable
  b) independent, or explanatory, variable
Scattergram; scatter diagram
Population regression line (PRL)
  a) conditional mean, or conditional expected, values
Population regression function (PRF)
Regression coefficients; parameters
  a) intercept
  b) slope
Conditional regression analysis
Stochastic, or random, error term; error term
  a) noise component
  b) stochastic, or statistical, PRF

  c) deterministic, or nonstochastic, PRF
Sample regression line (SRL)
Sample regression function (SRF)
Estimator; sample statistic
Estimate
Residual term e; residual
Linearity in variables
Linearity in parameters
  a) linear regression
Two-variable, or simple, regression vs. multiple linear regression
Estimation of parameters
  a) the method of ordinary least squares (OLS)
  b) the least squares principle
  c) residual sum of squares (RSS)
  d) normal equations
  e) OLS estimators

QUESTIONS

2.1. Explain carefully the meaning of each of the following terms:
  a. Population regression function (PRF).
  b. Sample regression function (SRF).
  c. Stochastic PRF.
  d. Linear regression model.
  e. Stochastic error term (u_i).
  f. Residual term (e_i).
  g. Conditional expectation.
  h. Unconditional expectation.
  i. Regression coefficients or parameters.
  j. Estimators of regression coefficients.
2.2. What is the difference between a stochastic population regression function (PRF) and a stochastic sample regression function (SRF)?
2.3. Since we do not observe the PRF, why bother studying it? Comment on this statement.
2.4. State whether the following statements are true, false, or uncertain. Give your reasons. Be precise.
  a. The stochastic error term u_i and the residual term e_i mean the same thing.
  b. The PRF gives the value of the dependent variable corresponding to each value of the independent variable.
  c. A linear regression model means a model linear in the variables.

      d. In the linear regression model the explanatory variable is the cause and the dependent variable is the effect.

      e. The conditional and unconditional mean of a random variable are the same thing.

      f. In Eq. (2.2) the regression coefficients, the B's, are random variables, whereas the b's in Eq. (2.4) are the parameters.

      g. In Eq. (2.1) the slope coefficient B_2 measures the slope of Y per unit change in X.

      h. In practice, the two-variable regression model is useless because the behavior of a dependent variable can never be explained by a single explanatory variable.

      i. The sum of the deviation of a random variable from its mean value is *always* equal to zero.

2.5. What is the relationship between

      a. B_1 and b_1; **b.** B_2 and b_2; and **c.** u_i and e_i? Which of these entities can be observed and how?

2.6. Can you rewrite Eq. (2.22) to express X as a function of Y? How would you interpret the converted equation?

2.7. The following table gives pairs of dependent and independent variables. In each case state whether you would expect the relationship between the two variables to be positive, negative, or uncertain. In other words, tell whether the slope coefficient will be positive, negative, or neither. Give a brief justification in each case.

Dependent variable	Independent variable
(a) GDP	Rate of interest
(b) Personal savings	Rate of interest
(c) Yield of crop	Rainfall
(d) U.S. defense expenditure	Soviet Union's defense expenditure
(e) Number of home runs hit by a star baseball player	Annual salary
(f) A president's popularity	Length of stay in office
(g) A student's first-year grade-point average	S.A.T. score
(h) A student's grade in econometrics	Grade in statistics
(i) Imports of Japanese cars	U.S. per capita income

PROBLEMS

2.8. State whether the following models are linear regression models:

      a. $Y_i = B_1 + B_2(1/X_i)$

      b. $Y_i = B_1 + B_2 \ln X_i + u_i$

      c. $\ln Y_i = B_1 + B_2 X_i + u_i$

      d. $\ln Y_i = B_1 + B_2 \ln X_i + u_i$

      e. $Y_i = B_1 + B_2 B_3 X_i + u_i$

      f. $Y_i = B_1 + B_2^3 X_i + u_i$

      Note: ln stands for the natural log, that is, log to the base e. (More on this in Chapter 4.)

2.9. Table 2-8 gives data on weekly family consumption expenditure (Y) (in dollars) and weekly family income (X) (in dollars).

TABLE 2-8 HYPOTHETICAL DATA ON WEEKLY CONSUMPTION EXPENDITURE AND WEEKLY INCOME

Weekly income ($)(X)	Weekly consumption expenditure ($) (Y)
80	55, 60, 65, 70, 75
100	65, 70, 74, 80, 85, 88
120	79, 84, 90, 94, 98
140	80, 93, 95, 103, 108, 113, 115
160	102, 107, 110, 116, 118, 125
180	110, 115, 120, 130, 135, 140
200	120, 136, 140, 144, 145
220	135, 137, 140, 152, 157, 160, 162
240	137, 145, 155, 165, 175, 189
260	150, 152, 175, 178, 180, 185, 191

a. For each income level, compute the mean consumption expenditure, $E(Y \mid X_i)$, that is, the conditional expected value.

b. Plot these data in a scattergram with income on the horizontal axis and consumption expenditure on the vertical axis.

c. Plot the conditional means derived in part (a) in the same scattergram created in part (b).

d. What can you say about the relationship between Y and X and between mean Y and X?

e. Write down the PRF and the SRF for this example.

f. Is the PRF linear or nonlinear?

2.10. From the data given in the preceding problem, a random sample of Y was drawn against each X. The result was as follows:

Y	70	65	90	95	110	115	120	140	155	150
X	80	100	120	140	160	180	200	220	240	260

a. Draw the scattergram with Y on the vertical axis and X on the horizontal axis.

b. What can you say about the relationship between Y and X?

c. What is the SRF for this example? Show all your calculations in the manner of Table 2-4.

d. On the same diagram, show the SRF and PRF.

e. Are the PRF and SRF identical? Why or why not?

2.11. Suppose someone has presented the following regression results for your consideration:

$$\hat{Y}_t = 2.6911 - 0.4795X_t$$

where Y = coffee consumption in the United States (cups per person per day)
 X = retail price of coffee ($ per pound)
 t = time period

a. Is this a time series regression or a cross-sectional regression?

b. Sketch the regression line.

c. What is the interpretation of the intercept in this example? Does it make economic sense?

d. How would you interpret the slope coefficient?

e. Is it possible to tell what the true PRF is in this example?

f. The *price elasticity* of demand is defined as the percentage change in the quantity demanded for a percentage change in the price. Mathematically, it is expressed as

$$\text{Elasticity} = \text{Slope}\left(\frac{X}{Y}\right)$$

That is, elasticity is equal to the product of the slope and the ratio of X to Y, where X = the price and Y = the quantity. From the regression results presented earlier, can you tell what the price elasticity of demand for coffee is? If not, what additional information would you need to compute the price elasticity?

2.12. Table 2-9 gives data on the Consumer Price Index (CPI) for all items (1982–1984 = 100) and the Standard & Poor's (S&P) index of 500 common stock prices (base of index: 1941–1943 = 10).

TABLE 2-9   CONSUMER PRICE INDEX (CPI) AND S&P 500 INDEX (S&P), UNITED STATES, 1978–1989

Year	CPI	S&P
1978	65.2	96.02
1979	72.6	103.01
1980	82.4	118.78
1981	90.9	128.05
1982	96.5	119.71
1983	99.6	160.41
1984	103.9	160.46
1985	107.6	186.84
1986	109.6	236.34
1987	113.6	286.83
1988	118.3	265.79
1989	124.0	322.84

Source: Economic Report of the President, 1990, Table C-58, for CPI and Table C-93 for the S&P index.

a. Plot the data on a scattergram with the S&P index on the vertical axis and CPI on the horizontal axis.

b. What can you say about the relationship between the two indexes? What does economic theory have to say about this relationship?

c. Consider the following regression model:

$$(S\&P)_t = B_1 + B_2 CPI_t + u_t$$

Use the method of least squares to estimate this equation from the preceding data and interpret your results.

d. Do the results obtained in part (c) make economic sense?

e. Do you know why the S&P index dropped in 1988?

2.13. Table 2-10 gives data on the nominal interest rate (Y) and the inflation rate (X) for the year 1988 for nine industrial countries.

TABLE 2-10   NOMINAL INTEREST RATE (Y) AND INFLATION (X) IN NINE INDUSTRIAL COUNTRIES FOR THE YEAR 1988

Country	Y (%)	X (%)
Australia	11.9	7.7
Canada	9.4	4.0
France	7.5	3.1
Germany	4.0	1.6
Italy	11.3	4.8
Mexico	66.3	51.7
Switzerland	2.2	2.0
United Kingdom	10.3	6.8
United States	7.6	4.4

Source: Rudiger Dornbusch and Stanley Fischer, *Macroeconomics,* 5th ed., McGraw-Hill, New York, 1990, p. 652. The original data are from various issues of *International Financial Statistics,* published by the International Monetary Fund (IMF).

a. Plot these data with the interest rate on the vertical axis and the inflation rate on the horizontal axis. What does the scattergram reveal?

b. Do an OLS regression of Y on X. Present all your calculations.

c. If the real interest rate is to remain constant, what must be the relationship between the nominal interest rate and the inflation rate? That is, what must be the value of the slope coefficient in the regression of Y on X and that of the intercept? Do your results suggest that this is the case? For a theoretical discussion of the relationship among the nominal interest rate, the inflation rate, and the real interest rate, see any textbook on macroeconomics and look up the topic of the Fisher equation, named after the famous American economist, Irving Fisher.

2.14. The real exchange rate (RE) is defined as the nominal exchange rate (NE) times the ratio of the domestic price to foreign price. Thus, RE for the United States against UK is

$$RE_{US} = NE_{US}(US_{CPI}/UK_{CPI})$$

a. From the data given in Table 1-3 of Problem 1.7, compute RE_{US}.

b. Using a regression package you are familiar with, estimate the following regression:

$$NE_{US} = B_1 + B_2 RE_{US} + u \tag{1}$$

c. A priori, what do you expect the relationship between the nominal and real exchange rates to be? You may want to read up on the purchasing power parity (PPP) theory from any text on international trade or macroeconomics.

d. Are the a priori expectations supported by your regression results? If not, what might be the reason?

*e. Run regression (1) in the following alternative form:

$$\ln NE_{US} = A_1 + A_2 \ln RE_{US} + u \qquad (2)$$

where ln stands for the natural logarithm, that is, log to the base e. Interpret the results of this regression. Are the results from regressions (1) and (2) qualitatively the same?

2.15. Refer to problem 2.12. In Table 2-11 we have data on CPI and the S&P 500 index for the years 1990 to 2007.

TABLE 2-11   CONSUMER PRICE INDEX (CPI) AND S&P 500 INDEX (S&P), UNITED STATES, 1990–2007

Year	CPI	S&P
1990	130.7	334.59
1991	136.2	376.18
1992	140.3	415.74
1993	144.5	451.41
1994	148.2	460.42
1995	152.4	541.72
1996	156.9	670.50
1997	160.5	873.43
1998	163.0	1085.50
1999	166.6	1327.33
2000	172.2	1427.22
2001	177.1	1194.18
2002	179.9	993.94
2003	184.0	965.23
2004	188.9	1130.65
2005	195.3	1207.23
2006	201.6	1310.46
2007	207.3	1477.19

Source: Economic Report of the President, 2008.

a. Repeat questions (*a*) to (*e*) from problem 2.12.

b. Do you see any difference in the estimated regressions?

c. Now combine the two sets of data and estimate the regression of the S&P index on the CPI.

d. Are there noticeable differences in the three regressions?

2.16. Table 2-12, found on the textbook's Web site, gives data on average starting pay (ASP), grade point average (GPA) scores (on a scale of 1 to 4), GMAT scores, annual tuition, percent of graduates employed at graduation, recruiter assessment score (5.0 highest), and percent of applicants accepted in the graduate business school for 47 well-regarded business schools in the United States for the year 2007–2008. *Note:* Northwestern University ranked 4th (in a tie with MIT and University of Chicago) but was removed from the data set because there was no information available about percent of applicants accepted.

a. Using a bivariate regression model, find out if GPA has any effect on ASP.

b. Using a suitable regression model, find out if GMAT scores have any relationship to ASP.

*Optional.

    c. Does annual tuition have any relationship to ASP? How do you know? If there is a positive relationship between the two, does that mean it pays to go to the most expensive business school? Can you argue that a high-tuition business school means a high-quality MBA program? Why or why not?

    d. Does the recruiter perception have any bearing on ASP?

2.17. Table 2-13 (found on the textbook's Web site) gives data on real GDP (Y) and civilian unemployment rate (X) for the United States for period 1960 to 2006.

    a. Estimate Okun's law in the form of Eq. (2.22). Are the regression results similar to the ones shown in (2.22)? Does this suggest that Okun's law is universally valid?

    b. Now regress percentage change in real GDP on change in the civilian unemployment rate and interpret your regression results.

    c. If the unemployment rate remains unchanged, what is the expected (percent) rate of growth in real GDP? (Use the regression in [b]). How would you interpret this growth rate?

2.18. Refer to Example 2.3, for which the data are as shown in Table 2-6 (on the textbook's Web site).

    a. Using a statistical package of your choice, confirm the regression results given in Eq. (2.24) and Eq. (2.25).

    b. For both regressions, get the estimated values of Y (i.e., $\hat{Y}_i$) and compare them with the actual Y values in the sample. Also obtain the residual values, e_i. From this can you tell which is a better model, Eq. (2.24) or Eq. (2.25)?

2.19. Refer to Example 2.5 on antique clock prices. Table 2-14 gives the underlying data.

    a. Plot clock prices against the age of the clock and against the number of bidders. Does this plot suggest that the linear regression models shown in Eq. (2.27) and Eq. (2.28) may be appropriate?

TABLE 2-14 AUCTION DATA ON PRICE, AGE OF CLOCK, AND NUMBER OF BIDDERS

Observations	Price	Age	Number of bidders	Observations	Price	Age	Number of bidders
1	1235	127	13	17	854	143	6
2	1080	115	12	18	1483	159	9
3	845	127	7	19	1055	108	14
4	1552	150	9	20	1545	175	8
5	1047	156	6	21	729	108	6
6	1979	182	11	22	1792	179	9
7	1822	156	12	23	1175	111	15
8	1253	132	10	24	1593	187	8
9	1297	137	9	25	1147	137	8
10	946	113	9	26	1092	153	6
11	1713	137	15	27	1152	117	13
12	1024	117	11	28	1336	126	10
13	2131	170	14	29	785	111	7
14	1550	182	8	30	744	115	7
15	1884	162	11	31	1356	194	5
16	2041	184	10	32	1262	168	7

b. Would it make any sense to plot the number of bidders against the age of the clock? What would such a plot reveal?

2.20. Refer to the math S.A.T. score example discussed in the text. Table 2-4 gives the necessary raw calculations to obtain the OLS estimators. Look at the columns Y (actual Y) and $\hat{Y}$ (estimated Y) values. Plot the two in a scattergram. What does the scattergram reveal? If you believe that the fitted model [Eq. (2.20)] is a "good" model, what should be the shape of the scattergram? In the next chapter we will see what we mean by a "good" model.

2.21. Table 2-15 (on the textbook's Web site) gives data on verbal and math S.A.T. scores for both males and females for the period 1972–2007.

    a. You want to predict the male math score (Y) on the basis of the male verbal score (X). Develop a suitable linear regression model and estimate its parameters.

    b. Interpret your regression results.

    c. Reverse the roles of Y and X and regress the verbal score on the math score. Interpret this regression

    d. Let a_2 be the slope coefficient in the regression of the math score on the verbal score and let b_2 be the slope coefficient of the verbal score on the math score. Multiply these two values. Compare the resulting value with the r^2 obtained from the regression of math score on verbal score or the r^2 value obtained from the regression of verbal score on math score. What conclusion can you draw from this exercise?

2.22. Table 2-16 (on the textbook's Web site) gives data on investment rate (ipergdp) and savings rate (spergdp), both measured as percent of GDP, for a cross-section of countries. These rates are averages for the period 1960–1974.*

    a. Plot the investment rate on the vertical axis and the savings rate on the horizontal axis.

    b. Eyeball a suitable curve from the scatter diagram in (*a*).

    c. Now estimate the following model

$$\text{ipergdp}_i = B_1 + B_2 \, \text{spergdp}_i + u_i$$

    d. Interpret the estimated coefficients.

    e. What general conclusion do you draw from your analysis?

    Note: Save your results for further analysis in the next chapter.

OPTIONAL QUESTIONS

2.23. Prove that $\Sigma e_i = 0$, and hence show that $\bar{e} = 0$.

2.24. Prove that $\Sigma e_i x_i = 0$.

2.25. Prove that $\Sigma e_i \hat{Y}_i = 0$, that is, that the sum of the product of residuals e_i and the estimated Y_i is always zero.

2.26. Prove that $\overline{Y} = \hat{\overline{Y}}$, that is, that the means of the actual Y values and the estimated Y values are the same.

*Source of data: Martin Feldstein and Charles Horioka, "Domestic Savings and International Capital Flows," *Economic Journal,* vol. 90, June 1980, pp. 314–329.

2.27. Prove that $\sum x_i y_i = \sum x_i y_i = \sum x_i y_i$, where $x_i = (X_i - \overline{X})$ and $y_i = (Y_i - \overline{Y})$.

2.28. Prove that $\sum x_i = \sum y_i = 0$, where x_i and y_i are as defined in Problem 2.27.

2.29. For the math S.A.T. score example data given in Table 2-4, verify that statements made in Question 2.23 hold true (save the rounding errors).

APPENDIX 2A: Derivation of Least-Squares Estimates

We start with Eq. (2.13):

$$\sum e_i^2 = \sum (Y_i - b_1 - b_2 X_1)^2 \tag{2A.1}$$

Using the technique of *partial differentiation* from calculus, we obtain:

$$\partial \sum e_i^2 / \partial b_1 = 2 \sum (Y_i - b_1 - b_2 X_i)(-1) \tag{2A.2}$$

$$\partial \sum e_i^2 / \partial b_2 = 2 \sum (Y_i - b_1 - b_2 X_i)(-X_i) \tag{2A.3}$$

By the first order condition of optimization, we set these two derivations to zero and simplify, which will give

$$\sum Y_i = nb_1 + b_2 \sum X_i \tag{2A.4}$$

$$\sum Y_i X_i = b_1 \sum X_i + b_2 \sum X_i^2 \tag{2A.5}$$

which are Eqs. (2.14) and (2.15), respectively, given in the text.

Solving these two equations simultaneously, we get the formulas given in Eqs. (2.16) and (2.17).

CHAPTER 3

THE TWO-VARIABLE MODEL: HYPOTHESIS TESTING

In Chapter 2 we showed how the method of least squares works. By applying that method to our math S.A.T. sample data given in Table 2-2, we obtained the following math S.A.T. score function:

$$\hat{Y}_i = 432.4138 + 0.0013X_i \qquad \textbf{(2.20)}$$

where Y represents math S.A.T. score and X represents annual family income, measured in dollars.

This example illustrated the estimation stage of statistical inference. We now turn our attention to its other stage, namely, hypothesis testing. The important question that we raise is: How "good" is the estimated regression line given in Equation (2.20)? That is, how can we tell that it really is a good estimator of the true population regression function (PRF)? How can we be sure just on the basis of a single sample given in Table 2-2 that the estimated regression function (i.e., the sample regression function [SRF]) is in fact a good approximation of the true PRF?

We cannot answer this question definitely unless we are a little more specific about our PRF, Eq. (2.2). As Eq. (2.2) shows, Y_i depends on both X_i and u_i. Now we have assumed that the X_i values are known or given—recall from Chapter 2 that our analysis is a conditional regression analysis, conditional upon the given X's. In short, we treat the X values as *nonstochastic*. The (nonobservable) error term u is of course random, or stochastic. (Why?) Since a stochastic term (u) is added to a nonstochastic term (X) to generate Y, Y becomes stochastic, too. This means that unless we are willing to assume how the stochastic u terms are generated, we will not be able to tell how good an SRF is as an estimate of the true PRF.

In deriving the ordinary least squares (OLS) estimators so far, we did not say how the u_i were generated, for the derivation of OLS estimators did not depend on any (probabilistic) assumption about the error term. But in testing statistical hypotheses based on the SRF, we cannot make further progress, as we will show shortly, unless we make some specific assumptions about how u_i are generated. This is precisely what the so-called **classical linear regression model (CLRM)** does, which we will now discuss. Again, to explain the fundamental ideas, we consider the two-variable regression model introduced in Chapter 2. In Chapter 4 we extend the ideas developed here to the multiple regression models.

3.1 THE CLASSICAL LINEAR REGRESSION MODEL

The CLRM makes the following assumptions:

A3.1.

The regression model is *linear in the parameters*; it may or may not be linear in the variables. That is, the regression model is of the following type.

$$Y_i = B_1 + B_2X_i + u_i \qquad (2.2)$$

As will be discussed in Chapter 4, this model can be extended to include more explanatory variables.

A3.2.

The explanatory variable(s) X is uncorrelated with the disturbance term u. However, if the X variable(s) is *nonstochastic* (i.e., its value is a fixed number), this assumption is automatically fulfilled. Even if the X value(s) is stochastic, with a large enough sample size this assumption can be related without severely affecting the analysis.[1]

This assumption is not a new assumption because in Chapter 2 we stated that our regression analysis is a *conditional regression analysis,* conditional upon the given X values. In essence, we are assuming that the X's are nonstochastic. Assumption (3.1) is made to deal with simultaneous equation regression models, which we will discuss in Chapter 11.

A3.3.

Given the value of X_i, the expected, or mean, value of the disturbance term u is zero. That is,

$$E(u \mid X_i) = 0 \qquad (3.1)$$

Recall our discussion in Chapter 2 about the nature of the random term u_i. It represents all those factors that are not specifically introduced in the model.

---

[1]For further discussion, see Gujarati and Porter, *Basic Econometrics,* 5th ed., McGraw-Hill, New York, 2009.

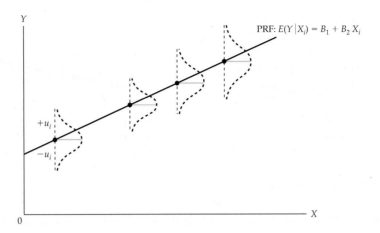

FIGURE 3-1   Conditional distribution of disturbances u_i

What Assumption (3.1) states is that these other factors or forces are not related to X_i (the variable explicitly introduced in the model) and therefore, given the value of X_i, *their mean value is zero.*[2] This is shown in Figure 3-1.

A3.4.

The variance of each u_i is constant, or **homoscedastic** (*homo* means equal and *scedastic* means variance). That is

$$\text{var}(u_i) = \sigma^2 \qquad\qquad (3.2)$$

Geometrically, this assumption is as shown in Figure 3-2(*a*). This assumption simply means that the conditional distribution of each Y population corresponding to the given value of X has the same variance; that is, the individual Y values are spread around their mean values with the same variance.[3] If this is not the case, then we have **heteroscedasticity,** or **unequal variance,** which is depicted in Figure 3-2(*b*).[4] As this figure shows, the variance of each Y population is different, which is in contrast to Figure 3-2(*a*), where each Y population has the same variance. The CLRM assumes that the variance of u is as shown in Figure 3-2(*a*).

---

[2]Note that Assumption (3.2) only states that X and u are uncorrelated. Assumption (3.3) adds that not only are X and u uncorrelated, but also that given the value of X, the mean of u (which represents umpteen factors) is zero.

[3]Since the X values are assumed to be given, or nonstochastic, the only source of variation in Y is from u. Therefore, given X_i, the variance of Y_i is the same as that of u_i. In short, the conditional variances of u_i and Y_i are the same, namely, σ^2. Note, however, that the unconditional variance of Y_i, as shown in Appendix B, is $E[Y_i - E(Y)]^2$. As we will see, if the variable X has any impact on Y, the conditional variance of Y will be smaller than the unconditional variance of Y. Incidentally, the sample counterpart of the unconditional variance of Y is $\Sigma(Y_i - \bar{Y})^2/(n-1)$.

[4]There is a debate in the literature regarding whether it is homoscedasticity or homoskedasticity and heteroscedasticity or heteroskedasticty. Both seem to be acceptable.

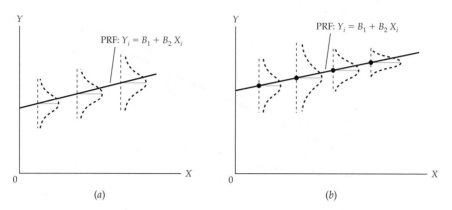

FIGURE 3-2   (a) Homoscedasticity (equal variance); (b) Heteroscedasticity (unequal variance)

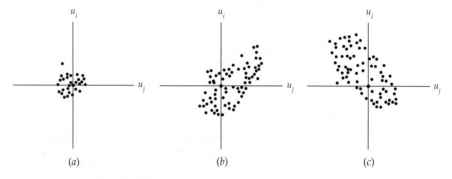

FIGURE 3-3   Patterns of autocorrelation: (a) No autocorrelation; (b) positive autocorrelation; (c) negative autocorrelation

A3.5.

There is no correlation between two error terms. This is the assumption of **no autocorrelation.**

Algebraically, this assumption can be written as

$$\text{cov}\,(u_i, u_j) = 0 \quad i \neq j \tag{3.3}$$

Here *cov* stands for covariance (see Appendix B) and i and j are any two error terms. (*Note:* If $i = j$, Equation (3.3) will give the variance of u, which by Eq. (3.2) is a constant).

Geometrically, Eq. (3.3) can be shown in Figure 3-3.

Assumption (3.5) means that there is no systematic relationship between two error terms. It does not mean that if one u is above the mean value, another error term u will also be above the mean value (for positive correlation), or that if one error term is below the mean value, another error term has to be above the mean value, or vice versa (negative correlation). In short, the assumption of no autocorrelation means the error terms u_i are random.

Since any two error terms are assumed to be uncorrelated, it means that any two Y values will also be uncorrelated; that is, $\text{cov}(Y_i, Y_j) = 0$. This is because $Y_i = B_1 + B_2 X_i + u_i$ and given that the B's are fixed numbers and that X is assumed to be fixed, Y will vary as u varies. So, if the u's are uncorrelated, the Y's will be uncorrelated also.

A3.6.

The regression model is correctly specified. Alternatively, there is no *specification bias* or *specification error* in the model used in empirical analysis.

What this assumption implies is that we have included all the variables that affect a particular phenomenon. Thus, if we are studying the demand for automobiles, if we only include prices of automobiles and consumer income and do not take into account variables such as advertising, financing costs, and gasoline prices, we will be committing model specification errors. Of course, it is not easy to determine the "correct" model in any given case, but we will provide some guidelines in Chapter 7.

You might wonder about all these assumptions. Why are they needed? How realistic are they? What happens if they are not true? How do we know that a particular regression model in fact satisfies all these assumptions? Although these questions are certainly pertinent, at this stage of the development of our subject matter, we cannot provide totally satisfactory answers to all of them. However, as we progress through the book, we will see the utility of these assumptions. As a matter of fact, all of Part II is devoted to finding out what happens if one or more of the assumptions of CLRM are not fulfilled.

But keep in mind that in any scientific inquiry we make certain assumptions because they facilitate the development of the subject matter in gradual steps, not because they are necessarily realistic. An analogy might help here. Students of economics are generally introduced to the model of perfect competition before they are introduced to the models of imperfect competition. This is done because the implications derived from this model enable us to better appreciate the models of imperfect competition, not because the model of perfect competition is necessarily realistic, although there are markets that may be reasonably perfectly competitive, such as the stock market or the foreign exchange market.

3.2 VARIANCES AND STANDARD ERRORS OF ORDINARY LEAST SQUARES ESTIMATORS

One immediate result of the assumptions just introduced is that they enable us to estimate the variances and standard errors of the ordinary least squares (OLS) estimators given in Eqs. (2.16) and (2.17). In Appendix D we discuss the basics of estimation theory, including the notions of (point) estimators, their sampling distributions, and the concepts of the variance and standard error of the estimators. Based on our knowledge of those concepts, we know that the

OLS estimators given in Eqs. (2.16) and (2.17) are *random variables,* for their values will change from sample to sample. Naturally, we would like to know something about the sampling variability of these estimators, that is, how they vary from sample to sample. These sampling variabilities, as we know now, are measured by the variances of these estimators, or by their *standard errors* (se), which are the square roots of the variances. The **variances** and **standard errors of the OLS estimators** given in Eqs. (2.16) and (2.17) are as follows:[5]

$$\text{var } (b_1) = \sigma_{b_1}^2 = \frac{\sum X_i^2}{n \sum x_i^2} \cdot \sigma^2 \tag{3.4}$$

(*Note:* This formula involves both small x and capital X.)

$$\text{se } (b_1) = \sqrt{\text{var } (b_1)} \tag{3.5}$$

$$\text{var } (b_2) = \sigma_{b_2}^2 = \frac{\sigma^2}{\sum x_i^2} \tag{3.6}$$

$$\text{se } (b_2) = \sqrt{\text{var } (b_2)} \tag{3.7}$$

where var = the variance and se = the standard error, and where σ^2 is the variance of the disturbance term u_i, which by the assumption of homoscedasticity is assumed to be the same for each u.

Once σ^2 is known, then all the terms on the right-hand sides of the preceding equations can be easily computed, which will give us the numerical values of the variances and standard errors of the OLS estimators. The homoscedastic σ^2 is estimated from the following formula:

$$\hat{\sigma}^2 = \frac{\sum e_i^2}{n - 2} \tag{3.8}$$

where $\hat{\sigma}^2$ is an estimator of σ^2 (recall we use ^ to indicate an estimator) and $\sum e_i^2$ is the **residual sum of squares (RSS),** that is, $\sum (Y_i - \hat{Y}_i)^2$, the sum of the squared difference between the actual Y and the estimated Y. (See the next to the last column of Table 2-4.)

The expression $(n - 2)$ is known as the *degrees of freedom* (d.f.), which, as noted in Appendix C, is simply the number of independent observations.[6]

Once e_i is computed, as shown in Table 2-4, $\sum e_i^2$ can be computed easily. Incidentally, in passing, note that

$$\hat{\sigma} = \sqrt{\hat{\sigma}^2} \tag{3.9}$$

---

[5]The proofs can be found in Gujarati and Porter, *Basic Econometrics,* 5th ed., McGraw-Hill, New York, 2009, pp. 93–94.

[6]Notice that we can compute e_i only when $\hat{Y}_i$ is computed. But to compute the latter, we must first obtain b_1 and b_2. In estimating these two unknowns, we lose 2 d.f. Therefore, although we have n observations, the d.f. are only $(n - 2)$.

TABLE 3-1   COMPUTATIONS FOR THE S.A.T. EXAMPLE

Estimator	Formula	Answer	Equation number
$\hat{\sigma}^2$	$\sum\left(\dfrac{e_i^2}{n-2}\right)$	975.1347	(3.10)
$\hat{\sigma}$	$\sqrt{\hat{\sigma}^2} = \sqrt{975.1347}$	31.2271	(3.11)
var (b_1)	$\left(\dfrac{\sum x_i^2}{n\sum x_i^2}\right)\sigma^2 = \dfrac{4.76 \times 10^{10}}{10(1.624 \times 10^{11})}(975.1347)$	285.8153	(3.12)
se (b_1)	$\sqrt{\text{var}(b_1)} = \sqrt{285.8153}$	16.9061	(3.13)
var (b_2)	$\dfrac{\sigma^2}{\sum x_i^2} = \dfrac{975.1347}{1.624 \times 10^{11}}$	6.0045×10^{-9}	(3.14)
se (b_2)	$\sqrt{\text{var}(b_2)} = \sqrt{6.0045 \times 10^{-9}}$	0.0000775	(3.15)

Note: The raw data underlying the calculations are given in Table 2-4. In computing the variances of the estimators, σ^2 has been replaced by its estimator, $\hat{\sigma}^2$.

which is known as the **standard error of the regression (SER)**, which is simply the standard deviation of the Y values about the estimated regression line.[7] This standard error of regression is often used as a summary measure of the *goodness of fit* of the estimated regression line, a topic discussed in Section 3.6. As you would suspect, the smaller the value of $\hat{\sigma}$, the closer the actual Y value is to its estimated value from the regression model.

Variances and Standard Errors of the Math S.A.T. Score Example

Using the preceding formulas, let us compute the variances and standard errors of our math S.A.T. score example. These calculations are presented in Table 3-1. (See Eqs. [3.10] to [3.15] therein.)

Summary of the Math S.A.T. Score Function

Let us express the estimated S.A.T. score function in the following form:

$$\hat{Y}_i = 432.4138 + 0.0013X_i$$

$$\text{se} = (16.9061)(0.000245)$$

(3.16)

where the figures in parentheses are the estimated standard errors. Regression results are sometimes presented in this format (but more on this in Section 3.8). Such a presentation indicates immediately the estimated parameters and their

---

[7]Note the difference between the standard error of regression $\hat{\sigma}$ and the standard deviation of Y. The latter is measured, as usual, from its mean value, as $S_y = \sqrt{\dfrac{\sum(Y_i - \bar{Y})^2}{n-1}}$, whereas the former is measured from the estimated value (i.e., $\hat{Y}_i$ from the sample regression). See also footnote 3.

standard errors. For example, it tells us that the estimated slope coefficient of the math S.A.T. score function (i.e., the coefficient of the annual family income variable) is 0.0013 and its standard deviation, or standard error, is 0.000245. This is a measure of variability of b_2 from sample to sample.

What use can we make of this finding? Can we say, for example, that our computed b_2 lies within a certain number of standard deviation units from the true B_2? If we can do that, we can state with some confidence (i.e., probability) how good the computed SRF, Equation (3.16), is as an estimate of the true PRF. This is, of course, the topic of hypothesis testing.

But before discussing hypothesis testing, we need a bit more theory. In particular, since b_1 and b_2 are random variables, we must find their **sampling, or probability, distributions.** Recall from Appendixes C and D that a random variable (r.v.) has a probability distribution associated with it. Once we determine the sampling distributions of our two estimators, as we will show in Section 3.4, the task of hypothesis testing becomes straightforward. But even before that we answer an important question: Why do we use the OLS method?

3.3 WHY OLS? THE PROPERTIES OF OLS ESTIMATORS

The method of OLS is used popularly not only because it is easy to use but also because it has some strong theoretical properties, which are summarized in the well-known **Gauss-Markov theorem.**

Gauss-Markov Theorem

Given the assumptions of the classical linear regression model, the OLS estimators have minimum variance in the class of linear estimators; that is, they are **BLUE** (best linear unbiased estimators).

We provide an overview of the **BLUE property** in Appendix D. In short, the OLS estimators have the following properties:[8]

1. b_1 and b_2 are linear estimators; that is, they are linear functions of the random variable Y, which is evident from Equations (2.16) and (2.17).
2. They are unbiased; that is, $E(b_1) = B_1$ and $E(b_2) = B_2$. Therefore, in repeated applications, on average, b_1 and b_2 will coincide with their true values B_1 and B_2, respectively.
3. $E(\hat{\sigma}^2) = \sigma^2$ that is, the OLS estimator of the error variance is unbiased. In repeated applications, on average, the estimated value of the error variance will converge to its true value.
4. b_1 and b_2 are *efficient* estimators; that is, var (b_1) is less than the variance of any other linear unbiased estimator of B_1, and var (b_2) is less than the

---

[8]For proof, see Gujarati and Porter, *Basic Econometrics,* 5th ed., McGraw-Hill, New York, 2009, pp. 95–96.

variance of any other linear unbiased estimator of B_2. Therefore, we will be able to estimate the true B_1 and B_2 more precisely if we use OLS rather than any other method that also gives linear unbiased estimators of the true parameters.

The upshot of the preceding discussion is that the OLS estimators possess many desirable statistical properties that we discuss in Appendix D. It is for this reason that the OLS method has been used popularly in regression analysis, as well as for its intuitive appeal and ease of use.

Monte Carlo Experiment

In theory the OLS estimators are unbiased, but how do we know that in practice this is the case? To find out, let us conduct the following Monte Carlo experiment.

Assume that we are given the following information:

$$Y_i = B_1 + B_2 X_i + u_i$$
$$= 1.5 + 2.0 X_i + u_i$$

where $u_i \sim N(0, 4)$.

That is, we are told that the true values of the intercept and slope coefficients are 1.5 and 2.0, respectively, and that the error term follows the normal distribution with a mean of zero and a variance of 4. Now suppose you are given 10 values of X: 1, 2, 3, 4, 5, 6, 7, 8, 9, 10.

Given this information, you can proceed as follows. Using any statistical package, you generate 10 values of u_i from a normal distribution with mean zero and variance 4. Given B_1, B_2, the 10 values of X, and the 10 values of u_i generated from the normal distribution, you will then obtain 10 values of Y from the preceding equation. Call this experiment or sample number 1. Go to the normal distribution table, collect another 10 values of u_i, generate another 10 values of Y, and call it sample number 2. In this manner obtain 21 samples.

For each sample of 10 values, regress Y_i generated above on the X values and obtain b_1, b_2, and $\hat{\sigma}^2$. Repeat this exercise for all 21 samples. Therefore, you will have 21 values each of b_1, b_2, and $\hat{\sigma}^2$. We conducted this experiment and obtained the results shown in Table 3-2.

From the data given in this table, we have computed the mean, or average, values of b_1, b_2, and $\hat{\sigma}^2$, which are, respectively, 1.4526, 1.9665, and 4.4743, whereas the true values of the corresponding coefficients, as we know, are 1.5, 2.0, and 4.0.

What conclusion can we draw from this experiment? It seems that if we apply the method of least squares time and again, *on average,* the values of the estimated parameters will be equal to their true (population parameter) values. That is, OLS estimators are unbiased. In the present example, had we conducted more than 21 sampling experiments, we would have come much closer to the true values.

TABLE 3-2 MONTE CARLO EXPERIMENT: $Y_i = 1.5 + 2X_i + u_i$;
$u \sim N(0, 4)$

b_1	b_2	$\hat{\sigma}^2$
2.247	1.840	2.7159
0.360	2.090	7.1663
−2.483	2.558	3.3306
0.220	2.180	2.0794
3.070	1.620	4.3932
2.570	1.830	7.1770
2.551	1.928	5.7552
0.060	2.070	3.6176
−2.170	2.537	3.4708
1.470	2.020	4.4479
2.540	1.970	2.1756
2.340	1.960	2.8291
0.775	2.050	1.5252
3.020	1.740	1.5104
0.810	1.940	4.7830
1.890	1.890	7.3658
2.760	1.820	1.8036
−0.136	2.130	1.8796
0.950	2.030	4.9908
2.960	1.840	4.5514
3.430	1.740	5.2258
$\bar{b}_1 = 1.4526$	$\bar{b}_2 = 1.9665$	$\bar{\hat{\sigma}}^2 = 4.4743$

3.4 THE SAMPLING, OR PROBABILITY, DISTRIBUTIONS OF OLS ESTIMATORS

Now that we have seen how to compute the OLS estimators and their standard errors and have examined some of the properties of these estimators, we need to find the sampling distributions of these estimators. Without that knowledge we will not be able to engage in hypothesis testing. The general notion of sampling distribution of an estimator is discussed in Appendix C (see Section C.2).

To derive the sampling distributions of the OLS estimators b_1 and b_2, we need to add one more assumption to the list of assumptions of the CLRM. This assumption is

A3.7.

In the PRF $Y_i = B_1 + B_2X_i + u_i$ the error term u_i follows the *normal distribution* with mean zero and variance σ^2. That is,

$$u_i \sim N(0, \sigma^2) \qquad \textbf{(3.17)}$$

What is the rationale for this assumption? There is a celebrated theorem in statistics, known as the **central limit theorem (CLT)**, which we discuss in Appendix C (see Section C.1), which states that:

Central Limit Theorem

If there is a large number of independent and identically distributed random variables, then, with a few exceptions,[9] the distribution of their sum tends to be a normal distribution as the number of such variables increases indefinitely.

Recall from Chapter 2 our discussion about the nature of the error term, u_i. As shown in Section 2.4, the error term represents the influence of all those forces that affect Y but are not specifically included in the regression model because there are so many of them and the individual effect of any one such force (i.e., variable) on Y may be too minor. If all these forces are random, and if we let u represent the sum of all these forces, then by invoking the CLT we can assume that the error term u follows the normal distribution. We have already assumed that the mean value of u_i is zero and that its variance, following the homoscedasticity assumption, is the constant σ^2. Hence, we have Equation (3.17).

But how does the assumption that u follows the normal distribution help us to find out the probability distributions of b_1 and b_2? Here we make use of another property of the normal distribution discussed in Appendix C, namely, *any linear function of a normally distributed variable is itself normally distributed.* Does this mean that if we prove that b_1 and b_2 are linear functions of the normally distributed variable u_i, they themselves are normally distributed? That's right! You can indeed prove that these two OLS estimators are in fact linear functions of the normally distributed u_i. (For proof, see Exercise 3.24).[10]

Now we know from Appendix C that a normally distributed r.v. has two parameters, the mean and the variance. What are the parameters of the normally distributed b_1 and b_2? They are as follows:

$$b_1 \sim N\left(B_1, \sigma_{b_1}^2\right) \tag{3.18}$$

$$b_2 \sim N\left(B_2, \sigma_{b_2}^2\right) \tag{3.19}$$

where the variances of b_1 and b_2 are as given in Eq. (3.4) and Eq. (3.6).

In short, b_1 and b_2 each follow the normal distribution with their means equal to true B_1 and B_2 and their variances given by Eqs. (3.4) and (3.6) developed previously. Geometrically, the distributions of these estimators are as shown in Figure 3-4.

---

[9]One exception is the Cauchy probability distribution, which has no mean or variance.
[10]It may also be noted that since $Y_i = B_1 + B_2X_i + u_i$ if $u_i \sim N(0, \sigma^2)$, then $Y_i \sim N(B_1 + B_2X_i, \sigma^2)$ because Y_i is a linear combination of u_i. (Note that B_1, B_2 are constants and X_i fixed).

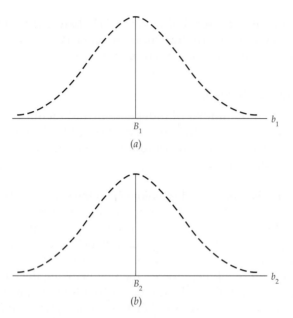

FIGURE 3-4   (Normal) sampling distributions of b_1 and b_2

3.5 HYPOTHESIS TESTING

Recall that estimation and hypothesis testing are the two main branches of statistical inference. In Chapter 2 we showed how OLS helps us to estimate the parameters of linear regression models. In this chapter the classical framework enabled us to examine some of the properties of OLS estimators. With the added assumption that the error term u_i is normally distributed, we were able to find the sampling (or probability) distributions of the OLS estimators, namely, the normal distribution. With this knowledge we are now equipped to deal with the topic of hypothesis testing in the context of regression analysis.

Let us return to our math S.A.T. example. The estimated math S.A.T. score function is given in Eq. (2.20). Suppose someone suggests that annual family income has no relationship to a student's math S.A.T. score.

$$H_0 : B_2 = 0$$

In applied regression analysis such a **"zero" null hypothesis,** the so-called **straw man hypothesis,** is deliberately chosen to find out whether Y is related to X at all. If there is no relationship between Y and X to begin with, then testing a hypothesis that $B_2 = -2$ or any other value is meaningless. Of course, if the zero null hypothesis is sustainable, there is no point at all in including X in the model. Therefore, if X really belongs in the model, you would fully expect to reject the zero null hypothesis H_0 in favor of the *alternative hypothesis H_1,* which says, for example, that $B_2 \neq 0$; that is, the slope coefficient is different from zero. It could be positive or it could be negative.

Our numerical results show that $b_2 = 0.0013$. You would therefore expect that the zero null hypothesis is not tenable in this case. But we cannot look at the numerical results alone, for we know that because of sampling fluctuations, the numerical value will change from sample to sample. Obviously, we need some formal testing procedure to reject or not reject the null hypothesis. How do we proceed?

This should not be a problem now, for in Equation (3.19) we have shown that b_2 follows the *normal distribution* with mean = B_2 and $\text{var}(b_2) = \sigma^2 / \sum x_i^2$. Then, following our discussion about hypothesis testing in Appendix D, Section D.5, we can use either:

1. The confidence interval approach or
2. The test of significance approach

to test any hypotheses about B_2 as well as B_1.

Since b_2 follows the normal distribution, with the mean and the variance stated in expression (3.19), we know that

$$Z = \frac{b_2 - B_2}{\text{se}(b_2)}$$

$$= \frac{b_2 - B_2}{\sigma \Big/ \sqrt{\sum x_i^2}} \sim N(0, 1) \tag{3.20}$$

follows the *standard normal distribution*. From Appendix C we know the properties of the standard normal distribution, particularly, the property that ≈ 95 percent of the area of the normal distribution lies within two standard deviation units of the mean value, where $\approx$ means approximately. Therefore, if our null hypothesis is $B_2 = 0$ and the computed $b_2 = 0.0013$, we can find out the probability of obtaining such a value from the Z, or standard normal, distribution (Appendix E, Table E-1). If this probability is very small, we can reject the null hypothesis, but if it is large, say, greater than 10 percent, we may not reject the null hypothesis. All this is familiar material from Appendixes C and D.

But, there is a hitch! To use Equation (3.20) we must know the true σ^2. This is not known, but we can estimate it by using $\hat{\sigma}^2$ given in Eq. (3.8). However, if we replace σ in Eq. (3.20) by its estimator $\hat{\sigma}$, then, as shown in Appendix C, Eq. (C.8), the right-hand side of Eq. (3.20) follows the *t distribution* with $(n - 2)$ d.f., not the standard normal distribution; that is,

$$\frac{b_2 - B_2}{\hat{\sigma} \Big/ \sqrt{\sum x_i^2}} \sim t_{n-2} \tag{3.21}$$

Or, more generally,

$$\frac{b_2 - B_2}{\text{se}(b_2)} \sim t_{n-2} \tag{3.22}$$

Note that we lose 2 d.f. in computing $\hat{\sigma}^2$ for reasons stated earlier.

Therefore, to test the null hypothesis in the present case, we have to use the t distribution in lieu of the (standard) normal distribution. But the procedure of hypothesis testing remains the same, as explained in Appendix D.

Testing $H_0:B_2 = 0$ versus $H_1: B_2 \neq 0$: The Confidence Interval Approach

For our math S.A.T. example we have 10 observations, hence the d.f. are $(10 - 2) = 8$. Let us assume that α, the level of significance or the probability of committing a type I error, is fixed at 5 percent. Since the alternative hypothesis is two-sided, from the t table given in Appendix E, Table E-2, we find that for 8 d.f.,

$$P(-2.306 \leq t \leq 2.306) = 0.95 \qquad \textbf{(3.23)}$$

That is, the probability that a t value (for 8 d.f.) lies between the limits $(-2.306, 2.306)$ is 0.95 or 95 percent; these, as we know, are the *critical t* values. Now by substituting for t from expression (3.21) into the preceding equation, we obtain

$$P\left(-2.306 \leq \frac{b_2 - B_2}{\hat{\sigma} \Big/ \sqrt{\sum x_i^2}} \leq 2.306 \right) = 0.95 \qquad \textbf{(3.24)}$$

Rearranging inequality (3.24), we obtain

$$P\left(b_2 - 2.306 \frac{\hat{\sigma}}{\sqrt{\sum x_i^2}} \leq B_2 \leq b_2 + 2.306 \frac{\hat{\sigma}}{\sqrt{\sum x_i^2}} \right) = 0.95 \qquad \textbf{(3.25)}$$

Or, more generally,

$$P[(b_2 - 2.306 \, se(b_2) \leq B_2 \leq b_2 + 2.306 \, se(b_2)] = 0.95 \qquad \textbf{(3.26)}$$

which provides *a 95% confidence interval for* B_2. In repeated applications 95 out of 100 such intervals will include the true B_2. As noted previously, in the language of hypothesis testing such a confidence interval is known as the *region of acceptance* (of H_0) and the area outside the confidence interval is known as the *rejection region* (of H_0).

Geometrically, the 95% confidence interval is shown in Figure 3-5(*a*).

Now following our discussion in Appendix D, if this interval (i.e., the acceptance region) includes the null-hypothesized value of B_2, we do not reject the hypothesis. But if it lies outside the confidence interval (i.e., it lies in the rejection region), we reject the null hypothesis, bearing in mind that in making either of these decisions we are taking a chance of being wrong a certain percent, say, 5 percent, of the time.

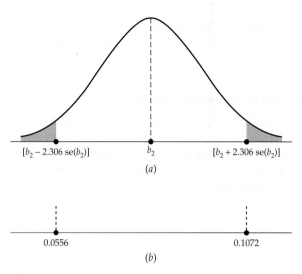

FIGURE 3-5   (a) 95% confidence interval for B_2 (8 d.f.); (b) 95% confidence interval for the slope coefficient of the math S.A.T. score example

All that remains to be done for our math S.A.T. score example is to obtain the numerical value of this interval. But that is now easy, for we have already obtained $se(b_2) = 0.000245$, as shown in Eq. (3.16). Substituting this value in Eq. (3.26), we now obtain the 95% confidence interval as shown in Figure 3-5(b).

$$0.0013 - 2.306(0.000245) \leq B_2 \leq 0.0013 + 2.306(0.000245)$$

That is,

$$0.00074 \leq B_2 \leq 0.00187 \qquad\qquad \textbf{(3.27)}$$

Since this interval does not include the null-hypothesized value of 0, we can reject the null hypothesis that annual family income is not related to math S.A.T. scores. Put positively, income does have a relationship to math S.A.T. scores.

A cautionary note: As noted in Appendix D, although the statement given in Eq. (3.26) is true, we *cannot say* that the probability is 95 percent that the particular interval in Eq. (3.27) includes the true B_2, for unlike Eq. (3.26), expression (3.27) is not a random interval; it is fixed. Therefore, the probability is either 1 or 0 that the interval in Eq. (3.27) includes B_2. We can only say that if we construct 100 intervals like the interval in Eq. (3.27), 95 out of 100 such intervals will include the true B_2; we cannot guarantee that this particular interval will necessarily include B_2.

Following a similar procedure exactly, the reader should verify that the 95% confidence interval for the intercept term B_1 is

$$393.4283 \leq B_1 \leq 471.3993 \qquad\qquad \textbf{(3.28)}$$

If, for example, $H_0 : B_1 = 0$ vs. $H_1 : B_1 \neq 0$, obviously this null hypothesis will be rejected too, for the preceding 95% confidence interval does not include 0.

On the other hand, if the null hypothesis were that the true intercept term is 400, we would not reject this null hypothesis because the 95% confidence interval includes this value.

The Test of Significance Approach to Hypothesis Testing

The key idea underlying this approach to hypothesis testing is that of a *test statistic* (see Appendix D) and the *sampling distribution* of the test statistic under the null hypothesis, H_0. The decision to accept or reject H_0 is made on the basis of the value of the test statistic obtained from the sample data.

To illustrate this approach, recall that

$$t = \frac{b_2 - B_2}{se(b_2)} \qquad (3.22)$$

follows the t distribution with $(n - 2)$ d.f. Now if we let

$$H_0 : B_2 = B_2^*$$

where B_2^* is a *specific numerical value* of B_2 (e.g., $B_2^* = 0$), then

$$t = \frac{b_2 - B_2^*}{se(b_2)}$$

$$= \frac{\text{estimator} - \text{hypothesized value}}{\text{standard error of the estimator}} \qquad (3.29)$$

can be readily computed from the sample data. Since all the quantities in Equation (3.29) are now known, we can use the t value computed from Eq. (3.29) as the test statistic, which follows the t distribution with $(n - 2)$ d.f. Appropriately, the testing procedure is called the **t test.**[11]

Now to use the t test in any concrete application, we need to know three things:

1. The d.f., which are always $(n - 2)$ for the two-variable model
2. The level of significance, α, which is a matter of personal choice, although 1, 5, or 10 percent levels are usually used in empirical analysis. Instead of arbitrarily choosing the α value, you can find the *p value* (the exact level of significance as described in Appendix D) and reject the null hypothesis if the computed *p value* is sufficiently low.
3. Whether we use a one-tailed or two-tailed test (see Table D-2 and Figure D-7).

---

[11]The difference between the confidence interval and the test of significance approaches lies in the fact that in the former we do not know what the true B_2 is and therefore try to guess it by establishing a $(1 - \alpha)$ confidence interval. In the test of significance approach, on the other hand, we hypothesize what the true B_2 ($=B_2^*$) is and try to find out if the sample value b_2 is sufficiently close to (the hypothesized) B_2^*.

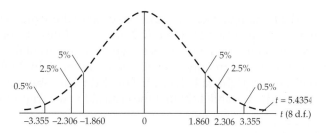

FIGURE 3-6   The t distribution for 8 d.f.

Math S.A.T. Example Continued

1. **A Two-Tailed Test** Assume that $H_0:B_2 = 0$ and $H_1:B_2 \neq 0$. Using Eq. (3.29), we find that

$$t = \frac{0.0013}{0.000245} = 5.4354 \tag{3.30}$$

Now from the t table given in Appendix E, Table E-2, we find that for 8 d.f. we have the following critical t values (two-tailed) (see Figure 3-6):

Level of significance	Critical t
0.01	3.355
0.05	2.306
0.10	1.860

In Appendix D, Table D-2 we stated that, in the case of the two-tailed t test, if the computed $|t|$, the absolute value of t, exceeds the critical t value at the chosen level of significance, we can reject the null hypothesis. Therefore, in the present case we can reject the null hypothesis that the true B_2 (i.e., the income coefficient) is zero because the computed $|t|$ of 5.4354 far exceeds the critical t value even at the 1% level of significance. We reached the same conclusion on the basis of the confidence interval shown in Eq. (3.27), which should not be surprising because *the confidence interval and the test of significance approaches to hypothesis testing are merely two sides of the same coin.*

Incidentally, in the present example the *p value* (i.e., probability value) of the t statistic of 5.4354 is about 0.0006. Thus, if we were to reject the null hypothesis that the true slope coefficient is zero at this *p value*, we would be wrong in six out of ten thousand occasions.

2. **A One-Tailed Test** Since the income coefficient in the math S.A.T. score function is expected to be positive, a realistic set of hypotheses would be $H_0:B_2 \leq 0$ and $H_1:B_2 > 0$; here the alternative hypothesis is one-sided.

The *t*-testing procedure remains exactly the same as before, except, as noted in Appendix D, Table D-2, the probability of committing a type I error is *not* divided equally between the two tails of the *t* distribution but is concentrated in only one tail, either left or right. In the present case it will be the right tail. (Why?) For 8 d.f. we observe from the *t* table (Appendix E, Table E-2) that the critical *t* value (right-tailed) is

Level of significance	Critical *t*
0.01	2.896
0.05	1.860
0.10	1.397

For the math S.A.T. example, we first compute the *t* value as if the null hypothesis were that $B_2 = 0$. We have already seen that this *t* value is

$$t = 5.4354 \tag{3.30}$$

Since this *t* value exceeds any of the critical values shown in the preceding table, following the rules laid down in Appendix D, Table D-2, we can reject the hypothesis that annual family income has no relationship to math S.A.T. scores; actually it has a positive effect (i.e., $B_2 > 0$) (see Figure 3-7).

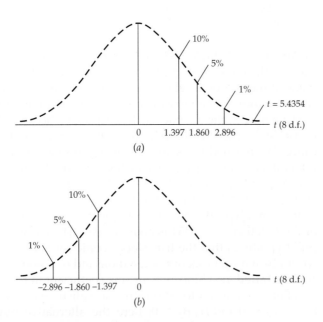

FIGURE 3-7   One-tailed *t* test: (*a*) Right-tailed; (*b*) left-tailed

3.6 HOW GOOD IS THE FITTED REGRESSION LINE: THE COEFFICIENT OF DETERMINATION, r^2

Our finding in the preceding section that on the basis of the t test both the estimated intercept and slope coefficients are *individually* statistically significant (i.e., significantly different from zero) suggests that the SRF, Eq. (3.16), shown in Figure 2-6 seems to "fit" the data "reasonably" well. Of course, not each actual Y value lies on the estimated PRF. That is, not all $e_i = (Y_i - \hat{Y}_i)$ are zero; as Table 2-4 shows, some e are positive and some are negative. Can we develop an overall measure of "goodness of fit" that will tell us how well the estimated regression line, Eq. (3.16), fits the actual Y values? Indeed, such a measure has been developed and is known as the **coefficient of determination,** denoted by the symbol r^2 (read as r squared). To see how r^2 is computed, we proceed as follows.

Recall that

$$Y_i = \hat{Y}_i + e_i \qquad \text{(Eq. 2.6)}$$

Let us express this equation in a slightly different but equivalent form (see Figure 3-8) as

$$\underset{\substack{\text{Variation in } Y_i \\ \text{from its mean value}}}{(Y_i - \overline{Y})} \;=\; \underset{\substack{\text{Variation in } Y_i \text{ explained} \\ \text{by } X(=\hat{Y}_i) \text{ around} \\ \text{its mean value} \\ (\text{Note:} \overline{Y} = \bar{\hat{Y}})}}{(\hat{Y}_i - \overline{Y})} \;+\; \underset{\substack{\text{Unexplained or} \\ \text{residual variation}}}{(Y_i - \hat{Y}_i)(\text{i.e., } e_i)} \qquad \textbf{(3.31)}$$

Now, letting small letters indicate deviations from mean values, we can write the preceding equation as

$$y_i = \hat{y}_i + e_i \qquad \textbf{(3.32)}$$

(*Note:* $y_i = (Y_i - \overline{Y})$, etc.) Also, note that $\bar{e} = 0$, as a result of which $\overline{Y} = \bar{\hat{Y}}$; that is, the mean values of the actual Y and the estimated Y are the same. Or

$$y_i = b_2 x_i + e_i \qquad \textbf{(3.33)}$$

since $\hat{y}_i = b_2 x_i$.

Now squaring Equation (3.33) on both sides and summing over the sample, we obtain, after simple algebraic manipulation,

$$\sum y_i^2 = \sum \hat{y}_i^2 + \sum e_i^2 \qquad \textbf{(3.34)}$$

Or, equivalently,

$$\sum y_i^2 = b_2^2 \sum x_i^2 + \sum e_i^2 \qquad \textbf{(3.35)}$$

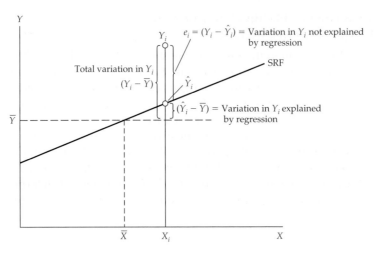

FIGURE 3-8   Breakdown of total variation in Y_i

This is an important relationship, as we will see. For proof of Equation (3.35), see Problem 3.25.

The various sums of squares appearing in Eq. (3.35) can be defined as follows:

$\sum y_i^2$ = the total variation[12] of the actual Y values about their sample mean $\overline{Y}$, which may be called the **total sum of squares (TSS).**

$\sum \hat{y}_i^2$ = the total variation of the estimated Y values about their mean value ($\hat{\overline{Y}} = \overline{Y}$), which may be called appropriately the *sum of squares due to regression* (i.e., due to the explanatory variable [s]), or simply the **explained sum of squares (ESS).**

$\sum e_i^2$ = as before, the residual sum of squares (RSS) or residual or unexplained variation of the Y values about the regression line.

Put simply, then, Eq. (3.35) is

$$\text{TSS} = \text{ESS} + \text{RSS} \qquad\qquad \textbf{(3.36)}$$

and shows that the total variation in the observed Y values about their mean value can be partitioned into two parts, one attributable to the regression line and the other to random forces, because not all actual Y observations lie on the fitted line. All this can be seen clearly from Figure 3-8 (see also Fig. 2-6).

Now if the chosen SRF fits the data quite well, ESS should be much larger than RSS. If all actual Y lie on the fitted SRF, ESS will be equal to TSS, and RSS will be zero. On the other hand, if the SRF fits the data poorly, RSS will be much larger than ESS. In the extreme, if X explains no variation at all in Y, ESS will be zero and RSS will equal TSS. These are, however, polar cases. Typically, neither

---

[12]The terms *variation* and *variance* are different. *Variation* means the sum of squares of deviations of a variable from its mean value. *Variance* is this sum divided by the appropriate d.f. In short, variance = variation/d.f.

ESS nor RSS will be zero. If ESS is relatively larger than RSS, the SRF will explain a substantial proportion of the variation in Y. If RSS is relatively larger than ESS, the SRF will explain only some part of the variation of Y. All these qualitative statements are intuitively easy to understand and can be readily quantified. If we divide Equation (3.36) by TSS on both sides, we obtain

$$1 = \frac{\text{ESS}}{\text{TSS}} + \frac{\text{RSS}}{\text{TSS}} \qquad (3.37)$$

Now let us define

$$r^2 = \frac{\text{ESS}}{\text{TSS}} \qquad (3.38)$$

The quantity r^2 thus defined is known as the (sample) coefficient of determination and is the most commonly used measure of the goodness of fit of a regression line. Verbally, r^2 *measures the proportion or percentage of the total variation in Y explained by the regression model.*

Two properties of r^2 may be noted:

1. It is a non-negative quantity. (Why?)
2. Its limits are $0 \le r^2 \le 1$ since a part (ESS) cannot be greater than the whole (TSS).[13] An r^2 of 1 means a "perfect fit," for the entire variation in Y is explained by the regression. An r^2 of zero means no relationship between Y and X whatsoever.

Formulas to Compute r^2

Using Equation (3.38), Equation (3.37) can be written as

$$1 = r^2 + \frac{\text{RSS}}{\text{TSS}}$$

$$= r^2 + \frac{\sum e_i^2}{\sum y_i^2} \qquad (3.39)$$

Therefore,

$$r^2 = 1 - \frac{\sum e_i^2}{\sum y_i^2} \qquad (3.40)$$

There are several equivalent formulas to compute r^2, which are given in Question 3.5.

---

[13]This statement assumes that an intercept term is included in the regression model. More on this in Chapter 5.

r^2 for the Math S.A.T. Example

From the data given in Table 2-4, and using formula (3.40), we obtain the following r^2 value for our math S.A.T. score example:

$$r^2 = 1 - \frac{7801.0776}{36610} \tag{3.41}$$
$$= 0.7869$$

Since r^2 can at most be 1, the computed r^2 is pretty high. In our math S.A.T. example X, the income variable, explains about 79 percent of the variation in math S.A.T. scores. In this case we can say that the sample regression (3.16) gives an excellent fit.

It may be noted that $(1 - r^2)$, the proportion of variation in Y not explained by X, is called, perhaps appropriately, the **coefficient of alienation.**

The Coefficient of Correlation, r

In Appendix B, we introduce the sample **coefficient of correlation, r,** as a measure of the strength of the linear relationship between two variables Y and X and show that r can be computed from formula (B.46), which can also be written as

$$r = \frac{\sum (X_i - \bar{X})(Y_i - \bar{Y})}{\sqrt{(X_i - \bar{X})^2 (Y_i - \bar{Y})^2}} \tag{3.42}$$

$$= \frac{\sum x_i y_i}{\sqrt{\sum x_i^2 \, \sum y_i^2}} \tag{3.43}$$

But this coefficient of correlation can also be computed from the coefficient of determination, r^2, as follows:

$$r = \pm \sqrt{r^2} \tag{3.44}$$

Since most regression computer packages routinely compute r^2, r can be computed easily. The only question is about the sign of r. However, that can be determined easily from the nature of the problem. In our math S.A.T. example, since math S.A.T. scores and annual family income are expected to be positively related, the r value in this case will be positive. In general, though, r has the same sign as the slope coefficient, which should be clear from formulas (2.17) and (3.43).

Thus, for the math S.A.T. example,

$$r = \sqrt{0.7869} = 0.8871 \tag{3.45}$$

In our example, math S.A.T. scores and annual family income are highly positively correlated, a finding that is not surprising.

Incidentally, if you use formula (3.43) to compute r between the actual Y values in the sample and the estimated Y_i values ($= \hat{Y}_i$) from the given model, and square this r value, the squared r is precisely equal to the r^2 value obtained from Eq. (3.42). For proof, see Question 3.5. You can verify this from the data given in Table 2-4. As you would expect, the closer the estimated Y values are to the actual Y values in the sample, the higher the r^2 value will be.

3.7   REPORTING THE RESULTS OF REGRESSION ANALYSIS

There are various ways of reporting the results of regression analysis. Until the advent of statistical software, regression results were presented in the format shown in Equation (3.46). Many journal articles still present regression results in this format. For our math S.A.T. score example, we have:

$$\hat{Y}_t = 432.4138 + 0.0013X_i$$
$$\text{se} = (16.9061)(0.000245)$$
$$t = (25.5774)(0.0006) \qquad r^2 = 0.7849 \tag{3.46}$$
$$p \text{ value} = (5.85 \times 10^{-9})(0.0006) \qquad \text{d.f.} = 8$$

In Equation (3.46) the figures in the first set of parentheses are the estimated standard errors (se) of the estimated regression coefficients. Those in the second set of parentheses are the estimated t values computed from Eq. (3.22) under the null hypothesis that the true population value of each regression coefficient individually is zero (i.e., the t values given are simply the ratios of the estimated coefficients to their standard errors). And those in the third set of parentheses are the p values of the computed t values.[14] As a matter of convention, from now on, if we do not specify a specific null hypothesis, then we will assume that it is the *zero null hypothesis* (i.e., the population parameter assumes zero value). And if we reject it (i.e., when the test statistic is significant), it means that the true population value is different from zero.

One advantage of reporting the regression results in the preceding format is that we can see at once whether each estimated coefficient is individually statistically significant, that is, significantly different from zero. By quoting the p values we can determine the exact level of significance of the estimated t value. Thus the t value of the estimated slope coefficient is 5.4354, whose p value is practically zero. As we note in Appendix D, *the lower the p value, the greater the evidence against the null hypothesis.*

A warning is in order here. When deciding whether to reject or not reject a null hypothesis, determine *beforehand* what level of the p value (call it the critical p value) you are willing to accept and then compare the computed p value with the critical p value. If the computed p value is smaller than the critical p value, the null hypothesis can be rejected. But if it is greater than the critical

---

[14]The t table in Appendix E of this book (Table E-2) can now be replaced by electronic tables that will compute the p values to several digits. This is also true of the normal, chi-square, and the F tables (Appendix E, Tables E-4 and E-3, respectively).

p value the null hypothesis may not be rejected. If you feel comfortable with the tradition of fixing the critical p value at the conventional 1, 5, or 10 percent level, that is fine. In Eq. (3.46), the actual p value (i.e., the exact level of significance) of the t coefficient of 5.4354 is 0.0006. If we had chosen the critical p value at 5 percent, obviously we would reject the null hypothesis, for the computed p value of 0.0006 is much smaller than 5 percent.

Of course, any null hypothesis (besides the zero null hypothesis) can be tested easily by making use of the t test discussed earlier. Thus, if the null hypothesis is that the true intercept term is 450 and if $H_1: B_1 \neq 450$, the t value will be

$$t = \frac{432.4138 - 450}{16.9061} = -1.0402$$

The p value of obtaining such a t value is about 0.3287, which is obtained from electronic tables. If you had fixed the critical p value at the 10 percent level, you would not reject the null hypothesis, for the computed p value is much greater than the critical p value.

The zero null hypothesis, as mentioned before, is essentially a kind of straw man. It is usually adopted for strategic reasons—to "dramatize" the statistical significance (i.e., importance) of an estimated coefficient.

3.8 COMPUTER OUTPUT OF THE MATH S.A.T. SCORE EXAMPLE

Since these days we rarely run regressions manually, it may be useful to produce the actual output of regression analysis obtained from a statistical software package. Below we give the selected output of our math S.A.T. example obtained from EViews.

Dependent Variable: Y
Method: Least Squares
Sample: 1 10
Included observations: 10

	Coefficient	Std. Error	t-Statistic	Prob.
C	432.4138	16.90607	25.57742	0.0000
X	0.001332	0.000245	5.435396	0.0006
R-squared		0.786914		
S.E. of regression		31.22715		
Sum squared resid		7801.078		

In this output, C denotes the constant term (i.e., intercept); Prob. is the p value; sum of squared resid is the RSS ($= \sum e_i^2$); and S.E. of regression is the standard error of the regression. The t values presented in this table are computed under the (null) hypothesis that the corresponding population regression coefficients are zero.

We also show (in Figure 3-9) how EViews presents the actual and estimated Y values as well as the residuals (i.e., e_i) in graphic form:

Actual Y_i	Fitted $\hat{Y}_i$	Residual e_i	Residual Plot (−) (0) (+)
410.000	439.073	−29.0733	●
420.000	452.392	−32.3922	●
440.000	465.711	−25.7112	●
490.000	479.030	10.9698	●
530.000	492.349	37.6509	●
530.000	505.668	24.3319	●
550.000	518.987	31.0129	●
540.000	532.306	07.69397	●
570.000	552.284	17.7155	●
590.000	632.198	−42.1983	●

FIGURE 3-9 Actual and fitted Y values and residuals for the math S.A.T. example

3.9 NORMALITY TESTS

Before we leave our math S.A.T. example, we need to look at the regression results given in Eq. (3.46). Remember that our statistical testing procedure is based on the assumption that the error term u_i is normally distributed. How do we find out if this is the case in our example, since we do not directly observe the true errors u_i? We have the residuals, e_i, which are proxies for u_i. Therefore, we will have to use the e_i to learn something about the normality of u_i. There are several tests of normality, but here we will consider only three comparatively simple tests.[15]

Histograms of Residuals

A histogram of residuals is a simple graphical device that is used to learn something about the shape of the probability density function (PDF) of a random variable. On the horizontal axis, we divide the values of the variable of interest (e.g., OLS residuals) into suitable intervals, and in each class interval, we erect rectangles equal in height to the number of observations (i.e., frequency) in that class interval.

If you mentally superimpose the bell-shaped normal distribution curve on this histogram, you might get some idea about the nature of the probability distribution of the variable of interest.

It is always a good practice to plot the histogram of residuals from any regression to get some rough idea about the likely shape of the underlying probability distribution.

[15]For a detailed discussion of various normality tests, see G. Barrie Wetherill, *Regression Analysis with Applications*, Chapman and Hall, London, 1986, Chap. 8.

Normal Probability Plot

Another comparatively simple graphical device to study the PDF of a random variable is the **normal probability plot (NPP)** which makes use of *normal probability paper,* a specially ruled graph paper. On the horizontal axis, (X-axis) we plot values of the variable of interest (say, OLS residuals e_i), and on the vertical axis (Y-axis), we show the expected values of this variable if its distribution were normal. Therefore, if the variable is in fact from the normal population, the NPP will approximate a straight line. MINITAB has the capability to plot the NPP of any random variable. MINITAB also produces the **Anderson-Darling normality test** known as the A^2 **statistic.** The underlying null hypothesis is that a variable is normally distributed. This hypothesis can be sustained if the computed A^2 is not statistically significant.

Jarque-Bera Test

A test of normality that has now become very popular and is included in several statistical packages is the **Jarque-Bera (JB) test.**[16] This is an *asymptotic,* or large sample, *test* and is based on OLS residuals. This test first computes the coefficients of *skewness, S* (a measure of asymmetry of a PDF), and *kurtosis, K* (a measure of how tall or flat a PDF is in relation to the normal distribution), of a random variable (e.g., OLS residuals) (see Appendix B). For a normally distributed variable, skewness is zero and kurtosis is 3 (see Figure B-4 in Appendix B).

Jarque and Bera have developed the following test statistic:

$$JB = \frac{n}{6}\left[S^2 + \frac{(K-3)^2}{4}\right] \qquad (3.47)$$

where n is the sample size, S represents skewness, and K represents kurtosis. They have shown that under the normality assumption the JB statistic given in Equation (3.47) *follows the chi-square distribution with 2 d.f. asymptotically* (i.e., in large samples). Symbolically,

$$JB_{asy} \sim \chi^2_{(2)} \qquad (3.48)$$

where asy means asymptotically.

As you can see from Eq. (3.47), if a variable is normally distributed, S is zero and $(K - 3)$ is also zero, and therefore the value of the JB statistic is zero ipso facto. But if a variable is not normally distributed, the JB statistic will assume increasingly larger values. What constitutes a large or small value of the JB statistic can be learned easily from the chi-square table (Appendix E, Table E-4). If the computed chi-square value from Eq. (3.47) exceeds the critical chi-square value for 2 d.f. at the chosen level of significance, we reject the null hypothesis of normal distribution; but if it does not exceed the critical chi-square value, we do

---

[16]See C. M. Jarque and A. K. Bera, "A Test for Normality of Observations and Regression Residuals," *International Statistical Review,* vol. 55, 1987, pp. 163–172.

not reject the null hypothesis. Of course, if we have the p value of the computed chi-square value, we will know the exact probability of obtaining that value.

We will illustrate these normality tests with the following example.

3.10   A CONCLUDING EXAMPLE: RELATIONSHIP BETWEEN WAGES AND PRODUCTIVITY IN THE U.S. BUSINESS SECTOR, 1959–2006

According to the marginal productivity theory of microeconomics, we would expect a positive relationship between wages and worker productivity. To see if this so, in Table 3-3 (on the textbook's Web site) we provide data on labor productivity, as measured by the index of output per hour of all persons, and wages, as measured by the index of real compensation per hour, for the business sector of the U.S. economy for the period 1959 to 2006. The base year of the index is 1992 and hourly real compensation is hourly compensation divided by the consumer price index (CPI).

Let *Compensation* (Y) = index of real compensation and *Productivity* (X) = index of output per hour of all persons. Plotting these data, we obtain the scatter diagram shown in Figure 3-10.

This figure shows a very close linear relationship between labor productivity and real wages. Therefore, we can use a (bivariate) linear regression to

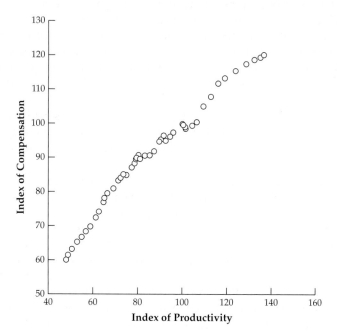

FIGURE 3-10   Relationship between compensation and productivity in the U.S. business sector, 1959–2006

model the data given in Table 3-3. Using EViews, we obtain the following results:

Dependent Variable: Compensation
Method: Least Squares
Sample: 1959 2006
Included observations: 48

	Coefficient	Std. Error	t-Statistic	Prob.
C	33.63603	1.400085	24.02428	0.0000
Productivity	0.661444	0.015640	42.29178	0.0000
R-squared	0.974926			
Adjusted R-squared	0.974381			
S.E. of regression	2.571761			
Sum squared resid	304.2420			
Durbin-Watson stat	0.146315			

Let us interpret the results. The slope coefficient of about 0.66 suggests that if the index of productivity goes up by a unit, the index of real wages will go up, on average, by 0.66 units. This coefficient is highly significant, for the t value of about 42.3 (obtained under the assumption that the true population coefficient is zero) is highly significant for the p value is almost zero. The intercept coefficient, C, is also highly significant, for the p value of obtaining a t value for this coefficient of as much as about 24 is practically zero.

The R^2 value of about 0.97 means that the index of productivity explains about 97 percent of the variation in the index of real compensation. This is a very high value, since an R^2 can at most be 1. For now neglect some of the information given in the preceding table (e.g., the Durbin-Watson statistic), for we will explain it at appropriate places.

Figure 3-11 gives the actual and estimated values of the index of real compensation, the dependent variable in our model, as well the differences between the two, which are nothing but the residuals e_i. These residuals are also plotted in this figure.

Figure 3-12 plots the histogram of the residuals shown in Figure 3-11 and also shows the JB statistics. The histogram and the JB statistic show that there is no reason to reject the hypothesis that the true error terms in the wages-productivity regression are normally distributed.

Figure 3-13 shows the normal probability plot of the residuals obtained from the compensation-productivity regression; this figure was obtained from MINITAB. As is clear from this figure, the estimated residuals lie approximately on a straight line, suggesting that the error terms (i.e., u_i) in this regression may be normally distributed. The computed AD statistic of 0.813 has a p value of about 0.03 or 3 percent. If we fix the critical p value, say, at the 5 percent level, the observed AD statistic is statistically significant, suggesting that the error terms are not normally distributed. This is in contrast to the conclusion reached on the basis of the JB

Actual Y_i	Fitted $\hat{Y}_i$	Residual e_i	Residual plot (−) (0) (+)
59.8710	65.4025	−5.53155	
61.3180	65.9575	−4.63950	
63.0540	67.0833	−4.02928	
65.1920	68.6145	−3.42252	
66.6330	69.9824	−3.34939	
68.2570	71.2113	−2.95435	
69.6760	72.5402	−2.86419	
72.3000	74.1191	−1.81906	
74.1210	75.0041	−0.88307	
76.8950	76.4163	0.47875	
78.0080	76.6253	1.38273	
79.4520	77.4799	1.97214	
80.8860	79.2856	1.60040	
83.3280	80.7593	2.56870	
85.0620	82.1926	2.86936	
83.9880	81.4300	2.55800	
84.8430	83.1068	1.73624	
87.1480	84.6631	2.48486	
88.3350	85.5296	2.80537	
89.7360	86.1018	3.63422	
89.8630	86.0919	3.77114	
89.5920	85.9900	3.60200	
89.6450	87.0662	2.57884	
90.6370	86.6495	3.98755	
90.5910	88.5366	2.05445	
90.7120	90.0003	0.71167	
91.9100	91.2683	0.64168	
94.8690	92.9497	1.91929	
95.2070	93.2540	1.95303	
96.5270	94.1621	2.36486	
95.0050	94.7588	0.24624	
96.2190	96.0664	0.15257	
97.4650	97.0705	0.39449	
100.0000	99.7804	0.21956	
99.7120	100.0360	−0.32376	
99.0240	100.6730	−1.64873	
98.6900	100.7690	−2.07930	
99.4780	102.7520	−3.27365	
100.5120	104.0650	−3.55328	
105.1730	106.0470	−0.87396	
108.0440	108.2650	−0.22145	
111.9920	110.4410	1.55106	
113.5360	112.4020	1.13388	
115.6940	115.6210	0.07329	
117.7090	118.7670	−1.05820	
118.9490	121.2050	−2.25562	
119.6920	122.9450	−3.25288	
120.4470	123.8600	−3.41265	

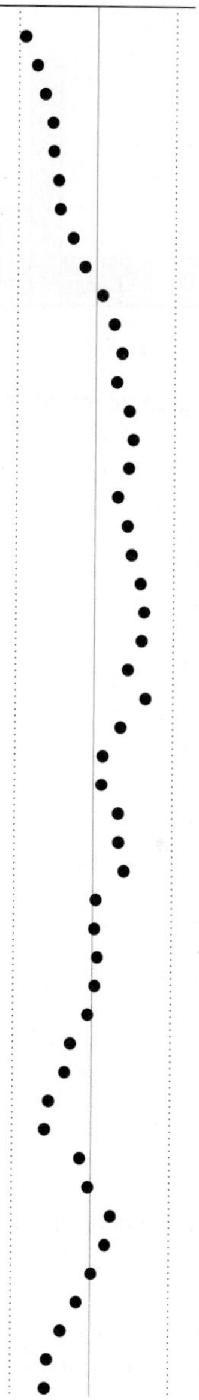

FIGURE 3-11   Actual Y, estimated Y, and residuals (regression of compensation on productivity)

Note: Y = Actual index of compensation

$\hat{Y}$ = Estimated index of compensation

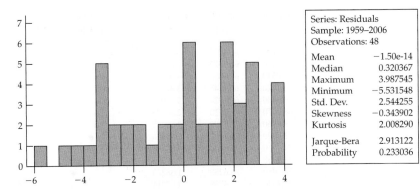

FIGURE 3-12   Histogram of residuals from the compensation-productivity regression

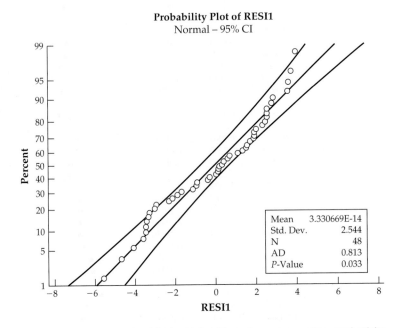

FIGURE 3-13   Normal probability plot of residuals obtained from the compensation-productivity regression

statistic. The problem here is that our sample of 10 observations is too small for using the JB and AD statistics, which are designed for large samples.

3.11   A WORD ABOUT FORECASTING

We noted in Chapter 2 that one of the purposes of regression analysis is to predict the mean value of the dependent variable, given the values of the explanatory variable(s). To be more specific, let us return to our math S.A.T. score example. Regression (3.46) presented the results of the math section of the S.A.T. based on the score data of Table 2-2. Suppose we want to find out the average math S.A.T. score by a person with a given level of annual family income. What is the expected math S.A.T. score at this level of annual family income?

To fix these ideas, assume that X (income) takes the value X_0, where X_0 is some *specified numerical value* of X, say $X_0 = \$78,000$. Now suppose we want to estimate $E(Y \mid X_0 = 78000)$, that is, the true mean math S.A.T. score corresponding to a family income of $\$78,000$. Let

$$\hat{Y}_0 = \text{the estimator of } E(Y \mid X_0) \qquad \text{(3.49)}$$

How do we obtain this estimate? Under the assumptions of the classical linear regression model (CLRM), it can be shown that Equation (3.49) can be obtained by simply putting the given X_0 value in Eq. (3.46), which gives:

$$\hat{Y}_{X=78000} = 432.4138 + 0.0013(78000)$$
$$= 533.8138 \qquad \text{(3.50)}$$

That is, the forecasted mean math S.A.T. score for a person with an annual family income of $\$78,000$ is about 534 points.

Although econometric theory shows that under CLRM $\hat{Y}_{\hat{X}=78000}$, or, more generally, $\hat{Y}_0$ is an unbiased estimator of the true mean value (i.e., a point on the population regression line), it is not likely to be equal to the latter in any given sample. (Why?) The difference between them is called the **forecasting, or prediction, error.** To assess this error, we need to find out the sampling distribution of $\hat{Y}_0$.[17] Given the assumptions of the CLRM, it can be shown that $\hat{Y}_0$ is *normally distributed* with the following mean and variance:

$$\text{Mean} = E(Y \mid X_0) = B_1 + B_2 X_0$$

$$\text{var} = \sigma^2 \left[\frac{1}{n} + \frac{(X_0 - \overline{X})^2}{\sum x_i^2} \right] \qquad \text{(3.51)}$$

where $\overline{X}$ = the sample mean of X values in the historical regression (3.46)
     $\sum x_i^2$ = their sum of squared deviations from $\overline{X}$
     σ^2 = the variance of u_i
     n = sample size

The positive square root of Equation (3.51) gives the standard error of $\hat{Y}_0$, $\text{se}(\hat{Y}_0)$.

Since in practice σ^2 is not known, if we replace it by its unbiased estimator $\hat{\sigma}^2$, $\hat{Y}_0$ follows the t distribution with $(n - 2)$ d.f. (Why?) Therefore, we can use the t distribution to establish a $100(1 - \alpha)\%$ confidence interval for the true (i.e., population) mean value of Y corresponding to X_0 in the usual manner as follows:

$$P[b_1 + b_2 X_0 - t_{a/2}\,\text{se}(\hat{Y}_0) \le B_1 + B_2 X_0 \le b_1 + b_2 X_0 + t_{a/2}\,\text{se}(\hat{Y}_0)] = (1 - \alpha) \qquad \text{(3.52)}$$

---

[17]Note that $\hat{Y}_0$ is an estimator and therefore will have a sampling distribution.

Let us continue with our math S.A.T. score example. First, we compute the variance of $\hat{Y}_{X=78000}$ from Equation (3.51).

$$\text{var}\left(\hat{Y}_{X=78000}\right) = 975.1347\left[\frac{1}{10} + \frac{(78,000 - 56,000)^2}{16,240,000,000}\right]$$

$$= 126.5754 \tag{3.53}$$

Therefore,

$$\text{se}\left(\hat{Y}_{X=78000}\right) = \sqrt{126.5754}$$

$$= 11.2506 \tag{3.54}$$

Note: In this example, $\overline{X} = 56000$, $\sum x_i^2 = 16,240,000,000$, and $\hat{\sigma}^2 = 975.1347$ (see Table 2-4).

The preceding result suggests that given the estimated annual family income = $78,000, the mean predicted math S.A.T. score, as shown in Equation (3.50), is 533.8138 points and the standard error of this predicted value is 11.2506 (points).

Now if we want to establish, say, a 95% confidence interval for the population mean math S.A.T. score corresponding to an annual family income of $78,000, we obtain it from expression (3.52) as

$$533.8138 - 2.306(11.2506) \leq E(Y \mid X = 78000) \leq 533.8138 + 2.306\,(11.2506)$$

That is,

$$507.8699 \leq E(Y \mid X = 78000) \leq 559.7577 \tag{3.55}$$

Note: For 8 d.f., the 5 percent two-tailed t value is 2.306.

Given the annual family income of $78,000, Equation (3.55) states that although the single best, or point, estimate of the mean math S.A.T. score is 533.8138, it is expected to lie in the interval 507.8699 to 559.7577 points, which is between about 508 and 560, with 95% confidence. Therefore, with 95% confidence, the forecast error will be between −25.9439 points (507.8699 − 533.8138) and 25.9439 points (559.7577 − 533.8138).

If we obtain a 95% confidence interval like Eq. (3.55) for each value of X shown in Table 2-2, we obtain what is known as a **confidence interval** or **confidence band** for the true mean math S.A.T. score for each level of annual family income, or for the entire population regression line (PRL). This can be seen clearly from Figure 3-14, obtained from EViews.

Notice some interesting aspects of Figure 3-14. The width of the confidence band is smallest when $X_0 = \overline{X}$, which should be apparent from the variance formula given in Eq. (3.51). However, the width widens sharply (i.e.,

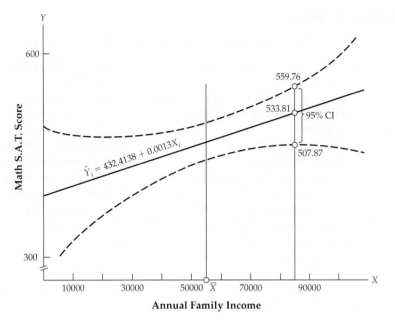

FIGURE 3-14   95% confidence band for the true math S.A.T. score function

the prediction error increases) as X_0 moves away from $\overline{X}$. This suggests that the predictive ability of the historical regression, such as regression (3.46), falls markedly as X_0 (the X value for which the forecast is made) departs progressively from $\overline{X}$. The message here is clear: *We should exercise great caution in "extrapolating" the historical regression line to predict the mean value of Y associated with any X that is far removed from the sample mean of X. In more practical terms, we should not use the math S.A.T. score regression (3.46) to predict the average math score for income well beyond the sample range on which the historical regression line is based.*

3.12   SUMMARY

In Chapter 2 we showed how to estimate the parameters of the two-variable linear regression model. In this chapter we showed how the estimated model can be used for the purpose of drawing inferences about the true population regression model. Although the two-variable model is the simplest possible linear regression model, the ideas introduced in these two chapters are the foundation of the more involved multiple regression models that we will discuss in ensuing chapters. As we will see, in many ways the multiple regression model is a straightforward extension of the two-variable model.

KEY TERMS AND CONCEPTS

The key terms and concepts introduced in this chapter are

Classical linear regression model (CLRM)
Homoscedasticity or equal variance
Heteroscedasticity or unequal variance
Autocorrelation and no autocorrelation
Variances of OLS estimators
Standard errors of OLS estimators
Residual sum of squares (RSS)
Standard error of the regression (SER)
Sampling, or probability, distributions of OLS estimators
Gauss-Markov theorem
BLUE property
Central limit theorem (CLT)

"Zero" null hypothesis; straw man hypothesis
t test of significance
  a) two-tailed t test
  b) one-tailed t test
Coefficient of determination, r^2
Total sum of squares (TSS)
Explained sum of squares (ESS)
Coefficient of alienation
Coefficient of correlation, r
Normal probability plot (NPP)
Anderson-Darling normality test (A^2 statistic)
Jarque-Bera (JB) test of normality
Forecasting, or prediction, error
Confidence interval; confidence band

QUESTIONS

3.1. Explain the meaning of
  a. Least squares.
  b. OLS estimators.
  c. The variance of an estimator.
  d. Standard error of an estimator.
  e. Homoscedasticity.
  f. Heteroscedasticity.
  g. Autocorrelation.
  h. Total sum of squares (TSS).
  i. Explained sum of squares (ESS).
  j. Residual sum of squares (RSS).
  k. r^2.
  l. Standard error of estimate.
  m. BLUE.
  n. Test of significance.
  o. t test.
  p. One-tailed test.
  q. Two-tailed test.
  r. Statistically significant.
3.2. State with brief reasons whether the following statements are true, false, or uncertain.
  a. OLS is an estimating procedure that minimizes the sum of the errors squared, $\sum u_i^2$.
  b. The assumptions made by the classical linear regression model (CLRM) are not necessary to compute OLS estimators.

c. The theoretical justification for OLS is provided by the Gauss-Markov theorem.

d. In the two-variable PRF, b_2 is likely to be a more accurate estimate of B_2 if the disturbances u_i follow the normal distribution.

e. The OLS estimators b_1 and b_2 each follow the normal distribution only if u_i follows the normal distribution.

f. r^2 is the ratio of TSS/ESS.

g. For a given alpha and d.f., if the computed $|t|$ exceeds the critical t value, we should accept the null hypothesis.

h. The coefficient of correlation, r, has the same sign as the slope coefficient b_2.

i. The p value and the level of significance, α, mean the same thing.

3.3. Fill in the appropriate gaps in the following statements:

a. If $B_2 = 0$, $b_2/\text{se}(b_2) = \ldots$

b. If $B_2 = 0$, $t = b_2/\ldots$

c. r^2 lies between ... and ...

d. r lies between ... and ...

e. TSS = RSS + ...

f. d.f. (of TSS) = d.f. (of ...) + d.f. (of RSS)

g. $\hat{\sigma}$ is called ...

h. $\sum y_i^2 = \sum(Y_i - \ldots)^2$

i. $\sum y_i^2 = b_2(\ldots)$

3.4. Consider the following regression:

$$\hat{Y}_i = -66.1058 + 0.0650X_i \qquad r^2 = 0.9460$$
$$\text{se} = (10.7509) \qquad (\quad) \qquad n = 20$$
$$t = (\quad) \qquad\qquad (18.73)$$

Fill in the missing numbers. Would you reject the hypothesis that true B_2 is zero at $\alpha = 5\%$? Tell whether you are using a one-tailed or two-tailed test and why.

3.5. Show that all the following formulas to compute r^2 are equivalent:

$$r^2 = 1 - \frac{\sum e_i^2}{\sum y_i^2}$$

$$= \frac{\sum \hat{y}_i^2}{\sum y_i^2}$$

$$= \frac{b_2^2 \sum x_i^2}{\sum y_i^2}$$

$$= \frac{\left(\sum y_i \hat{y}_i\right)^2}{\left(\sum y_i^2\right)\left(\sum \hat{y}_i^2\right)}$$

3.6. Show that $\sum e_i = n\overline{Y} - nb_1 - nb_2\overline{X} = 0$

PROBLEMS

3.7. Based on the data for the years 1962 to 1977 for the United States, Dale Bails and Larry Peppers[18] obtained the following demand function for automobiles:

$$\hat{Y}_t = 5807 + 3.24X_t \qquad r^2 = 0.22$$

$$se = \qquad (1.634)$$

where Y = retail sales of passenger cars (thousands) and X = the real disposable income (billions of 1972 dollars).

Note: The se for b_1 is not given.

a. Establish a 95% confidence interval for B_2.

b. Test the hypothesis that this interval includes $B_2 = 0$. If not, would you accept this null hypothesis?

c. Compute the t value under $H_0:B_2 = 0$. Is it statistically significant at the 5 percent level? Which t test do you use, one-tailed or two-tailed, and why?

3.8. The *characteristic line* of modern investment analysis involves running the following regression:

$$r_1 = B_1 + B_2 r_{mt} + u_t$$

where r = the rate of return on a stock or security

r_m = the rate of return on the market portfolio represented by a broad market index such as S&P 500, and

t = time

In investment analysis, B_2 is known as the *beta coefficient* of the security and is used as a measure of market risk, that is, how developments in the market affect the fortunes of a given company.

Based on 240 monthly rates of return for the period 1956 to 1976, Fogler and Ganapathy obtained the following results for IBM stock. The market index used by the authors is the market portfolio index developed at the University of Chicago:[19]

$$r_t = 0.7264 + 1.0598 r_{mt}$$

$$se = (0.3001) \ (0.0728) \quad r^2 = 0.4710$$

a. Interpret the estimated intercept and slope.

b. How would you interpret r^2?

c. A security whose beta coefficient is greater than 1 is called a volatile or aggressive security. Set up the appropriate null and alternative hypotheses and test them using the t test. *Note:* Use $\alpha = 5\%$.

3.9. You are given the following data based on 10 pairs of observations on Y and X.

$$\sum y_i = 1110 \quad \sum X_i = 1680 \quad \sum X_i Y_i = 204{,}200$$

$$\sum X_i^2 = 315{,}400 \quad \sum Y_i^2 = 133{,}300$$

[18]See Dale G. Bails and Larry C. Peppers, *Business Fluctuations: Forecasting Techniques and Applications,* Prentice-Hall, Englewood Cliffs, N.J., 1982, p. 147.

[19]H. Russell Fogler and Sundaram Ganapathy, *Financial Econometrics,* Prentice-Hall, Englewood-Cliffs, N.J., 1982, p. 13.

Assuming all the assumptions of CLRM are fulfilled, obtain

a. b_1 and b_2.

b. standard errors of these estimators.

c. r^2.

d. Establish 95% confidence intervals for B_1 and B_2.

e. On the basis of the confidence intervals established in (*d*), can you accept the hypothesis that $B_2 = 0$?

3.10. Based on data for the United States for the period 1965 to 2006 (found in Table 3-4 on the textbook's Web site), the following regression results were obtained:

$$GNP_t = -995.5183 + 8.7503M_{1t} \quad r^2 = 0.9488$$

$$se = (\quad) \qquad (0.3214)$$

$$t = (-3.8258) \qquad (\quad)$$

where GNP is the gross national product ($, in billions) and M_1 is the money supply ($, in billions).

Note: M_1 includes currency, demand deposits, traveler's checks, and other checkable deposits.

a. Fill in the blank parentheses.

b. The monetarists maintain that money supply has a significant positive impact on GNP. How would you test this hypothesis?

c. What is the meaning of the negative intercept?

d. Suppose M_1 for 2007 is $750 billion. What is the mean forecast value of GNP for that year?

3.11. *Political business cycle:* Do economic events affect presidential elections? To test this so-called political business cycle theory, Gary Smith[20] obtained the following regression results based on the U.S. presidential elections for the four yearly periods from 1928 to 1980 (i.e., the data are for years 1928, 1932, etc.):

$$\hat{Y}_t = 53.10 - 1.70X_t$$

$$t = (34.10)\,(-2.67) \qquad r^2 = 0.37$$

where Y is the percentage of the vote received by the incumbent and X is the unemployment rate change—unemployment rate in an election year minus the unemployment rate in the preceding year.

a. A priori, what is the expected sign of X?

b. Do the results support the political business cycle theory? Support your contention with appropriate calculations.

c. Do the results of the 1984 and 1988 presidential elections support the preceding theory?

d. How would you compute the standard errors of b_1 and b_2?

3.12. To study the relationship between capacity utilization in manufacturing and inflation in the United States, we obtained the data shown in Table 3-5 (found on the textbook's Web site). In this table, Y = inflation rate as measured by the

---

[20]Gary Smith, *Statistical Reasoning*, Allyn & Bacon, Boston, Mass., 1985, p. 488. Change in notation was made to conform with our format. The original data were obtained by Ray C. Fair, "The Effect of Economic Events on Votes for President," *The Review of Economics and Statistics*, May 1978, pp. 159–173.

percentage change in GDP implicit price deflator and X = capacity utilization rate in manufacturing as measured by output as a percent of capacity for the years 1960–2007.

   a. A priori, what would you expect to be the relationship between inflation rate and capacity utilization rate? What is the economic rationale behind your expectation?

   b. Regress Y on X and present your result in the format of Eq. (3.46).

   c. Is the estimated slope coefficient statistically significant?

   d. Is it statistically different from unity?

   e. The natural rate of capacity utilization is defined as the rate at which Y is zero. What is this rate for the period under study?

3.13. *Reverse regression*[21]: Continue with Problem 3.12, but suppose we now regress X on Y.

   a. Present the result of this regression and comment.

   b. If you multiply the slope coefficients in the two regressions, what do you obtain? Is this result surprising to you?

   c. The regression in Problem 3.12 may be called the *direct regression*. When would a reverse regression be appropriate?

   d. Suppose the r^2 value between X and Y is 1. Does it then make any difference if we regress Y on X or X on Y?

3.14. Table 3-6 gives data on X (net profits after tax in U.S. manufacturing industries [$, in millions]) and Y (cash dividend paid quarterly in manufacturing industries [$, in millions]) for years 1974 to 1986.

   a. What relationship, if any, do you expect between cash dividend and after-tax profits?

   b. Plot the scattergram between Y and X.

   c. Does the scattergram support your expectations in part (*a*)?

   d. If so, do an OLS regression of Y on X and obtain the usual statistics.

   e. Establish a 99% confidence interval for the true slope and test the hypothesis that the true slope coefficient is zero; that is, there is no relationship between dividend and the after-tax profit.

TABLE 3-6   CASH DIVIDEND (Y) AND AFTER-TAX PROFITS (X) IN U.S. MANUFACTURING INDUSTRIES, 1974–1986

Year	Y	X	Year	Y	X
	($, in millions)			($, in millions)	
1974	19,467	58,747	1981	40,317	101,302
1975	19,968	49,135	1982	41,259	71,028
1976	22,763	64,519	1983	41,624	85,834
1977	26,585	70,366	1984	45,102	107,648
1978	28,932	81,148	1985	45,517	87,648
1979	32,491	98,698	1986	46,044	83,121
1980	36,495	92,579			

Source: Business Statistics, 1986, U.S. Department of Commerce, Bureau of Economic Analysis, December 1987, p. 72.

[21]On this see G. S. Maddala, *Introduction to Econometrics,* 3rd ed., Wiley, New York, 2001, pp. 71–75.

3.15. Refer to the S.A.T. data given in Table 2-15 on the textbook's Web site. Suppose you want to predict the male math scores on the basis of the female math scores by running the following regression:

$$Y_t = B_1 + B_2 X_t + u_t$$

where Y and X denote the male and female math scores, respectively.

a. Estimate the preceding regression, obtaining the usual summary statistics.

b. Test the hypothesis that there is no relationship between Y and X whatsoever.

c. Suppose the female math score in 2008 is expected to be 490. What is the predicted (average) male math score?

d. Establish a 95% confidence interval for the predicted value in part (c).

3.16. Repeat the exercise in Problem 3.15 but let Y and X denote the male and the female critical reading scores, respectively. Assume a female critical reading score for 2008 of 505.

3.17. Consider the following regression results:[22]

$$\hat{Y}_t = -0.17 + 5.26 X_t \qquad \overline{R}^2 = 0.10, \text{ Durbin-Watson} = 2.01$$

$$t = (-1.73)(2.71)$$

where Y = the real return on the stock price index from January of the current year to January of the following year

X = the total dividends in the preceding year divided by the stock price index for July of the preceding year

t = time

Note: On Durbin-Watson statistic, see Chapter 10.

The time period covered by the study was 1926 to 1982.

Note: $\overline{R}^2$ stands for the adjusted coefficient of determination. The Durbin-Watson value is a measure of autocorrelation. Both measures are explained in subsequent chapters.

a. How would you interpret the preceding regression?

b. If the previous results are acceptable to you, does that mean the best investment strategy is to invest in the stock market when the dividend/price ratio is high?

c. If you want to know the answer to part (b), read Shiller's analysis.

3.18. Refer to Example 2.1 on years of schooling and average hourly earnings. The data for this example are given in Table 2-5 and the regression results are presented in Eq. (2.21). For this regression

a. Obtain the standard errors of the intercept and slope coefficients and r^2.

b. Test the hypothesis that schooling has no effect on average hourly earnings. Which test did you use and why?

c. If you reject the null hypothesis in (b), would you also reject the hypothesis that the slope coefficient in Eq. (2.21) is not different from 1? Show the necessary calculations.

---

[22]See Robert J. Shiller, *Market Volatility*, MIT Press, Cambridge, Mass., 1989, pp. 32–36.

3.19. Example 2.2 discusses Okun's law, as shown in Eq. (2.22). This equation can also be written as $X_t = B_1 + B_2Y_t$, where X = percent growth in real output, as measured by GDP and Y = change in the unemployment rate, measured in percentage points. Using the data given in Table 2-13 on the textbook's Web site,

    a. Estimate the preceding regression, obtaining the usual results as per Eq. (3.46).

    b. Is the change in the unemployment rate a significant determinant of percent growth in real GDP? How do you know?

    c. How would you interpret the intercept coefficient in this regression? Does it have any economic meaning?

3.20. For Example 2.3, relating stock prices to interest rates, are the regression results given in Eq. (2.24) statistically significant? Show the necessary calculations.

3.21. Refer to Example 2.5 about antique clocks and their prices. Based on Table 2-14, we obtained the regression results shown in Eqs. (2.27) and (2.28). For each regression obtain the standard errors, the t ratios, and the r^2 values. Test for the statistical significance of the estimated coefficients in the two regressions.

3.22. Refer to Problem 3.22. Using OLS regressions, answer questions (*a*), (*b*), and (*c*).

3.23. Table 3-7 (found on the textbook's Web site) gives data on U.S. expenditure on imported goods (*Y*) and personal disposable income (*X*) for the period 1959 to 2006.

    Based on the data given in this table, estimate an import expenditure function, obtaining the usual regression statistics, and test the hypothesis that expenditure on imports is unrelated to personal disposable income.

3.24. Show that the OLS estimators, b_1 and b_2, are linear estimators. Also show that these estimators are linear functions of the error term u_i (*Hint:* Note that $b_2 = \Sigma x_i y_i / \Sigma x_i^2 = \Sigma w_i y_i$, where $w_i = x_i / \Sigma x_i^2$ and note that the X's are nonstochastic).

3.25. Prove Eq. (3.35). (*Hint:* Square Eq. [3.33] and use some of the properties of OLS).

CHAPTER 4

MULTIPLE REGRESSION: ESTIMATION AND HYPOTHESIS TESTING

In the two-variable linear regression model that we have considered so far there was a single independent, or explanatory, variable. In this chapter we extend that model by considering the possibility that more than one explanatory variable may influence the dependent variable. A regression model with more than one explanatory variable is known as a **multiple regression model,** multiple because *multiple influences* (i.e., variables) may affect the dependent variable.

For example, consider the 1980s savings and loan (S&L) crisis resulting from the bankruptcies of some S&L institutions in several states. Similar events also occurred in the fall of 2008 as several banks were forced into bankruptcy. What factors should we focus on to understand these events? Is there a way to reduce the possibility that they will happen again? Suppose we want to develop a regression model to explain bankruptcy, the dependent variable. Now a phenomenon such as bankruptcy is too complex to be explained by a single explanatory variable; the explanation may entail several variables, such as the ratio of primary capital to total assets, the ratio of loans that are more than 90 days past due to total assets, the ratio of nonaccruing loans to total assets, the ratio of renegotiated loans to total assets, the ratio of net income to total assets, etc.[1] To include all these variables in a regression model to allow for the multiplicity of influences affecting bankruptcies, we have to consider a multiple regression model.

Needless to say, we could cite hundreds of examples of multiple regression models. In fact, most regression models are multiple regression models because very few economic phenomena can be explained by only a single explanatory variable, as in the case of the two-variable model.

[1]As a matter of fact, these were some of the variables that were considered by the Board of Governors of the Federal Reserve System in their internal studies of bankrupt banks.

93

In this chapter we discuss the multiple regression model seeking answers to the following questions:

1. How do we estimate the multiple regression model? Is the estimating procedure any different from that for the two-variable model?
2. Is the hypothesis-testing procedure any different from the two-variable model?
3. Are there any unique features of multiple regressions that we did not encounter in the two-variable case?
4. Since a multiple regression can have any number of explanatory variables, how do we decide how many variables to include in any given situation?

To answer these and other related questions, we first consider the simplest of the multiple regression models, namely, the three-variable model in which the behavior of the dependent variable Y is examined in relation to two explanatory variables, X_2 and X_3. Once the three-variable model is clearly understood, the extension to the four-, five-, or more variable case is quite straightforward, although the arithmetic gets a bit tedious. (But in this age of high-speed computers, that should not be a problem.) It is interesting that the three-variable model itself is in many ways a clear-cut extension of the two-variable model, as the following discussion reveals.

4.1   THE THREE-VARIABLE LINEAR REGRESSION MODEL

Generalizing the two-variable population regression function (PRF), we can write the three-variable PRF in its nonstochastic form as

$$E(Y_t) = B_1 + B_2 X_{2t} + B_3 X_{3t} \qquad \text{(4.1)}^2$$

and in the stochastic form as

$$Y_t = B_1 + B_2 X_{2t} + B_3 X_{3t} + u_t \qquad \text{(4.2)}$$

$$= E(Y_t) + u_t \qquad \text{(4.3)}$$

where Y = the dependent variable
X_2 and X_3 = the explanatory variables
u = the stochastic disturbance term
t = the tth observation

---

[2]Equation (4.1) can be written as: $E(Y_t) = B_1 X_{1t} + B_2 X_{2t} + B_3 X_{3t}$ with the understanding that $X_{1t} = 1$ for each observation. The presentation in Eq. (4.1) is for notational convenience in that the subscripts on the parameters or their estimators match the subscripts on the variables to which they are attached.

In case the data are cross-sectional, the subscript i will denote the ith observation. Note that we introduce u in the three-variable, or, more generally, in the multivariable model for the same reason that it was introduced in the two-variable case.

B_1 is the intercept term. It represents the average value of Y when X_2 and X_3 are set equal to zero. The coefficients B_2 and B_3 are called **partial regression coefficients;** their meaning will be explained shortly.

Following the discussion in Chapter 2, Equation (4.1) gives the *conditional mean* value of Y, conditional upon the given or fixed values of the variables X_2 and X_3. Therefore, as in the two-variable case, multiple regression analysis is *conditional regression* analysis, conditional upon the given or fixed values of the explanatory variables, and we obtain *the average, or mean, value of Y for the fixed values of the X variables.* Recall that the PRF gives the (conditional) means of the Y populations corresponding to the given levels of the explanatory variables, X_2 and X_3.[3]

The stochastic version, Equation (4.2), states that any individual Y value can be expressed as the sum of two components:

1. A systematic, or *deterministic,* component $(B_1 + B_2X_{2t} + B_3X_{3t})$, which is simply its mean value $E(Y_t)$ (i.e., the point on the population regression line, PRL),[4] and
2. u_t, which is the *nonsystematic,* or *random,* component, determined by factors other than X_2 and X_3.

All this is familiar territory from the two-variable case; the only point to note is that we now have two explanatory variables instead of one explanatory variable.

Notice that Eq. (4.1), or its stochastic counterpart Eq. (4.2), is a *linear regression model*—a model that is *linear in the parameters,* the B's. As noted in Chapter 2, our concern in this book is with regression models that are linear in the parameters; such models may or may not be linear in the variables (but more on this in Chapter 5).

The Meaning of Partial Regression Coefficient

As mentioned earlier, the regression coefficients B_2 and B_3 are known as **partial regression** or **partial slope coefficients.** The meaning of the partial regression coefficient is as follows: B_2 measures the *change* in the mean value of Y, $E(Y)$, per unit change in X_2, holding the value of X_3 constant. Likewise, B_3 measures the

---

[3]Unlike the two-variable case, we cannot show this diagrammatically because to represent the three variables Y, X_2, and X_3, we have to use a three-dimensional diagram, which is difficult to visualize in two-dimensional form. But by stretching the imagination, we can visualize a diagram similar to Figure 2-6.

[4]Geometrically, the PRL in this case represents what is known as a plane.

change in the mean value of Y per unit change in X_3, holding the value of X_2 constant. This is the unique feature of a multiple regression; in the two-variable case, since there was only a single explanatory variable, we did not have to worry about the presence of other explanatory variables in the model. In the multiple regression model we want to find out what part of the change in the average value of Y can be directly attributable to X_2 and what part to X_3. Since this point is so crucial to understanding the logic of multiple regression, let us explain it by a simple example. Suppose we have the following PRF:

$$E\,(Y_t) = 15 - 1.2X_{2t} + 0.8X_{3t} \tag{4.4}$$

Let X_3 be held constant at the value 10. Putting this value in Equation (4.4), we obtain

$$E(Y_t) = 15 - 1.2X_{2t} + 0.8(10)$$
$$= (15 + 8) - 1.2X_{2t}$$
$$= 23 - 1.2X_{2t} \tag{4.5}$$

Here the slope coefficient $B_2 = -1.2$ indicates that the mean value of Y decreases by 1.2 per unit increase in X_2 when X_3 is held constant—in this example it is held constant at 10 although any other value will do.[5] This slope coefficient is called the *partial regression coefficient*.[6] Likewise, if we hold X_2 constant, say, at the value 5, we obtain

$$E(Y_t) = 15 - 1.2(5) + 0.8X_{3t}$$
$$= 9 + 0.8X_{3t} \tag{4.6}$$

Here the slope coefficient $B_3 = 0.8$ means that the mean value of Y increases by 0.8 per unit increase in X_3 when X_2 is held constant—here it is held constant at 5, but any other value will do just as well. This slope coefficient too is a partial regression coefficient.

In short, then, a partial regression coefficient reflects the (partial) effect of one explanatory variable on the mean value of the dependent variable when the values of other explanatory variables included in the model are held constant. This unique feature of multiple regression enables us not only to include more than one explanatory variable in the model but also to "isolate" or "disentangle" the effect of each X variable on Y from the other X variables included in the model.

We will consider a concrete example in Section 4.5.

---

[5]As the algebra of Eq. (4.5) shows, it does not matter at what value X_3 is held constant, for that constant value multiplied by its coefficient will be a constant number, which will simply be added to the intercept.

[6]The mathematically inclined reader will notice at once that B_2 is the partial derivative of $E(Y)$ with respect to X_2 and that B_3 is the partial derivative of $E(Y)$ with respect to X_3.

4.2   ASSUMPTIONS OF THE MULTIPLE LINEAR REGRESSION MODEL

As in the two-variable case, our first order of business is to estimate the regression coefficients of the multiple regression model. Toward that end, we continue to operate within the framework of the classical linear regression model (CLRM) first introduced in Chapter 3 and to use the method of ordinary least squares (OLS) to estimate the coefficients.

Specifically, for model (4.2), we assume (cf. Section 3.1):

A4.1.

The regression model is linear in the parameters as in Eq. (4.1) and it is correctly specified.

A4.2.

X_2 and X_3 are uncorrelated with the disturbance term u. If X_2 and X_3 are nonstochastic (i.e., fixed numbers in repeated sampling), this assumption is automatically fulfilled.

However, if the X variables are random, or stochastic, they must be distributed independently of the error term u; otherwise, we will not be able to obtain unbiased estimates of the regression coefficients. But more on this in Chapter 11.

A4.3.

The error term u has a zero mean value; that is,

$$E(u_i) = 0 \qquad (4.7)$$

A4.4.

Homoscedasticity, that is, the variance of u, is constant:

$$\mathrm{var}(u_i) = \sigma^2 \qquad (4.8)$$

A4.5.

No autocorrelation exists between the error terms u_i and u_j:

$$\mathrm{cov}(u_i, u_j) \quad i \neq j \qquad (4.9)$$

A4.6.

No exact collinearity exists between X_2 and X_3; that is, there is no exact linear relationship between the two explanatory variables. This is a new assumption and is explained later.

A4.7.

For hypothesis testing, the error term u follows the normal distribution with mean zero and (homoscedastic) variance σ^2. That is,

$$u_i \sim N(0, \sigma^2) \tag{4.10}$$

Except for Assumption (4.6), the rationale for the other assumptions is the same as that discussed for the two-variable linear regression. As noted in Chapter 3, we make these assumptions to facilitate the development of the subject. In Part II we will revisit these assumptions and see what happens if one or more of them are not fulfilled in actual applications.

According to Assumption (4.6) there is no exact linear relationship between the explanatory variables X_2 and X_3, technically known as the assumption of *no collinearity,* or no **multicollinearity,** if more than one exact linear relationship is involved. This concept is new and needs some explanation.

Informally, no perfect collinearity means that a variable, say, X_2, cannot be expressed as an exact linear function of another variable, say, X_3. Thus, if we can express

$$X_{2t} = 3 + 2X_{3t}$$

or

$$X_{2t} = 4X_{3t}$$

then the two variables are **collinear,** for there is an **exact linear relationship** between X_2 and X_3. Assumption (4.6) states that this should not be the case. The logic here is quite simple. If, for example, $X_2 = 4X_3$, then substituting this in Eq. (4.1), we see that

$$E(Y_t) = B_1 + B_2(4X_{3t}) + B_3 X_{3t}$$
$$= B_1 + (4B_2 + B_3)X_{3t}$$
$$= B_1 + AX_{3t} \tag{4.11}$$

where

$$A = 4B_2 + B_3 \tag{4.12}$$

Equation (4.11) is a two-variable model, not a three-variable model. Now even if we can estimate Eq. (4.11) and obtain an estimate of A, there is no way that we can get individual estimates of B_2 or B_3 from the estimated A. Note that since Equation (4.12) is one equation with two unknowns we need two (independent) equations to obtain unique estimates of B_2 and B_3.

The upshot of this discussion is that in cases of perfect collinearity we cannot estimate the individual partial regression coefficients B_2 and B_3; in other words, we cannot assess the individual effect of X_2 and X_3 on Y. But this is hardly surprising, for we really do not have two independent variables in the model.

Although, in practice, the case of perfect collinearity is rare, the cases of **high** or **near perfect collinearity** abound. In a later chapter (see Chapter 8) we will examine this case more fully. For now we merely require that two or more explanatory variables do not have exact linear relationships among them.

4.3   ESTIMATION OF THE PARAMETERS OF MULTIPLE REGRESSION

To estimate the parameters of Eq. (4.2), we use the ordinary least squares (OLS) method whose main features have already been discussed in Chapters 2 and 3.

Ordinary Least Squares Estimators

To find the OLS estimators, let us first write the sample regression function (SRF) corresponding to the PRF Eq. (4.2), as follows:

$$Y_t = b_1 + b_2 X_{2t} + b_3 X_{3t} + e_t \tag{4.13}$$

where, following the convention introduced in Chapter 2, e is the *residual term,* or simply the *residual*—the sample counterpart of u—and where the b's are the *estimators* of the population coefficients, the B's. More specifically,

$$b_1 = \text{the estimator of } B_1$$
$$b_2 = \text{the estimator of } B_2$$
$$b_3 = \text{the estimator of } B_3$$

The sample counterpart of Eq. (4.1) is

$$\hat{Y}_t = b_1 + b_2 X_{2t} + b_3 X_{3t} \tag{4.14}$$

which is the *estimated* population regression line (PRL) (actually a plane).

As explained in Chapter 2, the OLS principle chooses the values of the unknown parameters in such a way that the residual sum of squares (RSS) $\sum e_t^2$ is as small as possible. To do this, we first write Equation (4.13) as

$$e_t = Y_t - b_1 - b_2 X_{2t} - b_3 X_{3t} \tag{4.15}$$

Squaring this equation on both sides and summing over the sample observations, we obtain

$$\text{RSS: } \sum e_t^2 = \sum (Y_t - b_1 - b_2 X_{2t} - b_3 X_{3t})^2 \tag{4.16}$$

And in OLS we minimize this RSS (which is simply the sum of the squared difference between actual Y_t and estimated Y_t).

The minimization of Equation (4.16) involves the calculus technique of differentiation. Without going into detail, this process of differentiation gives us the following equations, known as (least squares) *normal equations*, to help estimate the unknowns[7] (compare them with the corresponding equations given for the two-variable case in Equations [2.14] and [2.15]):

$$\overline{Y} = b_1 + b_2\overline{X}_2 + b_3\overline{X}_3 \tag{4.17}$$

$$\sum YX_{2t} = b_1\sum X_{2t} + b_2\sum X_{2t}^2 + b_3\sum X_{2t}X_{3t} \tag{4.18}$$

$$\sum Y_t X_{3t} = b_1\sum X_{3t} + b_2\sum X_{2t}X_{3t} + b_3\sum X_{3t}^2 \tag{4.19}$$

where the summation is over the sample range 1 to n. Here we have three equations in three unknowns; the knowns are the variables Y and the X's and the unknowns are the b's. Ordinarily, we should be able to solve three equations with three unknowns. By simple algebraic manipulations of the preceding equations, we obtain the three OLS estimators as follows:

$$b_1 = \overline{Y} - b_2\overline{X}_2 - b_3\overline{X}_3 \tag{4.20}$$

$$b_2 = \frac{\left(\sum y_t x_{2t}\right)\left(\sum x_{3t}^2\right) - \left(\sum y_t x_{3t}\right)\left(\sum x_{2t}x_{3t}\right)}{\left(\sum x_{2t}^2\right)\left(\sum x_{3t}^2\right) - \left(\sum x_{2t}x_{3t}\right)^2} \tag{4.21}$$

$$b_3 = \frac{\left(\sum y_t x_{3t}\right)\left(\sum x_{2t}^2\right) - \left(\sum y_t x_{2t}\right)\left(\sum x_{2t}x_{3t}\right)}{\left(\sum x_{2t}^2\right)\left(\sum x_{3t}^2\right) - \left(\sum x_{2t}x_{3t}\right)^2} \tag{4.22}$$

where, as usual, lowercase letters denote deviations from sample mean values (e.g., $y_t = Y_t - \overline{Y}$).

You will notice the similarity between these equations and the corresponding ones for the two-variable case given in Eqs. (2.16) and (2.17). Also, notice the following features of the preceding equations: (1) Equations (4.21) and (4.22) are symmetrical in that one can be obtained from the other by interchanging the roles of x_2 and x_3, and (2) the denominators of these two equations are identical.

Variance and Standard Errors of OLS Estimators

Having obtained the OLS estimators of the intercept and partial regression coefficients, we can derive the variances and standard errors of these estimators in the manner of the two-variable model. These variances or standard errors give us some idea about the variability of the estimators from sample to sample. As in the two-variable case, we need the standard errors for two main

---

[7]The mathematical details can be found in Appendix 4A.1.

purposes: (1) to establish confidence intervals for the true parameter values and (2) to test statistical hypotheses. The relevant formulas, stated without proof, are as follows:

$$\text{var}(b_1) = \left[\frac{1}{n} + \frac{\overline{X}_2^2 \sum x_{3t}^2 + \overline{X}_3^2 \sum x_{2t}^2 - 2\overline{X}_2\overline{X}_3 \sum x_{2t}x_{3t}}{\sum x_{2t}^2 \sum x_{3t}^2 - (\sum x_{2t}x_{3t})^2} \right] \cdot \sigma^2 \qquad (4.23)$$

$$\text{se}(b_1) = \sqrt{\text{var}(b_1)} \qquad (4.24)$$

$$\text{var}(b_2) = \frac{\sum x_{3t}^2}{\left(\sum x_{2t}^2\right)\left(\sum x_{3t}^2\right) - (\sum x_{2t} x_{3t})^2} \cdot \sigma^2 \qquad (4.25)$$

$$\text{se}(b_2) = \sqrt{\text{var}(b_2)} \qquad (4.26)$$

$$\text{var}(b_3) = \frac{\sum x_{2t}^2}{\left(\sum x_{2t}^2\right)\left(\sum x_{3t}^2\right) - (\sum x_{2t} x_{3t})^2} \cdot \sigma^2 \qquad (4.27)$$

$$\text{se}(b_3) = \sqrt{\text{var}(b_3)} \qquad (4.28)$$

In all these formulas σ^2 is the (homoscedastic) variance of the population error term u_t. The OLS estimator of this unknown variance is

$$\hat{\sigma}^2 = \frac{\sum e_t^2}{n - 3} \qquad (4.29)$$

This formula is a straightforward extension of its two-variable companion given in Equation (3.8) except that now the degrees of freedom (d.f.) are $(n-3)$. This is because in estimating RSS, $\sum e_t^2$, we must first obtain b_1, b_2, and b_3, which consume 3 d.f. This argument is quite general. In the four-variable case the d.f. will be $(n-4)$; in the five-variable case, $(n-5)$; etc.

Also, note that the (positive) square root of $\hat{\sigma}^2$

$$\hat{\sigma} = \sqrt{\hat{\sigma}^2} \qquad (4.30)$$

is the *standard error of the estimate,* or the *standard error of the regression,* which, as noted in Chapter 3, is the standard deviation of Y values around the estimated regression line.

A word about computing $\sum e_t^2$. Since $\sum e_t^2 = \sum(Y_t - \hat{Y}_t)^2$, to compute this expression, one has first to compute $\hat{Y}_t$, which the computer does very easily. But there is a shortcut to computing the RSS (see Appendix 4A.2), which is

$$\sum e_t^2 = \sum y_t^2 - b_2 \sum y_t x_{2t} - b_3 \sum y_t x_{3t} \qquad (4.31)$$

which can be readily computed once the partial slopes are estimated.

Properties of OLS Estimators of Multiple Regression

In the two-variable case we saw that under assumed conditions the OLS estimators are best linear unbiased estimators (BLUE). This property continues to hold for the multiple regression. Thus, each regression coefficient estimated by OLS is linear and unbiased—on the average it coincides with the true value. Among all such linear unbiased estimators, the OLS estimators have the least possible variance so that the true parameter can be estimated more accurately than by competing linear unbiased estimators. In short, the OLS estimators are efficient.

As the preceding development shows, in many ways the three-variable model is an extension of its two-variable counterpart, although the estimating formulas are a bit involved. These formulas get much more involved and cumbersome once we go beyond the three-variable model. In that case, we have to use matrix algebra, which expresses various estimating formulas more compactly. Of course, in this text matrix algebra is not used. Besides, today you rarely compute the estimates by hand; instead, you let the computer do the work.

4.4 GOODNESS OF FIT OF ESTIMATED MULTIPLE REGRESSION: MULTIPLE COEFFICIENT OF DETERMINATION, R^2

In the two-variable case we saw that r^2 as defined in Equation (3.38) measures the goodness of fit of the fitted sample regression line (SRL); that is, it gives the *proportion or percentage of the total variation in the dependent variable Y explained by the single explanatory variable X*. This concept of r^2 can be extended to regression models containing any number of explanatory variables. Thus, in the three-variable case we would like to know the proportion of the total variation in $Y(=\sum y_i^2)$ explained by X_2 and X_3 jointly. The quantity that gives this information is known as the **multiple coefficient of determination** and is denoted by the symbol R^2; conceptually, it is akin to r^2.

As in the two-variable case, we have the identity (cf. Eq. 3.36):

$$\text{TSS} = \text{ESS} + \text{RSS} \qquad (4.32)$$

where TSS = the total sum of squares of the dependent variable $Y(=\sum y_i^2)$
ESS = the explained sum of squares (i.e., explained by all the X variables)
RSS = the residual sum of squares

Also, as in the two-variable case, R^2 is defined as

$$R^2 = \frac{\text{ESS}}{\text{TSS}} \qquad (4.33)$$

That is, it is the ratio of the explained sum of squares to the total sum of squares; the only change is that the ESS is now due to more than one explanatory variable.

Now it can be shown that[8]

$$ESS = b_2 \sum y_t x_{2t} + b_3 \sum y_t x_{3t} \tag{4.34}$$

and, as shown before,

$$RSS = \sum y_t^2 - b_2 \sum y_t x_{2t} - b_3 \sum y_t x_{3t} \tag{4.35}$$

Therefore, R^2 can be computed as

$$R^2 = \frac{b_2 \sum y_t x_{2t} + b_3 \sum y_t x_{3t}}{\sum y_t^2} \tag{4.36}[9]$$

In passing, note that the positive square root of R^2, **R**, is known as the **coefficient of multiple correlation**, the two-variable analogue of r. Just as r measures the degree of linear association between Y and X, R can be interpreted as the degree of linear association between Y and all the X variables jointly. Although r can be positive or negative, R is always taken to be positive. In practice, however, R is of little importance.

4.5   ANTIQUE CLOCK AUCTION PRICES REVISITED

Let us take time out to illustrate all the preceding theory with the antique clock auction prices example we considered in Chapter 2 (See Table 2-14). Let Y = auction price, X_2 = age of clock, and X_3 = number of bidders. A priori, one would expect a positive relationship between Y and the two explanatory variables. The results of regressing Y on the two explanatory variables are as follows (the EViews output of this regression is given in Appendix 4A.4).

$$\hat{Y}_i = -1336.049 + 12.7413X_{2i} + 85.7640X_{3i}$$
$$se = (175.2725) \quad (0.9123) \quad (8.8019)$$
$$t = (-7.6226) \quad (13.9653) \quad (9.7437) \tag{4.37}$$
$$p = (0.0000)^* \quad (0.0000)^* \quad (0.0000)^*$$
$$R^2 = 0.8906; \quad F = 118.0585$$

Interpretation of the Regression Results

As expected, the auction price is positively related to both the age of the clock and the number of bidders. The interpretation of the slope coefficient of about 12.74 means that holding other variables constant, if the age of the clock goes up

[8]See Appendix 4A.2.

[9]R^2 can also be computed as $1 - \frac{RSS}{TSS} = 1 - \frac{\sum e_t^2}{\sum y_t^2}$.

*Denotes an extremely small value.

by a year, the average price of the clock will go up by about 12.74 marks. Likewise, holding other variables constant, if the number of bidders increases by one, the average price of the clock goes up by about 85.76 marks. The negative value of the intercept has no viable economic meaning. The R^2 value of about 0.89 means that the two explanatory variables account for about 89 percent of the variation in the auction bid price, a fairly high value. The F value given in Eq. (4.37) will be explained shortly.

4.6   HYPOTHESIS TESTING IN A MULTIPLE REGRESSION: GENERAL COMMENTS

Although R^2 gives us an overall measure of goodness of fit of the estimated regression line, by itself R^2 does not tell us whether the estimated partial regression coefficients are statistically significant, that is, statistically different from zero. Some of them may be and some may not be. How do we find out?

To be specific, let us suppose we want to entertain the hypothesis that age of the antique clock has no effect on its price. In other words, we want to test the null hypothesis: $H_0: B_2 = 0$. How do we go about it? From our discussion of hypothesis testing for the two-variable model given in Chapter 3, in order to answer this question we need to find out the sampling distribution of b_2, the estimator of B_2. What is the sampling distribution of b_2? And what is the sampling distribution of b_1 and b_3?

In the two-variable case we saw that the OLS estimators, b_1 and b_2, are normally distributed if we are willing to assume that the error term u follows the normal distribution. Now in Assumption (4.7) we have stated that even for multiple regression we will continue to assume that u is normally distributed with zero mean and constant variance σ^2. Given this and the other assumptions listed in Section 4.2, we can prove that b_1, b_2, and b_3 *each* follow the normal distribution with means equal to B_1, B_2, and B_3, respectively, and the variances given by Eqs. (4.23), (4.25), and (4.27), respectively.

However, as in the two-variable case, if we replace the true but unobservable σ^2 by its unbiased estimator $\hat{\sigma}^2$ given in Eq. (4.29), the OLS estimators follow the t distribution with $(n - 3)$ d.f., not the normal distribution. That is,

$$t = \frac{b_1 - B_1}{se(b_1)} \sim t_{n-3} \qquad (4.38)$$

$$t = \frac{b_2 - B_2}{se(b_2)} \sim t_{n-3} \qquad (4.39)$$

$$t = \frac{b_3 - B_3}{se(b_2)} \sim t_{n-3} \qquad (4.40)$$

Notice that the d.f. are now $(n - 3)$ because in computing the RSS, $\sum e_t^2$, and hence $\hat{\sigma}^2$, we first need to estimate the intercept and the two partial slope coefficients; so we lose 3 d.f.

We know that by replacing σ^2 with $\hat{\sigma}^2$ the OLS estimators follow the t distribution. Now we can use this information to establish confidence intervals as well as to test statistical hypotheses about the true partial regression coefficients. The actual mechanics in many ways resemble the two-variable case, which we now illustrate with an example.

4.7 TESTING HYPOTHESES ABOUT INDIVIDUAL PARTIAL REGRESSION COEFFICIENTS

Suppose in our illustrative example we hypothesize that

$$H_0: B_2 = 0 \quad \text{and} \quad H_1: B_2 \neq 0$$

That is, under the null hypothesis, the age of the antique clock has no effect whatsoever on its bid price, whereas under the alternative hypothesis, it is contended that age has some effect, positive or negative, on price. The alternative hypothesis is thus two-sided.

Given the preceding null hypothesis, we know that

$$t = \frac{b_2 - B_2}{\text{se}(b_2)}$$

$$= \frac{b_2}{\text{se}(b_2)} \qquad (\textit{Note: } B_2 = 0) \qquad (4.41)$$

follows the t distribution with $(n - 3) = 29$ d.f., since $n = 32$ in our example. From the regression results given in Eq. (4.37), we obtain

$$t = \frac{12.7413}{0.9123} \approx 13.9653 \qquad (4.42)$$

which has the t distribution with 29 d.f.

On the basis of the computed t value, do we reject the null hypothesis that the age of the antique clock has no effect on its bid price? To answer this question, we can either use the *test of significance approach* or the *confidence interval approach,* as we did for the two-variable regression.

The Test of Significance Approach

Recall that in the test of significance approach to hypothesis testing we develop a test statistic, find out its sampling distribution, choose a level of significance α, and determine the critical value(s) of the test statistic at the chosen level of significance. Then we compare the value of the test statistic obtained from the sample at hand with the critical value(s) and reject the null hypothesis if the computed value of the test statistic exceeds the critical value(s).[10] Alternatively,

---

[10]If the test statistic has a negative value, we consider its absolute value and say that if the absolute value of the test statistic exceeds the critical value, we reject the null hypothesis.

we can find the p value of the test statistic and reject the null hypothesis if the p value is smaller than the chosen α value. The approach that we followed for the two-variable case also carries over to the multiple regression.

Returning to our illustrative example, we know that the test statistic in question is the t statistic, which follows the t distribution with $(n - 3)$ d.f. Therefore, we use the *t test of significance.* The actual mechanics are now straightforward. Suppose we choose $\alpha = 0.05$ or 5%. Since the alternative hypothesis is two-sided, we have to find the critical t value at $\alpha/2 = 2.5\%$ (Why?) for $(n - 3)$ d.f., which in the present example is 29. Then from the t table we observe that for 29 d.f.,

$$(-2.045 \le t \le 2.045) = 0.95 \qquad \textbf{(4.43)}$$

That is, the probability that a t value lies between the limits -2.045 and $+2.045$ (i.e., the critical t values) is 95 percent.

From Eq. (4.42), we see that the computed t value under $H_0 : B_2 = 0$ is approximately 14, which obviously exceeds the critical t value of 2.045. We therefore reject the null hypothesis and conclude that age of an antique clock definitely has an influence on its bid price. This conclusion is also reinforced by the p value given in Eq. (4.37), which is practically zero. That is, if the null hypothesis that $B_2 = 0$ were true, our chances of obtaining a t value of about 14 or greater would be practically nil. Therefore, we can reject the null hypothesis more resoundingly on the basis of the p value than the conventionally chosen α value of 1% or 5%.

One-Tail or Two-Tail t Test?   Since, a priori, we expect the coefficient of the age variable to be positive, we should in fact use the one-tail t test here. The 5% critical t value for the one-tail test for 29 d.f. now becomes 1.699. Since the computed t value of about 14 is still so much greater than 1.699, we reject the null hypothesis and now conclude that the age of the antique clock *positively* impacts its bid price; the two-tail test, on the other hand, simply told us that age of the antique clock could have a positive or negative impact on its bid price. Therefore, be careful about how you formulate your null and alternative hypotheses. Let theory be the guide in choosing these hypotheses.

The Confidence Interval Approach to Hypothesis Testing

The basics of the confidence interval approach to hypothesis testing have already been discussed in Chapter 3. Here we merely illustrate it with our numerical example. We showed previously that

$$P(-2.045 \le t \le 2.045) = 0.95$$

We also know from Eq. (4.39) that

$$t = \frac{b_2 - B_2}{\text{se}(b_2)}$$

If we substitute this t value into Equation (4.43), we obtain

$$P\left(-2.045 \leq \frac{b_2 - B_2}{se(b_2)} \leq 2.045\right) = 0.95$$

Which, after rearranging becomes

$$P[b_2 - 2.045\ se(b_2) \leq B_2 \leq b_2 + 2.045\ se(b_2)] = 0.95 \qquad \textbf{(4.44)}$$

which is a 95% confidence interval for B_2 (cf. Eq. [3.26]). Recall that under the confidence interval approach, if the confidence interval, which we call the *acceptance region,* includes the null-hypothesized value, we do not reject the null hypothesis. On the other hand, if the null-hypothesized value lies outside the confidence interval, that is, in the *region of rejection,* we can reject the null hypothesis. But always bear in mind that in making either decision we are taking a chance of being wrong $\alpha\%$ (say, 5%) of the time.

For our illustrative example, Eq. (4.44) becomes

$$12.7413 - 2.045(0.9123) \leq B_2 \leq 12.7413 + 2.045(0.9123)$$

that is,

$$10.8757 \leq B_2 \leq 14.6069 \qquad \textbf{(4.45)}$$

which is a 95% confidence interval for true B_2. Since this interval does not include the null-hypothesized value, we can reject the null hypothesis: If we construct confidence intervals like expression (4.45), then 95 out of 100 such intervals will include the true B_2, but, as noted in Chapter 3, *we cannot say that the probability is 95% that the particular interval in Eq. (4.45) does or does not include the true B_2.*

Needless to say, we can use the two approaches to hypothesis testing to test hypotheses about any other coefficient given in the regression results for our illustrative example. As you can see from the regression results, the variable, number of bidders, is also statistically significant (i.e., significantly different from zero) because the estimated t value of about 8 has a p value of almost zero. Remember that the lower the p value, the greater the evidence against the null hypothesis.

4.8   TESTING THE JOINT HYPOTHESIS THAT $B_2 = B_3 = 0$ OR $R^2 = 0$

For our illustrative example we saw that *individually* the partial slope coefficients b_2 and b_3 are statistically significant; that is, *individually* each partial slope coefficient is significantly different from zero. But now consider the following null hypothesis:

$$H_0: B_2 = B_3 = 0 \qquad \textbf{(4.46)}$$

This null hypothesis is a **joint hypothesis** that B_2 and B_3 are *jointly* or *simultaneously* (and not individually or singly) equal to zero. This hypothesis states that the two explanatory variables *together* have no influence on Y. This is the same as saying that

$$H_0: R^2 = 0 \qquad \qquad \textbf{(4.47)}$$

That is, the two explanatory variables explain zero percent of the variation in the dependent variable (recall the definition of R^2). Therefore, the two sets of hypotheses (4.46) and (4.47) are equivalent; one implies the other. A test of either hypothesis is called a **test of the overall significance of the estimated multiple regression;** that is, whether Y is linearly related to both X_2 and X_3.

How do we test, say, the hypothesis given in Equation (4.46)? The temptation here is to state that since individually b_2 and b_3 are statistically different from zero in the present example, then jointly or collectively they also must be statistically different from zero; that is, we reject H_0 given in Eq. (4.46). In other words, since age of the antique clock and the number of bidders at the auction *each* has a significant effect on the auction price, *together* they also must have a significant effect on the auction price. But we should be careful here for, as we show more fully in Chapter 8 on multicollinearity, in practice, in a multiple regression one or more variables *individually* have no effect on the dependent variable but *collectively* they have a significant impact on it. *This means that the t-testing procedure discussed previously, although valid for testing the statistical significance of an individual regression coefficient, is not valid for testing the joint hypothesis.*

How then do we test a hypothesis like Eq. (4.46)? This can be done by using a technique known as **analysis of variance (ANOVA).** To see how this technique is employed, recall the following identity:

$$\text{TSS} = \text{ESS} + \text{RSS} \qquad \qquad \textbf{(4.32)}$$

That is,

$$\sum y_t^2 = b_2 \sum y_t x_{2t} + b_3 \sum y_t x_{3t} + \sum e_t^2 \qquad \qquad \textbf{(4.48)}^{11}$$

Equation (4.48) *decomposes* the TSS into two components, one explained by the (chosen) regression model (ESS) and the other not explained by the model (RSS). *A study of these components of TSS is known as the analysis of variance (ANOVA) from the regression viewpoint.*

As noted in Appendix C every sum of squares has associated with it its degrees of freedom (d.f.); that is, the number of independent observations on

---

[11]This is Equation (4.35) written differently.

TABLE 4-1   ANOVA TABLE FOR THE THREE-VARIABLE REGRESSION

Source of variation	Sum of squares (SS)	d.f.	MSS $= \frac{\text{SS}}{\text{d.f.}}$
Due to regression (ESS)	$b_2 \sum y_t x_{2t} + b_3 \sum y_t x_{3t}$	2	$\dfrac{b_2 \sum y_t x_{2t} + b_3 \sum y_t x_{3t}}{2}$
Due to residual (RSS)	$\sum e_t^2$	$n - 3$	$\dfrac{\sum e_t^2}{n - 3}$
Total (TSS)	$\sum y_t^2$	$n - 1$	

Note: MSS = mean, or average, sum of squares.

the basis of which the sum of squares is computed. Now each of the preceding sums of squares has these d.f.:

Sum of squares	d.f.
TSS	$n - 1$ (always, Why?)
RSS	$n - 3$ (three-variable model)
ESS	2 (three-variable model)*

*An easy way to find the d.f. for ESS is to subtract the d.f. for RSS from the d.f. for TSS.

Let us arrange all these sums of squares and their associated d.f. in a tabular form, known as the ANOVA table, as shown in Table 4-1.

Now given the assumptions of the CLRM (and Assumption 4.7) and the null hypothesis: $H_0: B_2 = B_3 = 0$, it can be shown that the variable

$$F = \frac{\text{ESS}/\text{d.f.}}{\text{RSS}/\text{d.f.}}$$

$$= \frac{\text{variance explained by } X_2 \text{ and } X_3}{\text{unexplained variance}} \qquad \textbf{(4.49)}$$

$$= \frac{(b_2 \sum y_t x_{2t} + b_3 \sum y_t x_{3t})/2}{\sum e_t^2/(n - 3)}$$

follows the F distribution with 2 and $(n - 3)$ d.f. in the numerator and denominator, respectively. (See Appendix C for a general discussion of the F distribution and Appendix D for some applications). *In general, if the regression model has k explanatory variables including the intercept term, the F ratio has $(k - 1)$ d.f. in the numerator and $(n - k)$ d.f. in the denominator.*[12]

How can we use the F ratio of Equation (4.49) to test the joint hypothesis that both X_2 and X_3 have no impact on Y? The answer is evident in Eq. (4.49). If the

---

[12] A simple way to remember this is that the numerator d.f. of the F ratio is equal to the number of *partial slope coefficients* in the model, and the denominator d.f. is equal to n minus the total number of parameters estimated (i.e., partial slopes plus the intercept).

TABLE 4-2   ANOVA TABLE FOR THE CLOCK AUCTION PRICE EXAMPLE

Source of variation	Sum of squares (SS)	d.f.	MSS $= \frac{SS}{d.f.}$
Due to regression (ESS)	4278295.3	2	4278295.3/2
Due to residual (RSS)	525462.2	29	525462.2/29
Total (TSS)	4803757.5	31	

$F = 2139147.6/18119.386 = 118.0585^*$

*Figures have been rounded.

numerator of Eq. (4.49) is larger than its denominator—if the variance of Y explained by the regression (i.e., by X_2 and X_3) is larger than the variance not explained by the regression—the F value will be greater than 1. Therefore, as the variance explained by the X variables becomes increasingly larger relative to the unexplained variance, the F ratio will be increasingly larger, too. *Thus, an increasingly large F value will be evidence against the null hypothesis that the two (or more) explanatory variables have no effect on Y.*

Of course, this intuitive reasoning can be formalized in the usual framework of hypothesis testing. As shown in Appendix C, Section C.4, we compute F as given in Eq. (4.49) and compare it with the critical F value for 2 and $(n - 3)$ d.f. at the chosen level of α, the probability of committing a type I error. *As usual, if the computed F value exceeds the critical F value, we reject the null hypothesis that the impact of all explanatory variables is simultaneously equal to zero. If it does not exceed the critical F value, we do not reject the null hypothesis that the explanatory variables have no impact whatsoever on the dependent variable.*

To illustrate the actual mechanics, let us return to our illustrative example. The numerical counterpart of Table 4-1 is given in Table 4-2.

The entries in this table are obtained from the EViews computer output given in Appendix 4A.4.[13] From this table and the computer output, we see that the estimated F value is 118.0585, or about 119. Under the null hypothesis that $B_2 = B_3 = 0$, and given the assumptions of the classical linear regression model (CLRM), we know that the computed F value follows the F distribution with 2 and 29 d.f. in the numerator and denominator, respectively. If the null hypothesis were true, what would be the probability of our obtaining an F value of as much as 118 or greater for 2 and 13 d.f.? The p value of obtaining an F value of 118 or greater is 0.000000, which is practically zero. Hence, we can reject the null hypothesis that age and number of bidders *together* has no effect on the bid price of antique clocks.[14]

In our illustrative example it so happens that not only do we reject the null hypothesis that B_2 and B_3 are *individually* statistically insignificant, but we also

---

[13]Unlike other software packages, EViews does not produce the ANOVA table, although it gives the F value. But it is very easy to construct this table, for EViews gives TSS and RSS from which ESS can be easily obtained.

[14]If you had chosen $\alpha = 1\%$, the critical F value for 2 and 30 (which is close to 29) d.f. would be 5.39. The F value of 118 is obviously much greater than this critical value.

reject the hypothesis that *collectively* they are insignificant. However, this need not happen all the time. We will come across cases where not all explanatory variables individually have much impact on the dependent variable (i.e., some of the t values may be statistically insignificant) yet all of them *collectively* influence the dependent variable (i.e., the F test will reject the null hypothesis that all partial slope coefficients are simultaneously equal to zero.) As we will see, this happens if we have the problem of multicollinearity, which we will discuss more in Chapter 8.

An Important Relationship between *F* and R^2

There is an important relationship between the coefficient of determination R^2 and the F ratio used in ANOVA. This relationship is as follows:

$$F = \frac{R^2/(k-1)}{(1-R^2)/(n-k)} \qquad (4.50)$$

where n = the number of observations and k = the number of explanatory variables including the intercept.

Equation (4.50) shows how F and R^2 are related. These two statistics vary directly. When $R^2 = 0$ (i.e., no relationship between Y and the X variables), F is zero ipso facto. The larger R^2 is, the greater the F value will be. In the limit when $R^2 = 1$, the F value is infinite.

Thus the **F test** discussed earlier, which is a measure of the overall significance of the estimated regression line, is also a test of significance of R^2; that is, whether R^2 is different from zero. In other words, testing the null hypothesis Eq. (4.46) is equivalent to testing the null hypothesis that (the population) R^2 is zero, as noted in Eq. (4.47).

One advantage of the F test expressed in terms of R^2 is the ease of computation. All we need to know is the R^2 value, which is routinely computed by most regression programs. Therefore, the overall F test of significance given in Eq. (4.49) can be recast in terms of R^2 as shown in Eq. (4.50), and the ANOVA Table 4-1 can be equivalently expressed as Table 4-3.

TABLE 4-3   ANOVA TABLE IN TERMS OF R^2

Source of variation	Sum of squares (SS)	d.f.	MSS $= \frac{SS}{d.f.}$
Due to regression (ESS)	$R^2\left(\sum y_i^2\right)$	2	$\frac{R^2\left(\sum y_i^2\right)}{2}$
Due to residual (RSS)	$(1-R^2)\left(\sum y_i^2\right)$	$n-3$	$\frac{(1-R^2)\left(\sum y_i^2\right)}{(n-3)}$
Total (TSS)	$\sum y_i^2$	$n-1$	

Note: In computing the F value, we do not need to multiply R^2 and $(1-R^2)$ by $\sum y_i^2$ since it drops out, as can be seen from Eq. (4.49).
In the k-variable model the d.f. will be $(k-1)$ and $(n-k)$, respectively.

For our illustrative example, $R^2 = 0.8906$. Therefore, the F ratio of Equation (4.50) becomes

$$F = \frac{0.8906/2}{(1 - 0.8906)/29} \approx 118.12 \tag{4.51}$$

which is about the same F as shown in Table 4-2, except for rounding errors.

It is left for you to set up the ANOVA table for our illustrative example in the manner of Table 4-3.

4.9   TWO-VARIABLE REGRESSION IN THE CONTEXT OF MULTIPLE REGRESSION: INTRODUCTION TO SPECIFICATION BIAS

Let us return to our example. In Example 2.5, we regressed auction price on the age of the antique clock and the number of bidders separately, as shown in Equations (2.27) and (2.28). These equations are reproduced here with the usual regression output.

$$\hat{Y}_i = -191.6662 + 10.4856 \, Age_i$$
$$se = (264.4393) + (1.7937) \tag{4.52}$$
$$t = (-0.7248) \quad (5.8457) \qquad r^2 = 0.5325; F = 34.1723$$

$$\hat{Y}_i = 807.9501 + 54.5724 \, Bidders$$
$$se = (231.9501) \quad (23.5724) \tag{4.53}$$
$$t = (3.4962) \quad (2.3455) \qquad r^2 = 0.1549; \; F = 5.5017$$

If we compare these regressions with the results of the multiple regression given in Eq. (4.37), we see several differences:

1. The slope values in Equations (4.52) and (4.53) are different from those given in the multiple regression (4.37), especially that of the number of bidders variable.
2. The intercept values in the three regressions are also different.
3. The R^2 value in the multiple regression is quite different from the r^2 values given in the two bivariate regressions. In a bivariate regression, however, R^2 and r^2 are basically indistinguishable.

As we will show, some of these differences are statistically significant and some others may not be.

Why the differences in the results of the two regressions? Remember that in Eq. (4.37), while deriving the impact of age of the antique clock on the auction price, we held the number of bidders constant, whereas in Eq. (4.52) we simply neglected the number of bidders. Put differently, in Eq. (4.37) the effect of a clock's age on auction price is *net* of the effect, or influence, of the number of bidders, whereas in Eq. (4.52) the effect of the number of bidders has *not* been netted out. Thus, the coefficient of the age variable in Eq. (4.52) reflects the *gross effect*—the *direct effect* of age as well as the *indirect effect* of the number of bidders. This difference between the results of regressions (4.37) and (4.52) shows very nicely the meaning of the "partial" regression coefficient.

We saw in our discussion of regression (4.37) that both the age of the clock and the number of bidders variables were *individually* as well as *collectively* important influences on the auction price. Therefore, by omitting the number of bidders variable from regression (4.52) we have committed what is known as a **(model) specification bias** or **specification error,** more specifically, the specification error of omitting a relevant variable from the model. Similarly, by omitting the age of the clock from regression (4.53), we also have committed a specification error.

Although we will examine the topic of specification errors in Chapter 7, what is important to note here is that you should be very careful in developing a regression model for empirical purposes. Take whatever help you can from the underlying theory and/or prior empirical work in developing the model. And once you choose a model, do not drop variables from the model arbitrarily.

4.10   COMPARING TWO R^2 VALUES: THE ADJUSTED R^2

By examining the R^2 values of our two-variable (Eq. [4.52] or Eq. [4.53]) and three-variable (Eq. [4.37]) regressions for our illustrative example, you will notice that the R^2 value of the former (0.5325 for Eq. [4.52] or 0.1549 for Eq. [4.53]) is smaller than that of the latter (0.8906). Is this always the case? Yes! An important property of R^2 is that the larger the number of explanatory variables in a model, the higher the R^2 will be. It would then seem that if we want to explain a substantial amount of the variation in a dependent variable, we merely have to go on adding more explanatory variables!

However, do not take this "advice" too seriously because the definition of $R^2 = \text{ESS}/\text{TSS}$ does not take into account the d.f. Note that in a k-variable model including the intercept term the d.f. for ESS is $(k - 1)$. Thus, if you have a model with 5 explanatory variables including the intercept, the d.f. associated with ESS will be 4, whereas if you had a model with 10 explanatory variables including the intercept, the d.f. for the ESS would be 9. But the conventional R^2 formula does not take into account the differing d.f. in the various models. Note that the d.f. for TSS is always $(n - 1)$. (Why?) *Therefore, comparing the R^2 values of two models with the same dependent variable but with differing numbers of explanatory variables is essentially like comparing apples and oranges.*

Thus, what we need is a measure of goodness of fit that is adjusted for (i.e., takes into account explicitly) the number of explanatory variables in the model. Such a measure has been devised and is known as the **adjusted R^2,** denoted by the symbol, $\overline{R}^2$. This $\overline{R}^2$ can be derived from the conventional R^2 (see Appendix 4A.3) as follows:

$$\overline{R}^2 = 1 - (1 - R^2)\frac{n - 1}{n - k} \qquad \textbf{(4.54)}$$

Note that the R^2 we have considered previously is also known as the *unadjusted* R^2 for obvious reasons.

The features of the adjusted R^2 are:

1. If $k > 1$, $\overline{R}^2 \leq R^2$; that is, as the number of explanatory variables increases in a model, the adjusted R^2 becomes increasingly smaller than the unadjusted R^2. There seems to be a "penalty" involved in adding more explanatory variables to a regression model.
2. Although the unadjusted R^2 is always positive, the adjusted R^2 can on occasion turn out to be negative. For example, in a regression model involving $k = 3$ and $n = 30$, if an R^2 is found to be 0.06, R^2 can be negative (-0.0096).

At present, most computer regression packages compute both the adjusted and unadjusted R^2 values. This is a good practice, for the adjusted R^2 will enable us to compare two regressions that have the *same dependent variable* but a different number of explanatory variables.[15] Even when we are not comparing two regression models, it is a good practice to find the adjusted R^2 value because it explicitly takes into account the number of variables included in a model.

For our illustrative example, you should verify that the adjusted R^2 value is 0.8830, which, as expected, is smaller than the unadjusted R^2 value of 0.8906. The adjusted R^2 values for regressions (4.52) and (4.53) are 0.5169 and 0.1268, respectively, which are slightly lower than the corresponding unadjusted R^2 values.

4.11   WHEN TO ADD AN ADDITIONAL EXPLANATORY VARIABLE TO A MODEL

In practice, in order to explain a particular phenomenon, we are often faced with the problem of deciding among several competing explanatory variables. The common practice is to add variables as long as the adjusted R^2 increases (even though its numerical value may be smaller than the unadjusted R^2). But when does adjusted R^2 increase? *It can be shown that $\overline{R}^2$ will increase if the $|t|$ (absolute t) value of the coefficient of the added variable is larger than 1, where the t value is computed under the null hypothesis that the population value of the said coefficient is zero.*[16]

To see this all clearly, let us first regress auction price on a constant only, then on a constant and the age of the clock, and then on a constant, the age of the clock, and the number of bidders. The results are given in Table 4-4.

---

[15]As we will see in Chapter 5, if two regressions have different dependent variables, we cannot compare their R^2 values directly, adjusted or unadjusted.

[16]Whether or not a particular t value is significant, the adjusted R^2 will increase so long as the $|t|$ of the coefficient of the added variable is greater than 1.

TABLE 4-4 A COMPARISON OF FOUR MODELS OF ANTIQUE CLOCK AUCTION PRICES

Dependent variable	Intercept	Age	# of Bidders	R^2	$\overline{R}^2$	F	
Auction price	1328.094	—	—	0.00	0.00	0	(1)
	(19.0850)						
Auction price	−191.6662	10.4856	—	0.5325	0.5169	34.1723	(2)
	(−0.7248)	(5.8457)					
Auction price	807.9501	—	54.5724	0.1549	0.1268	5.5017	(3)
	(3.4962)		(2.3455)				
Auction price	−1336.049	12.7413	85.7640	0.8906	0.8830	118.0585	(4)
	(−7.6226)	(13.9653)	(9.7437)				

Note: Figures in the parentheses are the estimated *t* values under the null hypothesis that the corresponding population values are zero.

Some interesting facts stand out in this exercise:

1. When we regress auction price on the intercept only, the $R^2, \overline{R}^2, and F$ values are all zero, as we would expect. But what does the intercept value represent here? It is nothing but the (sample) mean value of auction price. One way to check on this is to look at Eq. (2.16). If there is no X variable in this equation, the intercept is equal to the mean value of the dependent variable.

2. When we regress auction price on a constant and the age of the antique clock, we see that the *t* value of the age variable is not only greater than 1, but it is also statistically significant. Unsurprisingly, both $R^2 and \overline{R}^2$ values increase (although the latter is somewhat smaller than the former). But notice an interesting fact. If you square the *t* value of 5.8457, we get $(5.8457)^2 = 34.1722$, which is about the same as the *F* value of 34.1723 shown in Table 4-4. Is this surprising? No, because in Equation (C.15) in Appendix C we state that

$$t_k^2 = F_{1,k} \qquad\qquad \textbf{(4.55)} = \textbf{(C.15)}$$

That is, the square of the *t* statistic with *k* d.f. is equal to the *F* statistic with 1 d.f. in the numerator and *k* d.f. in the denominator. In our example, *k* = 30 (32 observations − 2, the two coefficients estimated in model [2]). The numerator d.f. is 1, because we have only one explanatory variable in this model.

3. When we regress auction price on a constant and the number of bidders, we see that the *t* value of the latter is 2.3455. If you square this value, you will get $(2.3455)^2 = 5.5013$, which is about the same as the *F* value shown in Table 4-4, which again verifies Eq. (4.55). Since the *t* value is greater than 1, both $R^2 and \overline{R}^2$ values have increased. The computed *t* value is also statistically significant, suggesting that the number of bidders variable should be added to model (1). A similar conclusion holds for model (2).

4. How do we decide if it is worth adding both age and number of bidders together to model (1)? We have already answered this question with the help of the ANOVA technique and the attendant F test. In Table 4.2 we showed that one could reject the hypothesis that $B_2 = B_3 = 0$; that is, the two explanatory variables together have no impact on the auction bid price.[17]

4.12   RESTRICTED LEAST SQUARES

Let us take another look at the regressions given in Table 4-4. There we saw the consequences of omitting relevant variables from a regression model. Thus, in regression (1) shown in this table we regressed antique clock auction price on the intercept only, which gave an R^2 value of 0, which is not surprising. Then in regression (4) we regressed auction price on the age of the antique clock as well as on the number of bidders present at the auction, which gave an R^2 value of 0.8906. On the basis of the F test we concluded that there was a specification error and that both the explanatory variables should be added to the model.

Let us call regression (1) the *restricted model* because it implicitly assumes that the coefficients of the age of the clock and the number of bidders are zero; that is, these variables do not belong in the model (i.e., $B_2 = B_3 = 0$). Let us call regression (4) the *unrestricted model* because it includes all the relevant variables. Since (1) is a restricted model, when we estimate it by OLS, we call it **restricted least squares (RLS).** Since (4) is an unrestricted model, when we estimate it by OLS, we call it **unrestricted least squares (URLS).** All the models we have estimated thus far have been essentially URLS, for we have assumed that the model being estimated has been correctly specified and that we have included all the relevant variables in the model. In Chapter 7 we will see the consequences of violating this assumption.

The question now is: How do we decide between RLS and URLS? That is, how do we find out if the restrictions imposed by a model, such as (1) in the present instance, are valid? This question can be answered by the F test. For this purpose, let R_r^2 denote the R^2 value obtained from the restricted model and R_{ur}^2 denote the R^2 value obtained from the unrestricted model. Now assuming that the error term u_i is normally distributed, it can be shown that

$$F = \frac{\left(R_{ur}^2 - R_r^2\right)/m}{\left(1 - R_{ur}^2\right)/(n - k)} \sim F_{m,n-k} \qquad (4.56)$$

follows the F distribution with m and $(n - k)$ d.f. in the numerator and denominator, respectively, where $R_r^2 = R^2$ obtained from the restricted regression,

---

[17]Suppose you have a model with four explanatory variables. Initially you only include two of these variables but then you want to find out if it is worth adding two more explanatory variables. This can be handled by an extension of the F test. For details, see Gujarati and Porter, *Basic Econometrics*, 5th ed., McGraw-Hill, New York, 2009, pp. 243–246.

$R_{ur}^2 = R^2$ obtained from the unrestricted regression, m = number of restrictions imposed by the restricted regression (two in our example), n = number of observations in the sample, and k = number of parameters estimated in the unrestricted regression (including the intercept). The null hypothesis tested here is that the restrictions imposed by the restricted model are valid. If the F value estimated from Equation (4.56) exceeds the critical F value at the chosen level of significance, we reject the restricted regression. That is, in this situation, the restrictions imposed by the (restricted) model are not valid.

Returning to our antique clock auction price example, putting the appropriate values in Eq. (4.56) from Table 4-4, we obtain:

$$F = \frac{(0.890 - 0)/2}{(1 - 0.890)/(32 - 3)} = \frac{0.445}{0.00379} = 117.414 \qquad \textbf{(4.57)}$$

The probability of such an F value is extremely small. Therefore, we reject the restricted regression. More positively, age of the antique clock as well as the number of bidders at auction both have a statistically significant impact on the auction price.

The formula (4.56) is of general application. The only precaution to be taken in its application is that in comparing the restricted and unrestricted regressions, the dependent variables must be in the same form. If they are not, we have to make them comparable using the method discussed in Chapter 5 (see Problem 5.16) or use an alternative that is discussed in Exercise 4.20.

4.13 ILLUSTRATIVE EXAMPLES

To conclude this chapter, we consider several examples involving multiple regressions. Our objective here is to show you how multiple regression models are used in a variety of applications.

Example 4.1. Does Tax Policy Affect Corporate Capital Structure?

To find out the extent to which tax policy has been responsible for the recent trend in U.S. manufacturing toward increasing use of debt capital in lieu of equity capital—that is, toward an increasing debt/equity ratio (called leverage in the financial literature)—Pozdena estimated the following regression model:[18]

$$Y_t = B_1 + B_2 X_{2t} + B_3 X_{3t} + B_4 X_{4t} + B_5 B X_{5t} + B_6 X_{6t} + u_t \qquad \textbf{(4.58)}$$

where Y = the leverage (= debt/equity) in percent
$\quad X_2$ = the corporate tax rate
$\quad X_3$ = the personal tax rate
$\quad X_4$ = the capital gains tax rate
$\quad X_5$ = nondebt-related tax shields
$\quad X_6$ = the inflation rate

[18]Randall Johnston Pozdena, "Tax Policy and Corporate Capital Structure," *Economic Review,* Federal Reserve Bank of San Francisco, Fall 1987, pp. 37–51.

TABLE 4-5   LEVERAGE IN MANUFACTURING CORPORATIONS, 1935–1982

Explanatory variable	Coefficient (t value in parentheses)
Corporate tax rate	2.4
	(10.5)
Personal tax rate	−1.2
	(−4.8)
Capital gains tax rate	0.3
	(1.3)
Non-debt-related tax shield	−2.4
	(−4.8)
Inflation rate	1.4
	(3.0)

$$n = 48 \text{ (number of observations)}$$
$$R^2 = 0.87$$
$$\bar{R}^2 = 0.85$$

Notes: 1. The author does not present the estimated intercept.
2. The adjusted R^2 is calculated using Eq. (4.54).
3. The standard errors of the various coefficients can be obtained by dividing the coefficient value by its *t* value (e.g., 2.4/10.5 = 0.2286 is the se of the corporate tax rate coefficient).
Source: Randall Johnston Pozdena, "Tax Policy and Corporate Capital Structure," *Economic Review*, Federal Reserve Bank of San Francisco, Fall 1987, Table 1, p. 45 (adapted).

Economic theory suggests that coefficients B_2, B_4, and B_6 will be positive and coefficients B_3 and B_5 will be negative.[19] Based on the data for U.S. manufacturing corporations for the years 1935 to 1982, Pozdena obtained the OLS results that are presented in tabular form (Table 4-5) rather than in the usual format (e.g., Eq. [4.37]). (Results are sometimes presented in this form for ease of reading.)

Discussion of Regression Results

The first fact to note about the preceding regression results is that all the coefficients have signs according to prior expectations. For instance, the corporate tax rate has a positive effect on leverage. Holding other things the same, as the corporate tax rate goes up by 1 percentage point, on the average, the leverage ratio (i.e., the debt/equity ratio) goes up by 2.4 percentage points. Likewise, if the inflation rate goes up by 1 percentage point, on the average, leverage goes up by 1.4 percentage points, other things remaining the same. (*Question:* Why would you expect a positive relation between leverage and inflation?) Other partial regression coefficients should be interpreted similarly.

Since the *t* values are presented underneath each partial regression coefficient under the null hypothesis that each population partial regression coefficient is

[19]See Pozdena's article (footnote 18) for the theoretical discussion of expected signs of the various coefficients. In the United States the interest paid on debt capital is tax deductible, whereas the income paid as dividends is not. This is one reason that corporations may prefer debt to equity capital.

individually equal to zero, we can easily test whether such a null hypothesis stands up against the (two-sided) alternative hypothesis that each true population coefficient is different from zero. Hence, we use the two-tail t test. The d.f. in this example are 42, which are obtained by subtracting from n (= 48) the number of parameters estimated, which are 6 in the present instance. (*Note:* The intercept value is not presented in Table 4-5, although it was estimated.) If we choose $\alpha = 0.05$ or 5%, the two-tail *critical t value* is about 2.021 for 40 d.f. (*Note:* This is good enough for present purposes since the t table does not give the precise t value for 42 d.f.) If α is fixed at 0.01 or a 1% level, the critical t value for 40 d.f. is 2.704 (two-tail). Looking at the t values presented in Table 4-5, we see that each partial regression coefficient, except that of the capital gains tax variable, is statistically significantly different from zero at the 1% level of significance. The coefficient of the capital gains tax variable is not significant at either the 1% or 5% level. Therefore, except for this variable, we can reject the *individual* null hypothesis that each partial regression coefficient is zero. In other words, all but one of the explanatory variables *individually* has an impact on the debt/equity ratio. In passing, note that *if an estimated coefficient is statistically significant at the 1% level, it is also significant at the 5% level, but the converse is not true.*

What about the overall significance of the estimated regression line? That is, do we reject the null hypothesis that all partial slopes are *simultaneously* equal to zero or, equivalently, is $R^2 = 0$? This hypothesis can be easily tested by using Eq. (4.50), which in the present case gives

$$
F = \frac{R^2/(k-1)}{(1-R^2)/(n-k)}
$$

$$
= \frac{0.87/5}{0.13/42} \qquad\qquad \textbf{(4.59)}
$$

$$
= 56.22
$$

This F value has an F distribution with 5 and 42 d.f. If α is set at 0.05, the F table (Appendix E, Table E-3) shows that for 5 and 40 d.f. (the table has no exact value of 42 d.f. in the denominator), the *critical F value* is 2.45. The corresponding value at $\alpha = 0.01$ is 3.51. The computed F of $\approx$ 56 far exceeds either of these critical F values. Therefore, we reject the null hypothesis that all partial slopes are simultaneously equal to zero or, alternatively, $R^2 = 0$. *Collectively,* all five explanatory variables influence the dependent variable. *Individually,* however, as we have seen, only four variables have an impact on the dependent variable, the debt/equity ratio. Example 4.1 again underscores the point made earlier that the (individual) t test and the (joint) F test are quite different.[20]

---

[20]In the two-variable linear regression model, as noted before, $t_k^2 = F_{1,k}$; that is, the square of a t value with k d.f. is equal to an F value with 1 d.f. in the numerator and k d.f. in the denominator.

Example 4.2. The Demand for Imports in Jamaica

To explain the demand for imports in Jamaica, J. Gafar[21] obtained the following regression based on annual data for 19 years:

$$\hat{Y}_t = -58.9 + 0.20X_{2t} - 0.10X_{3t}$$

$$se = \quad\quad\quad (0.0092) \quad (0.084) \quad\quad R^2 = 0.96 \quad\quad\quad\quad \textbf{(4.60)}$$

$$t = \quad\quad\quad (21.74) \quad (-1.1904) \quad \bar{R}^2 = 0.955$$

where Y = quantity of imports
$\quad\quad X_2$ = personal consumption expenditure
$\quad\quad X_3$ = import price/domestic price

Economic theory would suggest a positive relationship between Y and X_2 and a negative relationship between Y and X_3, which turns out to be the case. Individually, the coefficient of X_2 is statistically significant but that of X_3 is not at, say, the 5% level. But since the absolute t value of X_3 is greater than 1, R^2 for this example will drop if X_3 is dropped from the model. (Why?) Together, X_2 and X_3 explain about 96 percent of the variation in the quantity of imports into Jamaica.

Example 4.3. The Demand for Alcoholic Beverages in the United Kingdom

To explain the demand for alcoholic beverages in the United Kingdom, T. McGuinness[22] estimated the following regression based on annual data for 20 years:

$$\hat{Y}_t = -0.014 - 0.354X_{2t} + 0.0018X_{3t} + 0.657X_{4t} + 0.0059X_{5t}$$

$$se = (0.012) \quad (0.2688) \quad\quad (0.0005) \quad\quad (0.266) \quad\quad (0.0034)$$

$$t = (-1.16) \quad (1.32) \quad\quad\quad (3.39) \quad\quad\quad (2.47) \quad\quad (1.73) \quad \textbf{(4.61)}$$

$$R^2 = 0.689$$

where Y = the annual change in pure alcohol consumption per adult
$\quad\quad X_2$ = the annual change in the real price index of alcoholic drinks
$\quad\quad X_3$ = the annual change in the real disposable income per person
$$X_4 = \frac{\text{the annual change in the number of licensed premises}}{\text{the adult population}}$$
$\quad\quad X_5$ = the annual change in real advertising expenditure on alcoholic drinks per adult

Theory would suggest that all but the variable X_2 will be positively related to Y. This is borne out by the results, although not all coefficients are

[21]J. Gafar, "Devaluation and the Balance of Payments Adjustment in a Developing Economy: An Analysis Relating to Jamaica," *Applied Economics*, vol. 13, 1981, pp. 151–165. Notations were adapted. Adjusted R^2 computed.

[22]T. McGuinness, "An Econometric Analysis of Total Demand for Alcoholic Beverages in the United Kingdom," *Journal of Industrial Economics*, vol. 29, 1980, pp. 85–109. Notations were adapted.

individually statistically significant. For 15 d.f. (Why?), the 5% critical t value is 1.753 (one-tail) and 2.131 (two-tail). Consider the coefficient of X_5, the change in advertising expenditure. Since the advertising expenditure and the demand for alcoholic beverages are expected to be positive (otherwise, it is bad news for the advertising industry), we can entertain the hypothesis that $H_0 : B_5 = 0$ vs. $H_1 : B_5 > 0$ and therefore use the one-tail t test. The computed t value of 1.73 is very close to being significant at the 5% level.

It is left as an exercise for you to compute the F value for this example to test the hypothesis that all partial slope coefficients are simultaneously equal to zero.

Example 4.4. Civilian Labor Force Participation Rate, Unemployment Rate, and Average Hourly Earnings Revisited

In Chapter 1 we presented regression (1.5) without discussing the statistical significance of the results. Now we have the necessary tools to do that. The complete regression results are as follows:

$$\widehat{CLFPR}_t = 81.2267 - 0.6384 CUNR_t - 1.4449 AHE82_t$$

$$se = (3.4040) \quad (0.0715) \quad\quad (0.4148)$$

$$t = (23.88) \quad (-8.94) \quad\quad (-3.50) \quad\quad\quad \textbf{(4.62)}$$

$$p \text{ value} = (0.000)^* \quad (0.000)^* \quad\quad (0.002)$$

$$R^2 = 0.767; \quad \overline{R}^2 = 0.748; \quad F = 41.09$$

As these results show, each of the estimated regression coefficients is individually statistically highly significant, because the p values are so small. That is, each coefficient is significantly different from zero. Collectively, both $CUNR$ and $AHE82$ are also highly statistically significant, because the p value of the computed F value (for 2 and 25 d.f.) of 41.09 is extremely low.

As expected, the civilian unemployment rate has a negative relationship to the civilian labor force participation rate, suggesting that perhaps the discouraged-worker effect dominates the added-worker hypothesis. The theoretical reasoning behind this has already been explained in Chapter 1. The negative value of $AHE82$ suggests that perhaps the income effect dominates the substitution effect.

Example 4.5. Expenditure on Education in 38 Countries:[23]

Based on data taken from a sample of 38 countries (see Table 4-6, found on the textbook's Web site), we obtained the following regression:

$$Educ_i = 414.4583 + 0.0523 GDP_i - 50.0476 \, Pop$$

---

[23]The data used in this exercise are from Gary Koop, *Introduction to Econometrics*, John Wiley & Sons, England, 2008 and can be found on the following Web site: **www.wileyeurope.com/college/koop**.

*Denotes extremely small value.

$$se = (266.4583) \quad (0.0018) \quad (\ 9.9581)$$
$$t = (1.5538) \quad (28.2742) \quad (-5.0257)$$
$$p \text{ value} = (0.1292) \quad (0.0000) \quad (0.0000)$$
$$R^2 = 0.9616; \overline{R}^2 = 0.9594; F = 439.22; p \text{ value of } F = 0.000$$

where Educ = expenditure on education (millions of U.S. dollars), GDP = gross domestic product (millions of U.S. dollars), and Pop = population (millions of people). As you can see from the data, the sample includes a variety of countries in different stages of economic development.

It can be readily assessed that the GDP and Pop variables are individually highly significant, although the sign of the population variable may be puzzling. Since the estimated F is so highly significant, collectively the two variables have a significant impact on expenditure on education. As noted, the variables are also individually significant.

The R^2 and adjusted $\overline{R}^2$ square values are quite high, which is unusual in a cross-section sample of diverse countries.

We will explore these data further in later chapters.

4.14 SUMMARY

In this chapter we considered the simplest of the multiple regression models, namely, the three-variable linear regression model—one dependent variable and two explanatory variables. Although in many ways a straightforward extension of the two-variable linear regression model, the three-variable model introduced several new concepts, such as partial regression coefficients, adjusted and unadjusted multiple coefficient of determination, and multicollinearity.

Insofar as estimation of the parameters of the multiple regression coefficients is concerned, we still worked within the framework of the classical linear regression model and used the method of ordinary least squares (OLS). The OLS estimators of multiple regression, like the two-variable model, possess several desirable statistical properties summed up in the Gauss-Markov property of best linear unbiased estimators (BLUE).

With the assumption that the disturbance term follows the normal distribution with zero mean and constant variance σ^2, we saw that, as in the two-variable case, each estimated coefficient in the multiple regression follows the normal distribution with a mean equal to the true population value and the variances given by the formulas developed in the text. Unfortunately, in practice, σ^2 is not known and has to be estimated. The OLS estimator of this unknown variance is $\hat{\sigma}^2$. But if we replace σ^2 by $\hat{\sigma}^2$, then, as in the two-variable case, each estimated coefficient of the multiple regression follows the t distribution, not the normal distribution.

The knowledge that each multiple regression coefficient follows the t distribution with d.f. equal to $(n - k)$, where k is the number of parameters estimated (including the intercept), means we can use the t distribution to test statistical hypotheses about each multiple regression coefficient individually. This can be done on the basis of either the t test of significance or the confidence interval based on the t distribution. In this respect, the multiple regression model does not differ much from the two-variable model, except that proper allowance must be made for the d.f., which now depend on the number of parameters estimated.

However, when testing the hypothesis that all partial slope coefficients are simultaneously equal to zero, the individual t testing referred to earlier is of no help. Here we should use the analysis of variance (ANOVA) technique and the attendant F test. Incidentally, testing that all partial slope coefficients are simultaneously equal to zero is the same as testing that the multiple coefficient of determination R^2 is equal to zero. Therefore, the F test can also be used to test this latter but equivalent hypothesis.

We also discussed the question of when to add a variable or a group of variables to a model, using either the t test or the F test. In this context we also discussed the method of restricted least squares.

All the concepts introduced in this chapter have been illustrated by numerical examples and by concrete economic applications.

KEY TERMS AND CONCEPTS

The key terms and concepts introduced in this chapter are

Multiple regression model
  Partial regression coefficients; partial slope coefficients
Multicollinearity
Collinearity; exact linear relationship
  a) high or near perfect collinearity
Multiple coefficient of determination, R^2
Coefficient of multiple correlation, R
Individual hypothesis testing

Joint hypothesis testing or test of overall significance of estimated multiple regression
  a) analysis of variance (ANOVA)
  b) F test
Model specification bias (specification error)
Adjusted R^2 ($\overline{R}^2$)
Restricted least squares (RLS)
Unrestricted least squares (URLS)
Relationship between t and F tests

QUESTIONS

4.1. Explain carefully the meaning of
  a. Partial regression coefficient
  b. Coefficient of multiple determination, R^2
  c. Perfect collinearity
  d. Perfect multicollinearity
  e. Individual hypothesis testing
  f. Joint hypothesis testing
  g. Adjusted R^2

4.2. Explain step by step the procedure involved in
   a. Testing the statistical significance of a single multiple regression coefficient.
   b. Testing the statistical significance of all partial slope coefficients.

4.3. State with brief reasons whether the following statements are true (T), false (F), or uncertain (U).
   a. The adjusted and unadjusted R^2s are identical only when the unadjusted R^2 is equal to 1.
   b. The way to determine whether a group of explanatory variables exerts significant influence on the dependent variable is to see if any of the explanatory variables has a significant t statistic; if not, they are statistically insignificant as a group.
   c. When $R^2 = 1$, $F = 0$, and when $R^2 = 0$, $F =$ infinite.
   d. When the d.f. exceed 120, the 5% critical t value (two-tail) and the 5% critical Z (standard normal) value are identical, namely, 1.96.
   *e.** In the model $Y_i = B_1 + B_2X_{2i} + B_3X_{3i} + u_i$, if X_2 and X_3 are negatively correlated in the sample and $B_3 > 0$, omitting X_3 from the model will bias b_{12} downward [i.e., $E(b_{12}) < B_2$] where b_{12} is the slope coefficient in the regression of Y on X_2 alone.
   f. When we say that an estimated regression coefficient is statistically significant, we mean that it is statistically different from 1.
   g. To compute a critical t value, we need to know only the d.f.
   h. By the overall significance of a multiple regression we mean the statistical significance of any single variable included in the model.
   i. Insofar as estimation and hypothesis testing are concerned, there is no difference between simple regression and multiple regression.
   j. The d.f. of the total sum of squares (TSS) are always $(n - 1)$ regardless of the number of explanatory variables included in the model.

4.4. What is the value of $\hat{\sigma}^2$ in each of the following cases?
   a. $\Sigma e_i^2 = 880$, $n = 25$, $k = 4$ (including intercept)
   b. $\Sigma e_i^2 = 1220$, n = 14, k = 3 (excluding intercept)

4.5. Find the critical t value(s) in the following situations:

Degrees of freedom (d.f.)	Level of significance (%)	H_0
12	5	Two-tail
20	1	Right-tail
30	5	Left-tail
200	5	Two-tail

4.6. Find the critical F values for the following combinations:

Numerator d.f.	Denominator d.f.	Level of significance (%)
5	5	5
4	19	1
20	200	5

* Optional.

PROBLEMS

4.7. You are given the following data:

Y	X_2	X_3
1	1	2
3	2	1
8	3	-3

Based on these data, estimate the following regressions (*Note:* Do not worry about estimating the standard errors):

a. $Y_i = A_1 + A_2 X_{2i} + u_i$
b. $Y_i = C_1 + C_3 X_{3i} + u_i$
c. $Y_i = B_1 + B_2 X_{2i} + B_3 X_{3i} + u_i$
d. Is $A_2 = B_2$? Why or why not?
e. Is $C_3 = B_3$? Why or why not?
What general conclusion can you draw from this exercise?

4.8. You are given the following data based on 15 observations:

$$\bar{Y} = 367.693; \quad \bar{X}_2 = 402.760; \quad \bar{X}_3 = 8.0; \quad \sum y_i^2 = 66{,}042.269$$

$$\sum x_{2i}^2 = 84{,}855.096; \quad \sum x_{3i}^2 = 280.0; \quad \sum y_i x_{2i} = 74{,}778.346$$

$$\sum y_i x_{3i} = 4{,}250.9; \quad \sum x_{2i} x_{3i} = 4{,}796.0$$

where lowercase letters, as usual, denote deviations from sample mean values.
a. Estimate the three multiple regression coefficients.
b. Estimate their standard errors.
c. Obtain R^2 and $\bar{R}^2$.
d. Estimate 95% confidence intervals for B_2 and B_3.
e. Test the statistical significance of each estimated regression coefficient using $\alpha = 5\%$ (two-tail).
f. Test at $\alpha = 5\%$ that all partial slope coefficients are equal to zero. Show the ANOVA table.

4.9. A three-variable regression gave the following results:

Source of variation	Sum of squares (SS)	d.f.	Mean sum of squares (MSS)
Due to regression (ESS)	65,965	—	—
Due to residual (RSS)	—	—	—
Total (TSS)	66,042	14	

a. What is the sample size?
b. What is the value of the RSS?
c. What are the d.f. of the ESS and RSS?
d. What is R^2? And $\bar{R}^2$?
e. Test the hypothesis that X_2 and X_3 have zero influence on Y. Which test do you use and why?
f. From the preceding information, can you determine the individual contribution of X_2 and X_3 toward Y?

4.10. Recast the ANOVA table given in problem 4.9 in terms of R^2.

4.11. To explain what determines the price of air conditioners, B. T. Ratchford[24] obtained the following regression results based on a sample of 19 air conditioners:

$$\hat{Y}_i = -68.236 + 0.023X_{2i} + 19.729X_{3i} + 7.653X_{4i} \quad R^2 = 0.84$$

$$se = \qquad\qquad (0.005) \qquad (8.992) \qquad (3.082)$$

where Y = the price, in dollars
$\qquad$ X_2 = the BTU rating of air conditioner
$\qquad$ X_3 = the energy efficiency ratio
$\qquad$ X_4 = the number of settings
$\qquad$ se = standard errors

a. Interpret the regression results.
b. Do the results make economic sense?
c. At α = 5%, test the hypothesis that the BTU rating has no effect on the price of an air conditioner versus that it has a positive effect.
d. Would you accept the null hypothesis that the three explanatory variables explain a substantial variation in the prices of air conditioners? Show clearly all your calculations.

4.12. Based on the U.S. data for 1965-IQ to 1983-IVQ (n = 76), James Doti and Esmael Adibi[25] obtained the following regression to explain personal consumption expenditure (PCE) in the United States.

$$\hat{Y}_t = -10.96 + 0.93X_{2t} - 2.09X_{3t}$$

$$t = (-3.33)(249.06) \quad (-3.09) \qquad R^2 = 0.9996$$

$$F = 83,753.7$$

where Y = the PCE ($, in billions)
$\qquad$ X_2 = the disposable (i.e., after-tax) income ($, in billions)
$\qquad$ X_3 = the prime rate (%) charged by banks

a. What is the marginal propensity to consume (MPC)—the amount of additional consumption expenditure from an additional dollar's personal disposable income?
b. Is the MPC statistically different from 1? Show the appropriate testing procedure.
c. What is the rationale for the inclusion of the prime rate variable in the model? A priori, would you expect a negative sign for this variable?
d. Is b_3 significantly different from zero?
e. Test the hypothesis that $R^2 = 0$.
f. Compute the standard error of each coefficient.

[24]B. T. Ratchford, "The Value of Information for Selected Appliances," *Journal of Marketing Research*, vol. 17, 1980, pp. 14–25. Notations were adapted.
[25]James Doti and Esmael Adibi, *Econometric Analysis: An Applications Approach*, Prentice-Hall, Englewood Cliffs, N.J., 1988, p. 188. Notations were adapted.

4.13. In the illustrative Example 4.2 given in the text, test the hypothesis that X_2 and X_3 together have no influence on Y. Which test will you use? What are the assumptions underlying that test?

4.14. Table 4-7 (found on the textbook's Web site) gives data on child mortality (CM), female literacy rate (FLR), per capita GNP (PGNP), and total fertility rate (TFR) for a group of 64 countries.

    a. A priori, what is the expected relationship between CM and each of the other variables?

    b. Regress CM on FLR and obtain the usual regression results.

    c. Regress CM on FLR and PGNP and obtain the usual results.

    d. Regress CM on FLR, PGNP, and TFR and obtain the usual results. Also show the ANOVA table.

    e. Given the various regression results, which model would you choose and why?

    f. If the regression model in (*d*) is the correct model, but you estimate (*a*) or (*b*) or (*c*), what are the consequences?

    g. Suppose you have regressed CM on FLR as in (*b*). How would you decide if it is worth adding the variables PGNP and TFR to the model? Which test would you use? Show the necessary calculations.

4.15. Use formula (4.54) to answer the following question:

Value of R^2	n	k	$\bar{R}^2$
0.83	50	6	—
0.55	18	9	—
0.33	16	12	—
0.12	1,200	32	—

    What conclusion do you draw about the relationship between R^2 and $\bar{R}^2$?

4.16. For Example 4.3, compute the F value. If that F value is significant, what does that mean?

4.17. For Example 4.2, set up the ANOVA table and test that $R^2 = 0$. Use $\alpha = 1\%$.

4.18. Refer to the data given in Table 2-12 (found on the textbook's Web site) to answer the following questions:

    a. Develop a multiple regression model to explain the average starting pay of MBA graduates, obtaining the usual regression output.

    b. If you include both GPA and GMAT scores in the model, a priori, what problem(s) may you encounter and why?

    c. If the coefficient of the tuition variable is positive and statistically significant, does that mean it pays to go to the most expensive business school? What might the tuition variable be a proxy for?

    d. Suppose you regress GMAT score on GPA and find a statistically significant positive relationship between the two. What can you say about the problem of multicollinearity?

    e. Set up the ANOVA table for the multiple regression in part (*a*) and test the hypothesis that all partial slope coefficients are zero.

    f. Do the ANOVA exercise in part (*e*), using the R^2 value.

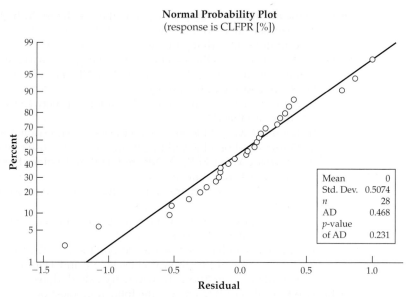

FIGURE 4-1 Normal probability plot for Example 4.4
AD = Anderson-Darling statistic

4.19. Figure 4-1 gives you the normal probability plot for Example 4.4.
  a. From this figure, can you tell if the error term in Eq. (4.62) follows the normal distribution? Why or why not?
  b. Is the observed Anderson-Darling A^2 value of 0.468 statistically significant? If it is, what does that mean? If it is not, what conclusion do you draw?
  c. From the given data, can you identify the mean and variance of the error term?

4.20. *Restricted least squares (RLS).* If the dependent variables in the restricted and unrestricted regressions are not the same, you can use the following variant of the F test given in Eq. (4.56)

$$ F = \frac{(RSS_r - RSS_{ur})/m}{RSS_{ur}/(n-k)} \sim F_{m,n-k} $$

where RSS_r = residual sum of squares from the restricted regression, RSS_{ur} = residual sum of squares from the unrestricted regression, m = number of restrictions, and $(n - k)$ = d.f. in the unrestricted regression.

　　Just to familiarize yourself with this formula, rework the model given in Table 4-4.

4.21. Refer to Example 4.5.
  a. Use the method of restricted least squares to find out if it is worth adding the Pop (population) variable to the model.
  b. Divide both Educ and GDP by Pop to obtain per capita Educ and per capita GDP. Now regress per capita Educ on per capita GDP and compare your

results with those given in Example 4.5. What conclusion can you draw from this exercise?

4.22. Table 4-8 (found on the textbook's Web site) contains variables from the Los Angeles 2008 Zagat Restaurant Guide. The variables are score values out of 30, with 30 being the best. For each restaurant listed, the table provides data for four categories: food, décor, service, and average price for a single meal at the establishment.

    a. Create a least squares regression model to predict Price based on the other three variables (Food, Décor, and Service). Are all the independent variables statistically significant?

    b. Does the normal probability plot indicate any problems?

    c. Create a scattergram of the residual values from the model versus the fitted values of the Price estimates. Does the plot indicate the residual values have constant variance? Retain this plot for use in future chapters.

APPENDIX 4A.1: Derivations of OLS Estimators Given in Equations (4.20) to (4.22)

Start with Eq. (4.16). Differentiate this equation partially with respect to b_1, b_2, and b_3, and set the resulting equations to zero to obtain:

$$\frac{\partial \sum e_i^2}{\partial \sum b_1} = 2\sum(Y_i - b_1 - b_2 X_{2i} - b_3 X_{3i})(-1) = 0$$

$$\frac{\partial \sum e_i^2}{\partial b_2} = 2\sum(Y_i - b_1 - b_2 X_2 - b_3 X_{3i})(-X_{2i}) = 0$$

$$\frac{\partial \sum e_i^2}{\partial b_3} = 2\sum(Y_i - b_1 - b_2 X_{2i} - b_3 X_3)(-X_{3i}) = 0$$

Simplifying these equations gives Eq. (4.17), (4.18), and (4.19). Using small letters to denote deviations from the mean values (e.g., $x_{2i} = X_{2i} - \overline{X}_2$), we can solve the preceding equations to obtain the formulas given in Eqs. (4.20), (4.21), and (4.22).

APPENDIX 4A.2: Derivation of Equation (4.31)

Note that the three-variable sample regression model

$$Y_i = b_1 + b_2 X_{2i} + b_3 X_{3i} + e_i \tag{4A.2.1}$$

can be expressed in the deviation form (i.e., each variable expressed as a deviation from the mean value and noting that $\bar{e} = 0$) as

$$y_i = b_2 x_{2i} + b_3 x_{3i} + e_i \tag{4A.2.2}$$

Therefore,

$$e_i = y_i - b_2 x_{2i} - b_3 x_{3i} \tag{4A.2.3}$$

Which we can write as

$$\sum e_i^2 = \sum (e_i e_i)$$

$$= \sum e_i (y_i - b_2 x_{2i} - b_3 x_{3i})$$

$$= \sum e_i y_i - b_2 \sum e_i x_{2i} - b_3 \sum e_i x_{3i}$$

$$= \sum e_i y_i \quad \text{since the last two terms are zero (why?)}$$

$$= \sum (y_i - b_2 x_{2i} - b_3 x_{3i})(y_i)$$

$$= \sum y_i^2 - b_2 \sum y_i x_{2i} - b_3 \sum y_i x_{3i}$$

$$= \sum y_i^2 - (b_2 \sum y_i x_{2i} + b_3 \sum y_i x_{3i})$$

$$= \text{TSS} - \text{ESS}$$

APPENDIX 4A.3: Derivation of Equation (4.50)

Recall that (see footnote 9)

$$R^2 = 1 - \frac{\text{RSS}}{\text{TSS}} \tag{4A.3.1}$$

Now $\overline{R}^2$ is defined as

$$\overline{R}^2 = 1 - \frac{\text{RSS}/(n-k)}{\text{TSS}/(n-1)} \tag{4A.3.2}$$

$$= 1 - \frac{\text{RSS}\,(n-1)}{\text{TSS}\,(n-k)}$$

Note how the degrees of freedom are taken into account.

Now substituting Equation (4A.3.1) into Equation (4A.3.2), and after algebraic manipulations, we obtain

$$\overline{R}^2 = 1 - (1 - R^2)\frac{n-1}{n-k}$$

Notice that if we do not take into account the d.f. associated with RSS $(= n - k)$ and TSS $(= n - 1)$, then, obviously $\overline{R}^2 = R^2$.

APPENDIX 4A.4: EViews Output of the Clock Auction Price Example

Method: Least Squares

Sample: 1 32
Included observations: 32

Variable	Coefficient	Std. Error	t-Statistic	Prob.
C	−1336.049	175.2725	−7.622698	0.0000
AGE	12.74138	0.912356	13.96537	0.0000
NOBID	85.76407	8.801995	9.743708	0.0000

R-squared	0.890614	Mean dependent var	1328.094
Adjusted R-squared	0.883070	S.D. dependent var	393.6495
S.E. of regression	134.6083	Akaike info criterion	12.73167
Sum squared resid	525462.2	Schwarz criterion	12.86909
Log likelihood	−200.7068	F-statistic	118.0585
Durbin-Watson stat	1.864656	Prob (F-statistic)	0.000000

Actual Y	Fitted ($\hat{Y}$)	Residual e_i	Residual Plot
1235.00	1397.04	−162.039	
1080.00	1158.38	−78.3786	
845.000	882.455	−37.4549	
1552.00	1347.03	204.965	
1047.00	1166.19	−119.191	
1979.00	1926.29	52.7127	
1822.00	1680.78	141.225	
1253.00	1203.45	49.5460	
1297.00	1181.40	115.603	
946.000	875.604	70.3963	
1713.00	1695.98	17.0187	
1024.00	1098.10	−74.0973	
2131.00	2030.68	100.317	
1550.00	1669.00	−118.995	
1884.00	1671.46	212.540	
2041.00	1866.01	174.994	
854.000	1000.55	−146.553	
1483.00	1461.71	21.2927	
1055.00	1240.72	−185.717	
1545.00	1579.81	−34.8054	
729.000	554.605	174.395	
1792.00	1716.53	75.4650	
1175.00	1364.71	−189.705	
1593.00	1732.70	−139.702	
1147.00	1095.63	51.3672	
1092.00	1127.97	−35.9668	
1152.00	1269.63	−117.625	
1336.00	1127.01	208.994	
785.000	678.593	106.407	
744.000	729.558	14.4417	
1356.00	1564.60	−208.599	
1262.00	1404.85	−142.852	

−   0   +

CHAPTER 5

FUNCTIONAL FORMS
OF REGRESSION MODELS

Until now we have considered models that were linear in parameters as well as in variables. But recall that in this textbook our concern is with models that are linear in *parameters*; the Y and X variables do not necessarily have to be linear. As a matter of fact, as we show in this chapter, there are many economic phenomena for which the linear-in-parameters/linear-in-variables (LIP/LIV, for short) regression models may not be adequate or appropriate.

For example, suppose for the LIP/LIV math S.A.T. score function given in Equation (2.20) we want to estimate the *score elasticity* of the math S.A.T., that is, the percentage change in the math S.A.T. score for a percentage change in annual family income. We cannot estimate this elasticity from Eq. (2.20) directly because the slope coefficient of that model simply gives the absolute change in the (average) math S.A.T. score for a unit (say, a dollar) change in the annual family income, but this is not elasticity. Such elasticity, however, can be readily computed from the so-called *log-linear* models that will be discussed in Section 5.1. As we will show, this model, although linear in the parameters, is not linear in the variables.

For another example, suppose we want to find out the *rate of growth*[1] over time of an economic variable, such as gross domestic product (GDP) or money supply, or unemployment rate. As we show in Section 5.4, this growth rate can

---

[1] If Y_t and Y_{t-1} are values of a variable, say, GDP, at time t and $(t-1)$, say, 2009 and 2008, then the rate of growth of Y in the two time periods is measured as $\dfrac{Y_t - Y_{t-1}}{Y_t} \cdot 100$, which is simply the relative, or proportional, change in Y multiplied by 100. It is shown in Section 5.4 how the semilog model can be used to measure the growth rate over a longer period of time.

be measured by the so-called *semilog* model which, while linear in parameters, is nonlinear in variables.

Note that even within the confines of the linear-in-parameter regression models, a regression model can assume a variety of *functional forms*. In particular, in this chapter we will discuss the following types of regression models:

1. Log-linear or constant elasticity models (Section 5.1).
2. Semilog models (Sections 5.4 and 5.5).
3. Reciprocal models (Section 5.6).
4. Polynomial regression models (Section 5.7).
5. Regression-through-the-origin, or zero intercept, model (Section 5.8).

An important feature of all these models is that they are linear in parameters (or can be made so by simple algebraic manipulations), but they are not necessarily linear in variables. In Chapter 2 we discussed the technical meaning of linearity in both variables and parameters. Briefly, for a regression model linear in explanatory variable(s) the rate of change (i.e., the slope) of the dependent variable remains constant for a unit change in the explanatory variable, whereas for regression models nonlinear in explanatory variable(s) the slope does not remain constant.

To introduce the basic concepts, and to illustrate them graphically, initially we will consider two-variable models and then extend the discussion to multiple regression models.

5.1 HOW TO MEASURE ELASTICITY: THE LOG-LINEAR MODEL

Let us revisit our math S.A.T. score function discussed in Chapters 2 and 3. But now consider the following model for the math S.A.T. score function. (To ease the algebra, we will introduce the error term u_i later.)

$$Y_i = AX_i^{B_2} \tag{5.1}$$

where Y is math S.A.T. score and X is annual family income.

This model is nonlinear in the variable X.[2] Let us, however, express Equation (5.1) in an alternative, but equivalent, form, as follows:

$$\ln Y_i = \ln A + B_2 \ln X_i \tag{5.2}$$

---

[2]Using calculus, it can be shown that

$$\frac{dY}{dX} = AB_2 X^{(B_2-1)}$$

which shows that the rate of change of Y with respect to X is not independent of X; that is, it is not constant. By definition, then, model (5.1) is not linear in variable X.

where ln = the natural log, that is, logarithm to the base e.[3] Now if we let

$$B_1 = \ln A \tag{5.3}$$

we can write Equation (5.2) as

$$\ln Y_i = B_1 + B_2 \ln X_i \tag{5.4}$$

And for estimating purposes, we can write this model as

$$\ln Y_i = B_1 + B_2 \ln X_i + u_i \tag{5.5}$$

This is a linear regression model, for the parameters B_1 and B_2 enter the model linearly.[4] It is of interest that this model is also linear in the logarithms of the variables Y and X. (*Note:* The original model [5.1] was nonlinear in X.) Because of this linearity, models like Equation (5.5) are called **double-log** (because both variables are in the log form) or **log-linear** (because of linearity in the logs of the variables) models.

Notice how an apparently nonlinear model (5.1) can be converted into a linear (in the parameter) model by suitable transformation, here the *logarithmic transformation*. Now letting $Y_i^* = \ln Y_i$ and $X_i^* = \ln X_i$, we can write model (5.5) as

$$Y_i^* = B_1 + B_2 X_i^* + u_i \tag{5.6}$$

which resembles the models we have considered in previous chapters; it is linear in both the parameters and the transformed variables Y^* and X^*.

If the assumptions of the classical linear regression model (CLRM) are satisfied for the transformed model, regression (5.6) can be estimated easily with the usual ordinary least squares (OLS) routine and the estimators thus obtained will have the usual best linear unbiased estimator (BLUE) property.[5]

One attractive feature of the double-log, or log-linear, model that has made it popular in empirical work is that the *slope coefficient B_2 measures the elasticity of Y with respect to X, that is, the percentage change in Y for a given (small) percentage change in X.*

[3]Appendix 5A discusses logarithms and their properties for the benefit of those who need it.

[4]Note that since $B_1 = \ln A$, A can be expressed as $A = $ antilog (B_1) which is, mathematically speaking, a nonlinear transformation. In practice, however, the intercept A often does not have much concrete meaning.

[5]Any regression package now routinely computes the logs of (positive) numbers. So there is no additional computational burden involved.

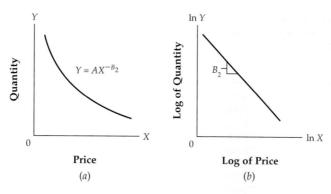

FIGURE 5-1 A constant elasticity model

Symbolically, if we let ΔY stand for a small change in Y and ΔX for a small change in X, we define the elasticity coefficient, E, as

$$
\begin{aligned}
E &= \frac{\% \text{ change in } Y}{\% \text{ change in } X} \\
&= \frac{\Delta Y/Y \cdot 100}{\Delta X/X \cdot 100} \\
&= \frac{\Delta Y}{\Delta X} \cdot \frac{X}{Y} \\
&= \text{slope} \left(\frac{X}{Y} \right)
\end{aligned}
\tag{5.7}^6
$$

Thus, if Y represents the quantity of a commodity demanded and X its unit price, B_2 measures the *price elasticity of demand*.

All this can be shown graphically.

Figure 5-1(a) represents the function (5.1), and Figure 5-1(b) shows its logarithmic transformation. The slope of the straight line shown in Figure 5-1(b) gives the estimate of price elasticity, $(-B_2)$. An important feature of the log-linear model should be apparent from Figure 5-1(b). Since the regression line is a straight line (in the logs of Y and X), its slope $(-B_2)$ is constant throughout. And since this slope coefficient is equal to the elasticity coefficient, for this

---

[6]In calculus notation

$$
E = \frac{dY}{dX} \cdot \frac{X}{Y}
$$

where dY/dX means the derivative of Y with respect to X, that is, the rate of change of Y with respect to X. $\Delta Y/\Delta X$ is an approximation of dY/dX. *Note:* For the transformed model (5.6),

$$
B_2 = \frac{\Delta Y^*}{\Delta X^*} = \frac{\Delta \ln Y}{\Delta \ln X} = \frac{\Delta Y/Y}{\Delta X/X} = \frac{\Delta Y}{\Delta X} \cdot \frac{X}{Y}
$$

which is the elasticity of Y with respect to X as per Equation (5.7). As noted in Appendix 5A, a change in the log of a number is a relative or proportional change. For example, $\Delta \ln Y = \frac{\Delta Y}{Y}$.

TABLE 5-1 MATH S.A.T. SCORE (Y) IN RELATION TO ANNUAL FAMILY INCOME (X) ($)

Y	X
410	5000
420	15000
440	25000
490	35000
530	45000
530	55000
550	65000
540	75000
570	90000
590	150000

model, the elasticity is also constant throughout—it does not matter at what value of X this elasticity is computed.[7]

Because of this special feature, the double-log or log-linear model is also known as the **constant elasticity model.** Therefore, we will use all of these terms interchangeably.

Example 5.1 Math S.A.T. Score Function Revisited

In Equation (3.46) we presented the linear (in variables) function for our math S.A.T. score example. Recall, however, that the scattergram showed that the relationship between math S.A.T. scores and annual family income was *approximately* linear because not all points were really on a straight line. Eq. (3.46) was, of course, developed for pedagogy. Let us see if the log-linear model fits the data given in Table 2-2, which for convenience is reproduced in Table 5-1.

The OLS regression based on the log-linear data gave the following results:

$$\widehat{\ln Y_i} = 4.8877 + 0.1258 \ln X_i$$

$$\text{se} = (0.1573) \qquad (0.0148)$$

$$t = (31.0740) \qquad (8.5095)$$

$$p = (1.25 \times 10^{-9})(2.79 \times 10^{-5}) \qquad r^2 = 0.9005$$

(5.8)

As these results show, the (constant) score elasticity is ≈ 0.13, suggesting that if the annual family income increases by 1 percent, the math S.A.T. score *on average* increases ≈ 0.13 percent. By convention, an elasticity coefficient less

---

[7]Note carefully, however, that in general, elasticity and slope coefficients are different concepts. As Eq. (5.7) makes clear, elasticity is equal to the slope times the ratio of X/Y. It is only for the double-log, or log-linear, model that the two are identical.

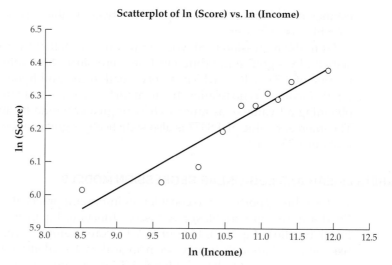

FIGURE 5-2 Log-linear model of math S.A.T. score

than 1 in absolute value is said to be inelastic, whereas if it is greater than 1, it is called elastic. An elasticity coefficient of 1 (in absolute value) has unitary elasticity. Therefore, in our example, the math S.A.T. score is inelastic; the math score increases proportionately less than the increase in annual family income.

The interpretation of the intercept of ≈ 4.89 means that the average value of ln Y is 4.89 if the value of ln X is zero. Again, this mechanical interpretation of the intercept may not have concrete economic meaning.[8]

The interpretation of $r^2 = 0.9005$ is that ≈ 90 percent of the variation in the log of Y is explained by the variation in the log of X.

The regression line in Equation (5.8) is sketched in Figure 5-2. Notice that this figure is quite similar to Figure 2-1.

Hypothesis Testing in Log-Linear Models

There is absolutely no difference between the linear and log-linear models insofar as hypothesis testing is concerned. Under the assumption that the error term follows the normal distribution with mean zero and constant variance σ^2, it follows that each estimated regression coefficient is normally distributed. Or, if we replace σ^2 by its unbiased estimator $\hat{\sigma}^2$, each estimator follows the t distribution with degrees of freedom (d.f.) equal to $(n-k)$, where k is the number of parameters

---

[8]Since ln $Y = 4.8877$ when ln X is zero, if we take the antilog of this number, we obtain ≈ 132.94. Thus, the average math S.A.T. score is about 133 points if the log of annual family income is zero. For the linear model given in Eq. (3.46), the intercept value was about 432.41 points when annual family income (not the log of income) was zero.

estimated, including the intercept. In the two-variable case, k is 2, in the three-variable case, $k = 3$, etc.

From the regression (5.8), you can readily check that the slope coefficient is statistically significantly different from zero since the t value of ≈ 8.51 has a p value of 2.79×10^{-5}, which is very small. If the null hypothesis that annual family income has no relationship to math S.A.T. score were true, our chances of obtaining a t value of as much as 8.51 or greater would be about 3 in 100,000! The intercept value of 4.8877 is also statistically significant because the p value is about 1.25×10^{-9}.

5.2   COMPARING LINEAR AND LOG-LINEAR REGRESSION MODELS

We take this opportunity to consider an important practical question. We have fitted a linear (in variables) S.A.T. score function, Eq. (3.46), as well as a log-linear function, Eq. (5.8), for our S.A.T. score example. Which model should we choose? Although it may seem logical that students with higher family income would tend to have higher S.A.T. scores, indicating a positive relationship, we don't really know which particular **functional form** defines the relationship between them.[9] That is, we may not know if we should fit the linear, log-linear, or some other model. The functional form of the regression model then becomes essentially an *empirical question*. Are there any guidelines or rules of thumb that we can follow in choosing among competing models?

One guiding principle is to plot the data. If the scattergram shows that the relationship between two variables looks reasonably linear (i.e., a straight line), the linear specification might be appropriate. But if the scattergram shows a nonlinear relationship, plot the log of Y against the log of X. If this plot shows an approximately linear relationship, a log-linear model may be appropriate. Unfortunately, this guiding principle works only in the simple case of two-variable regression models and is not very helpful once we consider multiple regressions; it is not easy to draw scattergrams in multiple dimensions. We need other guidelines.

Why not choose the model on the basis of r^2; that is, choose the model that gives the highest r^2? Although intuitively appealing, this criterion has its own problems. First, as noted in Chapter 4, *to compare the r^2 values of two models, the dependent variable must be in the same form.*[10] For model (3.46), the dependent variable is Y, whereas for the model (5.8), it is $\ln Y$, and these two dependent variables are obviously not the same. Therefore, $r^2 = 0.7869$ of the linear model (3.46) and $r^2 = 0.9005$ of the log-linear model are not directly comparable, even though they are approximately the same in the present case.

---

[9]A cautionary note here: Remember that regression models do not imply causation, so we are not implying that having a higher annual family income *causes* higher math S.A.T. scores, only that we would tend to see the two together. There may be several other reasons explaining this result. Perhaps students with higher family incomes are able to afford S.A.T. preparation classes or attend schools that focus more on material typically covered in the exam.

[10]It does not matter what form the independent or explanatory variables take; they may or may not be linear.

The reason that we cannot compare these two r^2 values is not difficult to grasp. By definition, r^2 measures the proportion of the variation in the dependent variable explained by the explanatory variable(s). In the linear model (3.46) r^2 thus measures the proportion of the variation in Y explained by X, whereas in the log-linear model (5.8) it measures the proportion of the variation in the log of Y explained by the log of X. Now the *variation in Y and the variation in the log of Y* are conceptually different. *The variation in the log of a number measures the relative or proportional change* (or percentage change if multiplied by 100), and the variation in a number measures the *absolute change*.[11] Thus, for the linear model (3.46), ≈ 79 percent of the variation in Y is explained by X, whereas for the log-linear model, ≈ 90 percent of the variation in the log of Y is explained by the log of X. If we want to compare the two r^2s, we can use the method discussed in Problem 5.16.

Even if the dependent variable in the two models is the same so that two r^2 values can be directly compared, you are well-advised against choosing a model on the basis of a **high r^2 value criterion.** This is because, as pointed out in Chapter 4, an r^2 ($=R^2$) can always be increased by adding more explanatory variables to the model. Rather than emphasizing the r^2 value of a model, you should consider factors such as the relevance of the explanatory variables included in the model (i.e., the underlying theory), the expected signs of the coefficients of the explanatory variables, their statistical significance, and certain derived measures like the elasticity coefficient. These should be the guiding principles in choosing between two competing models. If based on these criteria one model is preferable to the other, and if the chosen model also happens to have a higher r^2 value, then well and good. But *avoid the temptation of choosing a model only on the basis of the r^2 value alone.*

Comparing the results of the log-linear score function (5.8) versus the linear function (3.46), we observe that in both models the slope coefficient is positive, as per prior expectations. Also, both slope coefficients are statistically significant. However, we cannot compare the two slope coefficients directly, for in the LIV model it measures the absolute rate of change in the dependent variable, whereas in the log-linear model it measures elasticity of Y with respect to X.

If for the LIV model we can measure score elasticity, then it is possible to compare the two slope coefficients. To do this, we can use Equation (5.7), which shows that elasticity is equal to the slope times the ratio of X to Y. Although for the linear model the slope coefficient remains the same (Why?), which is 0.0013 in our S.A.T. score example, the elasticity changes from point to point on the linear curve because the ratio X/Y changes from point to point. From Table 5-1 we see that there are 10 different math S.A.T. score and annual family income figures. Therefore, in principle we can compute 10 different elasticity coefficients. In practice, however, the elasticity coefficient for the

---

[11]If a number goes from 45 to 50, the absolute change is 5, but the relative change is $(50 - 45)/45 \approx 0.1111$, or about 11.11 percent.

linear model is often computed at the sample mean values of X and Y to obtain a measure of *average elasticity*. That is,

$$\text{Average elasticity} = \frac{\Delta Y}{\Delta X} \cdot \frac{\overline{X}}{\overline{Y}} \tag{5.9}$$

where $\overline{X}$ and $\overline{Y}$ are sample mean values. For the data given in Table 5-1, $\overline{X} = 56{,}000$ and $\overline{Y} = 507$. Thus, the average elasticity for our sample is

$$\text{Average score elasticity} = (0.0013)\frac{56{,}000}{507} = 0.1436$$

It is interesting to note that for the log-linear function the score elasticity coefficient was 0.1258, which remains the same no matter at what income the elasticity is measured (see Figure 5-1[*b*]). This is why such a model is called a constant elasticity model. For the LIV, on the other hand, the elasticity coefficient changes from point to point on the score = family income curve.[12]

The fact that for the linear model the elasticity coefficient changes from point to point and that for the log-linear model it remains the same at all points on the demand curve means that we have to exercise some judgment in choosing between the two specifications, for, in practice, both these assumptions may be extreme. It is possible that over a small segment of the expenditure curve the elasticity remains constant but that over some other segment(s) it is variable.

5.3 MULTIPLE LOG-LINEAR REGRESSION MODELS

The two-variable log-linear model can be generalized easily to models containing more than one explanatory variable. For example, a three-variable log-linear model can be expressed as

$$\ln Y_i = B_1 + B_2 \ln X_{2i} + B_3 \ln X_{3i} + u_i \tag{5.10}$$

In this model the partial slope coefficients B_2 and B_3 are also called the partial elasticity coefficients.[13] Thus, B_2 measures the elasticity of Y with respect to X_2, holding the influence of X_3 constant; that is, it measures the percentage change in Y for a percentage change in X_2, holding the influence of X_3 constant. Since the influence of X_3 is held constant, it is called a partial elasticity. Similarly, B_3

[12]Notice this interesting fact: For the LIV model, the slope coefficient is constant but the elasticity coefficient is variable. However, for the log-linear model, the elasticity coefficient is constant but the slope coefficient is variable, which can be seen at once from the formula given in footnote 2.

[13]The calculus-minded reader will recognize that the partial derivative of $\ln Y$ with respect to $\ln X_2$ is

$$B_2 = \frac{\partial \ln Y}{\partial \ln X_2} = \frac{\partial Y/Y}{\partial X_2/X_2} = \frac{\partial Y}{\partial X_2} \cdot \frac{X_2}{Y}$$

which by definition is elasticity of Y with respect to X_2. Likewise, B_3 is the elasticity of Y with respect to X_3.

measures the (partial) elasticity of Y with respect to X_3, holding the influence of X_2 constant. In short, *in a multiple log-linear model, each partial slope coefficient measures the partial elasticity of the dependent variable with respect to the explanatory variable in question, holding all other variables constant.*

Example 5.2. The Cobb-Douglas Production Function

As an example of model (5.10), let Y = output, X_2 = labor input, and X_3 = capital input. In that case model (5.10) becomes a *production function*—a function that relates output to labor and capital inputs. As a matter of fact, regression (5.10) in this case represents the celebrated **Cobb-Douglas (C-D) production function.** As an illustration, consider the data given in Table 5-2, which relates to Mexico for the years 1955 to 1974. Y, the output, is measured by gross domestic product (GDP) (millions of 1960 pesos), X_2, the labor input, is measured by total employment (thousands of people), and X_3, the capital input, is measured by stock of fixed capital (millions of 1960 pesos).

TABLE 5-2 REAL GDP, EMPLOYMENT, AND REAL FIXED CAPITAL, MEXICO, 1955–1974

Year	GDP[a]	Employment[b]	Fixed capital[c]
1955	114043	8310	182113
1956	120410	8529	193745
1557	129187	8738	205192
1958	134705	8952	215130
1959	139960	9171	225021
1960	150511	9569	237026
1961	157897	9527	248897
1962	165286	9662	260661
1963	178491	10334	275466
1964	199457	10981	295378
1965	212323	11746	315715
1966	226977	11521	337642
1967	241194	11540	363599
1968	260881	12066	391847
1969	277498	12297	422382
1970	296530	12955	455049
1971	306712	13338	484677
1972	329030	13738	520553
1973	354057	15924	561531
1974	374977	14154	609825

Notes: [a]Millions of 1960 pesos.
[b]Thousands of people.
[c]Millions of 1960 pesos.
Source: Victor J. Elias, *Sources of Growth: A Study of Seven Latin American Economies,* International Center for Economic Growth, ICS Press, San Francisco, 1992. Data from Tables E5, E12, and E14.

Based on the data given in Table 5-2, the following results were obtained using the MINITAB statistical package:

$$\widehat{\ln Y_t} = -1.6524 + 0.3397 \ln X_{2t} + 0.8460 \ln X_{3t}$$

$$
\begin{array}{lll}
\text{se} = & (0.6062) \quad (0.1857) & (0.09343) \\
t = & (-2.73) \quad (1.83) & (9.06) \\
p \text{ value} = & (0.014) \quad (0.085) & (0.000)^*
\end{array}
$$

(5.11)

$$R^2 = 0.995$$

$$F = 1719.23 \quad (0.000)^{**}$$

The interpretation of regression (5.11) is as follows. The partial slope coefficient of 0.3397 measures the elasticity of output with respect to the labor input. Specifically, this number states that, holding the capital input constant, if the labor input increases by 1 percent, on the average, output goes up by about 0.34 percent. Similarly, holding the labor input constant, if the capital input increases by 1 percent, on the average, output goes up by about 0.85 percent. If we add the elasticity coefficients, we obtain an economically important parameter, called the **returns to scale parameter,** which gives the response of output to a proportional change in inputs. If the sum of the two elasticity coefficients is 1, we have **constant returns to scale** (i.e., doubling the inputs simultaneously doubles the output); if it is greater than 1, we have **increasing returns to scale** (i.e., doubling the inputs simultaneously more than doubles the output); if it is less than 1, we have **decreasing returns to scale** (i.e., doubling the inputs less than doubles the output).

For Mexico, for the study period, the sum of the two elasticity coefficients is 1.1857, suggesting that perhaps the Mexican economy was characterized by increasing returns to scale.

Returning to the estimated coefficients, we see that both labor and capital are individually statistically significant on the basis of the one-tail test although the impact of capital seems to be more important than that of labor. (*Note:* We use a one-tail test because both labor and capital are expected to have a positive effect on output.)

The estimated F value is so highly significant (because the p value is almost zero) we can strongly reject the null hypothesis that labor and capital together do not have any impact on output.

The R^2 value of 0.995 means that about 99.5 percent of the variation in the (log) of output is explained by the (logs) of labor and capital, a very high degree of explanation, suggesting that the model (5.11) fits the data very well.

Example 5.3. The Demand for Energy

Table 5-3 gives data on the indexes of aggregate final energy demand (Y), real GDP (X_2), and real energy price (X_3) for seven OECD countries (the

---

*Denotes extremely small value.
** p value of F, also extremely small.

TABLE 5-3   ENERGY DEMAND IN OECD COUNTRIES, 1960–1982

Year	Final demand	Real GDP	Real energy price
1960	54.1	54.1	111.9
1961	55.4	56.4	112.4
1962	58.5	59.4	111.1
1963	61.7	62.1	110.2
1964	63.6	65.9	109.0
1965	66.8	69.5	108.3
1966	70.3	73.2	105.3
1967	73.5	75.7	105.4
1968	78.3	79.9	104.3
1969	83.8	83.8	101.7
1970	88.9	86.2	97.7
1971	91.8	89.8	100.3
1972	97.2	94.3	98.6
1973	100.0	100.0	100.0
1974	97.4	101.4	120.1
1975	93.5	100.5	131.0
1976	99.1	105.3	129.6
1977	100.9	109.9	137.7
1078	103.9	114.4	133.7
1979	106.9	118.3	144.5
1980	101.2	119.6	179.0
1981	98.1	121.1	189.4
1982	95.6	120.6	190.9

Source: Richard D. Prosser, "Demand Elasticities in OECD: Dynamic Aspects," *Energy Economics,* January 1985, p. 10.

United States, Canada, Germany, France, the United Kingdom, Italy, and Japan) for the period 1960 to 1982. All indexes are with base $1973 = 100$. Using the data given in Table 5-3 and MINITAB we obtained the following log-linear energy demand function:

$$\widehat{\ln Y_t} = 1.5495 + 0.9972 \ln X_{2t} - 0.3315 \ln X_{3t}$$

$$\text{se} = (0.0903) \quad (0.0191) \qquad (0.0243)$$

$$t = (17.17) \quad (52.09) \qquad (13.61)$$

$$p \text{ value} = (0.000)^* \quad (0.000)^* \qquad (0.000)^*$$

$$R^2 = 0.994$$
$$\bar{R}^2 = 0.994$$
$$F = 1688$$

(5.12)

As this regression shows, energy demand is positively related to income (as measured by real GDP) and negatively related to real price; these findings

*Denotes extremely small value.

accord with economic theory. The estimated income elasticity is about 0.99, meaning that if real income goes up by 1 percent, the average amount of energy demanded goes up by about 0.99 percent, or just about 1 percent, ceteris paribus. Likewise, the estimated price elasticity is about −0.33, meaning that, holding other factors constant, if energy price goes up by 1 percent, the average amount of energy demanded goes down by about 0.33 percent. Since this coefficient is less than 1 in absolute value, we can say that the demand for energy is *price inelastic,* which is not very surprising because energy is a very essential item for consumption.

The R^2 values, both adjusted and unadjusted, are very high. The F value of about 1688 is also very high; the probability of obtaining such an F value, if in fact $B_2 = B_3 = 0$ is true, is almost zero. Therefore, we can say that income and energy price together strongly affect energy demand.

5.4   HOW TO MEASURE THE GROWTH RATE: THE SEMILOG MODEL

As noted in the introduction to this chapter, economists, businesspeople, and the government are often interested in finding out the rate of growth of certain economic variables. For example, the projection of the government budget deficit (surplus) is based on the projected rate of growth of the GDP, the single most important indicator of economic activity. Likewise, the Fed keeps a strong eye on the rate of growth of consumer credit outstanding (auto loans, installment loans, etc.) to monitor its monetary policy.

In this section we will show how regression analysis can be used to measure such growth rates.

Example 5.4. The Growth of the U.S. Population, 1975–2007

Table 5-4 gives data on the U.S. population (in millions) for the period 1975 to 2007.

We want to measure the rate of growth of the U.S. population (Y) over this period. Now consider the following well-known compound interest formula from your introductory courses in money, banking, and finance:

$$Y_t = Y_0(1 + r)^t \qquad (5.13)[14]$$

Y_0 = the beginning, or initial, value of Y
Y_t = Y's value at time t
r = the compound (i.e., over time) rate of growth of Y

---

[14]Suppose you deposit $Y_0 = \$100$ in a passbook account in a bank, paying, say, 6 percent interest per year. Here $r = 0.06$, or 6 percent. At the end of the first year this amount will grow to $Y_1 = 100(1 + 0.6) = 106$; at the end of the second year it will be $Y_2 = 106(1 + 0.06) = 100 (1 + 0.06)^2 = 112.36$ because in the second year you get interest not only on the initial $100 but also on the interest earned in the first year. In the third year this amount grows to $100(1 + 0.06)^3 = 119.1016$, etc.

TABLE 5-4   POPULATION OF UNITED STATES (MILLIONS OF PEOPLE), 1975–2007

U.S. population	Time	U.S. population	Time
215.973	1	256.894	18
218.035	2	260.255	19
220.239	3	263.436	20
222.585	4	266.557	21
225.055	5	269.667	22
227.726	6	272.912	23
229.966	7	276.115	24
232.188	8	279.295	25
234.307	9	282.430	26
236.348	10	285.454	27
238.466	11	288.427	28
240.651	12	291.289	29
242.804	13	294.056	30
245.021	14	296.940	31
247.342	15	299.801	32
250.132	16	302.045	33
253.493	17		

Note: 1975 = 1; 2007 = 33.
Source: Economic Report of the President, 2008, Table B34.

Let us manipulate Equation (5.13) as follows. Take the (natural) log of Eq. (5.13) on both sides to obtain

$$\ln Y_t = \ln Y_0 + t\ln(1 + r) \tag{5.14}$$

Now let

$$B_1 = \ln Y_0 \tag{5.15}$$

$$B_2 = \ln(1 + r) \tag{5.16}$$

Therefore, we can express model (5.14) as

$$\ln Y_t = B_1 + B_2 t \tag{5.17}$$

Now if we add the error term u_t to model (5.17), we will obtain[15]

$$\ln Y_t = B_1 + B_2 t + u_t \tag{5.18}$$

This model is like any other linear regression model in that parameters B_1 and B_2 are linear. The only difference is that the dependent variable is the logarithm of Y and the independent, or explanatory, variable is "time," which will take values of 1, 2, 3, etc.

---

[15]The reason we add the error term is that the compound interest formula will not exactly fit the data of Table 5-4.

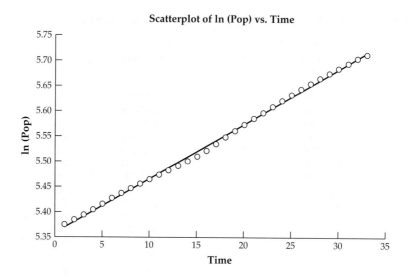

FIGURE 5-3   Semilog model

Models like regression (5.18) are called **semilog models** because only one variable (in this case the dependent variable) appears in the logarithmic form. How do we interpret semilog models like regression (5.18)? Before we discuss this, note that model (5.18) can be estimated by the usual OLS method, assuming of course that the usual assumptions of OLS are satisfied. For the data of Table 5-4, we obtain the following regression results:

$$\widehat{\ln(USpop)} = 5.3593 + 0.0107t \tag{5.19}$$

$$t = (3321.13)(129.779) \quad r^2 = 0.9982$$

Note that in Eq. (5.19) we have only reported the t values.

The estimated regression line is sketched in Figure 5-3.

The interpretation of regression (5.19) is as follows. The slope coefficient of 0.0107 means on the average the *log of Y* (U.S. population) has been increasing at the rate of 0.0107 per year. In plain English, Y has been increasing at the rate of 1.07 percent per year, for *in a semilog model like regression (5.19) the slope coefficient measures the proportional or relative change in Y for a given absolute change in the explanatory variable, time in the present case.*[16] If this relative change is multiplied by 100, we obtain the percentage change or the *growth*

---

[16]Using calculus it can be shown that

$$B_2 = \frac{d \ln Y}{dt} = \left(\frac{1}{Y}\right)\left(\frac{dY}{dt}\right)$$

$$= \frac{\frac{dY}{Y}}{dt} = \frac{\text{relative change in } Y}{\text{absolute change in } t}$$

rate (see footnote 1). In our example the relative change is 0.0107, and hence the growth rate is 1.07 percent.

Because of this, semilog models like Eq. (5.19) are known as growth models and such models are routinely used to measure the growth rate of many variables, whether economic or not.

The interpretation of the intercept term 5.3593 is as follows. From Eq. (5.15) it is evident that

$$b_1 = \text{the estimate of } \ln Y_0 = 5.3593$$

Therefore, if we take the antilog of 5.3593 we obtain

$$\text{antilog } (5.3593) \approx 212.5761$$

which is the value of Y when $t = 0$, that is, at the beginning of the period. Since our sample begins in 1975, we can interpret the value of ≈ 213 (millions) as the population figure at the end of 1974. But remember the warning given previously that often the intercept term has no particular physical meaning.

Instantaneous versus Compound Rate of Growth

Notice from Eq. (5.16) that

$$b_2 = \text{the estimate of } B_2 = \ln (1 + r)$$

Therefore,

$$\text{antilog } (b_2) = (1 + r)$$

which means that

$$r = \text{antilog } (b_2) - 1 \qquad \qquad \textbf{(5.20)}$$

And since r is the compound rate of growth, once we have obtained b_2 we can easily estimate the compound rate of growth of Y from Equation (5.20). For Example 5.4, we obtain

$$r = \text{antilog } (0.0107) - 1$$

$$= 1.0108 - 1 = 0.010757 \qquad \qquad \textbf{(5.21)}$$

That is, over the sample period, *the compound rate of growth of the U.S. population had been at the rate of 1.0757 percent per year.*

Earlier we said that the growth rate in Y was 1.07 percent but now we say it is 1.0757 percent. What is the difference? The growth rate of 1.07 percent (or, more generally, the slope coefficient in regressions like Eq. [5.19], multiplied by 100) gives the **instantaneous** (at a point in time) **growth rate,** whereas the growth rate of 1.0757 percent (or, more generally, that obtained from Equation [5.20]) is the **compound** (over a period of time) **growth rate.** In the present example the difference between the two growth rates may not sound important, but do not forget the power of compounding.

In practice, one generally quotes the instantaneous growth rate, although the compound growth rate can be easily computed, as just shown.

The Linear Trend Model

Sometimes, as a quick and ready method of computation, researchers estimate the following model:

$$Y_t = B_1 + B_2t + u_t \tag{5.22}$$

That is, regress Y on time itself, where time is measured chronologically. Such a model is called, appropriately, the **linear trend model,** and the time variable t is known as the **trend variable.**[17] If the slope coefficient in the preceding model is positive, there is an *upward trend* in Y, whereas if it is negative, there is a *downward trend* in Y.

For the data in Table 5-4, the results of fitting Equation (5.22) are as follows:

$$\widehat{USpop_t} = 209.6731 + 2.7570t$$
$$t = (287.4376)(73.6450) \quad r^2 = 0.9943 \tag{5.23}$$

As these results show, over the sample period the U.S. population had been increasing at the absolute (note, not the relative) rate of 2.757 million per year. Thus, over that period there was an upward trend in the U.S. population. The intercept value here probably represents the base population in the year 1974, which from this model it is about 210 million.

In practice, both the linear trend and growth models have been used extensively. For comparative purposes, however, the growth model is more useful. People are often interested in finding out the relative performance and not the absolute performance of economic measures, such as GDP, money supply, etc.

Incidentally, note that we cannot compare r^2 values of the two models because the dependent variables in the two models are not the same (but see Problem 5.16). Statistically speaking, both models give fairly good results, judged by the usual t test of significance.

Recall that for the log-linear, or double-log, model the slope coefficient gives the elasticity of Y with respect to the relevant explanatory variable. For the growth model and the linear trend models, we can also measure such elasticities. As a matter of fact, once the functional form of the regression model is known, we can compute elasticities from the basic definition of elasticity given in Eq. (5.7). Table 5-11 at the end of this chapter summarizes the elasticity coefficients for the various models we have considered in the chapter.

A cautionary note: The traditional practice of introducing the trend variable t in models such as (5.18) and (5.22) has recently been questioned by the new generation of time series econometricians. They argue that such a practice may be justifiable only if the error term u_t in the preceding models is *stationary.*

---

[17]By trend we mean a sustained upward or downward movement in the behavior of a variable.

Although the precise meaning of *stationarity* will be explained in Chapter 12, for now we state that u_t is stationary if its mean value and its variance do not vary systematically over time. In our classical linear regression model we have assumed that u_t has zero mean and constant variance σ^2. Of course, in an application we will have to check to see if these assumptions are valid. We will discuss this topic later.

5.5   THE LIN-LOG MODEL: WHEN THE EXPLANATORY VARIABLE IS LOGARITHMIC

In the previous section we considered the growth model in which the dependent variable was in the log form but the explanatory variable was in the linear form. For descriptive purposes, we can call such a model a **log-lin, or growth, model.** In this section we consider a model where the dependent variable is in the linear form but the explanatory variable is in the log form. Appropriately, we call this model the **lin-log model.**

We introduce this model with a concrete example.

Example 5.5. The Relationship between Expenditure on Services in Relation to Total Personal Consumption Expenditure in 1992 Billions of Dollars, 1975–2006

Consider the annual data given in Table 5-5 (found on the textbook's Web site) on consumer expenditure on various categories in relation to total personal consumption expenditure.

Suppose we want to find out how expenditure on services (Y) behaves if total personal consumption expenditure (X) increases by a certain percentage. Toward that end, suppose we consider the following model:

$$Y_t = B_1 + B_2 \ln X_{2t} + u_t \tag{5.24}$$

In contrast to the log-lin model in Eq. (5.18) where the dependent variable is in log form, the independent variable here is in log form. Before interpreting this model, we present the results based on this model; the results are based on MINITAB.

$$\hat{Y}_t = -12564.8 + 1844.22 \ln X_t$$

$$\text{se} = (916.351) \quad (114.32)$$

$$t = (-13.71) \quad (16.13) \tag{5.25}$$

$$p = (0.00) \quad (0.00) \quad r^2 = 0.881$$

Interpreted in the usual fashion, the slope coefficient of ≈ 1844 means that if the log of total personal consumption increases by a unit, the absolute change in the expenditure on personal services is $\approx \$1844$ billion. What does it mean in everyday language? Recall that a change in the log of a number is a relative change. Therefore, the slope coefficient in model (5.25) measures[18]

$$B_2 = \frac{\text{absolute change in } Y}{\text{relative change in } X}$$

$$= \frac{\Delta Y}{\Delta X / X}$$

(5.26)

where, as before, ΔY and ΔX represent (small) changes in Y and X. Equation (5.26) can be written, equivalently, as

$$\Delta Y = B_2 \left(\frac{\Delta X}{X} \right)$$

(5.27)

This equation states that the absolute change in $Y (= \Delta Y)$ is equal to B_2 times the relative change in X. If the latter is multiplied by 100, then Equation (5.27) gives the absolute change in Y for a percentage change in X. Thus, if $\Delta X / X$ changes by 0.01 unit (or 1 percent), the absolute change in Y is 0.01 (B_2). Thus, if in an application we find that $B_2 = 674$, the absolute change in Y is (0.01)(674), or 6.74. Therefore, when regressions like Eq. (5.24) are estimated by OLS, multiply the value of the estimated slope coefficient B_2 by 0.01, or what amounts to the same thing, divide it by 100.

Returning to our illustrative regression given in Equation (5.25), we then see that if aggregate personal expenditure increases by 1 percent, on the average, expenditure on services increases by $\approx$\$18.44 billion. (*Note:* Divide the estimated slope coefficient by 100.)

Lin-log models like Eq. (5.24) are thus used in situations that study the absolute change in the dependent variable for a percentage change in the independent variable. Needless to say, models like regression (5.24) can have more than one X variable in the log form. Each partial slope coefficient will then measure the absolute change in the dependent variable for a percentage change in the given X variable, holding all other X variables constant.

5.6 RECIPROCAL MODELS

Models of the following type are known as **reciprocal models:**

$$Y_i = B_1 + B_2 \left(\frac{1}{X_i} \right) + u_i$$

(5.28)

---

[18]If $Y = B_1 + B_2 \ln X$, using calculus it can be shown that $\frac{dY}{dX} = B_2 \left(\frac{1}{X} \right)$. Therefore, $B_2 = X \frac{dY}{dX} = \frac{dY}{dX / X} =$ Eq. (5.26).

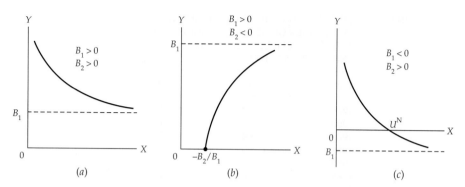

FIGURE 5-4   The reciprocal model: $Y_i = B_1 + B_2(1/X_i)$

This model is nonlinear in X because it enters the model *inversely* or *reciprocally*, but it is a linear regression model because the parameters are linear.[19]

The salient feature of this model is that as X increases indefinitely, the term $(1/X_i)$ approaches zero (Why?) and Y approaches the limiting or **asymptotic value** of B_1. Therefore, models like regression (5.28) have built into them an *asymptote* or *limit value* that the dependent variable will take when the value of the X variable increases indefinitely.

Some likely shapes of the curve corresponding to Eq. (5.28) are shown in Figure 5-4.

In Figure 5-4(*a*) if we let Y stand for the average fixed cost (AFC) of production, that is, the total fixed cost divided by the output, and X for the output, then as economic theory shows, AFC declines continuously as the output increases (because the fixed cost is spread over a larger number of units) and eventually becomes asymptotic at level B_1.

An important application of Figure 5-4(*b*) is the **Engel expenditure curve** (named after the German statistician Ernst Engel, 1821–1896), which relates a consumer's expenditure on a commodity to his or her total expenditure or income. If Y denotes expenditure on a commodity and X the total income, then certain commodities have these features: (1) There is some critical or *threshold* level of income below which the commodity is not purchased (e.g., an automobile). In Figure 5-4(*b*) this threshold level of income is at the level $-(B_2/B_1)$. (2) There is a satiety level of consumption beyond which the consumer will not go no matter how high the income (even millionaires do not generally own more than two or three cars at a time). This level is nothing but the asymptote B_1 shown in Figure 5-4(*b*). For such commodities, the reciprocal model of this figure is the most appropriate.

One important application of Figure 5-4(*c*) is the celebrated **Phillips curve** of macroeconomics. Based on the British data on the percent rate of change of money wages (Y) and the unemployment rate (X) in percent, Phillips obtained

---

[19]If we define $X^* = (1/X)$, then Equation (5.28) is linear in the parameters as well as the variables Y and X^*.

TABLE 5-6 YEAR-TO-YEAR PERCENTAGE CHANGE
IN THE INDEX OF HOURLY EARNINGS (Y)
AND THE UNEMPLOYMENT RATE (%) (X),
UNITED STATES, 1958–1969

Year	Y	X
1958	4.2	6.8
1959	3.5	5.5
1960	3.4	5.5
1961	3.0	6.7
1962	3.4	5.5
1963	2.8	5.7
1964	2.8	5.2
1965	3.6	4.5
1966	4.3	3.8
1967	5.0	3.8
1968	6.1	3.6
1969	6.7	3.5

Source: Economic Report of the President,
1989. Data on *X* from Table B-39, p. 352, and data
on *Y* from Table B-44, p. 358.

a curve similar to Figure 5-4(c).[20] As this figure shows, there is asymmetry in the response of wage changes to the level of unemployment. Wages rise faster for a unit change in unemployment if the unemployment rate is below U^N, which is called the *natural rate of unemployment* by economists, than they fall for an equivalent change when the unemployment rate is above the natural level, B_1 indicating the asymptotic floor for wage change. (See Figure 5-5 later.) This particular feature of the Phillips curve may be due to institutional factors, such as union bargaining power, minimum wages, or unemployment insurance.

Example 5.6. The Phillips Curve for the United States, 1958 to 1969

Because of its historical importance, and to illustrate the reciprocal model, we have obtained data, shown in Table 5-6, on percent change in the index of hourly earnings (Y) and the civilian unemployment rate (X) for the United States for the years 1958 to 1969.[21]

Model (5.28) was fitted to the data in Table 5-6, and the results were as follows:

$$\hat{Y}_t = -0.2594 + 20.5880 \left(\frac{1}{X_t}\right)$$

(5.29)

$$t = (-0.2572) \quad (4.3996) \qquad r^2 = 0.6594$$

This regression line is shown in Figure 5-5(a).

[20]A. W. Phillips, "The Relationship between Unemployment and the Rate of Change of Money Wages in the United Kingdom, 1861–1957," *Economica*, November 1958, pp. 283–299.
[21]We chose this period because until 1969 the traditional Phillips curve seems to have worked. Since then it has broken down, although many attempts have been made to resuscitate it with varying degrees of success.

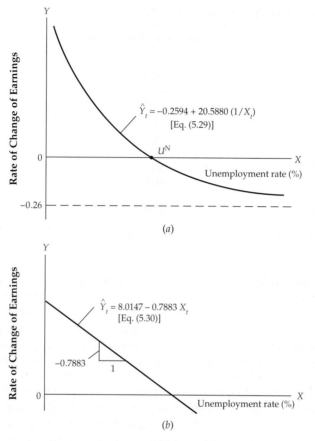

FIGURE 5-5   The Phillips curve for the United States, 1958–1969;
(a) reciprocal model; (b) linear model

As Figure 5-5 shows, the wage floor is −0.26 percent, which is not statistically different from zero. (Why?) Therefore, no matter how high the unemployment rate is, the rate of growth of wages will be, at most, zero.

For comparison we present the results of the following linear regression based on the same data (see Figure 5-5[b]):

$$\hat{Y}_t = 8.0147 - 0.7883X_t$$

$$t = (6.4625) \quad (-3.2605) \quad r^2 = 0.5153$$

(5.30)

Observe these features of the two models. In the linear model (5.30) the slope coefficient is negative, for the higher the unemployment rate is, the lower the rate of growth of earnings will be, ceteris paribus. In the reciprocal model, however, the slope coefficient is positive, which should be the case because the X variable enters inversely (two negatives make one positive). In other words, a positive slope in the reciprocal model is analogous to the negative slope in

TABLE 5-7 MANAGEMENT FEE SCHEDULE OF A MUTUAL FUND

Fee (%) Y	Net asset value ($, in billions) X
0.5200	0.5
0.5080	5.0
0.4840	10.0
0.4600	15.0
0.4398	20.0
0.4238	25.0
0.4115	30.0
0.4020	35.0
0.3944	40.0
0.3880	45.0
0.3825	55.0
0.3738	60.0

the linear model. The linear model suggests that as the unemployment rate increases by 1 percentage point, on the average, the percentage point change in the earnings is a constant amount of ≈ -0.79 no matter at what X we measure it. On the other hand, in the reciprocal model the percentage point rate of change in the earnings is not constant, but rather depends on at what level of X (i.e., the unemployment rate) the change is measured (see Table 5-11).[22] The latter assumption seems economically more plausible. Since the dependent variable in the two models is the same, we can compare the two r^2 values. The r^2 for the reciprocal model is higher than that for the linear model, suggesting that the former model fits the data better than the latter model.

As this example shows, once we go beyond the LIV/LIP models to those models that are still linear in the parameters but not necessarily so in the variables, we have to exercise considerable care in choosing a suitable model in a given situation. In this choice the theory underlying the phenomenon of interest is often a big help in choosing the appropriate model. *There is no denying that model building involves a good dose of theory, some introspection, and considerable hands-on experience.* But the latter comes with practice.

Before we leave reciprocal models, we discuss another application of such a model.

Example 5.7. Advisory Fees Charged for a Mutual Fund

The data in Table 5-7 relate to the management fees that a leading mutual fund in the United States pays its investment advisers to manage its assets. The fees depend on the net asset value of the fund. As you can see from Figure 5-6, the higher the net asset value of the fund, the lower the advisory fees are.

---

[22]As shown in Table 5-11, for the reciprocal model the slope is $-B_2(1/X^2)$.

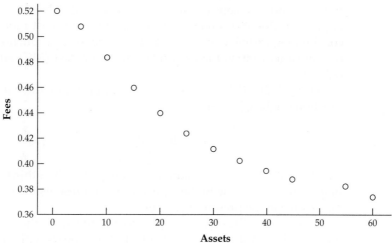

FIGURE 5-6   Management fees and asset size

The graph suggests that the relationship between the two variables is non-linear. Therefore, a model of the following type might be appropriate:

$$\text{Fees} = B_1 + B_2\left(\frac{1}{\text{assets}}\right) + u_i \tag{5.31}$$

Using the data in Table 5-7 and the EViews output in Figure 5-7, we obtained the following regression results:

Dependent Variable: Fees
Method: Least Squares

Sample: 1 12
Included observations: 12

Variable	Coefficient	Std. Error	t-Statistic	Prob.
C	0.420412	0.012858	32.69715	0.0000
1/assets	0.054930	0.022099	2.485610	0.0322

R-squared	0.381886	Mean dependent var	0.432317
Adjusted R-squared	0.320075	S.D. dependent var	0.050129
S.E. of regression	0.041335		
Sum squared resid	0.017086		
		F-statistic	6.178255
		Prob (F-statistic)	0.032232

FIGURE 5-7   EViews output of Equation (5.31)

It is left as an exercise for you to interpret these regression results (see Problem [5.20]).

5.7 POLYNOMIAL REGRESSION MODELS

In this section we consider regression models that have found extensive use in applied econometrics relating to production and cost functions. In particular, consider Figure 5-8, which depicts the total cost of production (TC) as a function of output as well as the associated marginal cost (MC) and the average cost (AC) curves.

Letting Y stand for TC and X for the output, mathematically, the total cost function can be expressed as

$$Y_i = B_1 + B_2X_i + B_3X_i^2 + B_4X_i^3 \qquad (5.32)$$

which is called a **cubic function,** or, more generally, a **third-degree polynomial** in the variable X—the highest power of X represents the degree of the polynomial (three in the present instance).

Notice that in these types of polynomial functions there is only one explanatory variable on the right-hand side, but it appears with various powers, thus making them multiple regression models.[23] (*Note:* We add the error term u_i to make model (5.32) a regression model.)

Although model (5.32) is nonlinear in the variable X, it is linear in the parameters, the B's, and is therefore a linear regression model. Thus, models like regression (5.32) can be estimated by the usual OLS routine. The only "worry" about the model is the likely presence of the problem of *collinearity* because the various powered terms of X are functionally related. But this concern is more apparent than real, for the terms X^2 and X^3 are *nonlinear functions of X* and do not violate the assumption of no perfect collinearity, that is, no perfect *linear* relationship between variables. In short, polynomial regression models can be estimated in the usual manner and do not present any special estimation problems.

Example 5.8. Hypothetical Total Cost Function

To illustrate the polynomial model, consider the hypothetical cost-output data given in Table 5-8.

The OLS regression results based on these data are as follows (see Figure 5-8):

$$\hat{Y}_i = 141.7667 + 63.4776X_i - 12.9615X_i^2 + 0.9396X_i^3$$

$$\text{se} = (6.3753) \quad (4.7786) \quad (0.9857) \quad (0.0591) \qquad \textbf{(5.33)}$$

$$R^2 = 0.9983$$

---

[23]Of course, one can introduce other X variables and their powers, if needed.

TABLE 5-8 HYPOTHETICAL COST-OUTPUT DATA

Y($)	193	226	240	244	257	260	274	297	350	420	Total cost
X	1	2	3	4	5	6	7	8	9	10	Output

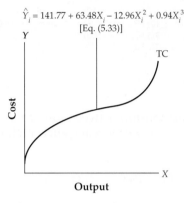
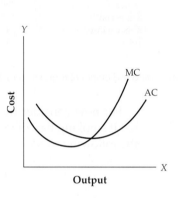

$$\hat{Y}_i = 141.77 + 63.48X_i - 12.96X_i^2 + 0.94X_i^3$$
[Eq. (5.33)]

FIGURE 5-8 Cost-output relationship

If cost curves are to have the U-shaped average and marginal cost curves shown in price theory texts, then the theory suggests that the coefficients in model (5.32) should have these a priori values:[24]

1. B_1, B_2, and B_4, each is greater than zero.
2. $B_3 < 0$.
3. $B_3^2 < 3B_2B_4$.

The regression results given in regression (5.33) clearly are in conformity with these expectations.

As a concrete example of polynomial regression models, consider the following example.

Example 5.9. Cigarette Smoking and Lung Cancer

Table 5-9, on the textbook's Web site, gives data on cigarette smoking and various types of cancer for 43 states and Washington, D.C., for 1960.

---

[24]For the economics of this, see Alpha C. Chiang, *Fundamental Methods of Mathematical Economics*, 3rd ed., McGraw-Hill, New York, 1984, pp. 205–252. The rationale for these restrictions is that to make economic sense the total cost curve must be upward-sloping (the larger the output is, the higher the total cost will be) and the marginal cost of production must be positive.

Predictor	Coef	SE Coef	T	P
Constant	−6.910	6.193	−1.12	0.271
CIG	1.5765	0.4560	3.46	0.001
CIGSQ	−0.019179	0.008168	−2.35	0.024

S = 2.75720   R-Sq = 56.4%   R-Sq (adj) = 54.3%

Analysis of Variance

Source	DF	SS	MS	F	P
Regression	2	403.89	201.94	26.56	0.000
Residual Error	41	311.69	7.60		
Total	43	715.58			

FIGURE 5-9   MINITAB output of regression (5.34)

For now consider the relationship between lung cancer and smoking. To see if smoking has an increasing or decreasing effect on lung cancer, consider the following model:

$$Y_i = B_1 + B_2 X_i + B_3 X_i^2 + u_i \tag{5.34}$$

where Y = number of deaths from lung cancer and X = the number of cigarettes smoked. The regression results using MINITAB are as shown in Figure 5-9.

These results show that the slope coefficient is positive but the coefficient of the cigarette-squared variable is negative. What this suggests is that cigarette smoking has an adverse impact on lung cancer, but that the adverse impact increases at a diminishing rate.[25] All the slope coefficients are statistically significant on the basis of the one-tail t test. We use the one-tail t test because medical research has shown that smoking has an adverse impact on lung and other types of cancer. The F value of 26.56 is also highly significant, for the estimated p value is practically zero. This would suggest that both variables belong in the model.

5.8   REGRESSION THROUGH THE ORIGIN

There are occasions when the regression model assumes the following form, which we illustrate with the two-variable model, although generalization to multiple regression models is straightforward.

$$Y_i = B_2 X_i + u_i \tag{5.35}$$

---

[25]Neglecting the error term, if you take the derivative of Y in Equation (5.34) with respect to X, you will obtain $\frac{\partial Y}{\partial X} = B_2 + 2B_3 X$, which in the present example gives $1.57 - 2(0.0192)X = 1.57 - 0.0384X$, which shows that the rate of change of lung cancer with respect to cigarette smoking is declining. If the coefficient of the cigsq variable were positive, then the effect of cigarette smoking on lung cancer would be increasing at an increasing rate. Here Y = incidence of lung cancer and X is the number of cigarettes smoked.

In this model the intercept is absent or zero, hence the name **regression through the origin.** We have already come across an example of this in Okun's law in Eq. (2.22). For Equation (5.35) it can be shown that[26]

$$b_2 = \frac{\sum X_i Y_i}{\sum X_i^2} \qquad (5.36)$$

$$\text{var}\,(b_2) = \frac{\sigma^2}{\sum X_i^2} \qquad (5.37)$$

$$\hat{\sigma}^2 = \frac{\sum e_i^2}{n-1} \qquad (5.38)$$

If you compare these formulas with those given for the two-variable model with intercept, given in Equations (2.17), (3.6), and (3.8), you will note several differences. *First*, in the model without the intercept, we use *raw* sums of squares and cross products, whereas in the intercept-present model, we use mean-adjusted sums of squares and cross products. *Second*, the d.f. in computing $\hat{\sigma}^2$ is now $(n-1)$ rather than $(n-2)$, since in Eq. (5.35) we have only one unknown. *Third*, the conventionally computed r^2 formula we have used thus far explicitly assumes that the model has an intercept term. Therefore, you should not use that formula. If you use it, sometimes you will get nonsensical results because the computed r^2 may turn out to be negative. *Finally*, for the model that includes the intercept, the sum of the estimated residuals, $\sum \hat{u}_i = \sum e_i$ is always zero, but this need not be the case for a model without the intercept term.

For all these reasons, one may use the zero-intercept model only if there is strong theoretical reason for it, as in Okun's law or some areas of economics and finance. An example is given in Problem 5.22. For now we will illustrate the zero-intercept model using the data given in Table 2-13, which relates to U.S. real GDP and the unemployment rate for the period 1960 to 2006. Similar to Equation (2.22), we add the variable representing the year and obtain the following results:

$$\hat{Y}_t = 0.00005 Year - 3.070 X_{t-1}$$
$$t = (2.55) \qquad\qquad (-2.92) \qquad (5.39)$$

where Y = change in the unemployment rate in percentage points and *Year*, X_{t-1} = percentage growth rate in real GDP from one year prior to the data in Y and *Year*.

---

[26]The proofs can be found in Gujarati and Porter, *Basic Econometrics*, 5th ed., McGraw-Hill, New York, 2009, pp. 182–183.

For comparison, we re-estimate Equation (5.39) with the intercept added.

$$\hat{Y}_t = 3.128 - 0.0015Year - 3.294X_{t-1}$$

$$t = (3.354)(-0.90) \qquad (-3.05) \qquad R^2 = 0.182 \qquad \textbf{(5.40)}$$

As you will notice, the intercept term is significant in Equation (5.40), but now the *Year* variable is not. Also notice that we have given the R^2 value for Eq. (5.40) but not for Eq. (5.39) for reasons stated before.[27]

5.9   A NOTE ON SCALING AND UNITS OF MEASUREMENT

Variables, economic or not, are expressed in various units of measurement. For example, we can express temperature in Fahrenheit or Celsius. GDP can be measured in millions or billions of dollars. Are regression results sensitive to the unit of measurement? The answer is that some results are and some are not. To show this, consider the data given in Table 5-10.

This table gives data on gross private domestic investment measured in billions of dollars (GDIB), the same data expressed in millions of dollars (GDIM), gross domestic product measured in billions of dollars (GDPB), and the same data expressed in millions of dollars (GDPM). Suppose we want to

TABLE 5-10   GROSS PRIVATE DOMESTIC INVESTMENT AND GROSS
DOMESTIC PRODUCT, UNITED STATES, 1997–2006

Year	GDPB	GDPM	GDIB	GDIM
1997	1389.8	1389800	8304.3	8304300
1998	1509.1	1509100	8747.0	8747000
1999	1625.7	1625700	9268.4	9268400
2000	1735.5	1735500	9817.0	9817000
2001	1614.3	1614300	10128.0	10128000
2002	1582.1	1582100	10469.6	10469600
2003	1664.1	1664100	10960.8	10960800
2004	1888.6	1888600	11685.9	11685900
2005	2077.2	2077200	12433.9	12433900
2006	2209.2	2209200	13194.7	13194700

Variables: GDPB = Gross private domestic product (billions of dollars).
GDPM = Gross private domestic product (millions of dollars).
GDIB = Gross private domestic investment (billions of dollars).
GDIM = Gross private domestic investment (millions of dollars).

---

[27]For Eq. (5.39) we can compute the so-called "raw" R^2, which is discussed in Problem 5.23.

find out how GDI behaves in relation to GDP. Toward that end, we estimate the following regression models:

$$\widehat{GDIB}_t = 461.511 + 5.8046GDPB_t$$
$$se = (1331.451)\,(0.762) \tag{5.41}$$
$$t = (0.3466) \quad (7.6143) \qquad r^2 = 0.8787$$

$$\widehat{GDIM}_t = 461511.076 + 5.8046GDPM_t$$
$$se = (1331451) \quad (0.762) \tag{5.42}$$
$$t = (0.3466) \quad (7.6143) \qquad r^2 = 0.8787$$

$$\widehat{GDIB}_t = 461.511 + 0.0058GDPM_t$$
$$se = (1331.451)\,(0.00076) \tag{5.43}$$
$$t = (0.3466) \quad (7.6143) \qquad r^2 = 0.8787$$

$$\widehat{GDIM}_t = 461511.076 + 5804.626GDPB_t$$
$$se = (1331451) \quad (762.335) \tag{5.44}$$
$$t = (0.3466) \quad (7.6143) \qquad r^2 = 0.8787$$

At first glance these results may look different. But they are not if we take into account the fact that 1 billion is equal to 1,000 million. All we have done in these various regressions is to express variables in different units of measurement. But keep in mind these facts. *First*, the r^2 value in all these regressions is the same, which should not be surprising because r^2 is a pure number, devoid of units in which the dependent variable (Y) and the independent variable (X) are measured. *Second*, the intercept term is always in the units in which the dependent variable is measured; recall that the intercept represents the value of the dependent variable when the independent variable takes the value of zero. *Third*, when Y and X are measured in the same units of measurement the slope coefficients as well as their standard errors remain the same (compare Equations [5.41] and [5.42]), although the intercept values and their standard errors are different. But the t ratios remain the same. *Third*, when the Y and X variables are measured in different units of measurement, the slope coefficients are different, but the interpretation does not change. Thus, in Equation (5.43) if GDP changes by a million, GDI changes by 0.0058 billions of dollars, which is 5.8 millions of dollars. Likewise, in Equation (5.44) if GDP increases by a billion dollars, GDI increases by 5804.6 millions. All these results are perfectly commonsensical.

5.10 REGRESSION ON STANDARDIZED VARIABLES

We saw in the previous section that the units in which the dependent variable (Y) and the explanatory variables (the X's) are measured affect the interpretation of the regression coefficients. This can be avoided if we express all the variables as *standardized variables.* A variable is said to be standardized if we subtract the mean value of the variable from its individual values and divide the difference by the standard deviation of that variable.

Thus, in the regression of Y on X, if we redefine these variables as

$$Y_i^* = \frac{Y - \overline{Y}}{S_Y} \tag{5.45}$$

$$X_i^* = \frac{X_i - \overline{X}}{S_X} \tag{5.46}$$

where $\overline{Y}$ = sample mean of Y
S_Y = sample standard deviation of Y
$\overline{X}$ = sample mean of X
S_X = sample standard deviation of X

the variables Y_i^* and X_i^* are called **standardized variables.**

An interesting property of a standardized variable is that its mean value is always zero and its standard deviation is always 1.[28]

As a result, it does not matter in what unit the Y and X variable(s) are measured. Therefore, instead of running the standard (bivariate) regression:

$$Y_i = B_1 + B_2 X_i + u_i \tag{5.47}$$

we could run the regression on the standardized variables as

$$\begin{aligned}
Y_i^* &= B_1^* + B_2^* X_i^* + u_i^* \\
&= B_2^* X_i^* + u_i^*
\end{aligned} \tag{5.48}$$

since it is easy to show that in the regression involving standardized variables the intercept value is always zero.[29] The regression coefficients of the standardized explanatory variables, denoted by *starred B* coefficients (B^*), are known in the literature as the **beta coefficients.** Incidentally, note that Eq. (5.48) is a regression through the origin.

How do we interpret the beta coefficients? The interpretation is that if the (standardized) regressor increases by one standard deviation, the average value of the (standardized) regressand increases by B_2^* standard deviation units. Thus, unlike the traditional model in Eq. (5.47), we measure the effect not in terms of the original units in which Y and X are measured, but in standard deviation units.

---

[28]For proof, see Gujarati and Porter, op.cit., pp. 183–184.
[29]Recall from Eq. (2.16) that Intercept − Mean value of Y − Slope × Mean value of X. But for the standardized variables, the mean value is always zero. This can be easily generalized to more than one X variable.

It should be added that if there is more than one X variable, we can convert each variable into the standardized form. To show this, let us return to the Cobb-Douglas production function data given for real GDP, employment, and real fixed capital for Mexico, 1955–1974, in Table 5-2. The results of fitting the logarithmic function are given in Eq. (5.11). The results of regressing the standardized logs of GDP on standardized employment and standardized fixed capital, using EViews, are as follows:

Dependent Variable: SLGDP
Method: Least Squares
Sample: 1955 1974
Included observations: 20

Variable	Coefficient	Std. Error	t-Statistic	Prob.
SLE	0.167964	0.089220	1.882590	0.0760
SLK	0.831995	0.089220	9.325223	0.0000
R-squared	0.995080	Mean dependent var		6.29E-06
Adjusted R-squared	0.994807	S.D. dependent var		0.999999
S.E. of regression	0.072063	Sum squared resid		0.093475

where SLGDP = standardized log of GDP
      SLE = standardized log of employment
      SLK = standardized log of capital

The interpretation of the regression coefficients is as follows: Holding capital constant, a standard deviation increase in employment increases the GDP, on average, by ≈0.17 standard deviation units. Likewise, holding employment constant, a one standard deviation increase in capital, on average, increases GDP by ≈0.83 standard deviation units. (Note that all variables are in the logarithmic form.) Relatively speaking, capital has more impact on GDP than employment. Here you will see the advantage of using standardized variables, for standardization puts all variables on equal footing because all standardized variables have zero means and unit variances.

Incidentally, we have not introduced the intercept term in the regression results. (Why?) If you include intercept in the model, its value will be almost zero.

5.11 SUMMARY OF FUNCTIONAL FORMS

In this chapter we discussed several regression models that, although linear in the parameters, were not necessarily linear in the variables. For each model, we noted its special features and also the circumstances in which it might be

TABLE 5-11   SUMMARY OF FUNCTIONAL FORMS

Model	Form	Slope $= \frac{dY}{dX}$	Elasticity $= \frac{dY}{dX} \cdot \frac{X}{Y}$
Linear	$Y = B_1 + B_2 X$	B_2	$B_2\left(\frac{X}{Y}\right)*$
Log-linear	$\ln Y = B_1 + B_2 \ln X$	$B_2\left(\frac{Y}{X}\right)$	B_2
Log-lin	$\ln Y = B_1 + B_2 X$	$B_2(Y)$	$B_2\,(X)*$
Lin-log	$Y = B_1 + B_2 \ln X$	$B_2\left(\frac{1}{X}\right)$	$B_2\left(\frac{1}{Y}\right)*$
Reciprocal	$Y = B_1 + B_2\left(\frac{1}{X}\right)$	$-B_2\left(\frac{1}{X^2}\right)$	$-B_2\left(\frac{1}{XY}\right)*$
Log-inverse	$\ln(Y) = B_1 - B_2\left(\frac{1}{X}\right)$	$B_2\left(\frac{Y}{X^2}\right)$	$B_2\left(\frac{1}{X}\right)$

Note: * Indicates that the elasticity coefficient is variable, depending on the value taken by X or Y or both. When no X and Y are specified, in practice, these elasticities are often measured at the mean values $\bar{X}$ and $\bar{Y}$.

appropriate. In Table 5-11 we summarize the various functional forms that we discussed in terms of a few salient features, such as the slope coefficients and the elasticity coefficients. Although for double-log models the slope and elasticity coefficients are the same, this is not the case for other models. But even for these models, we can compute elasticities from the basic definition given in Eq. (5.7).

As Table 5-11 shows, for the linear-in-variable (LIV) models, the slope coefficient is constant but the elasticity coefficient is variable, whereas for the log-log, or log-linear, model, the elasticity coefficient is constant but the slope coefficient is variable. For other models shown in Table 5-11, both the slope and elasticity coefficients are variable.

5.12 SUMMARY

In this chapter we considered models that are linear in parameters, or that can be rendered as such with suitable transformation, but that are not necessarily linear in variables. There are a variety of such models, each having special applications. We considered five major types of nonlinear-in-variable but linear-in-parameter models, namely:

1. The log-linear model, in which both the dependent variable and the explanatory variable are in logarithmic form.
2. The log-lin or growth model, in which the dependent variable is logarithmic but the independent variable is linear.
3. The lin-log model, in which the dependent variable is linear but the independent variable is logarithmic.
4. The reciprocal model, in which the dependent variable is linear but the independent variable is not.[30]

---

[30]The dependent variable can also be reciprocal and the independent variable linear, as in Problem 5.15. See also Problem 5.20.

5. The polynominal model, in which the independent variable enters with various powers.

Of course, there is nothing that prevents us from combining the features of one or more of these models. Thus, we can have a multiple regression model in which the dependent variable is in log form and some of the X variables are also in log form, but some are in linear form.

We studied the properties of these various models in terms of their relevance in applied research, their slope coefficients, and their elasticity coefficients. We also showed with several examples the situations in which the various models could be used. Needless to say, we will come across several more examples in the remainder of the text.

In this chapter we also considered the regression-through-the-origin model and discussed some of its features.

It cannot be overemphasized that in choosing among the competing models, the overriding objective should be the economic relevance of the various models and not merely the summary statistics, such as R^2. *Model building requires a proper balance of theory, availability of the appropriate data, a good understanding of the statistical properties of the various models, and the elusive quality that is called practical judgment.* Since the theory underlying a topic of interest is never perfect, there is no such thing as a perfect model. What we hope for is a reasonably good model that will balance all these criteria.

Whatever model is chosen in practice, we have to pay careful attention to the units in which the dependent and independent variables are expressed, for the interpretation of regression coefficients may hinge upon units of measurement.

KEY TERMS AND CONCEPTS

The key terms and concepts introduced in this chapter are

Double-log, log-linear, or constant elasticity model
Linear vs. log-linear regression model
  a) Functional form
  b) High r^2 value criterion
Cobb-Douglas (C-D) production function
  a) Returns to scale parameter
  b) Constant returns to scale
  c) Increasing and decreasing returns to scale
Semilog models
  a) Instantaneous growth rate
  b) Compound growth rate
Linear trend model
  a) trend variable

Log-lin, or growth, model
Lin-log model
Reciprocal models
  a) Asymptotic value
  b) Engel expenditure curve
  c) the Phillips curve
Polynomial regression models
  a) cubic function or third-degree polynomial
Regression through the origin
Scaling and units of measurement
Regression on standardized variables
  a) Standardized variables
  b) beta coefficients

QUESTIONS

5.1. Explain briefly what is meant by
  a. Log-log model
  b. Log-lin model
  c. Lin-log model
  d. Elasticity coefficient
  e. Elasticity at mean value

5.2. What is meant by a slope coefficient and an elasticity coefficient? What is the relationship between the two?

5.3. Fill in the blanks in Table 5-12.

TABLE 5-12   FUNCTIONAL FORMS OF REGRESSION MODELS

Model	When appropriate
$\ln Y_i = B_1 + B_2 \ln X_i$	—
$\ln Y_i = B_1 + B_2 X_i$	—
$Y_i = B_1 + B_2 \ln X_i$	—
$Y_i = B_1 + B_2 \left(\frac{1}{X_i}\right)$	—

5.4. Complete the following sentences:
  a. In the double-log model the slope coefficient measures . . .
  b. In the lin-log model the slope coefficient measures . . .
  c. In the log-lin model the slope coefficient measures . . .
  d. Elasticity of Y with respect to X is defined as . . .
  e. Price elasticity is defined as . . .
  f. Demand is said to be elastic if the absolute value of the price elasticity is . . . , but demand is said to be inelastic if it is . . .

5.5. State with reason whether the following statements are true (T) or false (F):
  a. For the double-log model, the slope and elasticity coefficients are the same.
  b. For the linear-in-variable (LIV) model, the slope coefficient is constant but the elasticity coefficient is variable, whereas for the log-log model, the elasticity coefficient is constant but the slope is variable.
  c. The R^2 of a log-log model can be compared with that of a log-lin model but not with that of a lin-log model.
  d. The R^2 of a lin-log model can be compared with that of a linear (in variables) model but not with that of a double-log or log-lin model.
  e. Model A: $\ln Y = -0.6 + 0.4X$; $r^2 = 0.85$
      Model B: $\hat{Y} = 1.3 + 2.2X$; $r^2 = 0.73$
      Model A is a better model because its r^2 is higher.

5.6. The *Engel expenditure curve* relates a consumer's expenditure on a commodity to his or her total income. Letting Y = the consumption expenditure on a commodity and X = the consumer income, consider the following models:
  a. $Y_i = B_1 + B_2 X_i + u_i$
  b. $Y_i = B_1 + B_2(1/X_i) + u_i$
  c. $\ln Y_i = B_1 + B_2 \ln X_i + u_i$

d. $\ln Y_i = B_1 + B_2(1/X_i) + u_i$

e. $Y_i = B_1 + B_2 \ln X_i + u_i$

f. $\ln(Y) = B_1 - B_2\left(\frac{1}{X}\right)$. This model is known as the log-inverse model.

Which of these models would you choose for the Engel curve and why? (*Hint:* Interpret the various slope coefficients, find out the expressions for elasticity of expenditure with respect to income, etc.)

5.7. The growth model Eq. (5.18) was fitted to several U.S. economic time series and the following results were obtained:

Time series and period	B_1	B_2	r^2
Real GNP (1954–1987) (1982 dollars)	7.2492 $t = (529.29)$	0.0302 (44.318)	0.9839
Labor force participation rate (1973–1987)	4.1056 $t = (1290.8)$	0.053 (15.149)	0.9464
S&P 500 index (1954–1987)	3.6960 $t = (57.408)$	0.0456 (14.219)	0.8633
S&P 500 index (1954–1987 quarterly data)	3.7115 $t = (114.615)$	0.0114 (27.819)	0.8524

a. In each case find out the instantaneous rate of growth.

b. What is the compound rate of growth in each case?

c. For the S&P data, why is there a difference in the two slope coefficients? How would you reconcile the difference?

PROBLEMS

5.8. Refer to the cubic total cost (TC) function given in Eq. (5.32).

a. The marginal cost (MC) is the change in the TC for a unit change in output; that is, it is the rate of change of the TC with respect to output. (Technically, it is the derivative of the TC with respect to X, the output.) Derive this function from regression (5.32).

b. The average variable cost (AVC) is the total variable cost (TVC) divided by the total output. Derive the AVC function from regression (5.32).

c. The average cost (AC) of production is the TC of production divided by total output. For the function given in regression (5.32), derive the AC function.

d. Plot the various cost curves previously derived and confirm that they resemble the stylized textbook cost curves.

5.9. Are the following models linear in the parameters? If not, is there any way to make them linear-in-parameter (LIP) models?

a. $Y_i = \dfrac{1}{B_1 + B_2 X_i}$

b. $Y_i = \dfrac{X_i}{B_1 + B_2 X_i^2}$

5.10. Based on 11 annual observations, the following regressions were obtained:

Model A: $\hat{Y}_t = 2.6911 - 0.4795 X_t$

$\qquad$ se $= (0.1216)\ (0.1140)\quad r^2 = 0.6628$

Model B: $\ln \hat{Y}_t = 0.7774 - 0.2530 \ln X_t$
$$se = (0.0152) \ (0.0494) \quad r^2 = 0.7448$$

where Y = the cups of coffee consumed per person per day and X = the price of coffee in dollars per pound.

a. Interpret the slope coefficients in the two models.

b. You are told that $\overline{Y} = 2.43$ and $\overline{X} = 1.11$. At these mean values, estimate the price elasticity for Model A.

c. What is the price elasticity for Model B?

d. From the estimated elasticities, can you say that the demand for coffee is price inelastic?

e. How would you interpret the intercept in Model B? (*Hint:* Take the antilog.)

f. Since the r^2 of Model B is larger than that of Model A, Model B is preferable to Model A. Comment on this statement.

5.11. Refer to the Cobb-Douglas production function given in regression (5.11).

a. Interpret the coefficient of the labor input X_2. Is it statistically different from 1?

b. Interpret the coefficient of the capital input X_3. Is it statistically different from zero? And from 1?

c. What is the interpretation of the intercept value of -1.6524?

d. Test the hypothesis that $B_2 = B_3 = 0$.

5.12. In their study of the demand for international reserves (i.e., foreign reserve currency such as the dollar or International Monetary Fund [IMF] drawing rights), Mohsen Bahami-Oskooee and Margaret Malixi[31] obtained the following regression results for a sample of 28 less developed countries (LDC):

$$\ln(R/P) = 0.1223 + 0.4079 \ln(Y/P) + 0.5040 \ln \sigma_{BP} - 0.0918 \ln \sigma_{EX}$$
$$t = (2.5128) \ (17.6377) \qquad (15.2437) \quad (-2.7449)$$
$$R^2 = 0.8268$$
$$F = 1151$$
$$n = 1120$$

where R = the level of nominal reserves in U.S. dollars

P = U.S. implicit price deflator for GNP

Y = the nominal GNP in U.S. dollars

σ_{BP} = the variability measure of balance of payments

σ_{EX} = the variability measure of exchange rates

(*Notes:* The figures in parentheses are t ratios. This regression was based on quarterly data from 1976 to 1985 (40 quarters) for each of the 28 countries, giving a total sample size of 1120.)

a. A priori, what are the expected signs of the various coefficients? Are the results in accord with these expectations?

b. What is the interpretation of the various partial slope coefficients?

---

[31]See Mohsen Bahami-Oskooee and Margaret Malixi, "Exchange Rate Flexibility and the LDCs Demand for International Reserves," *Journal of Quantitative Economics*, vol. 4, no. 2, July 1988, pp. 317–328.

      c. Test the statistical significance of each estimated partial regression coefficient (i.e., the null hypothesis is that *individually* each true or population regression coefficient is equal to zero).

      d. How would you test the hypothesis that all partial slope coefficients are simultaneously zero?

5.13. Based on the U.K. data on annual percentage change in wages (Y) and the percent annual unemployment rate (X) for the years 1950 to 1966, the following regression results were obtained:

$$\hat{Y}_t = -1.4282 + 8.7243\left(\frac{1}{X_t}\right)$$

$$se = (2.0675) \quad (2.8478) \quad r^2 = 0.3849$$

$$F(1,15) = 9.39$$

      a. What is the interpretation of 8.7243?

      b. Test the hypothesis that the estimated slope coefficient is not different from zero. Which test will you use?

      c. How would you use the F test to test the preceding hypothesis?

      d. Given that $\overline{Y} = 4.8$ percent and $\overline{X} = 1.5$ percent, what is the rate of change of Y at these mean values?

      e. What is the elasticity of Y with respect to X at the mean values?

      f. How would you test the hypothesis that the true $r^2 = 0$?

5.14. Table 5-13 gives data on the Consumer Price Index, $Y(1980 = 100)$, and the money supply, X (billions of German marks), for Germany for the years 1971 to 1987.

TABLE 5-13 CONSUMER PRICE INDEX (Y) (1980 = 100) AND THE MONEY SUPPLY (X) (MARKS, IN BILLIONS), GERMANY, 1971–1987

Year	Y	X
1971	64.1	110.02
1972	67.7	125.02
1973	72.4	132.27
1974	77.5	137.17
1975	82.0	159.51
1976	85.6	176.16
1977	88.7	190.80
1978	91.1	216.20
1979	94.9	232.41
1980	100.0	237.97
1981	106.3	240.77
1982	111.9	249.25
1983	115.6	275.08
1984	118.4	283.89
1985	121.0	296.05
1986	120.7	325.73
1987	121.1	354.93

Source: International Economic Conditions, annual ed., June 1988, The Federal Reserve Bank of St. Louis, p. 24.

a. Regress the following:
1. Y on X
2. $\ln Y$ on $\ln X$
3. $\ln Y$ on X
4. Y on $\ln X$
b. Interpret each estimated regression.
c. For each model, find the rate of change of Y with respect to X.
d. For each model, find the elasticity of Y with respect to X. For some of these models, the elasticity is to be computed at the mean values of Y and X.
e. Based on all these regression results, which model would you choose and why?

5.15. Based on the following data, estimate the model:

$$\left(\frac{1}{Y_i}\right) = B_1 + B_2 X_i + u_i$$

Y	86	79	76	69	65	62	52	51	51	48
X	3	7	12	17	25	35	45	55	70	120

a. What is the interpretation of B_2?
b. What is the rate of change of Y with respect to X?
c. What is the elasticity of Y with respect to X?
d. For the same data, run the regression

$$Y_i = B_1 + B_2\left(\frac{1}{X_i}\right) + u_i$$

e. Can you compare the r^2s of the two models? Why or why not?
f. How do you decide which is a better model?

5.16. *Comparing two r^2s when dependent variables are different.*[32] Suppose you want to compare the r^2 values of the growth model (5.19) with the linear trend model (5.23) of the consumer credit outstanding regressions given in the text. Proceed as follows:
a. Obtain $\ln Y_t$, that is, the estimated log value of each observation from model (5.19).
b. Obtain the antilog values of the values obtained in (a).
c. Compute r^2 between the values obtained in (b) and the actual Y values using the definition of r^2 given in Question 3.5.
d. This r^2 value is comparable with the r^2 value obtained from linear model (5.23).
Use the preceding steps to compare the r^2 values of models (5.19) and (5.23).

5.17. Based on the GNP/money supply data given in Table 5-14 (found on the textbook's Web site), the following regression results were obtained ($Y = $ GNP, $X = M2$):

---

[32]For additional details and numerical computation, see Gujarati and Porter, *Basic Econometrics*, 5th ed., McGraw-Hill, New York, 2009, pp. 203–205.

Model	Intercept	Slope	r^2
Log-linear	0.7826	0.8539	0.997
	$t = 11.40$	$t = 108.93$	
Log-lin	7.2392	0.0001	0.832
(growth model)	$t = 80.85$	$t = 14.07$	
Lin-log	−24299	3382.4	0.899
	$t = -15.45$	$t = 18.84$	
Linear	703.28	0.4718	0.991
(LIV model)	$t = 8.04$	$t = 65.58$	

a. For each model, interpret the slope coefficient.

b. For each model, estimate the elasticity of the GNP with respect to money supply and interpret it.

c. Are all r^2 values directly comparable? If not, which ones are?

d. Which model will you choose? What criteria did you consider in your choice?

e. According to the monetarists, there is a one-to-one relationship between the rate of changes in the money supply and the GDP. Do the preceding regressions support this view? How would you test this formally?

5.18. Refer to the energy demand data given in Table 5-3. Instead of fitting the log-linear model to the data, fit the following linear model:

$$Y_t = B_1 + B_2 X_{2t} + B_3 X_{3t} + u_t$$

a. Estimate the regression coefficients, their standard errors, and obtain R^2 and adjusted R^2.

b. Interpret the various regression coefficients

c. Are the estimated partial regression coefficients *individually* statistically significant? Use the p values to answer the question.

d. Set up the ANOVA table and test the hypothesis that $B_2 = B_3 = 0$.

e. Compute the income and price elasticities at the mean values of Y, X_2, and X_3. How do these elasticities compare with those given in regression (5.12)?

f. Using the procedure described in Problem 5.16, compare the R^2 values of the linear and log-linear regressions. What conclusion do you draw from these computations?

g. Obtain the normal probability plot for the residuals obtained from the linear-in-variable regression above. What conclusions do you draw?

h. Obtain the normal probability plot for the residuals obtained from the log-linear regression (5.12) and decide whether the residuals are approximately normally distributed.

i. If the conclusions in (g) and (h) are different, which regression would you choose and why?

5.19. To explain the behavior of business loan activity at large commercial banks, Bruce J. Summers used the following model:[33]

$$Y_t = \frac{1}{A + Bt} \qquad \text{(A)}$$

---

[33]See his article, "A Time Series Analysis of Business Loans at Large Commercial Banks," *Economic Review,* Federal Reserve Bank of St. Louis, May/June, 1975, pp. 8–14.

where Y is commercial and industrial (C&I) loans in millions of dollars, and t is time, measured in months. The data used in the analysis was collected monthly for the years 1966 to 1967, a total of 24 observations.

For estimation purposes, however, the author used the following model:

$$\frac{1}{Y_t} = A + Bt \tag{B}$$

The regression results based on this model for banks including New York City banks and excluding New York City banks are given in Equations (1) and (2), respectively:

$$\frac{1}{Y_t} = 52.00 - 0.2t$$

$$t = (96.13)\,(-24.52) \qquad \overline{R}^2 = 0.84 \tag{1}$$

$$\frac{\hat{1}}{Y_t} = 26.79 - 0.14t \qquad DW = 0.04^*$$

$$t = (196.70)\,(-66.52) \qquad \overline{R}^2 = 0.97 \tag{2}$$

$$DW = 0.03^*$$

*Durbin-Watson (DW) statistic (see Chapter 10).
a. Why did the author use Model (B) rather than Model (A)?
b. What are the properties of the two models?
c. Interpret the slope coefficients in Models (1) and (2). Are the two slope coefficients statistically significant?
d. How would you find out the standard errors of the intercept and slope coefficients in the two regressions?
e. Is there a difference in the behavior of New York City and the non–New York City banks in their C&I activity? How would you go about testing the difference, if any, formally?

5.20. Refer to regression (5.31).
a. Interpret the slope coefficient.
b. Using Table 5-11, compute the elasticity for this model. Is this elasticity constant or variable?

5.21. Refer to the data given in Table 5-5 (found on the textbook's Web site). Fit an appropriate Engle curve to the various expenditure categories in relation to total personal consumption expenditure and comment on the statistical results.

5.22. Table 5-15 gives data on the annual rate of return Y (%) on Afuture mutual fund and a return on a market portfolio as represented by the Fisher Index, X (%). Now consider the following model, which is known in the finance literature as the *characteristic line.*

$$Y_t = B_1 + B_2 X_i + u_i \tag{1}$$

TABLE 5-15   ANNUAL RATES OF RETURN (%) ON
AFUTURE FUND (*Y*) AND ON THE
FISHER INDEX (*X*), 1971–1980

Year	Y	X
1971	67.5	19.5
1972	19.2	8.5
1973	−35.2	−29.3
1974	−42.0	−26.5
1975	63.7	61.9
1976	19.3	45.5
1977	3.6	9.5
1978	20.0	14.0
1979	40.3	35.3
1980	37.5	31.0

Source: Haim Levy and Marshall Sarnat,
*Portfolio and Investment Selection: Theory
and Practice,* Prentice-Hall International,
Englewood Cliffs, N.J., 1984, pp. 730, 738.

In the literature there is no consensus about the prior value of B_1. Some studies have shown it to be positive and statistically significant and some have shown it to be statistically insignificant. In the latter case, Model (1) becomes a regression-through-the-origin model, which can be written as

$$Y_t = B_2 X_t + u_t \qquad (2)$$

Using the data given in Table 5-15, to estimate both these models and decide which model fits the data better.

5.23. *Raw R^2 for the regression-through-the-origin model.* As noted earlier, for the regression-through-the-origin regression model the conventionally computed R^2 may not be meaningful. One suggested alternative for such models is the so-called "raw" R^2, which is defined (for the two-variable case) as follows:

$$\text{Raw } r^2 = \frac{\left(\sum X_i Y_i\right)^2}{\sum X_i^2 \sum Y_i^2}$$

If you compare the raw R^2 with the traditional r^2 computed from Eq. (3.43), you will see that the sums of squares and cross-products in the raw r^2 are not mean-corrected.

For model (2) in Problem 5.22 compute the raw r^2. Compare this with the r^2 value that you obtained for Model (1) in Problem (5.22). What general conclusion do you draw?

5.24. For regression (5.39) compute the raw r^2 value and compare it with that given in Eq. (5.40).

5.25. Consider data on the weekly stock prices of Qualcomm, Inc., a digital wireless telecommunications designer and manufacturer, over the time period of 1995 to 2000. The complete data can be found in Table 5-16 on the textbook's Web site.

a. Create a scattergram of the closing stock price over time. What kind of pattern is evident in the plot?

b. Estimate a linear model to predict the closing stock price based on time. Does this model seem to fit the data well?

c. Now estimate a squared model by using both time and time-squared. Is this a better fit than in part (b)?

d. Now attempt to fit a cubic or third-degree polynomial to the data as follows:

$$Y_i = B_0 + B_1 X_i + B_2 X_i^2 + B_3 X_i^3 + u_i$$

where Y = stock price and X = time. Which model seems to be the best estimator for the stock prices?

5.26. Table 5-17 on the textbook's Web site contains data about several magazines. The variables are: magazine name, cost of a full-page ad, circulation (projected, in thousands), percent male among the predicted readership, and median household income of readership. The goal is to predict the advertisement cost.

a. Create scattergrams of the cost variable versus each of the three other variables. What types of relationships do you see?

b. Estimate a linear regression equation with all the variables and create a residuals versus fitted values plot. Does the plot exhibit constant variance from left to right?

c. Now estimate the following mixed model:

$$\ln Y_i = B_0 + B_1 \ln Circ + B_2 PercMale + B_3 MedIncome + u_i$$

and create another residual plot. Does this model fit better than the one in part (b)?

5.27. Refer to Example 4.5 (Table 4-6) about education, GDP, and population for 38 countries.

a. Estimate a linear (LIV) model for the data. What are the resulting equation and relevant output values (i.e., F statistic, t values, and R^2)?

b. Now attempt to estimate a log-linear model (where both of the independent variables are also in the natural log format).

c. With the log-linear model, what does the coefficient of the GDP variable indicate about education? What about the population variable?

d. Which model is more appropriate?

5.28. Table 5-18 on the textbook's Web site contains data on average life expectancy for 40 countries. It comes from the *World Almanac and Book of Facts, 1993,* by Pharos Books. The independent variables are the ratio of the number of people per television set and the ratio of number of people per physician.

a. Try fitting a linear (LIV) model to the data. Does this model seem to fit well?

b. Create two scattergrams, one of the natural log of life expectancy versus the natural log of people per television, and one of the natural log of life expectancy versus the natural log of people per physician. Do the graphs appear linear?

c. Estimate the equation for a log-linear model. Does this model fit well?

  d. What do the coefficients of the log-linear model indicate about the relation-ships of the variables to life expectancy? Does this seem reasonable?

5.29 Refer to Example 5.6 in the chapter. It was shown that the percentage change in the index of hourly earnings and the unemployment rate from 1958–1969 followed the traditional Phillips curve model. An updated version of the data, from 1965–2007, can be found in Table 5-19 on the textbook's Web site.

  a. Create a scattergram using the percentage change in hourly earnings as the Y variable and the unemployment rate as the X variable. Does the graph appear linear?

  b. Now create a scattergram as above, but use $1/X$ as the independent variable. Does this seem better than the graph in part (*a*)?

  c. Fit Eq. (5.29) to the new data. Does this model seem to fit well? Also create a regular linear (LIV) model as in Eq. (5.30). Which model is better? Why?

APPENDIX 5A: Logarithms

Consider the numbers 5 and 25. We know that

$$25 = 5^2 \tag{5A.1}$$

We say that the *exponent* 2 is the *logarithm* of 25 to the *base* 5. More formally, the logarithm of a number (e.g., 25) to a given base (e.g., 5) is the power (2) to which the base (5) must be raised to obtain the given number (25).

  More generally, if

$$Y = b^x \quad (b > 0) \tag{5A.2}$$

then

$$\log_b Y = X \tag{5A.3}$$

In mathematics the function (5A.2) is called an *exponential function* and (5A.3) is called the *logarithmic function*. As is clear from Eqs. (5A.2) and (5A.3), one function is the inverse of the other function.

  Although any (positive) base can be used, in practice, the two commonly used bases are 10 and the mathematical number $e = 2.71828 \ldots$.

  Logarithms to base 10 are called *common logarithms*. Thus,

$$\log_{10} 100 = 2 \quad \log_{10} 30 \approx 1.48$$

That is, in the first case $100 = 10^2$ and in the latter case $30 \approx 10^{1.48}$.

  Logarithms to the base e are called *natural logarithms*. Thus,

$$\log_e 100 \approx 4.6051 \quad \text{and} \quad \log_e 30 \approx 3.4012$$

All these calculations can be done routinely on a hand calculator.

  By convention, the logarithm to base 10 is denoted by the letters log and to the base e by ln. Thus, in the preceding example, we can write log 100 or log 30 or ln 100 or ln 30.

There is a fixed relationship between the common log and natural log, which is

$$\ln X = 2.3026 \log X \qquad \text{(5A.4)}$$

That is, the natural log of the number X is equal to 2.3026 times the log of X to the base 10. Thus,

$$\ln 30 = 2.3026 \log 30 = 2.3026(1.48) = 3.4012 \text{ (approx.)}$$

as before. Therefore, it does not matter whether one uses common or natural logs. But in mathematics the base that is usually preferred is e, that is, the natural logarithm. Hence, in this book all logs are natural logs, unless stated explicitly. Of course, we can convert the log of a number from one basis to the other using Eq. (5A.4).

Keep in mind that logarithms of negative numbers are not defined. Thus, the log of (-5) or the ln (-5) is not defined.

Some properties of logarithms are as follows: If A and B are any positive numbers, then it can be shown that:

1.
$$\ln (A \times B) = \ln A + \ln B \qquad \text{(5A.5)}$$

That is, the log of the product of two (positive) numbers A and B is equal to the sum of their logs.

2.
$$\ln (A/B) = \ln A - \ln B \qquad \text{(5A.6)}$$

That is, the log of the ratio of A to B is the difference in the logs of A and B.

3.
$$\ln (A \pm B) \neq \ln A \pm \ln B \qquad \text{(5A.7)}$$

That is, the log of the sum or difference of A and B is not equal to the sum or difference of their logs.

4.
$$\ln (A^k) = k \ln A \qquad \text{(5A.8)}$$

That is, the log of A raised to power k is k times the log of A.

5.
$$\ln e = 1 \qquad \text{(5A.9)}$$

That is, the log of e to itself as a base is 1 (as is the log of 10 to the base 10).

6.
$$\ln 1 = 0 \qquad \text{(5A.10)}$$

That is, the natural log of the number 1 is zero (so is the common log of number 1).

7.   If $Y = \ln X$,

$$\frac{dY}{dX} = \frac{1}{X} \qquad \text{(5A.11)}$$

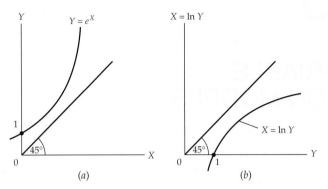

FIGURE 5A-1   Exponential and logarithmic functions: (a) exponential function; (b) logarithmic function

That is, the rate of change (i.e., the derivative) of Y with respect to X is 1 over X.

The exponential and (natural) logarithmic functions are depicted in Figure 5A.1.

Although the number whose log is taken is always positive, the logarithm of that number can be positive as well as negative. It can be easily verified that if

$$0 < Y < 1 \text{ then } \ln Y < 0$$
$$Y = 1 \text{ then } \ln Y = 0$$
$$Y > 1 \text{ then } \ln Y > 0$$

Also note that although the logarithmic curve shown in Figure 5A-1(b) is positively sloping, implying that the larger the number is, the larger its logarithmic value will be, the curve is increasing at a decreasing rate (mathematically, the second derivative of the function is negative). Thus, $\ln(10) = 2.3026$ (approx.) and $\ln(20) = 2.9957$ (approx.). That is, if a number is doubled, its logarithm does not double.

This is why the logarithm transformation is called a nonlinear transformation. This can also be seen from Equation (5A.11), which notes that if $Y = \ln X$, $dY/dX = 1/X$. This means that the slope of the logarithmic function depends on the value of X; that is, it is not constant (recall the definition of linearity in the variable).

Logarithms and percentages: Since $\frac{d(\ln X)}{dX} = \frac{1}{X}$, or $d(\ln X) = \frac{dX}{X}$, for very small changes the change in $\ln X$ is equal to the relative or proportional change in X. In practice, if the change in X is reasonably small, the preceding relationship can be written as the change in $\ln X \approx$ to the relative change in X, where $\approx$ means approximately.

Thus, for small changes,

$$(\ln X_t - \ln X_{t-1}) \approx \frac{(X_t - X_{t-1})}{X_{t-1}} = \text{relative change in } X$$

CHAPTER 6

DUMMY VARIABLE REGRESSION MODELS

In all the linear regression models considered so far the dependent variable Y and the explanatory variables, the X's, have been numerical or quantitative. But this may not always be the case; there are occasions when the explanatory variable(s) can be qualitative in nature. These **qualitative variables,** often known as **dummy variables,** have some alternative names used in the literature, such as *indicator variables, binary variables, categorical variables,* and *dichotomous variables.* In this chapter we will present several illustrations to show how the dummy variables enrich the linear regression model. For the bulk of this chapter we will continue to assume that the dependent variable is numerical.

6.1 THE NATURE OF DUMMY VARIABLES

Frequently in regression analysis the dependent variable is influenced not only by variables that can be quantified on some well-defined scale (e.g., income, output, costs, prices, weight, temperature) but also by variables that are basically qualitative in nature (e.g., gender, race, color, religion, nationality, strikes, political party affiliation, marital status). For example, some researchers have reported that, ceteris paribus, female college teachers are found to earn less than their male counterparts, and, similarly, that the average score of female students on the math part of the S.A.T. examination is less than their male counterparts (see Table 2-15, found on the textbook's Web site). Whatever the reason for this difference, qualitative variables such as gender should be included among the explanatory variables when problems of this type are encountered. Of course, there are other examples that also could be cited.

Such qualitative variables usually indicate the presence or absence of a "quality" or an attribute, such as male or female, black or white, Catholic or non-Catholic, citizens or non-citizens. One method of "quantifying" these attributes is by constructing *artificial variables* that take on values of 0 or 1, 0 indicating the absence of an attribute and 1 indicating the presence (or possession) of that attribute. For example, 1 may indicate that a person is a female and 0 may designate a male, or 1 may indicate that a person is a college graduate and 0 that he or she is not, or 1 may indicate membership in the Democratic party and 0 membership in the Republican party. Variables that assume values such as 0 and 1 are called **dummy variables.** We denote the dummy explanatory variables by the symbol D rather than by the usual symbol X to emphasize that we are dealing with a qualitative variable.

Dummy variables can be used in regression analysis just as readily as quantitative variables. As a matter of fact, a regression model may contain only dummy explanatory variables. Regression models that contain only dummy explanatory variables are called **analysis-of-variance (ANOVA) models.** Consider the following example of the ANOVA model:

$$Y_i = B_1 + B_2 D_i + u_i \tag{6.1}$$

where Y = annual expenditure on food (\$)
  $D_i = 1$ if female
    $= 0$ if male

Note that model (6.1) is like the two-variable regression models encountered previously except that instead of a quantitative explanatory variable X, we have a qualitative or dummy variable D. As noted earlier, from now on we will use D to denote a dummy variable.

Assuming that the disturbances u_i in model (6.1) satisfy the usual assumptions of the classical linear regression model (CLRM), we obtain from model (6.1) the following:[1]

Mean food expenditure, males:

$$E(Y_i \mid D_i = 0) = B_1 + B_2(0)$$

$$= B_1 \tag{6.2}$$

---

[1]Since dummy variables generally take on values of 1 or 0, they are nonstochastic; that is, their values are fixed. And since we have assumed all along that our X variables are fixed in repeated sampling, the fact that one or more of these X variables are dummies does not create any special problems insofar as estimation of model (6.1) is concerned. In short, dummy explanatory variables do not pose any new estimation problems and we can use the customary OLS method to estimate the parameters of models that contain dummy explanatory variables.

Mean food expenditure, females:

$$E(Y_i \mid D_i = 1) = B_1 + B_2(1)$$
$$= B_1 + B_2 \tag{6.3}$$

From these regressions we see that the intercept term B_1 gives the average or mean food expenditure of males (that is, the category for which the dummy variable gets the value of zero) and that the "slope" coefficient B_2 tells us by how much the mean food expenditure of females differs from the mean food expenditure of males; $(B_1 + B_2)$ gives the mean food expenditure for females. Since the dummy variable takes values of 0 and 1, it is not legitimate to call B_2 the slope coefficient, since there is no (continuous) regression line involved here. It is better to call it the **differential intercept coefficient** because it tells by how much the value of the intercept term differs between the two categories. In the present context, the differential intercept term tells by how much the mean food expenditure of females differs from that of males.

A test of the null hypothesis that there is no difference in the mean food expenditure of the two sexes (i.e., $B_2 = 0$) can be made easily by running regression (6.1) in the usual ordinary least squares (OLS) manner and finding out whether or not on the basis of the t test the computed b_2 is statistically significant.

Example 6.1. Annual Food Expenditure of Single Male and Single Female Consumers

Table 6-1 gives data on annual food expenditure ($) and annual after-tax income ($) for males and females for the year 2000 to 2001.

From the data given in Table 6-1, we can construct Table 6-2.

For the moment, just concentrate on the first three columns of this table, which relate to expenditure on food, the dummy variable taking the value of 1 for females and 0 for males, and after-tax income.

TABLE 6-1   FOOD EXPENDITURE IN RELATION TO AFTER-TAX INCOME, SEX, AND AGE

Age	Food expenditure, female ($)	After-tax income, female ($)	Food expenditure, male ($)	After-tax income, male ($)
<25	1983	11557	2230	11589
25–34	2987	29387	3757	33328
35–44	2993	31463	3821	36151
45–54	3156	29554	3291	35448
55–64	2706	25137	3429	32988
65>	2217	14952	2533	20437

Note: The food expenditure and after-tax income data are averages based on the actual number of people in various age groups. The actual numbers run into the thousands.
Source: Consumer Expenditure Survey, Bureau of Labor Statistics, **http://Stats.bls.gov/Cex/CSXcross.htm**.

TABLE 6-2   FOOD EXPENDITURE IN RELATION TO AFTER-TAX INCOME AND SEX

Observation	Food expenditure	After-tax income	Sex
1	1983.000	11557.00	1
2	2987.000	29387.00	1
3	2993.000	31463.00	1
4	3156.000	29554.00	1
5	2706.000	25137.00	1
6	2217.000	14952.00	1
7	2230.000	11589.00	0
8	3757.000	33328.00	0
9	3821.000	36151.00	0
10	3291.000	35448.00	0
11	3429.000	32988.00	0
12	2533.000	20437.00	0

Notes: Food expenditure = Expenditure on food in dollars.
After-tax income = After-tax income in dollars.
Sex = 1 if female, 0 if male.
Source: Extracted from Table 10-1.

Regressing food expenditure on the gender dummy variable, we obtain the following results.

$$\hat{Y}_i = 3176.833 - 503.1667 D_i$$

$$\text{se} = (233.0446)(329.5749) \tag{6.4}$$

$$t = (13.6318) \ (-1.5267) \qquad r^2 = 0.1890$$

where Y = food expenditure ($) and $D = 1$ if female, 0 if male.

As these results show, the mean food expenditure of males is ≈$3,177 and that of females is $(3176.833 - 503.1667) = 2673.6663$ or about $2,674. But what is interesting to note is that the estimated D_i is not statistically significant, for its t value is only about -1.52 and its p value is about 15 percent. This means that although the numerical values of the male and female food expenditures are different, statistically there is no significant difference between the two numbers. Does this finding make practical (as opposed to statistical) sense? We will soon find out.

We can look at this problem in a different perspective. If you simply take the averages of the male and female food expenditure figures separately, you will see that these averages are $3176.833 and $2673.6663. These numbers are the same as those that we obtained on the basis of regression (6.4). *What this means is that the dummy variable regression (6.4) is simply a device to find out if two mean values are different.* In other words, a regression on an intercept and a dummy variable is a simple way of finding out if the mean values of two groups differ. If the dummy coefficient B_2 is statistically significant (at the chosen level of significance level), we say that the two means are statistically different. If it is not statistically significant, we say that the two means are not statistically significant. In our example, it seems they are not.

Notice that in the present example the dummy variable "sex" has two categories. We have assigned the value of 1 to female consumers and the value of 0 to male consumers. The intercept value in such an assignment represents the mean value of the category that gets the value of 0, or male, in the present case. We can therefore call the category that gets the value of 0 the **base,** or **reference,** or **benchmark,** or **comparison, category.** To compute the mean value of food expenditure for females, we have to add the value of the coefficient of the dummy variable to the intercept value, which represents food expenditure of females, as shown before.

A natural question that arises is: Why did we choose male as the reference category and not female? If we have only two categories, as in the present instance, it does not matter which category gets the value of 1 and which gets the value of 0. If you want to treat female as the reference category (i.e., it gets the value of 0), Eq. (6.4) now becomes:

$$\hat{Y}_i = 2673.667 + 503.1667D_i$$

$$se = (233.0446) \quad (329.5749) \tag{6.5}$$

$$t = (11.4227) \quad (1.5267) \qquad r^2 = 0.1890$$

where $D_i = 1$ for male and 0 for female.

In either assignment of the dummy variable, the mean food consumption expenditure of the two sexes remains the same, as it should. Comparing Equations (6.4) and (6.5), we see the r^2 values remain the same, and the absolute value of the dummy coefficients and their standard errors remain the same. The only change is in the numerical value of the intercept term and its t value.

Another question: Since we have two categories, why not assign two dummies to them? To see why this is inadvisable, consider the following model:

$$Y_i = B_1 + B_2D_{2i} + B_3D_i + u_i \tag{6.6}$$

where Y is expenditure on food, $D_2 = 1$ for female and 0 for male, and $D_3 = 1$ for male and 0 for female. This model cannot be estimated because of perfect collinearity (i.e., perfect linear relationship) between D_2 and D_3. To see this clearly, suppose we have a sample of two females and three males. The **data matrix** will look something like the following.

	Intercept	D_2	D_3
Male Y_1	1	0	1
Male Y_2	1	0	1
Female Y_3	1	1	0
Male Y_4	1	0	1
Female Y_5	1	1	0

The first column in this data matrix represents the common intercept term, B_1. It is easy to verify that $D_2 = (1 - D_3)$ or $D_3 = (1 - D_2)$; that is, the two dummy variables are perfectly collinear. Also, if you add up columns D_2 and D_3, you will get the first column of the data matrix. In any case, we have the situation of perfect collinearity. As we noted in Chapter 3, in cases of perfect collinearity among explanatory variables, it is not possible to obtain unique estimates of the parameters.

There are various ways to mitigate the problem of perfect collinearity. If a model contains the (common) intercept, the simplest way is to assign the dummies the way we did in model (6.4), namely, to use only one dummy if a qualitative variable has two categories, such as sex. In this case, drop the column D_2 or D_3 in the preceding data matrix. *The general rule is: If a model has the common intercept, B_1, and if a qualitative variable has m categories, introduce only (m − 1) dummy variables.* In our example, sex has two categories, hence we introduced only a single dummy variable. If this rule is not followed, we will fall into what is known as the **dummy variable trap,** that is, the situation of **perfect collinearity** or **multicollinearity,** if there is more than one perfect relationship among the variables.[2]

Example 6.2. Union Membership and Right-to-Work Laws

Several states in the United States have passed *right-to-work laws* that prohibit union membership as a prerequisite for employment and collective bargaining. Therefore, we would expect union membership to be lower in those states that have such laws compared to those states that do not. To see if this is the case, we have collected the data shown in Table 6-3. For now concentrate only on the variable PVT (% of private sector employees in trade unions in 2006) and RWL, a dummy that takes a value of 1 if a state has a right-to-work law and 0 if a state does not have such a law. Note that we are assigning one dummy to distinguish the right- and non-right-to-work-law states to avoid the dummy variable trap.

The regression results based on the data for 50 states and the District of Columbia are as follows:

$$\widehat{PVT_i} = 15.480 - 7.161 RWL_i$$

$$se = (0.758) \quad (1.181)$$

$$t = (20.421)^* \quad (-6.062)^* \qquad r^2 = 0.429 \tag{6.7}$$

$$^*p \text{ values are extremely small}$$

Note: RWL = 1 for right-to-work-law states

In the states that do not have right-to-work laws, the average union membership is about 15.5 percent. But in those states that have such laws, the

---

[2]Another way to resolve the perfect collinearity problem is to keep as many dummies as the number of categories but to drop the common intercept term, B_1, from the model; that is, run the regression through the origin. But we have already warned about the problems involved in this procedure in Chapter 5.

TABLE 6-3   UNION MEMBERSHIP IN THE PRIVATE SECTOR AND
RIGHT-TO-WORK LAWS

PVT	RWL	PVT	RWL	PVT	RWL
10.6	1	11.1	0	7.6	1
24.7	0	6.5	1	15.4	0
9.7	0	13.8	0	8.5	1
6.5	1	14.5	0	15.4	0
17.8	0	14.0	0	16.6	0
9.2	0	20.6	0	15.8	0
16.6	0	17.0	0	5.9	1
12.8	0	8.9	1	7.7	1
13.6	0	11.9	0	6.4	1
7.3	1	15.6	0	5.7	0
5.4	1	9.7	1	6.8	1
24.2	0	17.7	1	12.2	0
6.4	1	11.2	0	4.8	1
15.2	0	20.6	0	21.4	0
12.9	1	11.4	0	14.7	0
13.1	1	26.3	0	15.4	0
8.7	1	3.9	1	9.4	1

Notes: PVT = Percent unionized in the private sector.
RWL = 1 for right-to-work-law states, 0 otherwise.
Sources: **http://www.dol.gov/esa/whd/state/righttowork.htm**.
http://www.bls.gov/news.release/union2.t05.htm.

average union membership is $(15.48 - 7.161)$ 8.319 percent. Since the dummy coefficient is statistically significant, it seems that there is indeed a difference in union membership between states that have the right-to-work laws and the states that do not have such laws.

It is instructive to see the scattergram of PVT and RWL, which is shown in Figure 6-1.

As you can see, the observations are concentrated at two extremes, 0 (no RWL states) and 1 (RWL states). For comparison, we have also shown the average level of unionization (%) in the two groups. The individual observations are scattered about their respective mean values.

ANOVA models like regressions (6.4) and (6.7), although common in fields such as sociology, psychology, education, and market research, are not that common in economics. In most economic research a regression model contains some explanatory variables that are quantitative and some that are qualitative. Regression models containing a combination of quantitative and qualitative variables are called **analysis-of-covariance (ANCOVA) models,** and in the remainder of this chapter we will deal largely with such models. ANCOVA models are an extension of the ANOVA models in that they provide a method of statistically controlling the effects of quantitative explanatory variables, called **covariates** or **control variables,** in a model that includes both quantitative and

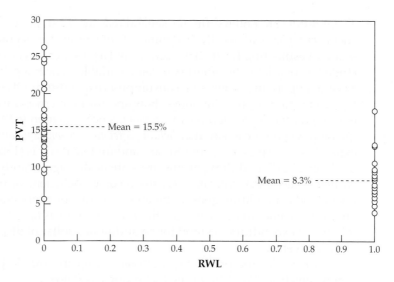

FIGURE 6-1 Unionization in private sector (PVT) versus right-to-work-law (RWL) states

qualitative, or dummy, explanatory variables. As we will show, if we exclude covariates from a model, the regression results are subject to model specification error.

6.2 ANCOVA MODELS: REGRESSION ON ONE QUANTITATIVE VARIABLE AND ONE QUALITATIVE VARIABLE WITH TWO CATEGORIES: EXAMPLE 6.1 REVISITED

As an example of the ANCOVA model, we reconsider Example 6.1 by bringing in disposable income (i.e., income after taxes), a *covariate*, as an explanatory variable.

$$Y_i = B_1 + B_2 D_i + B_3 X_i + u_i \qquad (6.8)$$

Y = expenditure on food (\$), X = after-tax income (\$), and $D = 1$ for female and 0 for male.

Using the data given in Table 6-2, we obtained the following regression results:

$$\hat{Y}_i = 1506.244 - 228.9868 D_i + 0.0589 X_i$$

$$\text{se} = (188.0096)(107.0582) \quad (0.0061)$$

$$t = (8.0115) \quad (-2.1388) \quad (9.6417) \qquad (6.9)$$

$$p = (0.000)^* \quad (0.0611) \quad (0.000)^*$$

$$R^2 = 0.9284$$

*Denotes extremely small values.

These results are noteworthy for several reasons. *First*, in Eq. (6.2), the dummy coefficient was statistically insignificant, but now it is significant. (Why?) It seems in estimating Eq. (6.2) we committed a specification error because we excluded a covariate, the after-tax income variable, which a priori is expected to have an important influence on consumption expenditure. Of course, we did this for pedagogic reasons. This shows how specification errors can have a dramatic effect(s) on the regression results. *Second,* since Equation (6.9) is a multiple regression, we now can say that *holding after-tax income constant,* the mean food expenditure for males is about $1,506, and for females it is (1506.244 − 228.9866) or about $1,277, and these means are statistically significantly different. *Third, holding gender differences constant,* the income coefficient of 0.0589 means the mean food expenditure goes up by about 6 cents for every additional dollar of after-tax income. In other words, the *marginal propensity of food consumption—* additional expenditure on food for an additional dollar of disposable income— is about 6 cents.

As a result of the preceding discussion, we can now derive the following regressions from Eq. (6.9) for the two groups as follows:

Mean food expenditure regression for females:

$$\hat{Y}_i = 1277.2574 + 0.0589X_i \tag{6.10}$$

Mean food expenditure regression for males:

$$\hat{Y}_i = 1506.2440 + 0.0589X_i \tag{6.11}$$

These two regression lines are depicted in Figure 6-2.

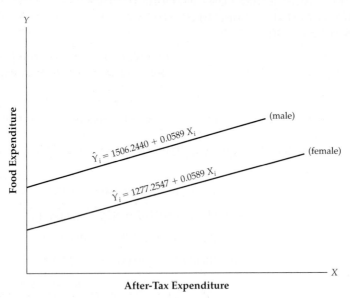

FIGURE 6-2   Food expenditure in relation to after-tax income

As you can see from this figure, the two regression lines differ in their intercepts but their slopes are the same. In other words, these two regression lines are parallel.

A question: By holding sex constant, we have said that the marginal propensity of food consumption is about 6 cents. Could there also be a difference in the marginal propensity of food consumption between the two sexes? In other words, could the slope coefficient B_3 in Equation (6.8) be statistically different for the two sexes, just as there was a statistical difference in their intercept values? If that turned out to be the case, then Eq. (6.8) and the results based on this model given in Eq. (6.9) would be suspect; that is, we would be committing another specification error. We explore this question in Section 6.5.

6.3 REGRESSION ON ONE QUANTITATIVE VARIABLE AND ONE QUALITATIVE VARIABLE WITH MORE THAN TWO CLASSES OR CATEGORIES

In the examples we have considered so far we had a qualitative variable with only two categories or classes—male or female, right-to-work laws or no right-to-work laws, etc. But the dummy variable technique is quite capable of handling models in which a qualitative variable has more than two categories.

To illustrate this, consider the data given in Table 6-4 on the textbook's Web site. This table gives data on the acceptance rates (in percents) of the top 65 graduate schools (as ranked by *U.S. News*), among other things. For the time being, we will concentrate only on the schools' acceptance rates. Suppose we are interested in finding out if there are statistically significant differences in the acceptance rates among the 65 schools included in the analysis. For this purpose, the schools have been divided into three regions: (1) South (22 states in all), (2) Northeast and North Central (32 states in all), and (3) West (10 states in all). The qualitative variable here is "region," which has the three categories just listed.

Now consider the following model:

$$Accept_i = B_1 + B_2 D_{2i} + B_3 D_{3i} + u_i \qquad (6.12)$$

where $D_2 = 1$ if the school is in the Northeastern or North Central region
$\qquad = 0$ otherwise (i.e., in one of the other 2 regions)
$\quad D_3 = 1$ if the school is in the Western region
$\qquad = 0$ otherwise (i.e., in one of the other 2 regions)

Since the qualitative variable region has three classes, we have assigned only two dummies. Here we are treating the South as the base or reference category. Table 6-4 includes these dummy variables.

From Equation (6.12) we can easily obtain the mean acceptance rate in the three regions as follows:

Mean acceptance rate for schools in the Northeastern and North Central region:

$$E(S_i \mid D_{2i} = 1, D_{3i} = 0) = B_1 + B_2 \qquad (6.13)$$

Mean acceptance rate for schools in the Western region:

$$E(S_i \mid D_{2i} = 0, D_{3i} = 1) = B_1 + B_2 \tag{6.14}$$

Mean acceptance rate for schools in the Southern region:

$$E(S_i \mid D_{2i} = 0, D_{3i} = 0) = B_1 + B_2 \tag{6.15}$$

As this exercise shows, the common intercept, B_1, represents the mean acceptance rate for schools that are assigned the dummy values of $(0, 0)$. Notice that B_2 and B_3, being the differential intercepts, tell us by how much the mean acceptance rates differ among schools in the different regions. Thus, B_2 tells us by how much the mean acceptance rates of the schools in the Northeastern and North Central region differ from those in the Southern region. Analogously, B_3 tells us by how much the mean acceptance rates of the schools in the Western region differ from those in the Southern region. To get the actual mean acceptance rate in the Northeastern and North Central region, we have to add B_2 to B_1, and the actual mean acceptance rate in the Western region is found by adding B_3 to B_1.

Before we present the statistical results, note carefully that we are treating the South as the reference region. Hence all acceptance rate comparisons are in relation to the South. If we had chosen the West as our reference instead, then we would have to estimate Eq. (6.12) with the appropriate dummy assignment. *Therefore, once we go beyond the simple dichotomous classification (female or male, union or nonunion, etc.), we must be very careful in specifying the base category, for all comparisons are in relation to it. Changing the base category will change the comparisons, but it will not change the substance of the regression results.* Of course, we can estimate Eq. (6.12) with any category as the base category.

The regression results of model (6.12) are as follows:

$$\widehat{Accept}_i = 44.541 - 10.680 D_{2i} - 12.501 D_{3i}$$
$$t = (14.38) \quad (-2.67) \quad \quad (-2.26) \tag{6.16}$$
$$p = (0.000) \quad (0.010) \quad \quad (0.028)$$
$$R^2 = 0.122$$

These results show that the mean acceptance rate in the South (reference category) was about 45 percent. The differential intercept coefficients of D_{2i} and D_{3i} are statistically significant (Why?). This suggests that there is a significant statistical difference in the mean acceptance rates between the Northeastern/North Central and the Southern schools, as well as between the Western and Southern schools.

In passing, note that the dummy variables will simply point out the differences, if they exist, but they will not suggest the reasons for the differences. Acceptance rates in the South may be higher for a variety of reasons.

As you can see, Eq. (6.12) and its empirical counterpart in Eq. (6.16) are ANOVA models. What happens if we consider an ANCOVA model by bringing

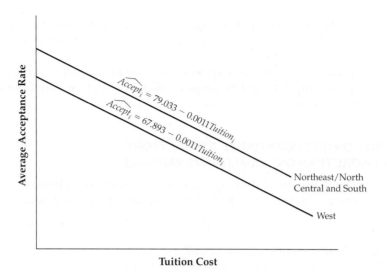

FIGURE 6-3 Average acceptance rates and tuition costs

in a quantitative explanatory variable, a covariate, such as the annual tuition per school? The data on this variable are already contained in Table 6-4. Incorporating this variable, we get the following regression (see Figure 6-3):

$$\widehat{Accept}_i = 79.033 - 5.670D_{2i} - 11.14D_{3i} - 0.0011\,Tuition$$

$$t = (15.53) \quad (-1.91) \quad (-2.79) \quad (-7.55)$$

$$p = (0.000)^* \quad (0.061)^{**} \quad (0.007)^* \quad (0.000)^*$$

$$R^2 = 0.546$$

(6.17)

A comparison of Equations (6.17) and (6.16) brings out a few surprises. Holding tuition costs constant, we now see that, at the 5 percent level of significance, there does not appear to be a significant difference in mean acceptance rates between schools in the Northeastern/North Central and the Southern regions (Why?). As we saw before, however, there still is a statistically significant difference in mean acceptance rates between the Western and Southern schools, even while holding the tuition costs constant. In fact, it appears that the Western schools' average acceptance rate is about 11 percent lower that that of the Southern schools while accounting for tuition costs. Since we see a difference in results between Eqs. (6.17) and (6.16), there is a chance we have committed a specification error in the earlier model by not including the tuition costs. This is similar to the finding regarding the food expenditure function with and without after-tax income. As noted before, omitting a covariate may lead to model specification errors.

*Statistically significant at the 5% level.
**Not statistically significant at the 5% level; however, at a 10% level, this variable would be significant.

The slope of −0.0011 suggests that if the tuition costs increase by $1, we should expect to see a decrease of about 0.11 percent in a school's acceptance rate, on average.

We also ask the same question that we raised earlier about our food expenditure example. Could the slope coefficient of tuition vary from region to region? We will answer this question in Section 6.5.

6.4   REGRESSION ON ONE QUANTIATIVE EXPLANATORY VARIABLE AND MORE THAN ONE QUALITATIVE VARIABLE

The technique of dummy variables can be easily extended to handle more than one qualitative variable. To that end, consider the following model:

$$Y_i = B_1 + B_2 D_{2i} + B_3 D_{3i} + B_4 X_i + u_i \tag{6.18}$$

where Y = hourly wage in dollars
X = education (years of schooling)
$D_2 = 1$ if female, 0 if male
$D_3 = 1$ if nonwhite and non-Hispanic, 0 if otherwise

In this model sex and race are qualitative explanatory variables and education is a quantitative explanatory variable.[3]

To estimate the preceding model, we obtained data on 528 individuals, which gave the following results.[4]

$$\hat{Y}_i = -0.2610 - 2.3606 D_{2i} - 1.7327 D_{3i} + 0.8028 X_i$$

$$t = (-0.2357)** \ (-5.4873)* \ (-2.1803)* \ (9.9094)* \tag{6.19}$$

$$R^2 = 0.2032; \ n = 528$$

*indicates p value less than 5%; **indicates p value greater than 5%

Let us interpret these results. *First,* what is the base category here, since we now have two qualitative variables? It is white and/or Hispanic male. *Second,* holding the level of education and race constant, on average, women earn less than men by about $2.36 per hour. Similarly, holding the level of education and sex constant, on average, nonwhite/non-Hispanics earn less than the base category by about $1.73 per hour. *Third,* holding sex and race constant, mean hourly wages go up by about 80 cents per hour for every additional year of education.

[3]If we were to define education as less than high school, high school, and more than high school, education would also be a dummy variable with three categories, which means we would have to use two dummies to represent the three categories.
[4]These data were originally obtained by Ernst Bernd and are reproduced from Arthur S. Goldberger, *Introductory Econometrics,* Harvard University Press, Cambridge, Mass., 1998, Table 1.1. These data were derived from the Current Population Survey conducted in May 1985.

Interaction Effects

Although the results given in Equation (6.19) make sense, implicit in Equation (6.18) is the assumption that the differential effect of the sex dummy D_2 is constant across the two categories of race and the differential effect of the race dummy D_3 is also constant across the two sexes. That is to say, if the mean hourly wage is higher for males than for females, this is so whether they are nonwhite/non-Hispanic or not. Likewise, if, say, nonwhite/non-Hispanics have lower mean wages, this is so regardless of sex.

In many cases such an assumption may be untenable. As a matter of fact, U.S. courts are full of cases charging all kinds of discrimination from a variety of groups. A female nonwhite/non-Hispanic may earn lower wages than a male nonwhite/non-Hispanic. In other words, there may be **interaction** between the qualitative variables, D_2 and D_3. Therefore, their effect on mean Y may not be simply **additive,** as in Eq. (6.18), but may be **multiplicative** as well, as in the following model:

$$Y_i = B_1 + B_2 D_{2i} + B_3 D_{3i} + B_3(D_{2i}D_{3i}) + B_4 X_i + u \qquad \text{(6.20)}$$

The dummy $D_{2i}D_3$, the product of two dummies, is called the **interaction dummy,** for it gives the joint, or simultaneous, effect of two qualitative variables.

From Equation (6.20) we can obtain:

$$E\,(Y_i \mid D_{2i} = 1, D_{3i} = 1, X_i) = (B_1 + B_2 + B_3 + B_4) + B_5 X_i \qquad \text{(6.21)}$$

which is the mean hourly wage function for female nonwhite/non-Hispanic workers. Observe that:

B_2 = differential effect of being female
B_3 = differential effect of being a nonwhite/non-Hispanic
B_4 = differential effect of being a female nonwhite/non-Hispanic

which shows that the mean hourly wage of female nonwhite/non-Hispanics is different (by B_4) from the mean hourly wage of females or nonwhite/non-Hispanics. Depending on the statistical significance of the various dummy coefficients, we can arrive at specific cases.

Using the data underlying Eq. (6.19), we obtained the following regression results:

$$\hat{Y}_i = -0.2610 \quad -2.3606 D_{2i} - 1.7327 D_{3i} + 2.1289 D_{2i}D_{3i} + 0.8028 X_i$$

$$t = (-0.2357)^{**} \;(-5.4873)^* \;(-2.1803)^*(1.7420)^! \qquad (9.9095)^* \qquad \text{(6.22)}$$

$$R^2 = 0.2032, \; n = 528$$

$^*p$ value below 5%, $^! = p$ value about 8%, $^{**}p$ value greater than 5%

Holding the level of education constant, if we add all the dummy coefficients, we obtain $(-2.3606 - 1.7327 + 2.1289) = -1.964$. This would suggest that the mean hourly wage of nonwhite/non-Hispanic female workers is lower by about $1.96, which is between the value of 2.3606 (sex difference alone) and 1.7327 (race difference alone). So, you can see how the interaction dummy modifies the effect of the two coefficients taken individually.

Incidentally, if you select 5% as the level of significance, the interaction dummy is not statistically significant at this level, so there is no interaction effect of the two dummies and we are back to Eq. (6.18).

A Generalization

As you can imagine, we can extend our model to include more than one quantitative variable and more than two qualitative variables. However, we must be careful that the *number of dummies for each qualitative variable is one less than the number of categories of that variable*. An example follows.

Example 6.3. Campaign Contributions by Political Parties

In a study of party contributions to congressional elections in 1982, Wilhite and Theilmann obtained the following regression results, which are given in tabular form (Table 6-5) using the authors' symbols. The *dependent variable* in this regression is PARTY$ (campaign contributions made by political parties to local congressional candidates). In this regression $GAP, VGAP, and PU are three quantitative variables and OPEN, DEMOCRAT, and COMM are three qualitative variables, each with two categories.

What do these results suggest? The larger the $GAP is (i.e., the opponent has substantial funding), the less the support by the national party to the local candidate is. The larger the VGAP is (i.e., the larger the margin by which the opponent won the previous election), the less money the national party is going to spend on this candidate. (This expectation is not borne out by the results for 1982.) An open race is likely to attract more funding from the national party to secure that seat for the party; this expectation is supported by the regression results. The greater the party loyalty (PU) is, the greater the party support will be, which is also supported by the results. Since the Democratic party has a smaller campaign money chest than the Republican party, the Democratic dummy is expected to have a negative sign, which it does (the intercept term for the Democratic party's campaign contribution regression will be smaller than that of its rival). The COMM dummy is expected to have a positive sign, for if you are up for election and happen to be a member of the national committees that distribute the campaign funds, you are more likely to steer proportionately larger amounts of money toward your own election.

TABLE 6-5 AGGREGATE CONTRIBUTIONS BY U.S.
POLITICAL PARTIES, 1982

Explanatory variable	Coefficient
$GAP	−8.189*
	(1.863)
VGAP	0.0321
	(0.0223)
OPEN	3.582*
	(0.7293)
PU	18.189*
	(0.849)
DEMOCRAT	−9.986*
	(0.557)
COMM	1.734*
	(0.746)
R^2	0.70
F	188.4

Notes: Standard errors are in parentheses.
*Means significant at the 0.01 level.
$GAP = A measure of the candidate's finances
VGAP = The size of the vote differential in the previous election
OPEN = 1 for open seat races, 0 if otherwise
PU = Party unity index as calculated by *Congressional Quarterly*
DEMOCRAT = 1 for members of the Democratic party, 0 if otherwise
COMM = 1 for representatives who are members of the Democratic Congressional Campaign Committee or the National Republican Congressional Committee
= 0 otherwise (i.e., those who are not members of such committees)
Source: Al Wilhite and John Theilmann, "Campaign Contributions by Political Parties: Ideology versus Winning," *Atlantic Economic Journal*, vol. XVII, June 1989, pp. 11–20. Table 2, p. 15 (adapted).

6.5 COMPARING TWO REGESSIONS[5]

Earlier in Sec. 6.2 we raised the possibility that not only the intercepts but also the slope coefficients could vary between categories. Thus, for our food expenditure example, are the slope coefficients of the after-tax income the same for

---

[5]An alternative approach to comparing two or more regressions that gives similar results to the dummy variable approach discussed below is popularly known as the *Chow test,* which was popularized by the econometrician Gregory Chow. The Chow test is really an application of the *restricted least-squares* method that we discussed in Chapter 4. For a detailed discussion of the Chow test, see Gujarati and Porter, *Basic Econometrics,* 5th ed., McGraw-Hill, New York, 2009, pp. 256–259.

both male and female? To explore this possibility, consider the following model:

$$Y_i = B_1 + B_2D_i + B_3X_i + B_4(D_iX_i) + u_i \qquad \textbf{(6.23)}$$

This is a modification of model (6.8) in that we have added an extra variable D_iX_i.

From this regression we can derive the following regression:

Mean food expenditure function, males ($D_i = 0$).

Taking the conditional expectation of Equation (6.23), given the values of D and X, we obtain

$$E\,(Y_i|D = 0, X_i) = B_1 + B_3X_i \qquad \textbf{(6.24)}$$

Mean food expenditure function, females ($D_i = 1$).

Again, taking the conditional expectation of Eq. (6.23), we obtain

$$E\,(Y_i|D_i = 1, X_i) = (B_1 + B_2D_i) + (B_3 + B_4D_i)X_i$$

$$= (B_1 + B_2) + (B_3 + B_4)X_i, \text{ since } D_i = 1 \qquad \textbf{(6.25)}$$

Just as we called B_2 the differential intercept coefficient, we can now call B_4 the **differential slope coefficient** (also called the **slope drifter**), for it tells by how much the slope coefficient of the income variable differs between the two sexes or two categories. Just as $(B_1 + B_2)$ gives the mean value of Y for the category that receives the dummy value of 1 when X is zero, $(B_3 + B_4)$ gives the slope coefficient of the income variable for the category that receives the dummy value of 1. Notice how the introduction of the dummy variable in the *additive form* enables us to distinguish between the intercept coefficients of the two groups and how the introduction of the dummy variable in the **interactive,** or **multiplicative, form** (D multiplied by X) enables us to differentiate between slope coefficients of the two groups.[6]

Now depending on the statistical significance of the differential intercept coefficient, B_2, and the differential slope coefficient, B_4, we can tell whether the female and male food expenditure functions differ in their intercept values or their slope values, or both. We can think of four possibilities, as shown in Figure 6-4.

Figure 6-4(*a*) shows that there is no difference in the intercept or the slope coefficients of the two food expenditure regressions. That is, the two regressions are identical. This is the case of **coincident regressions.**

Figure 6-4(*b*) shows that the two slope coefficients are the same, but the intercepts are different. This is the case of **parallel regressions.**

---

[6]In Eq. (6.20) we allowed for interactive dummies. But a dummy could also interact with a quantitative variable.

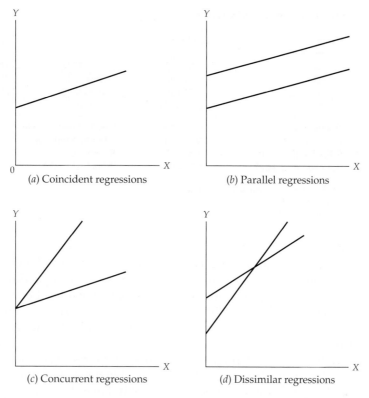

FIGURE 6-4   Comparing two regressions

Figure 6-4(c) shows that the two regressions have the same intercepts, but different slopes. This is the case of **concurrent regressions.**

Figure 6-4(d) shows that both the intercept and slope coefficients are different; that is, the two regressions are different. This is the case of **dissimilar regressions.**

Returning to our example, let us first estimate Eq. (6.23) and see which of the situations depicted in Figure 6-4 prevails. The data to run this regression are already given in Table 6-2. The regression results, using EViews, are as shown in Table 6-6.

It is clear from this regression that neither the differential intercept nor the differential slope coefficient is statistically significant, suggesting that perhaps we have the situation of coincident regressions shown in Figure 6-4(a). Are these results in conflict with those given in Eq. (6.8), where we saw that the two intercepts were statistically different? If we accept the results given in Eq. (6.8), then we have the situation shown in Figure 6-4(b), the case of parallel regressions (see also Fig. 6-3). What is an econometrician to do in situations like this?

It seems in going from Equations (6.8) to (6.23), we also have committed a specification error in that we seem to have included an unnecessary variable,

TABLE 6-6   RESULTS OF REGRESSION (6.23)

Variable	Coefficient	Std. Error	t-Statistic	Prob.
C	1432.577	248.4782	5.765404	0.0004
D	−67.89322	350.7645	−0.193558	0.8513
X	0.061583	0.008349	7.376091	0.0001
D.X	−0.006294	0.012988	−0.484595	0.6410
R-squared	0.930459	Mean dependent var		2925.250
Adjusted R-squared	0.904381	S.D. dependent var		604.3869
S.E. of regression	186.8903	F-statistic		35.68003
Sum squared resid	279423.9	Prob(F-statistic)		0.000056

Notes: Dependent Variable: FOODEXP
Sample: 1–12
Included observations: 12

D_iX_i. As we will see in Chapter 7, the consequences of including or excluding variables from a regression model can be serious, depending on the particular situation. As a practical matter, we should consider the most comprehensive model (e.g., model [6.23]) and then reduce it to a smaller model (e.g., Eq. [6.8]) after suitable diagnostic testing. We will consider this topic in greater detail in Chapter 7.

Where do we stand now? Considering the results of models (6.1), (6.8), and (6.23), it seems that model (6.8) is probably the most appropriate model for the food expenditure example. We probably have the case of parallel regression: The female and male food expenditure regressions only differ in their intercept values. Holding sex constant, it seems there is no difference in the response of food consumption expenditure in relation to after-tax income for men and women. But keep in mind that our sample is quite small. A larger sample might give a different outcome.

Example 6.4. The Savings-Income Relationship in the United States

As a further illustration of how we can use the dummy variables to assess the influence of qualitative variables, consider the data given in Table 6-7. These data relate to personal disposable (i.e., after-tax) income and personal savings, both measured in billions of dollars, in the United States for the period 1970 to 1995. Our objective here is to estimate a savings function that relates savings (Y) to personal disposable income (PDI) (X) for the United States for the said period.

To estimate this savings function, we could regress Y and X for the entire period. If we do that, we will be maintaining that the relationship between savings and PDI remains the same throughout the sample period. But that might be a tall assumption. For example, it is well known that in 1982 the United States suffered its worst peacetime recession. The unemployment rate that year reached 9.7 percent, the highest since 1948. An event such as this

TABLE 6-7 PERSONAL SAVINGS AND PERSONAL DISPOSABLE
INCOME, UNITED STATES, 1970–1995

Year	Personal savings	Personal disposable income (PDI)	Dummy variable	Product of the dummy variable and PDI
1970	61.0	727.1	0	0.0
1971	68.6	790.2	0	0.0
1972	63.6	855.3	0	0.0
1973	89.6	965.0	0	0.0
1974	97.6	1054.2	0	0.0
1975	104.4	1159.2	0	0.0
1976	96.4	1273.0	0	0.0
1977	92.5	1401.4	0	0.0
1978	112.6	1580.1	0	0.0
1979	130.1	1769.5	0	0.0
1980	161.8	1973.3	0	0.0
1981	199.1	2200.2	0	0.0
1982	205.5	2347.3	1*	2347.3
1983	167.0	2522.4	1	2522.4
1984	235.7	2810.0	1	2810.0
1985	206.2	3002.0	1	3002.0
1986	196.5	3187.6	1	3187.6
1987	168.4	3363.1	1	3363.1
1988	189.1	3640.8	1	3640.8
1989	187.8	3894.5	1	3894.5
1990	208.7	4166.8	1	4166.8
1991	246.4	4343.7	1	4343.7
1992	272.6	4613.7	1	4613.7
1993	214.4	4790.2	1	4790.2
1994	189.4	5021.7	1	5021.7
1995	249.3	5320.8	1	5320.8

Note: *Dummy variable = 1 for observations beginning in 1982.
Source: Economic Report of the President, 1997, data are in billions
of dollars and are from Table B-28, p. 332.

might disturb the relationship between savings and PDI. To see if this in fact
happened, we can divide our sample data into two periods, 1970 to 1981 and
1982 to 1995, the pre- and post-1982 recession periods.

In principle, we could estimate two regressions for the two periods in
question. Instead, we could estimate just one regression by adding a dummy
variable that takes a value of 0 for the period 1970 to 1981 and a value of 1 for
the period 1982 to 1995 and estimate a model similar to Eq. (6.23). To allow
for a different slope between the two periods, we have included the interaction term, as well. That exercise gives the results shown in Table 6-8.

As these results show, both the differential intercept and slope coefficients
are individually statistically significant, suggesting that the savings-income
relationship between the two time periods has changed. The outcome resembles Figure 6-4(*d*). From the data in Table 6-8, we can derive the following
savings regressions for the two periods:

TABLE 6-8   REGRESSION RESULTS OF SAVINGS-INCOME RELATIONSHIP

Variable	Coefficient	Std. Error	t-Statistic	Prob.
C	1.016117	20.16483	0.050391	0.9603
DUM	152.4786	33.08237	4.609058	0.0001
INCOME	0.080332	0.014497	5.541347	0.0000
DUM*INCOME	−0.065469	0.015982	−4.096340	0.0005
R-squared	0.881944	Mean dependent var		162.0885
Adjusted R-squared	0.865846	S.D. dependent var		63.20446
S.E. of regression	23.14996			

Notes: Dependent Variable: Savings
Sample: 1970–1995
Observations included: 26

Savings-Income regression: 1970–1981:

$$Savings_t = 1.0161 + 0.0803\ Income_t \tag{6.26}$$

Savings-Income regression: 1982–1995:

$$Savings_t = (1.0161 + 152.4786) + (0.0803 - 0.0655)\ Income_t$$

$$= 153.4947 + 0.0148\ Income_t \tag{6.27}$$

If we had disregarded the impact of the 1982 recession on the savings-income relationship and estimated this relationship for the entire period of 1970 to 1995, we would have obtained the following regression:

$$Savings_t = 62.4226 + 0.0376\ Income_t$$
$$t = (4.8917)\quad (8.8937)\qquad r^2 = 0.7672 \tag{6.28}$$

You can see significant differences in the **marginal propensity to save (MPS)**—additional savings from an additional dollar of income—in these regressions. The MPS was about 8 cents from 1970 to 1981 and only about 1 cent from 1982 to 1995. You often hear the complaint that Americans are poor savers. Perhaps these results may substantiate this complaint.

6.6   THE USE OF DUMMY VARIABLES IN SEASONAL ANALYSIS

Many economic time series based on monthly or quarterly data exhibit **seasonal patterns** (regular oscillatory movements). Examples are sales of department stores at Christmas, demand for money (cash balances) by households at holiday times, demand for ice cream and soft drinks during the summer, and demand for travel during holiday seasons. Often it is desirable to remove the

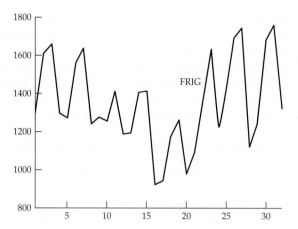

FIGURE 6-5   Sales of refrigerators, United States, 1978:1–1985:4

seasonal factor, or *component,* from a time series so that we may concentrate on the other components of times series, such as the *trend,*[7] which is a fairly steady increase or decrease over an extended time period. The process of removing the seasonal component from a time series is known as *deseasonalization,* or *seasonal adjustment,* and the time series thus obtained is called a *deseasonalized,* or *seasonally adjusted, time series.* The U.S. government publishes important economic time series on a seasonally adjusted basis.

There are several methods of deseasonalizing a time series, but we will consider only one of these methods, namely, the *method of dummy variables,*[8] which we will now illustrate.

Example 6.5. Refrigerator Sales and Seasonality

To show how dummy variables can be used for seasonal analysis, consider the data given in Table 6-9, found on the textbook's Web site.

This table gives data on the number of refrigerators sold (in thousands) for the United States from the first quarter of 1978 to the fourth quarter of 1985, a total of 32 quarters. The data on refrigerator sales are plotted in Fig. 6-5.

Figure 6-5 probably suggests that there is a seasonal pattern to refrigerator sales. To see if this is the case, consider the following model:

$$Y_t = B_1 + B_2 D_{2t} + B_3 D_{3t} + B_4 D_{4t} + u_t \qquad \textbf{(6.29)}$$

where Y = sales of refrigerators (in thousands), D_2, D_3, and D_4 are dummies for the second, third, and fourth quarter of each year, taking a value of 1 for

---

[7]A time series may contain four components: a *seasonal,* a *cyclical,* a *trend* (or long-term component), and one that is strictly random.

[8]For other methods of seasonal adjustment, see Paul Newbold, *Statistics for Business and Economics,* latest edition, Prentice-Hall, Englewood Cliffs, N.J.

the relevant quarter and a value of 0 for the first quarter. We are treating the first quarter as the reference quarter, although any quarter can serve as the reference quarter. Note that since we have four quarters (or four seasons), we have assigned only three dummies to avoid the dummy variable trap. The layout of the dummies is given in Table 6-9. Note that the refrigerator is classified as a durable goods item because it has a sufficiently long life.

The regression results of this model are as follows:

$$\hat{Y}_t = 1222.1250 + 245.3750D_{2t} + 347.6250D_{3t} - 62.1250D_{4t}$$

$$t = (20.3720)^* \quad (2.8922)^* \qquad (4.0974)^* \qquad (-0.7322)^{**} \qquad \textbf{(6.30)}$$

$$R^2 = 0.5318$$

*denotes a p value of less than 5%

**denotes a p value of more than 5%

Since we are treating the first quarter as the benchmark, the differential intercept coefficients (i.e., coefficients of the seasonal dummies) give the seasonal increase or decrease in the mean value of Y relative to the benchmark season. Thus, the value of about 245 means the average value of Y in the second quarter is greater by 245 than that in the first quarter, which is about 1222. The average value of sales of refrigerators in the second quarter is then about (1222 + 245) or about 1,467 thousands of units. Other seasonal dummy coefficients are to be interpreted similarly.

As you can see from Equation (6.30), the seasonal dummies for the second and third quarters are statistically significant but that for the fourth quarter is not. Thus, the average sale of refrigerators is the same in the first and the fourth quarters but different in the second and the third quarters. Hence, it seems that there is some seasonal effect associated with the second and third quarters but not the fourth quarter. Perhaps in the spring and summer people buy more refrigerators than in the winter and fall. Of course, keep in mind that all comparisons are in relation to the benchmark, which is the first quarter.

How do we obtain the deseasonalized time series for refrigerator sales? This can be done easily. Subtract the estimated value of Y from Eq. (6.30) from the actual values of Y, which are nothing but the residuals from regression (6.30). Then add to the residuals the mean value of Y. The resulting series is the deseasonalized time series. This series may represent the other components of the time series (cyclical, trend, and random).[9] This is all shown in Table 6-9.

---

[9] Of course, this assumes that the dummy variable technique is an appropriate method of deseasonalizing a time series (TS). A time series can be represented as $TS = s + c + t + u$, where s represents the seasonal, c the cyclical, t the trend, and u the random component. For other methods of deseasonalization, see Francis X. Diebold, *Elements of Forecasting*, 4th ed., South-Western Publishing, Cincinnati, Ohio, 2007.

In Example 6.5 we had quarterly data. But many economic time series are available on a monthly basis, and it is quite possible that there may be some seasonal component in the monthly data. To identify it, we could create 11 dummies to represent 12 months. This principle is general. If we have daily data, we could use 364 dummies, one less than the number of days in a year. Of course, you have to use some judgment in using several dummies, for if you use dummies indiscriminately, you will quickly consume degrees of freedom; you lose one d.f. for every dummy coefficient estimated.

6.7 WHAT HAPPENS IF THE DEPENDENT VARIABLE IS ALSO A DUMMY VARIABLE? THE LINEAR PROBABILITY MODEL (LPM)

So far we have considered models in which the dependent variable Y was quantitative and the explanatory variables were either qualitative (i.e., dummy), quantitative, or a mixture thereof. In this section we consider models in which the dependent variable is also dummy, or dichotomous, or binary.

Suppose we want to study the labor force participation of adult males as a function of the unemployment rate, average wage rate, family income, level of education, etc. Now a person is either in or not in the labor force. So whether a person is in the labor force or not can take only two values: 1 if the person is in the labor force and 0 if he is not. Other examples include: a country is either a member of the European Union or it is not; a student is either admitted to West Point or he or she is not; a baseball player is either selected to play in the majors or he is not.

A unique feature of these examples is that the dependent variable elicits a yes or no response, that is, it is dichotomous in nature.[10] How do we estimate such models? Can we apply OLS straightforwardly to such a model? The answer is that yes we can apply OLS but there are several problems in its application. Before we consider these problems, let us first consider an example.

Table 6-10, found on the textbook's Web site, gives hypothetical data on 40 people who applied for mortgage loans to buy houses and their annual incomes. Later we will consider a concrete application.

In this table $Y = 1$ if the mortgage loan application was accepted and 0 if it was not accepted, and X represents annual family income. Now consider the following model:

$$Y_i = B_1 + B_2X_i + u_i \tag{6.31}$$

where Y and X are as defined before.

---

[10]What happens if the dependent variable has more than two categories? For example, a person may belong to the Democratic party, the Republican party, or the Independent party. Here, party affiliation is a trichotomous variable. There are methods of handling models in which the dependent variable can take several categorical values. But this topic is beyond the scope of this book.

Model (6.31) looks like a typical linear regression model but it is not because we cannot interpret the slope coefficient B_2 as giving the rate of change of Y for a unit change in X, for Y takes only two values, 0 and 1. A model like Eq. (6.31) is called a **linear probability model (LPM)** because the conditional expectation of Y_i given X_i, $E\,(Y_i\,|\,X_i)$, can be interpreted as the *conditional probability* that the event will occur given X_i, that is, $P(Y_i = 1\,|\,X_i)$. Further, this conditional probability changes *linearly* with X. Thus, in our example, $E\,(Y_i\,|\,X_i)$ gives the probability that a mortgage applicant with income of X_i, say $60,000 per year, will have his or her mortgage application approved.

As a result, we now interpret the slope coefficient B_2 as a *change in the probability* that $Y = 1$, when X changes by a unit. The estimated Y_i value from Eq. (6.31), namely, $\hat{Y}_i$, is the predicted probability that Y equals 1 and b_2 is an estimate of B_2.

With this change in the interpretation of Eq. (6.31) when Y is binary can we then assume that it is appropriate to estimate Eq. (6.31) by OLS? The answer is yes, provided we take into account some problems associated with OLS estimation of Eq. (6.31). *First*, although Y takes a value of 0 or 1, there is no guarantee that the estimated Y values will necessarily lie between 0 and 1. In an application, some $\hat{Y}_i$ can turn out to be negative and some can exceed 1. *Second*, since Y is binary, the error term is also binary.[11] This means that we cannot assume that u_i follows a normal distribution. Rather, it follows the **binomial probability distribution.** *Third*, it can be shown that the error term is heteroscedastic; so far we are working under the assumption that the error term is homoscedastic. *Fourth*, since Y takes only two values, 0 and 1, the conventionally computed R^2 value is not particularly meaningful (for an alternative measure, see Problem 6.24).

Of course, not all these problems are insurmountable. For example, we know that if the sample size is reasonably large, the binomial distribution converges to the normal distribution. As we will see in Chapter 9, we can find ways to get around the heteroscedasticity problem. So the problem that remains is that some of the estimated Y values can be negative and some can exceed 1. In practice, if an estimated Y value is negative it is taken as zero, and if it exceeds 1, it is taken as 1. This may be convenient in practice if we do not have too many negative values or too many values that exceed 1.

But the major problem with LPM is that it assumes the *probability changes linearly with the X value;* that is, the incremental effect of X remains constant throughout. Thus if the Y variable is home ownership and the X variable is income, the LPM assumes that as X increases, the probability of Y increases linearly, whether $X = 1000$ or $X = 10,000$. In reality, we would expect the probability that $Y = 1$ to increase nonlinearly with X. At a low level of income, a family will not own a house, but at a sufficiently high level of income, a family most

---

[11]It is obvious from Eq. (6.31) that when $Y_i = 1$, we have $u_i = 1 - B_1 - B_2 X_i$ and when $Y_i = 0$, $u_i = -B_1 - B_2 X_i$.

likely will own a house. Beyond that income level, further increases in family income will have no effect on the probability of owning a house. Thus, at both ends of the income distribution, the probability of owning a house will be virtually unaffected by a small increase in income.

There are alternatives in the literature to the LPM model, such as the *logit* or *probit models*. A discussion of these models will, however, take us far afield and is better left for the references.[12] However, this topic is discussed in Chapter 12 for the benefit of those who want to pursue this subject further.

Despite the difficulties with the LPM, some of which can be corrected, especially if the sample size is large, the LPM is used in practical applications because of its simplicity. Very often it provides a benchmark against which we can compare the more complicated models, such as the logit and probit.

Let us now illustrate LPM with the data given in Table 6-10. The regression results are as follows:

$$\hat{Y}_i = -0.9456 + 0.0255X_i$$

$$t = (-7.6984)(12.5153) \qquad r^2 = 0.8047 \qquad \textbf{(6.32)}$$

The interpretation of this model is this: As income increases by a dollar, the probability of mortgage approval goes up by about 0.03. The intercept value here has no viable practical meaning. Given the warning about the r^2 values in LPM, we may not want to put much value in the observed high r^2 value in the present case. Sometimes we obtain a high r^2 value in such models if all the observations are closely bunched together either around zero or 1.

Table 6-10 gives the actual and estimated values of Y from LPM model (6.31). As you can observe, of the 40 values, 6 are negative and 6 are in excess of 1, which shows one of the problems with the LPM alluded to earlier. Also, the finding that the probability of mortgage approval increases linearly with income at a constant rate of about 0.03, may seem quite unrealistic.

To conclude our discussion of LPM, here is a concrete application.

Example 6.6. Discrimination in Loan Markets

To see if there is discrimination in getting mortgage loans, Maddala and Trost examined a sample of 750 mortgage applications in the Columbia, South Carolina, metropolitan area.[13] Of these, 500 applications were approved and 250 rejected. To see what factors determine mortgage approval, the authors developed an LPM and obtained the following results, which are given in tabular form. In this model the dependent variable is Y, which is binary, taking a value of 1 if the mortgage loan application was accepted and a value of 0 if it was rejected. Part of the objective of the study was to find out if there

---

[12]For an accessible discussion of these models, see Gujarati and Porter, 5th ed., McGraw-Hill, New York, 2009, Chapter 15.

[13]See G. S. Maddala and R. P. Trost, "On Measuring Discrimination in Loan Markets," *Housing Finance Review*, 1982, pp. 245–268.

was discrimination in the loan market on account of sex, race, and other qualitative factors.

Explanatory variable	Coefficient	t ratios
Intercept	0.501	not given
AI	1.489	4.69*
XMD	−1.509	−5.74*
DF	0.140	0.78**
DR	−0.266	−1.84*
DS	−0.238	−1.75*
DA	−1.426	−3.52*
NNWP	−1.762	0.74**
NMFI	0.150	0.23**
NA	−0.393	−0.134

Notes: AI = Applicant's and co-applicants' incomes ($ in thousands)
XMD = Debt minus mortgage payment ($ in thousands)
DF = 1 if female and 0 if male
DR = 1 if nonwhite and 0 if white
DS = 1 if single, 0 if otherwise
DA = Age of house (10^2 years)
NNWP = Percent nonwhite in the neighborhood ($\times 10^3$)
NMFI = Neighborhood mean family income (10^5 dollars)
NA = Neighborhood average age of home (10^2 years)
*p value 5% or lower, one-tail test.
**p value greater than 5%.

An interesting feature of the Maddala-Trost model is that some of the explanatory variables are also dummy variables. The interpretation of the dummy coefficient of DR is this: Holding all other variables constant, the probability that a nonwhite will have his or her mortgage loan application accepted is lower by 0.266 or about 26.6 percent compared to the benchmark category, which in the present instance is married white male. Similarly, the probability that a single person's mortgage loan application will be accepted is lower by 0.238 or 23.8 percent compared with the benchmark category, holding all other factors constant.

We should be cautious of jumping to the conclusion that there is race discrimination or discrimination against single people in the home mortgage market, for there are many factors involved in getting a home mortgage loan.

6.8 SUMMARY

In this chapter we showed how qualitative, or dummy, variables taking values of 1 and 0 can be introduced into regression models alongside quantitative variables. As the various examples in the chapter showed, the dummy variables are essentially a data-classifying device in that they divide a sample into various subgroups based on qualities or attributes (sex, marital status, race, religion, etc.) and *implicitly* run individual regressions for each subgroup. Now if there are differences in the responses of the dependent variable to the variation in the quantitative variables in the various subgroups, they will be reflected in the differences in the intercepts or slope coefficients of the various subgroups, or both.

Although it is a versatile tool, the dummy variable technique has to be handled carefully. *First*, if the regression model contains a constant term (as most models usually do), the number of dummy variables *must be one less than the number of classifications of each qualitative variable. Second*, the coefficient attached to the dummy variables *must always be interpreted in relation to the control, or benchmark, group—the group that gets the value of zero. Finally*, if a model has several qualitative variables with several classes, introduction of dummy variables can consume a large number of degrees of freedom (d.f.). Therefore, we should *weigh the number of dummy variables to be introduced into the model against the total number of observations in the sample.*

In this chapter we also discussed the possibility of committing a *specification error,* that is, of fitting the wrong model to the data. If intercepts as well as slopes are expected to differ among groups, we should build a model that incorporates both the *differential* intercept and slope dummies. In this case a model that introduces only the differential intercepts is likely to lead to a specification error. Of course, it is not always easy a priori to find out which is the true model. Thus, some amount of experimentation is required in a concrete study, especially in situations where theory does not provide much guidance. The topic of specification error is discussed further in Chapter 7.

In this chapter we also briefly discussed the linear probability model (LPM) in which the dependent variable is itself binary. Although LPM can be estimated by ordinary least square (OLS), there are several problems with a routine application of OLS. Some of the problems can be resolved easily and some cannot. Therefore, alternative estimating procedures are needed. We mentioned two such alternatives, the logit and probit models, but we did not discuss them in view of the somewhat advanced nature of these models (but see Chapter 12).

KEY TERMS AND CONCEPTS

The key terms and concepts introduced in this chapter are

Qualitative versus quantitative
   variables
Dummy variables
Analysis-of-variance (ANOVA)
   models
Differential intercept coefficients
Base, reference, benchmark, or
   comparison category
Data matrix
Dummy variable trap; perfect
   collinearity, multicollinearity
Analysis-of-covariance (ANCOVA)
   models
Covariates; control variables

Comparing two regressions
Interactive, or multiplicative
Additive
Interaction dummy
Differential slope coefficient, or
   slope drifter
Coincident regressions
Parallel regressions
Concurrent regressions
Dissimilar regressions
Marginal propensity to save (MPS)
Seasonal patterns
Linear probability model (LPM)
Binomial probability distribution

QUESTIONS

6.1. Explain briefly the meaning of:
   a. Categorical variables.
   b. Qualitative variables.
   c. Analysis-of-variance (ANOVA) models.
   d. Analysis-of-covariance (ANCOVA) models.
   e. The dummy variable trap.
   f. Differential intercept dummies.
   g. Differential slope dummies.
6.2. Are the following variables quantitative or qualitative?
   a. U.S. balance of payments.
   b. Political party affiliation.
   c. U.S. exports to the Republic of China.
   d. Membership in the United Nations.
   e. Consumer Price Index (CPI).
   f. Education.
   g. People living in the European Community (EC).
   h. Membership in General Agreement on Tariffs and Trade (GATT).
   i. Members of the U.S. Congress.
   j. Social security recipients.
6.3. If you have monthly data over a number of years, how many dummy variables will you introduce to test the following hypotheses?
   a. All 12 months of the year exhibit seasonal patterns.
   b. Only February, April, June, August, October, and December exhibit seasonal patterns.
6.4. What problems do you foresee in estimating the following models:

   a.
   $$Y_t = B_0 + B_1 D_{1t} + B_2 D_{2t} + B_3 D_{3t} + B_4 D_{4t} + u_t$$

   where $D_{it} = 1$ for observation in quarter i, $i = 1, 2, 3, 4$
   $\qquad\quad = 0$ otherwise

   b.
   $$GNP_t = B_1 + B_2 M_t + B_3 M_{t-1} + B_4 (M_t - M_{t-1}) + u_t$$

   where GNP_t = gross national product (GNP) at time t
   $\qquad M_t$ = the money supply at time t
   $\qquad M_{t-1}$ = the money supply at time $(t-1)$

6.5. State with reasons whether the following statements are true or false.
   a. In the model $Y_i = B_1 + B_2 D_i + u_i$, letting D_i take the values of (0, 2) instead of (0, 1) will *halve* the value of B_2 and will also *halve* the t value.
   b. When dummy variables are used, ordinary least squares (OLS) estimators are unbiased only in large samples.
6.6. Consider the following model:

$$Y_i = B_0 + B_1 X_i + B_2 D_{2i} + B_3 D_{3i} + u_i$$

where Y = annual earnings of MBA graduates
X = years of service
D_2 = 1 if Harvard MBA
     = 0 if otherwise
D_3 = 1 if Wharton MBA
     = 0 if otherwise

a. What are the expected signs of the various coefficients?
b. How would you interpret B_2 and B_3?
c. If $B_2 > B_3$, what conclusion would you draw?

6.7. Continue with Question 6.6 but now consider the following model:

$$Y_i = B_0 + B_1 X_i + B_2 D_{2i} + B_3 D_{3i} + B_4(D_{2i}X_i) + B_5(D_{3i}X_i) + u_i$$

a. What is the difference between this model and the one given in Question 6.6?
b. What is the interpretation of B_4 and B_5?
c. If B_4 and B_5 are individually statistically significant, would you choose this model over the previous one? If not, what kind of bias or error are you committing?
d. How would you test the hypothesis that $B_4 = B_5 = 0$?

PROBLEMS

6.8. Based on quarterly observations for the United States for the period 1961-I through 1977-II, H. C. Huang, J. J. Siegfried, and F. Zardoshty[14] estimated the following demand function for coffee. (The figures in parentheses are t values.)

$$\ln Q_t = 1.2789 - 0.1647 \ln P_t + 0.5115 \ln I_t + 0.1483 \ln P'_t$$

$$t = \qquad\qquad (-2.14) \quad (1.23) \qquad\quad (0.55)$$

$$-0.0089T - 0.0961 D_{1t} \quad -0.1570D_{2t} - 0.0097D_{3t} \qquad R^2 = 0.80$$

$$t = (-3.36) \qquad (-3.74) \qquad (-6.03) \qquad (-0.37)$$

where Q = pounds of coffee consumed per capita
P = the relative price of coffee per pound at 1967 prices
I = per capita PDI, in thousands of 1967 dollars
P' = the relative price of tea per quarter pound at 1967 prices
t = the time trend with $t = 1$ for 1961-I, to $t = 66$ for 1977-II
D_1 = 1 for the first quarter
D_2 = 1 for the second quarter
D_3 = 1 for the third quarter
$\ln$ = the natural log

---

[14]See H. C. Huang, J. J. Siegfried, and F. Zardoshty, "The Demand for Coffee in the United States, 1963–1977," *Quarterly Review of Economics and Business*, Summer 1980, pp. 36–50.

a. How would you interpret the coefficients of P, I, and P'?

b. Is the demand for coffee price elastic?

c. Are coffee and tea substitute or complementary products?

d. How would you interpret the coefficient of t?

e. What is the trend rate of growth or decline in coffee consumption in the United States? If there is a decline in coffee consumption, what accounts for it?

f. What is the income elasticity of demand for coffee?

g. How would you test the hypothesis that the income elasticity of demand for coffee is not significantly different from 1?

h. What do the dummy variables represent in this case?

i. How do you interpret the dummies in this model?

j. Which of the dummies are statistically significant?

k. Is there a pronounced seasonal pattern in coffee consumption in the United States? If so, what accounts for it?

l. Which is the benchmark quarter in this example? Would the results change if we chose another quarter as the base quarter?

m. The preceding model only introduces the *differential intercept* dummies. What implicit assumption is made here?

n. Suppose someone contends that this model is *misspecified* because it assumes that the slopes of the various variables remain constant between quarters. How would you rewrite the model to take into account *differential slope* dummies?

o. If you had the data, how would you go about reformulating the demand function for coffee?

6.9. In a study of the determinants of direct airfares to Cleveland, Paul W. Bauer and Thomas J. Zlatoper obtained the following regression results (in tabular form) to explain one-way airfare for first class, coach, and discount airfares. (The dependent variable is one-way airfare in dollars).

The explanatory variables are defined as follows:

Carriers = the number of carriers

Pass = the total number of passengers flown on route (all carriers)

Miles = the mileage from the origin city to Cleveland

Pop = the population of the origin city

Inc = per capita income of the origin city

Corp = the proxy for potential business traffic from the origin city

Slot = the dummy variable equaling 1 if the origin city has a slot-restricted airport
= 0 if otherwise

Stop = the number of on-flight stops

Meal = the dummy variable equaling 1 if a meal is served
= 0 if otherwise

Hub = the dummy variable equaling 1 if the origin city has a hub airline
= 0 if otherwise

EA = the dummy variable equaling 1 if the carrier is Eastern Airlines
= 0 if otherwise

CO = the dummy variable equaling 1 if the carrier is Continental Airlines
= 0 if otherwise

The results are given in Table 6-11.

a. What is the rationale for introducing both carriers and squared carriers as explanatory variables in the model? What does the negative sign for carriers and the positive sign for carriers squared suggest?

b. As in part (*a*), what is the rationale for the introduction of miles and squared miles as explanatory variables? Do the observed signs of these variables make economic sense?

TABLE 6-11 DETERMINANTS OF DIRECT AIR FARES TO CLEVELAND

Explanatory variable	First class	Coach	Discount
Carriers	−19.50	−23.00	−17.50
	*t = (−0.878)	(−1.99)	(−3.67)
Carriers^2	2.79	4.00	2.19
	(0.632)	(1.83)	(2.42)
Miles	0.233	0.277	0.0791
	(5.13)	(12.00)	(8.24)
Miles^2	−0.0000097	−0.000052	−0.000014
	(−0.495)	(−4.98)	(−3.23)
Pop	−0.00598	−0.00114	−0.000868
	(−1.67)	(−4.98)	(−1.05)
Inc	−0.00195	−0.00178	−0.00411
	(−0.686)	(−1.06)	(−6.05)
Corp	3.62	1.22	−1.06
	(3.45)	(2.51)	(−5.22)
Pass	−0.000818	−0.000275	0.853
	(−0.771)	(−0.527)	(3.93)
Stop	12.50	7.64	−3.85
	(1.36)	(2.13)	(−2.60)
Slot	7.13	−0.746	17.70
	(0.299)	(−0.067)	(3.82)
Hub	11.30	4.18	−3.50
	(0.90)	(0.81)	(−1.62)
Meal	11.20	0.945	1.80
	(1.07)	(0.177)	(0.813)
EA	−18.30	5.80	−10.60
	(−1.60)	(0.775)	(−3.49)
CO	−66.40	−56.50	−4.17
	(−5.72)	(−7.61)	(−1.35)
Constant term	212.00	126.00	113.00
	(5.21)	(5.75)	(12.40)
R^2	0.863	0.871	0.799
Number of observations	163	323	323

Note: *Figures in parentheses represent *t* values.
Source: Paul W. Bauer and Thomas J. Zlatoper, *Economic Review,* Federal Reserve Bank of Cleveland, vol. 25, no. 1, 1989, Tables 2, 3, and 4, pp. 6–7.

  c. The population variable is observed to have a negative sign. What is the implication here?

  d. Why is the coefficient of the per capita income variable negative in all the regressions?

  e. Why does the stop variable have a positive sign for first-class and coach fares but a negative sign for discount fares? Which makes economic sense?

  f. The dummy for Continental Airlines consistently has a negative sign. What does this suggest?

  g. Assess the statistical significance of each estimated coefficient. *Note:* Since the number of observations is sufficiently large, use the normal approximation to the t distribution at the 5% level of significance. Justify your use of one-tailed or two-tailed tests.

  h. Why is the slot dummy significant only for discount fares?

  i. Since the number of observations for coach and discount fare regressions is the same, 323 each, would you pull all 646 observations and run a regression similar to the ones shown in the preceding table? If you do that, how would you distinguish between coach and discount fare observations? (*Hint:* dummy variables.)

  j. Comment on the overall quality of the regression results given in the preceding table.

6.10. In a regression of weight on height involving 51 students, 36 males and 15 females, the following regression results were obtained:[15]

 1. $\widehat{Weight}_i = -232.06551 + 5.5662 height_i$
   $t = (-5.2066)$ (8.6246)

 2. $\widehat{Weight}_i = -122.9621 + 23.8238 dumsex_i + 3.7402 height_i$
   $t = (-2.5884)$ (4.0149) (5.1613)

 3. $\widehat{Weight}_i = -107.9508 + 3.5105 height_i + 2.0073 dumsex_i + 0.3263 dumht.$
   $t = (-1.2266)$ (2.6087) (0.0187) (0.2035)

where weight is in pounds, height is in inches, and where

$$Dumsex = 1 \text{ if male}$$
$$= 0 \text{ if otherwise}$$

$$Dumht. = \text{the interactive or differential slope dummy}$$

  a. Which regression would you choose, 1 or 2? Why?

  b. If 2 is in fact preferable but you choose 1, what kind of error are you committing?

  c. What does the dumsex coefficient in 2 suggest?

  d. In Model 2 the differential intercept dummy is statistically significant whereas in Model 3 it is statistically insignificant. What accounts for this change?

  e. Between Models 2 and 3, which would you choose? Why?

  f. In Models 2 and 3 the coefficient of the height variable is about the same, but the coefficient of the dummy variable for sex changes dramatically. Do you have any idea what is going on?

---

[15]A former colleague, Albert Zucker, collected these data and estimated the various regressions.

To answer questions (d), (e), and (f) you are given the following *correlation matrix.*

	Height	Dumsex	Dumht.
Height	1	0.6276	0.6752
Dumsex	0.6276	1	0.9971
Dumht.	0.6752	0.9971	1

The interpretation of this table is that the coefficient of correlation between height and dumsex is 0.6276 and that between dumsex and dumht. is 0.9971.

6.11. Table 6-12 on the textbook's Web site gives *nonseasonally* adjusted quarterly data on the retail sales of hobby, toy, and game stores (in millions) for the period 1992: I to 2008: II.
Consider the following model:

$$Sales_t = B_1 + B_2 D_{2t} + B_3 D_{3t} + B_4 D_{4t} + u_t$$

where $D_2 = 1$ in the second quarter, $= 0$ if otherwise
$\quad\quad D_3 = 1$ in the third quarter, $= 0$ if otherwise
$\quad\quad D_4 = 1$ in the fourth quarter, $= 0$ if otherwise

a. Estimate the preceding regression.
b. What is the interpretation of the various coefficients?
c. Give a logical reason for why the results are this way.
***d.** How would you use the estimated regression to deseasonalize the data?

6.12. Use the data of Problem 6.11 but estimate the following model:

$$Sales_t = B_1 D_{1t} + B_2 D_{2t} + B_3 D_{3t} + B_4 D_{4t} + u_t$$

In this model there is a dummy assigned to each quarter.
a. How does this model differ from the one given in Problem 6.11?
b. To estimate this model, will you have to use a regression program that suppresses the intercept term? In other words, will you have to run a regression through the origin?
c. Compare the results of this model with the previous one and determine which model you prefer and why.

6.13. Refer to Eq. (6.17) in the text. How would you modify this equation to allow for the possibility that the coefficient of *Tuition* also differs from region to region? Present your results.

6.14. How would you check that in Eq. (6.19) the slope coefficient of X varies by sex as well as race?

6.15. Reestimate Eq. (6.30) by assigning a dummy for each quarter and compare your results with those given in Eq. (6.30). In estimating such an equation, what precaution must you take?

*Optional.

6.16. Consider the following model:

$$Y_i = B_1 + B_2 D_{2i} + B_3 D_{3i} + B_4 (D_{2i} D_{3i}) + B_5 X_i + u_i$$

where Y = the annual salary of a college teacher
  X = years of teaching experience
  $D_2 = 1$ if male
    $= 0$ if otherwise
  $D_3 = 1$ if white
    $= 0$ if otherwise

a. The term $(D_{2i} D_{3i})$ represents the *interaction effect*. What does this expression mean?
b. What is the meaning of B_4?
c. Find $E(Y_i \mid D_2 = 1, D_3 = 1, X_i)$ and interpret it.

6.17. Suppose in the regression (6.1) we let

$$D_i = 1 \text{ for female}$$
$$= -1 \text{ for male}$$

Using the data given in Table 6-2, estimate regression (6.1) with this dummy setup and compare your results with those given in regression (6.4). What general conclusion can you draw?

6.18. Continue with the preceding problem but now assume that

$$D_i = 2 \text{ for female}$$
$$= 1 \text{ for male}$$

With this dummy scheme re-estimate regression (6.1) using the data of Table 6-2 and compare your results. What general conclusions can you draw from the various dummy schemes?

6.19. Table 6-13, found on the textbook's Web site, gives data on after-tax corporate profits and net corporate dividend payments ($, in billions) for the United States for the quarterly period of 1997:1 to 2008:2.
a. Regress dividend payments (Y) on after-tax corporate profits (X) to find out if there is a relationship between the two.
b. To see if the dividend payments exhibit any seasonal pattern, develop a suitable dummy variable regression model and estimate it. In developing the model, how would you take into account that the intercept as well as the slope coefficient may vary from quarter to quarter?
c. When would you regress Y on X, disregarding seasonal variation?
d. Based on your results, what can you say about the seasonal pattern, if any, in the dividend payment policies of U.S. private corporations? Is this what you expected a priori?

6.20. Refer to Example 6.6. What is the regression equation for an applicant who is an unmarried white male? Is it statistically different for an unmarried white single female?

6.21. Continue with Problem 6.20. What would the regression equation be if you were to include interaction dummies for the three qualitative variables in the model?

6.22. *The impact of product differentiation on rate of return on equity.* To find out whether firms selling differentiated products (i.e., brand names) experience higher rates of return on their equity capital, J. A. Dalton and S. L. Levin[16] obtained the following regression results based on a sample of 48 firms:

$$\hat{Y}_i = 1.399 + 1.490D_i + 0.246X_{2i} - 9.507X_{3i} - 0.016X_{4i}$$

se =	(1.380)	(0.056)	(4.244)	(0.017)	$R^2 = 0.26$
t =	(1.079)	(4.285)	(−2.240)	(−0.941)	
p value =	(0.1433)	(0.000)	(0.0151)	(0.1759)	

where Y = the rate of return on equity
    $D = 1$ for firms with high or moderate product differentiation
    X_2 = the market share
    X_3 = the measure of firm size
    X_4 = the industry growth rate

a. Do firms that product-differentiate earn a higher rate of return? How do you know?
b. Is there a statistical difference in the rate of return on equity capital between firms that do and do not product-differentiate? Show the necessary calculations.
c. Would the answer to (*b*) change if the authors had used differential slope dummies?
d. Write the equation that allows for both the differential intercept and differential slope dummies.

6.23. *What has happened to the United States Phillips curve?* Refer to Example 5.6. Extending the sample to 1977, the following model was estimated:

$$Y_t = B_1 + B_2D_t + B_3\left(\frac{1}{X_t}\right) + B_4D_t\left(\frac{1}{X_t}\right) + u_t$$

where Y = the year-to-year percentage change in the index of hourly earnings
    X = the percent unemployment rate
    $D_t = 1$ for observations through 1969
    $= 0$ if otherwise (i.e., for observations from 1970 through 1977)

The regression results were as follows:

$$\hat{Y}_t = 10.078 - 10.337D_t - 17.549\left(\frac{1}{X_t}\right) + 38.137D_t\left(\frac{1}{X_t}\right)$$

se = (1.4024)	(1.6859)	(8.3373)	(9.3999)	
t = (7.1860)	(−6.1314)	(−2.1049)	(4.0572)	$R^2 = 0.8787$
p value = (0.000)	(0.000)	(0.026)	(0.000)	

Compare these results with those given in Example 5.6.

a. Are the differential intercept and differential dummy coefficients statistically significant? If so, what does that suggest? Show the Phillips curve for the two periods separately.
b. Based on these results, would you say that the Phillips curve is dead?

---

[16]See J. A. Dalton and S. L. Levin, "Market Power: Concentration and Market Share," *Industrial Organization Review*, vol. 5, 1977, pp. 27–36. Notations were altered to conform with our notation.

6.24. *Count R^2.* Since the conventional R^2 value may not be appropriate for linear probability models, one suggested alternative is the *count R^2*, which is defined as:

$$Count\ R^2 = \frac{\text{number of correct predictions}}{\text{total number of observations}}$$

Since in LPM the dependent variable takes a value of 1 or 0, if the predicted probability is greater than 0.5, we classify that as 1, but if the predicted probability is less than 0.5, we classify that as 0. We then count the number of correct predictions and compute the count R^2 from the formula given above.

Find the count R^2 for the model (6.32). How does it compare with the conventional R^2 given in that equation?

6.25. Table 6-14, found on the textbook's Web site, gives quarterly data on real personal expenditure (PCE), real expenditure on durable goods (EXPDUR), real expenditure on nondurable goods (EXPNONDUR), and real expenditure on services (EXPSER), for the United States for the period 2000-1 to 2008-3. All data are in billions of (2000) dollars, and the quarterly data are at seasonally adjusted annual rates.

a. Plot the data on EXPDUR, EXPNONDUR, and EXPSER against PCE.

b. Suppose you regress each category of expenditure on PCE and the three dummies shown in Table 6-14. Would you expect the dummy variable coefficients to be statistically significant? Why or why not? Present your calculations.

c. If you do not expect the dummy variables to be statistically significant but you still include them in your model, what are the consequences of your action?

6.26. *The Phillips curve revisited again.* Refer to Example 5.6 and Problem 5.29 from Chapter 5. It was shown that the percentage change in the index of hourly earnings and the unemployment rate from 1958–1969 followed the traditional Phillips curve model. The updated version of the data, from 1965–2007, can be found in Table 5-19 on the textbook's Web site.

a. Create a dummy variable to indicate a possible break in the data in 1982. In other words, create a dummy variable that equals 0 from 1965 to 1982, then set it equal to 1 for 1983 to 2007.

b. Using the inverted "percent unemployment rate"$(1/X)$ variable created in Chapter 5, create an interaction variable between $(1/X)$ and the dummy variable from part (*a*).

c. Include both the dummy variable and the interaction term, along with $(1/X)$ on its own, in a regression to predict Y, the change in the hourly earnings index. What is your new model?

d. Which, if any, variables appear to be statistically significant?

e. Give a potential economic reason for this result.

6.27. Table 6-15 on the textbook's Web site contains data on 46 mid-level employees and their salaries. The available independent variables are:

Experience   = years of experience at the current job
Management = 0 for nonmanagers and 1 for managers
Education   = 1 for those whose highest education level is high school
                      2 for those whose highest education level is college
                      3 for those whose highest education level is graduate school

a. Does it make sense to utilize Education as it is listed in the data? What are the issues with leaving it this way?

b. After addressing the issues in part (*a*), run a linear regression using Experience, Management, and the changed Education variables. What is the new model? Are all the variables significant?

c. Now create a model to allow for the possibility that the increase in Salary may be different between managers and nonmanagers, with respect to their years of experience. What are the results?

*__d.__ Finally, create a model that incorporates the idea that Salary might increase, with respect to years of experience, at a different rate between employees with different education levels.

6.28. Based on the Current Population Survey (CPS) of March 1995, Paul Rudd extracted a sample of 1289 workers, aged 18 to 65, and obtained the following information on each worker:

Wage = hourly wage in $

Age = age in years

Female = 1 if female worker

Nonwhite = 1 if a nonwhite worker

Union = 1 if a union member

Education = years of schooling

Experience = potential labor market experience in years.[17]

The full data set can be found as Table 6-16 on the textbook's Web site.

a. Based on these data, estimate the following model, obtaining the usual regression statistics.

$$\ln Wage_i = B_1 + B_2\, Age + B_3\, Female + B_4\, Nonwhite + B_5\, Union + B_6\, Education + B_7\, Experience + u_i$$

where $\ln Wage$ = (natural logarithm of *Wage*)

b. How do you interpret each regression coefficient?

c. Which of these coefficients are statistically significant at the 5% level? Also obtain the *p* value of each estimated *t* value.

d. Do union workers, on average, earn a higher hourly wage?

e. Do female workers, on average, earn less than their male counterparts?

f. Is the average hourly wage of female nonwhite workers lower than the average hourly wage of female white workers? How do you know? (*Hint:* interaction dummy.)

g. Is the average hourly wage of female union workers higher than the average hourly wage of female non-union workers? How do you know?

h. Using the data, develop alternative specifications of the wage function, taking into account possible interactions between dummy variables and between dummy variables and quantitative variables.

*Optional.

[17]Paul R. Rudd, *An Introduction to Classical Econometric Theory*, Oxford University Press, New York, 2000, pp. 17–18. These data are derived from the Data Extraction System (DES) of the Census Bureau: **http://www.census.gov/DES/www/welcome.html**.

PART **II**

REGRESSION ANALYSIS
IN PRACTICE

In this part of the book, consisting of Chapters 7 through 10, we consider several practical aspects of the linear regression model. The classical linear regression model (CLRM) developed in Part I, although a versatile model, is based on several simplifying assumptions that may not hold in practice. In this part we find out what happens if one or more of these assumptions are relaxed or are not fulfilled in any given situation.

Chapter 7 on model selection discusses the assumption of the CLRM that the model chosen for investigation is the correct model. In this chapter we discuss the consequences of various types of misspecification of the regression model and suggest appropriate remedies.

Chapter 8 on multicollinearity tries to determine what happens if two or more explanatory variables are correlated. Recall that one of the assumptions of the CLRM is that explanatory variables do not have a perfect linear relationship(s) among themselves. This chapter shows that as long as explanatory variables are not perfectly linearly related, the ordinary least squares (OLS) estimators are still best linear unbiased estimators (BLUE).

Chapter 9 on heteroscedasticity discusses the consequences of violating the CLRM assumption that the error variance is constant. This chapter shows that if this assumption is violated, OLS estimators, although unbiased, are no longer efficient. In short, they are not BLUE. But this chapter shows how, with some simple transformations, we can eliminate the problem of heteroscedasticity.

Chapter 10 on autocorrelation considers yet another departure from the CLRM by examining the consequences of correlation in error terms. As in the case of heteroscedasticity, in the presence of autocorrelation the OLS estimators, although unbiased, are not efficient; that is, they are not BLUE. But we show in this chapter how, with suitable transformation of the data, we can minimize the problem of autocorrelation.

CHAPTER 7

MODEL SELECTION: CRITERIA AND TESTS

In the preceding chapters we considered several single-equation linear regression models, including the score function for math S.A.T. scores, the Phillips curve, and the Cobb-Douglas production function. In presenting these models we assumed implicitly, if not explicitly, that the chosen model represents "the truth, the whole truth, and nothing but the truth"; that is, that it correctly models the phenomenon under study. More technically, we assumed that there is no specification bias or specification error in the chosen model. A specification error occurs when instead of estimating the correct model we estimate another model, albeit unintentionally. In practice, however, searching for the true model can be like searching for the Holy Grail. We may never know what the true model is, but we hope to find a model that is a reasonably accurate representation of reality.

Because of its practical importance, we take a closer look at how to go about formulating an econometric model. Specifically, we consider the following questions:

1. What are the attributes of a "good" or "correct" model?
2. Suppose an omniscient econometrician has developed the "correct" model to analyze a particular problem. However, because of data availability, cost considerations, oversight, or sheer ignorance (which is not always bliss), the researcher uses another model, and thus, in relation to the "correct" model, commits a specification error. What type of specification errors are we likely to make in practice?
3. What are the consequences of the various specification errors?
4. How do we detect a specification error?
5. What remedies can we adopt to get back to the correct model if a specification error has been made?

7.1   THE ATTRIBUTES OF A GOOD MODEL

Whether a model chosen in empirical analysis is good, or appropriate, or the "right" model cannot be determined without some reference criteria, or guidelines. A. C. Harvey,[1] a noted econometrician, lists the following criteria by which we can judge a model.

Parsimony   A model can never completely capture the reality; some amount of abstraction or simplification is inevitable in any model building. The Occam's razor, or the **principle of parsimony,** suggests that a model be kept as simple as possible.

Identifiability   This means that, for a given set of data, the estimated parameters must have unique values or, what amounts to the same thing, there is only one estimate per parameter.

Goodness of Fit   Since the basic thrust of regression analysis is to explain as much of the variation in the dependent variable as possible by explanatory variables included in the model, a model is judged to be good if this explanation, as measured, say, by the adjusted R^2 $(=\overline{R}^2)$, is as high as possible.[2]

Theoretical Consistency   No matter how high the goodness of fit measures, a model may not be judged to be good if one or more coefficients have the wrong signs. Thus, in the demand function for a commodity, if the price coefficient has a positive sign (positively sloping demand curve!), or if the income coefficient has a negative sign (unless the good happens to be an inferior good), we must look at such results with great suspicion even if the R^2 of the model is high, say, 0.92. In short, in constructing a model we should have some theoretical underpinning to it; "measurement without theory" often leads to very disappointing results.

Predictive Power   As Milton Friedman, the Nobel laureate, notes: "The only relevant test of the validity of a hypothesis [model] is comparison of its prediction with experience."[3] Thus, in choosing between the monetarist and Keynesian models of the economy, by this criterion, we would choose the model whose theoretical predictions are borne out by actual experience.

Although there is no unique path to a good model, keep these criteria in mind in developing an econometric model.

---

[1]A. C. Harvey, *The Economic Analysis of Time Series*, Wiley, New York, 1981, pp. 5-7. The following discussion leans heavily on this material. See also D. F. Hendry and J. F. Richard, "On the Formulation of Empirical Models in Dynamic Econometrics," *Journal of Econometrics*, vol. 20, October 1982, pp. 3–33.

[2]Besides R^2, there are other criteria that have been used from time to time to judge the goodness of fit of a model. For an accessible discussion of these other criteria, see G. S. Maddala, *Introduction to Econometrics*, Macmillan, New York, 1988, pp. 425–429.

[3]Milton Friedman, "The Methodology of Positive Economics," *Essays in Positive Economics*, University of Chicago Press, 1953, p. 7.

7.2   TYPES OF SPECIFICATION ERRORS

As noted previously, a model should be parsimonious in that it should include key variables (called **core variables**) suggested by theory and should relegate minor influences (called **peripheral variables**) to the error term u. In this section we consider several ways in which a model can be deficient, which we label **specification errors.**

The topic of specification errors is vast. In this chapter we will discuss as succinctly as possible some of the major specification errors that a researcher may encounter in practice. In particular, we will discuss the following specification errors:

1. Omission of a relevant variable(s).
2. Inclusion of an unnecessary variable(s).
3. Adopting the wrong functional form.
4. Errors of measurement.

To keep the discussion simple, and to avoid matrix algebra, we will consider two- or three-variable models to drive home the essential nature of model specification errors. We will discuss each of the preceding topics separately.

Before we do that, note that the classical linear regression model (CLRM) that we have considered so far makes several simplifying assumptions. A violation of one or more of its assumptions may itself constitute a specification error. For example, the assumption that the error term u_i is uncorrelated (the assumption of no autocorrelation) or the assumption that the error variance is constant (the assumption of homoscedasticity) may not hold in practice. Because of their practical importance, we discuss these two topics in Chapters 9 and 10.

7.3   OMISSON OF RELEVANT VARIABLE BIAS: "UNDERFITTING" A MODEL

As noted in the introduction to this chapter, for a variety of reasons, a researcher may omit one or more explanatory variables that should have been included in the model. What are the consequences of such an omission for our ordinary least squares (OLS) estimating procedure?

To be specific, consider the data given in Problem 4.14 and consider the following model:

$$Y_i = B_1 + B_2X_{2i} + B_3X_{3i} + u_i \qquad (7.1)$$

where Y = child mortality rate, X_2 = per capita GNP, and X_3 = female literacy rate. All these variables are defined in Problem 4.14.

But instead of estimating the regression in Equation (7.1), we estimate the following function:

$$Y_t = A_1 + A_2X_{2t} + v_t \qquad (7.2)$$

which is the same as Equation (7.1), except that it excludes the "relevant" variable X_3. Note that v like u is a stochastic error term. Also, notice that we are using the B's to represent the parameters in the "true" regression and the A's to represent the parameters in the "incorrectly specified" regression: Equation (7.2) in relation to Eq. (7.1) is misspecified. What are the consequences of this misspecification, which can be called the **omitted variable bias?**

We first state the consequences of dropping the variable X_3 from the model in general terms and then illustrate them with the child mortality data.

The consequences of omitting X_3 are as follows:

1. If the omitted, or left-out, variable X_3 is correlated with the included variable X_2, a_1 and a_2 are *biased*; that is, their average, or expected, values do not coincide with the true values.[4] Symbolically,

$$E(a_1) \neq B_1 \quad \text{and} \quad E(a_2) \neq B_2$$

where E is the expectations operator. As a matter of fact, it can be shown that[5]

$$E(a_2) = B_2 + B_3 b_{32} \tag{7.3}$$
$$E(a_1) = B_1 + B_3(\overline{X}_3 - b_{32}\overline{X}_2) \tag{7.4}$$

where b_{32} is the slope coefficient in the regression of the omitted variable X_3 on the included variable X_2. Obviously, unless the last term in Equation (7.3) is zero, a_2 will be a biased estimator, the extent of the bias given by the last term. If both B_3 and b_{32} are positive, a_2 will have an *upward bias*—on the average it will overestimate the true B_2. But this result should not be surprising, for X_2 represents not only its *direct effect* on Y but also its *indirect effect* (via X_3) on Y. In short, X_2 gets credit for the influence that is rightly attributed to X_3, as shown in Figure 7-1.

On the other hand, if B_3 is positive and b_{32} is negative, or vice versa, a_2 will be *biased downward*—on the average it will underestimate the true B_2. Similarly, a_1 will be upward biased if the last term in model (7.4) is positive and downward biased if it is negative.

2. In addition a_1 and a_2 are also *inconsistent*; that is, no matter how large the sample size is, the bias does not disappear.

3. If X_2 and X_3 are uncorrelated, b_{32} will be zero. Then, as Eq. (7.3) shows, a_2 is unbiased. It is consistent as well. (As noted in Appendix D, if an estimator is unbiased [which is a small sample property], it is also *consistent* [which is a large sample property]. But the converse is not true; estimators can be consistent but may not be necessarily unbiased.) But a_1 still remains

---

[4]A technical point: Shouldn't X_2 and X_3 be uncorrelated by the "no multicollinearity" assumption? Recall from Chapter 4 that the assumption that there is no perfect collinearity among the X variables refers to the population regression (PRF) only; there is no guarantee that in a given sample the X's may not be correlated.

[5]The proof can be found in Gujarati and Porter, *Basic Econometrics*, 5th ed., McGraw-Hill, New York, 2009, pp. 519–520.

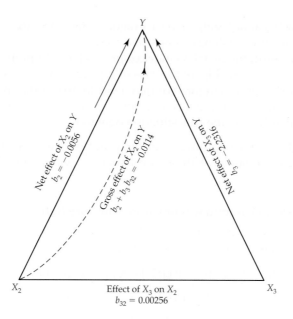

FIGURE 7-1 Net and gross effects of X_2 on Y

Note: Net means controlling the influence of other variables.
Gross means not controlling the influence of other variables.

biased, unless $\overline{X}_3$ is zero in Eq. (7.4). Even in this case the consequences mentioned in points (4) to (6) below hold true.

4. The error variance estimated from Eq. (7.2) is a biased estimator of the true error variance σ^2. In other words, the error variance estimated from the true model (7.1) and that estimated from the misspecified model (7.2) will not be the same; the former is an unbiased estimator of the true σ^2, but the latter is not.

5. In addition, the conventionally estimated variance of $a_2 (= \hat{\sigma}^2 / \Sigma x_2^2)$ is a biased estimator of the variance of the true estimator b_2. Even in the case where b_{32} is zero, that is, X_2 and X_3 are uncorrelated, this variance remains biased, for it can be shown that[6]

$$E[\text{var}\,(a_2)] = \text{var}\,(b_2) + \frac{B_3^2 \Sigma x_{3i}^2}{(n-2)\Sigma x_{2i}^2} \tag{7.5}$$

That is, the expected value of the variance of a_2 is not equal to the variance of b_2. Since the second term in Equation (7.5) will always be positive

---

[6]For proof, see Jan Kmenta, *Elements of Econometrics*, 2nd ed., Macmillan, New York, 1986, pp. 444–445. *Note:* This is true only when $b_{32} = 0$, which is not the case in our example, as can be seen from Equation (7.8), which follows.

(Why?), var (a_2) will, on the average, overestimate the true variance of b_2. This means it will have a positive bias.

6. As a result, the usual confidence interval and hypothesis-testing procedures are unreliable. In the case of Eq. (7.5), the confidence interval will be wider, and therefore we may tend to accept the hypothesis that the true value of the coefficient is zero (or any other null hypothesis) more frequently than the true situation demands.

Although we have not presented the proofs of the preceding propositions, we will illustrate some of these consequences with the child mortality rate example.

Example 7.1. Determinants of Child Mortality Rate

Using the data given in Table 4-7 (found on the textbook's Web site), the empirical counterpart of Eq. (7.1) is as follows:

$$\widehat{CM_i} = 263.6416 - 0.0056PGNP_i - 2.2316FLR_i$$

$$\text{se} = (11.5932) \quad (0.0019) \qquad\qquad (0.2099) \quad R^2 = 0.7077$$

$$(7.6)$$

The results of the misspecified equation (7.2) are as follows:

$$\widehat{CM_i} = 157.4244 - 0.0114PGNP_i$$

$$\text{se} = (9.8455) \quad (0.0032) \qquad\qquad r^2 = 0.1662$$

$$(7.7)$$

Note the following differences between the two regressions:

1. The misspecified Equation (7.7) shows that as per capita GNP (PGNP) increases by a dollar, on the average, the child mortality rate goes down by about 0.01. On the other hand, in the true model, if PGNP goes up by a dollar, the average child mortality rate (CM) goes down by only about 0.006. In the present instance, in absolute terms (i.e., disregarding the sign), the misspecified equation overestimates the true impact of PGNP on CM, that is, it is upward biased. The nature of this bias can be seen easily if we regress the female literacy rate (FLR) (the omitted variable) on PGNP, the included variable in the model. The results are as follows:

$$\widehat{FLR_i} = 47.5971 + 0.00256PGNP$$

$$\text{se} = (3.5553) \quad (0.0011) \qquad\qquad r^2 = 0.0721$$

$$(7.8)$$

Thus the slope coefficient $b_{32} = 0.00256$. Now from Equation (7.6) we can see that the estimated $B_2 = -0.0056$ and the estimated $B_3 - -2.2316$. Therefore, from Eq. (7.3) we obtain

$$\hat{B}_2 + \hat{B}_3 b_{32} = -0.0056 + (-2.2316)(0.00256) \approx -0.0114$$

which is just about what we obtain from the misspecified Eq. (7.7). Note that it is the product of B_3 (the true value of the omitted variable) and b_{32} (the slope coefficient in the regression of the omitted variable on the included variable) that determines the nature of the bias, upward or downward. Thus, by incorrectly dropping the FLR variable from the model, as in Eq. (7.2), or its empirical counterpart Eq. (7.7), we are not only neglecting the impact of FLR on CM (B_3) but also the impact of FLR on PGNP (b_{32}). The "lonely" variable PGNP included in the misspecified Eq. (7.7) model thus has to carry the "burden" of this omission, which, so to speak, prevents it from showing its true impact on CM (−0.0056 versus −0.0114). All this can be seen vividly in Figure 7-1.

2. The intercept term is also biased, but here it underestimates the true intercept term (157.42 versus 263.64).

3. The standard errors as well as the r^2's are also substantially different between the two regressions.

All these results are in accord with the theoretical results of misspecification discussed earlier. You can see at once that if we were to engage in hypothesis testing based upon the misspecified Eq. (7.7), our conclusions would be of dubious values, to say the least. Therefore, in developing a model, exercise utmost care. There is little doubt that dropping relevant variables from a model can have very serious consequences. This is why it is very important that in developing a model for empirical analysis, we should pay close attention to the appropriate theory underlying the phenomenon under study so that all theoretically relevant variables are included in the model. If such relevant variables are excluded from the model, then we are "underfitting" or "underspecifying" the model; in other words, we are omitting some important variables.

7.4 INCLUSION OF IRRELEVANT VARIABLES: "OVERFITTING" A MODEL

Sometimes researchers adopt the "kitchen sink" approach by including all sorts of variables in the model, whether or not they are theoretically dictated. The idea behind **overfitting** or overspecifying **the model** (i.e., including unnecessary variables) is the philosophy that so long as you include the theoretically relevant variables, inclusion of one or more unnecessary or "nuisance" variables will not hurt—unnecessary in the sense that there is no solid theory that says they should be included. Such irrelevant variables are often included inadvertently because the researcher is not sure about their role in the model. And this will happen if the theory underlying a particular phenomenon is not well developed. In that case inclusion of such variables will certainly increase R^2 (and adjusted R^2 if the absolute t value of the coefficient of the additional variable is greater than 1), which might increase the predictive power of the model.

What are the consequences of including unnecessary variables in the model, which may be called the (inclusion of) **irrelevant variable bias?** Again, to emphasize the point, we consider the case of simple two- and three-variable models. Now suppose that

$$Y_i = B_1 + B_2 X_{2i} + u_i \qquad (7.9)$$

is the correctly specified model, but a researcher adds the superfluous variable X_3 and estimates the following model:

$$Y_i = A_1 + A_2X_{2i} + A_3X_{3i} + v_i \qquad (7.10)$$

Here the specification error consists in overfitting the model, that is, including the unnecessary variable X_3, unnecessary in the sense that a priori it has no effect on Y. The consequences of estimating the regression (7.10) instead of the true model (7.9) are as follows:

1. The OLS estimators of the "incorrect" model (7.10) are *unbiased* (as well as consistent). That is, $E(a_1) = B_1$, $E(a_2) = B_2$, and $E(a_3) = 0$. This is not difficult to see. If X_3 does not belong in the model, B_3 is expected to be zero. Hence, in Eqs. (7.3) and (7.4) the B_3 term will drop out.
2. The estimator of σ^2 obtained from regression (7.10) is correctly estimated.
3. The standard confidence interval and hypothesis-testing procedure on the basis of the t and F tests remains valid.
4. However, the a's estimated from the regression (7.10) are *inefficient*— their variances will be generally larger than those of the b's estimated from the true model (7.9). As a result, the confidence intervals based on the standard errors of a's will be larger than those based on the standard errors of b's of the true model, even though the former are acceptable for the usual hypothesis-testing procedure. What will happen is that the true coefficients will not be estimated as precisely as if we had used the correct model (7.9). In short, the OLS estimators are LUE (linear unbiased estimators) but *not* BLUE.

Notice the difference between the two types of specification errors we have considered thus far. If we exclude a relevant variable (the case of underfitting), the coefficients of variables retained in the model are generally biased as well as inconsistent, the error variance is incorrectly estimated, the standard errors of estimators are biased, and therefore the usual hypothesis-testing procedure becomes invalid. On the other hand, including an irrelevant variable in the model (the case of overfitting), still gives us unbiased and consistent estimates of the coefficients of the true model, the error variance is correctly estimated, and the standard hypothesis-testing procedure is still valid. The major penalty we pay for the inclusion of the superfluous variable(s) is that the estimated variances of the coefficients are larger, and as a result, our probability inferences about the true parameters are less precise because the confidence intervals tend to be wider. In some cases we will accept the hypothesis that a true coefficient value is zero because of the wider confidence interval; that is, we will fail to recognize significant relationships between the dependent variable and the explanatory variable(s).

An unwarranted conclusion from the preceding discussion is that it is better to include irrelevant variables than to exclude the relevant ones. But this philosophy should not be encouraged because, as just noted, the addition of unnecessary variables will lead to a loss in the efficiency of the estimators (i.e., larger standard errors) and may also lead to the problem of multicollinearity (Why?), not to mention the loss of degrees of freedom.

In general, the best approach is to include only explanatory variables that on theoretical grounds *directly* influence the dependent variable and are not accounted for by other included variables.

Example 7.2.

In Chapter 6 we considered an example relating expenditure on food (Y) to income after tax (X) and the gender dummy D (1 if female and 0 if male). The regression results are given in Equation (6.9). Later we redid this model including differential intercept and differential slope dummies. The results are given in Table 6-6. As we saw, in the latter regression neither the differential intercept nor the differential slope coefficient was significant, whereas in Eq. (6.9) the differential intercept coefficient was significant. It is quite possible that the differential slope dummy variable was superfluous. That is to say, although the average level of food expenditure of the two sexes is different, it is quite possible that the rate of change of food expenditure in relation to after-tax income is the same for both sexes.

7.5 INCORRECT FUNCTIONAL FORM

We now consider a different type of specification error, that involving **incorrect** (wrong) **functional form bias.** Assume that variables Y, X_2, and X_3 included in the model are theoretically the correct variables. Now consider the following two specifications of the model:

$$Y_t = B_1 + B_2 X_{2t} + B_3 X_{3t} + u_t \tag{7.11}$$

$$\ln Y_t = A_1 + A_2 \ln X_{2t} + A_3 \ln X_{3t} + v_t \tag{7.12}$$

The variables that enter the model in Equation (7.11) also enter the regression (7.12), except the functional relationship between the variables is different; in the regression (7.12) the (natural) logarithm of Y is a linear function of the (natural) logarithms of X_2 and X_3; that is, it is a log-linear model. Note that in Eq. (7.12) A_2 measures the partial elasticity Y with respect to the X_2, whereas in Eq. (7.11) B_2 simply measures the rate of change (i.e., slope) of Y with respect to X_2. Similarly, in Eq. (7.12) A_3 measures the partial elasticity of Y with respect to X_3, whereas in Eq. (7.11) B_3 measures the rate of change of Y with respect to X_3. This is all familiar territory from Chapter 5. Note that not all the explanatory variables in Eq. (7.12) need to be in logarithmic form; some may be in logarithmic form and some may be in linear form, as in Equation (7.13) below.

Now the dilemma in choosing between the models (7.11) and (7.12) is that economic theory is usually not strong enough to tell us the functional form in which the dependent and explanatory variables are related. Therefore, if the regression (7.12) is in fact the true model and we fit Eq. (7.11) to the data, we are likely to commit as much of a specification error as if the situation were converse, although in both cases the economically relevant variables are included. Without going into theoretical fine points, if we choose the wrong functional form, the estimated coefficients may be biased estimates of the true coefficients.

Example 7.3. U.S. Expenditure on Imported Goods

To provide some insight into this problem, consider the data given in Table 3-7, found on the textbook Web site. These data relate to U.S. expenditure on imported goods (Y) and personal disposable income (X), both measured in billions of dollars, for the period 1959 to 2006.

Using these data, we obtained the following results:

$$\hat{Y}_t = 36295.3168 + 0.2975X_t - 18.5253\,Year$$
$$t = (6.3790)^* \qquad (20.5203)^* \quad (-6.4030)^* \tag{7.13}$$
$$R^2 = 0.9839;\ \overline{R}^2 = 0.9832;\ F = 1376.7802$$

where * signifies a p value less than 1%.
In this model year represents the trend variable.

$$\widehat{\ln Y}_t = 10.9327 + 1.4857\ln X_t - 0.0085\,Year$$
$$t = (0.7014) \quad (13.6501)^* \quad (-1.0215) \tag{7.14}$$
$$R^2 = 0.9959;\ \overline{R}^2 = 0.9957;\ F = 5421.7932$$

where * signifies a p value less than 1%.

Before deciding between the two models, let us look at the results briefly. In Equation (7.13) all the regression coefficients are individually as well as collectively significant (see the F value). The slope coefficient of 0.2975 means holding other variables constant, average expenditure on imported goods goes up by about 30 cents for every dollar increase in personal disposable income (PDI). Similarly, holding other variables constant (PDI here), the slope coefficient of -18.53 suggests that, on average over the sample period, expenditure on imported goods was decreasing by about 18.5 billions of dollars per year. In other words, there was a downward trend. The R^2 value is very high.

Turning to Equation (7.14), we see that the elasticity of import expenditure with respect to PDI was about 1.49, ceteris paribus. The coefficient of -0.0085 suggests that, holding other variables constant, on average, expenditure on imports was declining at the rate of about 0.85 percent (recall from Chapter 5 our discussion regarding logarithmic and semi-logarithmic models). The R^2 value of this model is also quite high.

How do we choose between Eqs. (7.13) and (7.14)? Although the R^2 values of the two models cannot be directly compared (Why?), they are both high. Also, both models are collectively significant (on the basis of the F test). For the linear model we can compute the elasticity of expenditure on imports with respect to PDI by using the mean values of these two variables.

Calculations will show that this value is 1.7807.[7] From the log model, we get this elasticity as 1.4857. Of course, the former elasticity is a kind of average, whereas the latter elasticity remains the same regardless of the value of X at which it is measured. So we cannot compare the two directly.

So where do we stand? Can we devise a test to choose between the two models? We will consider one such test in Section 7.7, and we will revisit this question then.

7.6   ERRORS OF MEASUREMENT

All along we have assumed implicitly that the dependent variable Y and the explanatory variables, the X's, are measured without any errors. Thus, in the regression of consumption expenditure on income and wealth of households, we assume that the data on these variables are accurate; they are not guess estimates, extrapolated, interpolated, or rounded off in any systematic manner, such as to the nearest hundredth dollar. Unfortunately, this ideal is not met in practice for a variety of reasons, such as nonresponse errors, reporting errors, and computing errors.

The consequences of errors of measurement depend upon whether such errors are in the dependent variable or the explanatory variables.

Errors of Measurement in the Dependent Variable

If there are errors of measurement in the dependent variable only, the following consequences ensue, which we state without proof:[8]

1. The OLS estimators are unbiased.
2. The variances of OLS estimators are also unbiased.
3. But the estimated variances of the estimators are larger than in the case where there are no errors of measurement. The reason that the estimated variances of the estimators are larger than necessary is because the error in the dependent variable gets added to the common error term, u_i.

So it seems that the consequences of measurement errors in the dependent variable may not matter much in practice.

Errors of Measurement in the Explanatory Variable(s)

In this case the consequence are as follows:

1. The OLS estimators are biased.
2. They are also inconsistent; that is, they remain biased even if the sample size increases indefinitely.

---

[7]Elasticity $= \frac{\partial Y}{\partial X} \cdot \frac{\overline{X}}{\overline{Y}} = 0.2975 \frac{3306.688}{552.447} = 1.7807.$

[8]For details, see Gujarati and Porter, *Basic Econometrics,* 5th ed., McGraw-Hill, New York, 2009, pp. 482–486.

Obviously, an error of measurement in the explanatory variable(s) is a serious problem. Of course, if there are measurement errors in both the dependent and explanatory variables, the consequences can be quite serious.

It is one thing to document the consequences of errors of measurement, but it is quite another thing to find the appropriate remedy because it may not be easy to detect such errors. For example, data on variables such as wealth are notoriously difficult to obtain. Similarly, data on income derived from activities such as the sale of illegal drugs or gambling are extremely difficult to obtain. In situations such as these not much can be done.

If there are errors of measurement in the explanatory variables, one suggested remedy is the use of **instrumental** or **proxy variables.** These variables, while highly correlated with original X variables, are uncorrelated with measurement errors and the usual regression term, u_i. In some situations such proxy variables can be found, but it is generally not that easy to find them.

The best practical advice is to make sure that the data on the X variables that you include in your model are measured as accurately as possible; avoid errors of recording, rounding, or omission. If there are changes in the definition of the variables over time, make sure that you use comparable data.

7.7   DETECTING SPECIFICATION ERRORS: TESTS OF SPECIFICATION ERRORS

To know the consequences of specification errors is one thing, but to find out that we have committed such errors is quite another thing, for we (hopefully) do not deliberately set out to commit such errors. Often specification errors arise inadvertently, perhaps because we have not formulated the model as precisely as possible because the underlying theory is weak, or we do not have the right kind of data to test the theoretically correct model, or the theory is silent about the functional form in which the dependent variable is related to explanatory variables. The practical issue is not that such errors are made, for they sometimes are, but how to detect them. Once it is found that specification errors have been made, the remedies often suggest themselves. If, for example, it can be shown that a variable is inappropriately omitted from a model, the obvious remedy is to include that variable in the analysis, assuming of course that data on that variable are available. We now consider several tests of specification errors.

Detecting the Presence of Unnecessary Variables

Suppose we have the following four-variable model:

$$Y_i = B_1 + B_2X_{2i} + B_3X_{3i} + B_4X_{4i} + u_i \tag{7.15}$$

Now if theory says that all three X variables determine Y, we should keep them in the model even though after empirical testing we find that the coefficient of one or more of the X variables is not statistically significant. Therefore, the question of irrelevant variables does not arise in this case. However, sometimes we

TABLE 7-1 MODELS OF LIFE EXPECTANCY

Explanatory variable	Model 1	Model 2	Model 3
Intercept	39.4380 (20.2392)	40.5082 (20.8204)	43.1662 (10.0172)
Income	0.0054 (4.4417)	0.0016 (3.4848)	0.0014 (2.6836)
Access	0.2833 (9.9599)	0.2499 (8.0803)	0.1491 (1.0010)
Income squared	—	−6.28E-08 (−2.4060)	−5.54E-08 (−1.9612)
Access squared	—	—	0.0008 (0.6918)
R^2	0.7741	0.7892	0.7904
F value	140.5332	101.0906	75.4496

Notes: Income = per capita income in U.S. dollars.
Access = an index of access to health care.
The figures in parentheses are the estimated t values.
−6.28E-08 is a short form for −0.0000000628.
The difference among these models is that Model 3 includes all the variables, whereas the other two drop one or more variables.

have *control variables* in the model that are only there to prevent omitted variable bias. It may then be the case that if the control variables are not statistically significant and dropping them does not substantially alter our point estimates or hypothesis test results, then dropping them may clarify the model. We can then drop them but mention that they were tried and made no difference.[9]

Suppose in the model (7.15) X_4 is the control variable in the sense that we are not absolutely sure whether it really belongs in the model. One simple way to find this out is to estimate the regression (7.15) and test the significance of b_4, the estimator of B_4. Under the null hypothesis that $B_4 = 0$, we know that $t = b_4 / \text{se}(b_4)$ follows the t distribution with $(n - 4)$ d.f. (Why?) Therefore, if the computed t value does not exceed the critical t value at the chosen level of significance, we do not reject the null hypothesis, in which case the variable X_4 is probably a superfluous variable.[10] Of course, if we reject the null hypothesis, the variable probably belongs in the model.

But suppose we are not sure that both X_3 and X_4 are relevant variables. In this case we would like to test the null hypothesis that $B_3 = B_4 = 0$. This can be done easily by the F test discussed in Chapter 4. (For details, see Section 4.12 on restricted least squares.)

Example 7.4. Life Expectancy in 85 Countries

To assess the impact of income and access to health care on life expectancy, we collected data on a sample of 85 countries and obtained the results shown in Table 7-1. The dependent variable in each case is life expectancy measured in years. (The raw data are given in Chapter 9, Table 9-6.)

[9]In this case the researcher should inform the reader that the results, including the dropped variables, could be made available on request.
[10]We say "probably" because if there is collinearity among X variables, then, as we show in Chapter 8, standard errors of the estimated parameters tend to be inflated relative to the values of the coefficients, thereby reducing the estimated t values.

A priori we would expect a positive relationship between income and life expectancy and between access and life expectancy. This expectation is borne out by Model 1. The addition of the income-squared variable in Model 2 is to find out if life expectancy increases at an increasing rate (in which case the squared income coefficient will be positive) or increases at a decreasing rate (in which case the squared income coefficient will be negative) with respect to income.[11] The results show that it is the latter case. Model 3 adds the variable access-squared to find out if life expectancy is increasing at an increasing rate or at a decreasing rate with respect to access. The results indicate that it is increasing at an increasing rate. However, this coefficient is not statistically significant. Not only that, when we add this variable, the access coefficient itself becomes statistically insignificant. Does this mean that access and access-squared variables are superfluous?

To see if this is the case, we can use the F test given in Equation (4.56), which gives the following result:

$$F = \frac{(R_{ur}^2 - R_r^2)/m}{(1 - R_{ur}^2)/(n - k)} \sim F_{2,80}$$

$$= \frac{(0.7904 - 0.7741)/2}{(1 - 0.7904)/(85 - 5)} = 3.1106$$

Note that in the present case $m = 2$, $R_{ur}^2 = 0.7904$, $R_r^2 = 0.7741$, and $k = 5$. For 2 d.f. in the numerator and 80 d.f. in the denominator, the probability of obtaining an F value of about 3.11 or greater is about 5 percent. It seems that access and access-squared are *not* superfluous variables. Is access-squared possibly a superfluous variable? Dropping this variable, we obtain Model 2, which shows that access has a statistically significant impact on life expectancy, which is not an unexpected result.

As this example shows, detecting the presence of an irrelevant variable(s) is not a difficult task. *But it is very important to remember that in carrying out these tests of specifications, we have a specific model in mind, which we accept as the "true" model.* Given that model, then, we can find out whether one or more X variables are really relevant by the usual t and F tests. However, bear in mind that we should not use t and F tests to build a model *iteratively;* that is, we cannot say that initially Y is related to X_2 because b_2 is statistically significant and then expand the model to include X_3 and decide to keep that variable in the model if b_3 turns out to be statistically significant. Such a procedure is known as **stepwise regression.**

---

[11]If you have a general quadratic equation like $Y = a + bX + cX^2$, then whether Y increases at an increasing or decreasing rate when X changes will generally depend on the signs of a, b, c and the value of X. On this, see Alpha C. Chang, *Fundamental Methods of Mathematical Economics*, 3rd ed., McGraw-Hill, New York, 1984, Chapter 9.

This strategy, called **data mining,** is generally not recommended, for if a priori X_3 belonged in the model to begin with, it should have been introduced. Excluding X_3 in the initial regression would then lead to the omission-of-relevant-variable bias with the potentially serious consequences that we have already discussed. This point cannot be overemphasized: *Theory must be the guide to model building; measurement without theory can lead up a blind alley.*

In our life expectancy example income and access to health care are obviously important variables in determining life expectancy, although we are not entirely sure of the form in which these variables enter the model. So to some extent some kind of experimentation (data mining, if you will) will be necessary to determine the appropriate functional form of the relationship between the dependent and explanatory variables. This is especially so if there are several explanatory variables in a model and we cannot graph them together to get a visual impression about the likely form of the relationship between them and the dependent variable.

Tests for Omitted Variables and Incorrect Functional Forms

The prescription that theory should be the underpinning of any model begs the question: What is theoretically the correct model? Thus, in our Phillips curve example discussed in an earlier chapter, although the rate of change of wages (Y) and the unemployment rate (X) are expected to be negatively related, they could be related in any of the following forms:

$$Y_t = B_1 + B_2 X_t + u_t \qquad B_2 < 0 \tag{7.16}$$

$$\ln Y_t = B_1 + B_2 \ln X_t + u_t \qquad B_2 < 0 \tag{7.17}$$

$$Y_t = B_1 + B_2 \frac{1}{X_t} + u_t \qquad B_2 > 0 \tag{7.18}$$

Or are they related in some other functional relationship?

As noted in the introduction to this chapter, this is one of those questions that cannot be answered definitely. Pragmatically, we proceed as follows. Based upon theory or introspection and prior empirical work, we develop a model that we believe captures the essence of the subject under study. We then subject the model to empirical testing. After we obtain the results, we begin the postmortem, keeping in mind the criteria of a good model discussed earlier. It is at this stage that we learn if the chosen model is adequate. In determining model adequacy, we look at some broad features of the results, such as:

1. R^2 and adjusted R^2 $(\overline{R}^2)$.
2. The estimated t ratios.
3. Signs of the estimated coefficients in relation to their prior expectations.

If these diagnostics are reasonably good, we accept the chosen model as a fair representation of reality.

By the same token, if the results do not look encouraging because the R^2 is too low, or because very few coefficients are statistically significant or have the correct signs, then we begin to worry about model adequacy and to look for remedies. Perhaps we have omitted an important variable or have used the wrong functional form. To help determine whether model adequacy is due to one or more of these problems, we can use some of the methods we are currently discussing.

Examination of Residuals   It is always a good practice to plot the residuals e_i (or e_t, in time series) of the fitted model, for such a plot may reveal specification errors, such as omission of an important variable or incorrect functional form. As we will see in Chapters 9 and 10, a residual plot is an invaluable tool to diagnose heteroscedasticity and autocorrelation.

To see this, return to model (7.13) where we regressed expenditure on imports on PDI and year. Suppose we erroneously drop the year or trend variable and estimate the following regression:

$$\hat{Y}_t = B_1 + B_2 X_t + v_t \tag{7.19}$$

The results are as follows:

$$\hat{Y}_t = -136.1649 + 0.2082 X_t$$
$$t = (-5.7782) \qquad (38.0911); \qquad r^2 = 0.9693 \tag{7.20}$$

Now if Eq. (7.13) is in fact the true model in that the trend variable X_3 belongs in the model, but we use model (7.19), then we are implicitly saying that the error term in the model (7.19) is

$$v_t = B_3 X_{3t} + u_t \tag{7.21}$$

because it will reflect not only the truly random term u, but also the variable X_3. No wonder in this case residuals estimated from Eq. (7.19) will show some systematic pattern, which may be due to the excluded variable X_3. This can be seen very vividly from Figure 7-2, which plots the residuals (S_1) from the inappropriately estimated regression (7.19). Also shown in this figure are the residuals (S_2) from the "correct" model (7.13).

The difference between the two residual series plotted in this figure is obvious. The residuals series S_2 may suggest that even if we include the trend variable in our import expenditure function the residuals may not be entirely randomly distributed. If that is the case, model (7.13) itself may not be correctly specified. Perhaps an index of import prices in relation to domestic prices has been left out or perhaps a quadratic term in the trend variable is missing.

In any case, an examination of residuals from the estimated model is often an extremely useful adjunct to model building.

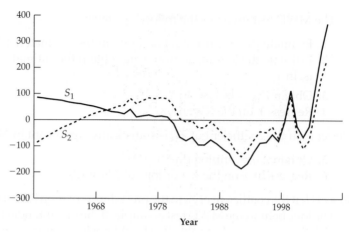

**Residuals from Regression of Y vs. X and
of Y vs. X and Year**

FIGURE 7-2   Residuals from regressions (7.13) and (7.20)

Notes: S_1 are residuals from model (7.20) and S_2 are residuals from model (7.13).

Besides examining the residuals, we can use several formal tests of model specification, such as: (1) the **MacKinnon-White-Davidson (MWD) test,** (2) **Ramsey's RESET (regression error specification) test,** (3) the Wald test, (4) the Lagrange Multiplier test, (5) the Hausman test, and (6) Box-Cox transformations (to determine the functional form of the regression model). A full discussion of these tests is beyond the scope of this book.[12] But we will discuss two of these tests, the MWD and RESET tests, in the sections that follow.

Choosing between Linear and Log-linear Regression Models: The MWD Test

Let us revisit the linear and log-linear specifications of the import expenditure function given in Equations (7.13) and (7.14), respectively. As we saw earlier, on the surface both models look reasonable, although the year variable is not statistically significant in Eq. (7.14). To see if one specification is better than the other, we can use the MWD test.[13]

We illustrate this test with our import expenditure example as follows:

H_0: *Linear Model*: Y is a linear function of the X's
H_1: *Log-linear Model*: ln Y is a linear function of the X's or a log of the X's

where, as usual, H_0 and H_1 denote the null and alternative hypotheses.

---

[12]For a somewhat elementary discussion of these tests, see Gujarati and Porter, *Basic Econometrics,* 5th ed., McGraw-Hill, New York, 2009, Chapter 13.

[13]J. MacKinnon, H. White, and R. Davidson,"Tests for Model Specification in the Presence of Alternative Hypotheses; Some Further Results," *Journal of Econometrics,* vol. 21, 1983.

The MWD test involves the following steps:

1. Estimate the linear model and obtain the estimated Y values, that is, $\hat{Y}_i$
2. Estimate the log-linear model and obtain the estimated $\ln Y_i$ values, that is, $\widehat{\ln Y_i}$
3. Obtain $Z_{1i} = \ln \hat{Y}_i - \widehat{\ln Y_i}$
4. Regress Y on the X's and Z_{1i}

Reject H_0 if the coefficient of Z_{1i} is statistically significant by the usual t test.

5. Obtain $Z_{2i} = \text{antilog}(\widehat{\ln Y_i}) - \hat{Y}_i$
6. Regress $\ln Y$ on the X's or logs of X's and Z_{2i}

Reject H_1 if the coefficient of Z_2 in the preceding equation is statistically significant.

The idea behind the MWD test is simple. If the linear model is in fact the correct model, the constructed variable Z_{1i} should not be significant, because in that case the estimated Y values from the linear model and those estimated from the log-linear model (after taking their antilog values for comparative purposes) should not be different. The same comment applies to the alternative hypothesis H_1.

Reverting to our import expenditure example, assume that the true import expenditure function is linear. Under this hypothesis, following the steps just outlined, we obtain the results shown in Table 7-2.

TABLE 7-2   ILLUSTRATION OF THE MWD TEST: LINEAR SPECIFICATION

Variable	Coefficient	Standard error	t statistic	p value
Intercept	49707.4561	5867.9548	8.4710	0.0000
X	0.3314	0.0149	22.2137	0.0000
Year	−25.3498	2.9844	−8.4940	0.0000
Z_1	−81.7933	19.8201	−4.1268	0.0002
R-squared	0.9884	F-statistic	1250.4978	

Notes: Dependent variable is Y.

These results would lead to the rejection of the null hypothesis H_0.

Let us see if H_1 is acceptable. Following the procedure just outlined, we obtain the regression results shown in Table 7-3.

TABLE 7-3   ILLUSTRATION OF THE MWD TEST: LOG-LINEAR SPECIFICATION

Variable	Coefficient	Standard error	t statistic	p value
Intercept	3.9653	14.0229	0.2828	0.7787
$\ln X$	1.4434	0.0977	14.7748	0.0000
Year	−0.0048	0.0074	−0.6417	0.5244
Z_2	0.0013	0.0004	3.5630	0.0009
R-squared	0.9968	F-statistic	4558.1058	

Notes: Dependent variable is $\ln(Y)$.

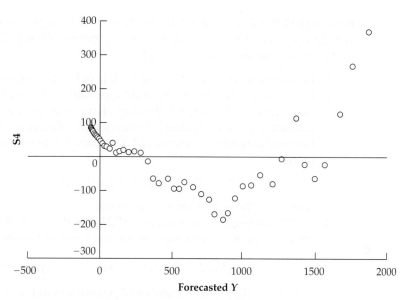

FIGURE 7-3   Residuals from regression of Y on X versus estimated Y

Notes: S4 = Residuals; Forecasted Y = $\hat{Y}$.

Since the coefficient of Z_2 is statistically significant, we reject H_1.

Looking at these results, it seems that either model is reasonable, although the trend variable, year, is not statistically significant in the log-linear model.

Regression Error Specification Test: RESET

To detect the omission of variables and/or the choice of inappropriate functional form, Ramsey has developed a general test of model misspecification.[14] To fix ideas, let us return to the import expenditure function, but now we regress expenditure on imports (Y) on personal disposable income only (X). This gives the following results:

$$\hat{Y}_t = -136.1649 + 0.2082X_t$$

$$t = (-5.7782) \qquad (38.0911); \qquad r^2 = 0.9693$$

(7.20) = (7.22)

If you plot the residuals from this model against $\hat{Y}_t$, we obtain Figure 7-3.

Although Σe_i and $\Sigma e_i \hat{Y}_i$ are necessarily zero because of the properties of OLS estimators discussed in Chapter 2, the residuals in this figure show a pattern (probably curvilinear) that might suggest that they vary in some fashion with the estimated Y values. This perhaps suggests that if we were to introduce $\hat{Y}_i$ in some form as an additional explanatory variable(s) in regression (7.22), it would increase R^2. And if the increase in R^2 were statistically significant (on the

---

[14]J. B. Ramsey, "Tests of Specification Errors in Classical Linear Least Squares Regression Analysis," *Journal of the Royal Statistical Society,* Series B, vol. 31, 1969, pp. 350–371.

basis of the F test discussed in Chapter 4), it would suggest that the initial model was misspecified. This is essentially the idea behind RESET. The steps involved in the application of RESET are as follows:

1. From the chosen model (e.g., Eq. [7.22]), obtain the estimated Y_i, namely, $\hat{Y}_i$.
2. Rerun the chosen model by adding powers of $\hat{Y}_i$, such as $\hat{Y}_i^2$, $\hat{Y}_i^3$, etc., to capture the systematic relationship, if any, between the residuals and the estimated Y_i. Since Figure 7-3 shows a curvilinear relationship between the residuals and the estimated Y values, let us consider the following model:

$$Y_t = B_1 + B_2 X_t + B_3 \hat{Y}_t^2 + B_4 \hat{Y}_t^3 + v_t \tag{7.23}$$

where v is the error term of this model.

3. Let R^2 obtained from Equation (7.23) be R^2_{new} and that obtained from Eq. (7.22) be R^2_{old}. Then we can use the F test of Equation (4.56), namely,

$$F = \frac{\left(R^2_{new} - R^2_{old}\right)/\text{number of new regressors}}{\left(1 - R^2_{new}\right)/(n - \text{number of parameters in the new model})} \tag{7.24}$$

to find out if the increase in R^2 from using Eq. (7.23) is statistically significant.

4. If the computed F value is statistically significant at the chosen level of significance, we can conclude that the initial model (such as Eq. [7.22]) is misspecified.

For our example, the empirical counterpart of Eq. (7.23) is as shown in Table 7-4:

TABLE 7-4   ILLUSTRATION OF RAMSEY'S RESET

Variable	Coefficient	Standard error	t statistic	p value
Intercept	−39.7720	15.1193	−2.6306	0.0117
X	0.1471	0.0133	11.0550	0.0000
$\hat{Y}^2$	0.0000	0.0001	−0.1458	0.8848
$\hat{Y}^3$	0.0000	0.0000	3.3763	0.0015
R-squared	0.9959			

Notes: Dependent variable is Y.

Now applying the F test given in Equation (7.24), we obtain:

$$F = \frac{(0.9959 - 0.9693)/2}{(1 - 0.9959)/(48 - 4)} = 142.7317 \tag{7.25}$$

For 2 d.f. in the numerator and 44 d.f. in the denominator, the 1% critical F value is 5.12263. Since the computed F value is much larger than this, the probability of obtaining an F value of as much as 142.7317 or greater must be very small.

Using statistical software packages or electronic tables we find that the actual probability of this is basically 0.0000.

The conclusion that we draw from this exercise is that the model (7.22) is misspecified. This is not surprising because we saw earlier that the trend variable belongs in this model. It is quite possible that not only the trend variable but perhaps a squared trend variable should also be included in the model. To find this out, see Problem 7.18.

One advantage of the RESET test is that it is easy to apply, for it does not require that we specify what the alternative model is. But that is also its disadvantage because knowing that a model is misspecified does not help us necessarily in choosing an alternative model. Therefore, we can regard the RESET test primarily as a diagnostic tool.[15]

7.8 SUMMARY

The major points discussed in this chapter can be summarized as follows:

1. The classical linear regression model assumes that the model used in empirical analysis is "correctly specified."
2. The term *correct specification* of a model can mean several things, including:
   a. No theoretically relevant variable has been excluded from the model.
   b. No unnecessary or irrelevant variables are included in the model.
   c. The functional form of the model is correct.
   d. There are no errors of measurement.
3. If a theoretically relevant variable(s) has been excluded from the model, the coefficients of the variables retained in the model are generally biased as well as inconsistent, and the error variance and the standard errors of the OLS estimators are biased. As a result, the conventional t and F tests remain of questionable value.
4. Similar consequences ensue if we use the wrong functional form.
5. The consequences of including irrelevant variables(s) in the model are less serious in that estimated coefficients still remain unbiased and consistent, the error variance and standard errors of the estimators are correctly estimated, and the conventional hypothesis-testing procedure is still valid. The major penalty we pay is that estimated standard errors tend to be relatively large, which means parameters of the model are estimated rather imprecisely. As a result, confidence intervals tend to be somewhat wider.
6. In view of the potential seriousness of specification errors, in this chapter we considered several diagnostic tools to help us find out if we have the specification error problem in any concrete situation. These tools include a graphical examination of the residuals and more formal tests, such as MWD and RESET.

---

[15]Note this technical point. Since $\hat{Y}_t$ is a random variable, its appearance as an explanatory variable in Eq. (7.23) means the use of t and F tests is justified only if the sample is reasonably large.

Since the search for a theoretically correct model can be exasperating, in this chapter we considered several practical criteria that we should keep in mind in this search, such as (1) parsimony, (2) identifiability, (3) goodness of fit, (4) theoretical consistency, and (5) predictive power.

As Granger notes, "In the ultimate analysis, model building is probably both an art and a science. A sound knowledge of theoretical econometrics and the availability of an efficient computer program are not enough to ensure success."[16]

KEY TERMS AND CONCEPTS

The key terms and concepts introduced in this chapter are:

Attributes of a good model
  a) Parsimony (principle of parsimony)
  b) Identifiability
  c) Goodness of fit
  d) Theoretical consistency
  e) Predictive power
Specification errors and model misspecification errors
  a) Core variables
  b) Peripheral variables
  c) Underfitting a model (omitted variable bias)
  d) Overfitting a model (inclusion of irrelevant variable bias)

  e) Incorrect (wrong) functional form bias
  f) Instrumental or proxy variables
Specification error tests
  a) Unnecessary variables (stepwise regression; data mining)
  b) Tests for omitted variables and incorrect functional forms
  c) MacKinnon-White-Davidson (MWD) test
  d) Ramsey's regression error specification (RESET) test

QUESTIONS

7.1.   What is meant by specification errors?

7.2.   What are the reasons for the occurrence of specification errors?

7.3.   What are the attributes of a "good" econometric model?

7.4.   What are different types of specification errors? Can one or more of these errors occur simultaneously?

7.5.   What are the consequences of omitting a relevant variable(s) from a model?

7.6.   When we say that a variable is "relevant" or "irrelevant," what do we mean?

7.7.   What are the consequences of including irrelevant variables in a model?

7.8.   Omitting a relevant variable(s) from a model is more dangerous than including an irrelevant variable(s). Do you agree? Why or why not?

[16]See C. W. J. Granger (ed.), *Modelling Economic Time Series: Readings in Econometric Methodology,* Clanrendon, Oxford, U.K., 1990, p. 2.

7.9. In looking for the simple Keynesian multiplier, you regress the GNP on investment and find that there is some relationship. Now, thinking that it cannot hurt much, you include the "irrelevant" variable "state and local taxes." To your surprise, the investment variable loses its significance. How can an irrelevant variable do this?

7.10. What would you do if you had to choose between a model that satisfies all statistical criteria but does not satisfy economic theory and a model that fits established economic theory but does not fit many statistical criteria?

PROBLEMS

7.11. Table 7-5, found on the textbook's Web site, gives data on the real gross product, labor input, and real capital input in the Taiwanese manufacturing sector for the years 1958 to 1972. Suppose the theoretically correct production function is of the Cobb-Douglas type, as follows:

$$\ln Y_t = B_1 + B_2 \ln X_{2t} + B_3 \ln X_{3t} + u_t$$

where $\ln$ = the natural log.

a. Given the data shown in Table 7-5, estimate the Cobb-Douglas production function for Taiwan for the sample period and interpret the results.

b. Suppose capital data were not initially available and therefore someone estimated the following production function:

$$\ln Y_t = C_1 + C_2 \ln X_{2t} + v_t$$

where v = an error term. What kind of specification error is incurred in this case? What are the consequences? Illustrate with the data in Table 7-5.

c. Now pretend that the data on labor input were not available initially and suppose you estimated the following model:

$$\ln Y_t = C_1 + C_2 \ln X_{3t} + w_t$$

where w = an error term. What are the consequences of this type of specification error? Illustrate with the data given in Table 7-5.

7.12. Consider the following models:
Model I: $\text{Consumption}_i = B_1 + B_2 \text{income}_i + u_i$
Model II: $\text{Consumption}_i = A_1 + A_2 \text{wealth}_i + v_i$

a. How would you decide which of the models is the "true" model?

b. Suppose you regress consumption on both income and wealth. How would this help you decide between the two models? Show the necessary details.

7.13. Refer to Equation 5.40 in Chapter 5, which discusses the regression-through-the-origin (i.e., zero-intercept) model. If there is in fact an intercept present in the model but you run it through the origin, what kind of specification error is committed? Document the consequences of this type of error with the data given in Table 2-13 (found on the textbook's Web site) in Chapter 2.

7.14. Table 7-6 (found on the textbook's Web site) gives data on the real rate of return (Y) on common stocks, the output growth (X_2), and inflation (X_3), all in percent for the United States for 1954 to 1981.

    a. Regress Y on X_3.

    b. Regress Y on X_2 and X_3.

    c. Comment on the two regression results in view of Professor Eugene Fama's observation that "the negative simple correlation between real stock returns and inflation is spurious (or false) because it is the result of two structural relationships: a positive relation between current real stock returns and expected output growth and a negative relationship between expected output growth and current inflation."

    d. Do the regression in part (*b*) for the period 1956 to 1976, omitting the data for 1954 and 1955 due to unusual stock return behavior in those years, and compare this regression with the one obtained in part (*b*). Comment on the difference, if any, between the two.

    e. Suppose you want to run the regression for the period 1956 to 1981 but want to distinguish between the periods 1956 to 1976 and 1977 to 1981. How would you run this regression? (*Hint:* Think of the dummy variables.)

7.15. Table 7-7 (found on the textbook's Web site) gives data on indexes of aggregate final energy demand (Y), the real gross domestic product, the GDP (X_2), and the real energy price (X_3) for the OECD countries—the United States, Canada, Germany, France, the United Kingdom, Italy, and Japan—for the period 1960 to 1982. (All indexes with base 1973 = 100.)

    a. Estimate the following models:

        Model A: $\ln Y_t = B_1 + B_2 \ln X_{2t} + B_3 \ln X_{3t} + u_{1t}$

        Model B: $\ln Y_t = A_1 + A_2 \ln X_{2t} + A_3 \ln X_{2(t-1)} + A_4 \ln X_{3t} + u_{2t}$

        Model C: $\ln Y_t = C_1 + C_2 \ln X_{2t} + C_3 \ln X_{3t} + C_4 \ln X_{3(t-1)} + u_{3t}$

        Model D: $\ln Y_t = D_1 + D_2 \ln X_{2t} + D_3 \ln X_{3t} + D_4 \ln Y_{(t-1)} + u_{4t}$

    where the u's are the error terms. *Note:* Models B and C are called *dynamic models*—models that explicitly take into account the changes of a variable over time. Models B and C are called *distributed lag models* because the impact of an explanatory variable on the dependent variable is spread over time, here over two time periods. Model D is called an *autoregressive model* because one of the explanatory variables is a lagged value of the dependent variable.

    b. If you estimate Model A only, whereas the true model is either B, C, or D, what kind of specification bias is involved?

    c. Since all the preceding models are log-linear, the slope coefficients represent elasticity coefficients. What are the income (i.e., with respect to GDP) and price elasticities for Model A? How would you go about estimating these elasticities for the other three models?

    d. What problems do you foresee with the OLS estimation of Model D since the lagged Y variable appears as one of the explanatory variables? (*Hint:* Recall the assumptions of the CLRM.)

7.16. Refer to Problem 7.11. Suppose you extend the Cobb-Douglas production function model by including the trend variable X_4, a surrogate for technology. Suppose further that X_4 turns out to be statistically significant. In that case, what type of specification error is committed? What if X_4 turns out to be statistically insignificant? Present the necessary calculations.

7.17. Table 7-8 on the textbook's Web site gives data on variables that might affect the demand for chickens in the United States. The dependent variable here is the per capita consumption of chickens, and the explanatory variables are per capita real disposable income and the prices of chicken and chicken substitutes (pork and beef).

    a. Estimate a log-linear model using these data.

    b. Estimate a linear model using these data.

    c. How would you choose between the two models? What test will you use? Show the necessary computations.

7.18. Suppose that we modify model (7.13) as follows:

$$Y_t = B_1 + B_2 X_t + B_3 Time + B_4 Time^2 + u_t$$

    a. Estimate this model.

    b. If the $Year^2$ in this model turns out to be statistically significant, what can you say about regression (7.13)?

    c. Is there a specification error involved here? If so, of what type? What are the consequences of this specification error?.

7.19. *Does more money help schools?* To answer this question, Rubén Hernández-Murillo and Deborah Roisman present the data given in Table 7-9 on the textbook's Web site.[17]

These data relate to several input and outcome variables for school districts in the St. Louis area and are for the academic year 1999 to 2000.

    a. Treating the Missouri Assessment Program (MAP) test score as the dependent variable, develop a suitable model to explain the behavior of MAP.

    b. Which variable(s) is crucial in determining MAP—economic or social?

    c. What is the rationale for the dummy variable?

    d. Would it be prudent to conclude from your analysis that spending per pupil and or smaller student/teacher ratio are unimportant determinants of test scores?

7.20. In *Bazemore* v. *Friday*, 478 U.S. 385 (1986), a case involving pay discrimination in the North Carolina Extension Service, the plaintiff, a group of black agents, submitted a multiple regression model showing that, on average, the black agents' salary was lower than that of their white counterparts. When the case reached the court of appeals, it rejected the plaintiff's case on the grounds that their regression had not included all the variables thought to have an effect on salary. The Supreme Court, however, reversed the appeals court. It stated:[18]

> The Court of Appeals erred in stating that petitioners' regression analyses were "unacceptable as evidence of discrimination," because they did not include all measurable variables thought to have an effect on salary level. The court's view of the evidentiary value of the regression analysis was plainly incorrect. While the omission of variables from a regression analysis may render the analysis less probative than it otherwise might be, it can hardly be said, absent some other infirmity, that an analysis which accounts for the major factors

---

[17]See their article, "Tough Lesson: More Money Doesn't Help Schools; Accountability Does," *The Regional Economist*, Federal Reserve Bank of St. Louis, April 2004, pp. 12–13.

[18]The following is reproduced from Michael O. Finkelstein and Bruce Levin, *Statistics for Lawyers*, Springer-Verlag, New York, 1989, p. 374.

"must be considered unacceptable as evidence of discrimination." *Ibid.* Normally, a failure to include variables will affect the analysis' probativeness, not its admissibility.

Do you think the Supreme Court was correct in this decision? Articulate your views fully, bearing in mind the theoretical consequences of specification errors and practical realities.

7.21. Table 7-10 on the textbook's Web site contains data about the manufacturing sector of all 50 states and the District of Columbia. The dependent variable is output, measured as "value added" in thousands of U.S. dollars, and the independent variables are worker hours and capital expenditures.

a. Predict output using a standard linear model. What is the function?

b. Create a log-linear model using the data as well. What is this function?

c. Use the MWD test to decide which model is more appropriate.

CHAPTER 8

MULTICOLLINEARITY: WHAT HAPPENS IF EXPLANATORY VARIABLES ARE CORRELATED?

In Chapter 4 we noted that one of the assumptions of the classical linear regression model (CLRM) is that there is no **perfect multicollinearity**—no exact linear relationships among explanatory variables, X's, included in a multiple regression. In that chapter we explained intuitively the meaning of perfect multicollinearity and reasons for assuming why it should not exist in the population regression function (PRF). In this chapter we take a closer look at the topic of multicollinearity. In practice, we rarely encounter perfect multicollinearity, but cases of **near** or **very high multicollinearity** where explanatory variables are *approximately* linearly related frequently arise in many applications. It is important to know what problems these correlated variables pose for the ordinary least squares (OLS) estimation of multiple regression models. Toward that end, in this chapter we will seek answers to the following questions:

1. What is the nature of multicollinearity?
2. Is multicollinearity really a problem?
3. What are the theoretical consequences of multicollinearity?
4. What are the practical consequences of multicollinearity?
5. In practice, how does one detect multicollinearity?
6. If it is desirable to eliminate the problem of multicollinearity, what remedial measures are available?

TABLE 8-1   THE DEMAND FOR WIDGETS

Y (quantity)	X_2 (price, \$)	X_3 (income per week, \$)	X_4 (earnings per week, \$)
49	1	298	297.5
45	2	296	294.9
44	3	294	293.5
39	4	292	292.8
38	5	290	290.2
37	6	288	289.7
34	7	286	285.8
33	8	284	284.6
30	9	282	281.1
29	10	280	278.8

8.1   THE NATURE OF MULTICOLLINEARITY: THE CASE OF PERFECT MULTICOLLINEARITY

To answer these various questions, we consider first a simple numerical example, which is specially constructed to emphasize some crucial points about multicollinearity. Consider the data given in Table 8-1.

This table gives data on demand for widgets (Y) in relation to price (X_2) and two measures of weekly consumer income, X_3, as estimated, say, by a researcher, and X_4, as estimated by another researcher. To distinguish between the two, we call X_3 income and X_4 earnings.

Since, besides the price, the income of the consumer is also an important determinant in the demand for most goods, we write the expanded demand function as

$$Y_i = A_1 + A_2X_{2i} + A_3X_{3i} + u_i \tag{8.1}$$

$$Y_i = B_1 + B_2X_{2i} + B_3X_{4i} + u_i \tag{8.2}$$

These demand functions differ in the measure of income used. A priori, or according to theory, A_2 and B_2 are expected to be negative (Why?), but A_3 and B_3 are expected to be positive (Why?).[1]

When an attempt was made to fit the regression (8.1) to the data in Table 8-1, the computer "refused" to estimate the regression.[2] What went wrong? Nothing. By plotting the variables price (X_2) and income (X_3), we get the diagram shown in Figure 8-1.

And by trying to regress X_3 on X_2, we obtain the following results:

$$X_{3i} = 300 - 2X_{2i} \qquad R^2(=r^2) = 1.00 \tag{8.3}$$

---

[1]According to economic theory, the income coefficient is expected to be positive for most normal economic goods. It is expected to be negative for what are called "inferior" goods.

[2]Usually, you will get a message saying that the X, or data, matrix is not positive definite; that is, it cannot be inverted. In matrix algebra such a matrix is called a singular matrix. Simply put, the computer cannot do the calculations.

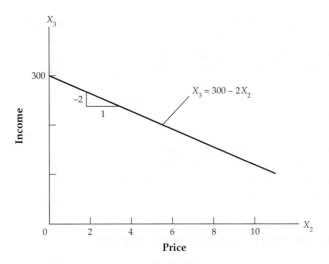

FIGURE 8-1 Scattergram between income (X_3) and price (X_2)

In other words, the income variable X_3 and the price variable X_2 are **perfectly linearly related;** that is, we have **perfect collinearity** (or **multicollinearity**).[3]

Because of the relationship in Equation (8.3), we cannot estimate the regression (8.1), for if we substitute Eq. (8.3) into Eq. (8.1), we obtain

$$Y_i = A_1 + A_2X_{2i} + A_3(300 - 2X_{2i}) + u_i$$
$$= (A_1 + 300A_3) + (A_2 - 2A_3)X_{2i} + u_i$$
$$= C_1 + C_2X_{2i} + u_i \qquad \textbf{(8.4)}$$

where
$$C_1 = A_1 + 300A_3 \qquad \textbf{(8.5)}$$
$$C_2 = A_2 - 2A_3 \qquad \textbf{(8.6)}$$

No wonder we could not estimate Eq. (8.1), for as Eq. (8.4) shows, we do not have a multiple regression but a simple two-variable regression between Y and X_2. Now, although we can estimate Eq. (8.4) and obtain estimates of C_1 and C_2, from these two values we cannot obtain estimates of the original parameters A_1, A_2, and A_3, for in Equations (8.5) and (8.6) we have only two equations but there are three unknowns to be estimated. (From school algebra we know that to estimate three unknowns we generally require three equations.)

The results of estimating the regression (8.4) are as follows:

$$\hat{Y}_i = 49.667 - 2.1576X_{2i}$$
$$se = (0.746)(0.1203) \qquad \textbf{(8.7)}$$
$$t = (66.538)(-17.935) \qquad r^2 = 0.9757$$

[3]Although the term *collinearity* refers to a single perfect linear relationship between variables and the term *multicollinearity* refers to more than one such relationship, from now on we will use the term *multicollinearity* in a generic sense to include both cases. The context will make it clear whether we have just one or more than one exact linear relationship.

As we can see, $C_1 = 49.667$ and $C_2 = -2.1576$. Try as we might, from these two values there is no way to retrieve the values of the three unknowns, A_1, A_2, and A_3.[4]

The upshot of the preceding discussion is that *in cases of perfect linear relationship or perfect multicollinearity among explanatory variables, we cannot obtain unique estimates of all parameters. And since we cannot obtain their unique estimates, we cannot draw any statistical inferences (i.e., hypothesis testing) about them from a given sample.*

To put it bluntly, in cases of perfect multicollinearity, estimation and hypothesis testing about individual regression coefficients in a multiple regression are not possible. It is a dead end issue. Of course, as Eqs. (8.5) and (8.6) show, we can obtain estimates of a linear combination (i.e., the sum or difference) of the original coefficients, but not of each of them individually.

8.2   THE CASE OF NEAR, OR IMPERFECT, MULTICOLLINEARITY

The case of perfect multicollinearity is a pathological extreme. In most applications involving economic data two or more explanatory variables are not exactly linearly related but can be approximately so. That is, collinearity can be high but not perfect. This is the case of **near, or imperfect,** or **high multicollinearity.** We will explain what we mean by "high" collinearity shortly. *From now on when talking about multicollinearity, we are refering to imperfect multicollinearity.* As we saw in Section 8.1, the case of perfect multicollinearity is a blind alley.

To see what we mean by near, or imperfect, multicollinearity, let us return to our data in Table 8-1, but this time, we estimate regression (8.2) with earnings as the income variable. The regression results are as follows:

$$\hat{Y}_i = 145.37 - 2.7975X_{2i} - 0.3191X_{4i}$$

$$se = (120.06) \quad (0.8122) \qquad (0.4003) \tag{8.8}$$

$$t = (1.2107) \quad (-3.4444) \qquad (-0.7971) \qquad R^2 = 0.9778$$

These results are interesting for several reasons:

1. Although the regression (8.1) cannot be estimated, we can estimate the regression (8.2), even though the difference between the two income variables is very small, which can be seen visually from the last two columns of Table 8-1.[5]

---

[4]Of course, if the value of one of A_1, A_2, and A_3 is fixed arbitrarily, then the values of the other two A's can be obtained from the estimated C's. But these values will not be unique, for they depend on the value arbitrarily chosen for one of the A's. To reiterate, there is no way of obtaining unique values of three unknowns (the three A's) from two knowns (the two C's).

[5]It is time to let the "cat out of the bag." The earnings figures reported in column 4 of Table 8-1 were constructed from the following relation: $X_{4i} = X_{3i} + u_i$, where the u's are random terms obtained from a random number table. The 10 values of u are as follows: $-0.5, -1.1, -0.5, 0.8, 0.2, 1.7, -0.2, 0.6, -0.9,$ and -1.2.

2. As expected, price coefficients are negative in both Equations (8.7) and (8.8), and the numerical difference between the two is not vast. Each price coefficient is statistically significantly different from zero (Why?), but notice that, relatively speaking, the $|t|$ value of the coefficient in Eq. (8.7) is much greater than the corresponding $|t|$ value in Eq. (8.8). Or what amounts to the same thing, comparatively, the standard error (se) of the price coefficient in Eq. (8.7) is much smaller than that in Eq. (8.8).

3. The R^2 value in Eq. (8.7) with one explanatory variable is 0.9757, whereas in Eq. (8.8) with two explanatory variables it is 0.9778, an increase of only 0.0021, which does not appear to be a great increase. It can be shown that this increase in the R^2 value is not statistically significant.[6]

4. The coefficient of the income (earnings) variable is statistically insignificant, but, more importantly, it has the wrong sign. For most commodities, income has a positive effect on the quantity demanded, unless the commodity in question happens to be an *inferior good*.

5. Despite the insignificance of the income variable, if we were to test the hypothesis that $B_2 = B_3 = 0$ (i.e., the hypothesis that $R^2 = 0$), the hypothesis could be rejected easily by applying the F test given in expression (4.49) or (4.50). In other words, collectively or together, price and earnings have a significant impact on the quantity demanded.

What explains these "strange" results? As a clue, let us plot X_2 against X_4, price against earnings. (See Figure 8-2.) Unlike Figure 8-1, we see that although

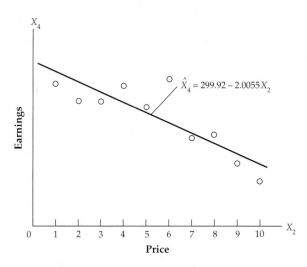

FIGURE 8-2   Earnings (X_4) and price (X_2) relationship

---

[6]This can be shown with the F test discussed in Chapter 4.

price and earnings are not perfectly linearly related, there is a high degree of dependency between the two.

This can be seen more clearly from the following regression:

$$X_{4i} = 299.92 - 2.0055X_{2i} + e_i$$

$$\text{se} = (0.6748) \quad (0.1088) \tag{8.9}$$

$$t = (444.44) \quad (-18.44) \qquad r^2 = 0.9770$$

As this regression shows, price and earnings are highly correlated; the coefficient of correlation is -0.9884 (which is the negative square root of r^2). This is the case of **near perfect linear relationship,** or near perfect multicollinearity. If the coefficient of correlation were -1, as in Eq. (8.3), this would be the case of perfect multicollinearity. Notice carefully, in Eq. (8.3) we have not added e_i because the linear relationship between X_{2i} and X_{3i} is perfect, whereas in Equation (8.9) we have added it to show that the linear relationship between X_{4i} and X_{2i} is not perfect.

In passing, note that if there are just two explanatory variables, the coefficient of correlation r can be used as a measure of the degree or strength of collinearity. But if more than two explanatory variables are involved, as we will show later, the coefficient of correlation may not be an adequate measure of collinearity.

8.3 THEORETICAL CONSEQUENCES OF MULTICOLLINEARITY

Now that we have discussed the nature of perfect and imperfect multicollinearity somewhat heuristically, let us state the consequences of multicollinearity a bit more formally. But keep in mind that from now on we consider only the case of *imperfect* multicollinearity, for perfect multicollinearity leads us nowhere.

As we know, given the assumptions of the CLRM, OLS estimators are best linear unbiased estimators (BLUE). In the class of all linear unbiased estimators, OLS estimators have the least possible variance. *It is interesting that so long as collinearity is not perfect, OLS estimators still remain BLUE even though one or more of the partial regression coefficients in a multiple regression can be individually statistically insignificant.* Thus, in Eq. (8.8), the income coefficient is statistically insignificant although the price coefficient is statistically significant. But OLS estimates presented in Eq. (8.8) still retain their BLUE property.[7] Then why all the fuss about multicollinearity? There are several reasons:

1. It is true that even in the presence of near collinearity, the OLS estimators are unbiased. But remember that *unbiasedness is a repeated sampling property.* What this says is that, keeping the values of the X variables fixed, if we obtain several samples and compute the OLS estimates for each of these samples, the average value of the estimates will tend to converge to the true population value of the estimates. But this says nothing about the properties of estimates given in any given sample. In reality, we rarely have the luxury of replicating samples.

---

[7]Since imperfect multicollinearity per se does not violate any of the assumptions listed in Chapter 4, OLS estimators retain the BLUE property.

2. It is also true that near collinearity does not destroy the minimum variance property of OLS estimators. In the class of all linear unbiased estimators, OLS estimators have minimum variance. This does not mean, however, that the variance of an OLS estimator will be small (in relation to the value of the estimator) in any given sample, as the regression (8.8) shows very clearly. It is true that the estimator of the income coefficient is BLUE, but in the sample at hand its variance is so large compared to the estimate that the computed t value (under the null hypothesis that the true income coefficient is zero) is only -0.7971. This would lead us to not reject the hypothesis that income has no effect on the quantity of widgets demanded. In short, *minimum variance does not mean the numerical value of the variance will be small.*

3. *Multicollinearity is essentially a sample (regression) phenomenon* in the sense that even if the X variables are not linearly related in the population (i.e., PRF), they can be so related in a particular sample, such as that of Table 8-1. When we postulate the PRF, we believe that all X variables included in the model have a separate or independent effect on the dependent variable Y. But it can happen that in any given sample that is used to estimate the PRF some or all X variables are so highly collinear that we cannot isolate their individual influence on Y. Our sample lets us down so to speak, although the theory says that all X's are important. And this happens because most economic data are not obtained in controlled laboratory experiments. Data on variables such as the gross domestic product (GDP), prices, unemployment, profits, and dividends are usually observed as they occur and are not obtained experimentally. If these data could be obtained experimentally to begin with, we would not allow collinearity to exist. Since data are usually obtained nonexperimentally, and if there is near collinearity in two or more explanatory variables, often we are in "the statistical position of not being able to make bricks without straw."[8]

For all these reasons, the fact that OLS estimators are BLUE despite (imperfect) multicollinearity is of little consolation in practice. Therefore, we must try to find out what happens or is likely to happen in any given sample. As noted, collinearity is usually a sample-specific phenomenon.

8.4 PRACTICAL CONSEQUENCES OF MULTICOLLINEARITY

In cases of near or high multicollinearity, as in our demand for widget regression (8.8), we are likely to encounter one or more of the following consequences:

1. *Large variances and standard errors of OLS estimators.* This is clearly seen from the widget regressions (8.7) and (8.8). As discussed earlier, because

---

[8]J. Johnston, *Econometric Methods*, 2nd ed., McGraw-Hill, New York, 1972, p. 164.

of high collinearity between price (X_2) and earnings (X_4), when both variables are included in the regression (8.8), the standard error of the coefficient of the price variable increases dramatically compared with the regression (8.7). As we know, if the standard error of an estimator increases, it becomes more difficult to estimate the true value of the estimator. That is, there is a fall in the *precision* of OLS estimators.

2. *Wider confidence intervals.* Because of large standard errors, confidence intervals for relevant population parameters tend to be large.

3. *Insignificant t ratios.* Recall that to test the hypothesis that in our regression (8.8) the true $B_3 = 0$ we use the t ratio $b_3/se(b_3)$ and compare the estimated t value with the critical t value from the t table. But as previously seen, in cases of high collinearity the estimated standard errors increase dramatically, thereby making t values smaller. Therefore, in such cases we will increasingly accept the null hypothesis that the relevant true population coefficient is zero. Thus, in the regression (8.8), since the t value is only -0.7971, we might jump to the conclusion that in the widget example income has no effect on the quantity demanded.

4. *A high R^2 value but few significant t ratios.* The regression (8.8) shows this clearly. The R^2 in this regression is quite high, about 0.98, but only the t ratio of the price variable is significant. And yet on the basis of the F ratio, as we have seen, we can reject the hypothesis that the price and earnings variables simultaneously have no effect on the quantity of widgets demanded.

5. *OLS estimators and their standard errors become very sensitive to small changes in the data; that is, they tend to be unstable.* To see this, return to Table 8-1. Suppose we change the data on the earnings variable X_4 slightly. The first, fifth, and tenth observations are now 295, 287, and 274, respectively. All other values remain intact. The result of this change gives the following regression:

$$\hat{Y}_i = 100.56 - 2.5164X_{2i} - 0.16995X_{4i}$$

$$se = (48.030) \quad (0.35906) \quad (0.1604) \tag{8.10}$$

$$t = (2.0936) \quad (-7.0083) \quad (-1.0597) \quad R^2 = 0.9791$$

Comparing Eq. (8.8) with regression (8.10), we observe that as a result of a very small change in the data, the regression results change quite substantially. Relatively speaking, standard errors have gone down in Eq. (8.10), and, as a result, t ratios have increased in absolute values and the income variable now has become less negative than before.

Why such a change? In the regression (8.8) the coefficient of correlation between X_2 and X_4 was -0.9884, whereas in the regression (8.10) it was -0.9431. In other words, the degree of collinearity between X_2 and X_4 has decreased in going from Eq. (8.8) to Eq. (8.10). Although the decrease in the correlation coefficient does not seem astounding, the change in regression results is noticeable. And this is precisely what happens in cases of near perfect collinearity.

6. *Wrong signs for regression coefficients.* As regressions (8.8) and (8.10) show, the earnings variable has the "wrong" sign, for economic theory would have us believe that for most commodities the income effect is positive. Of course, with an inferior good this is not a wrong sign. Therefore, we have to be careful in attributing the wrong sign to multicollinearity alone, but it should not be ruled out either.

7. *Difficulty in assessing the individual contributions of explanatory variables to the explained sum of squares (ESS) or R^2.* We can illustrate this point again with our widget example. In Eq. (8.7) we regressed quantity (Y) on price (X_2) alone, giving an R^2 value of 0.9757. In regression (8.8) we regressed Y on both price and earnings, obtaining an R^2 of 0.9778. Now if we regress Y on X_4 alone, we obtain the following results:

$$\hat{Y}_i = -263.74 + 1.0438X_{4i}$$

$$\text{se} = (26.929) \quad (0.0932) \tag{8.11}$$

$$t = (-9.794) \quad (11.200) \qquad R^2 = 0.9400$$

Lo and behold, earnings (X_4) alone explains 94 percent of the variation in the quantity demanded. In addition, the earnings coefficient is not only statistically significant, but it is also positive, in accord with theoretical expectations!

As shown previously, in the multiple regression (8.8) the R^2 value is 0.9778. What part of it is due to X_2 and what part is due to X_4? We cannot tell precisely because the two variables are so highly collinear that when one moves the other moves with it almost automatically, as the regression (8.9) so clearly demonstrates. Therefore, in cases of high collinearity it is futile to assess the contribution of each explanatory variable to the overall R^2.

A question: Can the consequences of multicollinearity that we have illustrated earlier be established rigorously? Yes indeed! But we will skip the proofs here since they can be found elsewhere.[9]

8.5   DETECTION OF MULTICOLLINEARITY

As demonstrated in the previous section, practical consequences of multicollinearity can be far-ranging, the BLUE property notwithstanding. So, what can we do about resolving the multicollinearity problem? Before resolving it, we must first find out if we have a collinearity problem to begin with. In short, how do we detect the presence of and severity of multicollinearity?

---

[9]The proofs are shown in Gujarati and Porter, *Basic Econometrics*, 5th ed., McGraw-Hill, New York, 2009, Chapter 10.

Now we have a problem, for as noted earlier, multicollinearity is **sample-specific;** it is a sample phenomenon. Here it is useful to keep in mind the following warning:[10]

1. Multicollinearity is a question of degree and not of kind. The meaningful distinction is not between the presence and the absence of multicollinearity, but between its various degrees.
2. Since multicollinearity refers to the condition of the explanatory variables that are assumed to be nonstochastic, it is a *feature of the sample* and not of the population.

Therefore, we do not "test for multicollinearity" but can, if we wish, measure its degree in any particular sample.

Having stated that, we must add that we do not have a single measure of multicollinearity, for in nonexperimentally collected data we can never be sure about the nature and degree of collinearity. What we have are some rules of thumb, or indicators, that will provide us with some clue about the existence of multicollinearity in concrete applications. Some of these indicators follow.

1. *High R^2 but few significant t ratios.* As noted earlier, this is the "classic" symptom of multicollinearity. If R^2 is high, say, in excess of 0.8, the F test in most cases will reject the null hypothesis that the partial slope coefficients are *jointly* or *simultaneously* equal to zero. But individual t tests will show that none or very few partial slope coefficients are statistically different from zero. Our widget regression (8.8) bears this out fully.
2. *High pairwise correlations among explanatory variables.* If in a multiple regression involving, say, six explanatory variables, we compute the coefficient of correlation between any pair of these variables using the formula (B.46) in Appendix B, and if some of these correlations are high, say, in excess of 0.8, there is the possibility that some serious collinearity exists. Unfortunately, this criterion is not often reliable, for pairwise correlations can be low (suggesting no serious collinearity) yet collinearity is suspected because very few t ratios are statistically significant.[11]
3. *Examination of partial correlations.* Suppose we have three explanatory variables, X_2, X_3, and X_4. Let r_{23}, r_{24}, and r_{34} represent the pairwise correlations between X_2 and X_3, between X_2 and X_4, and between X_3 and X_4, respectively. Suppose $r_{23} = 0.90$, indicating high collinearity between X_2 and X_3. Now consider the correlation coefficient, called the **partial correlation coefficient,** $r_{23.4}$, which is the coefficient of correlation between X_2 and X_3, *holding the influence of the variable X_4 constant* (the concept is similar to that of the partial regression coefficient discussed in Chapter 4). Suppose $r_{23.4} = 0.43$; that is, holding the influence of the variable X_4 constant, the correlation coefficient between X_2 and X_3 is only 0.43, whereas

[10]Jan Kmenta, *Elements of Econometrics*, 2nd ed., Macmillan, New York, 1986, p. 431.
[11]For technical details, see Gujarati and Porter, *Basic Econometrics*, 5th ed., McGraw-Hill, New York, 2009, Chapter 10.

not taking into account the influence of X_4, it is 0.90. Then, judged by the partial correlation, we cannot say that the collinearity between X_2 and X_3 is necessarily high.

As we can see, in the context of several explanatory variables, reliance on simple pairwise correlations as indicators of multicollinearity can be misleading. Unfortunately, the substitution of simple pairwise correlations by partial correlation coefficients does not provide a definitive indicator of the presence of multicollinearity or otherwise. The latter provides only another device to check the nature of multicollinearity.[12]

4. *Subsidiary, or auxiliary, regressions.* Since multicollinearity arises because one or more of the explanatory variables are exact or near exact linear combinations of other explanatory variables, one way of finding out which X variable is highly collinear with other X variables in the model is to regress each X variable on the remaining X variables and to compute the corresponding R^2. Each of these regressions is called a **subsidiary** or an **auxiliary regression,** auxiliary to the main regression of Y on all X's.

For example, consider the regression of Y on X_2, X_3, X_4, X_5, X_6, and X_7—six explanatory variables. If this regression shows that we have a problem of multicollinearity because, say, the R^2 is high but very few X coefficients are individually statistically significant, we then look for the "culprit," the variable(s) that may be a perfect or near perfect linear combination of the other X's. We proceed as follows:

(a) Regress X_2 on the remaining X's and obtain the coefficient of determination, say, R_2^2.
(b) Regress X_3 on the remaining X's and obtain its coefficient of determination, R_3^2.

Continue this procedure for the remaining X variables in the model. In the present example we will have six such auxiliary regressions, one for each explanatory variable.

How do we decide which of the X variables are collinear? The estimated R_i^2 will range between 0 and 1. (Why?) If an X variable is not a linear combination of the other X's, then the R_i^2 of that regression should not be statistically significantly different from zero. And from Chapter 4, Eq. (4.50), we know how to test the assumption that a particular coefficient of determination is statistically equal to zero.

Continuing with our hypothetical example involving six explanatory variables, suppose we want to test the hypothesis that $R_2^2 = 0$; that is, X_2 is not collinear with the remaining five X's. Now we use Eq. (4.50), which is

$$F = \frac{R^2/(k-1)}{(1-R^2)/(n-k)} \qquad \textbf{(4.50)}$$

[12]For technical details, see Gujarati and Porter, op. cit.

where n is the number of observations and k is the number of explanatory variables including the intercept. Let us illustrate.

In our hypothetical example involving six explanatory variables, suppose that we regress each of the X variables on the remaining X's in a sample involving 50 observations. The R^2 values obtained from the various auxiliary regressions are as follows:

$$R_2^2 = 0.90 \text{ (in the regression of } X_2 \text{ on other } X\text{'s)}$$

$$R_3^2 = 0.18 \text{ (in the regression of } X_3 \text{ on other } X\text{'s)}$$

$$R_4^2 = 0.36 \text{ (in the regression of } X_4 \text{ on other } X\text{'s)}$$

$$R_5^2 = 0.86 \text{ (in the regression of } X_5 \text{ on other } X\text{'s)}$$

$$R_6^2 = 0.09 \text{ (in the regression of } X_6 \text{ on other } X\text{'s)}$$

$$R_7^2 = 0.24 \text{ (in the regression of } X_7 \text{ on other } X\text{'s)}$$

The results of applying the F test given in Eq. (4.50) are given in Table 8-2.

As this table shows, the variables X_2, X_4, X_5, and X_7 seem to be collinear with the other X's, although the degree of collinearity, as measured by R^2, varies considerably. This example points out the important fact that a seemingly low R^2, such as 0.36, can still be statistically significantly different from zero. A concrete economic example of auxiliary regressions is given in Section 8.7.

One drawback of the auxiliary regression technique is the computational burden. If a regression contains several explanatory variables, we have to compute several subsidiary regressions, and therefore this method of detecting collinearity can be of limited practical value. But note that many computer packages now can compute the auxiliary regressions without much computational burden.

5. *The variance inflation factor (VIF).* Even if a model does not contain several explanatory variables, the R^2 values obtained from the various auxiliary

TABLE 8-2   TESTING THE SIGNIFICANCE OF R^2
(EQUATION [4.50])

Value of R^2	Value of F	Is F significant?
0.90	79.20	Yes*
0.18	1.93	No
0.36	4.95	Yes*
0.86	54.06	Yes*
0.09	0.87	No
0.24	2.78	Yes†

Notes: *Significant at the 1% level.
   †Significant at the 5% level.
   In this example $n = 50$ and $k = 6$.

regressions may not be a totally reliable indication of collinearity. This can be seen more clearly if we revert to the three-variable regression discussed more completely in Chapter 4. In Equations (4.25) and (4.27) we have been given the formulas to compute the variances of the two partial slopes b_2 and b_3. With simple algebraic manipulations, these variance formulas can be alternatively written as

$$\text{var}(b_2) = \frac{\sigma^2}{\sum x_{2i}^2\left(1 - R_2^2\right)}$$

$$= \frac{\sigma^2}{\sum x_{2i}^2} VIF \tag{8.12}$$

$$\text{var}(b_3) = \frac{\sigma^2}{\sum x_{3i}^2\left(1 - R_2^2\right)}$$

$$= \frac{\sigma^2}{\sum x_{3i}^2} VIF \tag{8.13}$$

(For proofs of these formulas, see Problem 8.21.) In these formulas R_2^2 is the coefficient of determination in the (auxiliary) regression of X_2 on X_3. (*Note:* The R^2 between X_2 and X_3 is the same as that between X_3 and X_2.)

In the preceding formulas

$$VIF = \frac{1}{\left(1 - R_2^2\right)} \tag{8.14}$$

The expression on the right-hand side of Equation (8.14) is called, very appropriately, the **variance inflation factor (VIF)** because as R^2 increases, the variance, and hence the standard error, of both b_2 and b_3 increases or inflates. (Do you see this?) In the extreme, when this coefficient of determination is 1 (i.e., perfect multicollinearity), these variances and standard errors are undefined. (Why?) Of course, if R^2 is zero, that is, there is no collinearity, the VIF will be 1 (Why?), and we do not have to worry about the large variances and standard errors that plague the collinearity situations.

Now an important question: Suppose an R_i^2 in an auxiliary regression is very high (but less than 1), suggesting a high degree of collinearity per the criterion discussed in the previous point 4. But as Eq. (8.12), (8.13), and (8.14) so clearly show, the variance of, say, b_2, not only depends upon the VIF but also upon the variance of u_i, σ^2, as well as on the variation in X_2, $\sum x_{2i}^2$. Thus, it is quite possible that an R_i^2 is very high, say, 0.91, but that either σ^2 is low or $\sum x_{2i}^2$ is high, or both, so that the variance of b_2 can still be lower and the t ratio higher. In other words, a high R^2 can be counterbalanced by a low σ^2 or a high $\sum x_{2i}^2$, or both. Of course, the terms *high* and *low* are used in a relative sense.

All this suggests that a high R^2 obtained from an auxiliary regression can be only a *surface* indicator of multicollinearity. It may not necessarily inflate the standard errors of the estimators, as the preceding discussion reveals. To put it more formally, "high R_i^2 is neither necessary nor sufficient to get high standard errors and thus multicollinearity by itself need not cause high standard errors."[13]

What general conclusions can we draw from the various multicollinearity diagnostics just discussed? That there are various indicators of multicollinearity and no single diagnostic will give us a complete answer to the collinearity problem. Remember that multicollinearity is a matter of degree and that it is a sample-specific phenomenon. In some situations it might be easy to diagnose, but in others one or more of the preceding methods will have to be used to find out the severity of the problem. There is no easy solution to the problem.

Research on multicollinearity diagnostics continues. There are some new techniques, such as the *condition index*, that have been developed. But they are beyond the scope of this book and are better left for the references.[14]

8.6   IS MULTICOLLINEARITY NECESSARILY BAD?

Before proceeding to consider remedial measures for the multicollinearity problem, we need to ask an important question: Is multicollinearity necessarily an "evil"? The answer depends on the purpose of the study. If the goal of the study is to use the model to predict or forecast the future mean value of the dependent variable, collinearity per se may not be bad.

Returning to our widget demand function Eq. (8.8), although the earnings variable is not individually statistically significant, the overall R^2 of 0.9778 is slightly higher than that of Eq. (8.7), which omits the earnings variable. Therefore, for prediction purposes Eq. (8.8) is marginally better than Eq. (8.7). Often forecasters choose a model on the basis of its explanatory power as measured by the R^2. Is this a good strategy? It may be if we assume that the collinearity observed between the price and earnings data given in Table 8-1 will also continue in the future. In Eq. (8.9) we have already shown how X_4 and X_2, earnings and price, are related. *If the same relationship is expected to continue into the future,* then Eq. (8.8) can be used to forecast. But that is a big *if.* If, in another sample, the degree of collinearity between the two variables is not that strong, obviously, a forecast based on Eq. (8.8) may be of little value.

On the other hand, if the objective of the study is not only prediction but also reliable estimation of the individual parameters of the chosen model, then serious collinearity may be bad, because we have seen that it leads to large standard errors of the estimators. However, as noted earlier, if the objective of the study is to estimate a group of coefficients (e.g., the sum or difference of two coefficients) fairly accurately, this can be done even in the presence of multicollinearity. In this case multicollinearity may not be a problem. Thus, in Eq. (8.7) the

[13]G. S. Maddala, *Introduction to Econometrics,* Macmillan, New York, 1988, p. 226. However, Maddala also says that "if R_i^2 is low, we would be better off."
[14]For a simple discussion of the condition index, see Gujarati and Porter, *Basic Econometrics,* 5th ed., McGraw-Hill, New York, 2009, pp. 339–340.

slope coefficient of -2.1576 is an estimate of $(A_2 - 2A_3)$ (see Eq. [8.6]), which can be measured accurately by the usual OLS procedure, although neither A_2 nor A_3 can be estimated individually.

There may be some "happy" situations where despite high collinearity the estimated R^2 and most individual regression coefficients are statistically significant on the basis of the usual t test at the conventional level of significance, such as 5%. As Johnston notes:

> This can arise if individual coefficients happen to be numerically well in excess of the true value, so that the effect still shows up in spite of the inflated standard error and/or because the true value itself is so large that even an estimate on the downside still shows up as significant.[15]

Before moving on, let us take time out to consider a concrete economic example illustrating several points discussed so far in this chapter.

8.7 AN EXTENDED EXAMPLE: THE DEMAND FOR CHICKENS IN THE UNITED STATES, 1960 TO 1982

Table 7-8 (found on the textbook's Web site) of Problem 7.17 gave data on the per capita consumption of chickens (Y), per capita real (i.e., adjusted for inflation) disposable income (X_2), the real retail price of chicken (X_3), the real retail price of pork (X_4), and the real retail price of beef (X_5) for the United States for the period 1960 to 1982.

Since in theory the demand for a commodity is generally a function of the real income of the consumer, the real price of the product, and real prices of competing or complementary products, the following demand function was estimated: The dependent variable (Y) is the natural log of per capita consumption of chickens in pounds.

Explanatory variable	Coefficient	Standard error (se)	t ratio	p value
Constant	2.1898	0.1557	14.063	0.0000
ln X_2	0.3426	0.0833	4.1140	0.0003
ln X_3	−0.5046	0.1109	−4.550	0.0001
ln X_4	0.1486	0.0997	1.4903	0.0767
ln X_5	0.0911	0.1007	0.9046	0.1878
$R^2 = 0.9823$;	$\bar{R}^2 = 0.9784$			

(8.15)

Since we have fitted a log-linear demand function, all slope coefficients are partial elasticities of Y with respect to the appropriate X variable. Thus, the income elasticity of demand is about 0.34 percent, the own-price elasticity of demand is about -0.50, the cross-(pork) price elasticity of demand is about 0.15, and the cross-(beef) price elasticity of demand is about 0.09.

---

[15]J. Johnston, *Econometric Methods,* 3rd ed., McGraw-Hill, New York, 1984, p. 249.

As the previous results show, individually the income and own-price elasticity of demand are statistically significant, but the two cross-price elasticities are not. Incidentally, note that chicken is not a luxury consumption item since the income elasticity is less than 1. The demand for chicken with respect to its own price is price inelastic because, in absolute terms, the elasticity coefficient is less than 1.

Although the two cross-price elasticities are positive, suggesting that the other two meats are competing with chicken, they are not statistically significant. Thus, it would seem that the demand for chicken is not affected by the variation in the prices of pork and beef. But this might be a hasty conclusion, for we have to guard against the possibility of multicollinearity. Let us therefore consider some of the multicollinearity diagnostics discussed in Section 8.5.

Collinearity Diagnostics for the Demand Function for Chickens (Equation [8.15])

The Correlation Matrix Table 8-3 gives the pairwise correlations among the (logs of the) four explanatory variables. As this table shows, the pairwise correlations between the explanatory variables are uniformly high; about 0.98 between the log of real income and the log of the price of beef, about 0.95 between the logs of pork and beef prices, about 0.91 between the log of real income and the log price of chicken, etc. Although such high pairwise correlations are no guarantee that our demand function suffers from the collinearity problem, the possibility exists.

The Auxiliary Regressions This seems to be confirmed when we regress each explanatory variable on the remaining explanatory variables, which can be seen from the results presented in Table 8-4. As this table shows, all regressions in this table have R^2 values in excess of 0.94; the F test shown in Eq. (4.50) shows that all these R^2's are statistically significant (see Problem 8.24), suggesting that each explanatory variable in the regression (8.15) is highly collinear with the other explanatory variables.

TABLE 8-3 PAIRWISE CORRELATIONS BETWEEN EXPLANATORY VARIABLES OF EQUATION (8.15)

	$\ln X_2$	$\ln X_3$	$\ln X_4$	$\ln X_5$
$\ln X_2$	1	0.9072	0.9725	0.9790
$\ln X_3$	0.9072	1	0.9468	0.9331
$\ln X_4$	0.9725	0.9468	1	0.9543
$\ln X_5$	0.9790	0.9331	0.9543	1

Note: The correlation matrix is symmetrical. Thus, the correlation between $\ln X_4$ and $\ln X_3$ is the same as that between $\ln X_3$ and $\ln X_4$.

TABLE 8-4   AUXILIARY REGRESSIONS

$$\ln X_2 = \underset{t=}{0.9460} \ \underset{(2.5564)}{} - \ \underset{(-3.4903)}{0.8324 \ln X_3} + \ \underset{(5.6590)}{0.9483 \ln X_4} + \ \underset{(6.7847)}{1.0176 \ln X_5}$$
$$R^2 = 0.9846$$

$$\ln X_3 = \underset{t=}{1.2332} \ \underset{(8.0053)}{} - \ \underset{(-3.4903)}{0.4692 \ln X_2} + \ \underset{(4.8652)}{0.6694 \ln X_4} + \ \underset{(3.7848)}{0.5955 \ln X_5}$$
$$R^2 = 0.9428$$

$$\ln X_4 = \underset{t=}{-1.0127} \ \underset{(-3.7107)}{} + \ \underset{(5.6590)}{0.6618 \ln X_2} + \ \underset{(4.8652)}{0.8286 \ln X_3} - \ \underset{(-2.2879)}{0.4695 \ln X_5}$$
$$R^2 = 0.9759$$

$$\ln X_5 = \underset{t=}{-0.7057} \ \underset{(-2.2362)}{} + \ \underset{(6.7847)}{0.6956 \ln X_2} + \ \underset{(3.7848)}{0.7219 \ln X_3} - \ \underset{(-2.2870)}{0.4598 \ln X_4}$$
$$R^2 = 0.9764$$

Therefore, it is quite possible that in the regression (8.15) we did not find the coefficients of the pork and beef price variables individually statistically significant. But this is all in accord with the theoretical consequences of high multicollinearity discussed earlier. It is interesting that despite high collinearity, the coefficients of the real income and own-price variables turned out to be statistically significant. This may very well be due to the fact mentioned by Johnston in footnote 15.

As this example shows, we must be careful about judging the individual significance of an explanatory variable in the presence of a high degree of collinearity. We will return to this example in the following section when we consider remedial measures for multicollinearity.

8.8 WHAT TO DO WITH MULTICOLLINEARITY: REMEDIAL MEASURES

Suppose on the basis of one or more of the diagnostic tests discussed in Section 8.5 that we find a particular problem is plagued by multicollinearity. What solution(s), if any, can be used to reduce the severity of the collinearity problem, if not eliminate it completely? Unfortunately, as in the case of collinearity diagnostics, there is no surefire remedy; there are only a few rules of thumb. This is so because multicollinearity is a feature of a particular sample and not necessarily a feature of the population. Besides, despite near collinearity, OLS estimators still retain their BLUE property. It is true that one or more regression coefficients can be individually statistically insignificant or that some of them can have the wrong signs. If the researcher is bent on reducing the severity of the collinearity problem, then he or she may try one or more of the following methods, keeping in mind that if the particular sample is "ill-conditioned," there is not much that can be done. With this caveat, let us consider the various remedies that have been discussed in the econometric literature.

Dropping a Variable(s) from the Model

Faced with severe multicollinearity, the simplest solution might seem to be to drop one or more of the collinear variables. Thus, in our demand function for chickens, the regression (8.15), since the three price variables are highly correlated, why not simply drop, say, the pork and beef price variables from the model?

But this remedy can be worse than the disease (multicollinearity). When formulating an economic model, such as the regression (8.15), we base the model on some theoretical considerations. In our example, following economic theory, we expect all three prices to have some effect on the demand for chicken since the three meat products are to some extent competing products. Therefore, economically speaking, the regression (8.15) is an appropriate demand function. Unfortunately, in our regression results based on the particular sample data given in Table 7-8 we were unable to detect the separate influence of the prices of pork and beef on the quantity of chicken demanded. But dropping those variables from the model will lead to what is known as **model specification error,** a topic that we discussed in Chapter 7. As we saw, if we drop a variable from a model simply to eliminate the collinearity problem and to estimate a model without that variable, the estimated parameters of the reduced model may turn out to be biased. To give some idea about this bias, let us present the results of the demand function for chickens without the pork and beef price variables:

$$\widehat{\ln Y} = 2.0328 + 0.4515 \ln X_2 - 0.3722 \ln X_3$$
$$t = (17.497) \quad (18.284) \quad (-5.8647) \tag{8.16}$$
$$R^2 = 0.9801; \overline{R}^2 = 0.9781$$

As these results show, compared to the regression (8.15), the income elasticity has gone up but the own-price elasticity, in absolute value, has declined. In other words, estimated coefficients of the reduced model seem to be biased.

As this discussion indicates, there may be a trade-off involved. In reducing the severity of the collinearity problem, we may be obtaining biased estimates of the coefficients retained in the model. *The best practical advice is not to drop a variable from an economically viable model just because the collinearity problem is serious.* Whether a chosen model is economically correct is, of course, an important issue, and we have listed in Chapter 7 the attributes of a good model. In passing, note that in regression (8.15) the t value of the pork price coefficient was in excess of 1. Therefore, following our discussion in Chapter 4, if we drop this variable from the model, the adjusted R^2 will decrease, which is the case in the present instance.

Acquiring Additional Data or a New Sample

Since multicollinearity is a sample feature, it is possible that in another sample involving the same variables, collinearity may not be as serious as in the first sample. The important practical question is whether we can obtain another sample, for collection of data can be costly.

Sometimes just acquiring additional data—increasing the sample size—can reduce the severity of the collinearity problem. This can be seen easily from formulas (8.12) and (8.13). For example, in the formula

$$\text{var}(b_3) = \frac{\sigma^2}{\sum x_{3i}^2 \left(1 - R_2^2\right)} \qquad (8.13)$$

for a given σ^2 and R^2, if the sample size of X_3 increases, $\sum x_{3i}^2$ will generally increase (Why?), as a result of which the variance of b_3 will tend to decrease, and with it the standard error of b_3.

As an illustration, consider the following regression of consumption expenditure (Y) on income (X_2) and wealth (X_3) based on 10 observations:[16]

$$\hat{Y}_i = 24.337 + 0.87164 X_{2i} - 0.0349 X_{3i}$$

$$\text{se} = (6.2801) \quad (0.31438) \qquad (0.0301) \qquad\qquad (8.17)$$

$$t = (3.875) \quad (2.7726) \qquad (-1.1595) \qquad R^2 = 0.9682$$

This regression shows that the wealth coefficient is not statistically significant, say, at the 5% level.

But when the sample size is increased to 40 observations, the following results are obtained:

$$\hat{Y}_i = 2.0907 + 0.7299 X_{2i} + 0.0605 X_{3i}$$

$$t = (0.8713) \quad (6.0014) \qquad (2.0641) \qquad R^2 = 0.9672 \qquad (8.18)$$

Now the wealth coefficient is statistically significant at the 5% level.

Of course, as in the case of obtaining a new sample, getting additional data on variables already in the sample may not be feasible because of cost and other considerations. But if these constraints are not very prohibitive, by all means this remedy is certainly feasible.

Rethinking the Model

Sometimes a model chosen for empirical analysis is not carefully thought out—maybe some important variables are omitted, or maybe the functional form of the model is incorrectly chosen. Thus, in our demand function for chicken, instead of the log-linear specification, the demand function is probably linear in variables (LIV). It is possible that in the LIV specification the extent of collinearity may not be as high as in the log-linear specification.

---

[16]I am indebted to Albert Zucker for providing the results given in regressions (8.17) and (8.18).

Returning to the demand function for chicken, we fitted the LIV model to the data given in Table 7-8, with the following results:

$$\hat{Y} = 37.232 - 0.00501X_2 - 0.6112X_3 + 0.1984X_4 + 0.0695X_5$$

$$t = (10.015)(1.0241) \qquad (-3.7530) \qquad (3.1137) \qquad (1.3631) \qquad \textbf{(8.19)}$$

$$R^2 = 0.9426;\ \overline{R}^2 = 0.9298$$

Compared to the regression (8.15), we now observe that in the LIV specification, the income coefficient is statistically insignificant but the pork price coefficient is statistically significant. What accounts for this change? Perhaps there is a high degree of collinearity between the income and the price variables. As a matter of fact, we found out from Table 8-4 that this was the case. As noted earlier, in the presence of a high degree of collinearity it is not possible to estimate a single regression coefficient too precisely (i.e., with a smaller standard error).

Prior Information about Some Parameters

Sometimes a particular phenomenon, such as a demand function, is investigated time and again. From prior studies it is possible that we can have some knowledge of the values of one or more parameters. This knowledge can be profitably used in the current sample. To be specific, let us suppose a demand function for widgets was estimated in the past and it was found that the income coefficient had a value of 0.9, which was statistically significant. But in the data of Table 8-1, as previously seen, we could not assess the individual impact of earnings (a measure of income) on the quantity demanded. If there is reason to believe that the past value of the income coefficient of 0.9 has not changed much, we could reestimate Eq. (8.8) as follows:

$$\text{Quantity} = B_1 + B_2\,\text{price} + B_3\,\text{earnings} + u_i$$

$$= B_1 + B_2\,\text{price} + 0.9\,\text{earnings} + u_i \qquad \textbf{(8.20)}$$

$$\text{Quantity} - 0.9\,\text{earnings} = B_1 + B_2\,\text{price} + u_i$$

where use is made of the prior information that $B_3 = 0.9$.

Assuming that the prior information is correct, we have resolved the collinearity problem, for on the right-hand side of Equation (8.20) we now have only one explanatory variable and no question of collinearity arises. To run Eq. (8.20), we only have to subtract from the quantity observation 0.9 times the corresponding earnings observation and treat the resulting difference as the dependent variable and regress it on price.[17]

---

[17]Note that multicollinearity is often encountered in times series data because economic variables tend to move with the business cycle. Here information from cross-sectional studies might be used to estimate one or more parameters in the models based on time series data.

Although an intuitively appealing method, the crux of the method lies in ob-taining extraneous, or prior, information, which is not always possible. But, more critically, even if we can obtain such information, to assume that the prior information continues to hold in the sample under study may be a "tall" as-sumption. Of course, if the income effect is not expected to vary considerably from sample to sample, and if we do have prior information on the income coefficient, this remedial measure can sometimes be employed.

Transformation of Variables

Occasionally, transformation of variables included in the model can minimize, if not solve, the problem of collinearity. For example, in a study of the aggregate consumption expenditure in the United States as a function of aggregate in-come and aggregate wealth we might express aggregate consumption expendi-ture on a per capita basis, that is, per capita consumption expenditure as a func-tion of per capita income and per capita wealth. It is possible that if there is serious collinearity in the aggregate consumption function, it may not be so se-vere in the per capita consumption function. Of course, there is no guarantee that such a transformation will always help, leaving aside for the moment the question of whether the aggregate or per capita consumption function to begin with is the appropriate model.

As an example of how a simple transformation of variables can reduce the severity of collinearity, consider the following regression based on the U.S. data for 1965 to 1980:[18]

$$\hat{Y}_t = -108.20 + 0.045X_{2t} + 0.931X_{3t}$$

$$t = \text{N.A.} \qquad (1.232) \qquad (1.844) \qquad R^2 = 0.9894$$

(8.21)

where N.A. = not available

Y = imports ($, in billions)

X_2 = the GNP ($, in billions)

X_3 = the Consumer Price Index (CPI)

In theory, imports are positively related to the GNP (a measure of income) and domestic prices.

The regression results show that neither the income nor the price coefficient is *individually* statistically significant at the 5% level (two-tailed).[19] But on the basis of the F test, we can easily reject the null hypothesis that the two (partial)

---

[18]See Dominick Salvatore, *Managerial Economics,* McGraw-Hill, New York, 1989, pp. 156–157. Notation is adapted.

[19]But note that the price coefficient is significant at the 5% level on the basis of the one-tailed t test.

slope coefficients are jointly equal to zero (check this out), strongly suggesting that the regression (8.21) is plagued by the collinearity problem. To resolve collinearity, Salvatore obtained the following regression:

$$\frac{\hat{Y}_t}{X_{3t}} = -1.39 + 0.202\frac{X_{2t}}{X_{3t}}$$

(8.22)

$$t = \text{N.A.} \qquad (12.22) \qquad R^2 = 0.9142$$

where N.A. = not available. This regression shows that real imports are statistically significantly positively related to real income, the estimated t value being highly significant. Thus, the "trick" of converting the nominal variables into "real" variables (i.e., transforming the original variables) has apparently eliminated the collinearity problem.[20]

Other Remedies

The preceding remedies are only suggestive. There are several other remedies suggested in the literature, such as combining time series and cross-sectional data, **factor** or **principal component analysis** and **ridge regression.** But a full discussion of these topics would not only take us far afield, it would also require statistical knowledge that is way beyond that assumed in this text.

8.9   SUMMARY

An important assumption of the classical linear regression model is that there is no exact linear relationship(s), or multicollinearity, among explanatory variables. Although cases of exact multicollinearity are rare in practice, situations of near exact or high multicollinearity occur frequently. In practice, therefore, the term *multicollinearity* refers to situations where two or more variables can be highly linearly related.

The consequences of multicollinearity are as follows. In cases of perfect multicollinearity we cannot estimate the individual regression coefficients or their standard errors. In cases of high multicollinearity individual regression coefficients can be estimated and the OLS estimators retain their BLUE property. But the standard errors of one or more coefficients tend to be large in relation to their coefficient values, thereby reducing t values. As a result, based on estimated t values, we can say that the coefficient with the low t value is not statistically different from zero. In other words, we cannot assess the *marginal* or

---

[20]Some authors warn against transforming variables routinely in this fashion. For details, see E. Kuh and J. R. Meyer, "Correlation and Regression Estimates When the Data Are Ratios," *Econometrica,* pp. 400–416, October 1955. Also, see G. S. Maddala, *Introduction to Econometrics,* Macmillan, New York, 1988, pp. 172–174.

individual contribution of the variable whose t value is low. Recall that in a multiple regression the slope coefficient of an X variable is the *partial regression coefficient*, which measures the (marginal or individual) effect of that variable on the dependent variable, holding all other X variables constant. However, if the objective of study is to estimate a group of coefficients fairly accurately, this can be done so long as collinearity is not perfect.

In this chapter we considered several methods of detecting multicollinearity, pointing out their pros and cons. We also discussed the various remedies that have been proposed to solve the problem of multicollinearity and noted their strengths and weaknesses.

Since multicollinearity is a feature of a given sample, we cannot foretell which method of detecting multicollinearity or which remedial measure will work in any given concrete situation.

KEY TERMS AND CONCEPTS

The key terms and concepts introduced in this chapter are

Perfect and imperfect collinearity
a) near or very high multicollinearity
b) perfectly linearly related
c) perfect collinearity or multicollinearity
d) near perfect linear relationship
Partial correlation coefficient
Subsidiary regression or auxiliary regression
Variance inflation factor (VIF)

Remedial measures for multicollinearity
a) dropping variables; model specification error
b) acquiring a new sample (or additional data)
c) rethinking the model
d) extraneous, or prior, information
e) transformation of variables
f) other—factor or principal component analysis; ridge regression

QUESTIONS

8.1. What is meant by collinearity? And by multicollinearity?
8.2. What is the difference between perfect and imperfect multicollinearity?
8.3. You include the subject's height, measured in inches, and the same subject's height measured in feet in a regression of weight on height. Explain intuitively why ordinary least squares (OLS) cannot estimate the regression coefficients in such a regression.
8.4. Consider the model

$$Y_i = B_1 + B_2 X_i + B_3 X_i^2 + B_4 X_i^3 + u_i$$

where Y = the total cost of production and X = the output. Since X^2 and X^3 are functions of X, there is perfect collinearity. Do you agree? Why or why not?

8.5. Refer to Equations (4.21), (4.22), (4.25), and (4.27). Let $x_{3i} = 2x_{2i}$. Show why it is impossible to estimate these equations.

8.6. What are the theoretical consequences of imperfect multicollinearity?

8.7. What are the practical consequences of imperfect multicollinearity?

8.8. What is meant by the variance inflation factor (VIF)? From the formula (8.14), can you tell the least possible and the highest possible value of the VIF?

8.9. Fill in the gaps in the following sentences:

  a. In cases of near multicollinearity, the standard errors of regression coefficients tend to be _____ and the t ratios tend to be _____.

  b. In cases of perfect multicollinearity, OLS estimators are _____ and their variances are _____.

  c. Ceteris paribus, the higher the VIF is, the higher the _____ of OLS estimators will be.

8.10. State with reasons whether the following statements are true or false:

  a. Despite perfect multicollinearity, OLS estimators are best linear unbiased estimators (BLUE).

  b. In cases of high multicollinearity, it is not possible to assess the individual significance of one or more partial regression coefficients.

  c. If an auxiliary regression shows that a particular R_i^2 is high, there is definite evidence of high collinearity.

  d. High pairwise correlations do not necessarily suggest that there is high multicollinearity.

  e. Multicollinearity is harmless if the objective of the analysis is prediction only.

8.11. In data involving economic time series such as unemployment, money supply, interest rate, or consumption expenditure, multicollinearity is usually suspected. Why?

8.12. Consider the following model:

$$Y_t = B_1 + B_2X_t + B_3X_{t-1} + B_4X_{t-2} + B_3X_{t-3} + u_t$$

where Y = the consumption
$\quad\quad X$ = the income
$\quad\quad t$ = the time

This model states that consumption expenditure at time t is a linear function of income not only at time t but also of income in three previous time periods. Such models are called *distributed lag models* and represent what are called *dynamic models* (i.e., models involving change over time).

  a. Would you expect multicollinearity in such models and why?

  b. If multicollinearity is suspected, how would you get rid of it?

PROBLEMS

8.13. Consider the following set of hypothetical data:

Y:	−10	−8	−6	−4	−2	0	2	4	6	8	10
X_2:	1	2	3	4	5	6	7	8	9	10	11
X_3:	1	3	5	7	9	11	13	15	17	19	21

Suppose you want to do a multiple regression of Y on X_2 and X_3.

a. Can you estimate the parameters of this model? Why or why not?

b. If not, which parameter or combination of parameters can you estimate?

8.14. You are given the annual data in Table 8-5 for the United States for the period 1971 to 1986. Consider the following aggregate demand function for passenger cars:

$$\ln Y_i = B_1 + B_2 \ln X_{2t} + B_3 \ln X_{3t} + B_4 \ln X_{4t} + B_5 \ln X_{5t} + B_6 \ln X_{6t} + u_t$$

where ln = the natural log

a. What is the rationale for the introduction of both price indexes X_2 and X_3?

b. What might be the rationale for the introduction of the "employed civilian labor force" (X_6) in the demand function?

c. How would you interpret the various partial slope coefficients?

d. Obtain OLS estimates of the preceding model.

8.15. Continue with Problem 8.14. Is there multicollinearity in the previous problem? How do you know?

8.16. If there is collinearity in Problem 8.14, estimate the various auxiliary regressions and find out which of the X variables are highly collinear.

TABLE 8-5   DEMAND FOR NEW PASSENGER CARS IN THE UNITED STATES, 1971 TO 1986

Year	Y	X_2	X_3	X_4	X_5	X_6
1971	10227	112.0	121.3	776.8	4.89	79367
1972	10872	111.0	125.3	839.6	4.55	82153
1973	11350	111.1	133.1	949.8	7.38	85064
1974	8775	117.5	147.7	1038.4	8.61	86794
1975	8539	127.6	161.2	1142.8	6.16	85846
1976	9994	135.7	170.5	1252.6	5.22	88752
1977	11046	142.9	181.5	1379.3	5.50	92017
1978	11164	153.8	195.4	1551.2	7.78	96048
1979	10559	166.0	217.4	1729.3	10.25	98824
1980	8979	179.3	246.8	1918.0	11.28	99303
1981	8535	190.2	272.4	2127.6	13.73	100397
1982	7980	197.6	289.1	2261.4	11.20	99526
1983	9179	202.6	298.4	2428.1	8.69	100834
1984	10394	208.5	311.1	2670.6	9.65	105005
1985	11039	215.2	322.2	2841.1	7.75	107150
1986	11450	224.4	328.4	3022.1	6.31	109597

Notes: Y = New passenger cars sold (thousands), seasonally unadjusted.
X_2 = New cars Consumer Price Index (1967 = 100), seasonally unadjusted.
X_3 = Consumer Price Index, all items, all urban consumers (1967 = 100), seasonally unadjusted.
X_4 = Personal disposable income (PDI) ($, in billions), unadjusted for seasonal variation.
X_5 = Interest rate (percent), finance company paper placed directly.
X_6 = Employed civilian labor force (thousands), unadjusted for seasonal variation.
Source: Business Statistics, 1986, a Supplement to the *Current Survey of Business,* U.S. Department of Commerce.

8.17. Continuing with the preceding problem, if there is severe collinearity, which variable would you drop and why? If you drop one or more X variables, what type of error are you likely to commit?

8.18. After eliminating one or more X variables, what is your final demand function for passenger cars? In what ways is this "final" model better than the initial model that includes all X variables?

8.19. What other variables do you think might better explain the demand for automobiles in the United States?

8.20. In a study of the production function of the United Kingdom bricks, pottery, glass, and cement industry for the period 1961 to 1981, R. Leighton Thomas obtained the following results:[21]

1. $\log Q = -5.04 + 0.887 \log K + 0.893 \log H$

   $\text{se} = \quad (1.40) \quad (0.087) \qquad (0.137) \qquad\qquad\qquad R^2 = 0.878$

2. $\log Q = -8.57 + 0.0272t + 0.460 \log K + 1.285 \log H$

   $\text{se} = \quad (2.99) \ (0.0204) \quad (0.333) \qquad (0.324) \qquad R^2 = 0.889$

where Q = the index of production at constant factor cost
$\qquad K$ = the gross capital stock at 1975 replacement cost
$\qquad H$ = hours worked
$\qquad t$ = the time trend, a proxy for technology

The figures in parentheses are the estimated standard errors.
   a. Interpret both regressions.
   b. In regression (1) verify that each partial slope coefficient is statistically significant at the 5% level.
   c. In regression (2) verify that the coefficients of t and $\log K$ are individually insignificant at the 5% level.
   d. What might account for the insignificance of $\log K$ variable in Model 2?
   e. If you were told that the correlation coefficient between t and $\log K$ is 0.980, what conclusion would you draw?
   f. Even if t and $\log K$ are individually insignificant in Model 2, would you accept or reject the hypothesis that in Model 2 all partial slopes are simultaneously equal to zero? Which test would you use?
   g. In Model 1, what are the returns to scale?

8.21. Establish Eqs. (8.12) and (8.13). (*Hint:* Find out the coefficient of correlation between X_2 and X_3, say, r^2_{23}.)

8.22. You are given the hypothetical data in Table 8-6 on weekly consumption expenditure (Y), weekly income (X_2), and wealth (X_3), all in dollars.
   a. Do an OLS regression of Y on X_2 and X_3.
   b. Is there collinearity in this regression? How do you know?
   c. Do separate regressions of Y on X_2 and Y on X_3. What do these regressions reveal?
   d. Regress X_3 on X_2. What does this regression reveal?
   e. If there is severe collinearity, would you drop one of the X variables? Why or why not?

[21]See R. Leighton Thomas, *Introductory Econometrics: Theory and Applications*, Longman, London, 1985, pp. 244–246.

TABLE 8-6   HYPOTHETICAL DATA ON CONSUMPTION
EXPENDITURE (Y), WEEKLY INCOME (X_2),
AND WEALTH (X_3)

Y	X_2	X_3
70	80	810
65	100	1009
90	120	1273
95	140	1425
110	160	1633
115	180	1876
120	200	2252
140	220	2201
155	240	2435
150	260	2686

8.23. Utilizing the data given in Table 8-1, estimate Eq. (8.20) and compare your
results.

8.24. Check that all R^2 values in Table 8-4 are statistically significant.

8.25. Refer to Problem 7.19 and the data given in Table 7-9. How would your
answer to this problem change knowing what you now know about multicollinearity? Present the necessary regression results.

8.26. Refer to Problem 2.16. Suppose you regress ASP on GPA, GMAT, acceptance
rate (%), tuition, and recruiter rating. A priori, would you face the multicollinearity problem? If so, how would you resolve it? Show all the necessary
regression results.

8.27. Based on the quarterly data for the U.K. for the period 1990-1Q to 1998-2Q,
the following results were obtained by Asteriou and Hall.[22] The dependent
variable in these regressions is Log(IM) = logarithm of imports (t ratios in
parentheses).

Explanatory variable	Model 1	Model 2	Model 3
Intercept	0.6318	0.2139	0.6857
	(1.8348)	(0.5967)	(1.8500)
Log(GDP)	1.9269	1.9697	2.0938
	(11.4117)	(12.5619)	(12.1322)
Log(CPI)	0.2742	1.0254	—
	(1.9961)	(3.1706)	0.1195
Log(PPI)	—	−0.7706	0.1195
		(−2.5248)	(0.8787)
Adjusted-R^2	0.9638	0.9692	0.9602

Notes: GDP = gross domestic product
CPI = Consumer Price Index
PPI = producer price index

[22]See Dimitrios Asteriou and Stephen Hall, *Applied Econometrics: A Modern Approach,*
Palgrave/Macmillan, New York, 2007, Chapter 6. Note that these results are summarized from various tables given in that chapter.

a. Interpret each equation.

b. In Model 1, which drops Log(PPI), the coefficient of Log(CPI) is positive and significant at about the 5% level. Does this make economic sense?

c. In Model 3, which drops Log(CPI), the coefficient of Log(PPI) is positive but statistically insignificant. Does this make economic sense?

d. Model 2 includes the logs of both price variables and their coefficients are individually statistically significant. However, the coefficient of Log(CPI) is positive and that of Log(PPI) is negative. How would you rationalize this result?

e. Do you think multicollinearity is the reason why some of these results are conflicting? Justify your answer.

f. If you were told that the correlation between PPI and CPI is 0.9819, would that suggest that there is a multicollinearity problem?

g. Of the three models given above, which would you choose and why?

8.28. Table 8-7 on the textbook's Web site gives data on imports, GDP, and the Consumer Price Index (CPI) for the United States over the period 1975–2005. You are asked to consider the following model:

$$\ln Imports_t = \beta_1 + \beta_2 \ln GDP_t + \beta_3 \ln CPI_t + u_t$$

a. Estimate the parameters of this model using the data given in the table.

b. Do you suspect that there is multicollinearity in the data?

c. Regress: (1) $\ln Imports_t = A_1 + A_2 \ln GDP_t$
              (2) $\ln Imports_t = B_1 + B_2 \ln CPI_t$
              (3) $\ln GDP_t = C_1 + C_2 \ln CPI_t$

On the basis of these regressions, what can you say about the nature of multicollinearity in the data?

d. Suppose there is multicollinearity in the data but $\hat{\beta}_2$ and $\hat{\beta}_3$ are individually significant at the 5% level and the overall F test is also significant. In this case, should we worry about the collinearity problem?

8.29. Table 8-8 on the textbook's Web site gives data on new passenger cars sold in the United States as a function of several variables.

a. Develop a suitable linear or log-linear model to estimate a demand function for automobiles in the United States.

b. If you decide to include all the regressors given in the table as explanatory variables, do you expect to face the multicollinearity problem? Why?

c. If you do expect to face the multicollinearity problem, how will you go about resolving the problem? State your assumptions clearly and show all calculations.

8.30. As cheese ages, several chemical processes take place that determine the taste of the final product. Table 8-9 on the textbook's Web site contains data on the concentrations of various chemicals in 30 samples of mature cheddar cheese and a subjective measure of taste for each sample. The variables *Acetic* and H2S are the natural logarithm of the concentration of acetic acid and hydrogen sulfide, respectively. The variable *lactic* has not been log-transformed.

a. Draw a scatterplot of the four variables.

b. Do a bivariate regression of taste on acetic and H2S and interpret your results.

     c. Do a bivariate regression of taste on lactic and H2S. How do interpret the results?

     d. Do a multiple regression of taste on acetic, H2S, and lactic. Interpret your results.

     e. Knowing what you know about multicollinearity, how would you decide among these regressions?

     f. What overall conclusions can you draw from your analysis?

8.31. Table 8-10 on the textbook's Web site gives data on the average salary of top managers (in thousands of Dutch guilders), profit (in millions of Dutch guilders), and turnover (in millions of Dutch guilders) for 84 of the largest firms in the Netherlands.[23] Let Y = salary, X_2 = profit, and X_3 = turnover.

     a. Estimate the following regression:

$$\ln Y_i = B_1 + B_2 \ln X_2 + B_3 \ln X_3 + u_i$$

     where ln = natural logarithm.

     b. Are all the slope coefficients *individually* statistically significant at the 5% level?

     c. Are the slope coefficients together statistically significant at the 5% level? Which test would you use and why?

     d. If the answer to (*b*) is yes, and the answer to (*a*) is no, what may be the reason(s)?

     e. If you suspect multicollinearity, how would you find that out? Which test(s) would you use?

     Note: Show all your calculations.

---

[23]These data are from Christiaan Heij, Paul de Boer, Philip Hans Franses, Teun Kloek, and Herman K. van Dijk, *Econometric Methods with Applications in Business and Economics,* Oxford University Press, 2004. See their Web site at **www.oup.com/uk/economics/cws**. The original data are for 100 large firms, but we have included the data for 84 firms because for 16 firms, data on one or more variables were not available.

CHAPTER 9

HETEROSCEDASTICITY: WHAT HAPPENS IF THE ERROR VARIANCE IS NONCONSTANT?

An important assumption of the classical linear regression model (CLRM) is that the disturbances u_i entering the population regression function (PRF) are *homoscedastic;* that is, they all have the same variance, σ^2. If this is not the case—if the variance of u_i is σ_i^2, indicating that it is varying from observation to observation (notice the subscript on σ^2)—we have the situation of *heteroscedasticity,* or *unequal,* or *nonconstant, variance.*

However, the assumption of homoscedasticity is imposed by the CLRM. There is no guarantee in practice that this assumption will always be fulfilled. Therefore, the major goal of this chapter is to find out what happens if this assumption is not fulfilled. Specifically, we seek answers to the following questions:

1. What is the nature of heteroscedasticity?
2. What are its consequences?
3. How do we detect that it is present in a given situation?
4. What are the remedial measures if heteroscedasticity is a problem?

9.1 THE NATURE OF HETEROSCEDASTICITY

To explain best the difference between homoscedasticity and heteroscedasticity, let us consider a two-variable linear regression model in which the dependent variable Y is personal savings and the explanatory variable X is personal disposable, or after-tax, income (PDI). Now consider the diagrams in Figure 9-1 (cf. Figure 3-2[a] and 3-2[b]).

Figure 9-1(a) shows that as PDI increases, the mean, or average, level of savings also increases, but the variance of savings around its mean value remains the same at all levels of PDI. Recall that the PRF gives the mean, or average, value of the

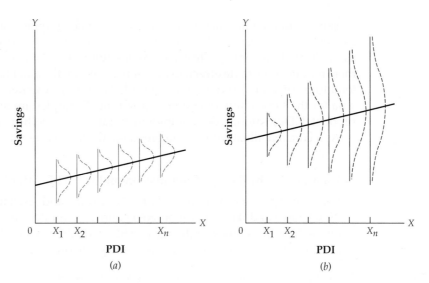

FIGURE 9-1   (*a*) Homoscedasticity; (*b*) heteroscedasticity

dependent variable for given levels of the explanatory variable(s). This is the case of **homoscedasticity,** or **equal variance.** On the other hand, as Figure 9-1(*b*) shows, although the average level of savings increases as the PDI increases, the variance of savings does not remain the same at all levels of PDI. Here it increases with PDI. This is the case of **heteroscedasticity,** or **unequal variance.** Put differently, Figure 9-1(*b*) shows that high-income people, on average, save more than low-income people, but there is also more variability in their savings. This is not only plausible; it is also borne out by a casual glance at U.S. savings and income statistics. After all, there is very little discretionary income left to save for people on the lower rung of the income distribution ladder. Therefore, in a regression of savings on income, error variances (i.e., variance of u_i) associated with high-income families are expected to be greater than those associated with low-income families.

Symbolically, we express heteroscedasticity as

$$E\left(u_i^2\right) = \sigma_i^2 \tag{9.1}$$

Notice again the subscript on σ^2, which is a reminder that the variance of u_i, is no longer constant but varies from observation to observation.

Researchers have observed that heteroscedasticity is usually found in **cross-sectional data** and not in time series data.[1] In cross-sectional data we generally deal with members of a population at *a given point in time,* such as individual

---

[1]This is, strictly speaking, not always true. In the autoregressive conditional heteroscedasticity (ARCH) models, heteroscedasticity can be observed in time series data also. But this is an involved topic and we will not discuss it in this text. For a discussion of the ARCH model, see Gujarati and Porter, *Basic Econometrics,* McGraw-Hill, 5th ed., New York, 2009, pp. 791–796.

consumers or their families; firms; industries; or geographical subdivisions, such as a state, county, or city. Moreover, these members may be of different sizes, such as small, medium, or large firms, or low, medium, or high income. In other words, there may be some **scale effect.** In time series data, on the other hand, the variables tend to be of similar orders of magnitude because researchers generally collect data for the same entity over a period of time. Examples are the gross domestic product (GDP), savings, or unemployment rate, say, over the period 1960 to 2008.

As a concrete illustration of heteroscedasticity, we present two examples.

Example 9.1. Brokerage Commission on the NYSE After Deregulation

Between April and May of 1975 the Securities and Exchange Commission (SEC) abolished the practice of fixed commission rates on stock transactions on the New York Stock Exchange (NYSE) and allowed stockbrokers to charge commission on a competitive basis. Table 9-1 presents data on the average

TABLE 9-1   COMMISSION RATE TRENDS, NEW YORK STOCK EXCHANGE, APRIL 1975–DECEMBER 1978

	X_1	X_2	X_3	X_4
April 1975	59.60	45.70	27.60	15.00
June	54.50	36.80	21.30	12.10
September	51.70	34.50	20.40	11.50
December	48.90	31.90	18.90	10.40
March 1976	50.30	33.80	19.00	10.80
June	50.00	33.40	19.50	10.90
September	46.70	31.10	18.40	10.20
December	47.00	31.20	17.60	10.00
March 1977	44.30	28.80	16.00	9.80
June	43.70	28.10	15.50	9.70
September	40.40	26.10	14.50	9.10
December	40.40	25.40	14.00	8.90
March 1978	40.20	25.00	13.90	8.10
June	43.10	27.00	14.40	8.50
September	42.50	26.90	14.40	8.70
December	40.70	24.50	13.70	7.80

Name	n	Mean	Standard deviation	Variance	Minimum	Maximum
X_1	16	46.500	5.6767	32.225	40.200	59.600
X_2	16	30.637	5.5016	30.268	24.500	45.700
X_3	16	17.444	3.7234	13.864	13.700	27.600
X_4	16	10.094	1.7834	3.1806	7.8000	15.000

Notes: X_1 = Commission rate, cents per share (for 0 to 199 shares)
X_2 = Commission rate, cents per share (for 200 to 299 shares)
X_3 = Commission rate, cents per share (for 1000 to 9999 shares)
X_4 = Commission rate, cents per share (for 10,000+ shares)
Source: S. Tinic and R. West, "The Securities Industry Under Negotiated Brokerage Commissions: Changes in the Structure and Performance of NYSE Member Firms," *The Bell Journal of Economics,* vol. 11, no. 1, Spring 1980.

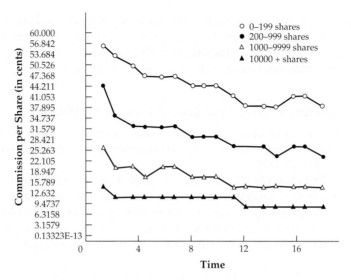

FIGURE 9-2 Commission per share, in cents, NYSE, April 1975 to December 1978
(based on Table 9-1 data)

per share commission (in cents) charged by the brokerage industry to
institutional investors for selected quarterly periods between April 1975 and
December 1978.

Notice two interesting features of this table. There is a downward trend in
the commission rate charged since the deregulation. But, more interestingly,
there is a substantial difference in the average commission charged and the
variance of commission among the four categories of institutional investors
shown in the table. The smallest institutional investors, those with share
transactions in the range of 0 to 199 shares, on average, paid a commission of
46.5 cents per share with a variance of 32.22, whereas the largest institutional
investors paid, on average, a rate of only 10.1 cents per share with a variance
of only 3.18. All this can be seen more vividly in Figure 9-2.

What explains this difference? Obviously, some scale effect seems to be
evident here—the larger the volume of the transaction is, the lower the total
cost of transacting is, and therefore the lower the average cost will be.
Economists would say that there are *economies of scale* in the brokerage industry data given in Table 9-1. (But this may not necessarily be so. See Example 9.8
in Section 9.6.) Even if there are scale economies in the brokerage industry,
why should the variance of the commission rate in the four categories be
different? In other words, why is there heteroscedasticity? To attract the
business of big institutional investors such as pension funds and mutual funds,
brokerage firms compete so intensely among themselves that there is not much
variability in the commission rates they charge. Small institutional investors
may not have the same bargaining clout as large institutions, and hence
have more variability in the commission rates that they pay. These and other
reasons may explain the heteroscedasticity observed in the data of Table 9-1.

Now if we were to develop a regression model to explain the commission rate as a function of the number of share transactions (and other variables), the error variance associated with high-transaction clients would be lower than that associated with low-transaction clients.

Example 9.2. Wage and Related Data for 523 Workers

As an example of purely cross-sectional data with potential for heteroscedasticity, consider the data given in Table 9-2, which is posted on the book's Web site.[2]

Data for 523 workers were collected on several variables, but to keep the illustration simple, in this example we will consider only the relationship between Wage (per hour, $), Education (years of schooling), and Experience (years of work experience). Let us suppose we want to find out how wages behave in relation to education, holding all other variables constant.

$$Wage_i = B_1 + B_2Edu_i + B_3Exper + u_i \qquad (9.2)$$

A priori, we would expect a positive relationship between wages and the two regressors. The results of this regression for our data are as follows:

Dependent Variable: WAGE
Method: Least Squares   (9.3)

Sample: 1 523
Included observations: 523

	Coefficient	Std. Error	t-Statistic	Prob.
C	−4.524472	1.239348	−3.650687	0.0003
EDUC	0.913018	0.082190	11.10868	0.0000
EXPER	0.096810	0.017719	5.463513	0.0000
R-squared	0.194953	Mean dependent var		9.118623
Adjusted R-squared	0.191856	S.D. dependent var		5.143200
S.E. of regression	4.623573	F-statistic		62.96235
Sum squared resid	11116.26	Prob (F-statistic)		0.000000
Durbin-Watson stat	1.867684			

Note: The Durbin-Watson statistic is discussed fully in Chapter 10. It is routinely produced as a part of standard regression output.

These results confirm our prior expectations: Wages are strongly positively related to education as well as work experience. The estimated coefficients of the two regressors are highly significant, assuming the classical assumptions hold.

[2]These data are obtained from **http://lib.stat.edu/datasets/CPS_85_wages** and supplemented from **http://www.economicswebinstitute.org.** The original data included 534 observations, but 11 observations had no work experience and so were dropped.

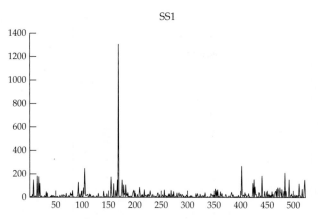

FIGURE 9-3   Squared residuals from regression (9.3)

Since we have data on 523 workers with diverse backgrounds, it is likely that the assumption of homoscedasticity may not hold. If that is the case, the estimated standard errors and t values may not be reliable. To see if this possibility exists, we plot the squared residuals obtained from regression (9.3), first by themselves (Figure 9-3) and then against each regressor (Figures 9-4[a] and [b]).

As Figures 9-4(a) and 9-4(b) show, there is considerable variability in the data, raising the possibility that our regression sufffers from heteroscedasticity.

A cautionary note: It is true that the residuals e_i are not the same thing as the disturbances u_i, although they are proxies. Therefore, from the observed variability of squared e_i we cannot categorically conclude that the variance of u_i is also variable.[3] But as we will show later, in practice we do not observe u_i, and thus we will have to make do with e_i. Therefore, by examining the pattern of e_i^2, we will have to infer something about the pattern of u_i^2. Also keep in mind that we estimate the variance of $u_i\ (= \sigma_u^2)$ as $\dfrac{\sum e_i^2}{n - k}$, where n is the sample size and k is the number of parameters estimated, and this is an unbiased estimate of σ_u^2.

Suppose in our wage regression we believe, say, on the basis of Figures 9-3 and 9-4, that we can have a heteroscedasticity situation. What then? Are the regression results given in the model (9.3), which are based explicitly on the assumption of homoscedasticity, useless?[4] To answer this question, we must find out what happens to the OLS method if there is heteroscedasticity, which is done in the following section.

---

[3]For the relationship between e_i and u_i, see E. Malinvaud, *Statistical Methods of Econometrics,* North-Holland, Amsterdam, 1970, pp. 88–89.

[4]As a practical matter, when running a regression, we generally assume that all assumptions of the CLRM are fulfilled. It is only when we examine the regression results that we begin to look for some clues which might tell us that one or more assumptions of the CLRM may not be tenable. This is not altogether a bad strategy. Why "look a gift horse in the mouth"?

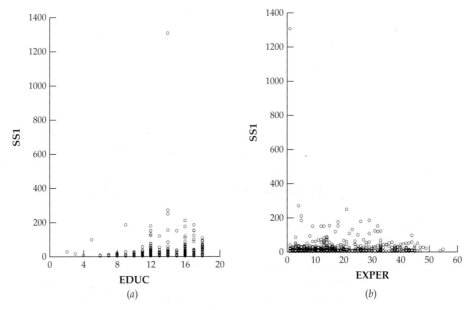

FIGURE 9-4   (a) Squared residuals versus education; (b) Squared residuals versus experience

9.2   CONSEQUENCES OF HETEROSCEDASTICITY

Recall that under the assumptions of the CLRM, ordinary least squares (OLS) estimators are best linear unbiased estimators (BLUE); that is, in the class of linear unbiased estimators least squares estimators have minimum variance—they are efficient. Now assume that all assumptions of CLRM hold except that we drop the assumption of homoscedasticity, allowing for the disturbance variance to be different from observation to observation. The following consequences are stated without proofs:[5]

1. OLS estimators are still linear.
2. They are still unbiased.
3. But they no longer have minimum variance; that is, they are no longer efficient. This is so even in large samples. In short, OLS estimators are no longer BLUE in small as well as in large samples (i.e., asymptotically).
4. The usual formulas to estimate the variances of OLS estimators are generally biased. A priori we cannot tell whether the bias will be positive (upward bias) or negative (downward bias). A positive bias occurs if OLS overestimates the true variances of estimators, and a negative bias occurs if OLS underestimates the true variances of estimators.

---

[5]Some of the proofs and references to other proofs can be found in Gujarati and Porter, *Basic Econometrics*, McGraw-Hill, 5th ed., New York, 2009, Chapter 11.

5. The bias arises from the fact that $\hat{\sigma}^2$, the conventional estimator of true σ^2, namely, $\sum e_i^2/\text{d.f.}$, is no longer an unbiased estimator of σ^2. (*Note:* The d.f. are $[n-2]$ in the two-variable case, $[n-3]$ in the three-variable case, etc.) Recall that $\hat{\sigma}^2$ enters into the calculations of the variances of OLS estimators.

6. As a result, the usual confidence intervals and hypothesis tests based on t and F distributions are unreliable. Therefore, every possibility exists of drawing wrong conclusions if conventional hypothesis-testing procedures are employed.

In short, in the presence of heteroscedasticity, the usual hypothesis-testing routine is not reliable, raising the possibility of drawing misleading conclusions.

Returning to our wage regression (9.3), if we have reason to believe that there is heteroscedasticity (the formal tests for the presence of heteroscedasticity are discussed in Section 9.3), we should be very careful about interpreting the results. In Eq. (9.3) the coefficient of education has a t value of about 11 and the coefficient of experience has a t value of about 5, both of which are "highly" significant. But these values were obtained under classical assumptions. What happens if the error variance is in fact heteroscedastic? As we noted previously, in that case the usual hypothesis-testing routine is not reliable, raising the possibility of drawing misleading conclusions.

As the preceding discussion indicates, heteroscedasticity is potentially a serious problem, for it might destroy the whole edifice of the standard, and so routinely used, OLS estimation and hypothesis-testing procedure. Therefore, it is important in any concrete study, especially one involving cross-sectional data, that we determine whether we have a heteroscedasticity problem.

Before turning to the task of detecting heteroscedasticity, however, we should know, at least intuitively, why OLS estimators are not efficient under heteroscedasticity.

Consider our simple two-variable regression model. Recall from Chapter 2 that in OLS we minimize the residual sum of squares (RSS):

$$\sum e_i^2 = \sum (Y_i - b_1 - b_2 X_i)^2 \qquad (2.13)$$

Now consider Figure 9-5.

This figure shows a hypothetical Y population against selected values of the X variable. As this diagram shows, the variance of each Y (sub) population corresponding to the given X is not the same throughout, suggesting heteroscedasticity. Suppose we choose at random a Y value against each X value. The Y's thus selected are encircled. As Equation (2.13) shows, in OLS each e_i^2 receives the same weight whether it comes from a population with a large variance or a small variance (compare points Y_n and Y_1). This does not seem sensible; ideally, we would like to give more *weight* to observations coming from populations

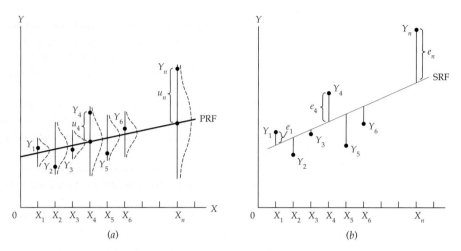

FIGURE 9-5   Hypothetical population and sample showing heteroscedasticity

with smaller variances than those coming from populations with larger variances. This will enable us to estimate the PRF more accurately. And this is precisely what the method of *weighted least squares* (WLS) does, a method we will discuss later.

9.3   DETECTION OF HETEROSCEDASTICITY: HOW DO WE KNOW WHEN THERE IS A HETEROSCEDASTICITY PROBLEM?

Although theoretically it is easy to document the consequences of heteroscedasticity, it is often not so easy to detect it in a concrete situation. This is understandable because σ_i^2 can be known only if we have the entire Y population corresponding to the chosen X's, as in the hypothetical population of our math S.A.T. score example given in Table 2-1. Unfortunately, however, we rarely have the entire population available for study. Most generally, we have a sample of some members of this population corresponding to the given values of the X variables. Typically, what we have is a single value of Y for given values of the X's. And there is no way to determine the variance of the conditional distribution of Y for the given X from a single Y value.[6]

Now we are "between the devil and the deep blue sea." If there is heteroscedasticity and we assume it away, we might be drawing misleading conclusions on the basis of the usual OLS procedure because OLS estimators are not BLUE. But since our data are mostly based on a sample, we have no way of

---

[6]Note that given the X's, the variance of u and the variance of Y are the same. In other words, the conditional variance of u (conditional on the given X's) is the same as the conditional variance of Y, as noted in footnote 3 of Chapter 3.

finding out the true error variance associated with each observation. If we could find out the true σ_i^2, it would be possible to solve the problem of heteroscedasticity, as is shown later in Section 9.4. What should we do?

As in the case of multicollinearity, we have no sure method of detecting heteroscedasticity; we only have several diagnostic tools that may aid us in detecting it. Some of the diagnostics follow.

Nature of the Problem

Often the nature of the problem under consideration suggests whether heteroscedasticity is likely to be present. For example, following the pioneering work of Prais and Houthakker[7] on family budget studies, in which they found that the residual variance around the regression of consumption on income increased with income, it is now generally assumed that in similar studies we can expect heteroscedasticity in the error term. As a matter of fact, in cross-sectional data involving heterogeneous units, heteroscedasticity may be the rule rather than the exception. Thus, in cross-sectional studies involving investment expenditure in relation to sales, the rate of interest, etc., heteroscedasticity is generally expected if small-, medium-, and large-sized firms are sampled together. Similarly, in a cross-sectional study of the average cost of production in relation to the output, heteroscedasticity is likely to be found if small-, medium-, and large-sized firms are included in the sample. (See Example 9.8 in Section 9.6.)

Graphical Examination of Residuals

In applied regression analysis it is always a good practice to examine the residuals obtained from the fitted regression line (or plane), for they may provide useful clues about the adequacy of the fitted model. Sometimes it is helpful to create a **residual plot** of the squared residuals, especially in the context of heteroscedasticity. The squared residuals can be plotted on their own (as in Figure 9-3) or they can be plotted against one or more explanatory variables (as in Figures 9-4[a] and 9-4[b]).

In Figure 9-6, we consider several likely patterns of squared residuals that one may encounter in applied work. Figure 9-6(a) has no discernible systematic pattern between e^2 and X, suggesting that perhaps there is no heteroscedasticity in the data. On the other hand, Figures 9-6(b) to (e) exhibit systematic relationships between the squared residuals and the explanatory variable X. For example, Figure 9-6(c) suggests a linear relationship between the two, whereas Figures 9-6(d) and (e) suggest a quadratic relationship.

---

[7]S. J. Prais and H. S. Houthakker, *The Analysis of Family Budgets,* Cambridge University Press, New York, 1955.

Therefore, if in an application the squared residuals exhibit one of the patterns shown in Figure 9-6(b) to (e), there is a possibility that heteroscedasticity is present in the data.

Keep in mind that the preceding graphical plots are simply diagnostic tools. Once the suspicion of heteroscedasticity is raised, we should proceed more cautiously to make sure that this suspicion is not just a "red herring." Shortly we will present some formal procedures to do exactly that.

Meanwhile we can pose a couple of practical questions. Suppose we have a multiple regression involving, say, four X variables. How do we proceed then? The most straightforward way to proceed is to plot e_i^2 against each X variable. It is possible that the patterns exhibited in Figure 9-6 can hold true of only one of the X variables. Sometimes we can resort to a shortcut. Instead of plotting e_i^2 against each X variable, plot them against $\hat{Y}_i$, the estimated mean value of Y. Since $\hat{Y}_i$ is a linear combination of the X's (Why?), a plot of squared residuals against $\hat{Y}_i$ might exhibit one of the patterns shown in Figures 9-6(b) to (e), suggesting that perhaps heteroscedasticity is present in the data. This avoids the need for plotting the squared residuals against individual X variables, especially if the number of explanatory variables in the model is very large.

Suppose we plot e_i^2 against one or more X variables or against $\hat{Y}_i$, and further suppose the plot suggests heteroscedasticity. What then? In Section 9.4 we

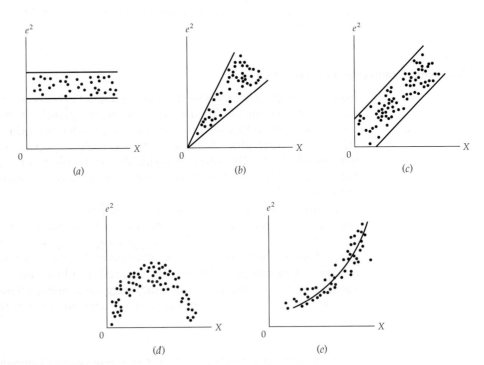

FIGURE 9-6 Hypothetical patterns of e^2

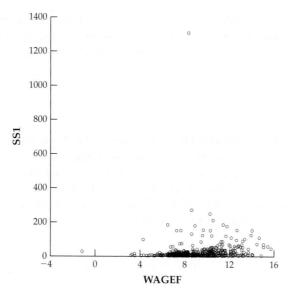

FIGURE 9-7 e_i^2 against estimated wages, wage regression (9.3)

will show how the knowledge that e_i^2 is related to an X variable or to $\hat{Y}_i$ enables us to transform the original data so that in the transformed data there is no heteroscedasticity.

Now let us return to our wage regression (9.3). In Figure 9-7 we plot the squared residuals estimated from regression (9.3) against the estimated wage values (Wagef) from this regression.[8]

This figure probably most closely resembles Figure 9-6(*b*), clearly suggesting that the squared residuals are systematically related to estimated wage values (which are linear combinations of education and experience), again supporting our earlier doubt that regression (9.3) suffers from the heteroscedasticity problem.

Also note that there is one observation (an outlier?) that is quite visible. In a sample of 523 observations, one outlier may not exert undue influence, but in small samples it can. So keep in mind that outliers also may be a cause of heteroscedasticity, especially in small samples.

Park Test[9]

The intuitively and visually appealing graphical test just presented can be formalized. If there is heteroscedasticity, the heteroscedastic variance σ_i^2 may

---

[8]Note that we are plotting e_i^2 and not e_i against X_i or $\hat{Y}_i$ because, as pointed out in Chapters 2 and 3, e_i has zero correlation with both X_i and $\hat{Y}_i$.

[9]R. E. Park, "Estimation with Heteroscedastic Error Terms," *Econometrica,* vol. 34, no. 4, October 1966, p. 888.

be systematically related to one or more explanatory variables. To see if this is the case, we can regress σ_i^2 on one or more of the X variables. For example, in the two-variable model we can run the following regression:

$$\ln \sigma_i^2 = B_1 + B_2 \ln X_i + v_i \qquad \textbf{(9.4)}$$

where v_i is a residual term. This is precisely what Park suggests. The particular functional form (9.4) that he chose was for convenience.

Unfortunately, regression (9.4) is not operational since we do not know the heteroscedastic variance σ_i^2. If we knew it, we could have solved the heteroscedasticity problem easily, as we will show in Section 9.4. Park suggests using e_i as proxies for u_i and running the following regression:

$$\ln e_i^2 = B_1 + B_2 \ln X_i + v_i \qquad \textbf{(9.5)}$$

Instead of regressing the log of the squared residuals on the log of the X variable(s), you can also regress the squared residuals on the X variable, especially if some of the X values are negative. Where do we obtain e_i^2? They are obtained from the original regression, such as the model (9.3).

The **Park test** therefore involves the following steps:

1. Run the original regression despite the heteroscedasticity problem, if any.
2. From this regression, obtain the residuals e_i, square them, and take their logs (most computer programs can do this routinely).
3. Run the regression (9.5) using an explanatory variable in the original model; if there is more than one explanatory variable, run the regression (9.5) against each X variable. Alternatively, run the regression (9.5) against $\hat{Y}_i$, the estimated Y.[10]
4. Test the null hypothesis that $B_2 = 0$; that is, there is no heteroscedasticity. If a statistically significant relationship exists between $\ln e_i^2$ and $\ln X_i$, the null hypothesis of no heteroscedasticity can be rejected, in which case we will have to take some remedial measure(s), which is discussed in Section 9.4.
5. If the null hypothesis is not rejected, then B_1 in the regression (9.5) can be interpreted as giving the value of the common, or homoscedastic, variance, σ^2.

---

[10]The choice of the appropriate functional form to run the regression (9.5) should also be considered. In some cases regressing e_i^2 on X_i might be the appropriate functional form; in some other cases $\ln e_i^2$ may be the appropriate dependent variable.

Example 9.3. Wage Regression and the Park Test

Let us illustrate the Park test with our wage example. Since there are two regressors, education and work experience, we have three options: We can regress wages on education only, or on experience only, or on both variables, as in Eq. (9.3), and obtain the squared residuals from these regressions. We can then regress the respective squared residuals on education only or on experience only or on both. We will use the third option, leaving the other two options for exercises at the end of the chapter.

Regressing squared residuals from Eq. (9.3) on the estimated wage values (Wagef) from this regression, we obtain the following empirical counterpart of the Park test:[11]

Dependent Variable: SS1
Method: Least Squares   (9.6)
Included observations: 523

	Coefficient	Std. Error	t-Statistic	Prob.
C	−10.35965	11.79490	−0.878316	0.3802
WAGEF	3.467020	1.255228	2.762063	0.0059
R-squared	0.014432	Mean dependent var		21.25480
Adjusted R-squared	0.012540	S.D. dependent var		65.53846
S.E. of regression	65.12624	F-statistic		7.628992
Sum squared resid	2209783.	Prob (F-statistic)		0.005947
Durbin-Watson stat	2.026039			

Note: SS1 are squared residuals from regression (9.3) and Wagef are the forecast values of wage from regression (9.3).

Since the Wagef coefficient is statistically significant, it seems that the Park test shows evidence of heteroscedasticity.

Before we accept the results of the Park test, we should note some of the problems associated with the test: The error term in regression (9.6), v_i, may itself be heteroscedastic.[12] In that case, we are back to square one. More testing may be needed before we can conclude that the wage regression (9.3) is free from heteroscedasticity.

Glejser Test[13]

The **Glejser test** is similar in spirit to the Park test. After obtaining residuals e_i from the original model, Glejser suggests regressing the absolute values of e_i, $|e_i|$, on the X variable that is thought to be closely associated with the

---

[11]Since one forecast value of wage from Eq. (9.3) was negative, we cannot use the log transform. We will therefore use squared residuals as the regressand.

[12]We tested the residuals from Eq. (9.6) for heteroscedasticity. On the basis of the Breusch-Pagan test (see Exercise 9.23 and the White test (discussed below) we saw no evidence of heteroscedasticity, but the Glejser test (discussed below) showed that there was heteroscedasticity.

[13]H. Glejser, "A New Test for Heteroscedasticity," *Journal of the American Statistical Association* (JASA), vol. 64, pp. 316–323.

heteroscedastic variance σ_i^2. Some functional forms that he has suggested for this regression are

$$|e_i| = B_1 + B_2 X_i + v_i \tag{9.7}$$

$$|e_i| = B_1 + B_2 \sqrt{X_i} + v_i \tag{9.8}$$

$$|e_i| = B_1 + B_2 \left(\frac{1}{X_i}\right) + v_i \tag{9.9}$$

The null hypothesis in each case is that there is no heteroscedasticity; that is, $B_2 = 0$. If this hypothesis is rejected, there is probably evidence of heteroscedasticity.

Example 9.4. Wage Regression and the Glejser Test

The results of estimating these models from the residuals obtained from regression (9.3) are as follows:

$$|e_i| = -0.3208 + 0.2829 Educ_i$$
$$t = (-0.4739)(5.5483) \qquad r^2 = 0.0557 \tag{9.10}$$

$$|e_i| = -3.1905 + 1.8263 \sqrt{Educ_i}$$
$$t = (-2.5068)(5.1764) \qquad r^2 = 0.0489 \tag{9.11}$$

$$|e_i| = 4.3879 - 12.6224 \frac{1}{Educ_i}$$

$$t = (10.6923)(-2.6561) \qquad r^2 = 0.133 \tag{9.12}$$

Note that we are using Educ as the regressor. In Exercise (9.22) you are asked to use Exper and Wagef as regressors and compare your results with Equations (9.10) to (9.12). It seems the Glejser test in various forms suggests that the wage regression (9.3) probably suffers from heteroscedasticity.

A *cautionary note regarding the Glejser test:* As in the case of the Park test, the error term v_i in the regressions suggested by Glejser can itself be heteroscedastic as well as serially correlated (see Chapter 10 on serial correlation). Glejser, however, has maintained that in large samples the preceding models are fairly good in detecting heteroscedasticity. Therefore, Glejser's test can be used as a diagnostic tool in large samples. Since the squared residuals, rather than the absolute residuals, capture the spirit of the variance, tests based on squared residuals (such as Parle, White, and Breusch-Pagan) may be preferable to the Glejser test, as various examples discussed in this chapter will show.

White's General Heteroscedasticity Test[14]

White's general test of heteroscedasticity is quite easy to apply. To see how the test is applied, suppose we have the following model:

$$Y_i = B_1 + B_2X_{2i} + B_3X_{3i} + u_i \qquad (9.13)$$

White's test proceeds as follows:

1. We first estimate regression (9.13) by OLS, obtaining the residuals, e_i.
2. We then run the following *auxiliary* regression:

$$e_i^2 = A_1 + A_2X_{2i} + A_3X_{3i} + A_4X_{2i}^2 + A_5X_{3i}^2 + A_6X_{2i}X_{3i} + v_i \qquad (9.14)$$

   That is, the residuals obtained from the original regression (9.13) are squared and regressed on all the original variables, their squared values, and their cross-products. Additional powers of the original X variables can also be added. The term v_i is the residual term in the auxiliary regression.
3. Obtain the R^2 value from the auxiliary regression (9.14). Under the null hypothesis that there is no heteroscedasticity (i.e., all the slope coefficients in Eq. [9.14] are zero), White has shown that the R^2 value obtained from regression (9.14) times the sample size (=n), follows the χ^2 distribution with d.f. equal to the number of explanatory variables in regression (9.14) (excluding the intercept term):

$$n.R^2 \sim \chi^2_{k-1} \qquad (9.15)$$

   where $(k-1)$ denotes d.f. In model (9.14) the d.f. are 5.
4. If the chi-square value obtained from Eq. (9.15) exceeds the critical chi-square value at the chosen level of significance, or if the p value of the computed chi-square value is reasonably low (say 1% or 5%), we can reject the null hypothesis of no heteroscedasticity. On the other hand, if the p value of the computed chi-square value is reasonably large (say above 5% or 10%), we do not reject the null hypothesis.

Example 9.5. Wage Regression and White's General Test of Heteroscedasticity

To illustrate White's test, we continue with the wage regression (9.3). The empirical counterpart of Eq. (9.14) is as follows:

Heteroscedasticity Test: White

F-statistic	2.269163	Prob. F(5,517)	0.0465
Obs*R-squared	11.23102	Prob. Chi-Square(5)	0.0470
Scaled explained SS	52.67924	Prob. Chi-Square(5)	0.0000

[14]H. White, "A Heteroscedasticity Consistent Covariance Matrix Estimator and a Direct Test of Heteroscedasticity," *Econometrica,* vol. 48, no. 4, 1980, pp. 817–818.

Test Equation:
Dependent Variable: RESID^2   (9.16)
Method: Least Squares
Included observations: 523

	Coefficient	Std. Error	t-Statistic	Prob.
C	14.38296	71.34726	0.201591	0.8403
EDUC	−1.183296	9.137968	−0.129492	0.8970
EDUC^2	0.168639	0.300676	0.560865	0.5751
EDUC*EXPER	0.022239	0.104117	0.213591	0.8309
EXPER	−1.401130	1.912126	−0.732760	0.4640
EXPER^2	0.027113	0.020969	1.293039	0.1966
R-squared	0.021474	Mean dependent var		21.25480
Adjusted R-squared	0.012011	S.D. dependent var		65.53846
S.E. of regression	65.14369	F-statistic		2.269163
Sum squared resid	2193993.	Prob (F-statistic)		0.046542
Durbin-Watson stat	2.016101			

For present purposes the important statistic is found through Eq. (9.15), which is 11.2310 in the present example. And this value is significant at the 5% level, again suggesting that the wage regression probably suffers from heteroscedasticity.

If we do not include the cross-product terms in the White test, we obtain $n.R^2 \approx 9.69$, with 2 d.f. This chi-square value has a probability of about 0.0078, which strongly suggests that the wage regression does suffer from heteroscedasticity.

As the various heteroscedasticity tests suggest, the overall conclusion seems to be that we do have the heteroscedasticity problem. This should not be a surprising finding, for in large cross-section data with heterogeneous units in the sample it is hard to maintain homogeneity.

Note: Although we have shown the various tests in detail, this labor can be reduced if we use statistical packages such as STATA and EViews. In EViews, for example, once you estimate a regression, you can click on the *View* button and choose the residuals test option. Once you invoke this option, EViews gives you a choice of several heteroscedasticity tests. Choosing one or more of these tests will provide the answer almost instantly.

Other Tests of Heteroscedasticity

The heteroscedasticity tests that we have discussed in this section by no means exhaust the list. We will now mention several other tests but will not discuss them here because a full discussion would take us far afield.

1. Spearman's rank correlation test (see Problem 9.13).
2. Goldfeld-Quandt test.
3. Bartlett's homogeneity-of-variance test.
4. Peak test.

5. Breusch-Pagan test.
6. CUSUMSQ test.

You may consult the references for details of these tests.[15]

9.4 WHAT TO DO IF HETEROSCEDASTICITY IS OBSERVED: REMEDIAL MEASURES

As we have seen, heteroscedasticity does not destroy the unbiasedness property of OLS estimators, but the estimators are no longer efficient, not even in large samples. This lack of efficiency makes the conventional OLS hypothesis-testing procedure of dubious value. Therefore, if heteroscedasticity is suspected or diagnosed, it is important to seek remedial measures.

For example, in our wage-education example, based on Figure 9-7, there was some indication that the wage regression given in Eq. (9.3) probably suffers from heteroscedasticity. This was confirmed by the Park, Glejser, and White tests. How can we solve this problem, if at all? Is there some way we can "transform" the model (9.3) so that there is homoscedasticity? But what kind of transformation? The answer depends on whether the true error variance, σ_i^2, is known or unknown.

When σ_i^2 Is Known: The Method of Weighted Least Squares (WLS)

To fix the ideas consider the two-variable PRF

$$Y_i = B_1 + B_2 X_i + u_i \qquad (9.17)$$

where Y is, say, hourly wage earnings and X is education, as measured by years of schooling. Assume for the moment that the true error variance σ_i^2 is known; that is, the error variance for each observation is known. Now consider the following "transformation" of the model (9.17):

$$\frac{Y_i}{\sigma_i} = B_1\left(\frac{1}{\sigma_i}\right) + B_2\left(\frac{X_i}{\sigma_i}\right) + \frac{u_i}{\sigma_i} \qquad (9.18)$$

All we have done here is to divide or "deflate" both the left- and right-hand sides of the regression (9.17) by the "known" σ_i, which is simply the square root of the variance σ_i^2.

Now let

$$u_i = \frac{u_i}{\sigma_i} \qquad (9.19)$$

We can call v_i the "transformed" error term. Is v_i homoscedastic? If it is, then the transformed regression (9.18) does not suffer from the problem of

---

[15]The Spearman's rank correlation, the Goldfeld-Quandt, and the Breusch-Pagan tests are discussed in Gujarati and Porter, *Basic Econometrics*, 5th ed., McGraw-Hill, New York, 2009, Chapter 11. This text also gives references to the other tests mentioned earlier. See also Problem 9.13.

heteroscedasticity. Assuming all other assumptions of the CLRM are fulfilled, OLS estimators of the parameters in Equation (9.18) will be BLUE and we can then proceed to statistical inference in the usual manner.

Now it is not too difficult to show that the error term v_i is homoscedastic. From Equation (9.19) we obtain

$$v_i^2 = \frac{v_i^2}{\sigma_i^2} \tag{9.20}$$

$$E(v_i^2) = E\left(\frac{u_i^2}{\sigma_i^2}\right)$$

$$= \frac{1}{\sigma_i^2}E(u_i^2), \text{ since } \sigma_i^2 \text{ is known}$$

Therefore,

$$= \left(\frac{1}{\sigma_i^2}\right)(\sigma_i^2) \text{ because of Eq. (9.1)}$$

$$= 1 \tag{9.21}$$

which is obviously a constant. In short, the transformed error term v_i is homoscedastic. As a result, the transformed model (9.18) does not suffer from the heteroscedasticity problem, and therefore it can be estimated by the usual OLS method.

To estimate the regression (9.18) actually, you will have to instruct the computer to divide each Y and X observation by the known σ_i and run OLS regression on the data thus transformed. (Most computer packages now can do this routinely.) The OLS estimators of B_1 and B_2 thus obtained are called **weighted least squares (WLS) estimators;** each Y and X observation is weighted (i.e., divided) by its own (heteroscedastic) standard deviation, σ_i. Because of this weighting procedure, the OLS method in this context is known as the *method of weighted least squares (WLS).*[16] (See Problem 9.14.)

When True σ_i^2 Is Unknown

Despite its intuitive simplicity, the WLS method of the model (9.18) begs an important question: How do we know or find out the true error variance, σ_i^2? As noted earlier, knowledge of the true error variance is a rarity. Therefore, if we want to use the method of WLS, we will have to resort to some ad hoc, although reasonably plausible, assumption(s) about σ_i^2 and transform the original regression model so that the transformed model satisfies the homoscedasticity

---

[16]Note this technical point about the regression (9.18). To estimate it, you will have to instruct the computer to run the *regression through the origin* because there is no "explicit" intercept in Eq. (9.18)—the first term in this regression is $B_1(1/\sigma_i)$. But the "slope" coefficient of $(1/\sigma_i)$ is, in fact, the intercept coefficient B_1. (Do you see this?) On the regression through the origin, see Chapter 5.

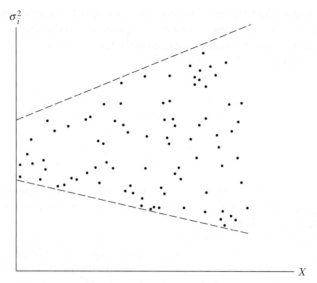

FIGURE 9-8 Error variance proportional to X

assumption. OLS can then be applied to the transformed model, for, as shown earlier, *WLS is simply OLS applied to the transformed data.*[17]

In the absence of knowledge about the true σ_i^2 the practical question then is, what assumption(s) can we make about the unknown error variance and how can we use the method of WLS? Here we consider several possibilities, which we discuss with the two-variable model (9.3); the extension to multiple regression models can be made straightforwardly.

Case 1: The Error Variance Is Proportional to X_i: The Square Root Transformation If after estimating the usual OLS regression we plot the residuals from this regression against the explanatory variable X and observe a pattern similar to that shown in Figure 9-8, the indication is that the error variance is linearly related, or proportional, to X.

That is,

$$E\left(u_i^2\right) = \sigma^2 X_i \qquad (9.22)$$

---

[17]Note that in OLS we minimize

$$\sum e_i^2 = \sum (Y_i - b_1 - b_2 X_i)^2$$

but in WLS we minimize

$$\sum \left(\frac{e_i}{\sigma_i}\right)^2 = \sum \left[\frac{Y_i - b_1 - b_2 X_i}{\sigma_i}\right]^2$$

provided σ_i is known. See how in WLS we "deflate" the importance of an observation with larger variance, for the larger the error variance, the larger the divisor will be.

which states that the heteroscedastic variance is proportional, or linearly related, to X_i; the constant σ^2 (no subscript on σ^2) is the factor of proportionality.

Given the assumption in Equation (9.22), suppose we transform the model (9.17) as follows:

$$\frac{Y_i}{\sqrt{X_i}} = B_1\frac{1}{\sqrt{X_i}} + B_2\frac{X_i}{\sqrt{X_i}} + \frac{u_i}{\sqrt{X_i}}$$

$$= B_1\frac{1}{\sqrt{X_i}} + B_2\sqrt{X_i} + v_i \qquad (9.23)$$

where $v_i = u_i/\sqrt{X_i}$. That is, we divide both sides of the model (9.17) by the square root of X_i. Equation (9.23) is an example of what is known as the **square root transformation.**

Following the development of Equation (9.21), it can be proved easily that the error variance v_i in the transformed regression is homoscedastic, and therefore we can estimate Eq. (9.23) by the usual OLS method. Actually we are using the WLS method here. (Why?)[18] *It is important to note that to estimate Eq. (9.23) we must use the regression-through-the-origin estimating procedure.* Most standard regression software packages do this routinely.

Example 9.6. Transformed Wage Regression

Let us illustrate with our wage regression (9.3). The empirical counterpart of Eq. (9.23) is as follows:

Dependent Variable: WAGE/(@SQRT(EDUC))
Method: Least Squares   (9.24)
Included observations: 523

	Coefficient	Std. Error	t-Statistic	Prob.
1/@SQRT(EDUC)	−2.645605	1.076890	−2.456708	0.0143
@SQRT(EDUC)	0.781380	0.071763	10.88840	0.0000
EXPER/(@SQRT(EDUC))	0.087698	0.016368	5.357896	0.0000
R-squared	0.084405	Mean dependent var		2.517214
Adjusted R-squared	0.080884	S.D. dependent var		1.316767
S.E. of regression	1.262392	Durbin-Watson stat		1.819673
Sum squared resid	828.6893			

Note: Suppress the intercept when you run this regression.

---

[18]Since $v_i = u_i/\sqrt{X_i}$, $v_i^2 = u_i^2/X_i$. Therefore,

$$E(v_i^2) = \frac{E(u_i^2)}{X_i} = \sigma^2\left(\frac{X_i}{X_i}\right) = \sigma^2$$

that is, homoscedasticity. Note that the X variable is nonstochastic.

To get back to the original (untransformed) wage equation, just multiply both sides of Eq. (9.24) by $\sqrt{Educ_i}$, which gives

$$Wage_i = -2.6456 + 0.7813\ Educ_i + 0.0876\ Exper_i \qquad \textbf{(9.25)}$$

If you compare this regression with the original regression (9.3), you will see that the estimated regression coefficients are not the same. The reason for the difference could be that we are using $\sqrt{Educ}$ as the deflator.

Incidentally, we tested the squared residuals from Eq. (9.24) for heteroscedasticity and found that, on the basis of the Breusch-Pagan and White tests, there was no evidence of heteroscedasticity. The Glejser test, however, showed that there was heteroscedasticity.

A question: What happens if there is more than one explanatory variable in the model? In this case we can transform the model as shown in Eq. (9.23) using any one of the X variables that, say, on the basis of graphical plot, seems the appropriate candidate (see Problem 9.7). But what if more than one X variable is a candidate? In this case instead of using any of the X's, we can use the $\hat{Y}_i$, the estimated mean value of Y_i, as the transforming variable, for as we know, $\hat{Y}_i$ is a linear combination of the X's.

Case 2: Error Variance Proportional to X_i^2 If the estimated residuals show a pattern similar to Figure 9-9, it suggests that the error variance is not linearly related to X but increases proportional to the square of X. Symbolically,

$$E\left(u_i^2\right) = \sigma^2 X_i^2 \qquad \textbf{(9.26)}$$

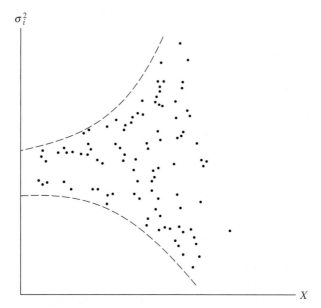

FIGURE 9-9   Error variance proportional to X^2

In this case the appropriate transformation of the two-variable model considered previously is to divide both sides of the model by X_i, rather than by the square root of X_i, as follows:

$$\frac{Y_i}{X_i} = B_1\left(\frac{1}{X_i}\right) + B_2 + \left(\frac{u_i}{X_i}\right)$$

$$= B_1\left(\frac{1}{X_i}\right) + B_2 + v_i \tag{9.27}$$

where $v_i = u_i/X_i$.

Following the earlier development, we can verify easily that the error term v in Equation (9.27) is homoscedastic. Hence, the OLS estimation of Eq. (9.27), which is actually a WLS estimation, will produce BLUE estimators. (Keep in mind that we are still keeping intact all the other assumptions of the CLRM.)

An interesting feature of Eq. (9.27) is that what was originally the slope coefficient now becomes the intercept, and what was originally the intercept now becomes the slope coefficient. But this change is only for estimation; once we estimate Eq. (9.27), multiplying by X_i on both sides, we get back to the original model.

The results of applying Eq. (9.27) to our wage-education model are as follows:

Dependent Variable: WAGE/EDUC
Method: Least Squares (9.27a)
Included observations: 523

	Coefficient	Std. Error	t-Statistic	Prob.
C	0.585431	0.051284	11.41551	0.0000
1/EDUC	0.090268	0.762246	0.118424	0.9058
EXPER/EDUC	0.070930	0.013836	5.126660	0.0000

R-squared	0.095542	Mean dependent var		0.705677
Adjusted R-squared	0.092063	S.D. dependent var		0.371773
S.E. of regression	0.354247	F-statistic		27.46492
Sum squared resid	65.25527	Prob (F-statistic)		0.000000
Durbin-Watson stat	1.755325			

Multiplying the preceding equation by Educ on both sides, we obtain:

$$Wage_i = 0.0902 + 0.5854\,Educ_i + 0.0709\,Exper_i$$

When this regression was tested for heteroscedasticity, we found that there was no evidence of it on the basis of the Breusch-Pagan and White tests, but the Glejser test did show heteroscedasticity.

Comparing this equation with Eq. (9.3), we can see that the coefficients of the two equations are not the same. This might very well be due to the particular deflator we have used on the transformation. As this example shows, it may not always be easy to find the right deflator. Some amount of trial and error is inevitable.

In Problem 9.24 you are asked to use Wagef instead of Educ as the deflator to see if the preceding conclusion changes. Since Wagef takes into account both Educ and Exper variables, the results based on this deflator may be more preferable.

Respecification of the Model

Instead of speculating about σ_i^2, sometimes a respecification of the PRF—choosing a different functional form (see Chapter 5)—can reduce heteroscedasticity. For example, instead of running the linear-in-variable (LIV) regression, if we estimate the model in the log form, it often reduces heteroscedasticity. That is, if we estimate

$$\ln Y_i = B_1 + B_2 \ln X_i + u_i \qquad (9.28)$$

the heteroscedasticity problem may be less serious in this transformation because the log transformation compresses the scales in which the variables are measured, thereby reducing a tenfold difference between two values to a twofold difference. Thus, the number 90 is 10 times the number 9, but ln 90 (= 4.4998) is only about 2 times as large as ln 9(= 2.1972).

An incidental advantage of the log-linear, or double-log, model, as we have seen in Chapter 5, is that the slope coefficient B_2 measures the elasticity of Y with respect to X, that is, the percentage change in Y for a percentage change in X.

Whether we should fit the LIV model or a log-linear model in a given instance has to be determined by theoretical and other considerations that we discussed in Chapter 7. But if there is no strong preference for either one, and if the heteroscedasticity problem is severe in the LIV model, we can try the double-log model.

Example 9.7. Log-linear Model for the Wage Data

For the wage-education data, the empirical counterpart of Eq. (9.28) is as follows:

Dependent Variable: LOG(WAGE)
Method: Least Squares   (9.29)
Included observations: 523

	Coefficient	Std. Error	t-Statistic	Prob.
C	−0.794552	0.259204	−3.065354	0.0023
LOG(EDUC)	0.957322	0.091702	10.43948	0.0000
LOG(EXPER)	0.166189	0.024690	6.731001	0.0000

R-squared	0.193841	Mean dependent var	2.072301
Adjusted R-squared	0.190740	S.D. dependent var	0.522545
S.E. of regression	0.470076	F-statistic	62.51699
Sum squared resid	114.9050	Prob (F-statistic)	0.000000
Durbin-Watson stat	1.772461		

Since this is a double-log model, the coefficients of log(Educ) and log(Exper) represent elasticities, elasticity of wage with respect to education and elasticity of wage with respect to experience, respectively. Both of these elasticities are highly significant, judged by their p values.

Before we accept these results, we need to check if regression (9.29) suffers from heteroscedasticity. Applying the Breusch-Pagan, Glejser, and White (no interaction terms) tests, we find no evidence of heteroscedasticity.

While the linear model (9.3) showed heteroscedasticity, the log-linear model shows the opposite. This shows that choosing the right model may be critical in resolving heteroscedasticity.

In Problem 9.9 you are asked to examine the preceding regression to find out if heteroscedasticity exists. If the regression (9.29) is not plagued by the heteroscedasticity problem, then this model is preferable to the LIV model, which had this problem present, necessitating the transformation of variables, as in the regression (9.24).

In passing, note that all the transformations we have discussed earlier to remove heteroscedasticity are known in the literature as **variance stabilizing transformations,** which is another name for obtaining homoscedastic variances.

To conclude our discussion on remedial measures, we should reiterate that all transformations discussed previously are to some extent ad hoc; in the absence of precise knowledge about true σ_i^2, we are essentially speculating about what it might be. Which of the transformations we have considered will work depends upon the nature of the problem and the severity of the heteroscedasticity. Also note that sometimes the error variance may not be related to any of the explanatory variables included in the model. Rather, it may be related to a variable that was originally a candidate for inclusion in the model but was not initially included. In this case the model can be transformed using that variable. Of course, if a variable logically belonged in the model, it should have been included in the first place, as we noted in Chapter 7.

9.5   WHITE'S HETEROSCEDASTICITY-CORRECTED STANDARD ERRORS AND t STATISTICS

As we have noted, in the presence of heteroscedasticity, the OLS estimators, although unbiased, are inefficient. As a result, the conventionally computed standard errors and t statistics of the estimators are suspect. White has developed an estimating procedure that produces standard errors of estimated regression coefficients that take into account heteroscedasticity. As a result, we can continue to use the t and F tests, except that they are now valid *asymptotically*, that is, in large samples. It should be pointed out that White's procedure does not change the values of the regression coefficients but only their standard errors.[19]

[19]The derivation of White's heteroscedasticity-corrected standard errors is beyond the scope of this book. Interested readers may refer to Jack Johnston and John DiNardo, *Econometrics Methods,* 4th ed., McGraw-Hill, New York, 1997, Chapter 6.

To see how the conventionally computed standard errors and t statistics can be misleading in the presence of heteroscedasticity, let us return to the wage regression (9.3). Using Eviews, we obtained the following results:

Dependent Variable: WAGE
Method: Least Squares   (9.30)

Sample: 1 533
Included observations: 533
White's Heteroscedasticity-Consistent Standard Errors and Covariance

	Coefficient	Std. Error	t-Statistic	Prob.
C	−4.857541	1.259182	−3.857695	0.0001
EDUC	0.923849	0.088110	10.48517	0.0000
EXPER	0.104346	0.018083	5.770424	0.0000
R-squared	0.200778	Mean dependent var		9.034709
Adjusted R-squared	0.197762	S.D. dependent var		5.138028
S.E. of regression	4.602016	F-statistic		66.57232
Sum squared resid	11224.63	Prob (F-statistic)		0.000000
Durbin-Watson stat	1.839859			

As noted, the regression coefficients of Eq. (9.3) and Eq. (9.30) are the same; the only difference is in their estimated standard errors and, therefore, the estimated t ratios. Since the standard errors of the slope coefficients under White's procedure are higher (and the t ratios lower), it seems Eq. (9.3) underestimated the true standard errors. Even then, the estimated t ratios under White's procedure are highly statistically significant, for their p values are practically zero.

This example shows that heteroscedasticity need not destroy the statistical significance of the estimated regression coefficients, provided we correct the standard errors once we find that we have the problem of heteroscedasticity.

9.6   SOME CONCRETE EXAMPLES OF HETEROSCEDASTICITY

We end this chapter by presenting three examples to show the importance of heteroscedasticity in applied work.

Example 9.8. Economies of Scale or Heteroscedasticity

The New York Stock Exchange (NYSE) was initially very much opposed to the deregulation of brokerage commission rates. As a matter of fact, in an econometric study presented to the Securities and Exchange Commission (SEC) before deregulation was introduced on May 1, 1975, the NYSE argued that there were economies of scale in the brokerage industry and therefore the (monopolistically determined) fixed rate commissions were justifiable.[20]

---

[20]Sometimes economists offer the economies of scale argument to justify monopolies in certain industries, especially in the so-called natural monopolies (e.g., the electric and gas-generating utilities).

The econometric study that the NYSE submitted basically revolved around the following regression:[21]

$$\hat{Y}_i = 476{,}000 + 31.348X_i - (1.083 \times 10^{-6})\, X_i^2$$

$$t = (2.98) \qquad (40.39) \qquad (-6.54) \qquad R^2 = 0.934$$

(9.31)

where Y = the total cost and X = the number of share transactions. From the model (9.31) we see that the total cost is positively related to the volume of transactions. But since the quadratic term in the transaction variable is negative and "statistically significant," it implies that the total cost is increasing at a decreasing rate. Therefore, argued the NYSE, there were economies of scale in the brokerage industry, justifying the monopoly status of the NYSE.

But the antitrust division of the U.S. Department of Justice argued that the so-called economies of scale claimed in model (9.31) are a mirage, for the regression (9.31) was plagued by the problem of heteroscedasticity. This was because in estimating the cost function in Eq. (9.31) the NYSE did not take into account that small and large firms were included in the sample. That is, it did not take into account the *scale factor.* Assuming that the error term was proportional to the volume of transaction (see Eq. [9.22]), the antitrust division reestimated Eq. (9.31), obtaining the following result:[22]

$$\hat{Y}_i = 342{,}000 + 25.57\, X_i + (4.34 \times 10^{-6})X_i^2$$

$$t = (32.3) \qquad (7.07) \qquad (0.503)$$

(9.32)

Lo and behold, not only is the quadratic term statistically insignificant, but also it has the wrong sign.[23] Thus, there are no economies of scale in the brokerage industry, demolishing the NYSE's argument for retaining its monopoly commission structure.

The preceding example shows dramatically how the assumption of homoscedasticity underlying Eq. (9.31) could have been potentially damaging. Imagine what would have happened if the SEC had accepted Eq. (9.31) on its face value and allowed the NYSE to fix the commission rates monopolistically, as before May 1, 1975!

[21]The results given in regressions (9.31) and (9.32) are reproduced from H. Michael Mann, "The New York Stock Exchange: A Cartel at the End of Its Reign" in Almarin Phillips (ed.), *Promoting Competition in Regulated Industries,* Brookings Institution, Washington D.C., 1975, p. 324.

[22]The actual mechanics consisted of estimating Eq. (9.23) shown in the text. Once this equation was estimated, it was multiplied by $\sqrt{X_i}$ to get back to the original equation, which is presented in Eq. (9.32).

[23]The NYSE in response said that the particular heteroscedasticity assumption used by the antitrust division was not valid. Substitution of other assumptions still supports the antitrust division's finding that there were no economies of scale in the brokerage industry. For details, see the Mann article cited in footnote 21.

TABLE 9-3 PER CAPITA INCOME GROWTH AND HIGHWAY CAPACITY

Explanatory variable	OLS	WLS^1	WLS^2	WLS^3
Constant	−7.69	−7.94	−8.19	−7.62
	se = (1.08)	(1.08)	(1.09)	(1.08)
ln X_2 (in 1960)	−1.59	−1.64	−1.69	−1.58
	se = (0.18)	(0.19)	(0.19)	(0.18)
ln X_3	0.30	0.30	0.31	0.30
	se = (0.06)	(0.06)	(0.06)	(0.06)
X_4	−0.009	−0.100	−0.011	−0.008
	se = (0.003)	(0.003)	(0.003)	(0.003)
D	−31.00	−32.00	−33.00	−31.00
	se = (0.08)	(0.08)	(0.08)	(0.08)
	$R^2 = 0.67$	0.49	0.46	0.73

Notes: Dependent variable Y: Average annual growth of per capita income (1972 $) from 1960 to 1980.
X_2 = The level of per capita income (1972 $) in the base year 1960
X_3 = The total existing road mileage, average over 1960 to 1985
X_4 = The percentage of highway mileage of deficient quality in 1982
D = Dummy = 1 if midwest region, 0 if otherwise
WLS^1 = Weighted least squares using the square root of X_2 (see Eq. [9.23])
WLS^2 = Weighted least squares using the level of X_2 (see Eq. [9.27])
WLS^3 = Weighted least squares using the level of ln X_2
Source: David A. Aschauer, "Highway Capacity and Economic Growth," *Economic Perspectives,* Federal Reserve Bank of Chicago, September/October 1990, Table 1, p. 18. Notation is adapted.

Example 9.9. Highway Capacity and Economic Growth

In support of his argument that economies with superior surface transportation infrastructure will benefit through higher productivity and per capita income growth, David A. Aschauer[24] obtained the results presented in Table 9-3. Since the study was conducted over a cross section of 48 states in the United States, "there is presumption that the error structure may not be homoskedastic" (p. 18).[25]

However, in the present instance the presumption of heteroscedasticity was just that since correcting for heteroscedasticity in various ways did not change OLS results much. But this example shows that if there is a presumption of heteroscedasticity, we should look into it rather than assume away the problem. As noted earlier, and as the NYSE economies of scale example so well demonstrates, heteroscedasticity is potentially a very serious problem and must not be taken lightly. It is better to err on the side of safety!

[24]This example and the statistical results presented in Table 9-3 are obtained from David A. Aschauer, "Highway Capacity and Economic Growth," *Economic Perspectives,* Federal Reserve Bank of Chicago, pp. 14–23, September/October 1990.
[25]A historical note: Is it heteroscedasticity or heteroskedasticity? It is the latter, but the former is so well established in the literature that we only occasionally find the word spelled with a k.

Example 9.10. An Extended Wage Model

For pedagogic reasons, we have presented a simple model of wage determination in this chapter. But using the data in Table 9-2, we now present a more refined model:

Dependent Variable: LOG(WAGE)
Method: Least Squares
Included observations: 523

	Coefficient	Std. Error	t-Statistic	Prob.
C	0.773947	0.123314	6.276238	0.0000
EDUC	0.091251	0.007923	11.51748	0.0000
EXPER	0.009712	0.001757	5.528884	0.0000
SEX	−0.244064	0.039288	−6.212101	0.0000
MARSTAT	0.069315	0.042214	1.641993	0.1012
REGION	−0.115626	0.042945	−2.692413	0.0073
UNION	0.183644	0.050956	3.603982	0.0003
R-squared	0.301086	Mean dependent var		2.072301
Adjusted R-squared	0.292959	S.D. dependent var		0.522545
S.E. of regression	0.439386	F-statistic		37.04803
Sum squared resid	99.61894	Prob (F-statistic)		0.000000
Durbin-Watson stat	1.861383			

(9.33)

Note: Sex = 1 for female; Marstat = 1 if married; Region = 1 if in the South; and Union = 1, if a union member.

In Equation (9.33) we have presented a semi-log model, with the wage variable in the logarithmic form and the regressors in the linear form. In the literature on wage modeling, the wage variable is often expressed in the log form. The coefficients of the Educ and Exper variables represent semi-elasticities. For example, the coefficient of Educ of about 0.091 means that, holding the other variables constant, if years of schooling increase by one year, on average, wages go up by about 9.1 percent. For the interpretation of the dummy variables, see Problem 9.25.

The estimated equation was tested for heteroscedasticity. On the basis of the Breusch-Pagan and White tests (with cross-product terms), there is no evidence of heteroscedasticity. This was confirmed when Eq. (9.33) was estimated with White's heteroscedasticity-corrected standard errors test. In fact, there was no difference between the OLS results and the White procedure standard errors.

9.7   SUMMARY

A critical assumption of the classical linear regression model is that the disturbances u_i all have the same (i.e., homoscedastic) variance. If this assumption is not satisfied, we have heteroscedasticity. Heteroscedasticity does not destroy the unbiasedness property of OLS estimators, but these estimators are no longer efficient. In other words, OLS estimators are no longer BLUE. If heteroscedastic variances σ_i^2 are known, then the method of weighted least squares (WLS) provides BLUE estimators.

Despite heteroscedasticity, if we continue to use the usual OLS method not only to estimate the parameters (which remain unbiased) but also to establish confidence intervals and test hypotheses, we are likely to draw misleading conclusions, as in the NYSE Example 9.8. This is because estimated standard errors are likely to be biased and therefore the resulting t ratios are likely to be biased, too. Thus, it is important to find out whether we are faced with the heteroscedasticity problem in a specific application. There are several diagnostic tests of heteroscedasticity, such as plotting the estimated residuals against one or more of the explanatory variables, the Park test, the Glejser test, or the rank correlation test (See Problem 9.13).

If one or more diagnostic tests reveal that we have the heteroscedasticity problem, remedial measures are called for. If the true error variance σ_i^2 is known, we can use the method of WLS to obtain BLUE estimators. Unfortunately, knowledge about the true error variance is rarely available in practice. As a result, we are forced to make some plausible assumptions about the nature of heteroscedasticity and to transform our data so that in the transformed model the error term is homoscedastic. We then apply OLS to the transformed data, which amounts to using WLS. Of course, some skill and experience are required to obtain the appropriate transformations. But without such a transformation, the problem of heteroscedasticity is insoluble in practice. However, if the sample size is reasonably large, we can use White's procedure to obtain heteroscedasticity-corrected standard errors.

KEY TERMS AND CONCEPTS

The key terms and concepts introduced in this chapter are

Homoscedasticity (or equal variance)
Heteroscedasticity (or unequal
   variance)
   a) cross-sectional data
   b) scale effect
Detection of heteroscedasticity
   a) residual plots
   b) Park test
   c) Glejser test
   d) White's general
      heteroscedasticity test
Other tests of heteroscedasticity
   a) Spearman's rank correlation test

b) Goldfeld-Quandt test
c) Bartlett's homogeneity-of-
   variance test
d) Peak test
e) Breusch-Pagan test
f) CUSUMSQ test
Weighted least squares (WLS)
   estimators
Square root transformation
Variance stabilizing transformations
White's heteroscedasticity-
   corrected standard errors and
   t statistics

QUESTIONS

9.1. What is meant by heteroscedasticity? What are its effects on the following?
   a. Ordinary least squares (OLS) estimators and their variances.
   b. Confidence intervals.
   c. The use of t and F tests of significance.

9.2. State with *brief reasons* whether the following statements are true or false:
   a. In the presence of heteroscedasticity OLS estimators are biased as well as inefficient.
   b. If heteroscedasticity is present, the conventional t and F tests are invalid.
   c. In the presence of heteroscedasticity the usual OLS method always overestimates the standard errors of estimators.
   d. If residuals estimated from an OLS regression exhibit a systematic pattern, it means heteroscedasticity is present in the data.
   e. There is no general test of heteroscedasticity that is free of any assumption about which variable the error term is correlated with.

9.3. Would you expect heteroscedasticity to be present in the following regressions?

Y	X	Sample
(a) Corporate profits	Net worth	Fortune 500
(b) Log of corporate profits	Log of net worth	Fortune 500
(c) Dow Jones industrial average	Time	1960–1990 (annual averages)
(d) Infant mortality rate	Per capita income	100 developed and developing countries
(e) Inflation rate	Money growth rate	United States, Canada, and 15 Latin American countries

9.4. Explain intuitively why the method of weighted least squares (WLS) is superior to OLS if heteroscedasticity is present.

9.5. Explain briefly the logic behind the following methods of detecting heteroscedasticity:
   a. The graphical method
   b. The Park test
   c. The Glejser test

PROBLEMS

9.6. In the two-variable population regression function (PRF), suppose the error variance has the following structure:

$$E(u_i^2) = \sigma^2 X_i^4$$

How would you transform the model to achieve homoscedastic error variance? How would you estimate the transformed model? List the various steps.

9.7. Consider the following two regressions based on the U.S. data for 1946 to 1975.[26] (Standard errors are in parentheses.)

$$C_t = 26.19 + 0.6248GNP_t - 0.4398D_t$$

$$\text{se} = (2.73) \ (0.0060) \qquad (0.0736) \qquad R^2 = 0.999$$

$$\left(\frac{C}{GNP}\right)_t = 25.92\frac{1}{GNP_t} + 0.6246 - 0.4315\frac{D}{GNP_t}$$

$$\text{se} = (2.22)(0.0068) \qquad (0.0597) \qquad R^2 = 0.875$$

where C = aggregate private consumption expenditure
$\quad GNP$ = gross national product
$\quad D$ = national defense expenditure
$\quad t$ = time

The objective of Hanushek and Jackson's study was to find out the effect of defense expenditure on other expenditures in the economy.
a. What might be the reason(s) for transforming the first equation into the second equation?
b. If the objective of the transformation was to remove or reduce heteroscedasticity, what assumption has been made about the error variance?
c. If there was heteroscedasticity, have the authors succeeded in removing it? How can you tell?
d. Does the transformed regression have to be run through the origin? Why or why not?
e. Can you compare the R^2 values of the two regressions? Why or why not?

9.8. In a study of population density as a function of distance from the central business district, Maddala obtained the following regression results based on a sample of 39 census tracts in the Baltimore area in 1970:[27]

$$\ln Y_i = 10.093 - 0.239X_i$$

$$t = (54.7)(-12.28) \qquad R^2 = 0.803$$

$$\frac{\ln Y_i}{\sqrt{X_i}} = 9.932\frac{1}{\sqrt{X_i}} - 0.2258\sqrt{X_i}$$

$$t = (47.87) \qquad (-15.10)$$

where Y = the population density in the census tract and X = the distance in miles from the central business district.
a. What assumption, if any, is the author making about heteroscedasticity in his data?

[26]These results are from Eric A. Hanushek and John E. Jackson, *Statistical Methods for Social Scientists,* Academic, New York, 1977, p. 160.
[27]G. S. Maddala, *Introduction to Econometrics,* Macmillan, New York, 1988, pp. 175–177.

    b. How can you tell from the transformed WLS regression that heteroscedasticity, if present, has been removed or reduced?

    c. How would you interpret the regression results? Do they make economic sense?

9.9. Refer to the wage data given in Table 9-2 (found on the textbook's Web site). Regression (9.30) gives the results of the regression of the log of wage on the log of education.

    a. Based on the data of Table 9-2, verify this regression.

    b. For this regression, obtain the absolute values of the residuals as well as their squared values and plot each against education. Is there any evidence of heteroscedasticity?

    c. Do the Park and Glejser tests on the residuals of this regression. What conclusions can you draw?

    d. If heteroscedasticity is found in the double-log model, what kind of WLS transformation would you recommend to eliminate it?

    e. For the linear regression (9.3) there was some evidence of heteroscedasticity. If for the log-log model there is no evidence of heteroscedasticity, which model would you choose and why?

    f. Can you compare the R^2s of the two regressions? Why not?

9.10. Continue with the wage data given in Table 9-2 (found on the textbook's Web site) and now consider the following regressions:

$$\text{wage}_i = A_1 + A_2 \text{ experience}_i + u_i$$

$$\ln \text{wage}_i = B_1 + B_2 \ln \text{experience}_i + u_i$$

    a. Estimate both regressions.

    b. Obtain the absolute and squared values of the residuals for each regression and plot them against the explanatory variable. Do you detect any evidence of heteroscedasticity?

    c. Verify your qualitative conclusion in part (*b*) with the Glejser and Park tests.

    d. If there is evidence of heteroscedasticity, how would you transform the data to reduce its severity? Show the necessary calculations.

9.11. Consider Figure 9-10, which plots the gross domestic product (GDP) growth, in percent, against the ratio of investment/GDP, in percent, for several countries for 1974 to 1985.[28] The various countries are divided into three groups—those that experienced positive real (i.e., inflation-adjusted) interest rates, those that experienced moderately negative real interest rates, and those that experienced strongly negative interest rates.

    a. Develop a suitable model to explain the percent GDP growth rate in relation to percent investment/GDP rate.

    b. From Figure 9-10, do you see any evidence of heteroscedasticity in the data? How would you test its presence formally?

    c. If heteroscedasticity is suspected, how would you transform your regression to eliminate it?

    d. Suppose you were to extend your model to take into account the qualitative differences in the three groups of countries by representing them with

[28] See *World Development Report, 1989*, the World Bank, Oxford University Press, New York, p. 33.

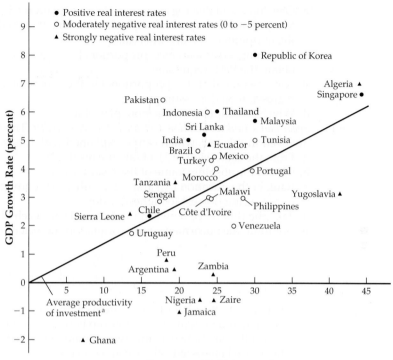

^{a} Line represents sample average.

FIGURE 9-10   Real interest rates, investment, productivity, and growth in 33 developing countries from 1974 to 1985

Source: World Development Report, 1989. Copyright © by the International Bank for Reconstruction & Development/The World Bank. Reprinted by permission of the Oxford University Press, Inc., p. 33.

dummy variables. Write the equation for this model. If you had the data and could estimate this expanded model, would you expect heteroscedasticity in the extended model? Why or why not?

9.12.   In a survey of 9,966 economists in 1964 the following data were obtained:

Age (years)	Median salary ($)	Age (years)	Median salary ($)
20–24	7,800	50–54	15,000
25–29	8,400	55–59	15,000
30–34	9,700	60–64	15,000
35–39	11,500	65–69	14,500
40–44	13,000	70+	12,000
45–49	14,800		

Source: "The Structure of Economists' Employment and Salaries," Committee on the National Science Foundation Report on the Economics Profession, *American Economics Review,* vol. 55, no. 4, December 1965, p. 36.

a. Develop a suitable regression model to explain median salary in relation to age. For the purpose of regression, assume that median salaries refer to the midpoint of the age interval.

b. Assuming error variance proportional to age, transform the data and obtain the WLS regression.

c. Now assume that it is proportional to the square of age. Obtain the WLS regression on this assumption.

d. Which assumption seems more plausible?

9.13. *Spearman's rank correlation test for heteroscedasticity.* The following steps are involved in this test, which can be explained with the wage regression (9.3):

a. From the regression (9.3), obtain the residuals e_i.

b. Obtain the absolute value of the residuals, $|e_i|$.

c. Rank both education (X_i) and $|e_i|$ in either descending (highest to lowest) or ascending (lowest to highest) order.

d. Take the difference between the two ranks for each observation, call it d_i.

e. Compute the Spearman's rank correlation coefficient r_s, defined as

$$r_s = 1 - 6\left[\frac{\sum d_i^2}{n(n^2 - 1)}\right]$$

where n = the number of observations in the sample.

If there is a systematic relationship between e_i and X_i, the rank correlation coefficient between the two should be statistically significant, in which case heteroscedasticity can be suspected.

Given the null hypothesis that the true population rank correlation coefficient is zero and that $n > 8$, it can be shown that

$$\frac{r_s\sqrt{(n - 2)}}{\sqrt{1 - r_s^2}} \sim t_{n-2}$$

follows Student's t distribution with $(n - 2)$ d.f.

Therefore, if in an application the rank correlation coefficient is significant on the basis of the t test, we do not reject the hypothesis that there is heteroscedasticity in the problem. Apply this method to the wage data given in the text to find out if there is evidence of heteroscedasticity in the data.

9.14. *Weighted least squares.* Consider the data in Table 9-4.

a. Estimate the OLS regression

$$Y_i = B_1 + B_2 X_i + u_i$$

b. Estimate the WLS

$$\frac{Y_i}{\sigma_i} = B_1\frac{1}{\sigma_i} + B_2\frac{X_i}{\sigma_i} + \frac{u_i}{\sigma_i}$$

(Make sure that you run the WLS through the origin.) Compare the results of the two regressions. Which regression do you prefer? Why?

9.15. Show that the error term v_i in Eq. (9.27) is homoscedastic.

TABLE 9-4   AVERAGE COMPENSATION IN RELATION TO PRODUCTIVITY
BY EMPLOYMENT SIZE, U.S. MANUFACTURING INDUSTRIES

Employment size (average number of employees) (1)	Average compensation Y ($) (2)	Average productivity X ($) (3)	Standard deviation of compensation σ_i ($) (4)
1–4	3,396	9,355	744
5–9	3,787	8,584	851
10–19	4,013	7,962	728
20–49	4,104	8,275	805
50–99	4,146	8,389	930
100–249	4,241	9,418	1,081
250–499	4,387	9,795	1,243
500–999	4,538	10,281	1,308
1,000–2,499	4,843	11,754	1,112

Source: Data from *The Census of Manufacturing,* U.S. Department of Commerce,
1958. (Figures in table computed by the author.)

9.16.   In a regression of average wages (W) on the number of employees (N) for a
random sample of 30 firms, the following regression results were obtained:[29]

$$\hat{W} = 7.5 + 0.009N$$

$$t = \text{N.A.}(16.10) \qquad\qquad R^2 = 0.90 \tag{1}$$

$$\frac{\hat{W}}{N} = 0.008 + 7.8\frac{1}{N}$$

$$t = (14.43)\ (76.58) \qquad\qquad R^2 = 0.99 \tag{2}$$

a. How would you interpret the two regressions?
b. What is the author assuming in going from Eq. (1) to (2)? Was he worried
about heteroscedasticity?
c. Can you relate the slopes and the intercepts of the two models?
d. Can you compare the R^2 values of the two models? Why or why not?

9.17.   From the total cost function given in the NYSE regression (9.31), how would
you derive the average cost function? And the marginal cost function? But if
Eq. (9.32) is the true (i.e., heteroscedasticity-adjusted) total cost function,
how would you derive the associated average and marginal cost functions? Explain the difference between the two models.

9.18.   Table 9-5, on the textbook's Web site, gives data on five socioeconomic
indicators for a sample of 20 countries, divided into four per-capita income
categories: low-income (up to $500 per year), lower-middle income (annual
income between $500 and $2200), upper-middle income (annual income between $2300 and $5500), and higher-income (over $5500 a year). The first five

---

[29]See Dominick Salvatore, *Managerial Economics,* McGraw-Hill, New York, 1989, p. 157.

countries in the table belong to the first income category, the second five countries to the second income category, and so on.

   a. Create a regression using all five independent variables. A priori, what do you expect the impact of the population growth rate (X_4) and daily calorie intake (X_5) will be on infant mortality rate (Y)?

   b. Estimate the preceding regression and see if your expectations were correct.

   c. If you encounter multicollinearity in the preceding regression, what can you do about it? You may undertake any corrective measures that you deem necessary.

9.19. The model from Ex. 9.18, without inclusion of X_4 and X_5, when tested for heteroscedasticity following the White test outlined in regression (9.14), yielded the following regression results. (*Note:* To save space, we have given only the t statistics and their p values. The results were obtained from the EViews statistical package.)

$$e_i^2 = -15.76 + 0.3810X_{2i} - 4.5641X_{3i} + 0.000005X_{2i}^2 + 0.1328X_{3i}^2 - 0.0050X_{2i}X_{3i}$$

$$t = (-0.01)\ (0.60) \qquad (-0.13) \qquad (0.87) \qquad (0.56) \qquad (-0.85)$$

$$p\ \text{value} = (0.989)(0.556) \qquad (0.895) \qquad (0.394) \qquad (0.581) \qquad (0.400)$$

$$R^2 = 0.23$$

   a. How do you interpret the preceding regression?

   b. Do these results suggest that the model above suffers from the problem of heteroscedasticity? How do you know?

   c. If the above regression suffers from heteroscedasticity, how would you get rid of it?

9.20. **a.** Use the data given in Table 9-5 (on the textbook's Web site) to develop a multiple regression model to explain daily calorie intake for the 20 countries shown in the table.

   b. Does this model suffer from heteroscedasticity? Show the necessary test(s).

   c. If there is heteroscedasticity, obtain White's heteroscedasticity-corrected standard errors and t statistics (see if your software does this) and compare and comment on the results obtained in part (*a*) above.

9.21. Refer to the life expectancy example (Example 7.4) discussed in Chapter 7. For the models considered in Table 7-1, find out if these models suffer from the problem of heteroscedasticity. The raw data are given in Table 9-6, found on the textbook's Web site. State the tests you use. How would you remedy the problem? Show the necessary calculations. Also, present the results based on White's heteroscedasticity-corrected standard errors. What general conclusion do you draw from this exercise?

9.22. Estimate the counterparts of Equations (9.10) to (9.12) using Exper and Wagef as the deflators.

9.23. Describe the Breusch-Pagan (BP) test. Verify that, on the basis of this test, Eq. (9.33) shows no evidence of heteroscedasticity.

9.24. Reestimate Eq. (9.27a) using Wagef as the deflator.

9.25. Interpret the dummy coefficients in Eq. (9.33).

9.26. Refer to Table 9-7 on the textbook's Web site. This data set considers R&D expenditure data in relation to sales.

a. Create a standard LIV (linear-in-variables) regression model and note the results.

b. Using the software package of your choice, obtain White's heteroscedasticity-corrected regression results. What are they?

c. Is there a substantial difference between the results obtained in parts (a) and (b)?

9.27. Table 9-8 (found on the textbook's Web site) gives data on salary and related data on 447 executives of Fortune 500 companies. Salary = 1999 salary and bonuses; totcomp = 1999 CEO total compensation; tenure = number of years as CEO (0 if less than 6 months); age = age of CEO; sales = total 1998 sales revenue of the firm; profits = 1998 profits for the firm; and assets = total assets of the firm in 1998.

a. Estimate the following regression from these data and obtain the Breusch-Pagan statistic to check for heteroscedasticity:

$$Salary_i = B_1 + B_2 tenure_i + B_3 age_i + B_4 sales_i + B_5 profits_i + B_6 assets_i + u_i$$

Does there seem to be a problem with heteroscedasticity?

b. Now create a second model using ln(Salary) as the dependent variable. Is there any improvement in the heteroscedasticity?

c. Create scattergrams of Salary versus each of the independent variables. Can you discern which variable(s) is (are) contributing to the issue? What suggestions would you make now to address this? What is your final model?

d. Now obtain (White's) robust standard errors. Are there any noticeable differences?

9.28. Table 9-9 (on the textbook's Web site) gives data on 81 cars regarding MPG (average miles per gallon), HP (engine horsepower), VOL (cubic feet of cab space), SP (top speed, miles per hour), and WT (vehicle weight in 100 lbs.).

a. Consider the following model:

$$MPG_i = B_1 + B_2 SP_i + B_3 HP_i + B_4 WT_i + u_i$$

Estimate the parameters of this model and interpret the results. Do they make economic sense?

b. Would you expect the error variance in the preceding model to be heteroscedastic? Why?

c. Use the White test to find out if the error variance is heteroscedastic.

d. Obtain White's heteroscedasticity-consistent standard errors and t values and compare your results with those obtained from OLS.

e. If heteroscedasticity is established, how would you transform the data so that in the transformed data the error variance is homoscedastic? Show the necessary calculations.

CHAPTER 10

AUTOCORRELATION: WHAT HAPPENS IF ERROR TERMS ARE CORRELATED?

In Chapter 9 we examined the consequences of relaxing one of the assumptions of the classical linear regression model (CLRM)—the assumption of homoscedasticity. In this chapter we consider yet another departure from the CLRM assumption, namely, that there is no **serial correlation** or **autocorrelation** among the disturbances u_i entering the population regression function (PRF). Although we discussed this assumption briefly in Chapter 3, we will take a long look at it in this chapter to seek answers to the following questions:

1. What is the nature of autocorrelation?
2. What are the theoretical and practical consequences of autocorrelation?
3. Since the assumption of no autocorrelation relates to u_i, which are not directly observable, how do we know that there is no autocorrelation in any concrete study? In short, how do we detect autocorrelation in practice?
4. How do we remedy the problem of autocorrelation if the consequences of not correcting for it are serious?

This chapter is in many ways similar to the preceding one on heteroscedasticity in that *under both heteroscedasticity and autocorrelation, ordinary least squares (OLS) estimators, although linear and unbiased, are not efficient; that is, they are not best linear unbiased estimators (BLUE).*

Since our emphasis in this chapter is on autocorrelation, we assume that all other assumptions of the CLRM remain intact.

10.1   THE NATURE OF AUTOCORRELATION

The term *autocorrelation* can be defined as "correlation between members of observations ordered in time (as in time series data) or space (as in cross-sectional data)."[1]

Just as heteroscedasticity is generally associated with cross-sectional data, autocorrelation is usually associated with time series data (i.e., data ordered in temporal sequence), although, as the preceding definition suggests, autocorrelation can occur in cross-sectional data also, in which case it is called **spatial correlation** (i.e., correlation in space rather than in time).

In the regression context the CLRM assumes that such correlation does not exist in disturbances u_i. Symbolically, no autocorrelation means

$$E(u_i u_j) = 0 \qquad i \neq j \qquad (10.1)$$

That is, the expected value of the product of two *different* error terms u_i and u_j is zero.[2] In plain English, this assumption means that the disturbance term relating to any observation is not related to or influenced by the disturbance term relating to any other observation. For example, in dealing with quarterly time series data involving the regression of output on labor and capital inputs (i.e., a production function), if, say, there is a labor strike affecting output in one quarter, there is no reason to believe that this disruption will be carried over to the next quarter. In other words, if output is lower this quarter, it will not necessarily be lower next quarter. Likewise, in dealing with cross-sectional data involving the regression of family consumption expenditure on family income, the effect of an increase of one family's income on its consumption expenditure is not expected to affect the consumption expenditure of another family.

But if there is such dependence, we have autocorrelation. Symbolically,

$$E(u_i u_j) \neq 0 \qquad i \neq j \qquad (10.2)$$

In this situation the disruption caused by a strike this quarter can affect output next quarter (it might in fact increase to catch up with the backlog) or the increase in the consumption expenditure of one family can pressure another family to increase its consumption expenditure if it wants to keep up with the Joneses (this is the case of *spatial correlation*).

It is interesting to visualize some likely patterns of autocorrelation and nonautocorrelation, which are given in Figure 10-1. In the figure the vertical axis shows both u_i (the population disturbances) and their sample counterparts, e_i (the residuals), for as in the case of heteroscedasticity, we do not observe the former and try to infer their behavior from the latter.

---

[1]Maurice G. Kendall and William R. Buckland, *A Dictionary of Statistical Terms*, Hafner, New York, 1971, p. 8.

[2]If $i = j$, Equation (10.1) becomes $E(u_i^2)$, the variance of u_i, which by the homoscedasticity assumption is equal to σ^2.

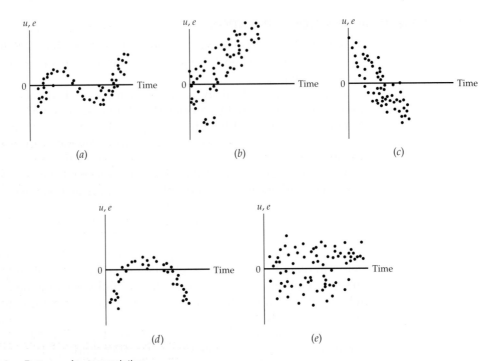

FIGURE 10-1   Patterns of autocorrelation

Figures 10-1(a) to (d) show a distinct pattern among the u's while Figure 10-1(e) shows no systematic pattern, which is the geometric counterpart of the assumption of no autocorrelation given in Equation (10.1).

Why does autocorrelation occur? There are several **reasons for autocorrelation,** some of which follow.

Inertia

A distinguishing feature of most economic time series is **inertia** or **sluggishness.** As is well known, time series such as the gross domestic product (GDP), production, employment, money supply, and price indexes exhibit *business cycles* (recurring and self-sustaining fluctuations in economic activity). Starting at the bottom of the recession, when economic recovery starts, most of these time series start moving upward. In this upswing the value of a series at one point in time is greater than its previous value. Thus, there is a momentum built into these time series and the upswing continues until something happens (e.g., an increase in taxes or interest rates, or both) to slow them down. Therefore, in regressions involving time series data successive observations are likely to be interdependent or correlated.

Model Specification Error(s)

Sometimes autocorrelation patterns such as those shown in Figures 10-1(*a*) to (*d*) occur not because successive observations are correlated but because the regression model is not "correctly" specified. As we saw in Chapter 7, by incorrect specification of a model we mean that either some important variables that should be included in the model are not included (this is the case of *underspecification*) or that the model has the wrong functional form—a linear-in-variable (LIV) model is fitted whereas a log-linear model should have been fitted. If such **model specification errors** occur, then the residuals from the incorrect model will exhibit a systematic pattern. A simple test of this is to include the excluded variable and to determine if the residuals still show a distinct pattern. If they do not, then the so-called serial correlation observed in the incorrect model was due to specification error.

The Cobweb Phenomenon

The supply of many agricultural commodities reflects the so-called **cobweb phenomenon,** where supply reacts to price with a *lag* of one time period because supply decisions take time to implement—the gestation period. Thus, at the beginning of this year's planting of crops farmers are influenced by the price prevailing last year so that their supply function is

$$\text{Supply}_t = B_1 + B_2 P_{t-1} + u_t \tag{10.3}$$

Suppose at the end of period t, price P_t turns out to be lower than P_{t-1}. Therefore, in period $(t + 1)$ farmers decide to produce less than they did in period t. Obviously, in this situation the disturbances u_t are not expected to be random, for if the farmers overproduce in year t, they are likely to underproduce in year $(t + 1)$, etc., leading to a cobweb pattern.

Data Manipulation

In empirical analysis the raw data are often "massaged" in a process referred to as **data manipulation.** For example, in time series regressions involving quarterly data, such data are often derived from the monthly data by simply adding three monthly observations and dividing the sum by 3. This averaging introduces "smoothness" into the data by dampening the fluctuations in the monthly data. Therefore, the graph plotting the quarterly data looks much smoother than the monthly data, and this smoothness can itself lend to a systematic pattern in the disturbances, thereby inducing autocorrelation.[3]

Before moving on, note that autocorrelation can be positive as well as negative, although economic time series generally exhibit positive autocorrelation

---

[3]It should be pointed out that sometimes the averaging or other data-editing procedures are used because the weekly or monthly data can be subject to substantial measurement errors. The averaging process, therefore, can produce more accurate estimates. But the unfortunate byproduct of this process is that it can induce autocorrelation.

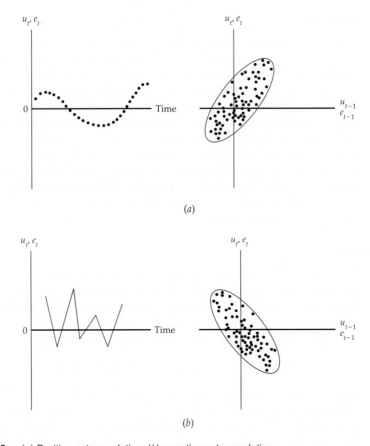

FIGURE 10-2   (a) Positive autocorrelation; (b) negative autocorrelation

because most of them either move upward or downward over extended time periods (possibly due to business cycles) and do not exhibit a constant up-and-down movement, such as that shown in Figure 10-2(b).

10.2   CONSEQUENCES OF AUTOCORRELATION

Suppose the error terms exhibit one of the patterns shown in Figures 10-1(a) to (d) or Figure 10-2. What then? In other words, what are the consequences of relaxing assumption (10.1) for the OLS methodology? These consequences are as follows.[4]

1. The least squares estimators are still linear and unbiased.
2. But they are not efficient; that is, they do not have minimum variance compared to the procedures that take into account autocorrelation. In

---

[4]The proofs can be found in Gujarati and Porter, *Basic Econometrics*, 5th ed., McGraw-Hill, New York, 2009, Chapter 12.

short, the usual ordinary least squares (OLS) estimators are not best linear unbiased estimators (BLUE).

3. The estimated variances of OLS estimators are biased. Sometimes the usual formulas to compute the variances and standard errors of OLS estimators seriously *underestimate* true variances and standard errors, thereby *inflating* t values. This gives the appearance that a particular coefficient is statistically significantly different from zero, whereas in fact that might not be the case.

4. Therefore, the usual t and F tests are not generally reliable.

5. The usual formula to compute the error variance, namely, $\hat{\sigma}^2 = \text{RSS}/\text{d.f.}$ (residual sum of squares/degrees of freedom), is a biased estimator of the true σ^2 and in some cases it is likely to underestimate the latter.

6. As a consequence, the conventionally computed R^2 may be an unreliable measure of true R^2.

7. The conventionally computed variances and standard errors of forecast may also be inefficient.

As you can see, these consequences are similar to those of heteroscedasticity, and just as serious in practice. Therefore, as with heteroscedasticity, we must find out if we have the autocorrelation problem in any given application.

10.3 DETECTING AUTOCORRELATION

When it comes to **detecting autocorrelation,** we face the same dilemma as in the case of heteroscedasticity. There, we did not know the true error variance σ_i^2 because the true u_i are unobservable. Here, too, not only do we not know what the true u_t are, but if they are correlated, we do not know what the true mechanism is that has generated them in a concrete situation. We only have their proxies, the e_t's. Therefore, as with heteroscedasticity, we have to rely on the e_t's obtained from the standard OLS procedure to learn something about the presence, or lack thereof, of autocorrelation. With this caveat, we will now consider several diagnostic tests of autocorrelation, which we will illustrate with an example.

Example 10.1. Relationship between Real Wages and Productivity, U.S. Business Sector, 1959–2006

From basic macroeconomics, one would expect a positive relationship between real wages and (labor) productivity—ceteris paribus, the higher the level of labor productivity, the higher the real wages. To shed some light on this, we explore the data in Table 10-1 (on the textbook's Web site), which contains data on real wages (real compensation per hour) and labor productivity (output per hour of all persons) for the business sector of the U.S. economy for the time period 1959 to 2006. (Recall that these data were also presented in Table 3-3, in our concluding example in Chapter 3.)

Regressing real wages on productivity, we obtain the following results; for discussion purposes we will call this the wages-productivity regression.

$$Realwages_i = 33.6360 + 0.6614\, Productivity_i$$
$$se = (1.4001) \quad (0.0156)$$
$$t = (24.0243) \quad (42.2928)$$
$$r^2 = 0.9749; \quad d = 0.1463$$

(10.4)

Note: d refers to the Durbin-Watson statistic that is discussed below.

Judged by the usual criteria, these results look good. As expected, there is a positive relationship between real wages and productivity. The estimated t ratios seem quite high and the R^2 value is quite high. Before we accept these results at their face value, we must guard against the possibility of autocorrelation, for in its presence, as we know, the results may not be reliable.

To test for autocorrelation, we consider three methods: (1) the graphical method, which is comparatively simple, (2) the celebrated Durbin-Watson d statistic, and (3) the runs test, which is discussed in Appendix 10A.

The Graphical Method

As in the case of heteroscedasticity, a simple visual examination of OLS residuals, e's, can give valuable insight about the likely presence of autocorrelation among the error terms, the u's. Now there are various ways of examining the residuals. We can plot them against time, as shown in Figure 10-3, which depicts the residuals obtained from regression (10.4) and shown in Table 10-2. Incidentally, such a plot is called a **time-sequence plot.**

An examination of Figure 10-3 shows that the residuals, e_t's, do not seem to be randomly distributed, as in Figure 10-1(*e*). As a matter of fact, they exhibit a

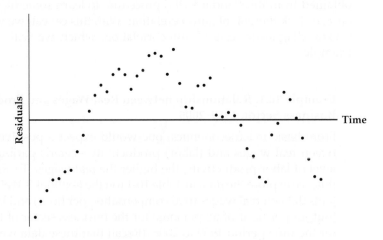

FIGURE 10-3   Residuals from the regression (10.4)

TABLE 10-2   RESIDUALS AND RELATED DATA FROM THE WAGES-PRODUCTIVITY REGRESSION

e_t	e_{t-1}	$D = e_t - e_{t-1}$	D^2	e_t^2	Sign of e
−5.5315	—	—	—	30.5980	−
−4.6395	−5.5315	0.8920	0.7958	21.5250	−
−4.0293	−4.6395	0.6102	0.3724	16.2351	−
−3.4225	−4.0293	0.6068	0.3682	11.7136	−
−3.3494	−3.4225	0.0731	0.0053	11.2184	−
−2.9543	−3.3494	0.3950	0.1561	8.7282	−
−2.8642	−2.9543	0.0902	0.0081	8.2036	−
−1.8191	−2.8642	1.0451	1.0923	3.3090	−
−0.8831	−1.8191	0.9360	0.8761	0.7798	−
0.4787	−0.8831	1.3618	1.8545	0.2292	+
1.3827	0.4787	0.9040	0.8172	1.9119	+
1.9721	1.3827	0.5894	0.3474	3.8894	+
1.6004	1.9721	−0.3717	0.1382	2.5613	+
2.5687	1.6004	0.9683	0.9376	6.5982	+
2.8694	2.5687	0.3007	0.0904	8.2332	+
2.5580	2.8694	−0.3114	0.0969	6.5434	+
1.7362	2.5580	−0.8218	0.6753	3.0145	+
2.4849	1.7362	0.7486	0.5604	6.1745	+
2.8054	2.4849	0.3205	0.1027	7.8701	+
3.6342	2.8054	0.8289	0.6870	13.2076	+
3.7711	3.6342	0.1369	0.0187	14.2215	+
3.6020	3.7711	−0.1691	0.0286	12.9744	+
2.5788	3.6020	−1.0232	1.0469	6.6504	+
3.9875	2.5788	1.4087	1.9845	15.9005	+
2.0544	3.9875	−1.9331	3.7369	4.2207	+
0.7117	2.0544	−1.3428	1.8030	0.5065	+
0.6417	0.7117	−0.0700	0.0049	0.4118	+
1.9193	0.6417	1.2776	1.6323	3.6837	+
1.9530	1.9193	0.0337	0.0011	3.8143	+
2.3649	1.9530	0.4118	0.1696	5.5926	+
0.2462	2.3649	−2.1186	4.4886	0.0606	+
0.1526	0.2462	−0.0937	0.0088	0.0233	+
0.3945	0.1526	0.2419	0.0585	0.1556	+
0.2196	0.3945	−0.1749	0.0306	0.0482	+
−0.3238	0.2196	−0.5433	0.2952	0.1048	−
−1.6487	−0.3238	−1.3250	1.7555	2.7183	−
−2.0793	−1.6487	−0.4306	0.1854	4.3235	−
−3.2736	−2.0793	−1.1943	1.4265	10.7168	−
−3.5533	−3.2736	−0.2796	0.0782	12.6258	−
−0.8740	−3.5533	2.6793	7.1787	0.7638	−
−0.2214	−0.8740	0.6525	0.4258	0.0490	−
1.5511	−0.2214	1.7725	3.1418	2.4058	+
1.1339	1.5511	−0.4172	0.1740	1.2857	+
0.0733	1.1339	−1.0606	1.1248	0.0054	+
−1.0582	0.0733	−1.1315	1.2803	1.1198	−
−2.2556	−1.0582	−1.1974	1.4338	5.0878	−
−3.2529	−2.2556	−0.9973	0.9945	10.5812	−
−3.4127	−3.2529	−0.1598	0.0255	11.6462	−

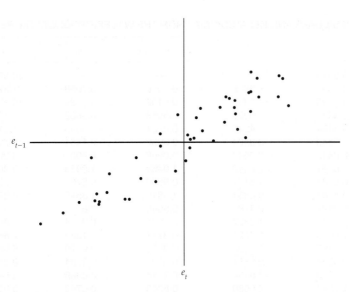

FIGURE 10-4   Residuals e_t against e_{t-1} from the regression (10.4)

distinct behavior. Initially they are negative, then they become positive, then negative, then positive, and then negative. This can be seen more vividly if we plot e_t given in column 1 of Table 10-2 against e_{t-1} given in column 2, as in Figure 10-4.

The general tenor of this figure is that successive residuals are positively correlated, suggesting positive autocorrelation; most residuals are bunched in the first (northeast) and the third (southwest) quadrants.

The Durbin-Watson *d* Test[5]

The most celebrated test for detecting autocorrelation is that developed by Durbin and Watson, popularly known as the **Durbin-Watson *d* statistic,** which is defined as

$$d = \frac{\sum\limits_{t=2}^{n}(e_t - e_{t-1})^2}{\sum\limits_{t=1}^{n} e_t^2} \qquad (10.5)$$

which is simply the ratio of the sum of squared differences in successive residuals to the RSS. Note that in the numerator of the *d* statistic the sample size is $(n - 1)$ because one observation is lost in taking successive differences.

[5]J. Durbin and G. S. Watson, "Testing for Serial Correlation in Least-Squares Regression," *Biometrika,* vol. 38, 1951, pp. 159–177.

A great advantage of the d statistic is its simplicity; it is based on the OLS residuals which are routinely computed by most regression packages. It is now common practice to report the Durbin-Watson d along with summary statistics, such as R^2, adjusted R^2, $(\bar{R}^2)$, t, F ratios, etc. (see Equation [10.4]).

For our illustrative regression, we can easily compute the d statistic from the data given in Table 10-2. First, subtract the lagged e's given in column 2 of that table from the e's given in column 1, square the difference, sum it, and divide the sum by the sum of squared e's given in column 5. The necessary raw data to compute d are presented in Table 10-2. Of course, this is now routinely done by the computer. For our example, the computed d value is 0.1463 (verify this).

Before proceeding to show how the computed d value can be used to determine the presence, or otherwise, of autocorrelation, it is *very important to note the assumptions underlying the d statistic:*

1. The regression model includes an intercept term. Therefore, it cannot be used to determine autocorrelation in models of regression through the origin.[6]
2. The X variables are nonstochastic; that is, their values are fixed in repeated sampling.
3. The disturbances u_t are generated by the following mechanism:

$$u_t = \rho u_{t-1} + v_t \qquad -1 \leq \rho \leq 1 \tag{10.6}$$

which states that the value of the disturbance, or error, term at time t depends on its value in time period $(t-1)$ and a purely random term (v_t), the extent of the dependence on the past value, is measured by ρ (rho). This is called the **coefficient of autocorrelation,** which lies between -1 and 1. (*Note:* A correlation coefficient always lies between -1 and 1.) The mechanism, Equation (10.6), is known as the **Markov first-order autoregressive scheme** or simply the *first-order autoregressive scheme,* usually denoted as the **AR(1) scheme.** The name autoregression is appropriate because Eq. (10.6) can be interpreted as the regression of u_t on itself lagged in one period. And this is first order because u_t and its immediate past value are involved; that is, the maximum lag is one time period.[7]

---

[6]However, R. W. Farebrother has calculated d values when the intercept is absent from the model. See his article "The Durbin-Watson Test for Serial Correlation When There Is No Intercept in the Regression," *Econometrica,* vol. 48, 1980, pp. 1553–1563.

[7]If the model were

$$u_t = \rho_1 u_{t-1} + \rho_2 u_{t-2} + v_t$$

it would be an AR(2) or second-order autoregressive scheme, etc. We note here that unless we are willing to assume some scheme by which the u's are generated, it is difficult to solve the problem of autocorrelation. This situation is similar to heteroscedasticity in which we also made some assumption about how the unobservable error variance σ_i^2 is generated. For autocorrelation, in practice, the AR(1) assumption has proven to be quite useful.

4. The regression does not contain the lagged value(s) of the dependent variable as one of the explanatory variables. In other words, the test is not applicable to models such as

$$Y_t = B_1 + B_2X_t + B_3Y_{t-1} + u_t \tag{10.7}$$

where Y_{t-1} is the one-period lagged value of the dependent variable Y. Models like regression (10.7) are known as **autoregressive models,** a regression of a variable on itself with a lag as one of the explanatory variables.

Assuming all these conditions are fulfilled, what can we say about autocorrelation in our wages-productivity regression with a d value of 0.1463? Before answering this question, we can show that for a large sample size Eq. (10.5) can be *approximately* expressed as (see Problem 10.19)

$$d \approx 2(1 - \hat{\rho}) \tag{10.8}$$

where $\approx$ means approximately and where

$$\hat{\rho} = \frac{\sum\limits_{t=2}^{n} e_t e_{t-1}}{\sum\limits_{t=1}^{n} e_t^2} \tag{10.9}$$

which is an estimator of the coefficient of autocorrelation ρ of the AR(1) scheme given in Equation (10.6). But since $-1 \le \hat{\rho} \le 1$, Equation (10.8) implies the following:

	Value of $\hat{\rho}$	Value of d (approx.)
1.	$\hat{\rho} = -1$ (perfect negative correlation)	$d = 4$
2.	$\hat{\rho} = 0$ (no autocorrelation)	$d = 2$
3.	$\hat{\rho} = 1$ (perfect positive correlation)	$d = 0$

In short,

$$0 \le d \le 4 \tag{10.10}$$

that is, the *computed d value must lie between 0 and 4.*

From the preceding discussion we can state that if a computed d value is closer to zero, there is evidence of positive autocorrelation, but if it is closer to 4, there is evidence of negative autocorrelation. And the closer the d value is to 2, the more the evidence is in favor of no autocorrelation. Of course, these are broad limits and some definite guidelines are needed as to when we can call a computed d value indicative of positive, negative, or no autocorrelation. In other words, is there a "critical" d value, as in the case of the t and F distributions, that will give us some definitive indication of autocorrelation?

Unfortunately, unlike t and F distributions, there is not one but two critical d values.[8] Durbin and Watson have provided a *lower limit* d_L and an upper limit d_U, such that if the d value computed from Equation (10.5) lies outside these bounds, a decision can be made regarding the presence of positive or negative serial correlation. These upper and lower limits, or upper and lower critical values, depend upon the number of observations, n, and the number of explanatory variables, k. These limits for n, from 6 to 200 observations, and for k, up to 20 explanatory variables, have been tabulated by Durbin and Watson for 1% and 5% significance levels and are reproduced in Appendix E, Table E-5. The actual mechanics of the Durbin-Watson test are best explained with Figure 10-5.

The steps involved in this test are as follows:

1. Run the OLS regression and obtain the residuals e_t.
2. Compute d from Eq. (10.5). (Most computer programs now do this routinely.)
3. Find out the critical d_L and d_U from the Durbin-Watson tables for the given sample size and the given number of explanatory variables.
4. Now follow the decision rules given in Table 10-3, which for ease of reference are also depicted in Figure 10-5.

Returning to Example 10.1, we have $d = 0.1463$. From the Durbin-Watson tables we see that for $n = 50$ (which is closest to our sample size of 48) and one explanatory variable, $d_L = 1.503$ and $d_U = 1.585$ at the 5% level of significance.

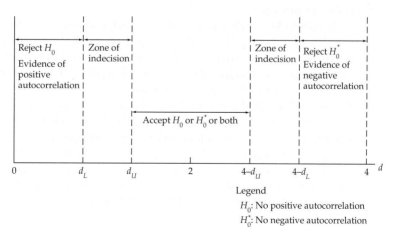

FIGURE 10-5   The Durbin-Watson d statistic

---

[8]Without going into technicalities, it should be mentioned that the exact critical value of d depends upon the value(s) taken by the explanatory variable(s), which will obviously vary from sample to sample.

TABLE 10-3   DURBIN-WATSON d TEST: DECISION RULES

Null hypothesis	Decision	If
No positive autocorrelation	Reject	$0 < d < d_L$
No positive autocorrelation	No decision	$d_L \leq d \leq d_U$
No negative autocorrelation	Reject	$4 - d_L < d < 4$
No negative autocorrelation	No decision	$4 - d_U \leq d \leq 4 - d_L$
No positive or negative autocorrelation	Do not reject	$d_U < d < 4 - d_U$

Since the computed d of 0.1463 is well below the lower bound value of 1.503, following the decision rules given in Table 10-3, we conclude that there is positive autocorrelation in our wages-productivity regression residuals. We reached the same conclusion on the basis of visual inspection of the residuals given in Figures 10-3 and 10-4.

Although popularly used, one drawback of the d test is that if it falls in the *indecisive zone,* or *region of ignorance* (see Figure 10-5), we cannot conclude whether or not autocorrelation exists. To solve this problem, several authors[9] have proposed modifications of the d test but they are involved and beyond the scope of this book. The computer program SHAZAM performs an exact d test (i.e., true critical value), and if you have access to the program you may want to use that test if the d statistic lies in the indecisive zone. Since the consequences of autocorrelation can be quite serious, as we have seen, if a d statistic lies in the indecisive zone, it might be prudent to assume that autocorrelation exists and proceed to correct the condition. Of course, the nonparametric runs test (discussed in Appendix 10A) and the visual graphics should also be invoked in this case.

To conclude our discussion of the d test, it should be reemphasized that this test should not be applied if the assumptions underlying this test discussed earlier do not hold. In particular, it should not be used to test for serial correlation in autoregressive models like the regression (10.7). If applied mistakenly in such cases, the computed d value is often found to be around 2, which is the value of d expected in the absence of AR(1). Hence, there is a built-in bias against discovering serial correlation in such models. But if such a model is used in empirical analysis, to test for autocorrelation in such models, Durbin has developed the so-called **h statistic,** which is discussed in Problem 10.16.

Before we move on, note that there are several other methods of detecting autocorrelation. We will discuss two such methods, the **runs test** and the **Breusch-Godfrey test,** in Appendixes 10A and 10B, respectively.[10]

[9]Some authors maintain that d_U, the upper limit of Durbin-Watson d, is approximately the true significance limit. Therefore, if the calculated d lies below d_U, we can assume that there is (positive) autocorrelation. See, for example, E. J. Hannan and R. D. Terrell, "Testing for Serial Correlation after Least Squares Regression," *Econometrica,* vol. 36, no. 2, 1968, pp. 133–150.

[10]For further details, see Gujarati and Porter, *Basic Econometrics,* 5th ed., McGraw-Hill, New York, 2009, Chapter 11.

10.4 REMEDIAL MEASURES

Since the consequences of serial correlation can be very serious and the cost of further testing can be high, and if on the basis of one or more diagnostic tests discussed earlier it is found that we have autocorrelation, we need to seek remedial measures. The remedy, however, depends upon what knowledge we have or can assume about the nature of interdependence in the error terms u_t. To keep the discussion as simple as possible, let us revert to our two-variable model:

$$Y_t = B_1 + B_2X_t + u_t \tag{10.11}$$

and assume that the error terms follow the AR(1) scheme:

$$u_t = \rho u_{t-1} + v_t \quad -1 \le \rho \le 1 \tag{10.6}$$

where the v's satisfy the usual OLS assumptions and ρ is known.

Now if somehow we can transform the model (10.11) so that in the transformed model the error term is serially independent, then applying OLS to the transformed model will give us the usual BLUE estimators, assuming of course that the other assumptions of CLRM are fulfilled. Recall that we used the same philosophy in the case of heteroscedasticity, where our objective was to transform the model so that in the transformed model the error term was homoscedastic.

To see how we can transform the regression (10.11) so that in the transformed model the error term does not have autocorrelation, write the regression (10.11) with a one-period lag as

$$Y_{t-1} = B_1 + B_2X_{t-1} + u_{t-1} \tag{10.12}$$

Multiply regression (10.12) by ρ on both sides to obtain

$$\rho Y_{t-1} = \rho B_1 + \rho B_2X_{t-1} + \rho u_{t-1} \tag{10.13}$$

Now subtract Equation (10.13) from Equation (10.11), to yield

$$(Y_t - \rho Y_{t-1}) = B_1(1 - \rho) + B_2(X_t - \rho X_{t-1}) + v_t \tag{10.14}$$

where use is made of Eq. (10.6).

Since the error term v_t in Equation (10.14) satisfies the standard OLS assumption, Eq. (10.14) provides the kind of transformation we are looking for which gives us a model free from serial correlation. If we write Eq. (10.14) as

$$Y_t^* = B_1^* + B_2X_t^* + v_t \tag{10.15}$$

where $Y_t^* = (Y_t - \rho Y_{t-1})$

$X_t^* = (X_t - \rho X_{t-1})$

$B_1^* = B_1(1 - \rho)$

and apply OLS to the transformed variables Y^* and X^*, the estimators thus obtained will have the desirable BLUE property.[11] Incidentally, note that when we apply OLS to transformed models, the estimators thus obtained are called **generalized least squares (GLS)** estimators. In the previous chapter on heteroscedasticity we also used GLS, except that there we called it WLS (weighted least squares).

We call Equations (10.14) and (10.15) **generalized difference equations;** specific cases of the generalized difference equation in which ρ takes a particular value will be discussed shortly. It involves regressing Y on X, not in the original form, but in the *difference form,* which is obtained by subtracting a portion ($= \rho$) of the value of a variable in the previous period from its value in the current time period. Thus, if $\rho = 0.5$, we subtract 0.5 times the value of the variable in the previous time period from its value in the current time period. In this differencing procedure we lose one observation because the first sample observation has no antecedent. To avoid this loss of one observation, the first observation of Y and X is transformed as follows:

$$Y_1^* = \sqrt{1 - \rho^2}(Y_1)$$
$$X_1^* = \sqrt{1 - \rho^2}(X_1)$$

(10.16)

This transformation is known as the **Prais-Winsten transformation.** In practice, though, if the sample size is very large, this transformation is not generally made and we use Eq. (10.14) with $(n - 1)$ observations. However, in small samples sometimes the results are sensitive if we exclude the first observation.

A couple of points about the generalized difference transformation Eq. (10.14) should be made here. *First,* although we have considered only a two-variable model, the transformation can be generalized to more than one explanatory variable (see Problem 10.18). *Second,* so far we have assumed only an AR(1) scheme, as in Eq. (10.6). But the transformation can be generalized easily to higher-order schemes, such as an AR(2), AR(3), etc.; no new principle is involved in the transformation except some tedious algebra.

It seems that we have a "solution" to the autocorrelation problem in the generalized difference equation (10.14). Alas, we have a problem. For the successful application of the scheme, we must know the true autocorrelation parameter, ρ. Of course, we do not know it, and to use Eq. (10.14), we must find ways to estimate the unknown ρ. The situation here is similar to that in the case of heteroscedasticity. There, we did not know the true σ_i^2 and therefore had to make some plausible assumptions as to what it might be. Of course, had we known it, we could have used weighted least squares (WLS) straightforwardly.

---

[11]A technical point may be noted here, since $B_1^* = B_1(1 - \rho)$, $B_1 = B_1^*/(1 - \rho)$, and so may not get unbiased estimation of the original intercept term. But as noted on several occasions, in most applications the intercept term may not have any concrete economic meaning.

10.5 HOW TO ESTIMATE ρ

There is no unique method of estimating ρ; rather, there are several approaches, some of which we present now.

ρ = 1: The First Difference Method

Since ρ lies between 0 and ±1, we can assume any value for ρ in the range −1 to 1 and use the generalized difference equation (10.14). As a matter of fact, Hildreth and Lu[12] proposed such a scheme. But which particular value of ρ? For even within the confines of the −1 to +1 range literally hundreds of values of ρ can be chosen. In applied econometrics one assumption that has been used extensively is that ρ = 1; that is, the error terms are perfectly positively autocorrelated, which may be true of some economic time series. If this assumption is acceptable, the generalized difference equation (10.14) reduces to the **first difference equation** as

$$Y_t - Y_{t-1} = B_2(X_t - X_{t-1}) + v_t$$

or

$$\Delta Y_t = B_2 \Delta X_t + v_t \qquad (10.17)$$

where Δ, called *delta*, is the first difference operator and is a symbol or operator (like the operator E for expected value) for successive differences of two values. In estimating Equation (10.17) all we have to do is to form the first differences of both the dependent and explanatory variable(s) and run the regression on the variable(s) thus transformed.

Note an important feature of the first difference model (10.17): *The model has no intercept.* Hence, to estimate Eq. (10.17), we have to use the regression-through-the-origin routine in the computer package. Naturally, we will not be able to estimate the intercept term in this case directly. (But note that $b_1 = \overline{Y} - b_2\overline{X}$.)

ρ Estimated from Durbin-Watson d Statistic

Recall earlier that we established the following approximate relationship between the d statistic and ρ:

$$d \approx 2(1 - \hat{\rho}) \qquad (10.8)$$

from which we can obtain

$$\hat{\rho} \approx 1 - \frac{d}{2} \qquad (10.18)$$

Since the d statistic is now routinely computed by most regression packages, we can easily obtain an approximate estimate of ρ from Equation (10.18).

---

[12]G. Hildreth and J. Y. Lu, "Demand Relations with Autocorrelated Disturbances," Michigan State University, *Agricultural Experiment Station,* Technical Bulletin 276, November 1960.

Once ρ is estimated from d as shown in Eq. (10.18), we can then use it to run the generalized difference equation (10.14) for the wages-productivity example, in which $d = 0.1463$. Therefore,

$$\hat{\rho} \approx 1 - \frac{0.1463}{2} = 0.9268 \qquad (10.19)$$

This ρ value is obviously different from $\rho = 1$ assumed for the first difference transformation. We can use this ρ value to transform the data as in Eq. (10.14).

This method of transformation is easy to use and generally gives good estimates of ρ if the sample size is reasonably large. For small samples, another estimate of ρ based on d is suggested by Theil and Nagar, which is discussed in Problem 10.20.

ρ Estimated from OLS Residuals, e_t

Recall the first-order autoregressive scheme

$$u_t = \rho u_{t-1} + v_t \qquad (10.6)$$

Since the u's are not directly observable, we can use their sample counterparts, the e's, and run the following regression:

$$e_t = \hat{\rho} e_{t-1} + v_t \qquad (10.20)$$

where $\hat{\rho}$ is an estimator of ρ. Statistical theory shows that although in small samples $\hat{\rho}$ is a biased estimator of true ρ, as the sample size increases the bias tends to disappear.[13] Hence, if the sample size is reasonably large, we can use $\hat{\rho}$ obtained from Equation (10.20) and use it to transform the data as shown in Eq. (10.14). An advantage of Eq. (10.20) is its simplicity, for we use the usual OLS method to obtain the residuals. The necessary data to run the regression are given in Table 10-2, and the results of the regression (10.20) are as follows:

$$\hat{e}_t = 0.8915 e_{t-1}$$
$$\text{se} = (0.0552) \qquad r^2 = 0.8499 \qquad (10.21)$$

Thus, the estimated ρ is about 0.89. (See Table 10-4.)

Other Methods of Estimating ρ

Besides the methods discussed previously, there are other ways of estimating ρ, which are as follows:

1. The Cochrane-Orcutt iterative procedure.
2. The Cochrane-Orcutt two-step method.
3. The Durbin two-step method.

---

[13]Technically, we say that $\hat{\rho}$ is a *consistent* estimator of ρ.

TABLE 10-4 WAGES-PRODUCTIVITY REGRESSION: ORIGINAL AND TRANSFORMED DATA ($\rho = 0.8915$)

RWAGES	RWAGES(−1)	RLAGY	YDIF	PRODUCT	PRODUCT(−1)	RLAGX	XDIF
59.8710	—	—	—	48.0260	—	—	—
61.3180	59.8710	53.3750	7.9430	48.8650	48.0260	42.8152	6.0498
63.0540	61.3180	54.6650	8.3890	50.5670	48.8650	43.5631	7.0039
65.1920	63.0540	56.2126	8.9794	52.8820	50.5670	45.0805	7.8015
66.6330	65.1920	58.1187	8.5143	54.9500	52.8820	47.1443	7.8057
68.2570	66.6330	59.4033	8.8537	56.8080	54.9500	48.9879	7.8201
69.6760	68.2570	60.8511	8.8249	58.8170	56.8080	50.6443	8.1727
72.3000	69.6760	62.1162	10.1838	61.2040	58.8170	52.4354	8.7686
74.1210	72.3000	64.4555	9.6656	62.5420	61.2040	54.5634	7.9786
76.8950	74.1210	66.0789	10.8161	64.6770	62.5420	55.7562	8.9208
78.0080	76.8950	68.5519	9.4561	64.9930	64.6770	57.6595	7.3335
79.4520	78.0080	69.5441	9.9079	66.2850	64.9930	57.9413	8.3437
80.8860	79.4520	70.8315	10.0545	69.0150	66.2850	59.0931	9.9219
83.3280	80.8860	72.1099	11.2181	71.2430	69.0150	61.5269	9.7161
85.0620	83.3280	74.2869	10.7751	73.4100	71.2430	63.5131	9.8969
83.9880	85.0620	75.8328	8.1552	72.2570	73.4100	65.4450	6.8120
84.8430	83.9880	74.8753	9.9677	74.7920	72.2570	64.4171	10.3749
87.1480	84.8430	75.6375	11.5105	77.1450	74.7920	66.6771	10.4679
88.3350	87.1480	77.6924	10.6426	78.4550	77.1450	68.7748	9.6802
89.7360	88.3350	78.7507	10.9853	79.3200	78.4550	69.9426	9.3774
89.8630	89.7360	79.9996	9.8634	79.3050	79.3200	70.7138	8.5912
89.5920	89.8630	80.1129	9.4791	79.1510	79.3050	70.7004	8.4506
89.6450	89.5920	79.8713	9.7737	80.7780	79.1510	70.5631	10.2149
90.6370	89.6450	79.9185	10.7185	80.1480	80.7780	72.0136	8.1344
90.5910	90.6370	80.8029	9.7881	83.0010	80.1480	71.4519	11.5491
90.7120	90.5910	80.7619	9.9501	85.2140	83.0010	73.9954	11.2186
91.9100	90.7120	80.8697	11.0403	87.1310	85.2140	75.9683	11.1627
94.8690	91.9100	81.9378	12.9312	89.6730	87.1310	77.6773	11.9957
95.2070	94.8690	84.5757	10.6313	90.1330	89.6730	79.9435	10.1895
96.5270	95.2070	84.8770	11.6500	91.5060	90.1330	80.3536	11.1524
95.0050	96.5270	86.0538	8.9512	92.4080	91.5060	81.5776	10.8304
96.2190	95.0050	84.6970	11.5220	94.3850	92.4080	82.3817	12.0033
97.4650	96.2190	85.7792	11.6858	95.9030	94.3850	84.1442	11.7588
100.0000	97.4650	86.8900	13.1100	100.0000	95.9030	85.4975	14.5025
99.7120	100.0000	89.1500	10.5620	100.3860	100.0000	89.1500	11.2360
99.0240	99.7120	88.8932	10.1308	101.3490	100.3860	89.4941	11.8549
98.6900	99.0240	88.2799	10.4101	101.4950	101.3490	90.3526	11.1424
99.4780	98.6900	87.9821	11.4959	104.4920	101.4950	90.4828	14.0092
100.5120	99.4780	88.6846	11.8274	106.4780	104.4920	93.1546	13.3234
105.1730	100.5120	89.6064	15.5666	109.4740	106.4780	94.9251	14.5489
108.0440	105.1730	93.7617	14.2823	112.8280	109.4740	97.5961	15.2319
111.9920	108.0440	96.3212	15.6708	116.1170	112.8280	100.5862	15.5308
113.5360	111.9920	99.8409	13.6951	119.0820	116.1170	103.5183	15.5637
115.6940	113.5360	101.2173	14.4767	123.9480	119.0820	106.1616	17.7864
117.7090	115.6940	103.1412	14.5678	128.7050	123.9480	110.4996	18.2054
118.9490	117.7090	104.9376	14.0114	132.3900	128.7050	114.7405	17.6495
119.6920	118.9490	106.0430	13.6490	135.0210	132.3900	118.0257	16.9953
120.4470	119.6920	106.7054	13.7416	136.4040	135.0210	120.3712	16.0328

Notes: RWAGES = Real wages
RWAGES(−1) = Real wages lagged one period
RLAGY = 0.8915 times rwages (−1)
YDIF = rwages − rlagy
PRODUCT = productivity
PRODUCT(−1) = productivity lagged one period
RLAGX = 0.8915 times product (−1)
XDIF = product − rlagX

TABLE 10-5   REGRESSION RESULTS OF WAGES AND PRODUCTIVITY BASED ON VARIOUS TRANSFORMATIONS

Method of transformation	ρ estimated from	Intercept	Slope	r^2	Autocorrelation?
Original regression	$\rho = 0$ (assumed)	33.6360 (1.4001)	0.6614 (0.0156)	0.9749	Yes
First difference	$\rho = 1$	*	0.6469 (0.0632)	0.6950**	No!
Eq. (10.21)!!	$\rho = 0.8915$	4.8131[†] (0.4783)	0.5617 (0.0413)	0.8040	No!
Eq. (10.21)!!!	$\rho = 0.8915$	2.9755 (0.7849)	0.7421 (0.0661)	0.7326	No!

Notes: Figures in the parentheses are the estimated standard errors.
*There is no intercept term in this regression. (Why?)
! Based on the runs test on the estimated residuals.
!! Excludes the first observation.
!!! Includes the first observation (i.e., Prais-Winsten transformation).
**The various r^2 values are not directly comparable.
†The intercept term in the transformed regression is $B_1^* = B_1(1 - \rho)$. The original intercept can be obtained as $B_1 = B_1^*/(1 - \rho)$.

4. The Hildreth-Lu search procedure.
5. The maximum likelihood method.

A discussion of all these methods will take us far afield and thus is left for the references.[14] (But see some of the problems at the end of the chapter.) Whichever method is employed, we use the ρ obtained from that method to transform our data as shown in Eq. (10.14) and run the usual OLS regression.[15] Although most computer software packages do the transformations with minimum instructions, we show in Table 10-4 how the transformed data will look.

Before concluding, let us consider the results of applying (1) the first difference transformation and (2) the transformation based on Eq. (10.21) to the wages-productivity regression. The results are summarized in Table 10-5 (see also Figures 10-6 and 10-7). Several observations can be made about these results.

1. The original regression was plagued by autocorrelation, but the various transformed regressions seem to be free from autocorrelation on the basis of the runs tests.[16]

---

[14]For a discussion of these methods, see Gujarati and Porter, *Basic Econometrics*, 5th ed., McGraw-Hill, New York, 2009, Chapter 12.

[15]In large samples the differences in the estimates of ρ produced by the various methods are generally small.

[16]We can obtain the Durbin-Watson d statistic for the transformed regressions too. But econometric theory suggests that the computed d statistic from the transformed regressions may not be appropriate to test for autocorrelation in such regressions because if we were to use it for that purpose, it would suggest that the original error term may not follow the AR(1) scheme. It could, for example, follow an AR(2) scheme. The runs test discussed in Appendix 10A does not suffer from this problem since it is a nonparametric test.

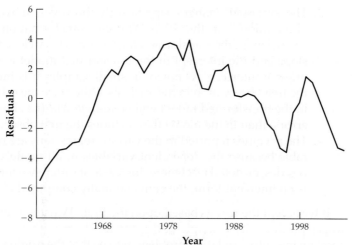

FIGURE 10-6   Residual from wages-productivity regression

2. Even though the ρ estimated from the first difference transformation and that estimated from Eq. (10.21) are not the same, the estimated slope coefficients do not differ substantially from one another if we do not include the first observation in the analysis. But the estimates of intercept and slope values are substantially different from the original OLS regression.

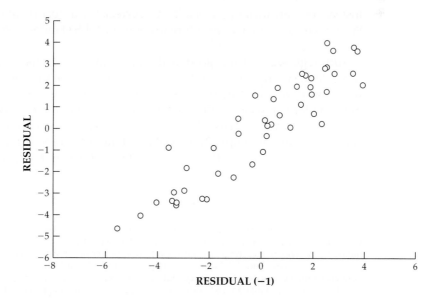

FIGURE 10-7   Residuals against lagged residual from the wages-productivity regression

3. The situation changes significantly, however, if we include the first observation via the Prais-Winsten transformation. Now the slope coefficient in the transformed regression is very close to the original OLS slope and the intercept in the transformed model is much closer to the original intercept. As noted, in small samples it is important to include the first observation in the analysis. Otherwise the estimated coefficients in the transformed model will be less *efficient* (i.e., have higher standard errors) than in the model that includes the first observation.

4. The r^2 values reported in the various regressions are not directly comparable because the dependent variables in all models are not the same. Besides, as noted elsewhere, for the first difference model in which there is no intercept term, the conventionally computed r^2 is not meaningful.

If we accept the results based upon the Prais-Winsten transformation for our wages-productivity example and compare them with the original regression beset by the autocorrelation problem, we see that the original t ratio of the slope coefficient, in absolute value, has decreased in the transformed regression. This is another way of saying that the original model underestimated the standard error. But this result is not surprising in view of our knowledge about theoretical consequences of autocorrelation. Fortunately, in this example even after correcting for autocorrelation, the estimated t ratio is statistically significant.[17] But that may not always be the case.

10.6   A LARGE SAMPLE METHOD OF CORRECTING OLS STANDARD ERRORS: THE NEWEY-WEST (NW) METHOD

Instead of transforming variables to correct for autocorrelation, Newey and West have developed a procedure to compute OLS standard errors that are corrected for autocorrelation.[18]

Although we will not go into the mathematics of this test,[19] it should be noted that, strictly speaking, this test is valid in large samples only. However, what constitutes a large sample is problem-specific. It should also be noted that most modern statistical software packages now include the NW test, which is popularly known as **HAC** (heteroscedasticity and autocorrelation-consistent) standard errors or simply **Newey-West standard errors.** *It is interesting to note that HAC does not change the values of the OLS estimator; it only corrects their standard errors.*

---

[17]Strictly speaking, this statement is correct if the sample size is reasonably large. This is because we do not know the true ρ and estimate it, and when we estimate ρ to transform the data, econometric theory shows that the usual statistical testing procedure is valid generally in large samples.

[18]W. K. Newey and K. West, "A Simple Positive Semi-Definite Heteroscedasticity and Autocorrelation Consistent Covariance Matrix," *Econometrica,* Vol. 55, 1987, pp. 703–708.

[19]For details, See Gujarati and Porter, *Basic Econometrics,* 5th ed., pp. 447–448.

To illustrate this test, we give in Table 10-6 (posted on the book's Web site) several macro-economic data for the U.S. from 1947-1Q to 2007-4Q, for a total of 244 quarterly observations. For our present purposes we will use data on corporate dividends paid and corporate profits (CP).

$$lDividend = B_1 + B_2 lCP + B_3 Time + u_t \qquad \text{(10.22)}$$

where l denotes natural logarithm.

The time or trend variable is included in the model to allow for the upward trend in the two time series. In Eq. (10.22) B_2 gives the elasticity of dividends with respect to profits and B_3 gives the relative, or if multiplied by 100, the percent growth in dividends over time.

Using EViews 6, we obtained the following results:

Dependent Variable: LDIVIDEND
Method: Least Squares

Sample: 1947Q1 2007Q4
Included observations: 244
Newey-West HAC Standard Errors & Covariance (lag truncation = 4)

	Coefficient	Std. error	t-Statistic	Prob.
C	0.435764	0.192185	2.267414	0.0243
LCP	0.424535	0.077733	5.461456	0.0000
Time	0.012691	0.001421	8.930795	0.0000
R-squared	0.991424	Mean dependent var	3.999717	
Adjusted R-squared	0.991353	S.D. dependent var	1.430724	
S.E. of regression	0.133041	Akaike info criterion	−1.184093	
Sum squared resid	4.265706	Schwarz criterion	−1.141095	
Log likelihood	147.4594	Hannan-Quinn criter.	−1.166776	
F-statistic	13930.73	Durbin-Watson stat	0.090181	
Prob (F-statistic)	0.000000			

Judged by the usual criteria, these results look "good." All the coefficients are individually highly significant (the p values are practically zero), and the R^2 is very high. The elasticity of dividends with respect to corporate profits is about 0.42 and the dividends have been increasing at the quarterly rate of about 1.26 percent. The only fly in the ointment is the low value of the Durbin-Watson statistic, which suggests a high degree of positive autocorrelation in the residuals. Therefore, we cannot trust these results without taking care of the autocorrelation problem.

Our sample of 244 observations covering a span of 61 years may be large enough to use the HAC procedure.

Using EViews 6, we obtained the following results:

Dependent Variable: LDIVIDEND
Method: Least Squares

Sample: 1947Q1 2007Q4
Included observations: 244
Newey-West HAC Standard Errors & Covariance (lag truncation = 4)

	Coefficient	Std. error	t-Statistic	Prob.
C	0.435764	0.192185	2.267414	0.0243
LCP	0.424535	0.077733	5.461456	0.0000
T	0.012691	0.001421	8.930795	0.0000
R-squared	0.991424	Mean dependent var		3.999717
Adjusted R-squared	0.991353	S.D. dependent var		1.430724
S.E. of regression	0.133041	Akaike info criterion		−1.184093
Sum squared resid	4.265706	Schwarz criterion		−1.141095
Log likelihood	147.4594	Hannan-Quinn criter.		−1.166776
F-statistic	13930.73	Durbin-Watson stat		0.090181
Prob (F-statistic)	0.000000			

The first thing to notice about these results is that the estimates of the regression coefficients remain the same under OLS as well as under HAC. However, the standard errors have changed substantially. It seems the OLS standard errors underestimated the true standard errors, thus inflating the t values. But even then the estimated regression coefficients are highly significant. *This example shows that autocorrelation need not necessarily negate the OLS results, but we should always check for the presence of autocorrelation in time series data.*

Incidentally, the HAC output still shows the same Durbin-Watson value as under OLS estimation. But do not worry about this, for HAC has already taken this into account in recalculating the standard errors.

10.7   SUMMARY

The major points of this chapter are as follows:

1. In the presence of autocorrelation OLS estimators, although unbiased, are not efficient. In short, they are not BLUE.
2. Assuming the Markov first-order autoregressive, the AR(1), scheme, we pointed out that the conventionally computed variances and standard errors of OLS estimators can be seriously biased.
3. As a result, standard t and F tests of significance can be seriously misleading.

4. Therefore, it is important to know whether there is autocorrelation in any given case. We considered three methods of detecting autocorrelation:
   a. graphical plotting of the residuals
   b. the runs test
   c. the Durbin-Watson d test
5. If autocorrelation is found, we suggest that it be corrected by appropriately transforming the model so that in the transformed model there is no autocorrelation. We illustrated the actual mechanics with several examples.

KEY TERMS AND CONCEPTS

The key terms and concepts introduced in this chapter are

Serial correlation or autocorrelation
   a) spatial correlation
Reasons for autocorrelation
   a) inertia or sluggishness
   b) model specification error
   c) cobweb phenomenon
   d) data manipulation
Detecting autocorrelation
   a) time-sequence plot
   b) the Durbin-Watson d test; coefficient of autocorrelation; the Markov first-order autoregressive or AR(1) scheme; autoregressive models; h statistic

Remedial measures for serial or autocorrelation
   a) generalized least squares (GLS) (generalized difference equation)
   b) Prais-Winsten transformation
Estimation of ρ
   a) first difference equation
   b) the Durbin-Watson d statistic
   c) OLS residuals
Large sample method of correcting OLS standard errors
   a) the Newey-West (NW) method; HAC; Newey-West standard errors

QUESTIONS

10.1. Explain briefly the meaning of
   a. Autocorrelation
   b. First-order autocorrelation
   c. Spatial correlation

10.2. What is the importance of assuming the Markov first-order, or AR(1), autocorrelation scheme?

10.3. Assuming the AR(1) scheme, what are the consequences of the CLRM assumption that the error terms in the PRF are uncorrelated?

10.4. In the presence of AR(1) autocorrelation, what is the method of estimation that will produce BLUE estimators? Outline the steps involved in implementing this method.

10.5. What are the various methods of estimating the autocorrelation parameter ρ in the AR(1) scheme?

10.6. What are the various methods of detecting autocorrelation? State clearly the assumptions underlying each method.

10.7. Although popularly used, what are some limitations of the Durbin-Watson d statistic?

10.8. State whether the following statements are true or false. Briefly justify your answers.

  a. When autocorrelation is present, OLS estimators are biased as well as inefficient.

  b. The Durbin-Watson d is useless in autoregressive models like the regression (10.7) where one of the explanatory variables is a lagged value(s) of the dependent variable.

  c. The Durbin-Watson d test assumes that the variance of the error term u_t is homoscedastic.

  d. The first difference transformation to eliminate autocorrelation assumes that the coefficient of autocorrelation ρ must be -1.

  e. The R^2 values of two models, one involving regression in the first difference form and another in the level form, are not directly comparable.

10.9. What is the importance of the Prais-Winsten transformation?

PROBLEMS

10.10. Complete the following table:

Sample size	Number of explanatory variables	Durbin-Watson d	Evidence of autocorrelation
25	2	0.83	Yes
30	5	1.24	—
50	8	1.98	—
60	6	3.72	—
200	20	1.61	—

10.11. Use the runs test to test for autocorrelation in the following cases. (Use the Swed-Eisenhart tables. See Appendix 10A.)

Sample size	Number of +	Number of −	Number of runs	Autocorrelation (?)
18	11	7	2	—
30	15	15	24	—
38	20	18	6	—
15	8	7	4	—
10	5	5	1	—

10.12. For the Phillips curve regression Equation (5.29) given in Chapter 5, the estimated d statistic would be 0.6394.

  a. Is there evidence of first-order autocorrelation in the residuals? If so, is it positive or negative?

    b. If there is autocorrelation, estimate the coefficient of autocorrelation from the d statistic.

    c. Using this estimate, transform the data given in Table 5-6 and estimate the generalized difference equation (10.15) (i.e., apply OLS to the transformed data).

    d. Is there autocorrelation in the regression estimated in part (c)? Which test do you use?

10.13. In studying the movement in the production workers' share in value added (i.e., labor's share) in manufacturing industries, the following regression results were obtained based on the U.S. data for the years 1949 to 1964[20] (t ratios in parentheses):

$$\text{Model A: } \hat{Y}_t = 0.4529 - 0.0041t; \quad r^2 = 0.5284; \quad d = 0.8252$$

$$t = \quad\quad\quad (-3.9608)$$

$$\text{Model B: } \hat{Y}_t = 0.4786 - 0.00127t + 0.0005t^2; \quad R^2 = 0.6629; \quad d = 1.82$$

$$t = \quad\quad\quad (-3.2724) \quad (2.7777)$$

where Y = labor's share and t = the time.

    a. Is there serial correlation in Model A? In Model B?

    b. If there is serial correlation in Model A but not in Model B, what accounts for the serial correlation in the former?

    c. What does this example tell us about the usefulness of the d statistic in detecting autocorrelation?

10.14. *Durbin's two-step method of estimating* ρ.[21] Write the generalized difference equation (10.14) in a slightly different but equivalent form as follows:

$$Y_t = B_1(1 - \rho) + B_2X_t - \rho B_2X_{t-1} + \rho Y_{t-1} + v_t$$

In *step 1* Durbin suggests estimating this regression with Y as the dependent variable and X_t, X_{t-1}, and Y_{t-1} as explanatory variables. The coefficient of Y_{t-1} will provide an estimate of ρ. The ρ thus estimated is a *consistent* estimator; that is, in large samples it provides a good estimate of true ρ.

In *step 2* use the ρ estimated from step 1 to transform the data to estimate the generalized difference equation (10.14).

Apply Durbin's two-step method to the U.S. import expenditure data discussed in Chapter 7 and compare your results with those shown for the original regression.

10.15. Consider the following regression model:[22]

$$\hat{Y}_t = -49.4664 + 0.88544X_{2t} + 0.09253X_{3t}; \quad\quad R^2 = 0.9979; d = 0.8755$$

$$t = (-2.2392) \quad (70.2936) \quad\quad (2.6933)$$

[20]See Damodar N. Gujarati, "Labor's Share in Manufacturing Industries," *Industrial and Labor Relations Review*, vol. 23, no. 1, October 1969, pp. 65–75.

[21]*Royal Statistical Society*, series B, vol. 22, 1960, pp. 139–153.

[22]See Dominick Salvatore, *Managerial Economics*, McGraw-Hill, New York, 1989, pp. 138, 148.

where Y = the personal consumption expenditure (1982 billions of dollars)
X_2 = the personal disposable income (1982 billions of dollars) (PDI)
X_3 = the Dow Jones Industrial Average Stock Index

The regression is based on U.S. data from 1961 to 1985.

a. Is there first-order autocorrelation in the residuals of this regression? How do you know?

b. Using the Durbin two-step procedure, the preceding regression was transformed per Eq. (10.15), yielding the following results:

$$Y_t^* = -17.97 + 0.89X_{2t}^* + 0.09X_{3t}^*; \qquad R^2 = 0.9816; d = 2.28$$

$$t = \qquad (30.72) \qquad (2.66)$$

Has the problem of autocorrelation been resolved? How do you know?

c. Comparing the original and transformed regressions, the t value of the PDI has dropped dramatically. What does this suggest?

d. Is the d value from the transformed regression of any value in determining the presence, or lack thereof, of autocorrelation in the transformed data?

10.16. *Durbin h statistic.* In autoregressive models like Eq. (10.7):

$$Y_t = B_1 + B_2X_t + B_3Y_{t-1} + v_t$$

the usual d statistic is not applicable to detect autocorrelation. For such models, Durbin has suggested replacing the d statistic by the h statistic defined as

$$h \approx \hat{\rho}\sqrt{\frac{n}{1 - n \cdot var(b_3)}}$$

where n = the sample size
$\hat{\rho}$ = the estimator of the autocorrelation coefficient ρ
$var(b_3)$ = the variance of the estimator of B_3, the coefficient of lagged Y variable

Durbin has shown that for *large samples,* and given the null hypothesis that true $\rho = 0$, the h statistic is distributed as

$$h \sim N(0, 1)$$

It follows the standard normal distribution, that is, normal distribution with zero mean and unit variance. Therefore, we would reject the null hypothesis that $\rho = 0$ if the computed h statistic exceeds the critical h value. If, e.g., the level of significance is 5%, the critical h value is -1.96 or 1.96. Therefore, if a computed h exceeds $|1.96|$, we can reject the null hypothesis; if it does not exceed this critical value, we do not reject the null hypothesis of no (first-order) autocorrelation. Incidentally, $\hat{\rho}$ entering the h formula can be obtained from any one of the methods discussed in the text.

Now consider the following demand for money function for India for the periods 1948 to 1949 and 1964 to 1965:

$$\widehat{\ln M_t} = 1.6027 - 0.1024 \ln R_t + 0.6869 \ln Y_t + 0.5284 \ln M_{t-1}$$

$$se = (1.2404) \quad (0.3678) \qquad (0.3427) \qquad (0.2007) \qquad R^2 = 0.9227$$

$$d = 1.8624$$

where M = real cash balances
R = the long-term interest rate
Y = the aggregate real national income

a. For this regression, find the h statistic and test the hypothesis that the preceding regression does not suffer from first-order autocorrelation.
b. As the regression results show, the Durbin-Watson d statistic is 1.8624. Tell why in this case it is inappropriate to use the d statistic. But note that you can use this d value to estimate ρ ($\hat{\rho} \approx 1 - d/2$).

10.17. Consider the data given in Table 10-7 (on the textbook's Web site) relating to stock prices and GDP for the period 1980–2006.
  a. Estimate the OLS regression

$$Y_t = B_1 + B_2 X_t + u_t$$

  b. Find out if there is first-order autocorrelation in the data on the basis of the d statistic.
  c. If there is, use the d value to estimate the autocorrelation parameter ρ.
  d. Using this estimate of ρ, transform the data per the generalized difference equation (10.14), and estimate this equation by OLS (1) by dropping the first observation and (2) by including the first observation.
  e. Repeat part (d), but estimate ρ from the residuals as shown in Eq. (10.20). Using this estimate of ρ, estimate the generalized difference equation (10.14).
  f. Use the first difference method to transform the model into Eq. (10.17) and estimate the transformed model.
  g. Compare the results of regressions obtained in parts (d), (e), and (f). What conclusions can you draw? Is there autocorrelation in the transformed regressions? How do you know?

10.18. Consider the following model:

$$Y_t = B_1 + B_2 X_{2t} + B_3 X_{3t} + B_4 X_{4t} + u_t$$

Suppose the error term follows the AR(1) scheme in Eq. (10.6). How would you transform this model so that there is no autocorrelation in the transformed model? (*Hint:* Extend Eq. [10.15].)

10.19. Establish Eq. (10.8). (*Hint:* Expand Eq. [10.5] and use Eq. [10.9]. Also, note that for a large sample size $\sum e_{t-1}^2$ and $\sum e_t^2$ are approximately the same.)

10.20. *The Theil-Nagar ρ based on d statistic.* Theil and Nagar have suggested that in small samples instead of estimating ρ as $(1 - d/2)$, it should be estimated as

$$\hat{\rho} = \frac{n^2(1 - d/2) + k^2}{n^2 - k^2}$$

where n = the sample size
d = the Durbin-Watson d
k = the number of coefficients (including the intercept) to be estimated

Show that for large n, this estimate of ρ is equal to the one obtained by the simpler formula $(1 - d/2)$.

10.21. Refer to Example 7.3 relating expenditure on imports (Y) to personal disposable income (X). Now consider the following models:

	Model 1	Model 2	Model 3
Intercept	−136.16	22.69	12.18
X	0.2082	0.2975	0.0382
Time	—	−18.525	−3.045
Y (−1)	—	—	0.9659
R^2	0.969	0.984	0.994
d	0.216	0.341	1.611

a. What do these results suggest about the nature of autocorrelation in this example?

b. How would you interpret the time and lagged Y terms in Model 3?
Note: The estimated coefficients in all the models, except for the X and Time coefficients in Model 3, were statistically significant at the 5% or lower level of significance.

10.22. *Monte Carlo experiment.* Consider the following model:

$$Y_t = 1.0 + 0.9X_t + u_t \tag{1}$$

where X takes values of 1, 2, 3, 4, 5, 6, 7, 8, 9, 10. Assume that

$$u_t = \rho u_{t-1} + v_t$$
$$= 0.9u_{t-1} + v_t \tag{2}$$

where $v_t \sim N(0, 1)$. Assume that $u_0 = 0$.
a. Generate 10 values of v_t and then 10 values of u_t per Equation (2).

     b. Using the 10 X values and the 10 u values generated in the preceding step, generate 10 values of Y.

     c. Regress the Y values generated in part (b) on the 10 X values, obtaining b_1 and b_2.

     d. How do the computed b_1 and b_2 compare with the true values of 1 and 0.9, respectively?

     e. What can you conclude from this experiment?

10.23. Continue with Problem 10.22. Now assume that $\rho = 0.1$ and repeat the exercise. What do you observe? What general conclusion can you draw from Problems 10.22 and 10.23?

APPENDIX 10A: The Runs Test

THE RUNS TEST[23]

To explain this test, simply note the sign ($+$ or $-$) of the residuals obtained from the estimated regression. Suppose in a sample of 20 observations, we obtained the following sequence of residuals

$$(++)(-\ -\ -\ -\ -\ -\ -\ -\ -\ -\ -\ -\ -)(+++++) \qquad \textbf{(10A.1)}$$

    We now define a **run** as an uninterrupted sequence of one symbol or attribute, such as $+$ or $-$. We further define the **length of the run** as the number of elements in the run. In the sequence shown in Equation (10A.1), there are 3 runs—a run of 2 pluses (i.e., of length 2), a run of 13 minuses (i.e., of length 13), and a run of 5 pluses (i.e., of length 5); for better visual effect we have put the various runs in parentheses.

    By examining how runs behave in a strictly random sequence of observations, we can derive a test of randomness of runs. The question we ask is: *Are the 3 runs observed in our example consisting of 20 observations too many or too few compared with the number of runs expected in a strictly random sequence of 20 observations?* If there are too many runs, it means that the e's change sign frequently, thus suggesting negative serial correlation (cf. Figure 10-2[b]). Similarly, if there are too few runs, it suggests positive autocorrelation, as in Figure 10-2(a).

        Now let N = total number of observations ($= N_1 + N_2$)

             N_1 = number of $+$ symbols (i.e., $+$ residuals)

             N_2 = number of $-$ symbols (i.e., $-$ residuals)

             k = number of runs

    Then under the null hypothesis that the successive outcomes (here, residuals) are independent, Swed and Eisenhart have developed special tables that give

---

[23]It is a nonparametric test because it makes no assumptions about the (probability) distribution from which the observations are taken.

critical values of the runs expected in a random sequence of N observations. These tables are given in Appendix E, Table E-6.

Swed-Eisenhart Critical Runs Test

To illustrate the use of these tables, let us revert to the sequence shown in Eq. (10A.1). We have $N = 20$, $N_1 = 7$ (7 pluses), $N_2 = 13$ (13 minuses), and $k = 3$ runs. For $N_1 = 7$ and $N_2 = 13$, the 5% critical values of runs are 5 and 15. Now, as noted in Appendix E, Table E-6, if the actual number of runs is equal to or less than 5 or equal to or greater than 15, we can reject the hypothesis that the observed sequence of the e's given in Eq. (10A.1) is random. In our example the actual number of runs is 3. Hence, we can conclude that the observed sequence in Eq. (10A.1) is not random.

Note that the Swed-Eisenhart table is for 40 observations at most—20 pluses and 20 minuses. If the actual sample size is greater, we cannot use these tables. But in that case it can be shown that if $N_1 > 10$ and $N_2 > 10$ and the null hypothesis is that the successive observations (residuals in our case) are independent, the number of runs k is *asymptotically (i.e., in large samples) normally distributed* with

$$\text{Mean: } E(k) = \frac{2N_1N_2}{N} + 1 \qquad \text{(10A.2)}$$

$$\text{Variance: } \sigma_k^2 = \frac{2N_1N_2(2N_1N_2 - N)}{N^2(N - 1)} \qquad \text{(10A.3)}$$

If the null hypothesis of randomness is sustainable, following the properties of the normal distribution, we should expect that

$$\text{Prob}[E(k) - 1.96\sigma_k \le k \le E(k) + 1.96\sigma_k] = 0.95 \qquad \text{(10A.4)}$$

That is, the probability is 95% that the preceding interval will include the observed k.

Decision Rule

Do not reject the null hypothesis of randomness with 95% confidence if k, the number of runs, lies in the interval of Eq. (10A.4); reject the null hypothesis if the estimated k lies outside these limits. (*Note:* You can choose any level of confidence you want.)

APPENDIX 10B: A General Test of Autocorrelation: The Breusch-Godfrey (BG) Test

A test of autocorrelation that is more general than some of the tests discussed so far is one developed by statisticians Breusch and Godfrey.[24] This test is general in that it allows for (1) stochastic regressors, such as the lagged values of the dependent variables, (2) higher-order autoregressive schemes, such as AR(1), AR(2), etc., and (3) simple or higher-order moving averages of the purely random error terms, such as v_{t-1}, v_{t-2}, etc.

To illustrate this test, we revert to the dividend–corporate profits example discussed in Section 10.6. In that example we regressed the logarithm of dividend on the logarithm of corporate profits and a trend variable. On the basis of the Durbin-Watson test, we found in that example that we did have the autocorrelation problem. This is also confirmed by the BG test, which proceeds as follows:

1. Run the dividend regression as shown in Eq. (10.22) and obtain residuals from this regression, e_t.

2. Now run the following regression:

$$e_t = A_1 + A_2 lCP_t + A_2\, Time + C_1 e_{t-1} + C_2 e_{t-2} + \cdots + C_k e_{t-k} + v_t$$

   That is, regress the residual at time t on the original regressors, including the intercept and the lagged values of the residuals up to time $(t - k)$, the value of k being determined by trial and error or on the basis of Akaike or Schwarz information criteria. Obtain the R^2 value of this regression. This is called the **auxiliary regression.**

3. Calculate nR^2, that is, obtain the product of the sample size n and the R^2 value obtained in (2). Under the null hypothesis that all the coefficients of the lagged residual terms are simultaneously equal to zero, it can be shown that in large samples

$$nR^2 \sim \chi_k^2$$

   That is, in large samples, the product of the sample size and R^2 follows the chi-square distribution with k degrees of freedom (i.e., the number of lagged residual terms). In econometrics literature, the BG test is known as the **Lagrange multiplier test.**

---

[24]T. S. Breusch, "Testing for Autocorrelation in Dynamic Linear Models," *Australian Economic Papers,* vol. 17, 1978, pp. 334–355, and L. G. Godfrey, "Testing Against General Autoregressive and Moving Average Error Models When the Regressand Includes Lagged Dependent Variables," *Econometrica,* vol. 46, 1978, pp. 1293–1302.

For our example, we obtained the following results (for illustrative purposes we have used three lagged values of the residuals, although only the first lagged value is statistically significant):

Breusch-Godfrey Serial Correlation LM Test:

F-statistic	823.0875	Prob. F(3,238)	0.0000
Obs*R-squared	222.5495	Prob. Chi-Square(3)	0.0000

Test Equation:
Dependent Variable: RESID
Method: Least Squares

Sample: 1947Q1 2007Q4
Included observations: 244
Presample missing value lagged residuals set to zero.

	Coefficient	Std. error	t-Statistic	Prob.
C	−0.020423	0.031482	−0.648726	0.5171
LCP	0.007548	0.012027	0.627611	0.5309
Time	−0.000121	0.000214	−0.565962	0.5720
RESID(−1)	0.907903	0.064654	14.04247	0.0000
RESID(−2)	−0.021374	0.087434	−0.244459	0.8071
RESID(−3)	0.074971	0.064785	1.157217	0.2483

R-squared	0.912088	Mean dependent var	−1.10E-15
Adjusted R-squared	0.910241	S.D. dependent var	0.132493
S.E. of regression	0.039694	Akaike info criterion	−3.590926
Sum squared resid	0.375005	Schwarz criterion	−3.504930
Log likelihood	444.0929	Hannan-Quinn criter.	−3.556291
F-statistic	493.8525	Durbin-Watson stat	2.021935
Prob (F-statistic)	0.000000		

As you can see, $nR^2 \sim 222.54 = \chi_3^2$. The probability of obtaining a chi-square value of as much as 222.54 or greater for 3 d.f. is practically zero. Therefore, we can reject the hypothesis that $C_1 = C_2 = C_3 = 0$. That is, there is evidence of autocorrelation in the error term. The BG test, therefore, confirms the finding on the basis of the Durbin-Watson test. But keep in mind that the BG test is of general applicability, whereas the Durbin-Watson test assumes only first-order serial correlation.

PART **III**

ADVANCED TOPICS IN ECONOMETRICS

In this part, consisting of two chapters, we discuss two topics that may be advanced for the beginner. But with an instructor's help, students can master them with some effort.

Chapter 11 discusses simultaneous equation models. Chapters in the previous two parts of the text were devoted to single equation regression models because such models are used extensively in empirical work in business and economics. In such models, as we have seen, one variable (the dependent variable, Y) is expressed as a linear function of one or more other variables (the explanatory variables, the X's). In such models an implicit assumption is that the cause-and-effect relationship, *if any*, between Y and the X's is unidirectional; the explanatory variables are the *cause*, and the dependent variable is the *effect*.

However, there are situations where there is a two-way flow, or influence, among economic variables; that is, one economic variable affects another economic variable(s) and is, in turn, affected by it (them). Thus in the regression of money (M) on the rate of interest (r), the single-equation methodology assumes implicitly that the rate of interest is fixed (say, by the Federal Reserve Bank) and tries to find out the change in the amount of money demanded in response to changes in the level of the interest rate. But what happens if the rate of interest depends on the demand for money? In this case, the conditional regression analysis made thus far in this book may not be appropriate because now M depends on r and r depends on M. This leads us to consider simultaneous equation models—models in which there is more than one regression equation, that is, one for each interdependent variable.

In this chapter we present a very elementary, and often heuristic, introduction to the vast and complex subject of *simultaneous equation models,* the details being left for the references.

Chapter 12 discusses a variety of topics in the field of time series econometrics, a field that is growing in importance. In regression analysis involving time series data we have to be careful in routinely using the standard classical linear regression assumptions. The critical concept in time series analysis is the concept of **stationary time series.** In this chapter we discuss this topic at an intuitive level and point out the importance of testing for stationarity.

In this chapter we also discuss the **logit model.** In Chapter 6 we considered several models in which one or more X variables were dummy variables, taking a value of 0 or 1. In logit models we try to model situations in which the dependent variable, Y, is a dummy variable. For example, admission to a graduate school is a dummy variable, for you are either accepted or rejected. Although such models can be estimated with the standard ordinary least squares (OLS) procedure, it is generally not recommended because of several estimation problems.

In these two chapters, as throughout the book, we illustrate the various concepts introduced with several concrete examples.

CHAPTER **11**

SIMULTANEOUS EQUATION MODELS

All the regression models we have considered so far have been *single equation* regression models in that a single dependent variable (Y) was expressed as a function of one or more explanatory variables (the X's). The underlying economic theory determined why Y was treated as the dependent variable and the X's as the determining or causal variables. In other words, in such single equation regression models the causality, if any, ran from the X's to Y. Thus, in our child mortality illustrative example considered earlier, it was socioeconomic theory that suggested that personal income (X_2) and female literacy rate (X_3) were the primary factors affecting child mortality (Y).

However, there are situations in which such a *unidirectional relationship* between Y and the X's cannot be maintained. It is quite possible that the X's not only affect Y, but that Y can also affect one or more X's. If that is the case, we have a *bilateral*, or *feedback, relationship* between Y and the X's. Obviously, if this is the case, the single equation modeling strategy that we have discussed in the previous chapters will not suffice, and in some cases it may be quite inappropriate because it may lead to biased (in the statistical sense) results. To take into account the bilateral relationship between Y and the X's, we will therefore need more than one regression equation. Regression models in which there is more than one equation and in which there are feedback relationships among variables are known as **simultaneous equation regression models.** In the rest of this chapter we will discuss the nature of such simultaneous equation models. Our treatment of the topic is heuristic. For a detailed treatment of this topic, consult the references.[1]

---

[1] An extended treatment of this subject can be found in Gujarati and Porter, *Basic Econometrics,* 5th ed., McGraw-Hill, New York, 2009, Chapters 18–20.

11.1   THE NATURE OF SIMULTANEOUS EQUATION MODELS

The best way to proceed is to consider some examples from economics.

Example 11.1. The Keynesian Model of Income Determination

A beginning student of economics is exposed to the simple Keynesian model of income determination. Using the standard macroeconomics textbook convention, let C stand for consumption (expenditure), Y for income, I for investment (expenditure), and S for savings. The simple Keynesian model of income determination consists of the following two equations:

$$\text{Consumption function: } C_t = B_1 + B_2 Y_t + u_t \qquad \textbf{(11.1)}$$

$$\text{Income identity: } Y_t = C_t + I_t \qquad \textbf{(11.2)}$$

where t is the time subscript, u is the stochastic error term, and $I_t = S_t$.

This simple Keynesian model assumes a *closed economy* (i.e., there is no foreign trade) and no government expenditure (recall that the income identity is generally written as $Y_t = C_t + I_t + G_t + NX_t$, where G is government expenditure and NX is net export [export − import]). The model also assumes that I, investment expenditure, is determined *exogenously*, say, by the private sector.

The consumption function states that consumption expenditure is linearly related to income; the stochastic error term is added to the function to reflect the fact that in empirical analysis the relation between the two is only approximate. The (national income) identity says that total income is equal to the sum of consumption expenditure and investment expenditure; the latter is equal to total savings. As we know, the slope coefficient B_2 in the consumption function is the *marginal propensity to consume (MPC),* the amount of extra consumption expenditure resulting from an extra dollar of income. Keynes assumed that MPC is positive but less than 1, which is reasonable because people may save part of their additional income.

Now we can see the feedback, or simultaneous, relationship between consumption expenditure and income. From Equation (11.1) we see that income affects consumption expenditure, but from Equation (11.2) we also see that consumption is a component of income. Thus, consumption expenditure and income are *interdependent*. The objective of analysis is to find out how consumption expenditure and income are determined simultaneously. Thus consumption and income are *jointly dependent* variables. In the language of simultaneous equation modeling, such jointly dependent variables are known as **endogenous variables.** In the simple Keynesian model, investment I is not an endogenous variable, for its value is determined independently; so it is called an **exogenous, or predetermined, variable.** In more refined Keynesian models, investment can also be made endogenous.

In general, an endogenous variable is a "variable that is an inherent part of the system being studied and that is determined within the system. In other words, a variable that is caused by other variables in a causal system," and an exogenous variable "is a variable entering from and determined from outside the system being studied. A causal system says nothing about its exogenous variables."[2]

Equations (11.1) and (11.2) represent a two-equation model involving two endogenous variables, C and Y. If there are more endogenous variables, there will be more equations, one for each of the endogenous variables. Some equations in the system are *structural*, or *behavioral, equations* and some are *identities*. Thus, in our simple Keynesian model, Eq. (11.1) is a **structural**, or **behavioral, equation,** for it depicts the structure or behavior of a particular sector of the economy, the consumption sector here. The coefficients (or parameters) of the structural equations, such as B_1 and B_2, are known as *structural coefficients*. Equation (11.2) is an **identity,** a relationship that is true by definition: Total income is equal to total consumption expenditure plus total investment.

Example 11.2. Demand and Supply Model

As every student of economics knows, the price P of a commodity and the quantity Q sold are determined by the intersection of the demand and supply curves for that commodity. Thus, assuming for simplicity that the demand and supply curves are linearly related to price and adding the stochastic, or random error, terms u_1 and u_2, we may write the empirical demand and supply functions as:

$$\text{Demand function: } Q_t^d = A_1 + A_2 P_t + u_{1t} \tag{11.3}$$

$$\text{Supply function: } Q_t^s = B_1 + B_2 P_t + u_{2t} \tag{11.4}$$

$$\text{Equilibrium condition: } Q_t^d = Q_t^s \tag{11.5}$$

where Q_t^d = quantity demanded, Q_t^s = quantity supplied, and t = time.

According to economic theory, A_2 is expected to be negative (downward-sloping demand curve) and B_2 is expected to be positive (upward-sloping supply curve). Equations (11.3) and (11.4) are both structural equations, the former representing the consumers and the latter the suppliers. The A's and B's are structural coefficients.

Now it is not too difficult to see why there is a simultaneous, or two-way, relationship between P and Q. If, for example, u_{1t} (in Eq. [11.3]) changes because of changes in other variables affecting demand (such as income, wealth, and tastes), the demand curve will shift upward if u_{1t} is positive and

[2]W. Paul Vogt, *Dictionary of Statistics and Methodology: A Nontechnical Guide for the Social Sciences,* Sage Publications, California, 1993, pp. 81, 85.

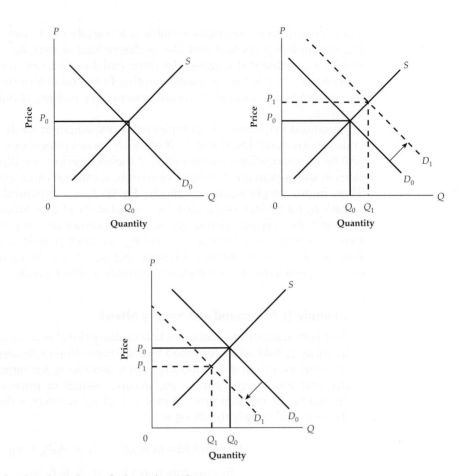

FIGURE 11-1   Interdependence of price and quantity

downward if u_{1t} is negative. As Figure 11-1 shows, a shift in the demand curve changes both P and Q. Similarly, a change in u_{2t} (because of strikes, weather, hurricanes) will shift the supply curve, again affecting both P and Q. Therefore, there is a bilateral, or simultaneous, relationship between the two variables; the P and Q variables are thus *jointly dependent*, or *endogenous*, *variables*. This is known as the **simultaneity problem.**

11.2   THE SIMULTANEOUS EQUATION BIAS: INCONSISTENCY OF OLS ESTIMATORS

Why is simultaneity a problem? To understand the nature of this problem, return to Example 11.1, which discusses the simple Keynesian model of income determination. Assume for the moment that we neglect the simultaneity between consumption expenditure and income and just estimate the consumption function (11.1) by the usual ordinary least squares (OLS) procedure. Using the usual OLS formula, we obtain

$$b_2 = \frac{\Sigma(C_t - \bar{C})(Y_t - \bar{Y})}{\Sigma(Y_t - \bar{Y})^2} = \frac{\Sigma c_t y_t}{\Sigma y_t^2} \tag{11.6}$$

Now recall from Chapter 3 that if we work within the framework of the classical linear regression model (CLRM), which is the framework we have used thus far, the OLS estimators are best linear unbiased estimators (BLUE). Is b_2 given in Equation (11.6) a BLUE estimator of the true marginal propensity to consume B_2? It can be shown that in the presence of the simultaneity problem the OLS estimators are generally not BLUE. In our case b_2 is not a BLUE estimator of B_2. In particular, b_2 is a *biased* estimator of B_2; on average, it underestimates or overestimates the true B_2. A formal proof of this statement is given in Appendix 11A. But intuitively it is easy to see why b_2 may not be BLUE.

As discussed in Section 3.1, one of the assumptions of the CLRM is that the stochastic error term u and the explanatory variable(s) *are not correlated*. Thus, in the Keynesian consumption function Y (income) and the error term u_t must not be correlated, if we want to use OLS to estimate the parameters of the consumption function (11.1). But that is not the case here. To see this, we proceed as follows:

$$\begin{aligned} Y_t &= C_t + I_t \\ &= (B_0 + B_1 Y_t + u_t) + I_t \qquad \text{substituting for } C_t \text{ from Eq. (11.1)} \\ &= B_0 + B_1 Y_t + u_t + I_t \end{aligned}$$

Therefore, transferring the $B_1 Y_t$ term to the left-hand side and simplifying, we obtain

$$Y_t = \frac{B_0}{1 - B_1} + \frac{1}{1 - B_1} I_t + \frac{1}{1 - B_1} u_t \tag{11.7}$$

Notice an interesting feature of this equation. National income Y not only depends on investment I but also on the stochastic error term u! Recall that the error term u represents all kinds of influences not explicitly included in the model. Let us suppose that one of these influences is consumer confidence as measured by, say, the consumer confidence index developed by the University of Michigan. Suppose consumers feel upbeat about the economy because of a boom in the stock market (as happened in the United States in 1996 and 1997). Therefore, consumers increase their consumption expenditure, which affects income Y in view of the income identity (11.2). This increase in income will lead to another round of increase in consumption because of the presence of Y in the consumption function (11.1), which will lead to further increases in income, and so on. What will the end result of this process be? Students familiar with elementary macroeconomics will recognize that the end result will depend on the value of the *multiplier* $(\frac{1}{1 - B_2})$. If, for example, the MPC (B_2) is 0.8 (i.e., 80 cents of every additional dollar's worth of income is spent on consumption), the multiplier will be 5.

The point to note is that Y and u in Eq. (11.1) are correlated, and hence we cannot use OLS to estimate the parameters of the consumption function (11.1). If we persist in using it, the estimators will be biased. Not only that, but as Appendix 11A shows, the estimators are not even *consistent*. As discussed in Appendix D.4, roughly speaking, an estimator is said to be an inconsistent estimator if it does not approach the true parameter value even if the sample size increases indefinitely. *In sum, then, because of the correlation between Y and u, the estimator b_2 is biased (in small samples) as well as inconsistent (in large samples).* This just about destroys the usefulness of OLS as an estimating method in the context of simultaneous equation models. Obviously, we need to explore other estimating methods. We discuss an alternative method in the following section. In passing, note that if an explanatory variable in a regression equation is correlated with the error term in that equation, that variable essentially becomes a random, or stochastic, variable. In most of the regression models considered previously, we either assumed that the explanatory variables assume fixed values, or if they were random, that they were uncorrelated with the error term. This is not the case in the present instance.

Before proceeding further, notice an interesting feature of Equation (11.7): It expresses Y (income) as a function of I (investment), which is given exogenously, and error term u. Such an equation, which expresses an *endogenous* variable solely as a function of an exogenous variable(s) and the error term, is known as a **reduced form equation** (regression). We will see the utility of such reduced form equations shortly.

If we now substitute Y from Eq. (11.7) into the consumption function (11.1), we obtain the reduced form equation for C as

$$C_t = \frac{B_1}{1 - B_2} + \frac{B_2}{1 - B_2}I_t + \frac{1}{1 - B_2}u_t \tag{11.8}$$

As in Eq. (11.7), this equation expresses the endogenous variable C (consumption) solely as a function of the exogenous variable I and the error term.

11.3   THE METHOD OF INDIRECT LEAST SQUARES (ILS)

For reasons just stated, we should not use OLS to estimate the parameters B_1 and B_2 of the consumption function (11.1) because of correlation between Y and u. What is the alternative? The alternative can be found in Equation (11.8). Why not simply regress C on I, using the method of OLS? We could do that, because I, being exogenous by assumption, is uncorrelated with u; this was not the case with the original consumption function (11.1).

But how does the regression (11.8) enable us to estimate the parameters of the original consumption function (11.1), the object of our primary interest? This is easy enough. Let us write Eq. (11.8) as

$$C_t = A_1 + A_2I_t + v_t \tag{11.9}$$

where $A_1 = B_1/(1 - B_2)$, $A_2 = B_2/(1 - B_2)$, and $v_t = u_t/(1 - B_2)$. Like u, v is also a stochastic error term; it is simply a rescaled u. The coefficients A_1 and A_2 are known as the *reduced form coefficients* because they are the coefficients attached to the reduced form (regression) equation. Observe that the reduced form coefficients are (nonlinear) combinations of the original structural coefficients of consumption function (11.1).

Now from the relationship between the A and B coefficients just given, it is easy to verify that

$$B_1 = \frac{A_1}{1 + A_2} \qquad \textbf{(11.10)}$$

$$B_2 = \frac{A_2}{1 + A_2} \qquad \textbf{(11.11)}$$

Therefore, once we estimate A_1 and A_2, we can easily "retrieve" B_1 and B_2 from them.

This method of obtaining the estimates of the parameters of the consumption function (11.1) is known as the method of **indirect least squares (ILS),** for we obtain the estimates of the original parameters indirectly by first applying OLS to the reduced form regression (11.9). What are the statistical properties of ILS estimators? We state (without proof) that the ILS estimators are *consistent* estimators; that is, as the sample size increases indefinitely, these estimators converge to their true population values. However, in small, or finite, samples, the ILS estimators may be biased. In contrast, the OLS estimators are biased as well as inconsistent.[3]

11.4 INDIRECT LEAST SQUARES: AN ILLUSTRATIVE EXAMPLE

As an application of the ILS, consider the data given in Table 11-1 on the textbook's Web site. The data on consumption, income, and investment are for the United States for the years 1959 to 2006 and are given in billions of dollars. It should be noted that the data on income is simply the sum of consumption and investment expenditure, in keeping with our simple Keynesian model of income determination.

Following our discussion of ILS, we first estimate the reduced form regression (11.8). Using the data given in Table 11-1, we obtain the following results; the results are given in the standard format as per Eq. (3.46).

$$\hat{C}_t = -97.4641 + 4.2767I_t$$

$$\text{se} = (69.4198) \quad (0.0729) \qquad \textbf{(11.12)}$$

$$t = (-1.4040) \quad (58.6475) \qquad r^2 = 0.9868$$

---

[3]For a proof of these statements, consult Gujarati and Porter, *Basic Econometrics,* 5th ed., McGraw-Hill, New York, 2009, Chapter 18.

Thus $a_1 = -97.4641$ and $a_2 = 4.2767$, which are respectively the estimates of A_1 and A_2, the parameters of the reduced form regression (11.8). Now we use Equations (11.10) and (11.11) to obtain the *estimates* of B_1 and B_2, the parameters of the consumption function (11.1):

$$b_1 = \frac{a_1}{1 + a_2} = \frac{-97.4641}{1 + 4.2767} = -18.4707 \tag{11.13}$$

$$b_2 = \frac{a_2}{1 + a_2} = \frac{4.2767}{1 + 4.2767} = 0.8105 \tag{11.14}$$

These are the ILS estimates of the parameters of the consumption function. And the estimated consumption function now is

$$\hat{C}_t = -18.4707 + 0.8105Y_t \tag{11.15}$$

Thus, the estimated marginal propensity to consume (MPC) is about 0.81.

For comparison, we give the results based on OLS, that is, the results obtained by directly regressing C on Y without the intermediary of the reduced form:

$$\hat{C}_t = -24.6841 + 0.8121Y_t$$
$$se = (12.8715) \quad (0.0026) \tag{11.16}$$
$$t = (-1.9177) \quad (312.8214) \quad r^2 = 0.9995$$

Note the difference between the ILS and OLS estimates of the parameters of the consumption function. Although the estimated marginal propensities to consume do not differ substantially, there is a difference in the estimated intercept values. Which results should we trust? We should trust the results obtained from the method of ILS, for we know that in the presence of the simultaneity problem, the OLS results are not only biased but are inconsistent as well.[4]

It would seem that we can always use the method of indirect least squares to estimate the parameters of simultaneous equation models. The question is whether we can retrieve the original structural parameters from these reduced form estimates. Sometimes we can, and sometimes we cannot. The answer depends on the so-called *identification problem*. In the following section we discuss this problem and then in the ensuing sections we discuss other methods of estimating the parameters of the simultaneous equation models.

---

[4]Notice that we have given standard errors and t values for the OLS regression (11.16) but not for the ILS regression (11.15). This is because the coefficients of the latter, obtained from Eqs. (11.13) and (11.14), are nonlinear functions of a_1 and a_2, and there is no *simple* method of obtaining standard errors of nonlinear functions.

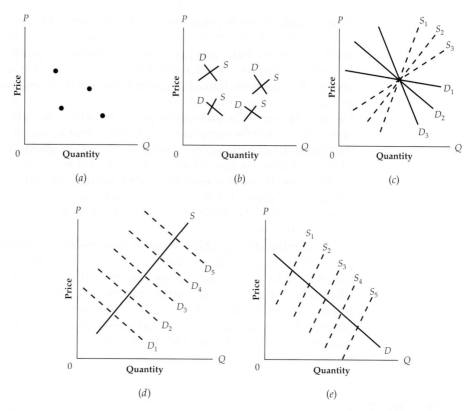

FIGURE 11-2   Hypothetical supply and demand functions and the identification problem

11.5   THE IDENTIFICATION PROBLEM: A ROSE BY ANY OTHER NAME MAY NOT BE A ROSE

Let us return to the supply and demand model of Example 11.2. Suppose we have data on P and Q only, and we want to estimate the demand function. Suppose we regress Q on P. How do we know that this regression in fact estimates a demand function? You might say that if the slope of the estimated regression is negative, it is a demand function because of the inverse relationship between price and quantity demanded. But suppose the slope coefficient turns out to be positive. What then? Do you then say that it must be a supply function because there is a positive relationship between price and quantity supplied?

You can see the potential problem involved in simply regressing quantity on price: A given P_t and Q_t combination represents simply the point of intersection of the appropriate supply and demand curves because of the equilibrium condition that demand is equal to supply. To see this more clearly, consider Figure 11-2.

Figure 11-2(a) gives a few scatterpoints relating P to Q. Each scatterpoint represents the intersection of a demand and supply curve, as shown in Figure 11-2(b).

Now consider a single point, such as that shown in Figure 11-2(c). There is no way we can be sure which demand and supply curve of the whole family of curves shown in that panel generated that particular point. Clearly, some additional information about the nature of the demand and supply curves is needed. For example, if the demand curve shifts over time because of a change in income or tastes, for example, but the supply curve remains relatively stable, as in Figure 11-2(d), the scatterpoints trace out a supply curve. In this situation, we say that *the supply curve is identified*; that is, we can uniquely estimate the parameters of the supply curve. By the same token, if the supply curve shifts over time because of weather factors (in the case of agricultural commodities) or other extraneous factors but the demand curve remains relatively stable, as in Figure 11-2(e), the scatterpoints trace out a demand curve. In this case, we say that the demand curve is identified; that is, we can uniquely estimate its parameters.

The **identification problem** therefore addresses whether we can estimate the parameters of the particular equation (be it a demand or a supply function) uniquely. If that is the case, we say that the particular equation is **exactly identified.** If we cannot estimate the parameters, we say that the equation is **unidentified** or **underidentified.** Sometimes it can happen that there is more than one numerical value for one or more parameters of the equation. In that case, we say that the equation is **overidentified.** We will now consider each of these cases briefly.

Underidentification

Consider once again Example 11.2. By the equilibrium condition that supply equals demand, we obtain

$$A_1 + A_2 P_t + u_{1t} = B_1 + B_2 P_t + u_{2t} \tag{11.17}$$

Solving Equation (11.17), we obtain the equilibrium price

$$P_t = \pi_1 + v_{1t} \tag{11.18}$$

where

$$\pi_1 = \frac{B_1 - A_1}{A_2 - B_2} \tag{11.19}$$

$$v_{1t} = \frac{u_{2t} - u_{1t}}{A_2 - B_2} \tag{11.20}$$

where v_1 is a stochastic error term, which is a linear combination of the u's. The symbol π is read as pi and is used here to represent a reduced form regression coefficient.

Substituting P_t from Equation (11.18) into either the supply or demand function of Example 11.2, we obtain the following equilibrium quantity:

$$Q_t = \pi_2 + u_{2t} \tag{11.21}$$

where

$$\pi_2 = \frac{A_2 B_1 - A_1 B_2}{A_2 - B_2} \tag{11.22}$$

$$v_{2t} = \frac{A_2 u_{2t} - B_2 u_{1t}}{A_2 - B_2} \tag{11.23}$$

where v_2 is also a stochastic, or random, error term.

Equations (11.19) and (11.21) are reduced form regressions. Now our demand and supply model has four structural coefficients, A_1, A_2, B_1, and B_2, but there is no unique way of estimating them from the two reduced form coefficients, π_1 and π_2. As elementary algebra teaches us, to estimate four unknowns we must have four (independent) equations. Incidentally, if we run the reduced form regressions (11.19) and (11.21) we see that there are no explanatory variables, only the constants, the π's, and these constants will simply give the mean values of P and Q. (Why?) There is no way of estimating the four structural coefficients from the two mean values. In short, both the demand and supply functions are *unidentified*.

Just or Exact Identification

We have already considered this case in the previous section where we discussed the estimation of the Keynesian consumption function using the method of indirect least squares. As shown there, from the reduced form regression (11.12), we were able to obtain unique values of the parameters of the consumption function, as can be seen from Eqs. (11.13) and (11.14).

To further illustrate exact identification, let us continue with our demand and supply example, but now we modify the model as follows:

$$\text{Demand function: } Q_t^d = A_1 + A_2 P_t + A_3 X_t + u_{1t} \tag{11.24}$$

$$\text{Supply function: } Q_t^s = B_1 + B_2 P_t + u_{2t} \tag{11.25}$$

where in addition to the variables already defined, $X =$ income of the consumer. Thus, the demand function states that the quantity demanded is a function of its price as well as the income of the consumer; economic theory of demand generally has price and income as its two main determinants. The inclusion of the income variable in the model will give us some additional information about consumer behavior. It is assumed that the income of the consumer is determined exogenously.

Using the market-clearing mechanism, quantity demanded = quantity supplied, we obtain

$$A_1 + A_2 P_t + A_3 X_t + u_{1t} = B_1 + B_2 P_t + u_{2t} \tag{11.26}$$

Solving Equation (11.26) provides the following equilibrium value of P_t:

$$P_t = \pi_1 + \pi_2 X_t + v_{1t} \tag{11.27}$$

where the reduced form coefficients are

$$\pi_1 = \frac{B_1 - A_1}{A_2 - B_2} \tag{11.28}$$

$$\pi_2 = -\frac{A_3}{A_2 - B_2} \tag{11.29}$$

$$v_{1t} = \frac{u_{2t} - u_{1t}}{A_2 - B_2} \tag{11.30}$$

Substituting the equilibrium value of P_t into the preceding demand or supply function, we obtain the following equilibrium, or market-clearing, quantity:

$$Q_t = \pi_3 + \pi_4 X_t + v_{2t} \tag{11.31}$$

where $\pi_3 = \dfrac{A_2 B_1 - A_1 B_2}{A_2 - B_2}$ (11.32)

$$\pi_4 = -\frac{A_3 B_2}{A_2 - B_2} \tag{11.33}$$

$$v_{2t} = \frac{A_2 u_{2t} - B_2 u_{1t}}{A_2 - B_2} \tag{11.34}$$

Since Equations (11.27) and (11.31) are both reduced form regressions, as noted before, OLS can always be applied to estimate their parameters. The question that remains is whether we can uniquely estimate the parameters of the structural equations from the reduced form coefficients.

Observe that the demand and supply models (11.24) and (11.25) contain five structural coefficients, A_1, A_2, A_3, B_1, and B_2. But we have only four equations to estimate them—the four reduced form coefficients, the four π's. So, we cannot obtain unique values of all five of the structural coefficients. But which of these coefficients can be uniquely estimated? The reader can verify that the parameters of the supply function can be uniquely estimated, for

$$B_1 = \pi_3 - B_2 \pi_1 \tag{11.35}$$

$$B_2 = \frac{\pi_4}{\pi_2} \tag{11.36}$$

Therefore, the supply function is exactly identified. But the demand function is unidentified because there is no unique way of estimating its parameters, the A coefficients.

Observe an interesting fact: *It is the presence of an additional variable in the demand function that enables us to identify the supply function.* Why? The inclusion of the income variable in the demand equation provides us with some additional information about the variability of the function, as indicated in Figure 11-2(*d*). The figure shows how the intersection of the stable supply curve with the shifting demand curve (due to changes in income) enables us to trace (identify) the supply curve.

How can the demand function be identified? Suppose we include P_{t-1}, the one-period lagged value of price as an additional variable in the supply function (11.25). This amounts to saying that the supply depends not only on the current price but also on the price prevailing in the previous period, not an unreasonable assumption for many agricultural commodities. Since at time t the value of P_{t-1} is already known, we can treat it as an exogenous, or predetermined, variable. Thus the new model is

$$\text{Demand function: } Q_t^d = A_1 + A_2 P_t + A_3 X_t + u_{1t} \qquad \textbf{(11.37)}$$

$$\text{Supply function: } Q_t^s = B_1 + B_2 P_t + B_3 P_{t-1} + u_{2t} \qquad \textbf{(11.38)}$$

Using Equations (11.37) and (11.38) and the market-clearing condition, obtain the reduced form regressions and verify that now both the demand and supply functions are identified; each reduced form regression will have X_t and P_{t-1} as explanatory variables, and since the values of these variables are determined outside the model, they are uncorrelated with the error terms. Once again notice how the inclusion or exclusion of a variable(s) from an equation helps us to identify that equation, that is, to obtain unique values of the parameters of that equation. Thus it is the exclusion of the P_{t-1} variable from the demand function that helps us to identify it, just as the exclusion of the income variable (X_t) from the supply function helps us to identify it. One implication is that an equation in a simultaneous equation system cannot be identified if it includes all the variables (endogenous as well as exogenous) in the system. Later we provide a simple rule of identification that generalizes this idea (see Section 11.6).

Overidentification

Although the exclusion of certain variables from an equation may enable us to identify it as we just showed, sometimes we can overdo it. This leads to the problem of *overidentification*, a situation in which there is more than one value for one or more parameters of an equation in the model. Let us see how this can happen.

Once again return to the demand-supply model and write it as

$$\text{Demand function: } Q_t^d = A_1 + A_2 P_t + A_3 X_t + A_4 W_t + u_{1t} \qquad \textbf{(11.39)}$$

$$\text{Supply function: } Q_t^s = B_1 + B_2 P_t + B_3 P_{t-1} + u_{2t} \qquad \textbf{(11.40)}$$

where in addition to the variables introduced previously, W_t stands for the wealth of the consumer. For many commodities, income as well as wealth are important determinants of demand. Compare the demand and supply models (11.37) and (11.38) with the models (11.39) and (11.40). Whereas originally the supply function excluded only the income variable, in the new model it excludes both the income and wealth variables. Before, the exclusion of the income variable from the supply function enabled us to identify it; now the exclusion of both the income and wealth variables from the supply function *overidentifies* it in the sense that we have two estimates of the supply parameter B_2, as we show below.

Equating models (11.39) and (11.40), we now obtain the following reduced form regressions:

$$P_t = \pi_1 + \pi_2 X_T + \pi_3 W_t + \pi_4 P_{t-1} + v_{1t} \tag{11.41}$$

$$Q_t = \pi_5 + \pi_6 X_t + \pi_7 W_t + \pi_8 P_{t-1} + v_{2t} \tag{11.42}$$

where
$$\pi_1 = \frac{B_1 - A_1}{A_2 - B_2} \qquad \pi_2 = -\frac{A_3}{A_2 - B_2}$$

$$\pi_3 = -\frac{A_4}{A_2 - B_2} \qquad \pi_4 = \frac{B_3}{A_2 - B_2}$$

$$\pi_5 = \frac{A_2 B_1 - A_1 B_2}{A_2 - B_2} \qquad \pi_6 = -\frac{A_3 B_2}{A_2 - B_2} \tag{11.43}$$

$$\pi_7 = \frac{A_4 B_2}{A_2 - B_2} \qquad \pi_8 = \frac{A_2 B_3}{A_2 - B_2}$$

$$v_{1t} = \frac{u_{2t} - u_{1t}}{A_2 - B_2} \qquad v_{2t} = \frac{A_2 u_{2t} - B_2 u_{1t}}{A_2 - B_2}$$

Remember that the supply and demand models we are considering have seven structural coefficients in all—the four A's and three B's. But there are eight reduced form coefficients in Equation (11.43). We have more equations than unknowns. Clearly, there is more than one solution to a parameter. You can readily verify that we have, in fact, two values for B_2:

$$B_2 = \frac{\pi_7}{\pi_3} \quad \text{or} \quad B_2 = \frac{\pi_6}{\pi_2} \tag{11.44}$$

And there is no reason to believe that these two estimates will be the same.

Since B_2 appears in the denominators of all the reduced form coefficients given in Eq. (11.43), the ambiguity in the estimation of B_2 will be transmitted to other structural coefficients also. Why do we obtain such a result? It seems that we have *too much information*—exclusion of either the income or wealth variable would have sufficed to identify the supply function. This is the opposite of the case of underidentification, where there was too little information. The point here is that more information may not always be better! Note, though, that the problem of overidentification occurs not because we are deliberately adding more variables. It is simply that sometimes theory tells us what variables to include or exclude from an equation, and the equation then ends up either unidentified or identified (either exactly or over).

In summary, an equation in a simultaneous equation model may be unidentified, exactly identified, or overidentified. There is nothing we can do about underidentification, assuming the model is correct. Underidentification is not a statistical problem that can be solved with a larger sample size. You can look at those four dots in Figure 11-2(*a*) all year long, but they will never tell you the slope of the supply and demand curves that generated them. If an equation is exactly identified, we can use the method of indirect least squares (ILS) to estimate its parameters. If an equation is overidentified, ILS will not provide unique estimates of the parameters. Fortunately, we can use the method of **two-stage least squares (2SLS)** to estimate the parameters of an overidentified equation. But before we turn to 2SLS, we would like to find out if there is a systematic way to determine whether an equation is underidentified, exactly identified, or overidentified; the method of reduced form regression to determine identification is rather cumbersome, especially if the model contains several equations.

11.6 RULES FOR IDENTIFICATION: THE ORDER CONDITION OF IDENTIFICATION

To understand the so-called **order condition of identification,** we introduce the following notations:

m = number of endogenous (or jointly dependent) variables in the model
k = total number of variables (endogenous and exogenous) *excluded* from the equation under consideration

Then,

1. If $k = m - 1$, the equation is exactly identified.
2. If $k > m - 1$, the equation is overidentified.
3. If $k < m - 1$, the equation is underidentified.

To apply the order condition, all we have to do is to count the number of endogenous variables (= number of equations in the model) and the total number of variables (endogenous as well as exogenous) excluded from the particular equation under consideration. Although the order condition of identification is only *necessary and not sufficient,* in most practical applications is has been found to be very helpful.

Thus, applying the order condition to the supply and demand models (11.39) and (11.40), we see that $m = 2$ and that the supply function excludes the variables X_t and W_t; that is, $k = 2$. Since $k > m - 1$, the supply equation is overidentified. As for the demand function, it excludes P_{t-1}. Since $k = m - 1$, the demand function is identified. But we now have a slight complication. If we try to estimate the parameters of the demand function from the reduced form coefficients given in Equation (11.43), the estimates will not be unique because B_2, which enters into the computations, takes two values, as shown in Equation (11.44). This complication can, however, be avoided if we use the method of 2SLS, which we will now discuss.

11.7 ESTIMATION OF AN OVERIDENTIFIED EQUATION: THE METHOD OF TWO-STAGE LEAST SQUARES

To illustrate the method of *two-stage least squares* (*2SLS*), consider the following model:

$$\text{Income function: } Y_t = A_1 + A_2 M_t + A_3 I_t + A_4 G_t + u_{1t} \tag{11.45}$$

$$\text{Money supply function: } M_t = B_1 + B_2 Y_t + u_{2t} \tag{11.46}$$

where Y = income

M = stock of money

I = investment expenditure

G = government expenditure on goods and services

u_1, u_2 = stochastic error terms

In this model, the variables I and G are assumed to be exogenous.

The *income function*, a hybrid of the quantity-theory and the Keynesian approaches to income determination, states that income is determined by the money supply, investment expenditure, and government expenditure. The *money supply function* states that the stock of the money supply is determined by the Federal Reserve System (FED) on the basis of the level of income. Obviously, we have a *simultaneity problem* here because of the feedback between income and money supply.

Applying the order condition of identification, we can check that the income equation is unidentified because it excludes no variable in the model, whereas the money supply function is overidentified because it excludes two variables in the system. (Note that $m = 2$ in this model.)

Since the income equation is underidentified, there is nothing we can do to estimate its parameters. What about the money supply function? Since it is overidentified, if we use ILS to estimate its parameters, we will not obtain unique estimates for the parameters; actually, B_2 will have two values. What about OLS? Because of the likely correlation between income Y and the stochastic error term u_2, OLS estimates will be inconsistent in view of our earlier discussion. What, then, is the alternative?

Suppose in the money supply function (11.46) we find a *surrogate* or *proxy* or an *instrumental variable* for Y such that, although resembling Y, it is uncorrelated with u_2. If we can find such a proxy, OLS can be used straightforwardly to estimate the parameters of the money supply function. (Why?) But how do we obtain such a proxy or instrumental variable? One answer is provided by the method of two-stage least squares (2SLS). As the name indicates, the method involves two successive applications of OLS. The process follows.

Stage 1 To get rid of the likely correlation between income Y and the error term u_2, first regress Y on *all* predetermined variables in the whole model, not just on that equation. In the present case, this means regressing Y on the predetermined variables I (gross private domestic investment) and G (government expenditure) as follows:

$$Y_t = \pi_1 + \pi_2 I_t + \pi_3 G_t + w_t \tag{11.47}$$

where w is a stochastic error term. From Equation (11.47), we obtain

$$\hat{Y}_t = \hat{\pi}_1 + \hat{\pi}_2 I_t + \hat{\pi}_3 G_t \tag{11.48}$$

where $\hat{Y}_t$ is the estimated mean value of Y, given the values of I and G. Note the ^ over the π coefficients indicates that these are the estimated values of the true π's.

Therefore we can write Eq. (11.47) as

$$Y_t = \hat{Y}_t + w_t \tag{11.49}$$

which shows that the (stochastic) Y consists of two parts: $\hat{Y}_t$, which from Equation (11.48) is a linear combination of the predetermined variables I and G and a random component w_t. Following OLS theory, $\hat{Y}$ and w are therefore uncorrelated. (Why? See Problem 2.25.)

Stage 2 The overidentified money supply function can now be written as

$$\begin{aligned} M_t &= B_1 + B_2(\hat{Y}_t + w_t) + u_{2t} \\ &= B_1 + B_2\hat{Y}_t + (u_{2t} + B_2 w_t) \\ &= B_1 + B_2\hat{Y}_t + v_t \end{aligned} \tag{11.50}$$

where $v_t = u_{2t} + B_2 w_1$

Comparing Equations (11.50) and (11.46), we see that they are very similar in appearance, the only difference being that Y is replaced by $\hat{Y}$, the latter being obtained from Eq. (11.48). What is the advantage of this? It can be shown that although Y in the original money supply function (11.46) is likely to be correlated with the stochastic error term u_2 (hence rendering OLS inappropriate), $\hat{Y}$ in Eq. (11.50) is uncorrelated with v_t *asymptotically,* that is, in a large sample (or, more accurately, as the sample size increases indefinitely). As a result, OLS can now be applied to Eq. (11.50), which will give *consistent estimates* of the parameters of the money supply function (11.46). This is an improvement over the direct application of OLS to Eq. (11.46), for in that situation the estimates are likely to be biased as well as inconsistent.[5]

11.8   2SLS: A NUMERICAL EXAMPLE

Let us continue with the money supply and income models of Equations (11.45) and (11.46). Table 11-2 in Problem 11.18 (found on the textbook's Web site), gives data on Y (income, as measured by GDP), M (money supply, as measured by the M2 measure of money supply), I (investment as measured by gross private domestic investment, GPDI), and G (federal government expenditure). The data are in billions of dollars, except the interest rate (as measured by the 6-month Treasury bill rate), which is a percentage. The data on interest rates are given for some problems at the end of the chapter. These data are annual and are for the period 1965–2006.

Stage 1 Regression   To estimate the parameters of the money supply function (11.46), we first regress the stochastic variable Y (income) on the proxy variables I and G, which are treated as exogenous or predetermined. The results of this regression are

$$\hat{Y}_t = -162.0426 + 2.6019I_t + 3.2250G_t$$

$$\text{se} = (54.0655) \qquad (0.3278) \qquad (0.2869) \tag{11.51}$$

$$t = (-2.9972) \qquad (7.9377) \qquad (11.2397) \qquad R^2 = 0.9975$$

Interpret these results in the usual manner. Notice that all the coefficients are statistically significant at the 5% level of significance.

Stage 2 Regression   We estimate the money supply function (11.46) by regressing M not on the original income Y but on the Y as estimated in Eq. (11.51). The results are

$$\hat{M}_t = 151.1360 + 0.5163\hat{Y}_t$$

$$\text{se} = (35.9740) \qquad (0.0057) \tag{11.52}^{[6]}$$

$$t = (4.2013) \qquad (89.9646) \qquad r^2 = 0.9951$$

Note: Observe that there is a ^ on Y on the right-hand side.

---

[5]For further discussion of this somewhat technical point, see Gujarati and Porter, *Basic Econometrics*, 5th ed., McGraw-Hill, New York, 2009, Chapter 20.

[6]These standard errors are corrected to reflect the nature of the error term v_t. This is a technical point. Consult Gujarati and Porter, *Basic Econometrics*, 5th ed., McGraw-Hill, New York, 2009, p. 736.

OLS Regression For a comparison, we give the results of the regression (11.46) based on the *inappropriately* applied OLS:

$$\hat{M}_t = 159.3544 + 0.5147Y_t$$

$$\text{se} = (47.7531) \quad (0.0076) \tag{11.53}$$

$$t = (3.3370) \quad (67.5898) \quad r^2 = 0.9913$$

Comparing the 2SLS and the OLS results, you might say that the results are not vastly different. This may be so in the present case, but there is no guarantee that this always will be the case. Besides, we know that in theory 2SLS is better than OLS, especially in large samples.

We conclude our somewhat nontechnical discussion of the simultaneous equation models by noting that besides ILS and 2SLS there are other methods of estimating such models. But a discussion of these methods (e.g., the method of full information maximum likelihood) is beyond the scope of this introductory book.[7] Our primary purpose in this chapter was to introduce readers to the bare bones of the topic of simultaneous equation models to make them aware that on occasion we may have to go beyond the single equation regression modeling considered in the previous chapters.

11.9 SUMMARY

In contrast to the single equation models discussed in the preceding chapters, in simultaneous equation regression models what is a dependent (endogenous) variable in one equation appears as an explanatory variable in another equation. Thus, there is a feedback relationship between the variables. This feedback creates the *simultaneity problem,* rendering OLS inappropriate to estimate the parameters of each equation individually. This is because the endogenous variable that appears as an explanatory variable in another equation may be correlated with the stochastic error term of that equation. This violates one of the critical assumptions of OLS that the explanatory variable be either fixed, or nonrandom, or if random, that it be uncorrelated with the error term. Because of this, if we use OLS, the estimates we obtain will be biased as well as inconsistent.

Besides the simultaneity problem, a simultaneous equation model may have an *identification problem.* An identification problem means we cannot uniquely estimate the values of the parameters of an equation. Therefore, before we estimate a simultaneous equation model, we must find out if an equation in such a model is identified.

One cumbersome method of finding out whether an equation is identified is to obtain the *reduced form* equations of the model. A reduced form equation expresses a dependent (or endogenous) variable solely as a function of *exogenous,*

---

[7]Refer to William H. Greene, *Econometric Analysis,* 3rd ed., Prentice-Hall, New Jersey, 1997, Chapter 16.

or *predetermined, variables*, that is, variables whose values are determined outside the model. If there is a one-to-one correspondence between the reduced form coefficients and the coefficients of the original equation, then the original equation is identified.

A shortcut to determining identification is via the *order condition of identification*. The order condition counts the number of equations in the model and the number of variables in the model (both endogenous and exogenous). Then, based on whether some variables are excluded from an equation but included in other equations of the model, the order condition decides whether an equation in the model is *underidentified, exactly identified*, or *overidentified*. An equation in a model is underidentified if we cannot estimate the values of the parameters of that equation. If we can obtain unique values of parameters of an equation, that equation is said to be exactly identified. If, on the other hand, the estimates of one or more parameters of an equation are not unique in the sense that there is more than one value of some parameters, that equation is said to be overidentified.

If an equation is underidentified, it is a dead-end case. There is not much we can do, short of changing the specification of the model (i.e., developing another model). If an equation is exactly identified, we can estimate it by the method of *indirect least squares (ILS)*. ILS is a two-step procedure. In step 1, we apply OLS to the reduced form equations of the model, and then we retrieve the original structural coefficients from the reduced form coefficients. ILS estimators are consistent; that is, as the sample size increases indefinitely, the estimators converge to their true values.

The parameters of the overidentified equation can be estimated by the method of *two-stage least squares (2SLS)*. The basic idea behind 2SLS is to replace the explanatory variable that is correlated with the error term of the equation in which that variable appears by a variable that is not so correlated. Such a variable is called a *proxy*, or *instrumental, variable*. 2SLS estimators, like the ILS estimators, are consistent estimators.

KEY TERMS AND CONCEPTS

The key terms and concepts introduced in this chapter are

Simultaneous equation regression
   model
Endogenous variable
Exogenous, or predetermined,
   variable
Structural or behavioral equation
Identity
Simultaneity problem
Reduced form equation

Indirect least squares (ILS)
Identification problem
   a) Exact identification
   b) Unidentification or
      underidentification
   c) Overidentification
Two-stage least squares (2SLS)
Identification rules
   a) Order condition of identification

QUESTIONS

11.1. What is meant by the simultaneity problem?

11.2. What is the meaning of endogenous and exogenous variables?

11.3. Why is OLS generally inappropriate to estimate an equation embedded in a simultaneous equation model?

11.4. What happens if OLS is applied to estimate an equation in a simultaneous equation model?

11.5. What is meant by a reduced form (regression) equation? What is its use?

11.6. What is the meaning of a structural, or behavioral, equation?

11.7. What is meant by indirect least squares? When is it used?

11.8. What is the nature of the identification problem? Why is it important?

11.9. What is the order condition of identification?

11.10. What may be meant by the statement that the order condition of identification is a necessary but not sufficient condition for identification?

11.11. Explain carefully the meaning of (1) underidentification, (2) exact identification, and (3) overidentification.

11.12. How do we estimate an underidentified equation?

11.13. What method(s) is used to estimate an exactly identified equation?

11.14. What is 2SLS used for?

11.15. Can 2SLS also be used to estimate an exactly identified equation?

PROBLEMS

11.16. Consider the following two-equation model:

$$Y_{1t} = A_1 + A_2Y_{2t} + A_3X_{1t} + u_{1t}$$
$$Y_{2t} = B_1 + B_2Y_{1t} + B_3X_{2t} + u_{2t}$$

where the Y's are the endogenous variables, the X's the exogenous variables, and the u's the stochastic error terms.

a. Obtain the reduced form regressions.

b. Determine which of the equations is identified.

c. For the identified equation, which method of estimation would you use and why?

d. Suppose, a priori, it is known that $A_3 = 0$. How would your answers to the preceding questions change? Why?

11.17. Consider the following model:

$$Y_{1t} = A_1 + A_2Y_{2t} + A_3X_{1t} + u_{1t}$$
$$Y_{2t} = B_1 + B_2Y_{1t} + u_{2t}$$

where the Y's are the endogenous variables, the X's the exogenous, and the u's the stochastic error terms. Based on this model, the following reduced form regressions are obtained

$$Y_{1t} = 6 + 8X_{1t}$$
$$Y_{2t} = 4 + 12X_{1t}$$

a. Which structural coefficients, if any, can be estimated from these reduced form equations?

b. How will our answer change if it is known a priori that (1) $A_2 = 0$ and (2) $A_1 = 0$?

11.18. Consider the following model:

$$R_t = A_1 + A_2 M_t + A_3 Y_t + u_{1t}$$
$$Y_t = B_1 + B_2 R_t + u_{2t}$$

where Y = income (measured by gross domestic product, GDP), R = interest rate (measured by 6-month Treasury bill rate, %), and M = money supply (measured by M2). Assume that M is determined exogenously.

a. What economic rationale lies behind this model? (*Hint:* See any macroeconomics textbook.)

b. Are the preceding equations identified?

c. Using the data given in Table 11-2 (on the textbook's Web site), estimate the parameters of the identified equation(s). Justify the method(s) you use.

11.19. Consider the following reformulation of the model given in Problem 11.18.

$$R_t = A_1 + A_2 M_t + A_3 Y_t + u_{1t}$$
$$Y_t = B_1 + B_2 R_t + B_3 I_t + u_{2t}$$

where in addition to the variables defined in the preceding problem, I stands for investment (measured by gross private domestic investment, GPDI). Assume that M and I are exogenous.

a. Which of the preceding equations is identified?

b. Using the data in Table 11-2 (on the textbook's Web site), estimate the parameters of the identified equation(s).

c. Comment on the difference in the results of this and the preceding problem.

11.20. Consider the wages data set used in Chapter 9 (see Table 9-2, on the textbook's Web site). As a reminder: Wage = \$, per hour; Occup = Occupation; Sector = 1 for manufacturing, 2 for construction, 0 for other; Union = 1 if union member, 0 otherwise; Education = years of schooling; Experience = work experience in years; Age = in years; Sex = 1 for female; Marital status = 1 if married; Race = 1 for other, 2 for Hispanic, 3 for white; Region = 1 if lives in the South.

Consider the following simple wage determination model:

$$\text{In } W = B_1 + B_2 Educ + B_3 Exper + B_4 Exper^2 + u_i \qquad (1)$$

Suppose education, like wages, is endogenous. How would you find out that in Equation (1) education is in fact endogenous? Use the data given in the table in your analysis.

11.21. Consider the following demand and supply model for loans of commercial banks to businesses:

$$\text{Demand: } Q_t = Q_t = \alpha_1 + \alpha_2 R_t + \alpha_2 RD_t + \alpha_4 IPI_t + u_{1t}$$
$$\text{Supply: } Q_t = \beta_1 + \beta_2 R_t + \beta_3 RS_t + \beta_4 TBD_t + u_{2t}$$

Where Q = total commercial bank loans ($ billion); R = average prime rate; RS = 3-month Treasury bill rate; RD = AAA corporate bond rate; IPI = Index of Industrial Production; and TBD = total bank deposits.

a. Collect data on these variables for the period 1980–2008 from various sources, such as **www.economagic.com**, the Web site of the Federal Reserve Bank of St. Louis, or any other source.

b. Are the demand and supply functions identified? List which variables are endogenous and which are exogenous.

c. How would you go about estimating the demand and supply functions listed above? Show the necessary calculations.

d. Why are both R and RS included in the model? What is the role of IPI in the model?

APPENDIX 11A: Inconsistency of OLS Estimators

To show that the OLS estimator of b_2 is an inconsistent estimator of B_2 because of correlation between Y_t and u_t, we start with the OLS estimator Eq. (11.6):

$$b_2 = \frac{\Sigma(C_t - \overline{C})(Y_t - \overline{Y})}{\Sigma(Y_t - \overline{Y})^2}$$

$$= \frac{\Sigma C_t y_t}{\Sigma y_t^2} \tag{11A.1}$$

where $y_t = (Y_t - \overline{Y})$.

Now substituting for C_t from Eq. (11.1), we obtain

$$b_2 = \frac{\Sigma(B_1 + B_2 Y_t + u_t)y_t}{\Sigma y_t^2}$$

$$= B_2 + \frac{\Sigma y_t u_t}{\Sigma y_t^2} \tag{11A.2}$$

where in the last step use is made of the fact that $\Sigma y_t = 0$ and $(\Sigma Y_t y_t / \Sigma y_t^2) = 1$. (Why?)

Taking the expectation of Equation (11A.2), we get

$$E(b_2) = B_2 + E\left[\frac{\Sigma y_t u_t}{\Sigma y_t^2}\right] \tag{11A.3}$$

Unfortunately, we cannot readily evaluate the expectation of the second term in Equation (11A.3), since the expectations operator E is a linear operator. (*Note:* $E[A/B] \neq E[A]/E[B]$.) But intuitively it should be clear that unless the second term in Eq. (11A.3) is zero, b_2 is a biased estimator of B_2.

Not only is b_2 biased, but it is inconsistent as well. An estimator is said to be consistent if its *probability limit (plim)* is equal to its true (population) value.[8] Using the properties of the plim, we can express[9]

$$\text{plim}(b_2) = \text{plim}(B_2) + \text{plim}\left[\frac{\Sigma y_t u_t}{\Sigma y_t^2}\right]$$

$$= B_2 + \text{plim}\left[\frac{\Sigma y_t u_t/n}{\Sigma y_t^2/n}\right]$$

$$= B_2 + \frac{p\lim\left(\Sigma y_t u_t/n\right)}{p\lim\left(\Sigma y_t^2/n\right)} \tag{11A.4}$$

where use is made of the properties of the plim operator that the plim of a constant (such as B_2) is that constant itself and that the plim of the ratio of two entities is the ratio of the plim of those entities.

Now as n increases indefinitely, it can be shown that

$$\text{plim}(b_2) = B_2 + \frac{1}{1 - B_2}\left(\frac{\sigma^2}{\sigma_y^2}\right) \tag{11A.5}$$

where σ^2 is the variance of u and σ_y^2 is the variance of Y.

Since B_2 (MPC) lies between 0 and 1, and since the two variance terms in Equation (11A.5) are positive, it is obvious from Eq. (11A.5) that plim (b_2) will always be greater than B_2; that is, b_2 will overestimate B_2 and the bias will not disappear no matter how large the sample size.

---

[8] If lim Probability $n \to \infty\{|b_2 - B_2| < d\} = 1$, where $d > 0$ and n is the sample size, we say that b_2 is a consistent estimator of B_2, which, for short, we write as $n \to \infty$ plim $(b_2) = B_2$. For further details, see Gujarati and Porter, *Basic Econometrics*, 5th ed., McGraw-Hill, New York, 2009, pp. 829–831.

[9] Although $E(A/B) \neq E(A)/E(B)$, we can write plim $(A/B) = \text{plim}(A)/\text{plim}(B)$.

CHAPTER 12

SELECTED TOPICS
IN SINGLE EQUATION
REGRESSION MODELS

In this chapter we will consider several topics that are useful in applied research. These topics are:

1. Dynamic economic models.
2. Spurious regression: Nonstationary time series.
3. Tests of stationarity.
4. Cointegrated time series.
5. The random walk model.
6. The logit model.

We will discuss the nature of these topics and illustrate them with several examples.

12.1 DYNAMIC ECONOMIC MODELS: AUTOREGRESSIVE AND DISTRIBUTED LAG MODELS

In all the regression models that we have considered up to this point we have assumed that the relationship between the dependent variable Y and the explanatory variables, the X's, is *contemporaneous*, that is, at the same point in time. This assumption may be tenable in cross-sectional data but not in time series data. Thus, in a regression of consumption expenditure on personal disposable income (PDI) involving time series data it is possible that consumption expenditure depends upon the PDI in the previous time period as well as upon the PDI in the current time period. That is, there may be a noncontemporaneous, or *lagged*, relationship between Y and the X's.

To illustrate, let Y_t = the consumption expenditure at time t, X_t = the PDI at time t, X_{t-1} = the PDI at time $(t-1)$, and X_{t-2} = the PDI at time $(t-2)$. Now consider the model

$$Y_t = A + B_0 X_t + B_1 X_{t-1} + B_2 X_{t-2} + u_t \qquad \text{(12.1)}$$

As this model shows, because of the lagged terms X_{t-1} and X_{t-2}, the relationship between consumption expenditure and PDI is not contemporaneous. Models like Equation (12.1) are called **dynamic models** (i.e., involving change over time) because the effect of a unit change in the value of the explanatory variable is felt over a number of time periods, three in the model of Eq. (12.1).

More technically, dynamic models like Eq. (12.1) are called **distributed lag models,** for the effect of a unit change in the value of the explanatory variable is spread over, or distributed over, a number of time periods. To illustrate this point further, consider the following hypothetical consumption function:

$$Y_t = \text{constant} + 0.4 X_t + 0.3 X_{t-1} + 0.2 X_{t-2} \qquad \text{(12.2)}$$

Suppose a person received a permanent salary increase of $1000 (permanent in the sense that the increase in the salary will be maintained). If his or her consumption function is as shown in Equation (12.2), then in the first year of the salary increase he or she increases his or her consumption expenditure by $400 (0.4 × 1000), by another $300 (0.3 × 1000) the next year, and by another $200 (0.2 × 1000) in the third year. Thus, by the end of the third year the level of his or her consumption expenditure will have increased by (200 + 300 + 400), or by $900; the remaining $100 goes into savings.

Contrast the consumption function Eq. (12.2) with the following consumption function:

$$Y_t = \text{constant} + 0.9 X_{t-1} \qquad \text{(12.3)}$$

Although the ultimate effect of a $1000 increase in income on consumption is the same in both cases, it takes place with a lag of one year in Equation (12.3), whereas in Eq. (12.2) it is distributed over a period of three years; hence the name *distributed lag model* for models like Eq. (12.2). This can be seen clearly from Figure 12-1.

Reasons for Lag

Before moving on, a natural question arises: Why do lags occur? That is, why does the dependent variable respond to a unit change in the explanatory variable(s) with a time lag? There are several reasons, which we discuss now.

Psychological Reasons   Due to the force of habit (inertia), people do not change their consumption habits immediately following a price decrease or an income increase, perhaps because the process of change involves some immediate disutility. Thus, those who become instant millionaires by winning lotteries may not change their lifestyles because they do not know how to react to

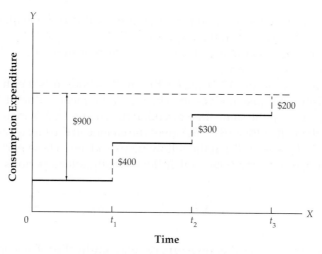

FIGURE 12-1   An example of a distributed lag model

such an immediate windfall, not to mention the hounding by financial planners, newly discovered relatives, tax lawyers, etc.

Technological Reasons   Every time a new-generation personal computer (PC) comes on the market, the prices of existing PCs drop dramatically. Some people who can still use existing PCs would therefore wait for the announcement of a new PC in the hope of purchasing an existing PC at a cheaper price. The same is true of automobiles. The moment, say, the 2010 models are on the market, the prices of 2009 models drop considerably. Consumers thinking of replacing their old cars may wait for the announcement of the new model in anticipation of buying a previous model at a lower price.

Institutional Reasons   Since most major collective bargaining agreements are multiyear contracts, union workers have to wait for the expiration of the existing contract to negotiate a new wage rate even though the inflation rate has increased substantially since the signing of the last contract. Likewise, a professional ball player has to wait until the expiration of his contract to negotiate a new one, even though his "productivity" has gone up since the contract was signed several years ago. Of course, some players try to renegotiate the existing contract and some do succeed.

For these and other reasons, lags occupy a central role in economics. This is clearly reflected in the short-run/long-run methodology of economics. In the short run the price or income elasticities are generally smaller in absolute value than their long-run counterparts because it takes time to make the necessary adjustment following a change in the values of explanatory variables.

Generalizing Eq. (12.1), we can write a *k-period distributed lag model* as

$$Y_t = A + B_0 X_t + B_1 X_{t-1} + B_2 X_{t-2} + \cdots + B_k X_{t-k} + u_t \qquad \textbf{(12.4)}$$

in which the effect of a unit change in the value of the explanatory variable is felt over k periods.[1] In the regression (12.4), Y responds to a unit change in the value of the X variable not only in the current time period but also in several previous time periods.

In the regression (12.4), the coefficient B_0 is known as the **short-run, or impact, multiplier** because it gives the change in the mean value of Y following a unit change in X in the same time period. If the change in X is maintained at the same level thereafter, then $(B_0 + B_1)$ gives the change in the mean value of Y in the next period, $(B_0 + B_1 + B_2)$ in the following period, etc. These partial sums are called **interim, or intermediate, multipliers.** Finally, after k periods, we obtain

$$\sum_{i=0}^{k} B_i = B_0 + B_1 + B_2 + \cdots + B_k \tag{12.5}$$

which is known as the **long-run, or total, multiplier.** Thus, in the consumption function given in the model (12.2), the short-run multiplier is 0.4, the interim multiplier is $(0.4 + 0.3) = 0.7$, and the long-run multiplier is $(0.4 + 0.3 + 0.2) = 0.9$. In the long run, here three periods, a unit change in PDI will lead, on average, to a 0.9 unit change in the consumption expenditure. In short, the long-run *marginal propensity to consume (MPC)* is 0.9, whereas the short-run MPC is only 0.4, 0.7 being the intermediate term MPC. Since the impact of the change in the value of the explanatory variable(s) in the distant past is probably less important than the impact in the immediate near future, we would expect that generally B_0 would be greater in value than B_1, which would be greater than B_2, etc. In other words, the values of the various B's are expected to decline from the first B onward, a fact that will be useful later when we estimate the distributed lag models.

Estimation of Distributed Lag Models

How do we estimate distributed models like regression (12.4)? Can we still use the usual ordinary least squares (OLS) method? In principle, yes, for if we assume that X_t is nonstochastic, or fixed in repeated sampling, so are X_{t-1} and all other lagged values of the X's. Therefore, model (12.4) per se does not violate any of the standard assumptions of the classical linear regression model (CLRM). However, there are some practical problems that need to be addressed.

1. The obvious problem is to determine how many **lagged values** of the explanatory variables to introduce, for economic theory is rarely robust enough to suggest the maximum length of the lag.
2. If we introduce too many lagged values, the degrees of freedom can become a serious problem. If we have 20 observations and introduce

---

[1]The term *period* is used generically; it can be a day, a week, a month, a quarter, a year, or any suitable time period.

10 lagged values, we will have only 8 degrees of freedom left—10 d.f. will be lost on account of the lagged values—one on account of the current value, and one for the intercept. Obviously, as the number of degrees of freedom dwindles, statistical inference becomes increasingly less reliable. The problem becomes all the more complex if we have more than one explanatory variable in the model, each with its own distributed lag structure. In this case we can consume degrees of freedom very fast. Note that for every coefficient estimated, we lose 1 d.f.

3. Even with a large sample where there is not much concern about the degrees of freedom problem, we may run into the problem of *multicollinearity*, for successive values of most economic variables tend to be correlated, sometimes very highly. As noted in Chapter 8, multicollinearity leads to imprecise estimation; that is, standard errors tend to be large in relation to estimated coefficients. As a result, based on the routinely computed t ratios, we tend to declare that a lagged coefficient(s) is statistically insignificant. Another problem that arises is that coefficients of successive lagged terms sometimes alternate in sign, which makes it difficult to interpret some coefficients, as the following example will show.

Example 12.1. An Illustrative Example: The St. Louis Model

To determine whether changes in the nominal gross national product (GNP) can be explained by changes in either the money supply (monetarism) or government expenditure (Keynesianism), the Federal Reserve Bank of St. Louis has developed a model, popularly known as the St. Louis model. One version of this model is

$$\dot{Y}_t = \text{constant} + \sum_{i=0}^{i=4} A_i \dot{M}_{t-i} + \sum_{i=0}^{i=4} B_i \dot{E}_{t-i} + u_t \tag{12.6}$$

where $\dot{Y}_t$ = the rate of growth of nominal GNP at time t
$\dot{M}_t$ = the rate of growth in the money supply (M_1 version) at time t
$\dot{E}_t$ = the rate of growth in full or high employment government expenditure at time t

By convention, a dot over a variable denotes growth rate (e.g., $\dot{Y}_t = \frac{1}{Y}\frac{dY}{dt}$; recall the log-lin model from Chapter 5).

The results based on the quarterly data from 1953-I to 1976-IV using four lagged values of $\dot{M}$ and $\dot{E}$ each follow.[2] For ease of reading, the results are presented in tabular form (Table 12-1).

---

[2]These results, with a change in notation, are from Keith M. Carlson, "Does the St. Louis Equation Now Believe in Fiscal Policy," *Review*, Federal Reserve Bank of St. Louis, vol. 60, no. 2, February 1978, Table IV, p. 17. Note: $\sum_{i=0}^{4} A_i \dot{M}_{t-i} = A_0\dot{M}_t + A_1\dot{M}_{t-1} + A_2\dot{M}_{t-2} + A_3\dot{M}_{t-3} + A_4\dot{M}_{t-4}$, and similarly for $\sum_{i=0}^{4} B_i \dot{E}_{t-i}$.

TABLE 12-1   THE ST. LOUIS MODEL

Coefficient	Estimate		Coefficient	Estimate	
A_0	0.40	(2.96)*	B_0	0.08	(2.26)*
A_1	0.41	(5.26)*	B_1	0.06	(2.52)*
A_2	0.25	(2.14)*	B_2	0.00	(0.02)
A_3	0.06	(0.71)	B_3	−0.06	(−2.20)
A_4	−0.05	(−0.37)	B_4	−0.07	(−1.83)*
	1.06	(5.59)*		0.01	(0.40)
	$R^2 = 0.40;$		$d = 1.78$		

Note: The figures in parentheses are *t* ratios.
*Significant at 5% level (one-tailed). The value of the intercept is not presented in the original article.

Notice several features of the results presented in Table 12-1.

1. Not all lagged coefficients are individually significant on the basis of the conventional *t* test. But we cannot tell whether this lack of significance is genuine or merely due to multicollinearity.

2. The fourth lagged value of $\dot{M}$ has a negative sign, which is difficult to interpret economically because all other lagged money coefficients have a positive impact on $\dot{Y}$. This negative value, however, is statistically insignificant, although we do not know if this is due to multicollinearity. The third and fourth lagged values of $\dot{E}$ are not only negative but are also statistically significant. Again, economically, it is difficult to interpret these negative values, for why should the rate of growth in government expenditure have a negative impact three and four periods in the past while the first two lagged values have a positive impact?

3. The immediate, or short-run, impact of a unit change in $\dot{M}$ is 0.40, whereas the long-term impact is 1.06 (which is the sum of the various A coefficients), and this is statistically significant. The interpretation is that a sustained 1 percent increase in the rate of growth of the money supply will be accompanied by $\approx$1 percent increase in the rate of growth of the nominal GNP in about five quarters. Similarly, the short-run impact of a 1 percent increase in the rate of growth of government expenditure is $\approx$0.08, which is statistically significant, but the long-term impact is only 0.01 (the sum of the B coefficients), which is statistically insignificant.

   The implication then is that changes in the growth rates in the money supply have a lasting impact on changes in the growth rate of the GNP (almost one for one) but changes in the growth rates of government expenditure do not. In short, the St. Louis model tends to support monetarism. That is why the St. Louis model is often called the *monetarist model*.

   From a statistical viewpoint the obvious question is why did the St. Louis model include only four lags of each explanatory variable? Can some insignificant coefficients be due to multicollinearity? These questions cannot be answered without examining the original data and determining what happens to the model if more lagged terms are introduced. But as you can well imagine, this will not be a particularly fruitful line of attack, for there is no way to avoid the problem of multicollinearity if more lagged terms are introduced. Clearly, we need an alternative that not only will rid us of the problem of multicollinearity but also will tell us how many lagged terms can be included legitimately in a model.

The Koyck, Adaptive Expectations, and Stock Adjustment Models Approach to Estimating Distributed Lag Models[3]

An ingenious approach to reducing both the number of lagged terms in the distributed lag models and the problem of multicollinearity is to adopt the approach used by the so-called **Koyck,** the **adaptive expectations,** and the **partial,** or **stock, adjustment models.** Without going into the technical details of these models, a remarkable feature of all of them is that distributed models like Eq. (12.4) can be reduced to the following "simple" model:[4]

$$Y_t = C_1 + C_2 X_t + C_3 Y_{t-1} + v_t \qquad (12.7)$$

where v is the error term. This model is called an **autoregressive model** (recall Chapter 10) because the lagged value of the dependent variable appears as an explanatory variable on the right-hand side of the equation. In the regression (12.4) we had to estimate the intercept, current, and k-lagged terms. So, if $k = 15$, we will have to estimate all 17 parameters, a considerable loss of degrees of freedom, especially if the sample size is not too large. But in the regression (12.7) we have to estimate only three unknowns, the intercept and the two slope coefficients, a tremendous savings in the degrees of freedom. So all lagged terms in the regression (12.4) are replaced by a single lagged value of Y.

Of course, there is no such thing as a "free lunch." In reducing the number of parameters to be estimated in the model (12.4) to only three, we have created some problems in the model (12.7). First, since Y_t is stochastic, or random, Y_{t-1} is random too. Therefore, to estimate the model (12.7) by OLS, we must make sure that the error term v_t and the lagged variable Y_{t-1} are not correlated; otherwise, as can be shown, *the OLS estimators are not only biased but are inconsistent as well.* If, however, v_t and Y_{t-1} are uncorrelated, it can be proved that the OLS estimators are biased (in small samples), but the bias tends to disappear as the sample size becomes increasingly large. That is, in a large sample (technically, asymptotically) the OLS estimators will be consistent. *Second,* if,

---

[3]See L. M. Koyck, *Distributed Lags and Investment Analysis,* North-Holland, Amsterdam, 1954; P. Cagan, "The Monetary Dynamics of Hyper Inflations," in M. Friedman (ed.), *Studies in the Quantity Theory of Money,* University of Chicago Press, Chicago, 1956 (for the adaptive expectations model); Marc Nerlove, *Distributed Lags and Demand for Agricultural and Other Commodities,* Handbook No. 141, U.S. Department of Agriculture, June 1958 (for the partial, or stock, adjustment model).
[4]For technical details, see Gujarati and Porter, *Basic Econometrics,* 5th ed., McGraw-Hill, New York, 2009, Chapter 17.

however, v_t is serially correlated (e.g., it follows the first-order Markov scheme: $v_t = \rho v_{t-1} + w_t$, where $-1 \le \rho \le 1$ and the error term w_t satisfies the usual OLS assumptions), OLS estimators are biased as well as inconsistent and the traditional t and F testing procedure becomes invalid. Therefore, in autoregressive models like Eq. (12.7) it is very important that we find out whether the error term v_t follows, say, the first-order Markov, or the AR(1) scheme, discussed in Chapter 10. *Third*, as we discussed in Chapter 10, in autoregressive models the conventional Durbin-Watson d test is not applicable. In such cases we can use the Durbin h statistic discussed in Problem 10.16 to detect first-order autocorrelation, or we can use the runs test.

Before we proceed to illustrate the model (12.7), it is interesting to note that the coefficient C_2 attached to X_t gives the *short-run impact* of a unit change in X_t on mean Y_t and $C_2/(1 - C_3)$ gives the *long-run impact* of a (sustained) unit change in X_t on mean Y_t; this is equivalent to summing the values of all B coefficients in the model (12.4), as shown in Eq. (12.5).[5] In other words, the lagged Y term in the regression (12.7) acts as the workhorse for all lagged X terms in the model (12.4).

Example 12.2. The Impact of Adjusted Monetary Base Growth Rate on Growth Rate of Nominal GNP, United States, 1960–1988

To see the relationship between the growth rate in the nominal GNP ($\dot{Y}$) and the growth rate in the adjusted monetary base (AMB),[6] Joseph H. Haslag and Scott E. Hein[7] obtained the following regression results. (*Note:* The authors did not present R^2. A dot over a variable represents its growth rate.)

$$\dot{Y}_t = 0.004 + 0.238 \text{AM}\dot{\text{B}}_{t-1} + 0.759 \dot{Y}_{t-1}$$

$$\text{se} = (0.004)\ (0.067) \qquad\qquad (0.054) \qquad\qquad \textbf{(12.8)}$$

$$t = (1.000)\ (3.552) \qquad\qquad (14.056)$$

$$Durbin\ h = 3.35$$

Before interpreting these results, notice that Haslag and Hein use a one-period (a year here) lagged value of the AMB as an explanatory variable and not the current period value, but this should cause no problem because AMB is largely determined by the Federal Reserve system. Besides, AMB_{t-1} is nonstochastic if

---

[5]The details can be found in Gujarati and Porter, *Basic Econometrics*, 5th ed., McGraw-Hill, New York, 2009, Chapter 17.

[6]The monetary base (MB), sometimes called *high-powered* money, in the United States consists of currency and total commercial bank reserves. The AMB takes into account the changes in the reserve ratio requirements of the Federal Reserve bank; in the United States all commercial banks are required to keep certain cash or cash equivalents against the deposits that customers keep with the banks. The reserve ratio is the ratio of cash and cash equivalents to the total deposits (which are liabilities of the banks). The Federal Reserve system changes this ratio from time to time to achieve some policy goals, such as containment of inflation or the rate of interest, etc.

[7]See Joseph H. Haslag and Scott E. Hein, "Reserve Requirements, the Monetary Base and Economic Activity," *Economic Review*, Federal Reserve Bank of Dallas, March 1989, p. 13. The regression results are presented to suit the format of model (3.46) in Chapter 3.

AMB_t is, which is what we usually assume about any explanatory variable in the standard CLRM. Now to the interpretation of model (12.8).

From Eq. (12.8) we observe that the *short-run* impact of AMB is 0.238; that is, a one percentage point change in AMB on the average leads to ≈0.238 percentage point change in the nominal GNP. This impact seems statistically significant because the computed t value is significant. However, the long-run impact is

$$\frac{0.238}{(1 - 0.759)} = 0.988$$

which is almost unity. Therefore, in the long run a (sustained) one percentage point change in the AMB leads to about a one percentage point change in the nominal GNP; so to speak, there is a one-to-one relationship between the growth rates of AMB and the nominal GNP.

The only problem with model (12.8) is that the estimated h value is statistically significant. As pointed out in Problem 10.16, in a large sample the h statistic follows the standard normal distribution. Therefore, the 5% two-tailed critical Z (standard normal) value is 1.96 and the 1% two-tailed critical Z value is ≈2.58. Since the observed h of 3.35 exceeds these critical values, it seems that the residuals in the regression (12.8) are autocorrelated, and therefore the results presented in model (12.8) should be taken with a grain of salt. But note that the h statistic is a large sample statistic and the sample size in the model (12.8) is 29, which may not be very large. In any case, Eq. (12.8) serves the pedagogical purpose of illustrating the mechanics of estimating distributed lag models via the Koyck, adaptive expectation, or stock adjustment models.

Example 12.3. Margin Requirements and Stock Market Volatility

To assess the short-run and long-run impact of a margin requirement (which restricts the amount of credit that brokers and dealers can extend to their customers), Gikas A. Hardouvelis[8] estimated the following regression (among several others) for the monthly data from December 1931 to December 1987, a total of 673 months, for the stocks included in the Standard & Poor's (S&P) index. (*Note:* The standard error, indicated by *, was not presented by the author.)

$$\hat{\sigma}_t = 0.112 - 0.112m_t + 0.186\sigma_{t-1}$$
$$se = (0.015) \quad (0.024) \quad (\quad)^* \quad R^2 = 0.44 \tag{12.9}$$

where σ_t = the standard deviation of the monthly excess nominal rate of return of stocks (the nominal rate of return minus the one-month T-bill rate at the end of the previous month) calculated from $(t - 11)$ to t (in decimals), which is taken as a measure of volatility; m_t = the average official margin requirement from $(t - 11)$ to t (in decimals); and the figures in parentheses are the estimated standard errors corrected for heteroscedasticity and autocorrelation.

[8]See Gikas A. Hardouvelis, "Margin Requirements and Stock Market Volatility," *Quarterly Review,* Federal Reserve Bank of New York, vol. 13, no. 2, Summer 1988, Table 4, p. 86, and footnote 21, p. 88.

Unfortunately, Hardouvelis does not present the standard error of the lagged volatility coefficient nor the h statistic. Note, though, that the author has corrected his results for autocorrelation.

As expected, the coefficient of the margin variable has a negative sign, suggesting that when margin requirements are increased, there is less speculative activity in the stock market, thereby reducing volatility. The value of -0.112 means that if the margin requirement is increased by, say, one percentage point, the volatility of S&P stocks decreases by ≈ 0.11 percentage points. This is, of course, the short-run impact. The long-run impact is

$$-\frac{0.112}{(1 - 0.186)} \approx -0.138$$

which obviously is higher (in absolute value) than the short-run impact, but not a lot higher.

Although the topic of dynamic modeling is vast and all kinds of newer econometric techniques to handle such models are currently available, the preceding discussion will give you the flavor of what dynamic modeling is all about. For additional details, consult the references.[9]

12.2   THE PHENOMENON OF SPURIOUS REGRESSION: NONSTATIONARY TIME SERIES

Regression models involving time series data sometimes give results that are *spurious*, or of dubious value, in the sense that superficially the results look good but on further investigation they look suspect. To explain this phenomenon of **spurious regression,** let us consider a concrete example. Table 12-2 (found on the textbook Web site) gives quarterly data for the United States on gross domestic product (GDP), personal disposable income (PDI), personal consumption expenditure (PCE), profits, and dividends for the period of 1970-I to 2008-IV (a total of 156 observations); all the data are in billions of 2000 dollars.

For now we will concentrate on PCE and PDI; the other data given in the table will be used in problems at the end of this chapter.

Using the data given in Table 12-2 and regressing PCE on PDI we obtain the following regression results:

$$\widehat{PCE_t} = -470.52 + 1.0006\ PDI_t \qquad R^2 = 0.998; \quad d = 0.3975$$
$$t = (-22.03) \quad (264.76) \tag{12.10}$$

These regression results look "fabulous": the R^2 is extremely high, the t value of PDI is extremely high, the marginal propensity to consume (MPC) out of PDI is positive and high. The only fly in the ointment is that the Durbin-Watson d is low. As Granger and Newbold have suggested, *an $R^2 > d$ is a good rule of thumb to suspect that the estimated regression suffers from spurious (or nonsense) regression;*

---

[9]A good reference is A. C. Harvey, *The Econometric Analysis of Time Series,* 2nd ed., MIT, Cambridge, Mass., 1990. Some parts of this book may be difficult for beginners.

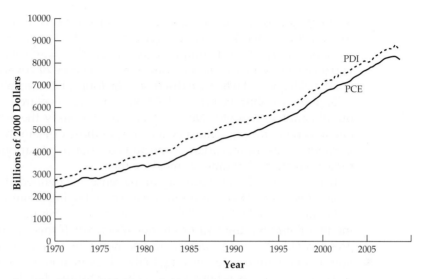

FIGURE 12-2   Quarterly PDI and PCE, United States, 1970–2008

that is, in actuality there may not be any meaningful relationship between PCE and PDI.[10]

Why may the regression results in Equation (12.10) be spurious? To understand this, we have to introduce the concept of a **stationary time series.** To explain this concept, let us first plot the data on PCE and PDI given in Table 12-2, as shown in Figure 12-2.

Looking at Figure 12-2, we can see that both the PCE and PDI time series are generally trending upward over the sample period. Such a picture generally indicates that such time series may be *nonstationary.* What does that mean?

Broadly speaking, a stochastic process is said to be *stationary* if its mean and variance are constant over time and the value of the covariance between two time periods depends only on the distance or lag between the two time periods and not on the actual time at which the covariance is computed.[11]

Symbolically, letting Y_t represent a stochastic time series, we say that it is stationary if the following conditions are satisfied:[12]

Mean: $E(Y_t) = \mu$ **(12.11)**

Variance: $E(Y_t - \mu)^2 = \sigma^2$ **(12.12)**

Covariance: $\gamma_k = E[(Y_t - \mu)(Y_{t+k} - \mu)]$ **(12.13)**

---

[10]C. W. J. Granger and P. Newbold, "Spurious Regression in Econometrics," *Journal of Econometrics,* vol. 2, no. 2, July 1974, pp. 111–120.

[11]Any time series data can be thought of as being generated by a *stochastic,* or *random, process* and a concrete set of data, such as that shown in Table 12-2, can be regarded as a (particular) *realization* (i.e., a sample) of the underlying stochastic process.

[12]In the time series literature such a stochastic process is called a *weakly stationary stochastic process.* In most applied work the assumption of weak stationarity has proved useful. In *strong stationarity* we consider higher moments of the PDF, that is, moments beyond the second.

where γ_k, the covariance (or autocovariance) at lag k, is the covariance between the values of Y_t and Y_{t+k}, that is, between two values of Y, k periods apart. If $k = 0$, we obtain γ_0, which is simply the variance of Y ($= \sigma^2$); if $k = 1$, γ_1 is the covariance between two adjacent values of Y, the type of covariance we encountered in Chapter 10 when we discussed the topic of autocorrelation.

Suppose we shift the origin of Y from Y_t to Y_{t+m} (say from 1970-I to 1974-I in our illustrative example). Now if Y_t is to be stationary, the mean, variance, and autocovariances of Y_{t+m} must be the same as those of Y_t. In short, if a time series is stationary, its mean, variance, and autocovariance (at various lags) remain the same no matter what time we measure them.

If a time series is not stationary in the sense just defined, it is called a *nonstationary time series*. (Keep in mind, we are only talking about weak stationarity.)

Looking at the PCE and PDI time series given in Figure 12-2, we get the feeling that these two time series are not stationary. If this is the case, then in regression (12.10) we are regressing one nonstationary time series on another nonstationary time series, leading to the phenomenon of *spurious regression*.

The question now is how do we verify our feeling that the PCE and PDI time series are in fact nonstationary? We will attempt to answer this question in the next section.

12.3   TESTS OF STATIONARITY

In the literature there are several tests of stationarity. Here we will consider the so-called **unit root test.** Without delving into the technicalities, this test can be described as follows.[13] Letting Y_t represent the stochastic time series of interest (such as PCE), we proceed like this.

1. Estimate the following regression:

$$\Delta Y_t = A_1 + A_2 t + A_3 Y_{t-1} + u_t \qquad (12.14)$$

where Δ represents the first difference operator that we encountered in Chapter 10, where t is the trend variable, taking values of 1, 2, and so on (156 for our illustrative example), and where Y_{t-1} is the one-period lagged value of the variable Y.[14]

2. The null hypothesis is that A_3, the coefficient of Y_{t-1}, is zero, which is another way of saying that the underlying time series is nonstationary. This is called the *unit root hypothesis*.[15]

---

[13]For details, see Gujarati and Porter, *Basic Econometrics,* 5th ed., McGraw-Hill, New York, 2009, Chapter 21.

[14]This regression can also be estimated without the intercept and the trend term, although they are generally included.

[15]To see intuitively why the term *unit root* is used, let us proceed as follows: $Y_t = A_1 + A_2 t + CY_{t-1} + u_t$. Now subtract Y_{t-1} from both sides of this equation to give $(Y_t - Y_{t-1}) = A_1 + A_2 t + CY_{t-1} - Y_{t-1}$, which then gives $\Delta Y_t = A_1 + A_2 t + (C-1)Y_{t-1} = A_1 + A_2 t + A_3 Y_{t-1}$, where $A_3 = (C-1)$. Thus, if C is in fact equal to 1, A_3 in regression (12.14) will in fact be zero, thus the name *unit root*.

3. To test that a_3, the estimated value of A_3, is zero, ordinarily we would use the now familiar t test. Unfortunately, we cannot do that because the t test is, strictly speaking, valid only if the underlying time series is stationary. However, we can use an alternative test called the τ *(tau) test,* whose critical values were tabulated by its creators on the basis of Monte Carlo simulations. In the literature, the **tau test** is known as the **Dickey-Fuller (DF) test,** in honor if its discoverers.[16] If in an application, the computed t (= tau) value of estimated A_3 is greater (in absolute value) than the critical Dickey-Fuller tau values, we reject the unit root hypothesis; that is, we conclude that the said time series is stationary. On the other hand, if the computed tau value is smaller (in absolute value) than the critical tau values, we do not reject the unit root hypothesis. In that case, the time series in question is nonstationary.

Let us apply the unit root test to the PCE and PDI time series given in Table 12-2. Corresponding to Equation (12.14), we obtain:

$$\widehat{\Delta \text{PCE}}_t = 42.04 + 0.6596t - 0.0117\,\text{PCE}_{t-1}$$
$$t(=\tau) = (2.83) \quad (2.18) \quad (-1.52) \qquad R^2 = 0.099$$

$$\widehat{\Delta \text{PDI}}_t = 74.19 + 1.0482t - 0.02209\,\text{PDI}_{t-1}$$
$$t(=\tau) = (1.88) \quad (1.58) \quad (-1.31) \qquad R^2 = 0.035$$

$$\text{(12.15)}$$

For the present purpose we are interested in the t value of the lagged PCE and PDI. The 1% and 5% critical DF, or tau, values from the table in Appendix E are about -4.04 and -3.45, respectively.[17] Since in absolute terms (i.e., disregarding sign), the tau values of the lagged PCE and PDI variables are much smaller than any of the preceding tau values, the conclusion is that the PCE and PDI time series are nonstationary (i.e., there is a unit root). In consequence, the OLS regression given in Eq. (12.10) may be spurious (i.e., not meaningful). Incidentally, note that if we had applied the usual t test to, say, the second regression in Eq. (12.15), we would have said that the t value of the lagged PDI variable is statistically significant. But on the basis of the correct tau test (in the presence of nonstationarity) this conclusion would be wrong.

12.4 COINTEGRATED TIME SERIES

The conclusion that the regression (12.10) may be spurious suggests to us that all time series regressions, such as regression (12.10), are spurious. If this were in fact the case, we would need to be very wary of doing regressions based on

[16]D. A. Dickey and W. A. Fuller, "Distribution of Estimators for Autoregressive Time Series with a Unit Root," *Journal of the American Statistical Association,* vol. 74, June 1979, pp. 427–431.
[17]J. G. MacKinnon, "Critical Values of Cointegration Tests," in R. F. Engle and C. W. J. Granger, eds., *Long-run Economic Relationships: Readings in Cointegration,* Oxford University Press, New York, 1991, Chapter 13. Computer packages, such as EViews, now compute the critical tau values routinely.

time series data. But there is no cause for despair. Even if the time series of PCE and PDI are nonstationary, it is quite possible that there is still a (long-run) stable or equilibrium relationship between the two. If that is indeed the case, we say that such time series are **cointegrated.**[18] But how do we find that out? This can be accomplished as follows.

Let us return to the PCE–PDI regression (12.10). From this regression, obtain the residuals, e_t; that is, obtain:

$$e_t = \text{PCE}_t + 470.52 - 1.0006\text{PDI}_t \qquad \textbf{(12.16)}$$

Treating e_t as a time series, we now apply the unit root test (see Eq. [12.14]), which gives the following results. (*Note:* there is no need to introduce intercept and the trend variable in this regression. Why?)

$$\Delta e_t = -0.2096\, e_{t-1}$$

$$t(= \tau) = (-4.35) \qquad r^2 = 0.1094 \qquad \textbf{(12.17)}$$

Now the critical tau values, as computed by Engle and Granger in Appendix E, are about -4.04 (1%), -3.37 (5%), and -3.03 (10%).[19] Since, in absolute terms, the computed tau of 4.35 exceeds any of these critical tau values, the conclusion is that the series e_t is stationary. Therefore, we can say that although PCE and PDI are individually nonstationary, their linear combination as shown in Eq. (12.16) is stationary. That is, the two time series are *cointegrated*, or, in other words, there seems to be a long-run or equilibrium relationship between the two variables. This is a very comforting finding because it means that the regression (12.10) is real and not spurious.

To sum up: *If we are dealing with time series data, we must make sure that the individual time series are either stationary or that they are cointegrated. If this is not the case, we may be open to the charge of engaging in spurious (or nonsense) regression analysis.*

We will conclude the discussion of nonstationary time series by considering another example of a nonstationary time series, the so-called *random walk model*, which has found quite useful applications in finance, investment, and international trade.

12.5 THE RANDOM WALK MODEL

Financial time series such as the S&P 500 stock index, the Dow-Jones index, and foreign exchange rates are often said to follow a "random walk" in the sense that knowing the values of these variables today will not enable us to predict

---

[18]The literature on cointegration is vast and quite technical. Our discussion here is heuristic. A commonly cited example of cointegration is the drunkard and his dog. Leaving the bar, the drunkard meanders in a haphazard way. His dog also meanders in his merry ways. But the dog never loses sight of his owner. So to speak, their meanderings are cointegrated.

[19]R. F. Engle and C. W. J. Granger, *Long-run Economic Relationships: Readings in Cointegration,* Oxford University Press, New York, 1991, Chapter 13.

what these values will be tomorrow. Thus, knowing the price of a stock (say, of Dell or IBM) today, it is hard to tell what it will be tomorrow. That is, the price behavior of stocks is essentially random—today's price is equal to yesterday's price plus a random shock.[20]

To see the anatomy of a **random walk model,** consider the following simple model:

$$Y_t = Y_{t-1} + u_t \tag{12.18}$$

where u_t is the *random error* term with zero mean and constant variance, σ^2. Let us suppose we start at time 0 with a value of Y_0. Now we can write:

$$Y_{t-1} = Y_{t-2} + u_{t-1} \tag{12.19}$$

Using the recursive relation (12.18) repeatedly as in Equation (12.19), we can write:

$$Y_t = Y_0 + \sum u_t \tag{12.20}$$

where the summation is from $t = 1$ to $t = T$, T being the total number of observations. Now it is easy to verify that

$$E(Y_t) = Y_0 \tag{12.21}$$

since the expected value of each u_t is zero. It is also easy to verify that

$$\text{var}(Y_t) = \text{var}(u_1 + u_2 + \cdots + u_T) = T\sigma^2 \tag{12.22}$$

where use is made of the fact that the u's are random, each with the same variance σ^2.

As Equation (12.22) shows, the variance of Y_t is not only not constant but also continuously increases with T. Therefore, by the definition of stationarity given earlier, the (random walk) variable Y_t given in Eq. (12.18) is nonstationary (here nonstationary in the variance). But notice an interesting feature of the random walk model given in Eq. (12.18). If you write it as:

$$\Delta Y_t = (Y_t - Y_{t-1}) = u_t \tag{12.23}$$

where, as usual, Δ is the first difference operator, we see that the first differences of Y are stationary, for $E(\Delta Y_t) = E(u_t) = 0$ and $\text{var}(\Delta Y_t) = \text{var}(u_t) = \sigma^2$. Therefore, if Y in Eq. (12.18) represents, say, share prices, then these prices may be nonstationary, but their first differences are purely random.

---

[20]The random walk is often compared with a drunkard's walk. Leaving the bar, the drunkard moves a random distance u_t at time t, and if he or she continues to walk indefinitely, he or she will eventually drift farther and farther away from the bar.

We can modify the random walk model (12.18) as follows:

$$Y_t = d + Y_{t-1} + u_t \tag{12.24}$$

where d is a constant. This is the **random walk model with drift**, d being the drift parameter.

We leave it as an exercise for you to show that for the model (12.24) we get

$$E(Y_t) = Y_0 + Td \tag{12.25}$$

$$\text{var}(Y_t) = T\sigma^2 \tag{12.26}$$

That is, for the random walk model with drift, both the mean and the variance continuously increase over time. Again, we have a random variable that is nonstationary both in the mean and the variance. If d is positive, we can see from model (12.24) that the mean value of Y will increase continuously over time; if d is negative, the mean value of Y will decrease continuously. In either case, the variance of Y increases continuously over time. A random variable whose mean value and variance are time-dependent is said to follow a **stochastic trend.** This is in contrast to the linear trend model that we discussed in Chapter 5 (see Equation [5.23]), where it was assumed that the variable Y followed a **deterministic trend.**

If we were to use the random walk models for forecasting purposes, we would obtain a picture such as is shown in Figure 12-3.

Figure 12-3(a) shows the random walk model without drift, and Figure 12-3(b) shows it with the drift. As you can see, in Figure 12-3(a) the mean forecast value remains the same at level Y_T all throughout the future, but, because of the increasing variance, the confidence interval around the mean value increases continuously. In Figure 12-3(b), assuming that the drift parameter d is positive, the mean value of forecast increases over time, and so does the forecast error.

In summary, the purpose of this section has been to warn you that regression models based on time series data need to be modeled carefully. If the dependent variable Y and the explanatory variable X(s) are nonstationary, high R^2 values and high t values may lull you into thinking that you have found a meaningful relationship between the two. In fact, a high R^2 may simply reflect the fact that the two variables share common trends, and, therefore, there may not be any true relationship between them. This is the phenomenon of spurious regression. Following Granger and Newbold, a tell-tale sign of spurious regression is that the R^2 value of a regression involving time series data is greater than the Durbin-Watson d value. Therefore, be on the lookout.

12.6 THE LOGIT MODEL

In Chapter 6 on dummy variables we briefly discussed the **linear probability model (LPM)** to estimate a model in which the dependent variable, Y, is binary, taking a value of 1 or 0, with 1 denoting the presence or possession of an attribute (e.g., married, female, in the labor force, etc.) and 0 denoting the absence

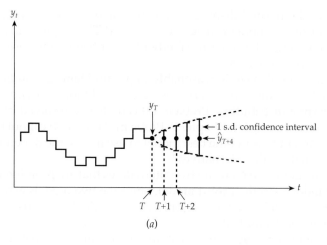

(a)

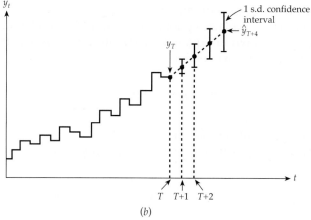

(b)

FIGURE 12-3   Forecasting with random walk models

Source: Adapted from Robert S. Pindyck and Daniel L. Rubinfeld, *Econometric Models and Economic Forecasts,* 4th ed., McGraw-Hill, New York, 1998, pp. 491–492.

of that attribute (e.g., unmarried, male, not in the labor force, etc.). The explanatory variables in the LPM can themselves be binary or dummy or quantitative or a mixture thereof.

Although such a model can be estimated by the usual OLS procedure, we warned against its blind application because of four major problems: (1) Although Y can take a value of 1 or 0, there is no guarantee that the estimated Y values will necessarily lie between 0 and 1; some estimated Y values may be negative and some may be in excess of 1, as we saw with the hypothetical home ownership example discussed in Chapter 6. (2) Since Y is binary, the error term in such a model is also binary. Actually, it follows the binomial distribution. Therefore, strictly speaking we cannot assume that the error term in such models follows the normal distribution, as we have assumed all along. (3) The error term in such a model is heteroscedastic. (4) The major weakness of the LPM is that it assumes that the probability of Y happening increases linearly with the explanatory variables.

If the sample size is reasonably large, problem (2) can be handled, for we know that as the sample size increases, the binomial distribution approaches the normal distribution. Problem (3) can also be resolved by using one of the methods discussed in Chapter 9. Problems (1) and (4) cannot be resolved easily. Therefore, LPM is not the best model to use in case the dependent variable is binary. What are the alternatives?

In the literature there are two alternatives that are prominently discussed, the **logit model** and the **probit model.** Since the two models generally give similar results, we will discuss here only the logit model because of its comparative mathematical simplicity.

We will continue with our home ownership example to explain the basic ideas underlying the logit model.

Recall that in explaining home ownership (Y) in relation to income (X), the LPM was as shown in Equation (6.31). But now consider the following representation of home ownership:

$$P_i = E(Y = 1|X_i) = \frac{1}{1 + e^{-(B_1 + B_2 X_i)}} \tag{12.27}$$

where P_i represents probability.

For ease of exposition, we write this equation as:

$$P_i = \frac{1}{1 + e^{-Z_i}} = \frac{e^z}{1 + e^z} \tag{12.28}$$

where $Z_i = B_1 + B_2 X_i$.

Equation (12.28) represents what is known in statistics as the (cumulative) **logistic distribution function,** which has been used extensively in analyzing growth phenomena, such as population, GDP, and money supply.

It is easy to verify that as Z_i ranges from $-\infty$ to $+\infty$, P_i ranges between 0 and 1, and that P_i is nonlinearly related to Z_i (i.e., X_i), thus remedying the problems facing the LPM.

But in remedying the defects of LPM, we have created an estimating problem because P_i is nonlinear not only in X but also in the parameters, the B's, which is clearly seen in Equation (12.27). This means we cannot use the familiar OLS procedure to estimate the parameters of Eq. (12.27). But this problem is more apparent than real because Eq. (12.27) can be linearized, as shown below.

If P_i, the probability of owning a house, is given by Eq. (12.28), then $(1 - P_i)$, the probability of not owning a house, is

$$1 - P_i = \frac{1}{1 + e^{Z_i}} \tag{12.29}$$

Therefore, we can write

$$\frac{P_i}{1 - P_i} = \frac{1 + e^{Z_i}}{1 + e^{-Z_i}} = e^{Z_i} \qquad (12.30)$$

Now $P_i/(1 - P_i)$ is simply the **odds ratio** in favor of owning a house—the ratio of the probability that a family will own a house to the probability that it will not own a house. Thus, if $P_i = 0.8$, it means the odds are 4 to 1 in favor of the family owning a house.

Now if we take the natural log (12.30), we obtain a very interesting result, namely,

$$L_i = \ln\left(\frac{P_i}{1 - P_i}\right) = Z_i = B_1 + B_2 X_i \qquad (12.31)$$

that is, L, the log of the odds ratio, is not only linear in X but also (from the estimation viewpoint) linear in the parameters. L is called the **logit**, and hence the name **logit model** for models like (12.31).

Notice several interesting features of the logit model.

1. As P goes from 0 to 1, (i.e., as Z varies from $-\infty$ to $+\infty$), the logit L goes from $-\infty$ to $+\infty$. That is, although the probabilities (of necessity) lie between 0 and 1, the logits are not so bounded.
2. Although L is linear in X, the probabilities themselves are not. This property is in contrast with the LPM where the probabilities increase linearly with X.
3. Although we have included a single X variable in Equation (12.31), we can add as many explanatory variables as may be dictated by the underlying theory. Some of these X's can be dummies.
4. If the logit L is positive, it means that when the value of the explanatory variable(s) increases, the odds that Y equals 1 (meaning some event of interest occurs) increase. If L is negative, the odds that Y equals 1 decrease as X increases. To state it differently, the logit becomes negative and increasingly large in magnitude as the odds ratio decreases from 1 to 0 and becomes large and increasingly positive as the odds ratio increases from 1 to infinity.
5. More formally, the interpretation of the logit model given in Eq. (12.31) is as follows: B_2, the slope, measures the change in L for a unit change in X; that is, it tells how the log-odds in favor of owning a house change as income changes by a unit, say, $1000. The intercept B_1 is the value of log-odds in favor of owning a house if income is zero. Like most interpretations of intercepts, this interpretation may not have any physical meaning.
6. Whereas the LPM assumes that P_i is linearly related to X_i, the logit model assumes that the log of the odds is linearly related to X_i.
7. Given a certain level of income, say, X^*, if we actually want to estimate not the odds but the probability of owning a house itself, this can be done directly from Eq. (12.28) once we estimate B_1 and B_2. But how do we estimate these parameters? The answer follows.

Estimation of the Logit Model

For estimation purposes, we write Eq. (12.31) as follows:

$$L_i = \ln\left(\frac{P_i}{1 - P_i}\right) = B_1 + B_2 X_i + u_i \qquad (12.32)$$

We will discuss the properties of the error term u_i shortly.

To estimate Equation (12.32), we need, apart from X_i, the values of the logit, L_i. This depends on the type of data we have for analysis. We distinguish two types of data: (1) *data at the individual, or micro, level*, and (2) *grouped or replicated data*.

Data at the Individual Level   If we have data on individual families, as in Table 6-10 (on the textbook's Web site), OLS estimation of Eq. (12.32) is infeasible. This is easy to see. In terms of the data given in Table 6-10, $P_i = 1$ if a family owns a house and $P_i = 0$ if it does not own a house. But if we put these values directly in the logit L_i, we get

$$L_i = \ln\left(\frac{1}{0}\right) \text{ if a family owns a house}$$

$$L_i = \ln\left(\frac{0}{1}\right) \text{ if a family does not own a house}$$

Obviously, these expressions are meaningless. Thus, if we have data at the individual level, we cannot estimate Eq. (12.32) by the standard OLS routine. In this situation we may have to resort to the **method of maximum likelihood (ML).** This method is somewhat involved and best left for the references.[21] Software packages, such as EViews, MINITAB, LIMDEP, SHAZAM, STATA, and MICROFIT, have routines to estimate the logit model at the individual level.

Grouped or Replicated Data   Consider the hypothetical data given in Table 12-3. This table gives data on several families *grouped* or *replicated* (repeat observations at a given X value) according to income level and the number of families owning a house at each level of income. Corresponding to each income level X_i, there are N_i families, n_i among whom are home owners ($n_i \leq N_i$). Therefore, if we compute

$$\hat{P}_i = \frac{n_i}{N_i} \qquad (12.33)$$

that is, the *relative frequency*, we can use it as an estimate of the true P_i corresponding to each X_i. If N_i is fairly large, $\hat{P}_i$ will be a reasonably good estimate of

---

[21]For details and applications, see Gujarati and Porter, *Basic Econometrics*, 5th ed., McGraw-Hill, New York, 2009, Chapter 15.

TABLE 12-3 HYPOTHETICAL DATA ON X_i (INCOME), N_i (NUMBER OF FAMILIES AT INCOME X_i), AND n_i (NUMBER OF FAMILIES OWNING A HOUSE)

X ($, in thousands) (1)	N_i (2)	n_i (3)	$P_i = \frac{n_i}{N_i}$ (4)
26	40	8	0.20
28	50	12	0.24
30	60	18	0.30
33	80	28	0.35
35	100	45	0.45
40	70	36	0.51
45	65	39	0.60
50	50	33	0.66
55	40	30	0.75
60	25	20	0.80
	580	269	

P_i, as we can see in Appendix A on probability. The estimated P_i are shown in Table 12-3. Using the estimated P_i, we can compute the estimated logit as:

$$\hat{L}_i = \ln\left(\frac{\hat{P}_i}{1 - \hat{P}_i}\right) \tag{12.34}$$

and then run the regression

$$\hat{L}_i = B_1 + B_2 X_i + u_i \tag{12.35}$$

Using the data given in Table 12-3, we estimated Equation (12.35) and obtained the following results:

$$\ln\frac{\hat{P}_i}{1 - \hat{P}_i} = -3.2438 + 0.0792\, X_i$$

$$se = (0.1708)\quad (0.0041) \tag{12.36}$$

$$t = (-18.992)\ (19.317)\qquad R^2 = 0.9791$$

As these results suggest, if income increases by a unit (here, $1000), the log of the odds in favor of owning a house goes up by ≈ 0.08 units. Of course, we can compute the probability of owning a house at any given level of income. For instance, letting $X = 26$, we obtain

$$\ln\left(\frac{P_i}{1 - P_i}\right) = -1.1846 \tag{12.37}$$

Therefore, following Eq. (12.28), we get

$$P_i \text{ (given } X = 26) = 0.2342 \qquad\qquad\qquad \textbf{(12.38)}$$

whereas the actual probability was 0.20 (see Table 12-3). Other probabilities can be computed similarly (see Problem 12.12).

Before we conclude our discussion of the (grouped) logit model, a technical point needs to be noted, which refers to the nature of the error term u_i given in Eq. (12.35). It can be shown that this error term is heteroscedastic with variance of $\left(\frac{1}{N_i P_i (1-P_i)}\right)$. As a result, we will have to correct for heteroscedasticity, using the method of weighted least squares discussed in Chapter 9.[22] The heteroscedasticity-corrected regression results in the present case do not differ vastly from those given in Eq. (12.36).

With the knowledge of the logit model, we can now easily handle models in which the dependent variable is dummy or binary. As a matter of fact, we can even run a regression in which the dependent variable as well as all explanatory variables are dummies. Not only that, but we can even consider regression models in which the dependent variable is not only dichotomous but also trichotomous (e.g., membership in the Republican party or the Democratic party or a third party), or even has more than three categories. Such models are called *multinominal regression models,* but they are beyond the scope of this book.[23]

We will now present a concrete application of the logit model.

Example 12.4. Predicting Bank Failure

Based on call report (i.e., bank examinations) data of 6869 calls between December 1982 and December 1984, Robert Avery and Terrence Belton estimated a *risk index* (i.e., a logit function) to predict bank failure. A bank was deemed to have failed if it failed within a year following the call—the bank examination. Their results are presented in Table 12-4.

As these results show, ceteris paribus, if KTA, the ratio of primary capital (i.e., shareholder equity) to total assets goes up by one percentage point, the log of the odds of bankruptcy goes down by 0.501, which is a sensible result. Similarly, if LNNACCA, the percent ratio of nonaccruing loans to total assets, goes up by a percentage point, the log of odds in favor of bankruptcy goes up by 4.310. The other coefficients are to be interpreted similarly. Statistically, RENEGA and NCOFSA are insignificant and NCOFSA has the wrong sign. (Why?)

---

[22]For details, see Gujarati and Porter, *Basic Econometrics,* 5th ed., McGraw-Hill, New York, 2009, pp. 557–558.

[23]For a general description of the logistic models, see David W. Hosmer and Stanley Lemesshow, *Applied Logistic Regression,* Wiley, New York, 1988.

TABLE 12-4   LOGIT MODEL: PREDICTING BANK FAILURE

Explanatory variable	Coefficient	t value
Constant	−2.420	3.07
KTA	−0.501	−4.89
PD090MA	0.428	5.16
LNNACCA	4.310	4.31
RENEGA	0.269	1.07
NCOFSA	0.223	1.60
NETINCA	0.331	2.68

Notes: KTA = Percent ratio of primary capital to total assets
PD090MA = Percent ratio of loans more than 90 days past due to total assets
LNNACCA = Percent ratio of nonaccruing loans to total assets
RENEGA = Percent ratio of renegotiated loans to total assets
NCOFSA = Percent ratio of net loan charge-offs (annualized) to total assets
NETINCA = Percent ratio of net income (annualized) to total assets
Source: Robert B. Avery and Terrence M. Belton, "Comparison of Risk-Based Capital and Risk-Based Deposit Insurance," *Economic Review*, Federal Reserve Bank of Cleveland, 1987, fourth quarter, pp. 20–30.

Avery and Belton conclude that:

> Although the overall fit of the model suggests that predicting bank failure is difficult, the failed banks in the sample had an average predicted probability of failure of 0.24, a number 69 times larger than the average predicted failure probability of nonfailed banks in the sample. Hence, the model clearly does have some ability to discriminate between high- and low-risk banks.

Note that logit models like the bank failure model just discussed have been used extensively in practice. Banks have used it to predict mortgage delinquencies, credit card companies have used it to predict credit card loan defaults, and several educational institutions have used it to predict admissions to higher education. It is rumored that the Internal Revenue Service (IRS) uses such a model to predict which tax payer is likely to be audited.

Example 12.5. To Smoke or Not to Smoke

We conclude our discussion of the logit model by considering the decision to smoke or not to smoke in a sample of 1196 individuals.[24] (See Table 12-5 on the textbook's Web site.) The dependent variable is binary, taking a value of 1 if a person smokes and zero if the person does not smoke. The explanatory variables are age, education (years of schooling), family income, and price of cigarettes in 1979.

[24]These data are from Michael P. Murray, *Econometrics: A Modern Approach*, Pearson/Addison Wesley, Boston, 2006, and can be downloaded from **www.aw-bc.com/murray**. These data are also posted on the textbook's Web site as Table 12-5.

Since the data are at the individual level, we have to use the maximum likelihood (ML) method to estimate the parameters of the model. Using EViews 6, we obtained the following results:

Dependent Variable: SMOKER
Method: ML—Binary Logit (Quadratic hill climbing)

Sample: 1 1196
Included observations: 1196
Convergence achieved after 3 iterations
Covariance matrix computed using second derivatives

	Coefficient	Std. Error	z-Statistic	Prob.
C	2.745077	0.829196	3.310529	0.0009
AGE	−0.020853	0.003739	−5.577290	0.0000
EDUC	−0.090973	0.020666	−4.402100	0.0000
INCOME	4.72E-06	7.17E-06	0.658284	0.5104
PCIGS79	−0.022319	0.012472	−1.789469	0.0735
McFadden R-squared	0.029748	Mean dependent var		0.380435
S.D. dependent var	0.485697	S.E. of regression		0.477407
Akaike info criterion	1.297393	Sum squared resid		271.4495
Schwarz criterion	1.318658	Log likelihood		−770.8409
Hannan-Quinn criter.	1.305405	Restr. log likelihood		−794.4748
LR statistic	47.26785	Avg. log likelihood		−0.644516
Prob (LR statistic)	0.000000			
Obs with Dep = 0	741	Total obs		1196
Obs with Dep = 1	455			

A priori, age, education, and the price of cigarettes have a negative impact on the logit and income has a positive impact. The results concur with these expectations, although the income coefficient is not statistically significant. The price of cigarettes coefficient is significant at about the 7 percent level of significance. Note that our sample of 1196 observations is quite large. Therefore, we use the Z (standard normal) rather than the t test. If we wanted to test the hypothesis that all the slope coefficients are simultaneously equal to zero, we would use the likelihood ratio (LR) test, which has a chi-square distribution with 4 d.f. If this hypothesis were true, the probability of obtaining an LR of about 47 would be practically zero. Hence we reject the null hypothesis; at least one regressor is statistically significant.

When the dependent variable takes only two values, 1 or 0, it is difficult to compute the equivalent of R^2 in the traditional regression analysis. The McFadden R^2 shown in the above table is a kind of R^2, but its practical importance should not be exaggerated.

Turning to the interpretation of the various slope coefficients presented in the preceding table, we cannot interpret them, as in the LPM, as the rate of change of probability for a unit change in the value of the regressor. The interpretation here is the change in the logit, or log of the odds ratio, for a unit change in the value of the regressor. Thus, the education coefficient of about −0.09 means if schooling goes up by one year, the logit goes down by about −0.09, holding other variables constant.

The logit language may be strange for most people. But we can talk in terms of the odds ratio in favor of smoking versus not smoking. We proceed as follows: Holding education, income, and the price of cigarettes constant, if we increase age by a unit (a year), the relative odds of

$$\frac{\text{Probability of smoking}}{\text{Probability of not smoking}}$$

is multiplied by $e^{-0.020852} = 0.9793$. Thus, there is a decrease in the probability of smoking of $(1 - 0.9793) = 0.0207$, or 2.07 percent. In similar fashion, we can compute the relative odds with respect to the other regressors, in each case holding the other variables constant.

It is left for the reader to verify that the relative odds with respect to education, income, and the price of cigarettes change by −8.7 percent, 0 percent, and −2.21 percent, respectively.

If you want to compute the probability of smoking rather than the odds, this can be obtained from Eq. (12.28) by entering the appropriate values of the regression coefficients and values of the regressors. This is of course tedious if you want to do it manually for 1196 observations. However, STATA and EViews can do this job routinely.

To conclude this example, we show the output of LPM for this example. It is left for the reader to compare the results of LPM with those obtained from the logit model.

Dependent Variable: SMOKER
Method: Least Squares

Sample: 1 1196
Included observations: 1196

	Coefficient	Std. Error	t-Statistic	Prob.
C	1.123089	0.188356	5.962575	0.0000
AGE	−0.004726	0.000829	−5.700952	0.0000
EDUC	−0.020613	0.004616	−4.465272	0.0000
INCOME	1.03E-06	1.63E-06	0.628522	0.5298
PCIGS79	−0.005132	0.002852	−1.799076	0.0723
R-squared	0.038770	F-statistic		12.00927
Adjusted R-squared	0.035541	Prob(F-statistic)		0.000000
S.E. of regression	0.476988			
Sum squared resid	270.9729			

The R^2 presented in the above table should be taken with a grain of salt, for the dependent variable takes only two values, 1 and zero. The F statistic given in the table tests the hypothesis that all the slope coefficients are simultaneously zero. This hypothesis can be soundly rejected, for the p value of the estimated F value is practically zero. Although some of the coefficients are individually insignificant, collectively they are all important in determining who smokes versus who does not.

12.7   SUMMARY

In this chapter we discussed several topics of considerable practical importance.

The first topic we discussed was dynamic modeling, in which time or lag explicitly enters into the analysis. In such models the current value of the dependent variable depends upon one or more lagged values of the explanatory variable(s). This dependence can be due to psychological, technological, or institutional reasons. These models are generally known as distributed lag models. Although the inclusion of one or more lagged terms of an explanatory variable does not violate any of the standard CLRM assumptions, the estimation of such models by the usual OLS method is generally not recommended because of the problem of multicollinearity and the fact that every additional coefficient estimated means a loss of degrees of freedom.

Therefore, such models are usually estimated by imposing some restrictions on the parameters of the models (e.g., the values of the various lagged coefficients decline from the first coefficient onward). This is the approach adopted by the Koyck, the adaptive expectations, and the partial, or stock, adjustment models. A unique feature of all these models is that they replace all lagged values of the explanatory variable by a single lagged value of the dependent variable. Because of the presence of the lagged value of the dependent variable among explanatory variables, the resulting model is called an autoregressive model. Although autoregressive models achieve economy in the estimation of distributed lag coefficients, they are not free from statistical problems. In particular, we have to guard against the possibility of autocorrelation in the error term because in the presence of autocorrelation and the lagged dependent variable as an explanatory variable, the OLS estimators are biased as well as inconsistent.

In discussing the dynamic models, we pointed out how they help us to assess the short- and long-run impact of an explanatory variable on the dependent variable.

The next topic we discussed related to the phenomenon of spurious, or nonsense, regression. Spurious regression arises when we regress a nonstationary random variable on one or more nonstationary random variables. A time series is said to be (weakly) stationary, if its mean, variance, and covariances at various lags are *not time dependent*. To find out whether a time series is stationary, we can use the unit root test. If the unit root test (or other tests) shows that the time series of interest is stationary, then the regression based on such time series may not be spurious.

We also introduced the concept of cointegration. Two or more time series are said to be cointegrated if there is a stable, long-term relationship between the two even though individually each may be nonstationary. If this is the case, regression involving such time series may not be spurious.

Next we introduced the random walk model, with or without drift. Several financial time series are found to follow a random walk; that is, they are non-stationary either in their mean value or their variance or both. Variables with these characteristics are said to follow stochastic trends. Stock prices are a prime example of a random walk. It is hard to tell what the price of a stock will be tomorrow just by knowing its price today. The best guess about tomorrow's price is today's price plus or minus a random error term (or shock, as it is called). If we could predict tomorrow's price fairly accurately, we would all be millionaires!

The next topic we discussed in this chapter was the dummy dependent variable, where the dependent variable can take values of either 1 or 0. Although such models can be estimated by OLS, in which case they are called linear probability models (LPM), this is not the recommended procedure since probabilities estimated from such models can sometimes be negative or greater than 1. Therefore, such models are usually estimated by the logit or probit procedures. In this chapter we illustrated the logit model with concrete examples. Thanks to excellent computer packages, estimation of logit and probit models is no longer a mysterious or forbidding task.

KEY TERMS AND CONCEPTS

The key terms and concepts introduced in this chapter are

Dynamic economic models
   a) distributed lag models
   b) short-run, or impact, multiplier
   c) interim, or intermediate, multiplier
   d) long-run, or total, multiplier
Estimating distributed lag models
   a) lagged values
   b) the Koyck model
   c) the adaptive expectations model
   d) the partial, or stock, adjustment model
   e) autoregressive model
Spurious regression

Stationary time series
Unit root test
Dickey-Fuller (DF) test (or tau test)
Cointegration
Random walk model
Random walk model with drift
Stochastic trend
Deterministic trend
Logit model and probit model
   a) Logistic distribution function
   b) odds ratio
   c) method of maximum likelihood (ML)

QUESTIONS

12.1. Explain the meaning of the following terms:
   a. Dynamic models
   b. Distributed lag models
   c. Autoregressive models

12.2. What are the reasons for the lag in the response of the dependent variable to one or more explanatory variables? Give some examples of distributed lag models.

12.3. What is wrong with the strategy of determining the number of lagged terms in a distributed lag model *sequentially,* that is, adding each successive lagged term if the t value of an added lagged term is statistically significant? In other words, you go on adding a lagged term as long as the t value of the added lagged term is statistically significant on the basis of the t test.

12.4. Since the successive lagged terms in a distributed lag model are likely to be collinear, in such models we should not worry about the statistical significance of any individual lagged coefficient but should consider the statistical significance of the sum of the lagged coefficients as a whole. Comment on this statement.

12.5. Although the logit and probit models may be superior to the LPM model, in practice, we should choose the LPM model because of its simplicity per Occam's razor principle. Do you agree with this statement? Why or why not?

12.6. True or false: The greater the value of the logit, the greater the probability that the particular event will occur.

12.7. What is the connection between cointegration and spurious regression?

PROBLEMS

12.8. Table 12-6 (on the textbook's Web site) gives data on personal consumption expenditure (PCE) and personal disposable income (PDI) for the United States for 1970 to 2007; all figures are in billions of dollars.
Estimate the following models:

$$PCE_t = A_1 + A_2 PDI_t + u_t$$
$$PCE_t = B_1 + B_2 PDI_t + B_3 PCE_{t-1} + v_t$$

a. Interpret the results of the two regressions.

b. What is the short- and long-run marginal propensity to consume (MPC)?

12.9. Use the data in Problem 12.8, but now consider the following models:

$$\ln PCE_t = A_1 + A_2 \ln PDI_t + u_t$$
$$\ln PCE_t = B_1 + B_2 \ln PDI_t + B_3 \ln PCE_{t-1} + v_t$$

where $\ln$ = the natural log.

a. Interpret these regressions.

b. What is the short- and long-run elasticity of PCE with respect to PDI?

12.10. To assess the impact of capacity utilization on inflation, Thomas A. Gittings[25] obtained the following regression for the United States for the period 1971 to 1988:

$$\hat{Y}_t = -30.12 + 0.1408 X_t + 0.2360 X_{t-1}$$
$$t = (-6.27) \quad (2.60) \qquad (4.26) \qquad R^2 = 0.727$$

where Y = GNP implicit deflator, % (a measure of the inflation rate)
X_t = Capacity utilization rate in manufacturing, %
X_{t-1} = Capacity utilization rate lagged over one year

[25]Thomas A. Gittings, "Capacity Utilization and Inflation," *Economic Perspectives,* Federal Reserve Bank of Chicago, May/June 1989, pp. 2–9.

TABLE 12-7   DATA FOR PROBLEM 12.11.

Concentration (mg per liter) X	log(X)	Total N_i	Deaths n_i	$P_i = \frac{n_i}{N_i}$
2.6	0.4150	50	6	0.120
3.8	0.5797	48	16	0.333
5.1	0.7076	46	24	0.522
7.7	0.8865	49	42	0.857
10.2	1.0086	50	44	0.880

Note: The log is a common log, that is, log to base 10.
Source: D. J. Finney, *Probit Analysis,* Cambridge University Press, London, 1964.

a. Interpret the preceding regression. A priori, why is there a positive relationship between inflation and capacity utilization?
b. What is the short-run impact of capacity utilization on inflation? And the long-run impact?
c. Is each slope coefficient individually statistically significant?
d. Will you reject the hypothesis that both slope coefficients are simultaneously equal to zero? Which test should you use?
e. Obtain more recent data and find out if the Gittings analysis still holds.

12.11. Table 12-7 gives data on the results of spraying rotenone of different concentrations on the chrysanthemum aphis in ≈50 batches. Develop a suitable model to express the probability of death as a function of the log of X, the log of dosage, and comment on the results.

12.12. From the regression (12.36), compute the probability of owning a house for each income level shown in Table 12-3.

12.13. Based on a sample of 20 couples, Barbara Bund Jackson[26] obtained the following regression. (*Note:* The author did not present standard errors.)

$$\ln \frac{P_i}{1 - P_i} = -9.456 + 0.3638\,\text{income}_i - 1.107\,\text{babysitter}_i$$

where P = the probability of restaurant usage, = 1 if went to a restaurant, 0 otherwise
Income = the income in thousands of dollars
Babysitter = 1 if needed a babysitter
0 if otherwise
Of the 20 couples, 11 regularly went to a restaurant, 6 regularly used a babysitter, and the income ranged from a low of $17,000 to a high of $44,000.
a. Interpret the preceding logit regression.
b. Find out the logit value of a couple with an income of $44,000 who needed a babysitter.
c. For the same couple, find out the probability of going to a restaurant.

[26]See Barbara Bund Jackson, *Multivariate Data Analysis: An Introduction,* Irwin, 1983, p. 92.

12.14. Refer to the data given in Table 12-2 (found on the textbook's Web site).
  a. Plot the data on profits and dividends and visually examine if the two time series are stationary.
  b. Apply the unit root test to the two series individually and determine if the two series are stationary.
  c. If the profits and dividends series are not stationary and if you regress dividends on profits, would the resulting regression be spurious? Why or why not? How do you decide? Show the necessary calculations.
  d. Take the first differences of the two time series and determine if the first difference time series are stationary.

12.15. *Monte Carlo experiment.* Consider the following random walk model:

$$Y_t = Y_{t-1} + u_t$$

Assume that $Y_0 = 0$ and u_t are normally and independently distributed with zero mean and variance of 9. Generate 100 values of u_t, and, using these values, generate 100 values of Y_t. Plot the Y values thus obtained. What can you say about the resulting graph?

12.16. *Monte Carlo experiment.* Now assume the following model:

$$Y_t = 4 + Y_{t-1} + u_t$$

where $Y_0 = 0$ and u_t are as stated in Problem 12.15. Repeat the procedure outlined in Problem 12.15. How does this experiment differ from the preceding one?

12.17. Refer to the data in Table 6.10 (found on the textbook's Web site). Since the data given in this table are at the individual level, if you want to fit a logit model to these data, you will have to use the maximum likelihood method to estimate the parameters. Using a package, such as EViews or MINITAB, estimate the logit model and comment on your results.

12.18. Table 12.8 (on the textbook's Web site) gives data on the dependent variable, the final grade on the intermediate macroeconomics examination (Y), such that $Y = 1$ if the final grade is an A and $Y = 0$ if the final grade is a B or C, and explanatory variables GPA = the entering grade-point average, TUCE = the score on an examination given at the beginning of the term to test macroeconomics knowledge of entering students, and PSI = 1 if the new method of personalized system of instructions is used and 0 if otherwise. These data pertain to 32 students. The primary objective of this study was to assess the effectiveness of PSI on the final grade.
  a. Estimate a linear probability model for the data given in Table 12-8.
  b. Using any computer software package (e.g., MINITAB, EViews, SHAZAM, etc.), estimate a logit model for the same data.
  c. Compare and comment on the results obtained in parts (*a*) and (*b*).

12.19. Obtain monthly data on the exchange rate between the U.S. dollar and the British pound for 1980 to 2007 and find out if this exchange rate follows a random walk. If it does, what are the implications for forecasting the U.S./U.K. exchange rate?

12.20. On the textbook's Web site, Table 12-9 contains data on the daily U.S./EU exchange rate from 2004 to 2008.
  a. Create a scatterplot of the rates over time. What pattern do you see?

b. Now take the first differences of the data and create a new plot. Based on this graph, do you think the original series is stationary?

c. Regress the differenced exchange rate on a (one-period) lagged version of the exchange rate as follows:

$$\Delta Y_t = A Y_{t-1} + u_t$$

Based on this model, do you think the original series is a random walk?

d. Now introduce a constant to the model:

$$\Delta Y_t = A_1 + A_2 Y_{t-1} + u_t$$

Do the results here indicate that Y_t is a random walk with drift?

e. Lastly, estimate the model using a drift parameter and a trend variable:

$$\Delta Y_t = A_1 + A_2 t + A_3 Y_{t-1} + u_t$$

f. What do all these results indicate about the stationarity of Y_t?

12.21. Table 12-10 on the textbook's Web site gives data for 2000 women regarding work (1 = a woman works, 0 = otherwise), age, marital status (1 = married, 0 = otherwise), number of children, and education (number of years of schooling). Out of a total of 2000 women, 657 were recorded as not being wage earners.

a. Using these data, estimate a logit model.

b. What are the marginal effects of each variable? Are all of the variables statistically significant?

12.22. Download the data set Benign, which is Table 12-11 on the textbook's Web site. The variable cancer is a dummy variable, where 1 = had breast cancer and 0 = did not have breast cancer.[27] Using the variables age (age of subject), HIGH (highest grade completed in school), CHK (= 0 if the subject did not undergo regular medical checkups and = 1 if the subject did undergo regular checkups), AGPI (age at first pregnancy), miscarriages (number of miscarriages), and weight (weight of subject), perform a logistic regression to conclude if these variables are statistically useful for predicting whether a woman will contract breast cancer or not.

---

[27]Data are provided on 50 women who were diagnosed as having benign breast disease and 150 age-matched controls, with three controls per case. Trained interviewers administered a standardized structured questionnaire to collect information from each subject (see Pastides, et al. [1983] and Pastides, et al. [1985]).

INTRODUCTION TO APPENDIXES A, B, C, AND D

BASICS OF PROBABILITY AND STATISTICS

Appendixes A, B, C, and D review the essentials of statistical theory that are needed to understand econometric theory and practice discussed in the main text of the book.

Appendix A discusses the fundamental concepts of probability, probability distributions, and random variables.

Appendix B discusses the characteristics of probability distributions such as the expected value, variance, covariance, correlation, conditional expectation, conditional variance, skewness, and kurtosis. This appendix shows how these characteristics are measured in practice.

Appendix C discusses four important probability distributions that are used extensively in practice: (1) the **normal** distribution, (2) the t distribution, (3) the **chi-square** distribution, and (4) the F distribution. In this appendix the main features of these distributions are outlined. With several examples, this appendix shows how these four probability distributions form the foundation of most statistical theory and practice.

Appendix D is devoted to a discussion of the two branches of classical statistics—**estimation** and **hypothesis testing.** A firm understanding of these two topics will make our study of econometrics in the main part of the text considerably easier.

These four appendixes are written in a very informal yet informative style so readers can brush up on their knowledge of elementary statistics. Since students coming to econometrics may have different statistics backgrounds, these four appendixes provide a fairly self-contained introduction to the subject.

All the concepts introduced in these appendixes are well illustrated with several practical examples.

APPENDIX A

REVIEW OF STATISTICS: PROBABILITY AND PROBABILITY DISTRIBUTIONS

The purpose of this and the following three appendixes is to review some fundamental statistical concepts that are needed to understand *Essentials of Econometrics*. These four appendixes will serve as a refresher course for those students who have had a basic course in statistics and will provide a unified framework for following discussions of the material in the main parts of this book for those whose knowledge of statistics has become somewhat rusty. Students who have had very little statistics should supplement these four appendixes with a good statistics book. (Some references are given at the end of this appendix.) Note that the discussion in Appendixes A through D is nonrigorous and is by no means a substitute for a basic course in statistics. It is simply an overview that is intended as a bridge to econometrics.

A.1 SOME NOTATION

In this appendix we come across several mathematical expressions that often can be expressed more conveniently in shorthand forms.

The Summation Notation

The Greek capital letter Σ (sigma) is used to indicate summation or addition. Thus,

$$\sum_{i=1}^{i=n} X_i = X_1 + X_2 + \cdots + X_n$$

where i is the index of summation and the expression on the left-hand side is the shorthand for "take the sum of the variable X from the first value ($i = 1$) to the

nth value $(i = n)$"; X_i stands for the ith value of the X variable.

$$\sum_{i=1}^{i=n} X_i \left(\text{or} \sum_{i=1}^{n} X_i\right)$$

is often abbreviated as

$$\sum X_i$$

where the upper and lower limits of the sum are known or can be easily determined or also expressed as

$$\sum_X X$$

which simply means take the sum of all the relevant values of X. We will use all these notations interchangeably.

Properties of the Summation Operator

Some important properties of $\sum$ are as follows:

1. Where k is a constant

$$\sum_{i=1}^{n} k = nk$$

That is, a constant summed n times is n times that constant. Thus,

$$\sum_{i=1}^{4} 3 = 4 \times 3 = 12$$

In this example $n = 4$ and $k = 3$.

2. Where k is a constant

$$\sum k X_i = k \sum X_i$$

That is, a constant can be pulled out of the summation sign and put in front of it.

3.
$$\sum (X_i + Y_i) = \sum X_i + \sum Y_i$$

That is, the summation of the sum of two variables is the sum of their individual summations.

4.
$$\sum (a + bX_i) = na + b \sum X_i$$

where a and b are constants and where use is made of properties 1, 2, and 3.

We will make extensive use of the summation notation in the remainder of this appendix and in the main parts of the book.

We now discuss several important concepts from probability theory.

A.2 EXPERIMENT, SAMPLE SPACE, SAMPLE POINT, AND EVENTS

Experiment

The first important concept is that of a **statistical** or **random experiment.** In statistics this term generally refers to any process of observation or measurement that has more than one possible outcome and for which there is uncertainty about which outcome will actually materialize.

Example A.1.

Tossing a coin, throwing a pair of dice, and drawing a card from a deck of cards are all experiments. Although it may seem completely different, the sales of Coca-Cola in a future quarter can also be considered an experiment since we don't know the outcome. Also, there are several possible values that could occur. It is implicitly assumed that in performing these experiments certain conditions are fulfilled, for example, that the coin or the dice are fair (not loaded). The outcomes of such experiments could be a head or a tail if a coin is tossed or any one of the numbers 1, 2, 3, 4, 5, or 6 if a die is thrown. The Coca-Cola sales figure could be any one of a seemingly infinite number of possibilities, depending on many factors. Note that the outcomes are unknown before the experiment is performed. The objectives of such experiments may be to establish a law (e.g., How many heads are you likely to obtain in a toss of, say, 1000 coins?) or to test the proposition that the coin is loaded (e.g., Would you regard a coin as being loaded if you obtained 70 heads in 100 tosses of a coin?).

Sample Space or Population

The set of all possible outcomes of an experiment is called the **population** or **sample space.** The concept of sample space was first introduced by von Mises, an Austrian mathematician and engineer, in 1931.

Example A.2.

Consider the experiment of tossing two fair coins. Let H denote a head and T a tail. Then we have these outcomes: HH, HT, TH, TT, where HH means a head on the first toss and a head on the second toss, HT means a head on the first toss and a tail on the second toss, etc.

In this example the totality of the outcomes, or sample space or population, is 4—no other outcomes are logically possible. (Don't worry about the coin landing on its edge.)

Example A.3.

The New York Mets are scheduled to play a doubleheader. Let O_1 indicate the outcome that they win both games, O_2 that they win the first game but lose the second, O_3 that they lose the first game but win the second, and O_4 that they lose both games. Here the sample space consists of four outcomes: O_1, O_2, O_3, and O_4.

Sample Point

Each member, or outcome, of the sample space or population is called a **sample point.** In Example A.2 each outcome, *HH, HT, TH,* and *TT,* is a sample point. In Example A.3 each outcome, $O_1, O_2, O_3,$ and $O_4,$ is a sample point.

Events

An **event** is a particular collection of outcomes and is thus a *subset* of the sample space.

Example A.4.

Let event *A* be the occurrence of one head and one tail in the coin-tossing experiment. From Example A.2 we see that only outcomes *HT* and *TH* belong to event *A*. (*Note: HT* and *TH* are a subset of the sample space *HH, HT, TH,* and *TT*). Let *B* be the event that two heads occur in a toss of two coins. Then, obviously, only the outcome *HH* belongs to event *B*. (Again, note that *HH* is a subset of the sample space *HH, HT, TH,* and *TT.*)

Events are said to be **mutually exclusive** if the occurrence of one event prevents the occurrence of another event at the same time. In Example A.3, if O_1 occurs, that is, the Mets win both the games, it rules out the occurrence of any of the other three outcomes. Two events are said to be **equally likely** if we are confident that one event is as likely to occur as the other event. In a single toss of a coin a head is as likely to appear as a tail. Events are said to be **collectively exhaustive** if they exhaust all possible outcomes of an experiment. In our coin-tossing example, since *HH, HT, TH,* and *TT* are the only possible outcomes, they are (collectively) exhaustive events. Likewise, in the Mets example, $O_1, O_2, O_3,$ and O_4 are the only possible outcomes, barring, of course, rain or natural calamities such as the earthquake that occurred during the 1989 World Series in San Francisco.

Venn Diagrams

A simple graphic device, called the **Venn diagram,** originally introduced by Venn in his book, *Symbolic Logic,* published in 1881, can be used to depict sample point, sample space, events, and related concepts, as shown in Figure A-1. In this figure each *rectangle represents the sample space S* and the two circles represent two events *A* and *B*. If there are more events, we can draw more circles to represent all those events. The various subfigures in this diagram depict various situations.

Figure A-1(*a*) shows outcomes that belong to *A* and the outcomes that do not belong to *A*, which are denoted by the symbol *A'*, which is called the *complement* of A.

Figure A-1(*b*) shows the *union* (i.e., sum) of *A* and *B*, that is the event whose outcomes belong to set *A* or set *B*. Using set theory notation, it is often denoted as $A \cup B$ (read as *A* union *B*), which is the equivalent of *A* + B.

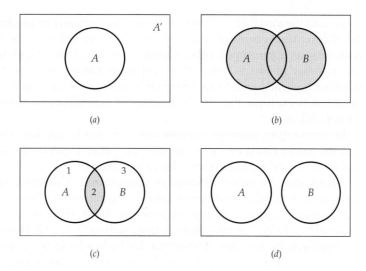

FIGURE A-1   Venn diagram

The shaded area in Figure A-1(*c*) denotes events whose outcomes belong to both set *A* and set *B*, which is represented as $A \cap B$ (read as *A* intersects *B*), and is the equivalent of the product *AB*.

Finally, Figure A-1(*d*) shows that the two events are *mutually exclusive* because they have no outcomes in common. In set notation, this means $A \cap B = 0$ (or that $AB = 0$).

A.3   RANDOM VARIABLES

Although the outcome(s) of an experiment can be described verbally, such as a head or a tail, or the ace of spades, it would be much simpler if the results of all experiments could be described numerically, that is, in terms of numbers. As we will see later, for statistical purposes such representation is very useful.

Example A.5.

Reconsider Example A.2. Instead of describing the outcomes of the experiment by *HH, HT, TH,* and *TT,* consider the "variable" number of heads in a toss of two coins. We have the following situation:

First coin	Second coin	Number of heads
T	*T*	0
T	*H*	1
H	*T*	1
H	*H*	2

We call the variable "number of heads" a **stochastic** or **random variable** (r.v., for short). *More generally, a variable whose (numerical) value is determined by the outcome of an experiment is called a random variable.* In the preceding example the r.v., number of heads, takes three different values, 0, 1, or 2, depending on whether no heads, one head, or two heads were obtained in a toss of two coins. In the Mets example the r.v., the number of wins, likewise takes three different values, 0, 1, or 2.

By convention, random variables are denoted by capital letters, X, Y, Z, etc., and the values taken by these variables are often denoted by small letters. Thus, if X is an r.v., x denotes a particular value taken by X.

An r.v. may be either **discrete** or **continuous**. A **discrete random variable** takes on only a finite number of values or countably infinite number of values (i.e., as many values as there are whole numbers). Thus, the number of heads in a toss of two coins can take on only three values, 0, 1, or 2. Hence, it is a discrete r.v. Similarly, the number of wins in a doubleheader is also a discrete r.v. since it can take only three values, 0, 1, or 2 wins. A **continuous random variable,** on the other hand, is an r.v. that can take on any value in some interval of values. Thus, the height of an individual is a continuous variable—in the range of, say, 60 to 72 inches it can take any value, depending on the precision of measurement. Similar factors such as weight, rainfall, or temperature also can be regarded as continuous random variables.

A.4 PROBABILITY

Having defined experiment, sample space, sample points, events, and random variables, we now consider the important concept of probability. First, we define the concept of probability of an event and then extend it to random variables.

Probability of an Event: The Classical or A Priori Definition

If an experiment can result in n *mutually exclusive* and *equally likely* outcomes, and if m of these outcomes are favorable to event A, then $P(A)$, the **probability** that A occurs, is the ratio m/n. That is,

$$P(A) = \frac{\text{number of outcomes favorable to A}}{\text{total number of outocmes}} \tag{A.1}$$

Note the two features of this definition: The outcomes must be *mutually exclusive* (that is, they cannot occur at the same time), and each outcome must have an *equal chance of occurring* (for example, in a throw of a die, any one of the six numbers has an equal chance of appearing).

Example A.6.

In a throw of a die numbered 1 through 6, there are six possible outcomes: 1, 2, 3, 4, 5, or 6. These outcomes are mutually exclusive since, in a single throw of the die, two or more numbers cannot turn up simultaneously. These six outcomes are also equally likely. Hence, by the classical definition, the probability that any of these six numbers will show up is 1/6—there are six total outcomes and each outcome has an equal chance of occurring. Here $n = 6$ and $m = 1$.

Similarly, the probability of obtaining a head in a single toss of a coin is 1/2 since there are two possible outcomes, H and T, and each has an equal chance of coming up. Likewise, in a deck of 52 cards, the probability of drawing any single card is 1/52. (Why?) The probability of drawing a spade, however, is 13/52. (Why?)

The preceding examples show why the classical definition is called an **a priori definition** since the probabilities are derived from purely *deductive* reasoning, or simply by the structure of the event. One doesn't have to throw a coin to state that the probability of obtaining a head or a tail is 1/2, since logically, these are the only possible outcomes.

But the classical definition has some deficiencies. What happens if the outcomes of an experiment are not finite or are not equally likely? What, for example, is the probability that the gross domestic product (GDP) next year will be a certain amount or what is the probability that there will be a recession next year? The classical definition is not equipped to answer these questions. A more widely used definition that can handle such cases is the relative frequency definition of probability, which we will now discuss.

Relative Frequency or Empirical Definition of Probability

To introduce this concept of probability, consider the following example.

Example A.7.

Table A-1 gives the distribution of marks received by 200 students on a microeconomics examination. Table A-1 is an example of a **frequency distribution** showing how the r.v. marks in the present example are distributed. The numbers in column 3 of the table are called **absolute frequencies,** that is, the number of occurrences of a given event. The numbers in column 4 are called **relative frequencies,** that is, the absolute frequencies divided by the total number of occurrences (200 in the present case). Thus, the absolute frequency of marks between 70 and 79 is 45 but the relative frequency is 0.225, which is 45 divided by 200.

Can we treat the relative frequencies as probabilities? Intuitively, it seems reasonable to consider the relative frequencies as probabilities provided the number of observations on which the relative frequencies are based is reasonably large. This is the essence of the *empirical,* or *relative frequency, definition of probability.*

TABLE A-1   THE DISTRIBUTION OF MARKS RECEIVED BY 200
STUDENTS ON A MICROECONOMICS EXAMINATION

Marks (1)	Midpoint of interval (2)	Absolute frequency (3)	Relative frequency (4) = (3)/200
0–9	5	0	0
10–19	15	0	0
20–29	25	0	0
30–39	35	10	0.050
40–49	45	20	0.100
50–59	55	35	0.175
60–69	65	50	0.250
70–79	75	45	0.225
80–89	85	30	0.150
90–99	95	10	0.050
Total		200	1.000

More formally, if in n trials (or observations), m of them are favorable to event A, then $P(A)$, the probability of event A, is simply the ratio m/n (i.e., the relative frequency) *provided n, the number of trials, is sufficiently large (technically, infinite)*.[1] Notice that, unlike the classical definition, we do not have to insist that the outcome be mutually exclusive and equally likely.

In short, if the number of trials is sufficiently large, we can treat the relative frequencies as fairly good measures of true probabilities. In Table A-1 we can, therefore, treat the relative frequencies given in column 4 as probabilities.[2]

Properties of Probabilities   The probability of an event as defined earlier has the following important properties:

1. The probability of an event always lies between 0 and 1. Thus, the probability of event A, $P(A)$, satisfies this relationship:

$$0 \leq P(A) \leq 1 \qquad \textbf{(A.2)}$$

$P(A) = 0$ means event A will not occur, whereas $P(A) = 1$ means event A will occur with certainty. Typically, the probability will lie somewhere between these numbers, as in the case of the probabilities shown in Table A-1.

---

[1]What constitutes a large or small number depends on the context of the problem. Sometimes a number as small as 30 can be regarded as reasonably large. In presidential elections in the United States, election polls based on a sample of about 800 people are fairly accurate in predicting the final outcome, although the actual number of voters runs into the millions.

[2]There is yet another definition of probability, called *subjective probability*, which is the foundation of *Bayesian statistics*, that is a rival to classical statistics. Under the subjective or "degrees of belief" definition of probability we can ask questions such as: What is the probability that Iraq will have a democratic government? What is the probability that the Chicago Cubs will win the World Series next year? Or what is the probability that there will be a stock market crash in the year 2010?

2. If A, B, C, ... are *mutually exclusive events,* the probability that any one of them will occur is equal to the sum of the probabilities of their individual occurrences. Symbolically,

$$P(A + B + C + \cdots) = P(A) + P(B) + P(C) + \cdots \qquad \textbf{(A.3)}$$

where the expression on the left-hand side of the equality means the probability of A or B or C, etc.[3]

3. If A, B, C, ... are *mutually exclusive* and *collectively exhaustive* sets of events, the sum of the probabilities of their individual occurrences is 1. Symbolically,

$$P(A + B + C + \cdots) = P(A) + P(B) + P(C) + \cdots = 1 \qquad \textbf{(A.4)}$$

Example A.8.

In Example A.6 we saw that the probability of obtaining any of the six numbers on a die is $1/6$ since there are six equally likely outcomes, and each one of them has an equal chance of turning up. Since the numbers 1, 2, 3, 4, 5, and 6 form an exhaustive set of events, $P(1 + 2 + 3 + 4 + 5 + 6) = 1$, where 1, 2, 3, ... means the probability of number 1 or number 2 or number 3, etc. And since 1, 2, ... 6 are mutually exclusive events in that two numbers cannot occur simultaneously in a throw of a single die, $P(1 + 2 + 3 + 4 + 5 + 6) = P(1) + P(2) + \cdots + P(6) = 1/6 + 1/6 + 1/6 + 1/6 + 1/6 + 1/6 = 1$.

In passing, note the following rules of probability that will come in handy later on.

1. If A, B, C, ... are any events, they are said to be *statistically independent* if the probability of their occurring together is equal to the product of their individual probabilities. Symbolically,

$$P(ABC \cdots) = P(A)\, P(B)\, P(C) \cdots \qquad \textbf{(A.5)}$$

where $P(ABC \cdots)$ means the probability of events $ABC \cdots$ occurring simultaneously or jointly.[4] Hence, it is called a *joint probability.* In relation to the joint probability $P(ABC \cdots)$, $P(A)$, $P(B)$, etc. are called *unconditional, marginal,* or *individual probabilities,* for reasons that will become clear in Section A.6.

Example A.9.

Suppose we throw two coins simultaneously. What is the probability of obtaining a head on the first coin and a head on the second coin? Let A denote the event of obtaining a head on the first coin and B on the second coin. We

---

[3]In set theory notation, this would be written as $P(A \cup B \cup C. \ldots)$.
[4]In set theory notation, this would be written as $P(A \cap B \cap C. \ldots)$.

therefore want to find the probability $P(AB)$. Common sense would suggest that the probability of obtaining a head on the first coin is independent of the probability of obtaining a head on the second coin. Hence, $P(AB) = P(A)P(B) = (1/2)(1/2) = 1/4$ since the probability of obtaining a head (or a tail) is $1/2$.

2. If events $A, B, C, \ldots$ are *not* mutually exclusive, Eq. (A.3) needs to be modified. Thus, if events A and B are not mutually exclusive, we have

$$P(A + B) = P(A) + P(B) - P(AB) \tag{A.6}$$

where $P(AB)$ is the joint probability that the two events occur together (see Fig. A-1[c]).[5] Of course, if A and B are mutually exclusive, $P(AB) = 0$ (Why?), and we are back to Eq. (A.3). Equation (A.6) can be easily generalized to more than two events.

3. For every event A there is an event A', called the **complement** of A, with these properties:
   a. $P(A + A') = 1$, and
   b. $P(AA') = 0$

These properties can be easily verified from Fig. A-1(a).

Example A.10.

A card is drawn from a deck of cards. What is the probability that it will be either a heart or a queen? Clearly a heart and a queen are not mutually exclusive events, for one of the four queens is a heart. Hence,

$$P \text{ (a heart or a queen)} = P(\text{heart}) + P(\text{queen}) - P(\text{heart and queen})$$

$$= 13/52 + 4/52 - 1/52$$

$$= 4/13$$

Let A and B be two events. Let us suppose we want to find out the probability that the event A occurs knowing that the event B has already occurred. This probability, called the **conditional probability of A**, *conditional on event B occurring*, and denoted by the symbol $P(A \mid B)$, is computed from the formula

$$P(A \mid B) = \frac{P(AB)}{P(B)}; \quad P(B) > 0 \tag{A.7}$$

That is, the conditional probability of A, given B, is equal to the ratio of their joint probability to the marginal probability of B. In like manner,

$$P(B \mid A) = \frac{P(AB)}{P(A)}; \quad P(A) > 0 \tag{A.8}$$

---

[5]To avoid the shaded area in Fig. A-1(c) being counted twice, we have to subtract $P(AB)$ on the right-hand side of this equation.

To visualize Eq. (A.7), we can resort to a Venn diagram, as shown in Figure A-1(c). As you can see from this figure, regions 2 and 3 represent event B and regions 1 and 2 represent event A. Because region 2 is common to both events, and since B has occurred, if we divide the area of region 2 by the sum of the areas of regions 2 and 3, we will get the (conditional) probability that event A has occurred, knowing that B has occurred. Simply put, the conditional probability is the fraction of the time that event A occurs when event B has occurred.

Example A.11.

In an introductory accounting class there are 500 students, of which 300 are males and 200 are females. Of these, 100 males and 60 females plan to major in accounting. A student is selected at random from this class, and it is found that this student plans to be an accounting major. What is the probability that the student is a male?

Let A denote the event that the student is a male and B that the student is an accounting major. Therefore, we want to find out $P(A \mid B)$. From the formula of conditional probability just given, this probability can be obtained as

$$P(A \mid B) = \frac{P(AB)}{P(B)}$$
$$= \frac{100/500}{160/500}$$
$$= 0.625$$

From the data given previously, it can be readily seen that $P(A) = 300/500 = 0.6$; that is, the unconditional probability of selecting a male student is 0.6, which is different from the preceding probability 0.625.

This example brings out an important point, namely, *conditional and unconditional probabilities in general are different.* However, if the two events are independent, then we can see from Eq. (A.7) that

$$P(A \mid B) = \frac{P(AB)}{P(B)} = \frac{P(A)P(B)}{P(B)} = P(A) \tag{A.9}$$

Note that $P(AB) = P(A)P(B)$ when the two events are independent, as noted earlier. In this case, the conditional probability of A given B is the same as the unconditional probability of A. In this case it does not matter if B occurs or not.

An interesting application of conditional probability is contained in the famous **Bayes' Theorem,** which was originally propounded by Thomas Bayes, a nonconformist minister in Turnbridge Wells, England (1701–1761). This theorem, published after Bayes' death, led to the so-called Bayesian School of Statistics, a rival to the school of classical statistics, which still predominates statistics teaching in most universities in the world. The knowledge that an event B has occurred can be used to revise or update the probability that an event A has occurred. This is the essence of Bayes' Theorem.

To explain this theorem, let A and B be two events, each with a positive probability. Bayes' Theorem then states that:[6]

$$P(A \mid B) = \frac{P(B \mid A)P(A)}{P(B \mid A)P(A) + P(B \mid A')P(A')} \tag{A.10}$$

where A', called the *complement of A*, means the event A does not occur.

In words, Bayes' Theorem shows how conditional probabilities of the form $P(B \mid A)$ may be combined with initial probability of A (i.e., P[A]) to obtain the final probability $P(A \mid B)$. Notice how the roles of conditioning event (B) and outcome event (A) have been interchanged. The following example will show how Bayes' Theorem works.

Example A.12. Bayes' Theorem

Suppose a woman has two coins in her handbag. One is a fair coin and one is two-headed. She takes a coin at random from her handbag and tosses it. Suppose a head shows up. What is the probability that the coin she tossed was two-headed?

Let A be the event that the coin is two-headed and A' the event that the coin is fair. The probability of selecting either of these coins is $P(A) = P(A') = 1/2$. Let B be the event that a head turns up. If the coin has two heads, B is certain to occur. Hence, $(B \mid A) = 1$. But if the coin is fair, $P(B \mid A') = 0.5$. Therefore by Bayes' Theorem we obtain

$$P(A \mid B) = \frac{P(B \mid A)P(A)}{P(B)} = \frac{(1)(0.5)}{0.75} = \frac{2}{3} \approx 0.66$$

Notice the particular feature of this theorem. Before the coin was tossed, the probability of selecting a regular or two-headed coin was the same, namely, 0.5. But knowing that a head was actually observed, the probability that the coin selected was two-headed is revised upwards to about 0.66.

In Bayesian language, $P(A)$ is called the **prior probability** (i.e., before the fact or evidence) and $P(A \mid B)$ is called the revised or **posterior probability** (after the fact or evidence). The knowledge that B has occurred leads us to reassess or revise the (prior) probability assigned to A.

---

[6]If the sample space is partitioned into A (event A occurs) and A' (event A does not occur), then for any event B, it is true that $P(B) = P(BA) + P(BA')$; that is, the probability that B occurs is the sum of the common outcomes between B and each partition of A. This result can be generalized if A is partitioned into several segments. This can be seen easily from a Venn diagram.

You might see this finding as somewhat puzzling. Intuitively you will think that this probability should be 1/2. But look at the problem this way. There are three ways in which heads can come up, and in two of these cases, the hidden face will also be heads.

Notice another interesting feature of the theorem. In classical statistics we assume that the coin is fair when we toss it. In Bayesian statistics we question that premise or hypothesis.

Probability of Random Variables

Just as we assigned probabilities to sample outcomes or events of a sample space, we can assign probabilities to random variables, for as we saw, random variables are simply numerical representations of the outcomes of the sample space, as shown in Example A.5. In this textbook we are largely concerned with random variables such as GDP, money supply, prices, and wages, and we should know how to assign probabilities to random variables. Technically, we need to study the *probability distributions* of random variables, a topic we will now discuss.

A.5 RANDOM VARIABLES AND THEIR PROBABILITY DISTRIBUTIONS

By probability distribution of a random variable we mean the possible values taken by that variable and the probabilities of occurrence of those values. To understand this clearly, we first consider the probability distribution of a discrete r.v., and then we consider the probability distribution of a continuous r.v., for there are differences between the two.

Probability Distribution of a Discrete Random Variable

As noted before, a discrete r.v. takes only a finite (or countably infinite) number of values.

Let X be an r.v. with distinct values of $x_1, x_2, \ldots$ The function f defined by

$$f(X = x_i) = P(X = x_i) \quad i = 1, 2, \ldots,$$
$$= 0 \text{ if } x \neq x_i$$

(A.11)

is called the **probability mass function (PMF)** or simply the **probability function (PF)**, where $P(X = x_i)$ means that the probability that the discrete r.v. X takes the numerical value of x_i.[7] Note these properties of the PMF given in Eq. (A.11):

$$0 \leq f(x_i) \leq 1$$

(A.12)

$$\sum_x f(x_i) = 1$$

(A.13)

---

[7]The values taken by a discrete r.v. are often call *mass points* and $f(X = x_i)$ denotes the mass associated with the mass point x_i.

where the summation extends over all the values of X. Notice the similarities of these properties with the properties of probabilities discussed earlier.

To see what this means, consider the following example.

Example A.13.

Let the r.v. X represent the number of heads obtained in two tosses of a coin. Now consider the following table:

Number of heads X	PF $f(X)$
0	1/4
1	1/2
2	1/4
Sum	1.00

In this example the r.v. X (the number of heads) takes three different values—$X = 0$, 1, or 2. The probability that X takes a value of zero (i.e., no heads are obtained in a toss of two coins) is 1/4, for of the four possible outcomes of throwing two coins (i.e., the sample space), only 1 is favorable to the outcome TT. Likewise, of the four possible outcomes, only one is favorable to the outcome of two heads; hence, its probability is also 1/4. On the other hand, two outcomes, HT and TH, are favorable to the outcome of one head; hence, its probability is $2/4 = 1/2$. Notice that in assigning these probabilities we have used the classical definition of probability.

Geometrically, the PMF of this example is as shown in Figure A-2.

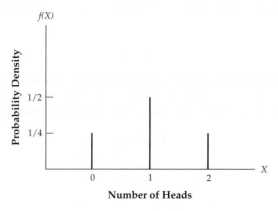

FIGURE A-2   The probability mass function (PMF) of the number of heads in two tosses of a coin (Example A.13)

Probability Distribution of a Continuous Random Variable

The probability distribution of a continuous random variable is conceptually similar to the probability distribution of a discrete r.v. except that we now measure the probability of such an r.v. over a certain range or interval. Instead of calling it a PMF, we call it a **probability density function (PDF).** An example will make the distinction between the two clear.

Let X represent the continuous r.v. height, measured in inches, and suppose we want to find out the probability that the height of an individual lies in the interval, say, 60 to 68 inches. Further, suppose that the r.v. height has the PDF as shown in Figure A-3.

The probability that the height of an individual lies in the interval 60 to 68 inches is given by the shaded area lying between 60 and 68 marked on the curve in Figure A-3. (How this probability is actually measured is shown in Appendix C.) In passing, note that since a continuous r.v. can take an uncountably infinite number of values, the probability that such an r.v. takes a particular numerical value (e.g., 63.00 inches) is always zero; *the probability for a continuous r.v. is always measured over an interval,* say, between 62.5 and 63.5 inches.

More formally, for a continuous r.v. X the probability density function (PDF), $f(X)$, is such that

$$P(x_1 < X < x_2) = \int_{x_1}^{x_2} f(x)\, dx \tag{A.14}$$

for all $x_1 < x_2$, where $\int$ is the integral symbol of calculus, which is the equivalent of the summation symbol (Σ) used for taking the sum of the values of a discrete random variable, and where dx stands for a small interval of x values.

A PDF has the following properties:

1. The total area under the curve $f(x)$ given in Eq. (A.14) is 1,
2. $P(x_1 < X < x_2)$ is the area under the curve between x_1 and x_2, where $x_2 > x_1$,

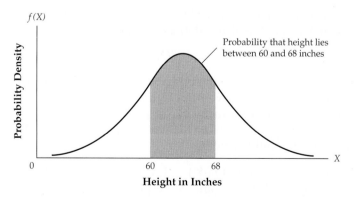

FIGURE A-3   The PDF of a continuous random variable

3. since the probability that a continuous r.v. takes a particular value is zero because probabilities for such a variable are measured over an area or interval, the left-hand side of Eq. (A.14) can be expressed in any of these forms:

$$P(x_1 \le X \le x_2) = P(x_1 < X \le x_2) = P(x_1 \le X < x_2) = P(x_1 < X < x_2)$$

An important example of a continuous PDF is the **normal probability density function,** which is discussed in Appendix C. We will use this function extensively in the later chapters.

Example A.14.

The PDF of a (continuous) r.v. X is given by

$$f(x) = \frac{x^2}{9} \qquad 0 \le x \le 3$$

What is the probability that $0 < x < 1$?

To get the answer, we have to evaluate the integral of the preceding PDF over the stated range. That is,

$$\int_0^1 \frac{x^2}{9} \, dx = \frac{1}{9} \int_0^1 x^2 \, dx = \frac{1}{9} \left[\frac{x^3}{3} \right]_0^1 = \frac{1}{27}$$

That is, the probability that x lies between 0 and 1 is $1/27$. (*Note:* The integral of x^2 is $(x^3/3)$, which can be checked easily by taking the derivative of the latter, which is $\frac{d}{dx} \left(\frac{x^3}{3} \right) = x^2$.)

Incidentally, if you evaluate the given PDF over the entire range of 0 to 3, you will see that $\int_0^3 \frac{x^2}{9} \, dx = 1$, as it should be. (Why?) Of course, $f(x) \ge 0$ for all x values in the range 0 to 3.

Cumulative Distribution Function (CDF)

Associated with the PMF or PDF of an r.v. X is its **cumulative distribution function (CDF),** $F(X)$, which is defined as follows:

$$F(X) = P(X \le x) \qquad\qquad\qquad \textbf{(A.15)}$$

where $P(X \le x)$ means the probability that the r.v. X takes a value less than or equal to x, where x is given. (Of course, for a continuous r.v., the probability that such an r.v. takes the exact value of x is zero.) Thus, $P(X \le 2)$ means the probability that the r.v. X takes a value less than or equal to 2. The following properties of CDF should be noted:

1. $F(-\infty) = 0$ and $F(\infty) = 1$, where $F(-\infty)$ and $F(\infty)$ are the limits of $F(x)$ as x tends to $-\infty$ and ∞, respectively.

2. $F(x)$ is a nondecreasing function such that if $x_2 > x_1$ then $F(x_2) \ge F(x_1)$.

3. $P(X \geq k) = 1 - F(k)$; that is, the probability that X assumes a value equal to or greater than k is 1 minus the probability that X takes a value below k.
4. $P(x_1 \leq X \leq x_2) = F(x_2) - F(x_1)$; that is, the probability that X lies between values x_1 and x_2 is the probability that X lies below x_2 *minus* the probability that X lies below x_1, a property that will help us in computing probabilities in practice.

Example A.15.

What are the PDF and CDF of the r.v. number of heads obtained in four tosses of a fair coin? These functions are as follows:

Number of heads (X)	PDF Value of X	PDF f(X)	CDF Value of X	CDF f(X)
0	$0 \leq X < 1$	1/16	$X \leq 0$	1/16
1	$1 \leq X < 2$	4/16	$X \leq 1$	5/16
2	$2 \leq X < 3$	6/16	$X \leq 2$	11/16
3	$3 \leq X < 4$	4/16	$X \leq 3$	15/16
4	$4 \leq X$	1/16	$X \leq 4$	1

As this example and the definition of CDF suggest, a CDF is merely an "accumulation" or simply the sum of the PDF for the values of X less than or equal to a given x. That is,

$$F(X) = \sum^{x} f(x) \tag{A.16}$$

where $\sum^{x} f(X)$ means the sum of the PDF for values of X less than or equal to the specified x, as shown in the preceding table. Thus, in this example the probability that X takes the value of less than 2 (heads) is 5/16, but the probability that it takes a value of less than 3 is 11/16. Of course, the probability that it takes a value of 4 or less than four heads is 1. (Why?)

Geometrically, the CDF of Example A.15 looks like Figure A-4. Since we are dealing with a discrete r.v. in Example A.15, its CDF is a discontinuous function, known as a **step function.** If we were dealing with the CDF of a continuous r.v., its CDF would be a continuous curve, as shown in Figure A-5.[8]

Example A.16.

Referring to Example A.15, what is the probability that X lies between 2 and 3? Here we want to find $F(X=3) - F(X=2)$. From the table given in Example A.15

---

[8]If x is continuous with a PDF of $f(x)$, then $F(x) = \int_{-\infty}^{x} f(x)\, dx$ and $f(x) = F'(x)$, where $F'(x)$ is the derivative of $F(x) = \frac{d}{dx} F(X)$.

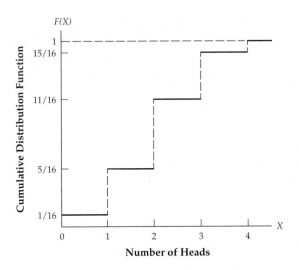

FIGURE A-4 The cumulative distribution function (CDF) of a discrete random variable (Example A.15)

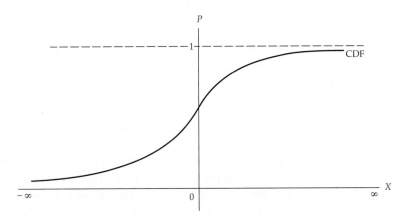

FIGURE A-5 The CDF of a continuous random variable

we find that $F(X \leq 3) = 15/16$ and that $F(X \leq 2) = 11/16$. Therefore, the probability that X lies between 2 and 3 is $4/16 = 1/4$.

A.6 MULTIVARIATE PROBABILITY DENSITY FUNCTIONS

So far we have been concerned with *single variable*, or *univariate*, probability distribution functions. Thus, the PMFs of Examples A.5 and A.13 are univariate PDFs, for we considered single random variables, such as the number of heads in a toss of two coins or the number of heads in a toss of four coins. However, we do not need to be so restrictive, for the outcomes of an experiment could be

TABLE A-2   THE FREQUENCY DISTRIBUTION OF TWO RANDOM VARIABLES:
NUMBER OF PCS SOLD (X) AND NUMBER OF PRINTERS SOLD (Y)

	Number of PCs Sold (X)					
	0	1	2	3	4	Total
Number of Printers Sold (Y)						
0	6	6	4	4	2	22
1	4	10	12	4	2	32
2	2	4	20	10	10	46
3	2	2	10	20	20	54
4	2	2	2	10	30	46
Total	16	24	48	48	64	200

described by more than one r.v., in which case we would like to find their prob-ability distributions. Such probability distributions are called **multivariate prob-ability distributions.** The simplest of these is the *bivariate,* or a two-variable PMF or PDF. Let us illustrate with an example.[9]

Example A.17.

A retail computer store sells personal computers (PCs) as well as printers. The number of computers and printers sold varies from day to day, but the store manager obtained the sales history over the past 200 days in the form of Table A-2.

In this example we have two random variables, X (number of PCs sold) and Y (number of printers sold). The table shows that of the 200 days, there were 30 days when the store sold 4 PCs and 4 printers, but on 2 days, although it sold 4 PCs, it sold no printers. Other entries in the table are to be interpreted simi-larly. Table A-2 provides an example of what is known as a **joint frequency dis-tribution;** it gives the number of times a combination of values is taken by the two variables. Thus, in our example the number of times 4 PCs and 4 printers were sold together is 30. Such a number is called an *absolute frequency.* All the numbers shown in Table A-2 are thus absolute frequencies.

Dividing the absolute frequencies given in the preceding table by 200, we obtain the relative frequencies, which are shown in Table A-3.

Since our sample is reasonably large, we can treat these (joint) relative fre-quencies as measures of joint probabilities, as per the frequency interpretation of probabilities. Thus, the probability that the store sells three PCs and three printers is 0.10, or about 10 percent. Other entries in the table are to be inter-preted similarly.

[9]This example is adapted from Ron C. Mittelhammer, *Mathematical Statistics for Economics and Business,* Springer, New York, 1995, p. 107.

TABLE A-3 THE BIVARIATE PROBABILITY DISTRIBUTION OF NUMBER OF PCS SOLD (X) AND NUMBER OF PRINTERS SOLD (Y)

	Number of PCs Sold (x)					
	0	1	2	3	4	Total $f(Y)$
Number of Printers Sold (y)						
0	0.03	0.03	0.02	0.02	0.01	0.11
1	0.02	0.05	0.06	0.02	0.01	0.16
2	0.01	0.02	0.10	0.05	0.05	0.23
3	0.01	0.01	0.05	0.10	0.10	0.27
4	0.01	0.01	0.01	0.05	0.15	0.23
Total $f(X)$ 0.08	0.12	0.24	0.24	0.32		1.00

Because the two variables are discrete, Table A-3 provides an example of what is known as **bivariate** or **joint probability mass function (PMF).**

More formally, let X and Y be two discrete random variables. Then the function

$$f(X, Y) = P(X = x \text{ and } Y = y)$$
$$= 0 \text{ when } X \neq x \text{ and } Y \neq y \tag{A.17}$$

is known as the joint PMF. This gives the joint probability that X takes the value of x and Y takes the value of y simultaneously, where x and y are some specific values of the two variables. Notice the following properties of the joint PMF:

1. $f(X, Y) \geq 0$ for all pairs of X and Y. This is so because all probabilities are nonnegative.
2. $\sum_x \sum_y f(X, Y) = 1$. This follows from the fact that the sum of the probabilities associated with all joint outcomes must equal 1.

Note that we have used the double summation sign because we are now dealing with two variables. If we were to deal with a three-variable joint PMF, we would be using the triple summation sign, and so on.

The joint probability of two continuous random variables (i.e., joint PDF) can be defined analogously, although the mathematical expressions are somewhat involved and are given by way of exercises for the benefit of the more mathematically inclined reader.

The discussion of joint PMF or joint PDF leads to a discussion of some related concepts, which we will now discuss.

Marginal Probability Functions

We have studied the univariate PFs, such as $f(X)$ or $f(Y)$, and the bivariate, or joint, PF $f(X, Y)$. Is there any relationship between the two? Yes, there is.

In relation to $f(X, Y)$, $f(X)$ and $f(Y)$ are called **univariate, unconditional, individual,** or **marginal PMFs or PDFs.** More technically, the probability that X

TABLE A-4   MARGINAL PROBABILITY DISTRIBUTIONS OF X (NUMBER OF PCS SOLD) AND Y (NUMBER OF PRINTERS SOLD)

Value of X	$f(X)$	Value of Y	$f(Y)$
0	0.08	0	0.11
1	0.12	1	0.16
2	0.24	2	0.23
3	0.24	3	0.27
4	0.32	4	0.23
Sum	1.00		1.00

assumes a given value (e.g., 2) *regardless of the values taken by Y* is called the marginal probability of X, and the distribution of these probabilities is called the marginal PMF of X. How do we compute these marginal PMFs or PDFs? That is easy. In Table A-3 we see from the column totals that the probability that X takes the value of 1 regardless of the values taken by Y is 0.12; the probability that it takes the value of 2 regardless of Y's value is 0.24, and so on. Therefore, the marginal PMF of X is as shown in Table A-4. Table A-4 also shows the marginal PMF of Y, which can be derived similarly. Note that the sum of each of the PFs, $f(X)$ and $f(Y)$, is 1. (Why?)

You will easily note that to obtain the marginal probabilities of X, we sum the joint probabilities corresponding to the given value of X regardless of the values taken by Y. *That is, we sum down the columns.* Likewise, to obtain the marginal probabilities of Y, we sum the joint probabilities corresponding to the given value of Y regardless of the values taken by X. *That is, we sum across the rows.* Once such marginal probabilities are computed, finding the marginal PMFs is straightforward, as we just showed. More formally, if $f(X, Y)$ is the joint PMF of random variables X and Y, then the marginal PFs of X and Y are obtained as follows:

$$f(X) = \sum_y f(X, Y) \text{ for all } X \qquad \textbf{(A.18)}$$

and

$$f(Y) = \sum_x f(X, Y) \text{ for all } Y \qquad \textbf{(A.19)}$$

If the two variables are continuous, we will replace the summation symbol with the integral symbol. For example, if $f(X, Y)$ represents a joint PDF, to find the marginal PDF of X, we will integrate the joint PDF with respect to Y values, and to find to marginal PDF of Y, we will integrate it with respect to the X values (see Problem A.20).

Conditional Probability Functions

Continuing with Example A.17, let us now suppose we want to find the probability that 4 printers were sold, knowing that 4 PCs were sold. In other words, what is the probability that $Y = 4$, conditional upon the fact that $X = 4$? This is known as **conditional probability** (recall our earlier discussion of conditional probability of an event). This probability can be obtained from the **conditional probability mass function** defined as

$$f(Y \mid X) = P(Y = y \mid X = x) \tag{A.20}$$

where $f(Y \mid X)$ stands for the *conditional PMF* of Y; it gives the probability that Y takes on the value of y (number of printers sold) conditional on the knowledge that X has assumed the value of x (number of PCs sold). Similarly,

$$f(X \mid Y) = P(X = x \mid Y = y) \tag{A.21}$$

gives the conditional PMF of X.

Note that the preceding two conditional PFs are for two discrete random variables, Y and X. Hence, they may be called *discrete conditional PMFs*. Conditional PDFs for continuous random variables can be defined analogously, although the mathematical formulas are slightly involved (see Problem A.20).

One simple method of computing the conditional PF is as follows:

$$
\begin{aligned}
f(Y \mid X) &= \frac{f(X, Y)}{f(X)} \\[2mm]
&= \frac{\text{joint probability of } X \text{ and } Y}{\text{marginal probability of } X}
\end{aligned}
\tag{A.22}
$$

$$
\begin{aligned}
f(X \mid Y) &= \frac{f(X, Y)}{f(Y)} \\[2mm]
&= \frac{\text{joint probability of } X \text{ and } Y}{\text{marginal probability of } Y}
\end{aligned}
\tag{A.23}
$$

In words, *the conditional PMF of one variable, given the value of the other variable, is simply the ratio of the joint probability of the two variables divided by the marginal or unconditional PF of the other (i.e., the conditioning) variable.* (Compare this with the conditional probability of an event A, given that event B has happened, i.e., $P[A \mid B]$.)

Returning to our example, we want to find out $f(Y = 4 \mid X = 4)$, which is

$$
\begin{aligned}
f(Y = 4 \mid X = 4) &= \frac{f(Y = 4 \text{ and } X = 4)}{f(X = 4)} \\[2mm]
&= \frac{0.15}{0.32} \text{ (from Table A-3)} \\[2mm]
&= \approx 0.47
\end{aligned}
\tag{A.24}
$$

From Table A-3 we observe that the marginal, or unconditional, probability that Y takes a value of 4 is 0.23, but knowing that 4 PCs were sold, the probability that 4 printers will be sold increases to ≈ 0.47. Notice how the knowledge about the other event, the conditioning event, changes our assessment of the probabilities. This is in the spirit of Bayesian statistics.

In regression analysis, as we show in Chapter 2, we are interested in studying the behavior of one variable, say, stock prices, conditional upon the knowledge of another variable, say, interest rates. Or, we may be interested in studying the female fertility rate, knowing a woman's level of education. Therefore, the knowledge of conditional PMFs or PDFs is very important for the development of regression analysis.

Statistical Independence

Another concept that is vital for the study of regression analysis is the concept of **independent random variables,** which is related to the concept of independence of events discussed earlier. We explain this with an example.

Example A.18.

A bag contains three balls numbered 1, 2, and 3, respectively. Two balls are drawn at random, with replacement, from the bag (i.e., every time a ball is drawn it is put back before another is drawn). Let the variable X denote the number on the first ball drawn and Y the number on the second ball. Table A-5 gives the joint as well as the marginal PMFs of the two variables.

Now consider the probabilities $f(X=1, Y=1)$, $f(X=1)$, and $f(Y=1)$. As Table A-5 shows, these probabilities are 1/9, 1/3, and 1/3, respectively. Now the first of these is a joint probability, whereas the last two are marginal probabilities. However, the joint probability in this case is equal to the product of the two marginal probabilities. When this happens, we say that the two variables are **statistically independent,** that is, the value taken by one variable has no effect on the value taken by the other variable. More formally, *two variables X and Y are statistically independent if and only if their joint PMF or PDF can be expressed as the product of their individual, or marginal, PMFs or PDFs for all combinations of X and Y values.* Symbolically,

$$f(X, Y) = f(X)\, f(Y) \tag{A.25}$$

TABLE A-5   STATISTICAL INDEPENDENCE OF TWO RANDOM VARIABLES

		X			
		1	2	3	$f(Y)$
	1	1/9	1/9	1/9	3/9
Y	2	1/9	1/9	1/9	3/9
	3	1/9	1/9	1/9	3/9
$f(X)$		3/9	3/9	3/9	1

You can easily verify that for any other combination of X and Y values given in Table A-5 the joint PF is the product of the respective marginal PFs; that is, the two variables are statistically independent. *Bear in mind that Equation (A.25) must be true for all combinations of X and Y values.*

Example A.19.

Are the number of PCs sold and the number of printers sold in Example A.17 independent random variables? To determine this, let us apply the definition of independence given in Eq. (A.25). Let $X = 3$ (3 computers sold) and $Y = 2$ (2 printers sold). From Table A-3 we see that $f(X = 3, Y = 2) = 0.05$; $f(X = 3) = 0.24$ and $f(Y = 2) = 0.23$. Obviously, in this case $0.05 \neq (0.24)(0.23)$. Hence, in the present case, the number of PCs sold and the number of printers sold are not independent variables. This may not be surprising, especially for those who buy a computer for the first time. Sometimes a store may offer a special discount if a customer buys both.

A.7 SUMMARY AND CONCLUSIONS

In econometrics, mathematical statistics plays a key role. And the foundation of mathematical statistics is based on probability theory. Therefore, without some background in probability, we will not be able to appreciate the theory behind several econometric techniques that we discuss in the main chapters of the book.

That is why in this appendix we introduced some fundamental concepts of probability, such as sample space, sample points, events, random variables, and probability distributions of random variables. Since in econometrics we deal with relationships between (economic) variables, we have to consider the joint probability distributions of such variables. This led to a discussion of concepts, such as joint events and joint variables and their probability distributions, conditional probability distributions, unconditional probability distributions, and statistical independence. An interesting application of the conditional probability distribution is Bayes' Theorem, which shows how experimental knowledge can be used to revise probabilities.

All the concepts discussed in this appendix are illustrated with several examples. You may want to refer to this appendix when these concepts are addressed in the econometric techniques explained in the main text of the book.

KEY TERMS AND CONCEPTS

The key terms and concepts introduced in this appendix are

Statistical or random experiment
Population or sample space
   a) sample point
   b) events—mutually exclusive;
    equally likely; collectively
    exhaustive

Venn diagram
Stochastic or random variable
   a) discrete random variable
   b) continuous random variable
Probability and features of
   probability

A priori definition (classical definition) of probability
Frequency distribution; absolute frequency; relative frequency
Complement
Conditional probability of *A*
Bayes' Theorem
     Prior probability
     Posterior probability
Probability mass function (PMF) or probability function (PF), and probability density function (PDF)
Normal probability density function
PMFs of discrete and PDFs of continuous random variable

Cumulative distribution function (CDF)
Step function
Multivariate PDF
    a) bivariate or joint PMF and PDF; joint frequency distribution
    b) marginal (or univariate, unconditional, or individual) PMF and PDF
    c) conditional probability; conditional PMF
Statistical independence; independent random variables

REFERENCES

As noted in the introduction to this appendix, the discussion presented here is, of necessity, brief and intuitive and not meant as a substitute for a basic course in statistics. Therefore, the reader is advised to keep on hand one or two of the many good books on statistics. The following short list of such references is only suggestive.

1. Newbold, Paul. *Statistics for Business and Economics* (latest ed.). Prentice-Hall, Englewood Cliffs, N.J. This is a comprehensive nonmathematical introduction to statistics with lots of worked-out examples.
2. Hoel, Paul G. *Introduction to Mathematical Statistics* (latest ed.). Wiley, New York. This book provides a fairly simple introduction to various aspects of mathematical statistics.
3. Mood, Alexander M., Franklin A. Graybill, and Duane C. Boes. *Introduction to the Theory of Statistics*. McGraw-Hill, New York, 1974. This is a standard but mathematically advanced book.
4. Mosteller, F., R. Rourke, and G. Thomas. *Probability with Statistical Applications* (latest ed.). Addison-Wesley, Reading, Mass.
5. DeGroot, Morris H. *Probability and Statistics* (3rd ed.). Addison-Wesley, Reading, Mass.
6. Ron C. Mittelhammer. *Mathematical Statistics for Economics and Business*. Springer, New York, 1999.

QUESTIONS

A.1. What is the meaning of
    a. sample space
    b. sample point
    c. events
    d. mutually exclusive events
    e. PMF and PDF
    f. joint PDF
    g. marginal PDF
    h. conditional PDF
    i. statistical independence

A.2. A and B are two events. Can they be mutually exclusive and independent simultaneously?

A.3. For every event A, there is the *complement of A*, denoted by A', which means that A does not occur. Are the following statements true or false?

a. $P(A + A')$ or $P(A \cup A') = 1$

b. $P(AA')$ or $P(A \cap A') = 0$

A.4. Four economists have predicted the following rates of growth of GDP (%) for the next quarter:

$E_1 =$ below 2%, $E_2 = 2$ or greater than 2% but below 4%, $E_3 = 4$ or greater than 4% but less than 6%, and $E_4 = 6\%$ or more.

Let A_i be the actual rate of % GDP growth rate according to the same four classifications as E_i (e.g., $A_1 =$ GDP growth rate of less than 2%).

a. Are the events E_1 through E_4 mutually exclusive? Are they collectively exhaustive?

b. What is the meaning of the events (1) E_1A_2 (or $E_1 \cap A_2$), (2) $E_3 + A_3$ (or $E_3 \cup A_3$), (3) $E_i + A_i$ (or $E_i \cup A_i$) where $I = 1$ through 4, and (4) E_iA_j (or $E_i \cap A_j$) where $i > j$?

A.5. What is the difference between a PDF and a PMF?

A.6. What is the difference between the CDFs of continuous and discrete random variables?

A.7. By the conditional probability formula, we have

1. $P(A \mid B) = \dfrac{P(AB)}{P(B)}$ and

2. $P(B \mid A) = \dfrac{P(AB)}{P(A)} \rightarrow P(AB) = P(B \mid A)P(A)$

where $\rightarrow$ means "implies." If you substitute for $P(AB)$ from the right-hand side of (2) into the numerator of (1), what do you get? How do you interpret this result?

PROBLEMS

A.8. What do the following stand for?

a. $\displaystyle\sum_{i=1}^{4} x^{i-1}$

e. $\displaystyle\sum_{i=1}^{4} (i + 4)$

b. $\displaystyle\sum_{i=2}^{6} ay_i$, a is a constant

f. $\displaystyle\sum_{i=1}^{3} 3^i$

c. $\displaystyle\sum_{i=1}^{2} (2x_i + 3y_i)$

g. $\displaystyle\sum_{i=1}^{10} 2$

d. $\displaystyle\sum_{i=1}^{3} \sum_{j=1}^{2} x_i y_j$

h. $\displaystyle\sum_{i=1}^{3} (4x^2 - 3)$

A.9. Express the following in the $\sum$ notation:

a. $x_1 + x_2 + x_3 + x_4 + x_5$

b. $x_1 + 2x_2 + 3x_3 + 4x_4 + 5x_5$

c. $\left(x_1^2 + y_1^2\right) + \left(x_2^2 + y_2^2\right) + \cdots + \left(x_k^2 + y_k^2\right)$

A.10. It can be shown that the sum of the first n positive numbers is:

$$\sum_{k=1}^{n} k = \frac{n(n+1)}{2}$$

Use the preceding formula to evaluate

a. $\sum_{k=1}^{500} k$ **b.** $\sum_{k=10}^{100} k$ **c.** $\sum_{k=10}^{100} 3k$

A.11. It can be proved that the sum of squares of the first n positive numbers is:

$$\sum_{k=1}^{n} k^2 = \frac{n(n+1)(2n+1)}{6}$$

Using this formula, obtain

a. $\sum_{k=1}^{10} k^2$ **b.** $\sum_{k=10}^{20} k^2$ **c.** $\sum_{k=11}^{19} k^2$ **d.** $\sum_{k=1}^{10} 4k^2$

A.12. An r.v. X has the following PDF:

TABLE A-6

X	f(X)
0	b
1	2b
2	3b
3	4b
4	5b

a. What is the value of b? Why?
b. Find the $P(X \le 2)$; $\text{prob}(X \le 3)$; $\text{prob}(2 \le X \le 3)$.

A.13. The following table gives the joint probability distribution, $f(X, Y)$, of two random variables X and Y.

TABLE A-7

Y	X 1	2	3
1	0.03	0.06	0.06
2	0.02	0.04	0.04
3	0.09	0.18	0.18
4	0.06	0.12	0.12

a. Find the marginal (i.e., unconditional) distributions of X and Y, namely, $f(X)$ and $f(Y)$.
b. Find the conditional PDF, $f(X | Y)$ and $f(Y | X)$.

A.14. Of 100 people, 50 are Democrats, 40 are Republicans, and 10 are Independents. The percentages of the people in these three categories who read *The Wall Street Journal* are known to be 30, 60, and 40 percent, respectively. If one of these people is observed reading the *Journal*, what is the probability that he or she is a Republican?

A.15. Let A denote the event that a person lives in New York City. Let $P(A) = 0.5$. Let B denote the event that the person does not live in New York City but works in the city. Let $P(B) = 0.4$. What is the probability that the person either lives in the city or does not live in the city but works there?

A.16. Based on a random sample of 500 married women, the following table gives the joint PMF of their work status in relation to the presence or absence of children in the household.[10]

TABLE A-8   CHILDREN AND WORK STATUS OF WOMEN IN THE UNITED STATES

	Works outside home	Does not work outside home	Total
Has children	0.2	0.3	0.5
Does not have children	0.4	0.1	0.5
Total	0.6	0.4	1.0

a. Are children and working outside of the home mutually exclusive?
b. Are working outside of the home and presence of children independent events?

A.17. The following table gives the joint probability of X and Y, where X represents a person's poverty status (below or above the poverty line as defined by the U.S. government), and Y represents the person's race (white, blacks only, and all Hispanic).

TABLE A-9   POVERTY IN THE UNITED STATES, 2007

Y	X	
	Below poverty line	Above poverty line
White	0.0546	0.6153
Black	0.0315	0.0969
Hispanic	0.0337	0.1228
Asian	0.0046	0.0406

Source: These data are derived from the U.S. Census Bureau, Current Population Reports, *Poverty in the United States: 2007*, September 2008, Table 1. Although the poverty line varies by several socioeconomic characteristics, for a family of four in 2007, the dividing line was about $21,302. Families below this income level can be classified as poor.

a. Compute $f(X|Y = white)$; $f(X|Y = black)$, $f(X|Y = Hispanic)$, and $f(X|Y = Asian)$, where X represents below the poverty line. What general conclusions can you draw from these computations?
b. Are race and poverty status independent variables? How do you know?

---

[10]Adapted from Barry R. Chiswick and Stephen J. Chiswick, *Statistics and Econometrics: A Problem Solving Approach,* University Park Press, Baltimore, 1975.

A.18. The following table gives joint probabilities relating cell phone usage to stopping properly at intersections.

    a. Compute the probability of failing to stop at an intersection, given the driver was on the cell phone.

    b. Compute the probability of failing to stop at an intersection, given the driver was not using a cell phone.

    c. Compute the probability of stopping properly at an intersection, given the driver was on the cell phone.

    d. Are cell phone usage and failing to stop at intersections independent of each other? Why or why not?

TABLE A-10

	Failed to stop at intersection	Stopped at intersection
On cell phone	0.047	0.016
Not using cell phone	0.201	0.736

    Source: David L. Strayer and Frank A. Drews, "Multitasking in the Automobile," Chapter 9.

*A.19. The PDF of a continuous random variable X is as follows:

$$f(X) = c(4x - 2x^2) \quad 0 \le x \le 2$$

$$= 0 \; otherwise$$

    a. For this to be a proper density function, what must be the value of c?

    b. Find $P(1 < x < 2)$

    c. Find $P(x > 2)$

*A.20. Consider the following joint PDF:

$$f(x, y) = \frac{12}{5}x(2 - x - y); \; 0 < x < 1; \; 0 < y < 1$$

$$= 0 \; otherwise$$

    a. Find $P(x > 0.5)$ and $P(y < 0.5)$

    b. What is the conditional density of X given that $Y = y$, where $0 < y < 1$?

*Optional.

APPENDIX B

CHARACTERISTICS OF PROBABILITY DISTRIBUTIONS

Although a PMF (PDF) indicates the values taken by a random variable (r.v.) and their associated probabilities, often we are not interested in the entire PMF. Thus, in the PMF of Example A.13 we may not want the individual probabilities of obtaining no heads, one head, or two heads. Rather, we may wish to find out the *average number* of heads obtained when tossing a coin several times. In other words, we may be interested in some summary **characteristics,** or more technically, the **moments** of a probability distribution. Two of the most commonly used summary measures or moments are the *expected value* (called the *first moment* of the probability distribution) and the *variance* (called the *second moment* of the probability distribution). On occasion, we will need higher moments of probability distributions, which we will discuss as we progress.

B.1 EXPECTED VALUE: A MEASURE OF CENTRAL TENDENCY

The **expected value** of a discrete r.v. X, denoted by the symbol $E(X)$ (read as E of X), is defined as follows:

$$E(X) = \sum_X x f(X) \tag{B.1}$$

where $f(X)$ is the PMF of X and where $\sum_X$ means the sum over all values of X.[1]

Verbally, the expected value of a random variable is the *weighted average* of its possible values, with the probabilities of these values [i.e., $f(X)$] serving as the *weights*. Equivalently, *it is the sum of products of the values taken by the r.v. and their corresponding probabilities.* The expected value of an r.v. is also known as its *average*

---

[1]The expected value of a continuous r.v. is defined similarly, with the summation symbol being replaced by the integral symbol. That is: $E(X) = \int x f(x)\,dx$, where the integral is over all the values of X.

TABLE B-1 THE EXPECTED VALUE OF A RANDOM VARIABLE X, THE NUMBER SHOWN ON A DIE

Number shown (1) X	Probability (2) $f(X)$	Number $\times$ Probability (3) $Xf(X)$
1	1/6	1/6
2	1/6	2/6
3	1/6	3/6
4	1/6	4/6
5	1/6	5/6
6	1/6	6/6
		$E(X) = 21/6 = 3.5$

or *mean* value, although, more correctly, it is called the **population mean value** for reasons to be discussed shortly.

Example B.1.

Suppose we roll a die numbered 1 through 6 several times. What is the expected value of the number shown? As given previously (see Example A.6), we have the situation shown in Table B-1.

Applying the definition of the expected value given in Eq. (B.1), we see that the expected value is 3.5.

Is it strange that we obtained this value, since the r.v. here is discrete and can take only one of the six values 1 through 6? The expected, or average, value of 3.5 in this example means that if we were to roll the die several times, then on the *average,* we would obtain the number 3.5, which is between 3 and 4. If, in a contest, someone were to give you as many dollars as the number shown on the die, then in several rolls of the die you would anticipate receiving on the average $3.50 per roll of the die.

Geometrically, the expected value of the preceding example is shown in Figure B-1.

Example B.2.

In the PC/printer sales example (Example A.17), what is the expected value of the number of PCs sold? This can be obtained easily from Table A-4 by multiplying the values of X (PCs sold) by their associated probabilities (i.e., $f[X]$) and summing the product. Thus,

$$E(X) = 0(0.08) + 1(0.12) + 2(0.24) + 3(0.24) + 4(0.32) = 2.60$$

That is, the average number of PCs sold per day is 2.60. Keep in mind that this is an average. On any given day the number of PCs sold will be any one of the numbers between 0 and 4.

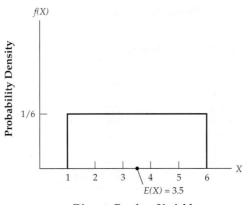

Discrete Random Variable

FIGURE B-1   The expected value, $E(X)$, of a discrete random variable (Example B.1)

You can easily verify that $E(Y) = 2.35$; that is, the average number of printers sold is 2.35.

Properties of Expected Value

The following properties of the expected value will prove very useful in the main chapters of the text:

1. The expected value of a constant is that constant itself. Thus, if b is a constant,

$$E(b) = b \qquad \text{(B.2)}$$

For example, if $b = 2$, $E(2) = 2$.

2. The expectation of the sum of two random variables is equal to the sum of the expectations of those random variables. Thus, for the random variables X and Y:[2]

$$E(X + Y) = E(X) + E(Y) \qquad \text{(B.3)}$$

3. However,

$$E(X/Y) \neq \frac{E(X)}{E(Y)} \qquad \text{(B.4)}$$

---

[2]This property can be generalized to more than two random variables. Thus, $E(X + Y + W + Z) = E(X) + E(Y) + E(W) + E(Z)$.

That is, the expected value of the ratio of two random variables is not equal to the ratio of the expected values of those random variables.

4. Also, in general,

$$E(XY) \neq E(X)E(Y) \qquad \text{(B.5)}$$

That is, in general, the expected value of the product of two random variables is not equal to the product of the expectations of those random variables. However, there is an exception to the rule. If X and Y are *independent random variables*, then it is true that

$$E(XY) = E(X)E(Y) \qquad \text{(B.6)}$$

Recall that X and Y are said to be independent if and only if $f(X, Y) = f(X)f(Y)$, for all values of X and Y, that is, when the joint PMF (PDF) is equal to the product of the individual PMFs (PDFs) of the two random variables for all values of the variables.

5. $$E(X^2) \neq [E(X)]^2 \qquad \text{(B.7)}$$

That is, the expected value of the square of X (or any random variable) is *not* equal to the square of the expected value of X.

6. If a is a constant, then

$$E(a X) = a E(X) \qquad \text{(B.8)}$$

That is, the expectation of a constant times an r.v. is equal to the constant times the expectation of the r.v.

7. If a and b are constants, then

$$E(a X + b) = a E(X) + E(b)$$
$$= a E(X) + b \qquad \text{(B.9)}$$

In deriving result (7), we use properties (1), (2), and (6). Thus,

$$E (4X + 7) = 4E(X) + E(7) = 4E(X) + 7$$

From Eq. (B.9) we see that E is a *linear operator*, which is also evident from Eq. (B.4).

Expected Value of Multivariate Probability Distributions

The concept of the expected value of a random variable can be extended easily to multivariate PMF or PDF. In the bivariate PMF, it can be shown that

$$E(XY) = \sum_x \sum_y xy f(X, Y) \qquad \text{(B.10)}$$

That is, we take each pair of X and Y values, multiply them by their joint probability, and sum over all the values of X and Y.

Example B.3.

Continuing with our PC/printer sales example, and applying Eq. (B.10), we get

$$E(XY) = (1)(1)(0.05) + (1)(2)(0.06) + (1)(3)(0.02) + (1)(4)(0.01) \cdots$$
$$+ (4)(1)(0.01) + 4(2)(0.01) + 4(3)(0.01) + (4)(3)(0.05) + (4)(4)(0.15)$$
$$= 7.06$$

which is the expected value of the product of the two random variables.

Recall that if two variables are independent, the expected value of their product is equal to the product of their individual expected values; that is, $E(XY) = E(X)E(Y)$. Is this the case in our illustrative example? As we saw in Example B.2, $E(X) = 2.60$ and $E(Y) = 2.35$. Therefore, $E(X)E(Y) = (2.60)(2.35) = 6.11 \neq E(XY) = 7.06$, showing that the two variables are not independent.

In passing, note that the formula for the expected value of the product of two random variables given in Eq. (B.10) is for two discrete random variables. In the case of two continuous random variables, in Eq. (B.10) we would replace the double summation sign by the double integral sign.

B.2 VARIANCE: A MEASURE OF DISPERSION

The expected value of an r.v. simply gives its *center of gravity*, but it does not indicate how the individual values are spread, dispersed, or distributed around this mean value. The most popular numerical measure of this spread is called the **variance**, which is defined as follows.

Let X be an r.v. and $E(X)$ be its expected value, which for notational simplicity may be denoted by μ_x (where μ is the Greek letter mu). Then the variance of X is defined as

$$\text{var}(X) = \sigma_x^2 = E(X - \mu_x)^2 \tag{B.11}$$

where $\mu_x = E(X)$ and where the Greek letter σ_x^2 (sigma squared) is the commonly used symbol for the variance. As Equation (B.11) shows, the variance of X (or any r.v.) is simply the expected value of the squared difference between an individual X value and its expected or mean value. The variance thus defined shows how the individual X values are spread or distributed around its expected, or mean, value. If all X values are precisely equal to $E(X)$, the variance will be zero, whereas if they are widely spread around the expected value, it will be relatively large, as shown in Figure B-2. Notice that the variance cannot be a negative number. (Why?)

The positive square root of σ_x^2, σ_x, is known as the **standard deviation (s.d.).** Equation (B.11) is the definition of variance. To compute the variance, we use the following formula:

$$\text{var}(X) = \sum_X (X - \mu_x)^2 f(X) \tag{B.12}$$

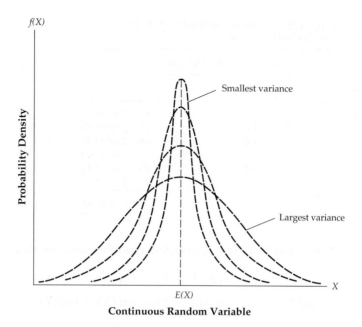

FIGURE B-2 Hypothetical PDFs of continuous random variables all with the same expected value

if X is a discrete r.v. In case of a continuous random variable, we replace the summation symbol by the integral symbol.

As Equation (B.12) shows, to compute the variance of a discrete r.v., we subtract the expected value of the variable from a given value of the variable, square the difference, and multiply the squared difference by the probability associated with that X value. We do this for each value assumed by the X variable and sum the products thus obtained. An example follows.

Example B.4.

We continue with Example B.1. There we showed that the expected value of the number in the repeated roll of a die is 3.5. To compute the variance for that problem, we set up Table B-2.

Thus, the variance of this example is 2.9167. Taking the positive square root of this value, we obtain a standard deviation (s.d.) of 1.7078.

Properties of Variance

The variance as defined earlier has the following properties, which we will find useful in our discussion of econometrics in the main chapters of the text.

1. The variance of a constant is zero. By definition, a constant has no variability.

TABLE B-2   THE VARIANCE OF A RANDOM VARIABLE X, THE
NUMBER SHOWN ON A DIE

X	Number Shown Probability $f(X)$	$(X - \mu_X)^2 f(X)$
1	1/6	$(1 - 3.5)^2 (1/6)$
2	1/6	$(2 - 3.5)^2 (1/6)$
3	1/6	$(3 - 3.5)^2 (1/6)$
4	1/6	$(4 - 3.5)^2 (1/6)$
5	1/6	$(5 - 3.5)^2 (1/6)$
6	1/6	$(6 - 3.5)^2 (1/6)$
		Sum $= 2.9167$

2. If X and Y are two *independent* random variables, then

$$\text{var}(X + Y) = \text{var}(X) + \text{var}(Y)$$

and
$$\text{var}(X - Y) = \text{var}(X) + \text{var}(Y) \qquad \textbf{(B.13)}$$

That is, the variance of the sum or difference of two independent random variables is equal to the sum of their individual variances.

3. If b is a constant, then

$$\text{var}(X + b) = \text{var}(X) \qquad \textbf{(B.14)}$$

That is, adding a constant number to (the values of) a variable does not change the variance of that variable. Thus, $\text{var}(X + 7) = \text{var}(X)$.

4. If a is constant, then

$$\text{var}(aX) = a^2\text{var}(X) \qquad \textbf{(B.15)}$$

That is, the variance of a constant times a variable is equal to the square of that constant times the variance of that variable. Thus, $\text{var}(5X) = 25\,\text{var}(X)$.

5. If a and b are constant, then

$$\text{var}(aX + b) = a^2\text{var}(X) \qquad \textbf{(B.16)}$$

which follows from properties (3) and (4). Thus,

$$\text{var}(5X + 9) = 25\,\text{var}(X)$$

6. If X and Y are *independent* random variables and a and b are constants, then

$$\text{var}(aX + bY) = a^2\text{var}(X) + b^2\text{var}(Y) \qquad \textbf{(B.17)}$$

This property follows from the previous properties. Thus,

$$\text{var}(3X + 5Y) = 9\,\text{var}(X) + 25\,\text{var}(Y)$$

7. For computational convenience, the variance formula Eq. (B.11) can also be written as

$$\text{var}(X) = E(X^2) - [E(X)]^2 \qquad\qquad \textbf{(B.18)}$$

which says that the variance of X is equal to the expected value of X squared minus the square of the expected value of X.[3] Note that

$$E(X^2) = \sum_x x^2 f(X) \qquad\qquad \textbf{(B.19)}$$

for a discrete r.v. For a continuous r.v., replace the summation sign with the integral sign.

The proofs of the various expressions above can be obtained from the basic definition of variance (see the optional exercises given at the end of this appendix).

Chebyshev's Inequality

How adequate are the expected value and variance of a random variable to describe a PMF or PDF of such a random variable? That is, knowing just these two summary numbers of a random variable, say X, can we compute the probability that X lies in a certain range? In a remarkable theorem, known as *Chebyshev's inequality*, the Russian mathematician Pafnuty Lvovich Chebyshev (1821–1894) showed that that is indeed possible.

Specifically, if X is a random variable with mean μ_x and a variance of σ_x^2, then for any positive constant c the probability that X lies *inside* the interval $[\mu_x - c\sigma_x, \mu_x + c\sigma_x]$ is at least $1 - \frac{1}{c^2}$, that is

$$P[|X - \mu_x| \le c\sigma_x] \le 1 - \frac{1}{c^2} \qquad\qquad \textbf{(B.20)}$$

where the symbol $|\ |$ means the absolute value of.[4]

---

[3]The proof is as follows:

$$E(X - \mu_x)^2 = E\left(X^2 - 2X\mu_x + \mu_x^2\right)$$
$$= E(X^2) - 2\mu_x E(X) + E\left(\mu_x^2\right)$$
$$= E(X^2) - 2\mu_x^2 + \mu_x^2 = E(X^2) - \mu_x^2$$

Keep in mind that μ_x is a constant.
[4]The inequality works quite well if $c > 1$.

In words this inequality states that at least the fraction $(1 - \frac{1}{c^2})$ of the total probability of X lies within c standard deviations of its mean or expected value. Put differently, the probability that a random variable deviates from its mean value by more than c standard deviations is less than or at the most equal to $1/c^2$.

What is remarkable about this inequality is that we do not need to know the actual PDF or PMF of a random variable. Of course, if we know the actual PDF or PMF, probabilities such as Eq. (B.20) can be computed easily, as we will show when we consider some specific probability distributions in Appendix C.

Example B.5. Illustration of Chebyshev's Inequality

The average number of donuts sold in a donut shop between 8 a.m. and 9 a.m. is 100 with a variance of 25. What is the probability that on a given day the number of donuts sold between 8 a.m. and 9 a.m. is between 90 and 110?

By Chebyshev's inequality, we have:

$$P[|X - \mu_x| \leq c\sigma_x] = 1 - \frac{1}{c^2}$$

$$P[|X - 100| \leq 5c] = 1 - \frac{1}{c^2}$$

(B.21)

Since $(110 - 100) = (100 - 90) = 10$, we see that $5c = 10$. Therefore, $c = 2$. It therefore follows that $(1 - \frac{1}{2^2}) = \frac{3}{4} = 0.75$. That is, the probability that between 90 and 110 donuts are sold between 8 a.m. and 9 a.m. is at least 75 percent. By the same token, the probability that the number of donuts sold between 8 a.m. and 9 a.m. exceeds 110 or is less than 90 is 25 percent.

Coefficient of Variation

Before moving on, note that since the standard deviation (or variance) depends on the units of measurement, it may be difficult to compare two or more standard deviations if they are expressed in different units of measurement. To get around this difficulty, use the **coefficient of variation (V),** a measure of *relative variation*, which is defined as follows:

$$V = \frac{\sigma_X}{\mu_X} \cdot 100$$

(B.22)

Verbally, the V is the ratio of the standard deviation of a random variable X to its mean value multiplied by 100. Since the standard deviation and the mean value of a random variable are measured in the same units of measurement, V is unitless; that is, it is a pure number. We can therefore compare the V values of two or more random variables directly.

Example B.6.

An instructor teaches two sections of an introductory econometrics class with 15 students in each class. On the midterm examination, class A scored an average of 83 points with a standard deviation of 10, and class B scored an average 88 points with a standard deviation of 16. Which class performed relatively better? If we use V as defined in Eq. (B.22), we get:

$$V_A = \frac{10}{83} \cdot 100 = 12.048 \quad and \quad V_B = \frac{16}{88} \cdot 100 = 18.181$$

Since the relative variability of class A is lower, we can say that class A did relatively better than class B.

B.3   COVARIANCE

The expected value and variance are the two most frequently used summary measures of a univariate PMF (or PDF). The former gives us the center of gravity, and the latter tells us how the individual values are distributed around the center of gravity. But once we go beyond the univariate probability distributions (e.g., the PMF of Example B.2), we need to consider, in addition to the mean and variance of each variable, some additional characteristics of multivariate PFs, such as the *covariance* and *correlation*, which we will now discuss.

Let X and Y be two random variables with means $E(X) = \mu_x$ and $E(Y) = \mu_y$. Then the covariance (cov) between the two variables is defined as

$$\text{cov}(X, Y) = E[(X - \mu_x)(Y - \mu_y)]$$
$$= E(XY) - \mu_x\mu_y \qquad \textbf{(B.23)}$$

As Equation (B.23) shows, a **covariance** is a special kind of expected value and is a measure of how two variables vary or move together (i.e., co-vary), as shown in Example B.7, which follows. In words, Eq. (B.23) states that to find the covariance between two variables, we must express the value of each variable as a deviation from its mean value and take the expected value of the product. How this is done in practice follows.

The covariance between two random variables can be *positive*, *negative*, or *zero*. If two random variables move in the same direction (i.e., if they both increase) as in Example B.7 below, then the covariance will be positive, whereas if they move in the opposite direction (i.e., if one increases and the other decreases), the covariance will be negative. If, however, the covariance between the two variables is zero, it means that there is no (linear) relationship between the two variables.

To compute the covariance as defined in Eq. (B.23), we use the following formula, assuming X and Y are discrete random variables:

$$\text{cov}(X, Y) = \sum_x \sum_y (X - \mu_X)(Y - \mu_y)f(X, Y)$$
$$= \sum_x \sum_y XYf(X, Y) - \mu_X\mu_y \qquad \textbf{(B.24)}$$
$$= E(XY) - \mu_X\mu_y$$

where $E(XY)$ is computed from Eq. (B.10).

Note the double summation sign in this expression because the covariance requires the summation of both variables over the range of their values. Using the integral notation of calculus, a similar formula can be devised to compute the covariance of two continuous random variables.

Example B.7.

Once again, return to our PC/printer sales example. To find out the covariance between computer sales (X) and printer sales (Y), we use formula (B.24). We have already computed the first term on the right-hand side of this equation in Example (B.3), which is 7.06. We have already found that $\mu_x = 2.60$ and $\mu_y = 2.35$. Therefore, the covariance in this example is

$$\text{cov}(X, Y) = 7.06 - (2.60)(2.35) = 0.95$$

which shows that PC sales and printer sales are positively related.

Properties of Covariance

The covariance as defined earlier has the following properties, which we will find quite useful in regression analysis in the main chapters of the text.

1. If X and Y are *independent* random variables, their covariance is zero. This is easy to verify. Recall that if two random variables are independent,

$$E(XY) = E(X)E(Y) = \mu_x\mu_y$$

Substituting this expression into Eq. (B.23), we see at once that the covariance of two *independent* random variables is zero.

2.
$$\text{cov}(a + bX, c + dY) = bd\,\text{cov}(X, Y) \qquad \text{(B.25)}$$

where a, b, c, and d are constants.

3.
$$\text{cov}(X, X) = \text{var}(X) \qquad \text{(B.26)}$$

That is, the covariance of a variable with itself is simply its variance, which can be verified from the definitions of variance and covariance given previously. Obviously, then, $\text{cov}(Y, Y) = \text{var}(Y)$.

4. If X and Y are two random variables but are not necessarily independent, then the variance formulas given in Eq. (B.13) need to be modified as follows:

$$\text{var}(X + Y) = \text{var}(X) + \text{var}(Y) + 2\,\text{cov}(X, Y) \qquad \text{(B.27)}$$

$$\text{var}(X - Y) = \text{var}(X) + \text{var}(Y) - 2\,\text{cov}(X, Y) \qquad \text{(B.28)}$$

Of course, if the two variables are independent, formulas (B.27) and (B.28) will coincide with Eq. (B.13).

B.4 CORRELATION COEFFICIENT

In the PC/printer sales example just considered we found that the covariance between PC sales and computer sales was 0.95, which suggests that the two variables are positively related. But the computed number of 0.95 does not give any idea of how strongly the two variables are positively related because the covariance is unbounded (i.e., $-\infty < \text{cov}[X, Y] < \infty$). We can find out how strongly any two variables are related in terms of what is known as the **(population) coefficient of correlation,** which is defined as follows:

$$\rho = \frac{\text{cov}(X, Y)}{\sigma_x \sigma_y}$$
(B.29)

where ρ (rho) denotes the coefficient of correlation.

As is clear from Equation (B.29), the **correlation** between two random variables X and Y is simply the ratio of the covariance between the two variables divided by their respective standard deviations. The correlation coefficient thus defined is a measure of *linear* association between two variables, that is, how strongly the two variables are linearly related.

Properties of Correlation Coefficient

The correlation coefficient just defined has the following properties:

1. Like the covariance, the correlation coefficient can be positive or negative. It is positive if the covariance is positive and negative if the covariance is negative. In short, it has the same sign as the covariance.
2. The correlation coefficient is a measure of *linear relationship* between two variables.
3. The correlation coefficient always lies between −1 and +1. Symbolically,

$$-1 \leq \rho \leq 1$$
(B.30)

If the correlation coefficient is +1, it means that the two variables are perfectly positively linearly related (as in $Y = B_1 + B_2X$), whereas if the correlation coefficient is −1, it means they are perfectly negatively linearly related. Typically, ρ lies between these limits.

4. The correlation coefficient is a *pure number*; that is, it is devoid of units of measurement. On the other hand, other characteristics of probability distributions, such as the expected value, variance, and covariance, depend on the units in which the original variables are measured.
5. If two variables are (statistically) independent, their covariance is zero. Therefore, the correlation coefficient will be zero. The converse, however, is not true. That is, if the correlation coefficient between two variables is zero, it does not mean that the two variables are independent. This is because the correlation coefficient is a measure of *linear association* or *linear relationship* between two variables, as noted previously. For example, if $Y = X^2$, the correlation between the two variables may be zero, but by no means are the two variables independent. Here Y is a *nonlinear* function of X.

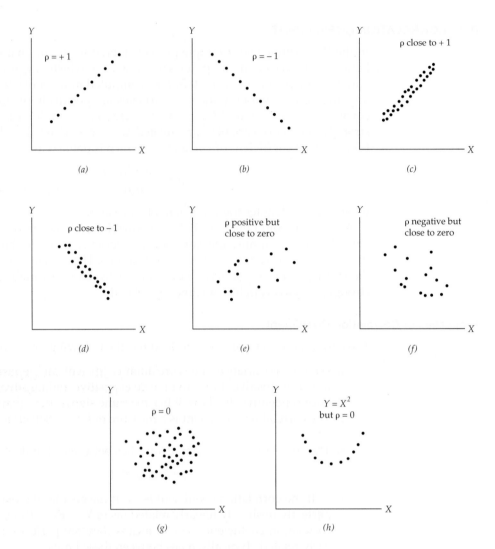

FIGURE B-3   Some typical patterns of the correlation coefficient, ρ

6. Correlation does not necessarily imply causality. If one finds a positive correlation between lung cancer and smoking, it does not necessarily mean that smoking causes lung cancer.

Figure B-3 gives some typical patterns of correlation coefficients.

Example B.8.

Let us continue with the PC/printer sales example. We have already seen that the covariance between the two variables is 0.95. From the data given in

Table A-4, we can easily verify that $\sigma_x = 1.2649$ and $\sigma_y = 1.4124$. Then, using formula (B.29), we obtain

$$\rho = \frac{0.95}{(1.2649)(1.4124)} = 0.5317$$

Thus, the two variables are positively correlated, although the value of the correlation coefficient is rather moderate. This probably is not surprising, for not everyone purchasing a PC buys a printer.

The use of the correlation coefficient in the regression context is discussed in Chapter 3.

Incidentally, Eq. (B.29) can also be written as:

$$\text{Cov}(X, Y) = \rho\sigma_x\sigma_y \qquad\qquad \textbf{(B.31)}$$

That is, the covariance between two variables is equal to the coefficient of correlation between the two times the product of the standard deviations of the two.

Variances of Correlated Variables

In Eq. (B.27) and Eq. (B.28) we gave formulas for the variance of variables that are not necessarily independent. Knowing the relationship between covariance and correlation, we can express these formulas alternatively as follows:

$$\text{var}(X + Y) = \text{var}(X) + \text{var}(Y) + 2\rho\sigma_x\sigma_y \qquad\qquad \textbf{(B.32)}$$

$$\text{var}(X - Y) = \text{var}(X) + \text{var}(Y) - 2\rho\sigma_x\sigma_y \qquad\qquad \textbf{(B.33)}$$

Of course, if the correlation between two random variables is zero, then $\text{var}(X + Y)$ and $\text{var}(X - Y)$ are both equal to $\text{var}(X) + \text{var}(Y)$, as we saw before. As an exercise, you can find the variance of $(X + Y)$ of our PC/printer example.

B.5 CONDITIONAL EXPECTATION

Another statistical concept that is especially important in regression analysis is the concept of **conditional expectation,** which is different from the expectation of an r.v. considered previously, which may be called the **unconditional expectation.** The difference between the two concepts of expectations can be explained as follows.

Return to our PC/printer sales example. In this example X is the number of PCs sold per day (ranging from 0 to 4) and Y is the number of printers sold per day (ranging from 0 to 4). We have seen that $E(X) = 2.6$ and $E(Y) = 2.35$. These are *unconditional* expected values, for in computing these values we have not put any restrictions on them.

But now consider this question: What is the average number of printers sold (Y) if it is known that on a particular day 3 PCs were sold? Put differently, what is the *conditional expectation* of Y given that $X = 3$? Technically, what is $E(Y \mid X = 3)$? This is known as the conditional expectation of Y. Similarly, we could ask: What is $E(Y \mid X = 1)$?

From the preceding discussion it should be clear that in computing the unconditional expectation of an r.v., we do not take into account information about any other r.v., whereas in computing the conditional expectation we do.

To compute such conditional expectations, we use the following definition of conditional expectation

$$E(X \mid Y = y) = \sum_X X f(X \mid Y = y) \tag{B.34}$$

which gives the conditional expectation of X, where X is a discrete r.v., $f(X \mid Y = y)$ is the conditional PDF of X given in Eq. (A.20), and $\sum_X$ means the sum over all values of X. In relation to Equation (B.34), $E(X)$, considered earlier, is called the *unconditional expectation*. Computationally, $E(X \mid Y = y)$ is similar to $E(X)$ except that instead of using the unconditional PDF of X, we use its conditional PDF, as seen clearly in comparing Eq. (B.34) with Eq. (B.1).

Similarly,

$$E(Y \mid X = x) = \sum_Y Y f(Y \mid X = x) \tag{B.35}$$

gives the conditional expectation of Y. Let us illustrate with an example.

Example B.9.

Let us compute $E(Y \mid X = 2)$ for our PC/printer sales example. That is, we want to find out the conditional expected value of printers sold, knowing that 2 PCs have been sold per day. Using formula (B.34), we have

$$
\begin{aligned}
E(Y \mid X = 2) &= \sum_0^4 Y f(Y \mid x = 2) \\
&= f(Y = 1 \mid X = 2) + 2f(Y = 2 \mid X = 2) \\
&\quad + 3f(Y = 3 \mid X = 2) + 4f(Y = 4 \mid X = 2) \\
&= 1.875
\end{aligned}
$$

Note: $f(Y = 1 \mid X = 2) = \frac{f(Y = 1, X = 2)}{f(X = 2)}$, and so on (see Table A-3).

As these calculations show, the conditional expectation of Y given that $X = 2$, is about 1.88, whereas, as shown previously, the unconditional expectation of Y was 2.35. Just as we saw previously that the conditional PDFs and marginal PDFs are generally different, the conditional and unconditional expectations in general are different too. Of course, if the two variables are independent, the conditional and unconditional expectations will be the same. (Why?)

Conditional Variance

Just as we can compute the conditional expectation of a random variable, we can also compute its **conditional variance,** $\text{var}(Y\,|\,X)$. For Example B.9, for instance, we may be interested in finding the variance of Y, given that $X = 2$, $\text{var}(Y\,|\,X = 2)$. We can use formula (B.11) for the variance of X, except that we now have to use the conditional expectation of Y and the conditional PDF. To see how this is actually done, see Optional Exercise B.23. Incidentally, the variance formula given in Eq. (B.11) may be called the **unconditional variance** of X.

Just as conditional and unconditional expectations of an r.v., in general, are different, the conditional and unconditional variances, in general, are different also. They will be the same, however, if the two variables are independent.

As we will see in Chapter 2 and in subsequent chapters, the concepts of conditional expectation and conditional variance will play an important role in econometrics. Referring to the civilian labor force participation rate (CLFPR) and the civilian unemployment rate (CUNR) example discussed in Chapter 1, will the unconditional expectation of CLFPR be the same as the conditional expectation of CLFPR, conditioned on the knowledge of CUNR? If they are the same, then, the knowledge of CUNR is not particularly helpful in predicting CLFPR. In such a situation, regression analysis is not very useful. On the other hand, if the knowledge of CUNR enables us to forecast CLFPR better than without that knowledge, regression analysis becomes a very valuable research tool, as we show in the main chapters of the text.

B.6 SKEWNESS AND KURTOSIS

To conclude our discussion of the characteristics of probability distributions, we discuss the concepts of *skewness* and *kurtosis* of a probability distribution, which tell us something about the *shape* of the probability distribution. **Skewness (S)** is a measure of asymmetry, and **kurtosis (K)** is a measure of tallness or flatness of a PDF, as can be seen in Figure B-4.

To obtain measures of skewness and kurtosis, we need to know the *third moment* and the *fourth moment* of a PMF (PDF). We have already seen that the first moment of the PMF (PDF) of a random variable X is measured by $E(X) = \mu_X$, the mean of X, and the second moment around the mean (i.e., the variance) is measured by $E(X - \mu_x)^2$. In like fashion, the third and fourth moments around the mean value can be expressed as:

$$\text{Third moment: } E(X - \mu_x)^3 \tag{B.36}$$

$$\text{Fourth moment: } E(X - \mu_x)^4 \tag{B.37}$$

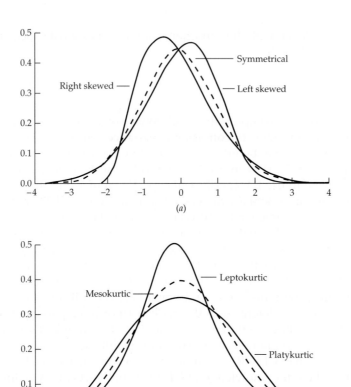

FIGURE B-4   (a) Skewness; (b) kurtosis

And, in general, the rth moment around the mean value can be expressed as

$$r\text{th moment: } E(X - \mu_x)^r \tag{B.38}$$

Given these definitions, the commonly used measures of skewness and kurtosis are as follows:

$$S = \frac{E(X - \mu_x)^3}{\sigma_x^3}$$

$$= \frac{\text{third moment about mean}}{\text{cube of standard deviation}} \tag{B.39}$$

Since for a symmetrical PDF the third (and all odd order) moments are zero, for such a PDF the S value is zero. The prime example is the normal distribution, which we will discuss more fully in Appendix C. If the S value is positive, the

PDF is right-, or positively, skewed, and if it is negative, it is left-, or negatively, skewed. (See Fig. B-4[a]).

$$K = \frac{E(X - \mu_X)^4}{[E(X - \mu_X)^2]^2}$$

$$= \frac{\text{fourth moment}}{\text{square of second moment}} \qquad \textbf{(B.40)}$$

PDFs with values of K less than 3 are called *platykurtic* (fat or short-tailed), and those with values of K greater than 3 are called *leptokurtic* (slim or long-tailed), as shown in Fig. B-4(b). For a normal distribution the K value is 3, and such a PDF is called *mesokurtic*.

Since we will be making extensive use of the normal distribution in the main text, the knowledge that for such a distribution the values of S and K are zero and 3, respectively, will help us to compare other PDFs with the normal distribution.

The computational formulas to obtain the third and fourth moments of a PDF are straightforward extensions of the formula given in Eq. (B.11), namely,

$$\text{Third moment: } \sum (X - \mu_x)^3 f(X) \qquad \textbf{(B.41)}$$

$$\text{Fourth moment: } \sum (X - \mu_x)^4 f(X) \qquad \textbf{(B.42)}$$

where X is a discrete r.v. For a continuous r.v. we will replace the summation sign by the integral sign ($\int$).

Example B.10.

Consider the PDF given in Table B-1. For this PDF we have already seen that $E(X) = 3.5$ and Var $(X) = 2.9167$. The calculations of the third and fourth moments about the mean value are as follows:

X	$f(X)$	$(X - \mu_X)^3 f(X)$	$(X - \mu_X)^4 f(X)$
1	1/6	$(1 - 3.5)^3 (1/6)$	$(1 - 3.5)^4 (1/6)$
2	1/6	$(2 - 3.5)^3 (1/6)$	$(2 - 3.5)^4 (1/6)$
3	1/6	$(3 - 3.5)^3 (1/6)$	$(3 - 3.5)^4 (1/6)$
4	1/6	$(4 - 3.5)^3 (1/6)$	$(4 - 3.5)^4 (1/6)$
5	1/6	$(5 - 3.5)^3 (1/6)$	$(5 - 3.5)^4 (1/6)$
6	1/6	$(6 - 3.5)^3 (1/6)$	$(6 - 3.5)^4 (1/6)$
	Sum =	0	14.732

From the definitions of skewness and kurtosis given before, verify that for the present example the skewness coefficient is zero (Is that surprising?) and that the kurtosis value is 1.7317. Therefore, although the PDF given above is symmetrical around its mean value, it is *platykurtic,* or much flatter than the normal distribution, which should be apparent from its shape in Fig. B-4(b).

B.7   FROM THE POPULATION TO THE SAMPLE

To compute the characteristics of probability distributions, such as the expected value, variance, covariance, correlation coefficient, and conditional expected value, we obviously need the PMF (PDF), that is, the whole sample space or population. Thus, to find out the average income of all the people living in New York City at a given time, obviously we need information on the population of the whole city. Although conceptually there is some finite population of New York City at any given time, it is simply not practical to collect information about each member of the population (i.e., outcome, in the language of probability). What is done in practice is to draw a "representative" or a "random" sample from this population and to compute the average income of the people sampled.[5]

But will the average income obtained from the sample be equal to the true average income (i.e., expected value of income) in the population as a whole? Most likely it will not. Similarly, if we were to compute the variance of the income in the sampled population, would that equal the true variance that we would have obtained had we studied the whole population? Again, most likely it would not.

How then could we learn about population characteristics like the expected value, variance, etc., if we only have one or two samples from a given population? And, as we will see throughout the main chapters of the book, in practice, invariably we have to depend on one or more samples from a given population.

The answer to this very important question will be the focus of our attention in Appendix D. But meanwhile, we must find the sample counterparts, the **sample moments,** of the various population characteristics that we discussed in the preceding sections.

Sample Mean

Let X denote the number of cars sold per day by a car dealer. Assume that the r.v. X follows some PDF. Further, suppose we want to find out the average number [i.e., $E(X)$] of cars sold by the dealer in the first 10 days of each month. Assume that the car dealer has been in business for 10 years but has no time to look up the sales figures for the first 10 days of each month for the past 10 years. Suppose that he decides to pick at random the past data for one month and notes the sales figures for the first 10 days of that month, which are as follows: 9, 11, 11, 14, 13, 9, 8, 9, 14, and 12. This is a sample of 10 values. Notice that he has data for 120 months, and if he had decided to choose another month, he probably would have obtained 10 other values.

If the dealer adds up the 10 sales values and divides the sum by 10 (i.e., the sample size), the number he would obtain is known as the **sample mean.**

---

[5]The precise meaning of a random sample will be explained in Appendix C.

The sample mean of an r.v. X is generally denoted by the symbol $\overline{X}$ (read as X bar) and is defined as

$$\overline{X} = \sum_{i=1}^{n} \frac{X_i}{n} \tag{B.43}$$

where $\sum_{i=1}^{n} X_i$, as usual, means the sum of the X values from 1 to n, where n is the sample size.

The sample mean thus defined is known as an **estimator** of $E(X)$, which we can now call the *population mean*. An *estimator is simply a rule or formula that tells us how to go about estimating a population quantity,* such as the population mean. In Appendix D we will show how $\overline{X}$ is related to $E(X)$.

For the sample just given, the sample mean is

$$\overline{X} = \frac{9 + 11 + 11 + \cdots + 12}{10} = \frac{110}{10} = 11$$

which we call an **estimate** of the population mean. *An estimate is simply the numerical value taken by an estimator,* 11 in the preceding example. In our example, the average number of cars sold in the first 10 days of the month is 11. But keep in mind that this number will not necessarily equal $E(X)$; to compute the latter, we will have to take into account the sales data for the first 10 days of each of the other 119 months. In short, we will have to consider the entire PDF of car sales. But as we show in Appendix D, often the estimate, such as 11, obtained from a given sample is a fairly good "proxy" for the true $E(X)$.

Sample Variance

The ten sample values given previously are not all equal to the sample mean of 11. The variability of the ten values from this sample mean can be measured by the **sample variance,** denoted by S_x^2, which is an *estimator* of σ_x^2, *which we can now call the population variance.* The sample variance is defined as

$$S_x^2 = \sum_{i=1}^{n} \frac{(X_i - \overline{X})^2}{n - 1} \tag{B.44}$$

which is simply the sum of the squared difference of an individual X value from its (sample) mean value divided by the total number of observations less one.[6] The expression $(n - 1)$ is known as the **degrees of freedom,** whose precise meaning will be explained in Appendix C. S_x, the positive square root of S_x^2, is called the **sample standard deviation (sample s.d.).**

---

[6]If the sample size is reasonably large, we can divide by n instead of $(n - 1)$.

For the sample of $10X$ values given earlier, the sample variance is

$$S_x^2 = \frac{(9 - 11)^2 + (11 - 11)^2 + \cdots + (12 - 11)^2}{9}$$

$$= \frac{44}{9} = 4.89$$

and the sample s.d. is $S_x = \sqrt{4.89} \approx 2.21$. Note that 4.89 is an *estimate* of the population variance and 2.21 is an *estimate* of the population s.d. Again, an estimate is a numerical value taken by an estimator in a given sample.

Sample Covariance

Example B.11.

Suppose we have a bivariate population of two variables Y (stock prices) and X (consumer prices). Suppose further that from this bivariate population we obtain the random sample shown in the first two columns of Table B-3. In this example, stock prices are measured by the Dow Jones average and consumer prices by the Consumer Price Index (CPI). The other entries in this table are discussed later.

TABLE B-3 SAMPLE COVARIANCE AND SAMPLE CORRELATION COEFFICIENT BETWEEN DOW JONES AVERAGE (Y) AND CONSUMER PRICE INDEX (X) OVER THE PERIOD 1998–2007

Year	Dow Y (1)	CPI X (2)	$(Y - \bar{Y})(X - \bar{X})$ (3)
1998	8,625.52	163.00	$(8625.5 - 10367.8)(163 - 183.6)$
1999	10,464.88	166.60	$(10464.9 - 10367.8)(166.6 - 183.6)$
2000	10,734.90	172.20	—	—
2001	10,189.13	177.10	—	—
2002	9,226.43	179.90	—	—
2003	8,993.59	184.00	—	—
2004	10,317.39	188.90	—	—
2005	10,547.67	195.30	—	—
2006	11,408.67	201.60	$(11408.7 - 10367.8)(201.6 - 183.6)$
2007	13,169.98	207.34	$(13170 - 10367.8)(207.3 - 183.6)$
Sum	103,678.16	1,835.94	$\approx 121,992.73$

$\bar{Y} = \dfrac{103,678.16}{10} = 10367.8$ Sample var(Y) = 1,708,150

$\bar{X} = \dfrac{1,835.94}{10} = 183.594$ Sample var(X) = 216.898

Source: Data on X and Y are from the *Economic Report of the President*, 2008, Tables B-95, B-96, and B-60, respectively.

Analogous to the population covariance defined in Eq. (B.23), the **sample covariance** between two random variables X and Y is defined as

$$\text{Sample cov } (X, Y) = \frac{\Sigma(X_i - \overline{X})(Y_i - \overline{Y})}{n - 1} \qquad \text{(B.45)}$$

which is simply the sum of the cross products of the two random variables expressed as deviations from their (sample) mean values and divided by the degrees of freedom, $(n - 1)$. (If the sample size is large, we may use n as the divisor.) The sample covariance defined in Equation (B.45) is thus the estimator of the population covariance. Its numerical value in a given instance will provide an *estimate* of the population covariance, as in the following example.

In Table B-3 we have given the necessary quantities to compute the sample covariance, which in the present case is

$$\text{Sample cov } (X, Y) = \frac{121{,}992.73}{9} = 13{,}554.75$$

Thus, in the present case the covariance between stock prices and consumer prices is positive. Some analysts believe that investment in stocks is a hedge against inflation; that is, as inflation increases, stock prices increase, too. Apparently, for the period 1998 to 2007 that seems to be the case, although empirical evidence on this subject is not unequivocal.

Sample Correlation Coefficient

In Eq. (B.29) we defined the population correlation coefficient between two random variables. Its sample analogue, or estimator, which we denote by the symbol r, is as follows:

$$r = \frac{\Sigma_{i=1}^{n}(X_i - \overline{X})(Y_i - \overline{Y})/(n - 1)}{S_x S_y}$$

$$= \frac{\text{sample cov } (X, Y)}{\text{s.d.}(X)\text{s.d.}(Y)} \qquad \text{(B.46)}$$

The **sample correlation** coefficient thus defined has the same properties as the population correlation coefficient ρ; they both lie between -1 and $+1$.

For the data given in Table B-3 you can easily compute the sample standard deviations of Y and X, and therefore can compute the sample correlation coefficient r, an estimate of ρ, which turns out to be

$$r = \frac{13{,}554.75}{(14.727)(1306.962)}$$

$$= 0.7042$$

Thus, in our example stock prices and consumer prices are pretty positively correlated because the computed value is close to 1.

Sample Skewness and Kurtosis

To compute **sample skewness** and **sample kurtosis** values, we use the sample third and fourth moments (compare with Eqs. [B.36] and [B.37]). The sample third moment (compare with the formula for sample variance) is

$$\frac{\Sigma(X - \overline{X})^3}{(n - 1)} \tag{B.47}$$

and the sample fourth moment is

$$\frac{\Sigma(X - \overline{X})^4}{(n - 1)} \tag{B.48}$$

Using the data given in Table B-3, calculate the sample third and fourth moments and divide them by the standard deviation value to the third and fourth powers, respectively. Verify that the sample skewness and kurtosis measures for the Dow Jones average are 0.6873 and 2.9447, respectively, suggesting that the distribution of the Dow Jones average is positively skewed and that it is flatter than a normal distribution.

B.8 SUMMARY

After introducing several fundamental concepts of probability, random variables, probability distributions, etc., in Appendix A, in this appendix we discussed some major characteristics or moments of probability distributions of random variables, such as the expected value, variance, covariance, correlation, skewness, kurtosis, conditional expectation, and conditional variance. We also discussed the famous Chebyshev's inequality. The discussion of these concepts has been somewhat intuitive, for our objective here is not to teach statistics per se but simply to review some of its major concepts that are needed to follow the various topics discussed in the main chapters of this book.

In this appendix we also presented several important formulas. These formulas tell us how to compute the probabilities of random variables and how to estimate the characteristics of probability distributions (i.e., the moments), such as the expected or mean value, variance, covariance, correlation, and conditional expectation. In presenting these formulas, we made a careful distinction between the *population moments* and *sample moments* and gave the appropriate computing formulas. Thus, $E(X)$, the expected value of the r.v. X, is a population moment, that is, the mean value of X if the entire population of the X values were known. On the other hand, $\overline{X}$ is a sample moment, that is, the average value of X if it is based on sample values of X and not on the entire population. In statistics the dichotomy between the population and the sample is very important, for in most applications we have only one or two samples from some population of interest and often we want to draw inferences about the population moments on the basis of the sample moments. We will explain how this is done in Appendixes C and D.

KEY TERMS AND CONCEPTS

The key terms and concepts introduced in this appendix are

Characteristics (moments) of
univariate PMFs
   a) expected value (population
      mean value)
   b) variance
   c) standard deviation (s.d.)
   d) coefficient of variation (V)
Characteristics of multivariate PDFs
   a) covariance
   b) (population) coefficient of
      correlation
   c) correlation
   d) conditional expectation
   e) unconditional expectation
   f) conditional variance

   g) unconditional variance
   h) skewness (S)
   i) kurtosis (K)
Population vs. sample
   a) sample moments
   b) sample mean
   c) estimator; estimate
   d) sample variance
   e) degrees of freedom
   f) sample standard deviation
      (sample s.d.)
   g) sample covariance
   h) sample correlation
   i) sample skewness
   j) sample kurtosis

QUESTIONS

B.1. What is meant by the moments of a PDF? What are the most frequently used moments?

B.2. Explain the meaning of
   a. expected value
   b. variance
   c. standard deviation
   d. covariance
   e. correlation
   f. conditional expectation

B.3. Explain the meaning of
   a. sample mean
   b. sample variance
   c. sample standard deviation
   d. sample covariance
   e. sample correlation

B.4. Why is it important to make the distinction between population moments and sample moments?

B.5. Fill in the gaps in the manner of (a) below.
   a. The expected value or mean is a measure of central tendency.
   b. The variance is a measure of . . .
   c. The covariance is a measure of . . .
   d. The correlation is a measure of . . .

B.6. A random variable (r.v.) X has a mean value of $50 and its standard deviation (s.d.) is $5. Is it correct to say that its variance is $25 squared? Why or why not?

B.7. Explain whether the following statements are true or false. Give reasons.
   a. Although the expected value of an r.v. can be positive or negative, its variance is always positive.

b. The coefficient of correlation will have the same sign as that of the covariance between the two variables.

c. The conditional and unconditional expectations of an r.v. mean the same thing.

d. If two variables are independent, their correlation coefficient will always be zero.

e. If the correlation coefficient between two variables is zero, it means that the two variables are independent.

f. $E\left(\frac{1}{X}\right) = \frac{1}{E(X)}$

g. $E[X - \mu_X]^2 = [E(X - \mu_X)]^2$

PROBLEMS

B.8. Refer to Problem A.12.

    a. Find the expected value of X.

    b. What is the variance and standard deviation of X?

    c. What is the coefficient of variation of X?

    d. Find the skewness and kurtosis values of X.

B.9. The following table gives the anticipated 1-year rates of return from a certain investment and their probabilities.

TABLE B-4 ANTICIPATED 1-YEAR RATE OF RETURN FROM A CERTAIN INVESTMENT

Rate of return (X) %	$f(X)$
-20	0.10
-10	0.15
10	0.45
25	0.25
30	0.05
Total	1.00

    a. What is the expected rate of return from this investment?

    b. Find the variance and standard deviation of the rate of return.

    c. Find the skewness and kurtosis coefficients.

    d. Find the cumulative distribution function (CDF) and obtain the probability that the rate of return is 10 percent or less.

B.10. The following table gives the joint PDF of random variables X and Y, where X = the first-year rate of return (%) expected from investment A, and Y = the first-year rate of return (%) expected from investment B.

TABLE B-5 RATES OF RETURN ON TWO INVESTMENTS

Y(%)	X (%)			
	-10	0	20	30
20	0.27	0.08	0.16	0.00
50	0.00	0.04	0.10	0.35

a. Find the marginal distributions of Y and X.
b. Calculate the expected rate of return from investment B.
c. Find the conditional distribution of Y, given $X = 20$.
d. Are X and Y independent random variables? How do you know? Hint:

$$E(XY) = \sum_{X=1}^{4} \sum_{Y=1}^{2} X_i Y_i f(X_i, Y_i)$$

B.11. You are told that $E(X) = 8$ and var $(X) = 4$. What are the expected values and variances of the following expressions?
   a. $Y = 3X + 2$
   b. $Y = 0.6X - 4$
   c. $Y = X/4$
   d. $Y = aX + b$, where a and b are constants
   e. $Y = 3X^2 + 2$
   How would you express these formulas verbally?

B.12. Consider formulas (B.32) and (B.33). Let X stand for the rate of return on a security, say, IBM, and Y the rate of return on another security, say, General Foods. Let $s_X^2 = 16$, $s_Y^2 = 9$, and $r = -0.8$. What is the variance of $(X + Y)$ in this case? Is it greater than or smaller than var (X) + var (Y)? In this instance, is it better to invest equally in the two securities (i.e., diversify) than in either security exclusively? This problem is the essence of the *portfolio theory* of finance. (See, for example, Richard Brealey and Stewart Myers, *Principles of Corporate Finance,* McGraw-Hill, New York, latest edition.)

B.13. Table B-6 gives data on the number of new business incorporations (Y) and the number of business failures (X) for the United States from 1984 to 1995.
   a. What is the average value of new business incorporations? And the variance?
   b. What is the average value of business failures? And the variance?
   c. What is the covariance between Y and X? And the correlation coefficient?

TABLE B-6 NUMBER OF NEW BUSINESS
INCORPORATIONS (Y) AND NUMBER OF
BUSINESS FAILURES (X), UNITED STATES,
1984–1995

YEAR	Y	X
1984	634,991	52,078
1985	664,235	57,253
1986	702,738	61,616
1987	685,572	61,111
1988	685,095	57,097
1989	676,565	50,361
1990	647,366	60,747
1991	628,604	88,140
1992	666,800	97,069
1993	706,537	86,133
1994	741,778	71,558
1995	766,988	71,128

Source: Economic Report of the President, 2004,
Table B-96, p. 395.

d. Are the two variables independent?

e. If there is correlation between the two variables, does this mean that one variable causes the other variable? That is, do new incorporations cause business failures, or vice versa?

B.14. For Problem A.13, find out the var $(X + Y)$. How would you interpret this variance?

B.15. Refer to Table 1-2 given in Problem 1.6.

a. Compute the covariances between the S&P 500 index and the CPI and between the three-month Treasury bill rate and the CPI. Are these population or sample covariances?

b. Compute the correlation coefficients between the S&P 500 index and the CPI and between the three-month Treasury bill rate and the CPI. A priori, would you expect these correlation coefficients to be positive or negative? Why?

c. If there is a positive relationship between the CPI and the three-month Treasury bill rate, does that mean *inflation*, as measured by the CPI, is the *cause* of higher T bill rates?

B.16. Refer to Table 1-3 in Problem 1.7. Let ER stand for U.K. pound/$ exchange rate (i.e., the number of U.K. pounds per U.S. dollar) and RPR stand for the ratio of the U.S. CPI/U.K. CPI. Is the correlation between ER and RPR expected to be positive or negative? Why? Show your computations. Would your answer change if you found correlation between ER and (1/RPR)? Why?

OPTIONAL EXERCISES

B.17. Find the expected value of the following PDF:

$$f(X) = \frac{X^2}{9} \quad 0 \le x \le 3$$

B.18. Show that

a. $E(X^2) \ge [E(X)]^2$ *Hint:* Recall the definition of variance.

b. cov $(X, Y) = E[(X - \mu_X)(Y - \mu_Y)]$
$$= E(XY) - \mu_X\mu_Y$$
where $\mu_X = E(X)$ and $\mu_Y = E(Y)$.
How would you express these formulas verbally?

B.19. Establish Eq. (B.15). *Hint:* Var $(aX) = E[aX - E(aX)]^2$ and simplify.

B.20. Establish Eq. (B.17). *Hint:* Var $(aX + bY) = E[(aX + bY) - E(aX + bY)]^2$ and simplify.

B.21. According to Chebyshev's inequality, what percentage of any set of data must lie within c standard deviations on either side of the mean value if (a) $c = 2.5$ and (b) $c = 8$?

B.22. Show that $E(X - k)^2 = $ var $(X) + [E(X) - k]^2$. For what value of k will $E(X - k)^2$ be minimum? And what is that value of k?

B.23. For the PC/printer sales example discussed in this appendix compute the conditional variance of Y (printers sold) given that X (PCs sold) is 2. *Hint:* Use the conditional expectation given in Example B.9 and use the formula:

$$\text{var } (Y \mid X = 2) = \sum[Y_i - E(Y \mid X = 2)]^2 f(Y \mid X = 2)$$

B.24. Compute the expected value and variance for the PDF given in Problem A.19.

APPENDIX C

SOME IMPORTANT PROBABILITY DISTRIBUTIONS

In Appendix B we noted that a random variable (r.v.) can be described by a few characteristics, or moments, of its probability function (PDF or PMF), such as the expected value and variance. This, however, presumes that we know the PDF of that r.v., which is a tall order since there are all kinds of random variables. In practice, however, some random variables occur so frequently that statisticians have determined their PDFs and documented their properties. For our purpose, we will consider only those PDFs that are of direct interest to us. But keep in mind that there are several other PDFs that statisticians have studied which can be found in any standard statistics textbook. In this appendix we will discuss the following four probability distributions:

1. The normal distribution
2. The t distribution
3. The chi-square (χ^2) distribution
4. The F distribution

These probability distributions are important in their own right, but for our purposes they are especially important because they help us to find out the probability distributions of estimators (or *statistics*), such as the sample mean and sample variance. Recall that estimators are random variables. Equipped with that knowledge, we will be able to draw inferences about their true population values. For example, if we know the probability distribution of the sample mean, $\overline{X}$, we will be able to draw inferences about the true, or population, mean μ_X. Similarly, if we know the probability distribution of the sample variance S_X^2, we will be able to say something about the true population variance, σ_X^2. This is the essence of *statistical inference*, or drawing conclusions about some characteristics (i.e., moments) of the population on the basis of the sample at hand. We will discuss in depth how this is accomplished in Appendix D. For now we discuss the salient features of the four probability distributions.

461

C.1   THE NORMAL DISTRIBUTION

Perhaps the single most important probability distribution involving a continuous r.v. is the **normal distribution.** Its *bell-shaped* picture, as shown in Figure A-3, should be familiar to anyone with a modicum of statistical knowledge. Experience has shown that the normal distribution is a reasonably good model for a continuous r.v. whose value depends on a number of factors, each factor exerting a comparatively small positive or negative influence. Thus, consider the r.v. body weight. It is likely to be normally distributed because factors such as heredity, bone structure, diet, exercise, and metabolism are each expected to have some influence on weight, yet no single factor dominates the others. Likewise, variables such as height and grade-point average are also found to be normally distributed.

For notational convenience, we express a normally distributed r.v. X as

$$X \sim N\left(\mu_X, \sigma_X^2\right) \tag{C.1}[1]$$

where $\sim$ means distributed as, N stands for the normal distribution, and the quantities inside the parentheses are the *parameters* of the distribution, namely, its (population) mean or expected value μ_X and its variance σ_X^2. Note that X is a continuous r.v. and may take any value in the range $-\infty$ to ∞.

Properties of the Normal Distribution

1. The normal distribution curve, as Figure A-3 shows, is symmetrical around its mean value μ_X.
2. The PDF of a normally distributed r.v. is highest at its mean value but tails off at its extremities (i.e., in the tails of the distribution). That is, the probability of obtaining a value of a normally distributed r.v. far away from its mean value becomes progressively smaller. For example, the probability of someone exceeding the height of 7.5 feet is very small.
3. As a matter of fact, *approximately* 68 percent of the area under the normal curve lies between the values of $(\mu_X \pm \sigma_X)$, approximately 95 percent of the area lies between $(\mu_X \pm 2\sigma_X)$, and approximately 99.7 percent of the area lies between $(\mu_X \pm 3\sigma_X)$, as shown in Figure C-1. As noted in Appendix A, and

---

[1]For the mathematically inclined student, here is the mathematical equation for the PDF of a normally distributed r.v. X:

$$f(X) = \frac{1}{\sigma_X \sqrt{2\pi}} \exp\left\{-\frac{1}{2}\left(\frac{X - \mu_X}{\sigma_X}\right)^2\right\}$$

where exp{ } means e raised to the power the expression inside { }, $e \approx 2.71828$ (the base of natural logarithm), and $\pi \approx 3.14159$. μ_X and σ_X^2, known as the parameters of the distribution, are, respectively, the mean, or expected value, and the variance of the distribution.

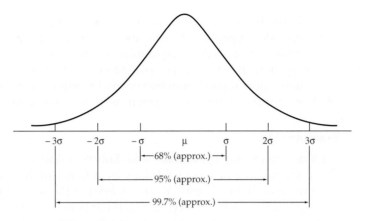

FIGURE C-1   Areas under the normal curve

discussed further subsequently, these areas can be used as measures of probabilities. The total area under the curve is 1, or 100 percent.

4. A normal distribution is *fully described by its two parameters,* μ_X and σ_X^2. That is, once the values of these two parameters are known, we can find out the probability of X lying within a certain interval from the mathematical formula given in footnote 1. Fortunately, we do not have to compute the probabilities from this formula because these probabilities can be obtained easily from the specially prepared table in Appendix E (Table E-1). We will explain how to use this table shortly.

5. A *linear combination (function) of two (or more) normally distributed random variables is itself normally distributed*—an especially important property of the normal distribution in econometrics. To illustrate, let

$$X \sim N\left(\mu_X, \sigma_X^2\right)$$

$$Y \sim N\left(\mu_Y, \sigma_Y^2\right)$$

and assume that X and Y are *independent*.[2]

Now consider the linear combination of these two variables: $W = aX + bY$, where a and b are constant (e.g., $W = 2X + 4Y$); then

$$W \sim N[\mu_W, \sigma_W^2] \qquad \text{(C.2)}$$

where

$$\mu_W = (a\mu_X + b\mu_Y)$$
$$\sigma_W^2 = \left(a^2\sigma_X^2 + b^2\sigma_Y^2\right) \qquad \text{(C.3)}$$

[2]Recall that two variables are independently distributed if their joint PDF (PMF) is the product of their marginal PDFs, that is, $f(X, Y) = f(X)f(Y)$, for all values of X and Y.

Note that in Eq. (C.3) we have used some of the properties of the expectation operator E and the variances of independent random variables discussed in Appendix B. (See Section B.2.)[3] Incidentally, expression (C.2) can be extended straightforwardly to a linear combination of more than two normal random variables.

6. For a normal distribution, skewness (S) is zero and kurtosis (K) is 3.

Example C.1.

Let X denote the number of roses sold daily by a florist in uptown Manhattan and Y the number of roses sold daily by a florist in downtown Manhattan. Assume that both X and Y are *independently* normally distributed as $X \sim N(100, 64)$ and $Y \sim N(150, 81)$. What is the average value of the roses sold in two days by the two florists and the corresponding variance of sale? Here $W = 2X + 2Y$. Therefore, following expression (C.3), we have $E(W) = E(2X + 2Y) = 500$ and $\text{var}(W) = 4 \text{ var}(X) + 4 \text{ var}(Y) = 580$. Therefore, W is distributed normally with a mean value of 500 and a variance of 580: [$W \sim N(500, 580)$].

The Standard Normal Distribution

Although a normal distribution is fully specified by its two parameters, (population) mean or expected value and variance, one normal distribution can differ from another in either its mean or variance, or both, as shown in Figure C-2.

How do we compare the various normal distributions shown in Figure C-2? Since these normal distributions differ in either their mean values or variances, or both, let us define a new variable, Z, as follows:

$$Z = \frac{X - \mu_X}{\sigma_X} \tag{C.4}$$

If the variable X has a mean μ_X and a variance σ_X^2, it can be shown that the Z variable defined previously has a mean value of zero and a variance of 1 (or unity). (For proof, see Problem C.26). In statistics such a variable is known as a **unit** or **standardized variable.**

If $X \sim N(\mu_X, \sigma_X^2)$, then Z as defined in Eq. (C.4) is known as a **unit** or **standard normal variable**, that is, a normal variable with zero mean and unit (or 1) variance. We write such a normal variable as:

$$Z \sim N(0, 1) \tag{C.5}[4]$$

---

[3]Note that if X and Y are normally distributed but are not independent, W is still normally distributed with the mean given in Eq. (C.3) but with the following variance (cf. Eq. B.27): $\sigma_w^2 = a^2 \sigma_X^2 + b^2 \sigma_y^2 + 2ab \text{ cov } (X, Y)$.

[4]This can be proved easily by noting the property of the normal distribution that a linear function of a normally distributed variable is itself normally distributed. Note that given μ_X and σ_X^2, Z is a linear function of X.

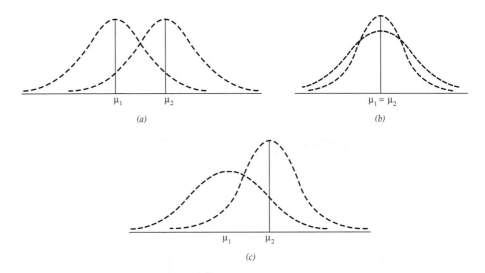

FIGURE C-2 (*a*) Different means, same variance; (*b*) same mean, different variances; (*c*) different means, different variances

Thus, *any normally distributed r.v. with a given mean and variance can be converted to a standard normal variable,* which greatly simplifies our task of computing probabilities, as we will show shortly.

The PDF and CDF (cumulative distribution function) of the standard normal distribution are shown in Figures C-3(*a*) and C-3(*b*), respectively. (See Section A.5 on the definitions of PDF and CDF. See also Tables E-1(*a*) and E-1(*b*) in Appendix E.) The CDF, like any other CDF, gives the probability that the standard normal variable takes a value equal to or less than *z*, that is, $P(Z \leq z)$, where *z* is a specific numerical value of Z.

To illustrate how we use the standard normal distribution to compute various probabilities, we consider several concrete examples.

Example C.2.

It is given that *X*, the daily sale of bread in a bakery, follows the normal distribution with a mean of 70 loaves and a variance of 9; that is, $X \sim N(70, 9)$. What is the probability that on any given day the sale of bread is greater than 75 loaves?

Since *X* follows the normal distribution with the stated mean and variance, it follows that

$$Z = \frac{75 - 70}{3} = \approx 1.67$$

follows the standard normal distribution. Therefore, we want to find[5]

$$P(Z > 1.67)$$

[5]*Note:* Whether we write $P(Z > 1.67)$ or $P(Z \geq 1.67)$ is immaterial because, as noted in Appendix A, the probability that a continuous r.v. takes a particular value (e.g., 1.67) is always zero.

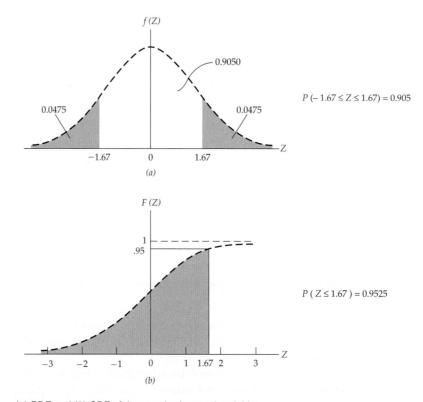

FIGURE C-3   (a) PDF and (b) CDF of the standard normal variable

Now Table E-1(*b*) in Appendix E gives the CDF of the standard normal distribution between the values of $Z = -3.0$ to $Z = 3.0$. For example, this table shows that the probability that Z lies between -3.0 to $Z = 1.67 = 0.9525$. Therefore,

$$P(Z > 1.67) = 1 - 0.9525 = 0.0475$$

That is, the probability of the daily sale of bread exceeding 75 loaves of bread is 0.0475 or about 4.75 percent. (See Figure C-3[*a*].)

Example C.3.

Continue with Example C.2, but suppose we now want to find out the probability of a daily sale of bread of 75 or fewer loaves. The answer is obvious from the previous example, namely, that this probability is 0.9525 which is shown in Figure C-3(*b*).

Example C.4.

Continue with Example C.2, but now suppose we want to find out the probability that the daily sale of bread is between 65 and 75 loaves. To compute this probability, we first compute

$$Z_1 = \frac{65 - 70}{3} = \approx -1.67$$

$$Z_2 = \frac{75 - 70}{3} = \approx 1.67$$

Now from Table E-1 we see that

$$P(-3.0 \leq Z \leq -1.67) = 0.0475$$

and

$$P(-3.0 \leq Z \leq 1.67) = 0.9525$$

Therefore,

$$P(-1.67 \leq Z \leq 1.67) = 0.9525 - 0.0475 = 0.9050$$

That is, the probability is 90.5 percent that the sales volume will lie between 65 and 75 loaves of bread per day, as shown in Figure C-3(a).

Example C.5.

Continue with the preceding example but now assume that we want to find the probability that the sale of bread either exceeds 75 loaves or is less than 65 loaves per day. If you have mastered the previous examples, you can see easily that this probability is 0.0950, as shown in Figure C-3(a).

As the preceding examples show, once we know that a particular r.v. follows the normal distribution with a given mean and variance, all we have to do is convert that variable into the standard normal variable and compute the relevant probabilities from the standard normal table (Table E-1). It is indeed remarkable that just one standard normal distribution table suffices to deal with any normally distributed variable regardless of its specific mean and variance values.

As we have remarked earlier, the normal distribution is probably the single most important theoretical probability distribution because several (continuous) random variables are found to be normally distributed or at least approximately so. We will show this in Section C.2. But before that, we consider some practical problems in dealing with the normal distribution.

TABLE C-1   25 RANDOM NUMBERS FROM $N(0, 1)$ AND $N(2, 4)$

$N(0, 1)$	$N(2, 4)$	$N(0, 1)$	$N(2, 4)$
−0.48524	4.25181	0.22968	0.21487
0.46262	0.01395	−0.00719	−0.47726
2.23092	0.09037	−0.71217	1.32007
−0.23644	1.96909	−0.53126	−1.25406
1.10679	1.62206	−1.02664	3.09222
−0.82070	1.17653	−1.29535	1.05375
0.86553	2.78722	−0.61502	0.58124
−0.40199	2.41138	−1.80753	1.55853
1.13667	2.58235	0.20687	1.71083
−2.05585	0.40786	−0.19653	0.90193
2.98962	0.24596	2.49463	−0.14726
0.61674	−3.45379	0.94602	−3.69238
−0.32833	3.29003		

Random Sampling from a Normal Population

Since the normal distribution is used so extensively in theoretical and practical statistics, it is important to know how we can obtain a random sample from such a population. Suppose we wish to draw a random sample of 25 observations from a normal probability distribution with a mean of zero and variance of 1 [i.e., the standard normal distribution, $N(0, 1)$]. How do we obtain such a sample?

Most statistical packages have routines, called **random number generators,** to obtain random samples from the most frequently used probability distributions. For example, using the MINITAB statistical package, we obtained 25 random numbers from an $N(0, 1)$ normal population. These are shown in the first column of Table C-1. Also shown in column 2 of the table is another random sample of 25 observations obtained from a normal population with mean 2 and variance 4 (i.e., $N(2, 4)$).[6] Of course, you can generate as many samples as wanted by the procedure just described.

The Sampling or Probability Distribution of the Sample Mean $\bar{X}$

In Appendix B we introduced the sample mean (see Eq. [B.43]) as an estimator of the population mean. But since the sample mean is based on a given sample, its value will vary from sample to sample; that is, the sample mean can be treated as an r.v., which will have its own PDF. Can we find out the PDF of the sample mean? The answer is yes, provided the sample is drawn randomly.

---

[6]MINITAB will generate a random sample from a normal population with a given mean variance. Actually, once we obtain a random sample from the standard normal distribution [i.e., $N(0, 1)$], we can easily convert this sample to a normal population with a different mean and variance. Let $Y = a + bZ$, where Z is $N(0, 1)$, and where a and b are constants. Since Y is a linear combination of a normally distributed variable, Y is itself normally distributed with $E(Y) = E(a + bZ) = a$, since $E(Z) = 0$ and var $(a + bZ) = b^2$ var $(Z) = b^2$, since var $(Z) = 1$. Hence, $Y \sim N(a, b^2)$. Therefore, if you multiply the values of Z by b and add a to it, you will have a sample from a normal population with mean a and variance b^2. Thus, if $a = 2$ and $b = 2$, we have $Y \sim N(2, 4)$.

In Appendix B we described the notion of random sampling in an intuitive way by letting each member of the population have an equal chance of being included in the sample. In statistics, however, the term **random sampling** is used in a rather special sense. *We say that $X_1, X_2, \ldots, X_n$ constitutes a random sample of size n if all these X's are drawn independently from the same probability distribution (i.e., each X_i has the same PDF).* The X's thus drawn are known as **i.i.d.** (*independently and identically distributed*) **random variables.** In the remainder of this appendix and the main chapters of the text, therefore, the term *random sample* will denote a sample of i.i.d. random variables. For brevity, sometimes we will use the term an *i.i.d. sample* to mean a random sample in the sense just described.

Thus, if each $X_i \sim N(\mu_X, \sigma_X^2)$ and if each X_i value is drawn independently, then we say that $X_1, X_2, \ldots, X_n$ are i.i.d. random variables, the normal PDF being their common probability distribution. Note two things about this definition: First, each X included in the sample must have the *same* PDF and, second, each X included in the sample is drawn independently of the others.

Given the very important concept of random sampling, we now develop another very important concept in statistics, namely, the concept of the **sampling,** or **probability, distribution of an estimator,** such as, say, the sample mean, $\overline{X}$. A firm comprehension of this concept is absolutely essential to understand the topic of statistical inference in Appendix D and for our discussion of econometrics in the main chapters of the text. Since many students find the concept of sampling distribution somewhat bewildering, we will explain it with an example.

Example C.6.

Consider a normal distribution with a mean value of 10 and a variance of 4, that is, $N(10, 4)$. From this population we obtain 20 random samples of 20 observations each. For each sample thus drawn, we obtain the sample mean value, $\overline{X}$. Thus we have a total of 20 sample means. These are collected in Table C-2.

Let us group these 20 means in a frequency distribution, as shown in Table C-3.

The frequency distribution of the sample means given in Table C-3 may be called the *empirical sampling,* or *probability, distribution* of the sample means.[7] Plotting this empirical distribution, we obtain the bar diagram shown in Figure C-4.

If we connect the heights of the various bars shown in the figure, we obtain the *frequency polygon,* which *resembles* the shape of the normal distribution. If we had drawn many more such samples, would the frequency polygon take the familiar bell-shaped curve of the normal distribution? That is, would the sampling distribution of the sample mean in fact follow the normal distribution? Indeed, this is the case.

[7]The sampling distribution of an estimator is like the probability distribution of any random variable, except that the random variable in this case happens to be an estimator or a statistic. Put differently, a *sampling distribution is a probability distribution where the random variable is an estimator,* such as the sample mean or sample variance.

TABLE C-2 20 SAMPLE MEANS FROM $N(10, 4)$

Sample means ($\bar{X}_i$)	
9.641	10.134
10.040	10.249
9.174	10.321
10.840	10.399
10.480	9.404
11.386	8.621
9.740	9.739
9.937	10.184
10.250	9.765
10.334	10.410

Sum of 20 sample means = 201.05

$$\bar{\bar{X}} = \frac{201.05}{20} = 10.052$$

$$\text{Var}(\bar{X}_i) = \frac{\Sigma(\bar{X}_i - \bar{\bar{X}})^2}{19}$$

$$= 0.339 \quad \textit{Note: } \bar{\bar{X}} = \frac{\Sigma\bar{X}_i}{n}$$

TABLE C-3 FREQUENCY DISTRIBUTION OF 20 SAMPLE MEANS

Range of sample mean	Absolute frequency	Relative frequency
8.5–8.9	1	0.05
9.0–9.4	1	0.05
9.5–9.9	5	0.25
10.0–10.4	8	0.40
10.5–10.9	4	0.20
11.0–11.4	1	0.05
Total	20	1.00

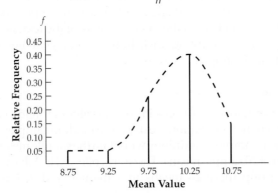

FIGURE C-4 Distribution of 20 sample means from $N(10, 4)$ population

Here we rely on statistical theory: If $X_1, X_2, \ldots, X_n$ is a *random sample* from a normal population with mean μ_X and variance σ_X^2, then the sample mean, $\bar{X}$, also follows the normal distribution with the same mean μ_X but with variance $\frac{\sigma_X^2}{n}$, that is,

$$\bar{X} \sim N\left(\mu_X, \frac{\sigma_X^2}{n}\right) \tag{C.6}$$

In other words, the sampling (or probability) distribution of the sample mean, $\bar{X}$ the estimator of μ_X, also follows the normal distribution with the same mean as that of each X_i but with variance equal to the variance of $X_i(= \sigma_X^2)$ *divided by the sample size n* (for proof, see Problem C.25). As you can see for $n > 1$, the variance of the sample mean will be much smaller than the variance of any X_i. To see this graphically, go to **www.ruf.rice.edu/~lane/stat_sim** and ruin the sampling distribution applet. This will demonstrate how the distribution of sample means changes for different population distributions and different sample sizes.

If we take the (positive) square root of the variance of $\overline{X}$, we obtain $\frac{\sigma_X}{\sqrt{n}}$, which is called the **standard error** (se) of $\overline{X}$, which is akin to the concept of standard deviation. Historically, the square root of the variance of a random variable is called the standard deviation and the square root of the variance of an estimator is called the standard error. Since an estimator is also a random variable, there is no need to distinguish the two terms. But we will keep the distinction because it is so well entrenched in statistics.

Returning to our example, then, the expected value of $\overline{X}_i$, $E(\overline{X}_i)$, should be 10, and its variance should be $4/20 = 0.20$. If we take the mean value of the 20 sample means given in Table C-2, call it the *grand mean* $\overline{\overline{X}}$, it should be about equal to $E(\overline{X}_i)$, and if we compute the sample variance of these 20 sample means, it should be about equal to 0.20. As Table C-2 shows, $\overline{\overline{X}} = 10.052$, about equal to the expected value of 10 and var$(\overline{X}_i) = 0.339$, which is not quite close to 0.20. Why the difference?

Notice that the data given in Table C-2 is based only on 20 samples. As noted, if we had many more samples (each based on 20 observations), we would come close to the theoretical result of mean 10 and variance of 0.20. It is comforting to know that we have such a useful theoretical result. As a consequence, we do not have to conduct the type of sampling experiment shown in Table C-2, which can be time-consuming. Just based on one random sample from the normal distribution, we can say that the expected value of the sample mean is equal to the true mean value of μ_X. As we will show in Appendix D, knowledge that a particular estimator follows a particular probability distribution will immensely help us in relating a sample quantity to its population counterpart. In passing, note that as a result of Eq. (C.6), it follows at once that

$$Z = \frac{(\overline{X} - \mu_X)}{\frac{\sigma_X}{\sqrt{n}}} \sim N(0, 1) \tag{C.7}$$

that is, a standard normal variable. Therefore, you can easily compute from the standard normal distribution table the probabilities that a given sample mean is greater than or less than a given population mean. An example follows.

Example C.7.

Let X denote the number of miles per gallon achieved by cars of a particular model. You are told that $X \sim N(20, 4)$. What is the probability that, for a random sample of 25 cars, the average gallons per mile will be

  a. greater than 21 miles
  b. less than 18 miles
  c. between 19 and 21 miles?

Since X follows the normal distribution with mean $= 20$ and variance $= 4$, we know that $\overline{X}$ also follows the normal distribution with mean $= 20$ and variance $= 4/25$. As a result, we know that

$$Z = \frac{\overline{X} - 20}{\sqrt{4/25}} = \frac{\overline{X} - 20}{0.4} \sim N(0, 1)$$

That is, Z follows the standard normal distribution. Therefore, we want to find

$$P(\overline{X} > 21) = P\left(Z > \frac{21 - 20}{0.4}\right)$$

$$= P(Z > 2.5)$$

$$= 0.062 \text{ (From Table E } = 1[b])$$

$$P(\overline{X} < 18) = P\left(Z < \frac{18 - 20}{0.4}\right)$$

$$= P(Z < -5) \approx 0$$

$$P(19 \le \overline{X} \le 21) = P(-2.5 \le Z \le 2.5)$$

$$= 0.9876$$

Before moving on, note that the sampling experiment we conducted in Table C-2 is an illustration of the so-called **Monte Carlo experiments** or **Monte Carlo simulations**. They are a very inexpensive method of studying properties of various statistical models, especially when conducting real experiments would be time-consuming and expensive (see Problems C.21, C.22, and C.23).

The Central Limit Theorem (CLT)

We have just shown that the sample mean of a sample drawn from a normal population also follows the normal distribution. But what about samples drawn from other populations? There is a remarkable theorem in statistics—the **central limit theorem (CLT)**—originally proposed by the French mathematician Laplace, which states that if $X_1, X_2, \ldots, X_n$ is a random sample from *any* population (i.e., probability distribution) with mean μ_X and σ_X^2, the sample mean $\overline{X}$ tends to be normally distributed with mean μ_X and variance $\frac{\sigma_X^2}{n}$ *as the sample size increases indefinitely* (technically, infinitely).[8] Of course, if the X_i happen to be from the normal population, the sample mean follows the normal distribution regardless of the sample size. This is shown in Figure C-5.

---

[8]In practice, no matter what the underlying probability distribution is, the sample mean of a sample size of at least 30 observations will be approximately normal.

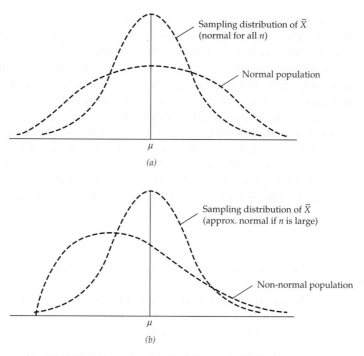

FIGURE C-5   The central limit theorem: (a) Samples drawn from a normal population; (b) samples drawn from a non-normal population

C.2   THE *t* DISTRIBUTION

The probability distribution that we use most intensively in this book is the **t distribution,** also known as **Student's t distribution.**[9] It is closely related to the normal distribution.

To introduce this distribution, recall that if $\overline{X} \sim N(\mu_X, \sigma_X^2/n)$, the variable

$$Z = \frac{(\overline{X} - \mu_X)}{\sigma_X/\sqrt{n}} \sim N(0, 1)$$

that is, the standard normal distribution. This is so provided that both μ_X and σ_X^2 are known. But suppose we only know μ_X and estimate σ_X^2 by its (sample) estimator $S_x^2 = \frac{\Sigma(X_i - \overline{X})^2}{n-1}$, given in Eq. (B.44). Replacing σ_X by S_x, that is, replacing the population standard deviation (s.d.) by the sample s.d., in Equation (C.7), we obtain a new variable

$$t = \frac{\overline{X} - \mu_X}{S_x/\sqrt{n}} \tag{C.8}$$

[9]*Student* was the pseudonym of W. S. Gosset, who used to work as a statistician for the Guinness Brewery in Dublin. He discovered this probability distribution in 1908.

Statistical theory shows that the t variable thus defined follows Student's t distribution with $(n-1)$ d.f. Just as the mean and variance are the parameters of the normal distribution, the t distribution has a single parameter, namely, the d.f., which in the present case are $(n-1)$. *Note:* Before we compute S_x^2 (and hence S_x), we must first compute $\overline{X}$. But since we use the same sample to compute $\overline{X}$, we have $(n-1)$, not n, independent observations to compute S^2; so to speak, we lose 1 d.f.

In sum, if we draw random samples from a normal population with mean μ_X and variance σ_X^2 but replace σ_X^2 by its estimator S_x^2, the sample mean $\overline{X}$ follows the t distribution. A t-distributed r.v. is often designated as t_k, where k denotes the d.f. (To avoid confusion with the sample size n, we use the subscript k to denote the d.f. in general.) Table E-2 in Appendix E tabulates the t distribution for various d.f. We will demonstrate the use of this table shortly.

Properties of the t Distribution

1. The t distribution, like the normal distribution, is symmetric, as shown in Figure C-6.
2. The mean of the t distribution, like the standard normal distribution, is zero, but its variance is $k/(k-2)$. Therefore, the variance of the t distribution is defined for d.f. greater than 2.

We have already seen that for the standard normal distribution the variance is always 1, which means that the variance of the t distribution is larger than the variance of the standard normal distribution, as shown in Figure C-6. In other words, the t distribution is flatter than the normal distribution. But as k increases, the variance of the t distribution approaches the variance of the standard normal distribution, namely, 1. Thus, if the d.f. are $k = 10$, the variance of the t distribution is $10/8 = 1.25$; if $k = 30$, the variance becomes $30/28 = 1.07$; and when $k = 100$, the variance becomes $100/98 = 1.02$, which is not much greater than 1. As a result, *the t distribution approaches the standard normal distribution as the d.f. increase.* But notice that even for k as small as 30, there is not a

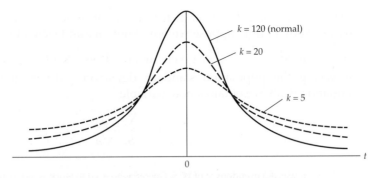

FIGURE C-6   The t distribution for selected degrees of freedom (d.f.)

great difference in the variances of the t and the standard normal variable. Therefore, the sample size does not have to be enormously large for the t distribution to approximate the normal distribution.

To illustrate the t table (Table E-2) given in Appendix E, we now consider a few examples.

Example C.8.

Let us revisit Example C.2. In a period of 15 days the sale of bread averaged 74 loaves with a (sample) s.d. of 4 loaves. What is the probability of obtaining such a sale given that the true average sale is 70 loaves a day?

If we had known the true σ, we could have used the standard normal Z variable to answer this question. But since we know its estimator, S, we can use Eq. (C.8) to compute the t value and use Table E-2 in Appendix E to answer this question as follows:

$$t = \frac{74 - 70}{4/\sqrt{15}}$$

$$= 3.873$$

Notice that in this example the d.f. are $14 = (15 - 1)$. (Why?)

As Table E-2 shows, for 14 d.f. the probability of obtaining a t value of 2.145 or greater is 0.025 (2.5 percent), of 2.624 or greater is 0.01 (1 percent), and of 3.787 or greater is 0.001 (0.1 percent). Therefore, the probability of obtaining a t value of as much as 3.873 or greater must be much smaller than 0.001.

Example C.9.

Let us keep the setup of Example C.8 intact except to assume that the sale of bread averages 72 loaves in the said 15-day period. Now what is the probability of obtaining such a sales figure?

Following exactly the same line of reasoning, the reader can verify that the computed t value is ~1.936. Now from Table E-2 we observe that for 14 d.f. the probability of obtaining a t value of 1.761 or greater is ~0.05 (or 5 percent) and that of 2.145 or greater is 0.025 (or 2.5 percent). Therefore, the probability of obtaining a t value of 1.936 or greater lies somewhere between 2.5 and 5 percent.

Example C.10.

Now assume that in a 15-day period the average sale of bread was 68 loaves with an s.d. of 4 loaves a day. If the true mean sales are 70 loaves a day, what is the probability of obtaining such a sales figure?

Plugging in the relevant numbers in Equation (C.8), we find that the t value in this case is −1.936. But since the t distribution is symmetric, the probability of obtaining a t value of -1.936 or smaller is the same as that of obtaining a t value of $+1.936$ or greater, which, as we saw earlier, is somewhere between 2.5 and 5 percent.

Example C.11.

Again, continue with the previous example. What is the probability that the average sale of bread in the said 15-day period was either greater than 72 loaves or less than 68 loaves?

From Examples C.9 and C.10 we know that the probability of the average sale exceeding 72 or being less than 68 is the same as the probability that a t value either exceeds 1.936 or is smaller than -1.936.[10] These probabilities, as we saw previously, are each between 0.025 and 0.05. Therefore, the total probability will be between 0.05 or 0.10 (or between 5 and 10 percent). In cases like this we would, therefore, compute the probability that $|t| > 1.936$, where $|t|$ means the absolute value of t, that is, the t value disregarding the sign. (For example, the absolute value of 2 is 2 and the absolute value of -2 is also 2.)

From the preceding examples we see that once we compute the **t value** from Eq. (C.8), and once we know the d.f., computing the probabilities of obtaining a given t value involves simply consulting the t table. We will consider further uses of the t table in the regression context at appropriate places in the text.

Example C.12.

For the years 1972 to 2007 the Scholastic Aptitude Test (S.A.T.) scores were as follows:

	Male	Female
Critical reading (average)	510.03	503.00
	(36.54)	(51.09)
Math (average)	524.83	486.36
	(48.31)	(102.07)

Note: The figures in parentheses are the variances.

A random sample of 10 male S.A.T. scores on the critical reading test gave the (sample) mean value of 510.12 and the (sample) variance of 41.08. What is the probability of obtaining such a score knowing that for the entire 1972–2007 period the (true) average score was 510.03?

With the knowledge of the t distribution, we can now answer this question easily. Substituting the relevant values in Eq. (C.8), we obtain

$$t = \frac{510.12 - 510.03}{\sqrt{\frac{41.08}{10}}} = 0.0444$$

[10] Be careful here. The number -2.0 is smaller than -1.936, and the number -2.3 is smaller than -2.0.

This t value has the t distribution with 9 d.f. (Why?) From Table E-2 we observe that the probability of obtaining such a t value is greater than 0.25 or 25 percent.

A note on the use of the t table (Table E-2): With the advent of user-friendly statistical software packages and electronic statistical tables, Table E-2 is now of limited value because it gives probabilities for a few selected d.f. This is also true of the other statistical tables given in Appendix E. Therefore, if you have access to one or more statistical software packages, you can compute probabilities for any given degrees of freedom much more accurately than using those given in the tables in Appendix E.

C.3   THE CHI-SQUARE (χ^2) PROBABILITY DISTRIBUTION

Now that we have derived the sampling distribution of the sample mean $\overline{X}$, (normal if the true standard deviation is known or the t distribution if we use the sample standard deviation) can we derive the sampling distribution of the sample variance, $S^2 = \frac{\Sigma(X_i - \overline{X})^2}{n-1}$, since we use the sample mean and sample variance very frequently in practice? The answer is yes, and the probability distribution that we need for this purpose is the **chi-square (χ^2) probability distribution,** which is very closely related to the normal distribution. Note that just as the sample mean will vary from sample to sample, so will the sample variance. That is, like the sample mean, the sample variance is also a random variable. Of course, when we have a specific sample, we have a specific sample mean and a specific sample variance value.

We already know that if a random variable (r.v.) X follows the normal distribution with mean μ_X and variance σ_X^2, that is, $X \sim N(\mu_X, \sigma_X^2)$, then the r.v. $Z = (X - \mu_X)/\sigma_X$ is a standard normal variable, that is, $Z \sim N(0, 1)$. Statistical theory shows that the *square of a standard normal variable is distributed as a chi-square (χ^2) probability distribution with one degree of freedom (d.f.).* Symbolically,

$$Z^2 = \chi^2_{(1)} \qquad\qquad \textbf{(C.9)}$$

where the subscript (1) of χ^2 shows the **degrees of freedom (d.f.)**—1 in the present case. As in the case of the t distribution, the d.f. is the parameter of the chi-square distribution. In Equation (C.9) there is only 1 d.f. since we are considering only the square of one standard normal variable.

A note on degrees of freedom: In general, the number of d.f. means the number of independent observations available to compute a statistic, such as the sample mean or sample variance. For example, the sample variance of an r.v. X is defined as $S^2 = \Sigma(X_i - \overline{X})^2/(n - 1)$. In this case we say that the number of d.f. is $(n - 1)$ because if we use the same sample to compute the sample mean $\overline{X}$, around which we measure the sample variance, so to speak, we lose one d.f.; that is, we have only $(n - 1)$ independent observations. An example will clarify this further. Consider three X values: 1, 2, and 3. The sample mean is 2. Now since $\Sigma(X_i - \overline{X}) = 0$ always, of the three deviations $(1 - 2)$, $(2 - 2)$, and $(3 - 2)$,

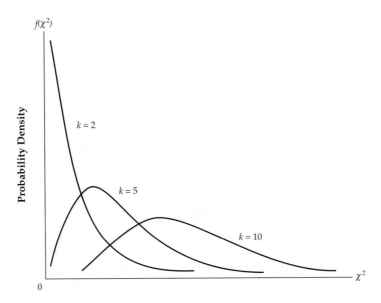

FIGURE C-7   Density function of the χ^2 variable

only two can be chosen arbitrarily; the third must be fixed in such a way that the condition $\sum(X_i - \overline{X}) = 0$ is satisfied.[11] Therefore, in this case, although there are three observations, the d.f. are only 2.

Now let $Z_1, Z_2, \ldots, Z_k$ be k *independent* unit normal variables (i.e., each Z is a normal r.v. with zero mean and unit variance). If we square each of these Z's, we can show that the sum of the squared Z's also follows a chi-square distribution with k d.f. That is,

$$\sum Z_i^2 = Z_1^2 + Z_2^2 + \cdots Z_k^2 \sim \chi_{(k)}^2 \tag{C.10}$$

Note that the d.f. are now k since there are k independent observations in the sum of squares shown in Equation (C.10).

Geometrically, the χ^2 distribution appears as in Figure C-7.

Properties of the Chi-square Distribution

1. As Figure C-7 shows, unlike the normal distribution, the chi-square distribution takes only positive values (after all, it is the distribution of a squared quantity) and ranges from 0 to infinity.
2. As Figure C-7 also shows, unlike the normal distribution, the chi-square distribution is a *skewed distribution,* the degree of the skewness depending on the d.f. For comparatively few d.f. the distribution is highly skewed to

---

[11]Note that $\sum(X_i - \overline{X}) = \sum X_i - \sum \overline{X} = n\overline{X} - n\overline{X} = 0$, because $\overline{X} = \sum X_i/n$ and $\sum \overline{X} = n\overline{X}$, because $\overline{X}$ is a constant, given a particular sample.

the right, but as the d.f. increase, the distribution becomes increasingly symmetrical and approaches the normal distribution.

3. The expected, or mean, value of a chi-square r.v. is k and its variance is $2k$, where k is the d.f. *This is a noteworthy property of the chi-square distribution in that its variance is twice its mean value.*

4. If Z_1 and Z_2 are two *independent* chi-square variables with k_1 and k_2 d.f., then their sum $(Z_1 + Z_2)$ is also a chi-square variable with d.f. $= (k_1 + k_2)$.

Table E-4 in Appendix E tabulates the probabilities that a particular χ^2 value exceeds a given number, assuming the d.f. underlying the chi-square value are known or given. Although specific applications of the chi-square distribution in regression analysis will be considered in later chapters, for now we will look at how to use the table.

Example C.13.

For 30 d.f., what is the probability that an observed chi-square value is greater than 13.78? Or greater than 18.49? Or greater than 50.89?

From Table E-4 in Appendix E we observe that these probabilities are 0.995, 0.95, and 0.01, respectively. Thus, for 30 d.f. the probability of obtaining a chi-square value of approximately 51 is very small, only about 1 percent, but for the same d.f. the probability of obtaining a chi-square value of approximately 14 is very high, about 99.5 percent.

Example C.14.

If S^2 is the sample variance obtained from a random sample of n observations from a normal population with the variance of σ^2, statistical theory shows that the quantity

$$(n - 1)\left(\frac{S^2}{\sigma^2}\right) \sim \chi^2_{(n-1)} \tag{C.11}$$

That is, the ratio of the sample variance to population variance multiplied by the d.f. $(n-1)$ follows the chi-square distribution with $(n-1)$ d.f. Suppose a random sample of 20 observations from a normal population with $\sigma^2 = 8$ gave a sample variance of $S^2 = 16$. What is the probability of obtaining such a sample variance?

Putting the appropriate numbers in the preceding expression, we find that $19(16/8) = 38$ is a chi-square variable with 19 d.f. And from Table E-4 in Appendix E we find that for 19 d.f. if the true σ^2 were 8, the probability of finding a chi-square value of ≈ 38 is ≈ 0.005, a very small probability. There is doubt whether the particular random sample came from a population with a variance value of 8. But we will discuss this more in Appendix D.

In Appendix D we will show how Eq. (C.11) enables us to test hypotheses about σ^2 if we have knowledge only about the sample variance S^2.

C.4 THE F DISTRIBUTION

Another probability distribution that we find extremely useful in econometrics is the **F distribution.** The motivation behind this distribution is as follows. Let $X_1, X_2, \ldots, X_m$ be a random sample of size m from a normal population with mean μ_X and variance σ_X^2, and let $Y_1, Y_2, \ldots, Y_n$ be a random sample of size n from a normal population with mean μ_y and variance σ_y^2. Assume that these two samples are independent and are drawn from populations that are normally distributed. Suppose we want to find out if the variances of the two normal populations are the same, that is, whether $\sigma_X^2 = \sigma_y^2$. Since we cannot directly observe the two population variances, let us suppose we obtain their estimators as follows:

$$S_X^2 = \sum \frac{(X_i - \overline{X})^2}{m - 1} \tag{C.12}$$

$$S_Y^2 = \sum \frac{(Y_i - \overline{Y})^2}{n - 1} \tag{C.13}$$

Now consider the following ratio:

$$F = \frac{S_X^2}{S_Y^2}$$
$$= \frac{\sum(X_i - \overline{X})^2/(m - 1)}{\sum(Y_i - \overline{Y})^2/(n - 1)} \tag{C.14}[12]$$

If the two population variances are in fact equal, the F ratio given in Equation (C.14) should be about 1, whereas if they are different, the F ratio should be different from 1; the greater the difference between the two variances, the greater the F value will be.

Statistical theory shows that if $\sigma_X^2 = \sigma_y^2$ (i.e., the two population variances are equal), the F ratio given in Eq. (C.14) follows the F *distribution* with $(m - 1)$ (numerator) d.f. and $(n - 1)$ (denominator) d.f.[13] And since the F distribution is often used to compare the variances of two (approximately normal) populations, it is also known as the **variance ratio distribution.** The F ratio is often designated

[12]By convention, in computing the F value the variance with the larger numerical value is put in the numerator. That is why the F value is always 1 or greater than 1. Also, note that if a variable, say, W, follows the F distribution with m and n d.f. in the numerator and denominator, respectively, then the variable $(1/W)$ also follows the F distribution but with n and m d.f. in the numerator and denominator, respectively. More specifically,

$$F_{(1-\alpha),m,n} = \frac{1}{F_{\alpha,n,m}}$$

where α denotes the level of significance, which we will discuss in Appendix D.

[13]To be precise, $\frac{S_x^2/\sigma_X^2}{S_y^2/\sigma_y^2}$ follows the F distribution. But if $\sigma_X^2 = \sigma_y^2$, we have the F ratio given in Eq. (C.14). Note that in computing the two sample variances we lose 1 d.f. for each, because in each case, we use the same sample to compute the sample mean, which consumes 1 d.f.

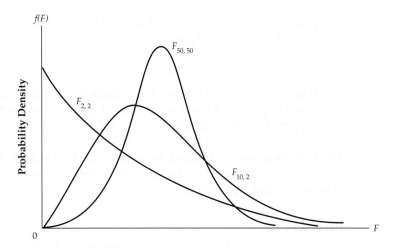

FIGURE C-8   The *F* distribution for various d.f.

as F_{k_1,k_2}, where the double subscript indicates the parameters of the distribution, namely, the **numerator and the denominator d.f.** (in the preceding example, $k_1 = [m-1]$ and $k_2 = [n-1]$).[14]

Properties of the *F* Distribution

1. Like the chi-square distribution, the *F* distribution is also skewed to the right and also ranges between 0 and infinity (see Figure C-8).
2. Also, like the *t* and chi-square distributions, the *F* distribution approaches the normal distribution as k_1 and k_2, the d.f., become large (technically, infinite).
3. The square of a *t*-distributed r.v. with *k* d.f. has an *F* distribution with 1 and *k* d.f. in the numerator and denominator, respectively. That is,

$$t_k^2 = F_{1,k} \tag{C.15}$$

We will see the usefulness of this property in Chapter 4.

4. Just as there is a relationship between the *F* and *t* distributions, there is a relationship between the *F* and chi-square distributions, which is

$$F_{(m,n)} = \frac{\chi^2}{m} \qquad as\ n \to \infty \tag{C.16}$$

That is, a chi-square variable divided by its d.f., *m*, approaches the *F* variable with *m* d.f. in the numerator and very large (technically, infinite) d.f. in the denominator. Therefore, in very large samples, we can use the

---

[14]The *F* distribution has two sets of d.f. because statistical theory shows that the *F* distribution is the distribution of the ratio of two *independent chi-square* random variables divided by their respective d.f.

χ^2 distribution instead of the F distribution, and vice versa. We can write Eq. (C.16) alternatively as

$$m \cdot F_{(m,n)} = \chi_m^2 \qquad \text{as } n \to \infty \qquad \text{(C.17)}$$

That is, numerator d.f. times $F_{(m,n)}$ equals a chi-square value with numerator d.f., provided the denominator degrees of freedom are sufficiently large (technically, infinite).

The F distribution is tabulated in Table E-3 in Appendix E. We will consider its specific uses in the context of regression analysis in the text, but in the meantime let us see how this table is used.

Example C.15.

Let us return to the S.A.T. example (Example C.12). Assume that the critical reading scores for males and females are each normally distributed. Further assume that average scores and their variances given in the preceding table represent sample values from a much larger population. Based on the two sample variances, can we assume that the two population variances are the same?

Since the critical reading scores of the male and female populations are assumed to be normally distributed random variables, we can compute the F ratio given in Eq. (C.14) as

$$F = \frac{51.09}{36.54} = 1.3982$$

which has the F distribution with 35 d.f. in the numerator and 35 d.f. in the denominator. (*Note:* In computing the F value, we are putting the larger of the two variances in the numerator.) Although Table E-3 in Appendix E does not give the F value corresponding to d.f. of 35, if we use 30 d.f. for both the numerator and the denominator, the probability of obtaining an F value of about 1.40 lies somewhere between 10 and 25 percent. Since this probability is not very low (more about this in Appendix D), we could say there does not seem to be enough evidence to claim the two population variances are unequal. Therefore, we decide there is not a difference in the population variances of male and female scores on the critical reading part of the S.A.T. test. Remember that if the two population variances are the same, the F value will be 1, but if they are different, the F value will be increasingly greater than 1.

Example C.16.

An instructor gives the same econometrics examination to two classes, one consisting of 100 students and the other consisting of 150 students. He draws a random sample of 25 students from the first class and a random sample of 31 students from the other class and observes that the sample variances of the grade-point average in the two classes are 100 and 132, respectively. It is assumed that the r.v., grade-point average, in the two classes is normally distributed. Can we assume that the variances of grade-point average in the two classes are the same?

Since we are dealing with two independent random samples drawn from two normal populations, applying the F ratio given in Eq. (C.14), we find that

$$F = \frac{132}{100} = 1.32$$

follows the F distribution with 30 and 24 d.f., respectively. From the F values given in Table E-3 we observe that for 30 numerator d.f. and 24 denominator d.f. the probability of obtaining an F value of as much as 1.31 or greater is 25 percent. If we regard this probability as reasonably high, we can conclude that the (population) variances in the two econometrics classes are (statistically) the same.

C.5 SUMMARY

In Appendix A we discussed probability distributions in general terms. In this appendix, we considered four specific probability distributions—the normal, the t, the chi-square, and the F—and the special features of each distribution, in particular, the situations in which these distributions can be useful. As we will see in the main chapters of this book, these four PDFs play a very pivotal role in econometric theory and practice. Therefore, a solid grasp of the fundamentals of these distributions is essential to follow the text material. You may want to return to this appendix from time to time to consult specific points of these distributions when they are referred to in the main chapters.

KEY TERMS AND CONCEPTS

The key terms and concepts introduced in this appendix are

The normal distribution
    a) unit or standardized variable
    b) unit or standard normal variable
Random number generators
Random sampling; i.i.d. random variables
Sampling, or probability, distribution of an estimator (e.g., the sample mean)
Standard error (se)

Monte Carlo experiments or simulations
Central limit theorem (CLT)
t distribution (Student's t distribution)
Chi-square (χ^2) probability distribution
Degrees of freedom (d.f.)
F distribution
    a) variance ratio distribution
    b) numerator and denominator degrees of freedom (d.f.)

QUESTIONS

C.1. Explain the meaning of
  a. Degrees of freedom.
  b. Sampling distribution of an estimator.
  c. Standard error.

C.2. Consider a random variable (r.v.) $X \sim N(8, 16)$. State whether the following statements are true or false:
  a. The probability of obtaining an X value of greater than 12 is about 0.16.
  b. The probability of obtaining an X value between 12 and 14 is about 0.09.
  c. The probability that an X value is more than 2.5 standard deviations from the mean value is 0.0062.

C.3. Continue with Question C.2.
  a. What is the probability distribution of the sample mean $\overline{X}$ obtained from a random sample from this population?
  b. Does your answer to (*a*) depend on the sample size? Why or why not?
  c. Assuming a sample size of 25, what is the probability of obtaining an $\overline{X}$ of 6?

C.4. What is the difference between the t distribution and the normal distribution? When should you use the t distribution?

C.5. Consider an r.v. that follows the t distribution.
  a. For 20 degrees of freedom (d.f.), what is the probability that the t value will be greater than 1.325?
  b. What is the probability that the t value in C.5(*a*) will be less than -1.325?
  c. What is the probability that a t value will be greater than or less than 1.325?
  d. Is there a difference between the statement in C.5(*c*) and the statement, "What is the probability that the absolute value of t, $|t|$, will be greater than 1.325?"

C.6. *True or false.* For a sufficiently large d.f., the t, the chi-square, and the F distributions all approach the unit normal distribution.

C.7. For a sufficiently large d.f., the chi-square distribution can be approximated by the standard normal distribution as: $Z = \sqrt{2\chi^2} - \sqrt{2k-1} \sim N(0, 1)$. Let $k = 50$.
  a. Use the chi-square table to find out the probability that a chi-square value will exceed 80.
  b. Determine this probability by using the preceding normal approximation.
  c. Assume that the d.f. are now 100. Compute the probability from the chi-square table as well as from the given normal approximation. What conclusions can you draw from using the normal approximation to the chi-square distribution?

C.8. What is the importance of the central limit theorem in statistics?

C.9. Give examples where the chi-square and F probability distributions can be used.

PROBLEMS

C.10. Profits (X) in an industry consisting of 100 firms are normally distributed with a mean value of $1.5 million and a standard deviation (s.d.) of $120,000. Calculate
  a. $P(X < \$1 \text{ million})$
  b. $P(\$800{,}000 \leq X \leq \$1{,}300{,}000)$

C.11. In Problem C.10, if 10 percent of the firms are to exceed a certain profit, what is that profit?

C.12. The grade-point average in an econometrics examination was normally distributed with a mean of 75. In a sample of 10 percent of students it was found that the grade-point average was greater than 80. Can you tell what the s.d. of the grade-point average was?

C.13. The amount of toothpaste in a tube is normally distributed with a mean of 6.5 ounces and an s.d. of 0.8 ounces. The cost of producing each tube is 50 cents. If in a quality control examination a tube is found to weigh less than 6 ounces, it is to be refilled to the mean value at a cost of 20 cents per tube. On the other hand, if the tube weighs more than 7 ounces, the company loses a profit of 5 cents per tube.

If 1000 tubes are examined,

a. How many tubes will be found to contain less than 6 ounces?

b. In that case, what will be the total cost of the refill?

c. How many tubes will be found to contain more than 7 ounces? In that case, what will be the amount of profits lost?

C.14. If $X \sim N(10, 3)$ and $Y \sim N(15, 8)$, and if X and Y are independent, what is the probability distribution of

  a. $X + Y$ **b.** $X - Y$ **c.** $3X$ **d.** $4X + 5Y$

C.15. Continue with Problem C.14, but now assume that X and Y are positively correlated with a correlation coefficient of 0.6.

C.16. Let X and Y represent the rates of return (in percent) on two stocks. You are told that $X \sim N(15, 25)$ and $Y \sim N(8, 4)$, and that the correlation coefficient between the two rates of return is -0.4. Suppose you want to hold the two stocks in your portfolio in equal proportion. What is the probability distribution of the return on the portfolio? Is it better to hold this portfolio or to invest in only one of the two stocks? Why?

C.17. Return to Example C.12. A random sample of 10 female S.A.T. scores on the math test gave a sample variance of 142. Knowing that the true variance is 102.07, what is the probability of obtaining such a sample value? Which probability distribution will you use to answer this question? What are the assumptions underlying that distribution?

C.18. The 10 economic forecasters of a random sample were asked to forecast the rate of growth of the real gross national product (GNP) for the coming year. Suppose the probability distribution of the r.v.—forecast—is normal.

  a. The probability is 0.10 that the sample variance of the forecast is more than X percent of the population variance. What is the value of X?

  b. If the probability is 0.95 so that the sample variance is between X and Y percent of the population variance, what will be the values of X and Y?

C.19. When a sample of 10 cereal boxes of a well-known brand was reweighed, it gave the following weights (in ounces):

16.13	16.02	15.90	15.83	16.00
15.79	16.01	16.04	15.96	16.20

  a. What is the sample mean? And the sample variance?

  b. If the true mean weight per box was 16 ounces, what is the probability of obtaining such a (sample) mean? Which probability distribution did you use and why?

C.20. The same microeconomics examination was given to students at two different universities. The results were as follows:

$$\overline{X}_1 = 75, \qquad S_1^2 = 9.0, \qquad n_1 = 50$$

$$\overline{X}_2 = 70, \qquad S_2^2 = 7.2, \qquad n_2 = 40$$

where the $\overline{X}$'s denote the grade averages in the two samples, the S^2's, the two sample variances; and the n's, the sample sizes. How would you test the hypothesis that the population variances of the test scores in the two universities are the same? Which probability distribution would you use? What are the assumptions underlying that distribution?

C.21. *Monte Carlo Simulation.* Draw 25 random samples of 25 observations from the t distribution with $k = 10$ d.f. For each sample compute the sample mean. What is the sampling distribution of these sample means? Why? You may use graphs to illustrate your answer.

C.22. Repeat Problem C.21, but this time use the χ^2 distribution with 8 d.f.

C.23. Repeat Problem C.21, but use the F distribution with 10 and 15 d.f. in the numerator and denominator, respectively.

C.24. Using Eq. (C.16), compare the values of $\chi^2_{(10)}$ with $F_{10,10}$, $F_{10,20}$, and $F_{10,60}$. What general conclusions do you draw?

C.25. Given $X \sim N(\mu_X, \sigma_X^2)$, prove that $\overline{X} \sim N(\mu_X, \sigma_X^2/n)$. *Hint:* var $(\overline{X}) = \mathrm{var}\left(\dfrac{X_1 + X_2 + \cdots + X_n}{n}\right)$. Expand this, recalling some of the properties of the variance discussed in Appendix B and the fact that the X_i are i.i.d.

C.26. Prove that $Z = \left(\dfrac{X - \mu_X}{\sigma_X}\right)$, has zero mean and unit variance. Note that this is true whether Z is normal or not. *Hint:* $E(Z) = E\left(\dfrac{X - \mu_X}{\sigma_X}\right) = \dfrac{1}{\sigma_X} E\left(X - \mu_X\right)$.

STATISTICAL INFERENCE: ESTIMATION AND HYPOTHESIS TESTING

Equipped with the knowledge of probability; random variables; probability distributions; and characteristics of probability distributions, such as expected value, variance, covariance, correlation, and conditional expectation, in this appendix we are now ready to undertake the important task of **statistical inference.** Broadly speaking, statistical inference is concerned with drawing conclusions about the nature of some population (e.g., the normal) on the basis of a random sample that has supposedly been drawn from that population. Thus, if we believe that a particular sample has come from a normal population and we compute the sample mean and sample variance from that sample, we may want to know what the true (population) mean is and what the variance of that population may be.

D.1 THE MEANING OF STATISTICAL INFERENCE[1]

As noted previously, the concepts of *population* and *sample* are extremely important in statistics. *Population,* as defined in Appendix A, is the totality of all possible outcomes of a phenomenon of interest (e.g., the population of New York City). A *sample* is a subset of a population (e.g., the people living in Manhattan, which is one of the five boroughs of the city). Statistical inference, loosely speaking, is the study of the relationship between a population and a sample drawn from that population. To understand what this means, let us consider a concrete example.

---

[1]Broadly speaking, there are two approaches to statistical inference, Bayesian and classical. The classical approach, as propounded by statisticians Neyman and Pearson, is generally the approach that a beginning student in statistics first encounters. Although there are basic philosophical differences in the two approaches, there may not be gross differences in the inferences that result.

TABLE D-1 PRICE TO EARNINGS (P/E) RATIOS OF 28 COMPANIES
ON THE NEW YORK STOCK EXCHANGE (NYSE)

Company	P/E	Company	P/E
AA	27.96	INTC	36.02
AXP	22.90	IBM	22.94
T	8.30	JPM	12.10
BA	49.78	JNJ	22.43
CAT	24.68	MCD	22.13
C	14.55	MRK	16.48
KO	28.22	MSFT	33.75
DD	28.21	MMM	26.05
EK	34.71	MO	12.21
XOM	12.99	PG	24.49
GE	21.89	SBC	14.87
GM	9.86	UTX	14.87
HD	20.26	WMT	27.84
HON	23.36	DIS	37.10
Mean = 23.25, variance = 90.13, standard deviation = 9.49			

Source: **www.stockselector.com**.

Table D-1 gives data on the *price to earnings ratio*—the famous P/E ratio—for 28 companies listed on the New York Stock Exchange (NYSE) for February 2, 2004 (at about 3 p.m.).[2] Assume that this is a random sample from the universe (population) of stocks listed on the NYSE, some 3000 or so. The P/E ratio of 27.96 for Alcoa (AA) listed in this table, for example, means that on that day the stock was selling at about 28 times its annual earnings. The P/E ratio is one of the key indicators for investors in the stock market.

Suppose our primary interest is not in any single P/E ratio, but in the *average* P/E ratio in the entire population of the NYSE listed stocks. Since we can obtain data on the P/E ratios of all the stocks listed on the NYSE, in principle, we can easily compute the average P/E ratio. In practice, that would be time-consuming and expensive. Could we use the data given in Table D-1 to compute the *average* P/E ratio of the 28 companies listed in this table and use this (sample) average as an *estimate* of the average P/E ratio in the entire population of the stocks listed on the NYSE? Specifically, if we let X = P/E ratio of a stock and $\overline{X}$ = the average P/E ratio of the 28 stocks given in Table D-1, can we tell what the expected P/E ratio, $E(X)$, is in the NYSE population as a whole? *This process of generalizing from the sample value (e.g., $\overline{X}$) to the population value (e.g., $E[X]$) is the essence of statistical inference.* We will now discuss this topic in some detail.

---

[2]Since the price of the stock varies from day to day, the P/E ratio will vary from day to day, even though the earnings do not change. The stocks given in this table are members of the so-called Dow 30. In reality stock prices change very frequently when the stock market is open, but most newspapers quote the P/E ratios as of the end of the business day.

D.2   ESTIMATION AND HYPOTHESIS TESTING: TWIN BRANCHES OF STATISTICAL INFERENCE

From the preceding discussion it can be seen that statistical inference proceeds along the following lines. There is some population of interest, say, the stocks listed on the NYSE, and we are interested in studying some aspect of this population, say, the P/E ratio. Of course, we may not want to study each and every P/E ratio, but only the average P/E ratio. Since collecting information on all the NYSE P/E ratios needed to compute the average P/E ratio is expensive and time-consuming, we may obtain a *random sample* of only a few stocks to get the P/E ratio of each of these sampled stocks and compute the sample average P/E ratio, say, $\overline{X}$. $\overline{X}$ is an **estimator,** also known as a (sample) *statistic,* of the population average P/E ratio, $E(X)$, which is called the (population) **parameter.** (Refer to the discussion in Appendix B). For example, the mean and variance are the parameters of the normal distribution. A particular numerical value of the estimator is called an *estimate* (e.g., an $\overline{X}$ value of 23). Thus, *estimation is the first step in statistical inference.* Having obtained an estimate of a parameter, we next need to find out how good that estimate is, for an estimate is not likely to equal the true parameter value. If we obtain two or more random samples of 28 stocks each and compute $\overline{X}$ for each of these samples, the two estimates will probably not be the same. This variation in estimates from sample to sample is known as *sampling variation* or *sampling error.*[3] Are there any criteria by which we can judge the "goodness" of an estimator? In Section D.4 we discuss some of the commonly used criteria to judge the goodness of an estimator.

Whereas estimation is one side of statistical inference, hypothesis testing is the other. In *hypothesis testing* we may have prior judgment or expectation about what value a particular parameter may assume. For example, prior knowledge or an expert opinion tells us that the true average P/E ratio in the population of NYSE stocks is, say, 20. Suppose a particular random sample of 28 stocks gives this estimate as 23. Is this value of 23 close to the *hypothesized value* of 20? Obviously, the number 23 is different from the number 20. But the important question here is this: Is 23 *statistically different* from 20? We know that because of sampling variation there is likely to be a difference between a (sample) estimate and its population value. It is possible that statistically the number 23 may not be very different from the number 20, in which case we may not reject the hypothesis that the true average P/E ratio is 20. But how do we decide that? This is the essence of the topic of *hypothesis testing,* which we will discuss in Section D.5.

With these preliminaries, let us examine the twin topics of estimation and hypothesis testing in some detail.

---

[3]Notice that this sampling error is not deliberate, but it occurs because we have a random sample and the elements included in the sample will vary from sample to sample. This is inevitable in any analysis based on a sample.

D.3 ESTIMATION OF PARAMETERS

In Appendix C we considered several theoretical probability distributions. Often we know or are willing to assume that a random variable X follows a particular distribution, but we do not know the value(s) of the parameter(s) of the distribution. For example, if X follows the normal distribution, we may want to know the values of its two parameters, namely, the mean $E(X) = \mu_X$ and the variance σ_X^2. To estimate these unknowns, the usual procedure is to assume that we have a *random sample* of size n from the known probability distribution and to use the sample to estimate the unknown parameters. Thus, we can use the sample mean as an estimate of the population mean (or expected value) and the sample variance as an estimate of the population variance. This procedure is known as the *problem of estimation.* The problem of estimation can be broken down into two categories: point estimation and interval estimation.

To fix the ideas, assume that the random variable (r.v.), X (P/E ratio), is normally distributed with a certain mean and a certain variance, but for now we do not know the values of these parameters. Suppose, however, we have a random sample of 28 P/E ratios (28 X's) from this normal population, as shown in Table D-1.

How can we use these sample data to compute the population mean value $\mu_X = E(X)$ and the population variance σ_X^2? More specifically, suppose our immediate interest is in finding out μ_X.[4] How do we go about it? An obvious choice is the sample mean $\overline{X}$ of the 28 P/E ratios shown in Table D-1, which is 23.25. We call this *single numerical value* the **point estimate** of μ_X, and the formula $\overline{X} = \Sigma_1^{28} X_i/n$ that we used to compute this point estimate is called the *point estimator, or statistic.* Notice that a *point estimator, or a statistic, is an r.v., as its value will vary from sample to sample.* (Recall our sampling experiment in Example C-6.) Therefore, how reliable is a specific estimate such as 23.25 of the true μ_X? In other words, how can we rely on just one estimate of the true population mean? Would it not be better to state that although $\overline{X}$ is the single best guess of the true population mean, the interval, say, from 19 to 24, most likely includes the true μ_X? This is essentially the idea behind **interval estimation.** We will now consider the actual mechanics of obtaining interval estimates.

The key idea underlying interval estimation is the notion of **sampling,** or **probability, distribution** of an estimator such as the sample mean $\overline{X}$, which we have already discussed in Appendix C. In Appendix C we saw that if an r.v. $X \sim N(\mu_X, \sigma_X^2)$, then

$$\overline{X} \sim \left(\mu_X, \ \frac{\sigma_X^2}{n} \right) \tag{D.1}$$

or

$$Z = \frac{(\overline{X} - \mu_X)}{\sigma_X/\sqrt{n}} \sim N(0, 1) \tag{D.2}$$

---

[4]This discussion can be easily extended to estimate σ_X^2.

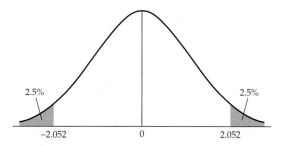

FIGURE D-1 The *t* distribution for 27 d.f.

That is, the sampling distribution of the sample mean $\overline{X}$ also follows the normal distribution with the stated parameters.[5]

As pointed out in Appendix C, $\sigma_{\overline{X}}^2$ is not generally known, but if we use its estimator $S_{\overline{x}}^2 = \Sigma(X_i - \overline{X})^2/(n - 1)$, then we know that

$$t = \frac{(\overline{X} - \mu_X)}{S_x/\sqrt{n}} \tag{D.3}$$

follows the *t* distribution with $(n - 1)$ degrees of freedom (d.f.).

To see how Equation (D.3) helps us to obtain an interval estimation of the μ_X of our P/E example, note that we have a total of 28 observations and, therefore, 27 d.f. Now if we consult the *t* table (Table E-2) given in Appendix E, we notice that for 27 d.f.,

$$P(-2.052 \le t \le 2.052) = 0.95 \tag{D.4}$$

as shown in Figure D-1. That is, for 27 d.f., the probability is 0.95 (or 95 percent) that the interval $(-2.052, 2.052)$ will include the *t* value computed from Eq. (D.3).[6] These *t* values, as we will see shortly, are known as **critical *t* values;** they show what percentage of the area under the *t* distribution curve (see Figure D-1) lies between those values (note that the total area under the curve is 1); $t = -2.052$ is called the *lower critical t value* and $t = 2.052$ is called the *upper critical t value*.

Now substituting the *t* value from Eq. (D.3) into Eq. (D.4), we obtain

$$P\left(-2.052 \le \frac{(\overline{X} - \mu_X)}{S_x/\sqrt{n}} \le 2.052\right) \tag{D.5}$$

Simple algebraic manipulation will show that Equation (D.5) can be expressed *equivalently* as

$$P\left(\overline{X} - 2.052\frac{S_x}{\sqrt{n}} \le \mu_X \le \overline{X} + 2.052\frac{S_x}{\sqrt{n}}\right) = 0.95 \tag{D.6}$$

---

[5]Note that if X does not follow the normal distribution, $\overline{X}$ will follow the normal distribution à la the central limit theorem if n, the sample size, is sufficiently large.

[6]Needless to say, these values will depend on the d.f. as well as on the level of probability used. For example, for the same d.f. $P(-2.771 \le t \le 2.771) = 0.99$.

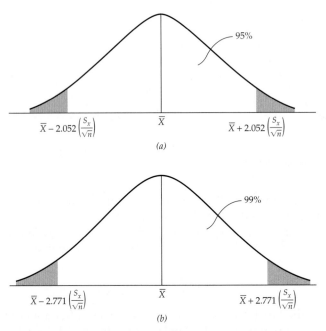

FIGURE D-2 (*a*) 95% and (*b*) 99% confidence intervals for μ_X for 27 d.f.

Equation (D.6) provides an *interval estimator* of the true μ_X.

In statistics we call Eq. (D.6) a 95% **confidence interval (CI)** for the true but unknown population mean μ_X and 0.95 is called the **confidence coefficient.** In words, Eq. (D.6) says that the *probability is 0.95 that the random interval* $(\overline{X} \pm 2.052 S_x/\sqrt{n})$ *contains the true* μ_X. $(\overline{X} - 2.052 S_x/\sqrt{n})$ is called the **lower limit** of the interval and $(\overline{X} + 2.0096 S_x/\sqrt{n})$ is the **upper limit** of the interval. See Figure D-2.

Before proceeding further, note this important point: The interval given in Eq. (D.6) is a **random interval** because it is based on $\overline{X}$ and $S_x/\sqrt{n}$, which will vary from sample to sample. The true or population mean μ_X, although unknown, is some fixed number and therefore is not random. Thus, *one should not say that the probability is 0.95 that* μ_X *lies in this interval. The correct statement, as noted earlier, is that the probability is 0.95 that the random interval, Eq. (D.6), contains the true* μ_X. *In short, the interval is random and not the parameter* μ_X.

Returning to our P/E example of Table D-1, we have $n = 28$, $\overline{X} = 23.25$, and $S_x = 9.49$. Plugging these values into Eq. (D.6), we obtain

$$23.25 - \frac{(2.052)(9.49)}{\sqrt{28}} \le \mu_X \le 23.25 + \frac{(2.052)(9.49)}{\sqrt{28}}$$

which yields

$$19.57 \le \mu_X \le 26.93 \ (approx) \tag{D.7}$$

as the 95% confidence interval for μ_X.

Equation (D.7) says, in effect, that if we construct intervals like Eq. (D.7), say, 100 times, then 95 out of 100 such intervals will include the true μ_X.[7] Incidentally, note that for our P/E example the lower limit of the interval is 19.57 and the upper limit is 26.93.

Thus, *interval estimation, in contrast to point estimation (such as 23.25), provides a range of values that will include the true value with a certain degree of confidence or probability (such as 0.95).* If we have to give one best estimate of the true mean, it is the point estimate 23.25, but if we want to be less precise we can give the interval (19.57 to 26.93) as the range that most probably includes the true mean value with a certain degree of confidence (95 percent in the present instance).

More generally, suppose X is an r.v. with some probability distribution function (PDF). Suppose further that we want to estimate a parameter of this distribution, say, its mean value μ_X. Toward that end, we obtain a random sample of n values, $X_1, X_2, \cdots, X_n$, and compute two statistics (or estimators) L and U from this sample such that

$$P(L \leq \mu_X \leq U) = 1 - \alpha \quad 0 < \alpha < 1 \qquad \textbf{(D.8)}$$

That is, the probability is $(1 - \alpha)$ that the *random interval* from L to U contains the true μ_X. L is called the lower limit of the interval and U is called the upper limit. This interval is known as a *confidence interval* of size $(1 - \alpha)$ for μ_X (or any parameter for that matter), and $(1 - \alpha)$ is known as the *confidence coefficient.* If $\alpha = 0.05$, $(1 - \alpha) = 0.95$, meaning that if we construct a confidence interval with a confidence coefficient of 0.95, then in repeated such constructions, 95 out of 100 intervals can be expected to include the true μ_X. In practice, $(1 - \alpha)$ is often multiplied by 100 to express it in percent form (e.g., 95 percent). In statistics alpha (α) is known as the **level of significance,** or, alternatively, **the probability of committing a type I error,** which is defined and discussed in Section D.5.

Now that we have seen how to establish confidence intervals, what do we do with them? As we will see in Section D.5, confidence intervals make our task of testing hypotheses—the twin of statistical inference—much easier.

D.4   PROPERTIES OF POINT ESTIMATORS

In the P/E example we used the sample mean $\overline{X}$ as a point estimator of μ_X, as well as to obtain an interval estimator of μ_X. But why did we use $\overline{X}$? It is well

---

[7]Be careful again. We cannot say that the probability is 0.95 that the particular interval in Eq. (D.7) includes the true μ_X; it may or may not. Therefore, statements like $P(19.5 \leq \mu_X \leq 26.93) = 0.95$ *are not permissible under the classical approach to hypothesis testing.* Intervals like those in Eq. (D.7) are to be interpreted in the repeated sampling sense that if we construct such intervals a large number of times, then 95 percent of such intervals will include the true mean value; the particular interval in Eq. (D.7) is just one realization of the interval estimator in Eq. (D.6).

known that besides the sample mean, the (sample) median or the (sample) mode also can be used as point estimators of μ_X.[8]

In practice, the sample mean is the most frequently used measure of the population mean because it satisfies several properties that statisticians deem desirable. Some of these properties are:

1. Linearity
2. Unbiasedness
3. Minimum variance
4. Efficiency
5. Best linear unbiased estimator (BLUE)
6. Consistency

We will now discuss these properties somewhat heuristically.

Linearity

An estimator is said to be a **linear estimator** *if it is a linear function of the sample observations.* The sample mean is obviously a linear estimator because

$$\overline{X} = \sum_{i=1}^{n} \frac{X_i}{n} = \frac{1}{n}(X_1 + X_2 + \cdots + X_n)$$

is a linear function of the observations, the X's. (*Note:* The X's appear with an index or power of 1 only.)

In statistics a linear estimator is generally much easier to deal with than a nonlinear estimator.

Unbiasedness

If there are several estimators of a population parameter (i.e., several methods of estimating that parameter), and if one or more of these estimators *on the average* coincide with the true value of the parameter, we say that such estimators are **unbiased estimators** of that parameter. Put differently, if in repeated applications of a method the *mean* value of the estimators coincides with the true parameter value, that estimator is called an unbiased estimator. More formally, an estimator, say, $\overline{X}$, is an unbiased estimator of μ_X if

$$E(\overline{X}) = \mu_X \tag{D.9}$$

[8]The *median* is that value of a random variable that divides the total PDF into two halves such that half the values in the population exceed it and half are below it. To compute the median from a sample, arrange the observations in increasing order; the median is the middle value in this order. For example, if we have observations 7, 3, 6, 11, 5 and rearrange them in increasing order, we obtain 3, 5, 6, 7, 11. The median, or the middlemost value, here is 6. The *mode* is the most popular or frequent value of the random variable. For example, if we have observations 3, 5, 7, 5, 8, 5, 9, the *modal value* is 5 since it occurs most frequently.

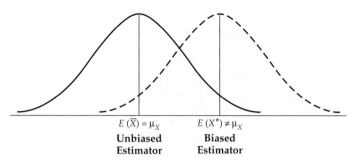

$$E(\overline{X}) = \mu_X \qquad E(X^*) \neq \mu_X$$

Unbiased   **Biased**
Estimator   **Estimator**

FIGURE D-3   Biased (X^*) and unbiased ($\overline{X}$) estimators of population mean value, μ_X

as shown in Figure D-3. If this is not the case, however, then we call that estimator a *biased estimator,* such as the estimator X^* shown in Figure D-3.

Example D.1.

Let $X_i \sim N(\mu_X, \sigma_X^2)$, then, as we saw in Appendix C. $\overline{X}$, based on a random sample of size n from this population, is distributed with mean $E(\overline{X}) = \mu_X$ and var $(\overline{X}) = \sigma_X^2/n$. Thus, the sample mean $\overline{X}$ is an unbiased estimator of true μ_X. If we draw repeated samples of size n from this normal population and compute $\overline{X}$ for each sample, then on the average, $\overline{X}$ will coincide with μ_X. But notice carefully that we cannot say that in a single sample, such as the one in Table D-1, the computed mean of 23.25 will necessarily coincide with the true mean value.

Example D.2.

Again, let $X_i \sim N(\mu_X, \sigma_X^2)$, and suppose we draw a random sample of size n from this population. Let X_{med} represent the median value of this sample. It can be shown that $E(X_{\text{med}}) = \mu_X$. In words, the median from this population is also an unbiased estimator of the true mean. Notice also that unbiasedness is a *repeated sampling property;* that is, if we draw several samples of size n from this population and compute the median value for each sample, then the average of the median values obtained will tend to approach μ_X.

Minimum Variance

Figure D-4 shows the sampling distributions of three estimators of μ_X, obtained from three different estimators, $\hat{\mu}_1$, $\hat{\mu}_2$ and $\hat{\mu}_3$.

Now an estimator of, say, μ_X, is said to be a **minimum-variance** estimator if its variance is smaller than any other estimator of μ_X. As you can see from Fig. D-4, the variance of $\hat{\mu}_3$ is the smallest of the three estimators shown there. Hence, it is a minimum-variance estimator. But note that $\hat{\mu}_3$ is a biased estimator. (Why?)

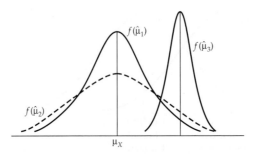

FIGURE D-4   Distribution of three estimators of μ_X

Efficiency

The property of unbiasedness, although desirable, is not adequate by itself. What happens if we have two or more estimators of a parameter and they are all unbiased? How do we choose among them?

Suppose we have a random sample of n values of an r.v. X such that each $X \sim N(\mu_X, \sigma_X^2)$. Let $\overline{X}$ and X_{med} be the mean and median values obtained from this sample. We already know that

$$\overline{X} \sim N(\mu_X, \sigma^2/n) \tag{D.10}$$

It can also be shown that *if the sample size is large,*

$$X_{\text{med}} \sim N(\mu_X, (\pi/2)(\sigma^2/n)) \tag{D.11}$$

where $\pi = 3.142$ (approx.). That is, in large samples, the median computed from a random sample of a normal population also follows a normal distribution with the same mean μ_X but with a variance that is larger than the variance of $\overline{X}$ by the factor $\pi/2$, which can be visualized from Figure D-5. As a matter of fact, by forming the ratio

$$\frac{\text{var}(X_{\text{med}})}{\text{var}(\overline{X})} = \frac{\pi}{2}\frac{\sigma^2/n}{\sigma^2/n} = \frac{\pi}{2} = 1.571 \quad \text{(approx)} \tag{D.12}$$

we show that the variance of the sample median is ≈ 57 percent larger than the variance of the sample mean.

Now given Figure D-5 and the preceding discussion, which estimator would you choose? Common sense suggests that we choose $\overline{X}$ over X_{med}, for although both estimators are unbiased, $\overline{X}$ has a smaller variance than X_{med}. Therefore if we use $\overline{X}$ in repeated sampling, we will estimate μ_X more accurately than if we were to use the sample median. In short, $\overline{X}$ provides a more *precise* estimate of the population mean than the median X_{med}. In statistical language we say that $\overline{X}$ is an **efficient estimator.** Stated more formally, *if we consider only unbiased estimators of a parameter, the one with the smallest variance is called the best, or efficient, estimator.*

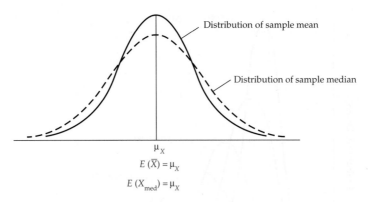

FIGURE D-5   An example of an efficient estimator (sample mean)

Best Linear Unbiased Estimator (BLUE)

In econometrics the property that is frequently encountered is the property **best linear unbiased estimator,** or **BLUE** for short. *If an estimator is linear, is unbiased, and has minimum variance in the class of all linear unbiased estimators of a parameter, it is called a best linear unbiased estimator.* Obviously, this property combines the properties of linearity, unbiasedness, and minimum variance. In Chapters 3 and 4 we will see the importance of this property.

Consistency

To explain the property of consistency, suppose $X \sim N(\mu_X, \sigma_X^2)$ and we draw a random sample of size n from this population. Now consider two estimators of μ_X.

$$\overline{X} = \sum \frac{X_i}{n} \tag{D.13}$$

$$X^* = \sum \frac{X_i}{n + 1} \tag{D.14}$$

The first estimator is the usual sample mean. Now, as we already know

$$E(\overline{X}) = \mu_X$$

and it can be shown that

$$E(X^*) = \left(\frac{n}{n + 1}\right)\mu_X \tag{D.15}$$

Since $E(X^*)$ is not equal to μ_X, X^* is obviously a *biased estimator*. (For proof, see Problem D. 21.)

But suppose we increase the sample size. What would you expect? The estimators $\overline{X}$ and X^* differ only in that the former has n in the denominator whereas the latter has $(n + 1)$. But as the sample increases, we should not find

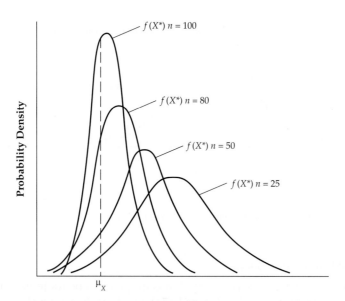

FIGURE D-6   The property of consistency. The behavior of the estimator X^* of population mean μ_X as the sample size increases

much difference between the two estimators. That is, as the sample size increases, X^* also will approach the true μ_X. In statistics such an estimator is known as a **consistent estimator.** Stated more formally, *an estimator (e.g., X^*) is said to be a consistent estimator if it approaches the true value of the parameter as the sample size gets larger and larger.* As we will see in the main chapters of the text, sometimes we may not be able to obtain an unbiased estimator, but we can obtain a consistent estimator.[9] The property of consistency is depicted in Figure D-6.

D.5   STATISTICAL INFERENCE: HYPOTHESIS TESTING

Having studied in some detail the estimation branch of statistical inference, we will now consider its twin, hypothesis testing. Although the general nature of hypothesis testing was discussed earlier, we study it here in some detail.

Let us return to the P/E example given in Table D-1. In Section D.3, based on a random sample of 28 P/E ratios, we established a 95% confidence interval for μ_X, the true but unknown average P/E ratio in the population of the stocks listed on the NYSE. Now let us reverse our strategy. Instead of establishing a

---

[9]Note the critical difference between an unbiased and a consistent estimator. If we fix the sample size and draw several random samples of an r.v. from some probability distribution to estimate a parameter of this distribution, then unbiasedness requires that *on the average* we should be able to obtain the true parameter value. In establishing consistency, on the other hand, we see the behavior of an estimator as the sample size increases. If a sample size is reasonably large and the estimator based on that sample size approaches the true parameter value, then that estimator is a consistent estimator.

confidence interval, suppose we *hypothesize* that the true μ_X takes a particular numerical value (e.g., $\mu_X = 18.5$). Our task now is to test this hypothesis.[10] How do we test this hypothesis—that is, support or refute it?

In the language of hypothesis testing a hypothesis such as $\mu_X = 18.5$ is called a **null hypothesis** and is generally denoted by the symbol H_0. Thus, H_0: $\mu_X = 18.5$. The null hypothesis is usually tested against an **alternative hypothesis,** denoted by the symbol H_1. The alternative hypothesis can take one of these forms:

H_1:$\mu_X > 18.5$, which is called a **one-sided** or **one-tailed** alternative hypothesis, or

H_1:$\mu_X < 18.5$, also a **one-sided** or **one-tailed** alternative hypothesis, or
H_1:$\mu_X \neq 18.5$, which is called a **composite, two-sided,** or **two-tailed** alternative hypothesis. That is, the true mean value is either greater than or less than 18.5.[11]

To test the null hypothesis (against the alternative hypothesis), we use the sample data (e.g., the sample average P/E ratio of 23.25 obtained from the sample in Table D-1) and statistical theory to develop decision rules that will tell us whether the sample evidence supports the null hypothesis. If the sample evidence supports the null hypothesis, we do not reject H_0, but if it does not, we reject H_0. In the latter case we may accept the alternative hypothesis, H_1.

How do we develop these decision rules? There are two complementary approaches: (1) confidence interval and (2) test of significance. We illustrate each with the aid of our P/E example. Assume that

$$H_0:\mu_X = 18.5$$

$$H_1:\mu_X \neq 18.5 \ (a\ two\text{-}sided\ hypothesis)$$

The Confidence Interval Approach to Hypothesis Testing

To test the null hypothesis, suppose we have the sample data given in Table D-1. From these data we computed the sample mean of 23.25. We know from our discussion in Section D.3 that the sample mean is distributed normally with mean μ_X and variance σ_X^2/n. But since the true variance is unknown, we replace it with the sample variance, in which case we know that the sample mean follows the t distribution, as shown in Eq. (D.3). Based on the t distribution, we obtain the following 95% confidence interval for:

$$19.57 \leq \mu_X \leq 26.93 \qquad \textbf{(D.16)} = \textbf{(D.7)}$$

We know that confidence intervals provide a range of values that may include the true μ_X with a certain degree of confidence, such as 95 percent. Therefore, if

---

[10]A *hypothesis* is "something considered to be true for the purpose of investigation or argument" (*Webster's*), or a "supposition made as a basis for reasoning, or as a starting point for further investigation from known facts" (*Oxford English Dictionary*).
[11]There are various ways of stating the null and alternative hypotheses. For example, we could have H_0:$\mu_X \geq 13$ and H_1: $\mu_X < 13$.

this interval does not include a particular null hypothesized value such as $\mu_X = 18.5$, could we not reject this null hypothesis? Yes, we can, with 95% confidence.

From the preceding discussion it should be clear that the topics of confidence interval and hypothesis testing are intimately related. In the language of hypothesis testing, the 95% confidence interval shown in inequality (D.7) (see Fig. D-2) is called the **acceptance region** and the area outside the acceptance region is called the **critical region,** or **the region of rejection,** of the null hypothesis. The lower and upper limits of the acceptance region are called **critical values.** In this language, if the acceptance region includes the value of the parameter under H_0, we do not reject the null hypothesis. But if it falls outside the acceptance region (i.e., it lies within the rejection region), we reject the null hypothesis. In our example we reject the null hypothesis that $\mu_X = 18.5$ since the acceptance region given in Eq. (D.7) does not include the null-hypothesized value. It should be clear now why the boundaries of the acceptance region are called critical values, for they are the dividing line between accepting and rejecting a null hypothesis.

Type I and Type II Errors: A Digression

In our P/E example we rejected $H_0:\mu_X = 18.5$ because our sample evidence of $\overline{X} = 23.25$ does not seem to be compatible with this hypothesis. Does this mean that the sample shown in Table D-1 did not come from a normal population whose mean value was 18.5? We cannot be absolutely sure, for the confidence interval given in inequality (D.7) is 95 and not 100 percent. If that is the case, we would be making an error in rejecting $H_0:\mu_X = 18.5$. In this case we are said to commit a **type I error,** that is, *the error of rejecting a hypothesis when it is true.* By the same token, suppose $H_0:\mu_X = 21$, in which case, as inequality (D.7) shows, we would not reject this null hypothesis. But quite possibly the sample in Table D-1 did not come from a normal distribution with a mean value of 21. Thus, we are said to commit a **type II error,** that is, *the error of accepting a false hypothesis.* Schematically,

	Reject H_0	Do not reject H_0
H_0 is true	Type I error	Correct decision
H_0 is false	Correct decision	Type II error

Ideally, we would like to minimize both these errors. But, unfortunately, for *any given sample size,*[12] it is not possible to minimize both errors simultaneously. The classical approach to this problem, embodied in the work of statisticians Neyman and Pearson, is to assume that a type I error is likely to be more serious in practice than a type II error. Therefore, we should try to keep the probability

[12]The only way to decrease a type II error without increasing a type I error is to increase the sample size, which may not always be easy.

of committing a type I error at a fairly low level, such as 0.01 or 0.05, and then try to minimize a type II error as much as possible.[13]

In the literature the probability of committing a type I error is designated as α and is called the **level of significance,**[14] and the probability of committing a type II error is designated as β. Symbolically,

$$\text{Type I error} = \alpha = \text{prob. } (\textit{rejecting } H_0 \mid H_0 \textit{ is true})$$

$$\text{Type II error} = \beta = \text{prob. } (\textit{accepting } H_0 \mid H_0 \textit{ is false})$$

The probability of *not* committing a type II error, that is, rejecting H_0 when it is false, is $(1 - \beta)$, which is called the **power of the test.**

The standard, or classical, approach to hypothesis testing is to fix α at levels such as 0.01 or 0.05 and then try to maximize the power of the test; that is, to minimize β. How this is actually accomplished is involved, and so we leave the subject for the references.[15] Suffice it to note that, in practice, the classical approach simply specifies the value of α without worrying too much about β. But keep in mind that, in practice, in making a decision there is a trade-off between the significance level and the power of the test. That is, for a *given sample size,* if we try to reduce the probability of a type I error, we ipso facto increase the probability of a type II error and therefore reduce the power of the test. Thus, instead of using $\alpha = 5$ percent, if we were to use $\alpha = 1$ percent, we may be very confident when we reject H_0, but we may not be so confident when we do not reject it.

Since the precedent point is important, let us illustrate. For our P/E ratio example, in Eq. (D.7) we established a 95% confidence. Let us still assume that $H_0 : \mu_X = 18.5$ but now fix $\alpha = 1$ percent and obtain the 99% confidence interval, which is (noting that for 99% CI, the critical t values are $(-2.771, 2.771)$ for 27 d.f.):

$$18.28 \leq \mu_X \leq 28.22 \tag{D.17}$$

This 99% confidence interval is also shown in Fig. D-2. Obviously, this interval is wider than the 95% confidence interval. Since this interval includes the hypothesized value of 18.5, we do not reject the null hypothesis, whereas in Eq. (D.7) we rejected the null hypothesis on the basis of a 95% confidence interval. What now? By reducing a type I error from 5 percent to 1 percent, we have increased the probability of a type II error. That is, in not rejecting the null hypothesis on the basis of Eq. (D.17), we may be falsely accepting the hypothesis

---

[13]To Bayesian statisticians this procedure sounds rather arbitrary because it does not consider carefully the relative seriousness of the two types of errors. For further discussion of this and related points, see Robert L. Winkler, *Introduction to Bayesian Inference and Decision*, Holt, Rinehart and Winston, New York, 1972, Chap. 7.

[14]α is also known as the *size of the (statistical) test.*

[15]For a somewhat intuitive discussion of this topic, see Gujarati and Porter, *Basic Econometrics*, 5th ed., McGraw-Hill, New York, 2009, pp. 833–835. Statistical packages, such as MINITAB, can calculate the power of a test of size α.

that the true μ_X is 18.5. So, always keep in mind the trade-off involved between type I and type II errors.

You will recognize that the **confidence coefficient** $(1 - \alpha)$ discussed earlier is simply 1 minus the probability of committing a type I error. Thus, a 95% confidence coefficient means that we are prepared to accept at most a 5 percent probability of committing a type I error—we do not want to reject the true hypothesis by more than 5 out of 100 times. *In short, a 5% level of significance or a 95% level or degree of confidence means the same thing.*

Let us consider another example to illustrate further the confidence interval approach to hypothesis testing.

Example D.3.

The number of peanuts contained in a jar follows the normal distribution, but we do not know its mean and standard deviation, both of which are measured in ounces. Twenty jars were selected randomly and it was found that the sample mean was 6.5 ounces and the sample standard deviation was 2 ounces. Test the hypothesis that the true mean value is 7.5 ounces against the hypothesis that it is different from 7.5. Use $\alpha = 1\%$.

Answer: Letting X denote the number of peanuts in a jar, we are given that $X \sim N(\mu_X, \sigma_X^2)$, both parameters being unknown. Since the true variance is unknown, if we use its estimator S_x^2, it follows that

$$t = \frac{\overline{X} - \mu_X}{S_x/\sqrt{n}} \sim t_{19}$$

That is, the t distribution with 19 d.f.

From the t distribution table given in Table E-2 in Appendix E, we observe that for 19 d.f.,

$$P(-2.861 \leq t \leq 2.861) = 0.99$$

Then from expression (D.6) we obtain

$$P\left(\overline{X} - 2.861\frac{S_x}{\sqrt{20}} \leq \mu_X \leq \overline{X} + 2.861\frac{S_x}{\sqrt{20}}\right) = 0.99$$

Substituting $\overline{X} = 6.5$, $S_x = 2$, and $n = 20$ into this inequality, we obtain

$$5.22 \leq \mu_X \leq 7.78 \quad \text{(approx.)} \tag{D.18}$$

as the 99% confidence interval for μ_X. Since this interval includes the hypothesized value of 7.5, we do not reject the null hypothesis that the true $\mu_X = 7.5$.

The null hypothesis in our P/E example was $\mu_X = 18.5$ and the alternative hypothesis was that $\mu_X \neq 18.5$, which is a two-sided, or composite, hypothesis.

How do we handle one-sided alternative hypotheses such as $\mu_X < 18.5$ *or* $\mu_X > 18.5$? Although the confidence interval approach can be easily adapted to construct one-sided confidence intervals, in practice it is much easier to use the test of significance approach to hypothesis testing, which we will now discuss.

The Test of Significance Approach to Hypothesis Testing

The test of significance is an alternative, but complementary and perhaps shorter, approach to hypothesis testing. To see the essential points involved, return to the P/E example and Eq. (D.3). We know that

$$t = \frac{\overline{X} - \mu_X}{S_x/\sqrt{n}} \qquad \text{(D.19) = (D.3)}$$

follows the t distribution with $(n - 1)$ d.f. In any concrete application we will know the values of $\overline{X}, S_x$, and n. The only unknown value is μ_X. But if we specify a value for μ_X, as we do under H_0, then the right-hand side of Eq. (D.3) is known, and therefore we will have a unique t value. And since we know that the t of Eq. (D.3) follows the t distribution with $(n - 1)$, we simply look up the t table to find out the probability of obtaining such a t value.

Observe that if the difference between $\overline{X}$ and μ_X is small (in absolute terms), then, as Eq. (D.3) shows, the $|t|$ value will also be small, where $|t|$ means the absolute t value. In the event that $\overline{X} = \mu_X$, t will be zero, in which case we do not reject the null hypothesis. *Therefore, as the $|t|$ value increasingly deviates from zero, we will tend to reject the null hypothesis.* As the t table shows, for any given d.f., the probability of obtaining an increasingly higher $|t|$ value becomes progressively smaller. *Thus, as $|t|$ gets larger, we will be more and more inclined to reject the null hypothesis.* But how large must $|t|$ be before we can reject the null hypothesis? The answer, as you would suspect, depends on α, the probability of committing a type I error, as well as on the d.f., as we will demonstrate shortly.

This is the general idea behind the test of significance approach to hypothesis testing. The key idea here is the **test statistic**—the t statistic—and its probability distribution under the hypothesized value of μ_X. Appropriately, in the present instance the test is known as the t **test** since we use the t distribution. (For details of the t distribution, see Section C.2).

In our P/E example $\overline{X} = 23.25$, $S_x = 9.49$ and $n = 28$. Let $H_0{:}\mu_X = 18.5$ and $H_1{:}\mu_X \neq 18.5$, as before. Therefore,

$$t = \frac{23.25 - 18.5}{9.49/\sqrt{28}} = 2.6486 \qquad \text{(D.20)}$$

Is the computed t value such that we can reject the null hypothesis? We cannot answer this question without first specifying what chance we are willing to take if we reject the null hypothesis when it is true. In other words, to answer this question, we must specify α, the probability of committing a type I error. Suppose we fix α at 5 percent. Since the alternative hypothesis is two-sided, we want to divide the risk of a type I error equally between the two tails of the

t distribution—the two critical regions—so that if the computed t value lies in either of the rejection regions, we can reject the null hypothesis.

Now for 27 d.f., as we saw earlier, the 5% *critical t values* are -2.052 and $+2.052$, as shown in Fig. D-1. The probability of obtaining a t value equal to or smaller than -2.0096 is 2.5 percent and that of obtaining a t value equal to or greater than $+2.0096$ is also 2.5 percent, giving the total probability of committing a type I error of 5 percent.

As Fig. D-1 also shows, the computed t value for our example is about 2.6, which obviously lies in the right tail critical region of the t distribution. We therefore reject the null hypothesis that the true average P/E ratio is 18.5. If that hypothesis were true, we would not have obtained a t value as large as 2.6 (in absolute terms); the probability of our obtaining such a t value is much smaller than 5 percent—our prechosen probability of committing a type I error. Actually, the probability is much smaller than 2.5 percent. (Why?)

In the language of the test of significance we frequently come across the following two terms:

1. A test (statistic) is *statistically significant.*
2. A test (statistic) is *statistically insignificant.*

When we say that a test is statistically significant, we generally mean that we can reject the null hypothesis. That is, the probability that the observed difference between the sample value and the hypothesized value is due to mere chance is small, less than α (the probability of a type I error). By the same token, when we say that a test is statistically insignificant, we do not reject the null hypothesis. In this case, the observed difference between the sample value and the hypothesized value could very well be due to sampling variation or due to mere chance (i.e., the probability of the difference is much greater than α).

When we reject the null hypothesis, we say that our finding is *statistically significant.* On the other hand, when we do not reject the null hypothesis, we say that our finding is *not statistically significant.*

One or Two-Tailed Test?   In all the examples considered so far the alternative hypothesis was two-sided, or two-tailed. Thus, if the average P/E ratio were equal to 18.5 under H_0, it was either greater than or less than 18.5 under H_1. In this case if the test statistic fell in either tail of the distribution (i.e., the rejection region), we rejected the null hypothesis, as is clear from Figure D-7(a).

However, there are occasions when the null and alternative hypotheses are one-sided, or one-tailed. For example, if for the P/E example we had $H_0{:}\mu_X \leq 18.5$ and $H_1{:}\mu_X > 18.5$, the alternative hypothesis is one-sided. How do we test this hypothesis?

The testing procedure is exactly the same as that used in previous cases except instead of finding out two critical values, we determine only a single critical value of the test statistic, as shown in Fig. D-7. As this figure illustrates, the probability of committing a type I error is now concentrated only in one tail of the probability distribution, t in the present case. For 27 d.f. and $\alpha = 5$ percent, the t table will

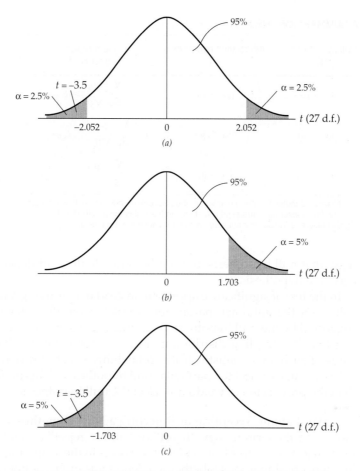

FIGURE D-7   The *t* test of significance: (*a*) Two-tailed; (*b*) right-tailed; (*c*) left-tailed

show that the one-tailed critical *t* value is 1.703 (right tail) or −1.703 (left tail), as shown in Fig. D-7. For our P/E example, as noted before, the computed *t* value is about 2.43. Since the *t* value lies in the critical region of Fig. D-7(*b*), this *t* value is statistically significant. That is, we reject the null hypothesis that the true average P/E ratio is equal to (or less than) 18.5; the chances of that happening are much smaller than our prechosen probability of committing a type I error of 5 percent.

Table D-2 summarizes the *t* test of significance approach to testing the two-tailed and one-tailed null hypothesis.

In practice, whether we use the confidence interval approach or the test of significance approach to hypothesis testing is a matter of personal choice and convenience.

In the confidence interval approach we specify a plausible range of values (i.e., confidence interval) for the true parameter and find out if the confidence interval includes the hypothesized value of that parameter. If it does, we do not

TABLE D-2 A SUMMARY OF THE *t* TEST

Null hypothesis H_0	Alternative hypothesis H_1	Critical region Reject H_0 if
$\mu_X = \mu_0$	$\mu_X > \mu_0$	$t = \dfrac{\overline{X} - \mu_0}{S_x/\sqrt{n}} > t_{\alpha,d.f.}$
$\mu_X = \mu_0$	$\mu_X < \mu_0$	$t = \dfrac{\overline{X} - \mu_0}{S_x/\sqrt{n}} < -t_{\alpha,d.f.}$
$\mu_X = \mu_0$	$\mu_X \neq \mu_0$	$|t| = \dfrac{\overline{X} - \mu_0}{S_x/\sqrt{n}} > t_{\alpha/2,d.f.}$

Note: μ_0 denotes the particular value of μ_X assumed under the null hypothesis. The first subscript on the *t* statistic shown in the last column is the level of significance, and the second subscript is the d.f. These are the critical *t* values.

reject that null hypothesis, but if it lies outside the confidence interval, we can reject the hypothesis.

In the test of significance approach, instead of specifying a range of plausible values for the unknown parameter, we pick a specific value of the parameter suggested by the null hypothesis; compute a test statistic, such as the *t* statistic; and find its sampling distribution and the probability of obtaining a specific value of such a test statistic. If this probability is very low, say, less than $\alpha = 5$ or 1 percent, we reject the particular null hypothesis. If this probability is greater than the preselected α, we do not reject the null hypothesis.

A Word about Accepting or Rejecting a Null Hypothesis   In this book we have used the terminology "reject" or "do not reject" a null hypothesis rather than "reject" or "accept" a hypothesis. This is in the same spirit as a jury verdict in a court trial that says whether a defendant is guilty or not guilty rather than guilty or innocent. The fact that a person is not found guilty does not necessarily mean that he or she is innocent. Similarly, the fact that we do not reject a null hypothesis does not necessarily mean that the hypothesis is true, because another null hypothesis may be equally compatible with the data. For our P/E example, for instance, from Eq. (D.7) it is obvious any value of μ_X between 19.57 and 26.93 would be an "acceptable" hypothesis.

A Word on Choosing the Level of Significance, α, and the *p* Value

The Achilles heel of the classical approach to hypothesis testing is its arbitrariness in selecting α. Although 1, 5, and 10 percent are the commonly used values of α, there is nothing sacrosanct about these values. As noted earlier, unless we examine the consequences of committing both type I and type II errors, we cannot make the appropriate choice of α. In practice, it is preferable to find the **p value** (i.e., the probability value), also known as the *exact significance level*, of the test statistic. This may be defined as *the lowest significance level at which a null hypothesis can be rejected*.

To illustrate, in an application involving 20 d.f. a t value of 3.552 was obtained. The t table given in Appendix E (Table E-2) shows that the p value for this t is 0.001 (one-tailed) or 0.002 (two-tailed). That is, this t value is statistically significant at the 0.001 (one-tailed) or 0.002 (two-tailed) level.

For our P/E example under the null hypothesis that the true P/E ratio is 18.5, we found that $t = 2.43$. If the alternative hypothesis is that the true P/E ratio is greater than 18.5, we find from Table E-1 in Appendix E that $P(t > 2.43)$ is about .01 This is the p value of the t statistic. We say that this t value is statistically significant at the 0.01 or 1 percent level. Put differently, if we were to fix $\alpha = 0.01$, at that level we can reject the null hypothesis that the true $\mu_X = 18.5$. Of course, this is a much smaller probability, smaller than the conventional α value, such as 5 percent. Therefore, we can reject the null hypothesis much more emphatically than if we were to choose, say, $\alpha = 0.05$. *As a rule, the smaller the p value, the stronger the evidence against the null hypothesis.*

One virtue of quoting the p value is that it avoids the arbitrariness involved in fixing α at artificial levels, such as 1, 5, or 10 percent. If, for example, in an application the p value of a test statistic (such as t) is, say, 0.135, and if you are willing to accept an $\alpha = 13.5$ percent, this p value is statistically significant (i.e., you reject the null hypothesis at this level of significance). Nothing is wrong if you want to take a chance of being wrong 13.5 percent of the time if you reject the true null hypothesis.

Nowadays several statistical packages routinely compute the p values of various test statistics, and *it is recommended that you report these p values.*

The χ^2 and *F* Tests of Significance

Besides the t test of significance discussed previously, in the main chapters of the text we will need tests of significance based on the χ^2 and the F probability distributions considered in Appendix C. Since the philosophy of testing is the same, we will simply present here the actual mechanism with a couple of illustrative examples; we will present further examples in the main text.

The χ^2 test of significance In Appendix C (see Example C.14) we showed that if S^2 is the sample variance obtained from a random sample of n observations from a normal population with variance σ^2, then the quantity

$$(n - 1)\left(\frac{S^2}{\sigma^2}\right) \sim \chi^2_{(n-1)} \qquad \textbf{(D.21)}$$

That is, the ratio of the sample variance to population variance multiplied by the d.f. $(n - 1)$ follows the χ^2 distribution with $(n - 1)$ d.f. If the d.f. and S^2 are known but σ^2 is not known, we can establish a $(1 - \alpha)$% confidence interval for the true but unknown σ^2 using the χ^2 distribution. The mechanism is similar to that for establishing confidence intervals on the basis of the t test.

But if we are given a specific value of σ^2 under H_0, we can directly compute the χ^2 value from expression (D.21) and test its significance against the critical χ^2 values given in Table E-4 in Appendix E. An example follows.

Example D.4.

Suppose a random sample of 31 observations from a normal population gives a (sample) variance of $S^2 = 12$. Test the hypothesis that the true variance is 9 against the hypothesis that it is different from 9. Use $\alpha = 5\%$. Here

$$H_0{:}\sigma^2 = 9 \quad \text{and} \quad H_1{:}\sigma^2 \neq 9$$

Answer: Putting the appropriate numbers in expression (D.21), we obtain: $\chi^2 = 30(12/9) = 40$, which has 30 d.f. From Table E-4 in Appendix E, we observe that the probability of obtaining a χ^2 value of about 40 or higher (for 30 d.f.) is 0.10 or 10 percent. Since this probability is greater than our level of significance of 5 percent, we do not reject the null hypothesis that the true variance is 9.

Table D-3 summarizes the χ^2 **test** for the various types of null and alternative hypotheses.

The *F* Test of Significance In Appendix C we showed that if we have two randomly selected samples from two normal populations, X and Y, with m and n observations, respectively, then the variable

$$F = \frac{S_X^2}{S_Y^2}$$

$$= \frac{\Sigma(X_i - \overline{X})^2/(m - 1)}{\Sigma(Y_i - \overline{Y})^2/(n - 1)} \tag{D.22}$$

follows the F distribution with $(m - 1)$ and $(n - 1)$ d.f., *provided the variances of the two normal populations are equal.* In other words, the H_0 is $\sigma_X^2 = \sigma_Y^2$. To test this hypothesis, we use the ***F* test** given in Eq. (D.22). An example follows.

Example D.5.

Refer to the S.A.T. math scores for male and female students given in Examples C.12 and C.15. The variances of these scores were (48.31) for the

TABLE D-3 A SUMMARY OF THE χ^2 TEST

Null hypothesis H_0	Alternative hypothesis H_1	Critical region Reject H_0 if
$\sigma_X^2 = \sigma_0^2$	$\sigma_X^2 > \sigma_0^2$	$\dfrac{(n-1)S^2}{\sigma_0^2} > \chi^2_{\alpha,(n-1)}$
$\sigma_X^2 = \sigma_0^2$	$\sigma_X^2 < \sigma_0^2$	$\dfrac{(n-1)S^2}{\sigma_0^2} < \chi^2_{(1-\alpha),(n-1)}$
$\sigma_X^2 = \sigma_0^2$	$\sigma_X^2 \neq \sigma_0^2$	$\dfrac{(n-1)S^2}{\sigma_0^2} > \chi^2_{\alpha/2,(n-1)}$
		or $< \chi^2_{(1-\alpha/2),(n-1)}$

Note: σ_0^2 is the value of σ_X^2 under the null hypothesis. The first subscript on χ^2 in the last column is the level of significance and the second subscript is the d.f. These are critical χ^2 values.

male students and (102.07) for the female students. The number of observations were 36 or 35 d.f. each. Assuming that these variances represent a sample from a much larger population of S.A.T. scores, test the hypothesis that the male and female population variances on the math part of the S.A.T. scores are the same. Use $\alpha = 1\%$.

Answer: Here the *F* value is $102.07/48.31 = 2.1128$ (approx.). This *F* value has the *F* distribution with 35 d.f. each. Now from Table E-3 in Appendix E we see that for 30 d.f. (35 d.f. is not given in the table), the *critical F* value at the 1% level of significance is 2.39. Since the observed *F* value of 2.1128 is less than 2.39, it is not statistically significant. That is, at $\alpha = 1\%$, we do not reject the null hypothesis that the two population variances are the same.

Example D.6.

In the preceding example, what is the *p* value of obtaining an *F* value of 2.1128? Using MINITAB, we can find that for 35 d.f. in the numerator and denominator, the probability of obtaining an *F* value of 2.1128 or greater is about 0.01492 or about 10.5 percent. This is the *p* value of obtaining an *F* value of as much as 2.1128 or greater. In other words, this is the lowest level of probability at which we can reject the null hypothesis that the two variances are the same. Therefore, in this case if we reject the null hypothesis that the two variances are the same, we are taking the chance of being wrong 1.5 out of 100 times.

Examples D.5 and D.6 suggest a practical strategy. We may fix α at some level (e.g., 1, 5, or 10 percent) and also find out the *p* value of the test statistic. If the estimated *p* value is smaller than the chosen level of significance, we can reject the null hypothesis under consideration. On the other hand, if the estimated *p* value is greater than the preselected level of significance, we may not reject the null hypothesis.

Table D-4 summarizes the *F* test.

TABLE D-4 A SUMMARY OF THE *F* STATISTIC

Null hypothesis H_0	Alternative hypothesis H_1	Critical region Reject H_0 if
$\sigma_1^2 = \sigma_2^2$	$\sigma_1^2 > \sigma_2^2$	$\dfrac{S_1^2}{S_2^2} > F_{\alpha,ndf,\,ddf}$
$\sigma_1^2 = \sigma_2^2$	$\sigma_1^2 \neq \sigma_2^2$	$\dfrac{S_1^2}{S_2^2} > F_{\alpha/2,ndf,ddf}$ or $< F_{(1-\alpha/2),ndf,ddf}$

Notes:
1. σ_1^2 and σ_2^2 are the two population variances.
2. S_1^2 and S_2^2 are the two sample variances.
3. *ndf* and *ddf* denote, respectively, the numerator and denominator d.f.
4. In computing the *F* ratio, put the larger S^2 value in the numerator.
5. The critical *F* values are given in the last column. The first subscript of *F* is the level of significance and the second subscript is the numerator and denominator d.f.
6. Note that $F_{(1-\alpha/2),ndf,ddf} = \dfrac{1}{F_{\alpha/2,ddf,ndf}}$.

To conclude this appendix, we summarize the steps involved in testing a statistical hypothesis:

Step 1: State the null hypothesis H_0 and the alternative hypothesis H_1 (e.g., $H_0 : \mu_X = 18.5$ and $H_1 : \mu_X \neq 18.5$ for our P/E example).
Step 2: Select the test statistic (e.g., $\overline{X}$).
Step 3: Determine the probability distribution of the test statistic (e.g., $\overline{X} \sim N(\mu_X, \sigma_X^2/n)$.
Step 4: Choose the level of significance α, that is, the probability of committing a type I error. (But keep in mind our discussion about the p value.)
Step 5: Choose the confidence interval or the test of significance approach.

The Confidence Interval Approach Using the probability distribution of the test statistic, establish a $100(1 - \alpha)\%$ confidence interval. If this interval (i.e., the acceptance region) includes the *null-hypothesized value*, do not reject the null hypothesis. But if this interval does not include it, reject the null hypothesis.

The Test of Significance Approach Alternatively, you can follow this approach by obtaining the relevant test statistic (e.g., the t statistic) under the null hypothesis and find out the p value of obtaining a specified value of the test statistic from the appropriate probability distribution (e.g., the t, F, or the χ^2 distribution). If this probability is less than the prechosen value of α, you can reject the null hypothesis. But if it is greater than α, do not reject it. If you do not want to preselect α, just present the p value of the statistic.

Whether you choose the confidence interval or the test of significance approach, *always keep in mind that in rejecting or not rejecting a null hypothesis you are taking a chance of being wrong α (or p value) percent of the time.*

Further uses of the various tests of significance discussed in this appendix will be illustrated throughout the rest of this book.

D.6 SUMMARY

Estimating population parameters on the basis of sample information and testing hypotheses about them in light of the sample information are the two main branches of (classical) statistical inference. In this appendix we examined the essential features of these branches.

KEY TERMS AND CONCEPTS

The key terms and concepts introduced in this appendix are

Statistical inference
Parameter estimation
  a) point estimation
  b) interval estimation
Sampling (probability) distribution

Critical t values
Confidence interval (CI)
  a) confidence coefficient
  b) random interval (lower limit, upper limit)

Level of significance
Probability of committing a type I error
Properties of estimators
   a) linearity (linear estimator)
   b) unbiasedness (unbiased
     estimator)
   c) minimum variance (minimum-
     variance estimator)
   d) efficiency (efficient estimator)
   e) best linear unbiased estimator
     (BLUE)
   f) consistency (consistent
     estimator)
Hypothesis testing
   a) null hypothesis
   b) alternative hypothesis
   c) one-sided; one-tailed
     hypothesis

   d) two-sided; two-tailed;
     composite hypothesis
Confidence interval (approach to
   hypothesis testing)
   a) acceptance region
   b) critical region; region of
     rejection
   c) critical values
Type I error (α); level of significance;
   confidence coefficient $(1 - \alpha)$
Type II error (β)
   power of the test $(1 - \beta)$
Tests of significance (approach to
   hypothesis testing)
   a) Test statistic; t statistic; t test
   b) χ^2 test
   c) F test
The p value

QUESTIONS

D.1. What is the distinction between each of the following pairs of terms?
   a. Point estimator and interval estimator.
   b. Null and alternative hypotheses.
   c. Type I and type II errors.
   d. Confidence coefficient and level of significance.
   e. Type II error and power.
D.2. What is the meaning of
   a. Statistical inference.   **e.** Critical value of a test.
   b. Sampling distribution.   **f.** Level of significance.
   c. Acceptance region.   **g.** The p value.
   d. Test statistic.
D.3. Explain carefully the meaning of
   a. An unbiased estimator.   **d.** A linear estimator.
   b. A minimum variance estimator.   **e.** A best linear unbiased estimator (BLUE).
   c. A best, or efficient, estimator.
D.4. State whether the following statements are true, false, or uncertain. Justify your answers.
   a. An estimator of a parameter is a random variable, but the parameter is non-random, or fixed.
   b. An unbiased estimator of a parameter, say, μ_X, means that it will always be equal to μ_X.
   c. An estimator can be a minimum variance estimator without being unbiased.
   d. An efficient estimator means an estimator with minimum variance.
   e. An estimator can be BLUE only if its sampling distribution is normal.
   f. An acceptance region and a confidence interval for any given problem means the same thing.

g. A type I error occurs when we reject the null hypothesis even though it is false.

h. A type II error occurs when we reject the null hypothesis even though it may be true.

i. As the degrees of freedom (d.f.) increase indefinitely, the t distribution approaches the normal distribution.

j. The central limit theorem states that the sample mean is always distributed normally.

k. The terms *level of significance* and *p value* mean the same thing.

D.5. Explain carefully the difference between the confidence interval and test of significance approaches to hypothesis testing.

D.6. Suppose in an example with 40 d.f. that you obtained a t value of 1.35. Since its p value is somewhere between a 5 and 10 percent level of significance (one-tailed), it is not statistically very significant. Do you agree with this statement? Why or why not?

PROBLEMS

D.7. Find the critical Z values in the following cases:
a. $\alpha = 0.05$ (two-tailed test)   c. $\alpha = 0.01$ (two-tailed test)
b. $\alpha = 0.05$ (one-tailed test)   d. $\alpha = 0.02$ (one-tailed test)

D.8. Find the critical t values in the following cases:
a. $n = 4$, $\alpha = 0.05$ (two-tailed test)   d. $n = 14$, $\alpha = 0.01$ (one-tailed test)
b. $n = 4$, $\alpha = 0.05$ (one-tailed test)   e. $n = 60$, $\alpha = 0.05$ (two-tailed test)
c. $n = 14$, $\alpha = 0.01$ (two-tailed test)   f. $n = 200$, $\alpha = 0.05$ (two-tailed test)

D.9. Assume that the per capita income of residents in a country is normally distributed with mean $\mu = \$1000$ and variance $\sigma^2 = 10,000$ ($\$$ squared).
a. What is the probability that the per capita income lies between $800 and $1200?
b. What is the probability that it exceeds $1200?
c. What is the probability that it is less than $800?
d. Is it true that the probability of per capita income exceeding $5000 is practically zero?

D.10. Continuing with problem D.9, based on a random sample of 1000 members, suppose that you find the sample mean income, $\overline{X}$, to be $900.
a. Given that $\mu = \$1000$, what is the probability of obtaining such a sample mean value?
b. Based on the sample mean, establish a 95% confidence interval for μ and find out if this confidence interval includes $\mu = \$1000$. If it does not, what conclusions would you draw?
c. Using the test of significance approach, decide whether you want to accept or reject the hypothesis that $\mu = \$1000$. Which test did you use and why?

D.11. The number of peanuts contained in a jar follows the normal distribution with mean μ and variance σ^2. Quality control inspections over several periods show that 5 percent of the jars contain less than 6.5 ounces of peanuts and 10 percent contain more than 6.8 ounces.
a. Find μ and σ^2.
b. What percentage of bottles contain more than 7 ounces?

D.12. The following random sample was obtained from a normal population with mean μ and variance $= 2$.

$$8, 9, 6, 13, 11, 8, 12, 5, 4, 14$$

a. Test: $\mu = 5$ against $\mu \neq 5$

b. Test: $\mu = 5$ against $\mu > 5$

  Note: use $\alpha = 5\%$.

c. What is the p value in part (*a*) of this problem?

D.13. Based on a random sample of 10 values from a normal population with mean μ and standard deviation σ, you calculated that $\overline{X} = 8$ and the sample standard deviation $= 4$. Estimate a 95% confidence interval for the population mean. Which probability distribution did you use? Why?

D.14. You are told that $X \sim N(\mu_X = 8, \sigma_X^2 = 36)$. Based on a sample of 25 observations, you found that $\overline{X} = 7.5$.

a. What is the sampling distribution of $\overline{X}$?

b. What is the probability of obtaining an $\overline{X} = 7.5$ or less?

c. From your answer in part (*b*) of this problem, could such a sample value have come from the preceding population?

D.15. Compute the p values in the following cases:

a. $t \geq 1.72$, d.f. $= 24$

b. $Z \geq 2.9$

c. $F \geq 2.59$, d.f. $= 3$ and 20, respectively

d. $\chi^2 \geq 19$, d.f. $= 30$

  Note: If you cannot get an exact answer from the various probability distribution tables, try to obtain them from a program such as MINITAB or Excel.

D.16. In an application involving 30 d.f. you obtained a t statistic of 0.68. Since this t value is not statistically significant even at the 10% level of significance, you can safely accept the relevant hypothesis. Do you agree with this statement? What is the p value of obtaining such a statistic?

D.17. Let $X \sim N(\mu_X, \sigma_X^2)$. A random sample of three observations was obtained from this population. Consider the following estimators of μ_X:

$$\hat{\mu}_1 = \frac{X_1 + X_2 + X_3}{3} \quad \text{and} \quad \hat{\mu}_2 = \frac{X_1}{6} + \frac{X_2}{3} + \frac{X_3}{2}$$

a. Is $\hat{\mu}_1$ an unbiased estimator of μ_X? What about $\hat{\mu}_2$?

b. If both estimators are unbiased, which one would you choose? (*Hint:* Compare the variances of the two estimators.)

D.18. Refer to Problem C.10 in Appendix C. Suppose a random sample of 10 firms gave a mean profit of $900,000 and a (sample) standard deviation of $100,000.

a. Establish a 95% confidence interval for the true mean profit in the industry.

b. Which probability distribution did you use? Why?

D.19. Refer to Example C.14 in Appendix C.

a. Establish a 95% confidence interval for the true σ^2.

b. Test the hypothesis that the true variance is 8.2.

D.20. Sixteen cars are first driven with a standard fuel and then with Petrocoal, a gasoline with a methanol additive. The results of the nitrous oxide emissions (NO_x) test are as follows:

Type of fuel	Average NO_x	Standard deviation of NO_x
Standard	1.075	0.5796
Petrocoal	1.159	0.6134

Source: Michael O. Finkelstein and Bruce Levin, *Statistics for Lawyers*, Springer-Verlag, New York, 1990, p. 230.

     a. How would you test the hypothesis that the two population standard deviations are the same?

     b. Which test did you use? What are the assumptions underlying that test?

D.21. Show that the estimator given in Eq. (D.14) is biased. (*Hint:* Expand Eq. (D.14), and take the expectation of each term, keeping in mind that the expected value of each X_i is μ_X).

D.22. *One-sided confidence interval.* Return to the P/E example in this appendix and look at the two-sided 95% confidence interval given in Eq. (D.7). Suppose you want to establish a one-sided confidence interval only, either an upper bound or a lower bound. How would you go about establishing such an interval? (*Hint:* Find the one-tail critical t value.)

APPENDIX E

STATISTICAL TABLES

TABLE E-1a   AREAS UNDER THE STANDARDIZED NORMAL DISTRIBUTION

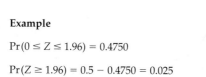

Example

$\Pr(0 \le Z \le 1.96) = 0.4750$

$\Pr(Z \ge 1.96) = 0.5 - 0.4750 = 0.025$

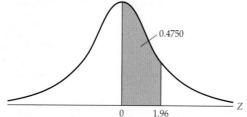

Z	.00	.01	.02	.03	.04	.05	.06	.07	.08	.09
0.0	.0000	.0040	.0080	.0120	.0160	.0199	.0239	.0279	.0319	.0359
0.1	.0398	.0438	.0478	.0517	.0557	.0596	.0636	.0675	.0714	.0753
0.2	.0793	.0832	.0871	.0910	.0948	.0987	.1026	.1064	.1103	.1141
0.3	.1179	.1217	.1255	.1293	.1331	.1368	.1406	.1443	.1480	.1517
0.4	.1554	.1591	.1628	.1664	.1700	.1736	.1772	.1808	.1844	.1879
0.5	.1915	.1950	.1985	.2019	.2054	.2088	.2123	.2157	.2190	.2224
0.6	.2257	.2291	.2324	.2357	.2389	.2422	.2454	.2486	.2517	.2549
0.7	.2580	.2611	.2642	.2673	.2704	.2734	.2764	.2794	.2823	.2852
0.8	.2881	.2910	.2939	.2967	.2995	.3023	.3051	.3078	.3106	.3133
0.9	.3159	.3186	.3212	.3238	.3264	.3289	.3315	.3340	.3365	.3389
1.0	.3413	.3438	.3461	.3485	.3508	.3531	.3554	.3577	.3599	.3621
1.1	.3643	.3665	.3686	.3708	.3729	.3749	.3770	.3790	.3810	.3830
1.2	.3849	.3869	.3888	.3907	.3925	.3944	.3962	.3980	.3997	.4015
1.3	.4032	.4049	.4066	.4082	.4099	.4115	.4131	.4147	.4162	.4177
1.4	.4192	.4207	.4222	.4236	.4251	.4265	.4279	.4292	.4306	.4319
1.5	.4332	.4345	.4357	.4370	.4382	.4394	.4406	.4418	.4429	.4441
1.6	.4452	.4463	.4474	.4484	.4495	.4505	.4515	.4525	.4535	.4545
1.7	.4454	.4564	.4573	.4582	.4591	.4599	.4608	.4616	.4625	.4633
1.8	.4641	.4649	.4656	.4664	.4671	.4678	.4686	.4693	.4699	.4706
1.9	.4713	.4719	.4726	.4732	.4738	.4744	.4750	.4756	.4761	.4767
2.0	.4772	.4778	.4783	.4788	.4793	.4798	.4803	.4808	.4812	.4817
2.1	.4821	.4826	.4830	.4834	.4838	.4842	.4846	.4850	.4854	.4857
2.2	.4861	.4864	.4868	.4871	.4875	.4878	.4881	.4884	.4887	.4890
2.3	.4893	.4896	.4898	.4901	.4904	.4906	.4909	.4911	.4913	.4916
2.4	.4918	.4920	.4922	.4925	.4927	.4929	.4931	.4932	.4934	.4936
2.5	.4938	.4940	.4941	.4943	.4945	.4946	.4948	.4949	.4951	.4952
2.6	.4953	.4955	.4956	.4957	.4959	.4960	.4961	.4962	.4963	.4964
2.7	.4965	.4966	.4967	.4968	.4969	.4970	.4971	.4972	.4973	.4974
2.8	.4974	.4975	.4976	.4977	.4977	.4978	.4979	.4979	.4980	.4981
2.9	.4981	.4982	.4982	.4983	.4984	.4984	.4985	.4985	.4986	.4986
3.0	.4987	.4987	.4987	.4988	.4988	.4989	.4989	.4989	.4990	.4990

Note: This table gives the area in the right-hand tail of the distribution (i.e., $Z \ge 0$). But since the normal distribution is symmetrical about $Z = 0$, the area in the left-hand tail is the same as the area in the corresponding right-hand tail. For example, $P(-1.96 \le Z \le 0) = 0.4750$. Therefore, $P(-1.96 \le Z \le 1.96) = 2(0.4750) = 0.95$.

TABLE E-1b CUMULATIVE PROBABILITIES OF THE STANDARD NORMAL DISTRIBUTION

Entry is area A under the standard normal curve from $-\infty$ to $Z(A)$

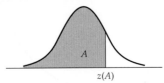

$z(A)$

z	.00	.01	.02	.03	.04	.05	.06	.07	.08	.09
.0	.5000	.5040	.5080	.5120	.5160	.5199	.5239	.5279	.5319	.5359
.1	.5398	.5438	.5478	.5517	.5557	.5596	.5636	.5675	.5714	.5753
.2	.5793	.5832	.5871	.5910	.5948	.5987	.6026	.6064	.6103	.6141
.3	.6179	.6217	.6255	.6293	.6331	.6368	.6406	.6443	.6480	.6517
.4	.6554	.6591	.6628	.6664	.6700	.6736	.6772	.6808	.6844	.6879
.5	.6915	.6950	.6985	.7019	.7054	.7088	.7123	.7157	.7190	.7224
.6	.7257	.7291	.7324	.7357	.7389	.7422	.7454	.7486	.7517	.7549
.7	.7580	.7611	.7642	.7673	.7704	.7734	.7764	.7794	.7823	.7852
.8	.7881	.7910	.7939	.7967	.7995	.8023	.8051	.8078	.8106	.8133
.9	.8159	.8186	.8212	.8238	.8264	.8289	.8315	.8340	.8365	.8389
1.0	.8413	.8438	.8461	.8485	.8508	.8531	.8554	.8577	.8599	.8621
1.1	.8643	.8665	.8686	.8708	.8729	.8749	.8770	.8790	.8810	.8830
1.2	.8849	.8869	.8888	.8907	.8925	.8944	.8962	.8980	.8997	.9015
1.3	.9032	.9049	.9066	.9082	.9099	.9115	.9131	.9147	.9162	.9177
1.4	.9192	.9207	.9222	.9236	.9251	.9265	.9279	.9292	.9306	.9319
1.5	.9332	.9345	.9357	.9370	.9382	.9394	.9406	.9418	.9429	.9441
1.6	.9452	.9463	.9474	.9484	.9495	.9505	.9515	.9525	.9535	.9545
1.7	.9554	.9564	.9573	.9582	.9591	.9599	.9608	.9616	.9625	.9633
1.8	.9641	.9649	.9656	.9664	.9671	.9678	.9686	.9693	.9699	.9706
1.9	.9713	.9719	.9726	.9732	.9738	.9744	.9750	.9756	.9761	.9767
2.0	.9772	.9778	.9783	.9788	.9793	.9798	.9803	.9808	.9812	.9817
2.1	.9821	.9826	.9830	.9834	.9838	.9842	.9846	.9850	.9854	.9857
2.2	.9861	.9864	.9868	.9871	.9875	.9878	.9881	.9884	.9887	.9890
2.3	.9893	.9896	.9898	.9901	.9904	.9906	.9909	.9911	.9913	.9916
2.4	.9918	.9920	.9922	.9925	.9927	.9929	.9931	.9932	.9934	.9936
2.5	.9938	.9940	.9941	.9943	.9945	.9946	.9948	.9949	.9951	.9952
2.6	.9953	.9955	.9956	.9957	.9959	.9960	.9961	.9962	.9963	.9964
2.7	.9965	.9966	.9967	.9968	.9969	.9970	.9971	.9972	.9973	.9974
2.8	.9974	.9975	.9976	.9977	.9977	.9978	.9979	.9979	.9980	.9981
2.9	.9981	.9982	.9982	.9983	.9984	.9984	.9985	.9985	.9986	.9986
3.0	.9987	.9987	.9987	.9988	.9988	.9989	.9989	.9989	.9990	.9990
3.1	.9990	.9991	.9991	.9991	.9992	.9992	.9992	.9992	.9993	.9993
3.2	.9993	.9993	.9994	.9994	.9994	.9994	.9994	.9995	.9995	.9995
3.3	.9995	.9995	.9995	.9996	.9996	.9996	.9996	.9996	.9996	.9997
3.4	.9997	.9997	.9997	.9997	.9997	.9997	.9997	.9997	.9997	.9998

Selected Percentiles

Cumulative probability A:	.90	.95	.975	.98	.99	.995	.999
Z(A):	1.282	1.645	1.960	2.054	2.326	2.576	3.090

TABLE E-2   PERCENTAGE POINTS OF THE t DISTRIBUTION

Example

$\Pr(t > 2.086) = 0.025$

$\Pr(t > 1.725) = 0.05$ for d.f. = 20

$\Pr(|t| > 1.725) = 0.10$

Pr d.f.	0.25 0.50	0.10 0.20	0.05 0.10	0.025 0.05	0.01 0.02	0.005 0.010	0.001 0.002
1	1.000	3.078	6.314	12.706	31.821	63.657	318.31
2	0.816	1.886	2.920	4.303	6.965	9.925	22.327
3	0.765	1.638	2.353	3.182	4.541	5.841	10.214
4	0.741	1.533	2.132	2.776	3.747	4.604	7.173
5	0.727	1.476	2.015	2.571	3.365	4.032	5.893
6	0.718	1.440	1.943	2.447	3.143	3.707	5.208
7	0.711	1.415	1.895	2.365	2.998	3.499	4.785
8	0.706	1.397	1.860	2.306	2.896	3.355	4.501
9	0.703	1.383	1.833	2.262	2.821	3.250	4.297
10	0.700	1.372	1.812	2.228	2.764	3.169	4.144
11	0.697	1.363	1.796	2.201	2.718	3.106	4.025
12	0.695	1.356	1.782	2.179	2.681	3.055	3.930
13	0.694	1.350	1.771	2.160	2.650	3.012	3.852
14	0.692	1.345	1.761	2.145	2.624	2.977	3.787
15	0.691	1.341	1.753	2.131	2.602	2.947	3.733
16	0.690	1.337	1.746	2.120	2.583	2.921	3.686
17	0.689	1.333	1.740	2.110	2.567	2.898	3.646
18	0.688	1.330	1.734	2.101	2.552	2.878	3.610
19	0.688	1.328	1.729	2.093	2.539	2.861	3.579
20	0.687	1.325	1.725	2.086	2.528	2.845	3.552
21	0.686	1.323	1.721	2.080	2.518	2.831	3.527
22	0.686	1.321	1.717	2.074	2.508	2.819	3.505
23	0.685	1.319	1.714	2.069	2.500	2.807	3.485
24	0.685	1.318	1.711	2.064	2.492	2.797	3.467
25	0.684	1.316	1.708	2.060	2.485	2.787	3.450
26	0.684	1.315	1.706	2.056	2.479	2.779	3.435
27	0.684	1.314	1.703	2.052	2.473	2.771	3.421
28	0.683	1.313	1.701	2.048	2.467	2.763	3.408
29	0.683	1.311	1.699	2.045	2.462	2.756	3.396
30	0.683	1.310	1.697	2.042	2.457	2.750	3.385
40	0.681	1.303	1.684	2.021	2.423	2.704	3.307
60	0.679	1.296	1.671	2.000	2.390	2.660	3.232
120	0.677	1.289	1.658	1.980	2.358	2.617	3.160
∞	0.674	1.282	1.645	1.960	2.326	2.576	3.090

Note: The smaller probability shown at the head of each column is the area in one tail; the larger probability is the area in both tails.

Source: From E. S. Pearson and H. O. Hartley, eds., *Biometrika Tables for Statisticians,* vol. 1, 3rd ed., Table 12, Cambridge University Press, New York, 1966. Reproduced by permission of the editors and trustees of *Biometrika*.

TABLE E-3 UPPER PERCENTAGE POINTS OF THE *F* DISTRIBUTION

Example

$\Pr(F > 1.59) = 0.25$

$\Pr(F > 2.42) = 0.10$ for d.f. $N_1 = 10$

$\Pr(F > 3.14) = 0.05$ and $N_2 = 9$

$\Pr(F > 5.26) = 0.01$

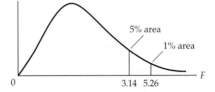

d.f. for denominator N_2	Pr	\multicolumn{12}{c}{d.f. for numerator N_1}
		1	2	3	4	5	6	7	8	9	10	11	12
1	.25	5.83	7.50	8.20	8.58	8.82	8.98	9.10	9.19	9.26	9.32	9.36	9.41
	.10	39.90	49.50	53.60	55.80	57.20	58.20	58.90	59.40	59.90	60.20	60.50	60.70
	.05	161.00	200.00	216.00	225.00	230.00	234.00	237.00	239.00	241.00	242.00	243.00	244.00
2	.25	2.57	3.00	3.15	3.23	3.28	3.31	3.34	3.35	3.37	3.38	3.39	3.39
	.10	8.53	9.00	9.16	9.24	9.29	9.33	9.35	9.37	9.38	9.39	9.40	9.41
	.05	18.50	19.00	19.20	19.20	19.30	19.30	19.40	19.40	19.40	19.40	19.40	19.40
	.01	98.50	99.00	99.20	99.20	99.30	99.30	99.40	99.40	99.40	99.40	99.40	99.40
3	.25	2.02	2.28	2.36	2.39	2.41	2.42	2.43	2.44	2.44	2.44	2.45	2.45
	.10	5.54	5.46	5.39	5.34	5.31	5.28	5.27	5.25	5.24	5.23	5.22	5.22
	.05	10.10	9.55	9.28	9.12	9.01	8.94	8.89	8.85	8.81	8.79	8.76	8.74
	.01	34.10	30.80	29.50	28.70	28.20	27.90	27.70	27.50	27.30	27.20	27.10	27.10
4	.25	1.81	2.00	2.05	2.06	2.07	2.08	2.08	2.08	2.08	2.08	2.08	2.08
	.10	4.54	4.32	4.19	4.11	4.05	4.01	3.98	3.95	3.94	3.92	3.91	3.90
	.05	7.71	6.94	6.59	6.39	6.26	6.16	6.09	6.04	6.00	5.96	5.94	5.91
	.01	21.20	18.00	16.70	16.00	15.50	15.20	15.00	14.80	14.70	14.50	14.40	14.40
5	.25	1.69	1.85	1.88	1.89	1.89	1.89	1.89	1.89	1.89	1.89	1.89	1.89
	.10	4.06	3.78	3.62	3.52	3.45	3.40	3.37	3.34	3.32	3.30	3.28	3.27
	.05	6.61	5.79	5.41	5.19	5.05	4.95	4.88	4.82	4.77	4.74	4.71	4.68
	.01	16.30	13.30	12.10	11.40	11.00	10.70	10.50	10.30	10.20	10.10	9.96	9.89
6	.25	1.62	1.76	1.78	1.79	1.79	1.78	1.78	1.78	1.77	1.77	1.77	1.77
	.10	3.78	3.46	3.29	3.18	3.11	3.05	3.01	2.98	2.96	2.94	2.92	2.90
	.05	5.99	5.14	4.76	4.53	4.39	4.28	4.21	4.15	4.10	4.06	4.03	4.00
	.01	13.70	10.90	9.78	9.15	8.75	8.47	8.26	8.10	7.98	7.87	7.79	7.72
7	.25	1.57	1.70	1.72	1.72	1.71	1.71	1.70	1.70	1.69	1.69	1.69	1.68
	.10	3.59	3.26	3.07	2.96	2.88	2.83	2.78	2.75	2.72	2.70	2.68	2.67
	.05	5.59	4.74	4.35	4.12	3.97	3.87	3.79	3.73	3.68	3.64	3.60	3.57
	.01	12.20	9.55	8.45	7.85	7.46	7.19	6.99	6.84	6.72	6.62	6.54	6.47
8	.25	1.54	1.66	1.67	1.66	1.66	1.65	1.64	1.64	1.63	1.63	1.63	1.62
	.10	3.46	3.11	2.92	2.81	2.73	2.67	2.62	2.59	2.56	2.54	2.52	2.50
	.05	5.32	4.46	4.07	3.84	3.69	3.58	3.50	3.44	3.39	3.35	3.31	3.28
	.01	11.30	8.65	7.59	7.01	6.63	6.37	6.18	6.03	5.91	5.81	5.73	5.67
9	.25	1.51	1.62	1.63	1.63	1.62	1.61	1.60	1.60	1.59	1.59	1.58	1.58
	.10	3.36	3.01	2.81	2.69	2.61	2.55	2.51	2.47	2.44	2.42	2.40	2.38
	.05	5.12	4.26	3.86	3.63	3.48	3.37	3.29	3.23	3.18	3.14	3.10	3.07
	.01	10.60	8.02	6.99	6.42	6.06	5.80	5.61	5.47	5.35	5.26	5.18	5.11

				d.f. for numerator N_1										d.f. for denominator N_2
15	20	24	30	40	50	60	100	120	200	500	∞	Pr	
9.49	9.58	9.63	9.67	9.71	9.74	9.76	9.78	9.80	9.82	9.84	9.85	.25	
61.20	61.70	62.00	62.30	62.50	62.70	62.80	63.00	63.10	63.20	63.30	63.30	.10	1
246.00	248.00	249.00	250.00	251.00	252.00	252.00	253.00	253.00	254.00	254.00	254.00	.05	
3.41	3.43	3.43	3.44	3.45	3.45	3.46	3.47	3.47	3.48	3.48	3.48	.25	
9.42	9.44	9.45	9.46	9.47	9.47	9.47	9.48	9.48	9.49	9.49	9.49	.10	2
19.40	19.40	19.50	19.50	19.50	19.50	19.50	19.50	19.50	19.50	19.50	19.50	.05	
99.40	99.40	99.50	99.50	99.50	99.50	99.50	99.50	99.50	99.50	99.50	99.50	.01	
2.46	2.46	2.46	2.47	2.47	2.47	2.47	2.47	2.47	2.47	2.47	2.47	.25	
5.20	5.18	5.18	5.17	5.16	5.15	5.15	5.14	5.14	5.14	5.14	5.13	.10	3
8.70	8.66	8.64	8.62	8.59	8.58	8.57	8.55	8.55	8.54	8.53	8.53	.05	
26.90	26.70	26.60	26.50	26.40	26.40	26.30	26.20	26.20	26.20	26.10	26.10	.01	
2.08	2.08	2.08	2.08	2.08	2.08	2.08	2.08	2.08	2.08	2.08	2.08	.25	
3.87	3.84	3.83	3.82	3.80	3.80	3.79	3.78	3.78	3.77	3.76	3.76	.10	4
5.86	5.80	5.77	5.75	5.72	5.70	5.69	5.66	5.66	5.65	5.64	5.63	.05	
14.20	14.00	13.90	13.80	13.70	13.70	13.70	13.60	13.60	13.50	13.50	13.50	.01	
1.89	1.88	1.88	1.88	1.88	1.88	1.87	1.87	1.87	1.87	1.87	1.87	.25	
3.24	3.21	3.19	3.17	3.16	3.15	3.14	3.13	3.12	3.12	3.11	3.10	.10	5
4.62	4.56	4.53	4.50	4.46	4.44	4.43	4.41	4.40	4.39	4.37	4.36	.05	
9.72	9.55	9.47	9.38	9.29	9.24	9.20	9.13	9.11	9.08	9.04	9.02	.01	
1.76	1.76	1.75	1.75	1.75	1.75	1.74	1.74	1.74	1.74	1.74	1.74	.25	
2.87	2.84	2.82	2.80	2.78	2.77	2.76	2.75	2.74	2.73	2.73	2.72	.10	6
3.94	3.87	3.84	3.81	3.77	3.75	3.74	3.71	3.70	3.69	3.68	3.67	.05	
7.56	7.40	7.31	7.23	7.14	7.09	7.06	6.99	6.97	6.93	6.90	6.88	.01	
1.68	1.67	1.67	1.66	1.66	1.66	1.65	1.65	1.65	1.65	1.65	1.65	.25	
2.63	2.59	2.58	2.56	2.54	2.52	2.51	2.50	2.49	2.48	2.48	2.47	.10	7
3.51	3.44	3.41	3.38	3.34	3.32	3.30	3.27	3.27	3.25	3.24	3.23	.05	
6.31	6.16	6.07	5.99	5.91	5.86	5.82	5.75	5.74	5.70	5.67	5.65	.01	
1.62	1.61	1.60	1.60	1.59	1.59	1.59	1.58	1.58	1.58	1.58	1.58	.25	
2.46	2.42	2.40	2.38	2.36	2.35	2.34	2.32	2.32	2.31	2.30	2.29	.10	8
3.22	3.15	3.12	3.08	3.04	2.02	3.01	2.97	2.97	2.95	2.94	2.93	.05	
5.52	5.36	5.28	5.20	5.12	5.07	5.03	4.96	4.95	4.91	4.88	4.86	.01	
1.57	1.56	1.56	1.55	1.55	1.54	1.54	1.53	1.53	1.53	1.53	1.53	.25	
2.34	2.30	2.28	2.25	2.23	2.22	2.21	2.19	2.18	2.17	2.17	2.16	.10	9
3.01	2.94	2.90	2.86	2.83	2.80	2.79	2.76	2.75	2.73	2.72	2.71	.05	
4.96	4.81	4.73	4.65	4.57	4.52	4.48	4.42	4.40	4.36	4.33	4.31	.01	

TABLE E-3   UPPER PERCENTAGE POINTS OF THE *F* DISTRIBUTION (CONTINUED)

d.f. for denominator N_2	Pr	1	2	3	4	5	6	7	8	9	10	11	12
10	.25	1.49	1.60	1.60	1.59	1.59	1.58	1.57	1.56	1.56	1.55	1.55	1.54
	.10	3.29	2.92	2.73	2.61	2.52	2.46	2.41	2.38	2.35	2.32	2.30	2.28
	.05	4.96	4.10	3.71	3.48	3.33	3.22	3.14	3.07	3.02	2.98	2.94	2.91
	.01	10.00	7.56	6.55	5.99	5.64	5.39	5.20	5.06	4.94	4.85	4.77	4.71
11	.25	1.47	1.58	1.58	1.57	1.56	1.55	1.54	1.53	1.53	1.52	1.52	1.51
	.10	3.23	2.86	2.66	2.54	2.45	2.39	2.34	2.30	2.27	2.25	2.23	2.21
	.05	4.84	3.98	3.59	3.36	3.20	3.09	3.01	2.95	2.90	2.85	2.82	2.79
	.01	9.65	7.21	6.22	5.67	5.32	5.07	4.89	4.74	4.63	4.54	4.46	4.40
12	.25	1.46	1.56	1.56	1.55	1.54	1.53	1.52	1.51	1.51	1.50	1.50	1.49
	.10	3.18	2.81	2.61	2.48	2.39	2.33	2.28	2.24	2.21	2.19	2.17	2.15
	.05	4.75	3.89	3.49	3.26	3.11	3.00	2.91	2.85	2.80	2.75	2.72	2.69
	.01	9.33	6.93	5.95	5.41	5.06	4.82	4.64	4.50	4.39	4.30	4.22	4.16
13	.25	1.45	1.55	1.55	1.53	1.52	1.51	1.50	1.49	1.49	1.48	1.47	1.47
	.10	3.14	2.76	2.56	2.43	2.35	2.28	2.23	2.20	2.16	2.14	2.12	2.10
	.05	4.67	3.81	3.41	3.18	3.03	2.92	2.83	2.77	2.71	2.67	2.63	2.60
	.01	9.07	6.70	5.74	5.21	4.86	4.62	4.44	4.30	4.19	4.10	4.02	3.96
14	.25	1.44	1.53	1.53	1.52	1.51	1.50	1.49	1.48	1.47	1.46	1.46	1.45
	.10	3.10	2.73	2.52	2.39	2.31	2.24	2.19	2.15	2.12	2.10	2.08	2.05
	.05	4.60	3.74	3.34	3.11	2.96	2.85	2.76	2.70	2.65	2.60	2.57	2.53
	.01	8.86	6.51	5.56	5.04	4.69	4.46	4.28	4.14	4.03	3.94	3.86	3.80
15	.25	1.43	1.52	1.52	1.51	1.49	1.48	1.47	1.46	1.46	1.45	1.44	1.44
	.10	3.07	2.70	2.49	2.36	2.27	2.21	2.16	2.12	2.09	2.06	2.04	2.02
	.05	4.54	3.68	3.29	3.06	2.90	2.79	2.71	2.64	2.59	2.54	2.51	2.48
	.01	8.68	6.36	5.42	4.89	4.56	4.32	4.14	4.00	3.89	3.80	3.73	3.67
16	.25	1.42	1.51	1.51	1.50	1.48	1.47	1.46	1.45	1.44	1.44	1.44	1.43
	.10	3.05	2.67	2.46	2.33	2.24	2.18	2.13	2.09	2.06	2.03	2.01	1.99
	.05	4.49	3.63	3.24	3.01	2.85	2.74	2.66	2.59	2.54	2.49	2.46	2.42
	.01	8.53	6.23	5.29	4.77	4.44	4.20	4.03	3.89	3.78	3.69	3.62	3.55
17	.25	1.42	1.51	1.50	1.49	1.47	1.46	1.45	1.44	1.43	1.43	1.42	1.41
	.10	3.03	2.64	2.44	2.31	2.22	2.15	2.10	2.06	2.03	2.00	1.98	1.96
	.05	4.45	3.59	3.20	2.96	2.81	2.70	2.61	2.55	2.49	2.45	2.41	2.38
	.01	8.40	6.11	5.18	4.67	4.34	4.10	3.93	3.79	3.68	3.59	3.52	3.46
18	.25	1.41	1.50	1.49	1.48	1.46	1.45	1.44	1.43	1.42	1.42	1.41	1.40
	.10	3.01	2.62	2.42	2.29	2.20	2.13	2.08	2.04	2.00	1.98	1.96	1.93
	.05	4.41	3.55	3.16	2.93	2.77	2.66	2.58	2.51	2.46	2.41	2.37	2.34
	.01	8.29	6.01	5.09	4.58	4.25	4.01	3.84	3.71	3.60	3.51	3.43	3.37
19	.25	1.41	1.49	1.49	1.47	1.46	1.44	1.43	1.42	1.41	1.41	1.40	1.40
	.10	2.99	2.61	2.40	2.27	2.18	2.11	2.06	2.02	1.98	1.96	1.94	1.91
	.05	4.38	3.52	3.13	2.90	2.74	2.63	2.54	2.48	2.42	2.38	2.34	2.31
	.01	8.18	5.93	5.01	4.50	4.17	3.94	3.77	3.63	3.52	3.43	3.36	3.30
20	.25	1.40	1.49	1.48	1.46	1.45	1.44	1.43	1.42	1.41	1.40	1.39	1.39
	.10	2.97	2.59	2.38	2.25	2.16	2.09	2.04	2.00	1.96	1.94	1.92	1.89
	.05	4.35	3.49	3.10	2.87	2.71	2.60	2.51	2.45	2.39	2.35	2.31	2.28
	.01	8.10	5.85	4.94	4.43	4.10	3.87	3.70	3.56	3.46	3.37	3.29	3.23

d.f. for numerator N_1

				d.f. for numerator N_1									d.f. for denominator N_2
15	20	24	30	40	50	60	100	120	200	500	∞	Pr	
1.53	1.52	1.52	1.51	1.51	1.50	1.50	1.49	1.49	1.49	1.48	1.48	.25	
2.24	2.20	2.18	2.16	2.13	2.12	2.11	2.09	2.08	2.07	2.06	2.06	.10	10
2.85	2.77	2.74	2.70	2.66	2.64	2.62	2.59	2.58	2.56	2.55	2.54	.05	
4.56	4.41	4.33	4.25	4.17	4.12	4.08	4.01	4.00	3.96	3.93	3.91	.01	
1.50	1.49	1.49	1.48	1.47	1.47	1.47	1.46	1.46	1.46	1.45	1.45	.25	
2.17	2.12	2.10	2.08	2.05	2.04	2.03	2.00	2.00	1.99	1.98	1.97	.10	11
2.72	2.65	2.61	2.57	2.53	2.51	2.49	2.46	2.45	2.43	2.42	2.40	.05	
4.25	4.10	4.02	3.94	3.86	3.81	3.78	3.71	3.69	3.66	3.62	3.60	.01	
1.48	1.47	1.46	1.45	1.45	1.44	1.44	1.43	1.43	1.43	1.42	1.42	.25	
2.10	2.06	2.04	2.01	1.99	1.97	1.96	1.94	1.93	1.92	1.91	1.90	.10	12
2.62	2.54	2.51	2.47	2.43	2.40	2.38	2.35	2.34	2.32	2.31	2.30	.05	
4.01	3.86	3.78	3.70	3.62	3.57	3.54	3.47	3.45	3.41	3.38	3.36	.01	
1.46	1.45	1.44	1.43	1.42	1.42	1.42	1.41	1.41	1.40	1.40	1.40	.25	
2.05	2.01	1.98	1.96	1.93	1.92	1.90	1.88	1.88	1.86	1.85	1.85	.10	13
2.53	2.46	2.42	2.38	2.34	2.31	2.30	2.26	2.25	2.23	2.22	2.21	.05	
3.82	3.66	3.59	3.51	3.43	3.38	3.34	3.27	3.25	3.22	3.19	3.17	.01	
1.44	1.43	1.42	1.41	1.41	1.40	1.40	1.39	1.39	1.39	1.38	1.38	.25	
2.01	1.96	1.94	1.91	1.89	1.87	1.86	1.83	1.83	1.82	1.80	1.80	.10	14
2.46	2.39	2.35	2.31	2.27	2.24	2.22	2.19	2.18	2.16	2.14	2.13	.05	
3.66	3.51	3.43	3.35	3.27	3.22	3.18	3.11	3.09	3.06	3.03	3.00	.01	
1.43	1.41	1.41	1.40	1.39	1.39	1.38	1.38	1.37	1.37	1.36	1.36	.25	
1.97	1.92	1.90	1.87	1.85	1.83	1.82	1.79	1.79	1.77	1.76	1.76	.10	15
2.40	2.33	2.29	2.25	2.20	2.18	2.16	2.12	2.11	2.10	2.08	2.07	.05	
3.52	3.37	3.29	3.21	3.13	3.08	3.05	2.98	2.96	2.92	2.89	2.87	.01	
1.41	1.40	1.39	1.38	1.37	1.37	1.36	1.36	1.35	1.35	1.34	1.34	.25	
1.94	1.89	1.87	1.84	1.81	1.79	1.78	1.76	1.75	1.74	1.73	1.72	.10	16
2.35	2.28	2.24	2.19	2.15	2.12	2.11	2.07	2.06	2.04	2.02	2.01	.05	
3.41	3.26	3.18	3.10	3.02	2.97	2.93	2.86	2.84	2.81	2.78	2.75	.01	
1.40	1.39	1.38	1.37	1.36	1.35	1.35	1.34	1.34	1.34	1.33	1.33	.25	
1.91	1.86	1.84	1.81	1.78	1.76	1.75	1.73	1.72	1.71	1.69	1.69	.10	17
2.31	2.23	2.19	2.15	2.10	2.08	2.06	2.02	2.01	1.99	1.97	1.96	.05	
3.31	3.16	3.08	3.00	2.92	2.87	2.83	2.76	2.75	2.71	2.68	2.65	.01	
1.39	1.38	1.37	1.36	1.35	1.34	1.34	1.33	1.33	1.32	1.32	1.32	.25	
1.89	1.84	1.81	1.78	1.75	1.74	1.72	1.70	1.69	1.68	1.67	1.66	.10	18
2.27	2.19	2.15	2.11	2.06	2.04	2.02	1.98	1.97	1.95	1.93	1.92	.05	
3.23	3.08	3.00	2.92	2.84	2.78	2.75	2.68	2.66	2.62	2.59	2.57	.01	
1.38	1.37	1.36	1.35	1.34	1.33	1.33	1.32	1.32	1.31	1.31	1.30	.25	
1.86	1.81	1.79	1.76	1.73	1.71	1.70	1.67	1.67	1.65	1.64	1.63	.10	19
2.23	2.16	2.11	2.07	2.03	2.00	1.98	1.94	1.93	1.91	1.89	1.88	.05	
3.15	3.00	2.92	2.84	2.76	2.71	2.67	2.60	2.58	2.55	2.51	2.49	.01	
1.37	1.36	1.35	1.34	1.33	1.33	1.32	1.31	1.31	1.30	1.30	1.29	.25	
1.84	1.79	1.77	1.74	1.71	1.69	1.68	1.65	1.64	1.63	1.62	1.61	.10	20
2.20	2.12	2.08	2.04	1.99	1.97	1.95	1.91	1.90	1.88	1.86	1.84	.05	
3.09	2.94	2.86	2.78	2.69	2.64	2.61	2.54	2.52	2.48	2.44	2.42	.01	

TABLE E-3   UPPER PERCENTAGE POINTS OF THE *F* DISTRIBUTION (CONTINUED)

d.f. for denominator N_2	Pr	\multicolumn{12}{c}{d.f. for numerator N_1}
		1	2	3	4	5	6	7	8	9	10	11	12
22	.25	1.40	1.48	1.47	1.45	1.44	1.42	1.41	1.40	1.39	1.39	1.38	1.37
	.10	2.95	2.56	2.35	2.22	2.13	2.06	2.01	1.97	1.93	1.90	1.88	1.86
	.05	4.30	3.44	3.05	2.82	2.66	2.55	2.46	2.40	2.34	2.30	2.26	2.23
	.01	7.95	5.72	4.82	4.31	3.99	3.76	3.59	3.45	3.35	3.26	3.18	3.12
24	.25	1.39	1.47	1.46	1.44	1.43	1.41	1.40	1.39	1.38	1.38	1.37	1.36
	.10	2.93	2.54	2.33	2.19	2.10	2.04	1.98	1.94	1.91	1.88	1.85	1.83
	.05	4.26	3.40	3.01	2.78	2.62	2.51	2.42	2.36	2.30	2.25	2.21	2.18
	.01	7.82	5.61	4.72	4.22	3.90	3.67	3.50	3.36	3.26	3.17	3.09	3.03
26	.25	1.38	1.46	1.45	1.44	1.42	1.41	1.39	1.38	1.37	1.37	1.36	1.35
	.10	2.91	2.52	2.31	2.17	2.08	2.01	1.96	1.92	1.88	1.86	1.84	1.81
	.05	4.23	3.37	2.98	2.74	2.59	2.47	2.39	2.32	2.27	2.22	2.18	2.15
	.01	7.72	5.53	4.64	4.14	3.82	3.59	3.42	3.29	3.18	3.09	3.02	2.96
28	.25	1.38	1.46	1.45	1.43	1.41	1.40	1.39	1.38	1.37	1.36	1.35	1.34
	.10	2.89	2.50	2.29	2.16	2.06	2.00	1.94	1.90	1.87	1.84	1.81	1.79
	.05	4.20	3.34	2.95	2.71	2.56	2.45	2.36	2.29	2.24	2.19	2.15	2.12
	.01	7.64	5.45	4.57	4.07	3.75	3.53	3.36	3.23	3.12	3.03	2.96	2.90
30	.25	1.38	1.45	1.44	1.42	1.41	1.39	1.38	1.37	1.36	1.35	1.35	1.34
	.10	2.88	2.49	2.28	2.14	2.05	1.98	1.93	1.88	1.85	1.82	1.79	1.77
	.05	4.17	3.32	2.92	2.69	2.53	2.42	2.33	2.27	2.21	2.16	2.13	2.09
	.01	7.56	5.39	4.51	4.02	3.70	3.47	3.30	3.17	3.07	2.98	2.91	2.84
40	.25	1.36	1.44	1.42	1.40	1.39	1.37	1.36	1.35	1.34	1.33	1.32	1.31
	.10	2.84	2.44	2.23	2.09	2.00	1.93	1.87	1.83	1.79	1.76	1.73	1.71
	.05	4.08	3.23	2.84	2.61	2.45	2.34	2.25	2.18	2.12	2.08	2.04	2.00
	.01	7.31	5.18	4.31	3.83	3.51	3.29	3.12	2.99	2.89	2.80	2.73	2.66
60	.25	1.35	1.42	1.41	1.38	1.37	1.35	1.33	1.32	1.31	1.30	1.29	1.29
	.10	2.79	2.39	2.18	2.04	1.95	1.87	1.82	1.77	1.74	1.71	1.68	1.66
	.05	4.00	3.15	2.76	2.53	2.37	2.25	2.17	2.10	2.04	1.99	1.95	1.92
	.01	7.08	4.98	4.13	3.65	3.34	3.12	2.95	2.82	2.72	2.63	2.56	2.50
120	.25	1.34	1.40	1.39	1.37	1.35	1.33	1.31	1.30	1.29	1.28	1.27	1.26
	.10	2.75	2.35	2.13	1.99	1.90	1.82	1.77	1.72	1.68	1.65	1.62	1.60
	.05	3.92	3.07	2.68	2.45	2.29	2.17	2.09	2.02	1.96	1.91	1.87	1.83
	.01	6.85	4.79	3.95	3.48	3.17	2.96	2.79	2.66	2.56	2.47	2.40	2.34
200	.25	1.33	1.39	1.38	1.36	1.34	1.32	1.31	1.29	1.28	1.27	1.26	1.25
	.10	2.73	2.33	2.11	1.97	1.88	1.80	1.75	1.70	1.66	1.63	1.60	1.57
	.05	3.89	3.04	2.65	2.42	2.26	2.14	2.06	1.98	1.93	1.88	1.84	1.80
	.01	6.76	4.71	3.88	3.41	3.11	2.89	2.73	2.60	2.50	2.41	2.34	2.27
∞	.25	1.32	1.39	1.37	1.35	1.33	1.31	1.29	1.28	1.27	1.25	1.24	1.24
	.10	2.71	2.30	2.08	1.94	1.85	1.77	1.72	1.67	1.63	1.60	1.57	1.55
	.05	3.84	3.00	2.60	2.37	2.21	2.10	2.01	1.94	1.88	1.83	1.79	1.75
	.01	6.63	4.61	3.78	3.32	3.02	2.80	2.64	2.51	2.41	2.32	2.25	2.18

					d.f. for numerator N_1									d.f. for denominator N_2
15	20	24	30	40	50	60	100	120	200	500	∞	Pr	
1.36	1.34	1.33	1.32	1.31	1.31	1.30	1.30	1.30	1.29	1.29	1.28	.25	
1.81	1.76	1.73	1.70	1.67	1.65	1.64	1.61	1.60	1.59	1.58	1.57	.10	22
2.15	2.07	2.03	1.98	1.94	1.91	1.89	1.85	1.84	1.82	1.80	1.78	.05	
2.98	2.83	2.75	2.67	2.58	2.53	2.50	2.42	2.40	2.36	2.33	2.31	.01	
1.35	1.33	1.32	1.31	1.30	1.29	1.29	1.28	1.28	1.27	1.27	1.26	.25	
1.78	1.73	1.70	1.67	1.64	1.62	1.61	1.58	1.57	1.56	1.54	1.53	.10	24
2.11	2.03	1.98	1.94	1.89	1.86	1.84	1.80	1.79	1.77	1.75	1.73	.05	
2.89	2.74	2.66	2.58	2.49	2.44	2.40	2.33	2.31	2.27	2.24	2.21	.01	
1.34	1.32	1.31	1.30	1.29	1.28	1.28	1.26	1.26	1.26	1.25	1.25	.25	
1.76	1.71	1.68	1.65	1.61	1.59	1.58	1.55	1.54	1.53	1.51	1.50	.10	26
2.07	1.99	1.95	1.90	1.85	1.82	1.80	1.76	1.75	1.73	1.71	1.69	.05	
2.81	2.66	2.58	2.50	2.42	2.36	2.33	2.25	2.23	2.19	2.16	2.13	.01	
1.33	1.31	1.30	1.29	1.28	1.27	1.27	1.26	1.25	1.25	1.24	1.24	.25	
1.74	1.69	1.66	1.63	1.59	1.57	1.56	1.53	1.52	1.50	1.49	1.48	.10	28
2.04	1.96	1.91	1.87	1.82	1.79	1.77	1.73	1.71	1.69	1.67	1.65	.05	
2.75	2.60	2.52	2.44	2.35	2.30	2.26	2.19	2.17	2.13	2.09	2.06	.01	
1.32	1.30	1.29	1.28	1.27	1.26	1.26	1.25	1.24	1.24	1.23	1.23	.25	
1.72	1.67	1.64	1.61	1.57	1.55	1.54	1.51	1.50	1.48	1.47	1.46	.10	30
2.01	1.93	1.89	1.84	1.79	1.76	1.74	1.70	1.68	1.66	1.64	1.62	.05	
2.70	2.55	2.47	2.39	2.30	2.25	2.21	2.13	2.11	2.07	2.03	2.01	.01	
1.30	1.28	1.26	1.25	1.24	1.23	1.22	1.21	1.21	1.20	1.19	1.19	.25	
1.66	1.61	1.57	1.54	1.51	1.48	1.47	1.43	1.42	1.41	1.39	1.38	.10	40
1.92	1.84	1.79	1.74	1.69	1.66	1.64	1.59	1.58	1.55	1.53	1.51	.05	
2.52	2.37	2.29	2.20	2.11	2.06	2.02	1.94	1.92	1.87	1.83	1.80	.01	
1.27	1.25	1.24	1.22	1.21	1.20	1.19	1.17	1.17	1.16	1.15	1.15	.25	
1.60	1.54	1.51	1.48	1.44	1.41	1.40	1.36	1.35	1.33	1.31	1.29	.10	60
1.84	1.75	1.70	1.65	1.59	1.56	1.53	1.48	1.47	1.44	1.41	1.39	.05	
2.35	2.20	2.12	2.03	1.94	1.88	1.84	1.75	1.73	1.68	1.63	1.60	.01	
1.24	1.22	1.21	1.19	1.18	1.17	1.16	1.14	1.13	1.12	1.11	1.10	.25	
1.55	1.48	1.45	1.41	1.37	1.34	1.32	1.27	1.26	1.24	1.21	1.19	.10	120
1.75	1.66	1.61	1.55	1.50	1.46	1.43	1.37	1.35	1.32	1.28	1.25	.05	
2.19	2.03	1.95	1.86	1.76	1.70	1.66	1.56	1.53	1.48	1.42	1.38	.01	
1.23	1.21	1.20	1.18	1.16	1.14	1.12	1.11	1.10	1.09	1.08	1.06	.25	
1.52	1.46	1.42	1.38	1.34	1.31	1.28	1.24	1.22	1.20	1.17	1.14	.10	200
1.72	1.62	1.57	1.52	1.46	1.41	1.39	1.32	1.29	1.26	1.22	1.19	.05	
2.13	1.97	1.89	1.79	1.69	1.63	1.58	1.48	1.44	1.39	1.33	1.28	.01	
1.22	1.19	1.18	1.16	1.14	1.13	1.12	1.09	1.08	1.07	1.04	1.00	.25	
1.49	1.42	1.38	1.34	1.30	1.26	1.24	1.18	1.17	1.13	1.08	1.00	.10	∞
1.67	1.57	1.52	1.46	1.39	1.35	1.32	1.24	1.22	1.17	1.11	1.00	.05	
2.04	1.88	1.79	1.70	1.59	1.52	1.47	1.36	1.32	1.25	1.15	1.00	.01	

TABLE E-4 UPPER PERCENTAGE POINTS OF THE χ^2 DISTRIBUTION

Example

$\Pr(\chi^2 > 10.85) = 0.95$
$\Pr(\chi^2 > 23.83) = 0.25$ for d.f. $= 20$
$\Pr(\chi^2 > 31.41) = 0.05$

Degrees of Freedom \ Pr	.995	.990	.975	.950	.900
1	392704×10^{-10}	157088×10^{-9}	982069×10^{-9}	393214×10^{-8}	.0158
2	.0100	.0201	.0506	.1026	.2107
3	.0717	.1148	.2158	.3518	.5844
4	.2070	.2971	.4844	.7107	1.0636
5	.4117	.5543	.8312	1.1455	1.6103
6	.6757	.8721	1.2373	1.6354	2.2041
7	.9893	1.2390	1.6899	2.1674	2.8331
8	1.3444	1.6465	2.1797	2.7326	3.4895
9	1.7349	2.0879	2.7004	3.3251	4.1682
10	2.1559	2.5582	3.2470	3.9403	4.8652
11	2.6032	3.0535	3.8158	4.5748	5.5778
12	3.0738	3.5706	4.4038	5.2260	6.3038
13	3.5650	4.1069	5.0087	5.8919	7.0415
14	4.0747	4.6604	5.6287	6.5706	7.7895
15	4.6009	5.2294	6.2621	7.2609	8.5468
16	5.1422	5.8122	6.9077	7.9616	9.3122
17	5.6972	6.4078	7.5642	8.6718	10.0852
18	6.2648	7.0149	8.2308	9.3905	10.8649
19	6.8440	7.6327	8.9066	10.1170	11.6509
20	7.4339	8.2604	9.5908	10.8508	12.4426
21	8.0337	8.8972	10.2829	11.5913	13.2396
22	8.6427	9.5425	10.9823	12.3380	14.0415
23	9.2604	10.1957	11.6885	13.0905	14.8479
24	9.8862	10.8564	12.4011	13.8484	15.6587
25	10.5197	11.5240	13.1197	14.6114	16.4734
26	11.1603	12.1981	13.8439	15.3791	17.2919
27	11.8076	12.8786	14.5733	16.1513	18.1138
28	12.4613	13.5648	15.3079	16.9279	18.9392
29	13.1211	14.2565	16.0471	17.7083	19.7677
30	13.7867	14.9535	16.7908	18.4926	20.5992
40	20.7065	22.1643	24.4331	26.5093	29.0505
50	27.9907	29.7067	32.3574	34.7642	37.6886
60	35.5346	37.4848	40.4817	43.1879	46.4589
70	43.2752	45.4418	48.7576	51.7393	55.3290
80	51.1720	53.5400	57.1532	60.3915	64.2778
90	59.1963	61.7541	65.6466	69.1260	73.2912
100*	67.3276	70.0648	74.2219	77.9295	82.3581

*For d.f. greater than 100 the expression $\sqrt{2\chi^2} - \sqrt{(2k-1)} = Z$ follows the standardized normal distribution, where k represents the degrees of freedom.

.750	.500	.250	.100	.050	.025	.010	.005
.1015	.4549	1.3233	2.7055	3.8415	5.0239	6.6349	7.8794
.5754	1.3863	2.7726	4.6052	5.9915	7.3778	9.2103	10.5966
1.2125	2.3660	4.1084	6.2514	7.8147	9.3484	11.3449	12.8381
1.9226	3.3567	5.3853	7.7794	9.4877	11.1433	13.2767	14.8602
2.6746	4.3515	6.6257	9.2364	11.0705	12.8325	15.0863	16.7496
3.4546	5.3481	7.8408	10.6446	12.5916	14.4494	16.8119	18.5476
4.2549	6.3458	9.0372	12.0170	14.0671	16.0128	18.4753	20.2777
5.0706	7.3441	10.2188	13.3616	15.5073	17.5346	20.0902	21.9550
5.8988	8.3428	11.3887	14.6837	16.9190	19.0228	21.6660	23.5893
6.7372	9.3418	12.5489	15.9871	18.3070	20.4831	23.2093	25.1882
7.5841	10.3410	13.7007	17.2750	19.6751	21.9200	24.7250	26.7569
8.4384	11.3403	14.8454	18.5494	21.0261	23.3367	26.2170	28.2995
9.2991	12.3398	15.9839	19.8119	22.3621	24.7356	27.6883	29.8194
10.1653	13.3393	17.1170	21.0642	23.6848	26.1190	29.1413	31.3193
11.0365	14.3389	18.2451	22.3072	24.9958	27.4884	30.5779	32.8013
11.9122	15.3385	19.3688	23.5418	26.2962	28.8454	31.9999	34.2672
12.7919	16.3381	20.4887	24.7690	27.5871	30.1910	33.4087	35.7185
13.6753	17.3379	21.6049	25.9894	28.8693	31.5264	34.8053	37.1564
14.5620	18.3376	22.7178	27.2036	30.1435	32.8523	36.1908	38.5822
15.4518	19.3374	23.8277	28.4120	31.4104	34.1696	37.5662	39.9968
16.3444	20.3372	24.9348	29.6151	32.6705	35.4789	38.9321	41.4010
17.2396	21.3370	26.0393	30.8133	33.9244	36.7807	40.2894	42.7956
18.1373	22.3369	27.1413	32.0069	35.1725	38.0757	41.6384	44.1813
19.0372	23.3367	28.2412	33.1963	36.4151	39.3641	42.9798	45.5585
19.9393	24.3366	29.3389	34.3816	37.6525	40.6465	44.3141	46.9278
20.8434	25.3364	30.4345	35.5631	38.8852	41.9232	45.6417	48.2899
21.7494	26.3363	31.5284	36.7412	40.1133	43.1944	46.9630	49.6449
22.6572	27.3363	32.6205	37.9159	41.3372	44.4607	48.2782	50.9933
23.5666	28.3362	33.7109	39.0875	42.5569	45.7222	49.5879	52.3356
24.4776	29.3360	34.7998	40.2560	43.7729	46.9792	50.8922	53.6720
33.6603	39.3354	45.6160	51.8050	55.7585	59.3417	63.6907	66.7659
42.9421	49.3349	56.3336	63.1671	67.5048	71.4202	76.1539	79.4900
52.2938	59.3347	66.9814	74.3970	79.0819	83.2976	88.3794	91.9517
61.6983	69.3344	77.5766	85.5271	90.5312	95.0231	100.425	104.215
71.1445	79.3343	88.1303	96.5782	101.879	106.629	112.329	116.321
80.6247	89.3342	98.6499	107.565	113.145	118.136	124.116	128.299
90.1332	99.3341	109.141	118.498	124.342	129.561	135.807	140.169

TABLE E-5a DURBIN-WATSON d STATISTIC: SIGNIFICANCE POINTS OF d_L AND d_U AT 0.05 LEVEL OF SIGNIFICANCE

	$k'=1$		$k'=2$		$k'=3$		$k'=4$		$k'=5$		$k'=6$		$k'=7$		$k'=8$		$k'=9$		$k'=10$	
n	d_L	d_U	d_L	d_U	d_L	d_U	d_L	d_U	d_L	d_U	d_L	d_U	d_L	d_U	d_L	d_U	d_L	d_U	d_L	d_U
6	0.610	1.400	—	—	—	—	—	—	—	—	—	—	—	—	—	—	—	—	—	—
7	0.700	1.356	0.467	1.896	—	—	—	—	—	—	—	—	—	—	—	—	—	—	—	—
8	0.763	1.332	0.559	1.777	0.368	2.287	—	—	—	—	—	—	—	—	—	—	—	—	—	—
9	0.824	1.320	0.629	1.699	0.455	2.128	0.296	2.588	—	—	—	—	—	—	—	—	—	—	—	—
10	0.879	1.320	0.697	1.641	0.525	2.016	0.376	2.414	0.243	2.822	—	—	—	—	—	—	—	—	—	—
11	0.927	1.324	0.658	1.604	0.595	1.928	0.444	2.283	0.316	2.645	0.203	3.005	—	—	—	—	—	—	—	—
12	0.971	1.331	0.812	1.579	0.658	1.864	0.512	2.177	0.379	2.506	0.268	2.832	0.171	3.149	—	—	—	—	—	—
13	1.010	1.340	0.861	1.562	0.715	1.816	0.574	2.094	0.445	2.390	0.328	2.692	0.230	2.985	0.147	3.266	—	—	—	—
14	1.045	1.350	0.905	1.551	0.767	1.779	0.632	2.030	0.505	2.296	0.389	2.572	0.286	2.848	0.200	3.111	0.127	3.360	—	—
15	1.077	1.361	0.946	1.543	0.814	1.750	0.685	1.977	0.562	2.220	0.447	2.472	0.343	2.727	0.251	2.979	0.175	3.216	0.111	3.438
16	1.106	1.371	0.982	1.539	0.857	1.728	0.734	1.935	0.615	2.157	0.502	2.388	0.398	2.624	0.304	2.860	0.222	3.090	0.155	3.304
17	1.133	1.381	1.015	1.536	0.897	1.710	0.779	1.900	0.664	2.104	0.554	2.318	0.451	2.537	0.356	2.757	0.272	2.975	0.198	3.184
18	1.158	1.391	1.046	1.535	0.933	1.696	0.820	1.872	0.710	2.060	0.603	2.257	0.502	2.461	0.407	2.667	0.321	2.873	0.244	3.073
19	1.180	1.401	1.074	1.536	0.967	1.685	0.859	1.848	0.752	2.023	0.649	2.206	0.549	2.396	0.456	2.589	0.369	2.783	0.290	2.974
20	1.201	1.411	1.100	1.537	0.998	1.676	0.894	1.828	0.792	1.991	0.692	2.162	0.595	2.339	0.502	2.521	0.416	2.704	0.336	2.885
21	1.221	1.420	1.125	1.538	1.026	1.669	0.927	1.812	0.829	1.964	0.732	2.124	0.637	2.290	0.547	2.460	0.461	2.633	0.380	2.806
22	1.239	1.429	1.147	1.541	1.053	1.664	0.958	1.797	0.863	1.940	0.769	2.090	0.677	2.246	0.588	2.407	0.504	2.571	0.424	2.734
23	1.257	1.437	1.168	1.543	1.078	1.660	0.986	1.785	0.895	1.920	0.804	2.061	0.715	2.208	0.628	2.360	0.545	2.514	0.465	2.670
24	1.273	1.446	1.188	1.546	1.101	1.656	1.013	1.775	0.925	1.902	0.837	2.035	0.751	2.174	0.666	2.318	0.584	2.464	0.506	2.613
25	1.288	1.454	1.206	1.550	1.123	1.654	1.038	1.767	0.953	1.886	0.868	2.012	0.784	2.144	0.702	2.280	0.621	2.419	0.544	2.560
26	1.302	1.461	1.224	1.553	1.143	1.652	1.062	1.759	0.979	1.873	0.897	1.992	0.816	2.117	0.735	2.246	0.657	2.379	0.581	2.513
27	1.316	1.469	1.240	1.556	1.162	1.651	1.084	1.753	1.004	1.861	0.925	1.974	0.845	2.093	0.767	2.216	0.691	2.342	0.616	2.470
28	1.328	1.476	1.255	1.560	1.181	1.650	1.104	1.747	1.028	1.850	0.951	1.958	0.874	2.071	0.798	2.188	0.723	2.309	0.650	2.431
29	1.341	1.483	1.270	1.563	1.198	1.650	1.124	1.743	1.050	1.841	0.975	1.944	0.900	2.052	0.826	2.164	0.753	2.278	0.682	2.396
30	1.352	1.489	1.284	1.567	1.214	1.650	1.143	1.739	1.071	1.833	0.998	1.931	0.926	2.034	0.854	2.141	0.782	2.251	0.712	2.363
31	1.363	1.496	1.297	1.570	1.229	1.650	1.160	1.735	1.090	1.825	1.020	1.920	0.950	2.018	0.879	2.120	0.810	2.226	0.741	2.333
32	1.373	1.502	1.309	1.574	1.244	1.650	1.177	1.732	1.109	1.819	1.041	1.909	0.972	2.004	0.904	2.102	0.836	2.203	0.769	2.306
33	1.383	1.508	1.321	1.577	1.258	1.651	1.193	1.730	1.127	1.813	1.061	1.900	0.994	1.991	0.927	2.085	0.861	2.181	0.795	2.281
34	1.393	1.514	1.333	1.580	1.271	1.652	1.208	1.728	1.144	1.808	1.080	1.891	1.015	1.979	0.950	2.069	0.885	2.162	0.821	2.257
35	1.402	1.519	1.343	1.584	1.283	1.653	1.222	1.726	1.160	1.803	1.097	1.884	1.034	1.967	0.971	2.054	0.908	2.144	0.845	2.236
36	1.411	1.525	1.354	1.587	1.295	1.654	1.236	1.724	1.175	1.799	1.114	1.877	1.053	1.957	0.991	2.041	0.930	2.127	0.868	2.216
37	1.419	1.530	1.364	1.590	1.307	1.655	1.249	1.723	1.190	1.795	1.131	1.870	1.071	1.948	1.011	2.029	0.951	2.112	0.891	2.198
38	1.427	1.535	1.373	1.594	1.318	1.656	1.261	1.722	1.204	1.792	1.146	1.864	1.088	1.939	1.029	2.017	0.970	2.098	0.912	2.180
39	1.435	1.540	1.382	1.597	1.328	1.658	1.273	1.722	1.218	1.789	1.161	1.859	1.104	1.932	1.047	2.007	0.990	2.085	0.932	2.164
40	1.442	1.544	1.391	1.600	1.338	1.659	1.285	1.721	1.230	1.786	1.175	1.854	1.120	1.924	1.064	1.997	1.008	2.072	0.952	2.149
45	1.475	1.566	1.430	1.615	1.383	1.666	1.336	1.720	1.287	1.776	1.238	1.835	1.189	1.895	1.139	1.958	1.089	2.022	1.038	2.088
50	1.503	1.585	1.462	1.628	1.421	1.674	1.378	1.721	1.335	1.771	1.291	1.822	1.246	1.875	1.201	1.930	1.156	1.986	1.110	2.044
55	1.528	1.601	1.490	1.641	1.452	1.681	1.414	1.724	1.374	1.768	1.334	1.814	1.294	1.861	1.253	1.909	1.212	1.959	1.170	2.010
60	1.549	1.616	1.514	1.652	1.480	1.689	1.444	1.727	1.408	1.767	1.372	1.808	1.335	1.850	1.298	1.894	1.260	1.939	1.222	1.984
65	1.567	1.629	1.536	1.662	1.503	1.696	1.471	1.731	1.438	1.767	1.404	1.805	1.370	1.843	1.336	1.882	1.301	1.923	1.266	1.964
70	1.583	1.641	1.554	1.672	1.525	1.703	1.494	1.735	1.464	1.768	1.433	1.802	1.401	1.837	1.369	1.873	1.337	1.910	1.305	1.948
75	1.598	1.652	1.571	1.680	1.543	1.709	1.515	1.739	1.487	1.770	1.458	1.801	1.428	1.834	1.399	1.867	1.369	1.901	1.339	1.935
80	1.611	1.662	1.586	1.688	1.560	1.715	1.534	1.743	1.507	1.772	1.480	1.801	1.453	1.831	1.425	1.861	1.397	1.893	1.369	1.925
85	1.624	1.671	1.600	1.696	1.575	1.721	1.550	1.747	1.525	1.774	1.500	1.801	1.474	1.829	1.448	1.857	1.422	1.886	1.396	1.916
90	1.635	1.679	1.612	1.703	1.589	1.726	1.566	1.751	1.542	1.776	1.518	1.801	1.494	1.827	1.469	1.854	1.445	1.881	1.420	1.909
95	1.645	1.687	1.623	1.709	1.602	1.732	1.579	1.755	1.557	1.778	1.535	1.802	1.512	1.827	1.489	1.852	1.465	1.877	1.442	1.903
100	1.654	1.694	1.634	1.715	1.613	1.736	1.592	1.758	1.571	1.780	1.550	1.803	1.528	1.826	1.506	1.850	1.484	1.874	1.462	1.898
150	1.720	1.746	1.706	1.760	1.693	1.774	1.679	1.788	1.665	1.802	1.651	1.817	1.637	1.832	1.622	1.847	1.608	1.862	1.594	1.877
200	1.758	1.778	1.748	1.789	1.738	1.799	1.728	1.810	1.718	1.820	1.707	1.831	1.697	1.841	1.686	1.852	1.675	1.863	1.665	1.874

	k' = 11		k' = 12		k' = 13		k' = 14		k' = 15		k' = 16		k' = 17		k' = 18		k' = 19		k' = 20	
n	d_L	d_U	d_L	d_U	d_L	d_U	d_L	d_U	d_L	d_U	d_L	d_U	d_L	d_U	d_L	d_U	d_L	d_U	d_L	d_U
16	0.098	3.503	—	—	—	—	—	—	—	—	—	—	—	—	—	—	—	—	—	—
17	0.138	3.378	0.087	3.557	—	—	—	—	—	—	—	—	—	—	—	—	—	—	—	—
18	0.177	3.265	0.123	3.441	0.078	3.603	—	—	—	—	—	—	—	—	—	—	—	—	—	—
19	0.220	3.159	0.160	3.335	0.111	3.496	0.070	3.642	—	—	—	—	—	—	—	—	—	—	—	—
20	0.263	3.063	0.200	3.234	0.145	3.395	0.100	3.542	0.063	3.676	—	—	—	—	—	—	—	—	—	—
21	0.307	2.976	0.240	3.141	0.182	3.300	0.132	3.448	0.091	3.583	0.058	3.705	—	—	—	—	—	—	—	—
22	0.349	2.897	0.281	3.057	0.220	3.211	0.166	3.358	0.120	3.495	0.083	3.619	0.052	3.731	—	—	—	—	—	—
23	0.391	2.826	0.322	2.979	0.259	3.128	0.202	3.272	0.153	3.409	0.110	3.535	0.076	3.650	0.048	3.753	—	—	—	—
24	0.431	2.761	0.362	2.908	0.297	3.053	0.239	3.193	0.186	3.327	0.141	3.454	0.101	3.572	0.070	3.678	0.044	3.773	—	—
25	0.470	2.702	0.400	2.844	0.335	2.983	0.275	3.119	0.221	3.251	0.172	3.376	0.130	3.494	0.094	3.604	0.065	3.702	0.041	3.790
26	0.508	2.649	0.438	2.784	0.373	2.919	0.312	3.051	0.256	3.179	0.205	3.303	0.160	3.420	0.120	3.531	0.087	3.632	0.060	3.724
27	0.544	2.600	0.475	2.730	0.409	2.859	0.348	2.987	0.291	3.112	0.238	3.233	0.191	3.349	0.149	3.460	0.112	3.563	0.081	3.658
28	0.578	2.555	0.510	2.680	0.445	2.805	0.383	2.928	0.325	3.050	0.271	3.168	0.222	3.283	0.178	3.392	0.138	3.495	0.104	3.592
29	0.612	2.515	0.544	2.634	0.479	2.755	0.418	2.874	0.359	2.992	0.305	3.107	0.254	3.219	0.208	3.327	0.166	3.431	0.129	3.528
30	0.643	2.477	0.577	2.592	0.512	2.708	0.451	2.823	0.392	2.937	0.337	3.050	0.286	3.160	0.238	3.266	0.195	3.368	0.156	3.465
31	0.674	2.443	0.608	2.553	0.545	2.665	0.484	2.776	0.425	2.887	0.370	2.996	0.317	3.103	0.269	3.208	0.224	3.309	0.183	3.406
32	0.703	2.411	0.638	2.517	0.576	2.625	0.515	2.733	0.457	2.840	0.401	2.946	0.349	3.050	0.299	3.153	0.253	3.252	0.211	3.348
33	0.731	2.382	0.668	2.484	0.606	2.588	0.546	2.692	0.488	2.796	0.432	2.899	0.379	3.000	0.329	3.100	0.283	3.198	0.239	3.293
34	0.758	2.355	0.695	2.454	0.634	2.554	0.575	2.654	0.518	2.754	0.462	2.854	0.409	2.954	0.359	3.051	0.312	3.147	0.267	3.240
35	0.783	2.330	0.722	2.425	0.662	2.521	0.604	2.619	0.547	2.716	0.492	2.813	0.439	2.910	0.388	3.005	0.340	3.099	0.295	3.190
36	0.808	2.306	0.748	2.398	0.689	2.492	0.631	2.586	0.575	2.680	0.520	2.774	0.467	2.868	0.417	2.961	0.369	3.053	0.323	3.142
37	0.831	2.285	0.772	2.374	0.714	2.464	0.657	2.555	0.602	2.646	0.548	2.738	0.495	2.829	0.445	2.920	0.397	3.009	0.351	3.097
38	0.854	2.265	0.796	2.351	0.739	2.438	0.683	2.526	0.628	2.614	0.575	2.703	0.522	2.792	0.472	2.880	0.424	2.968	0.378	3.054
39	0.875	2.246	0.819	2.329	0.763	2.413	0.707	2.499	0.653	2.585	0.600	2.671	0.549	2.757	0.499	2.843	0.451	2.929	0.404	3.013
40	0.896	2.228	0.840	2.309	0.785	2.391	0.731	2.473	0.678	2.557	0.626	2.641	0.575	2.724	0.525	2.808	0.477	2.892	0.430	2.974
45	0.988	2.156	0.938	2.225	0.887	2.296	0.838	2.367	0.788	2.439	0.740	2.512	0.692	2.586	0.644	2.659	0.598	2.733	0.553	2.807
50	1.064	2.103	1.019	2.163	0.973	2.225	0.927	2.287	0.882	2.350	0.836	2.414	0.792	2.479	0.747	2.544	0.703	2.610	0.660	2.675
55	1.129	2.062	1.087	2.116	1.045	2.170	1.003	2.225	0.961	2.281	0.919	2.338	0.877	2.396	0.836	2.454	0.795	2.512	0.754	2.571
60	1.184	2.031	1.145	2.079	1.106	2.127	1.068	2.177	1.029	2.227	0.990	2.278	0.951	2.330	0.913	2.382	0.874	2.434	0.836	2.487
65	1.231	2.006	1.195	2.049	1.160	2.093	1.124	2.138	1.088	2.183	1.052	2.229	1.016	2.276	0.980	2.323	0.944	2.371	0.908	2.419
70	1.272	1.986	1.239	2.026	1.206	2.066	1.172	2.106	1.139	2.148	1.105	2.189	1.072	2.232	1.038	2.275	1.005	2.318	0.971	2.362
75	1.308	1.970	1.277	2.006	1.247	2.043	1.215	2.080	1.184	2.118	1.153	2.156	1.121	2.195	1.090	2.235	1.058	2.275	1.027	2.315
80	1.340	1.957	1.311	1.991	1.283	2.024	1.253	2.059	1.224	2.093	1.195	2.129	1.165	2.165	1.136	2.201	1.106	2.238	1.076	2.275
85	1.369	1.946	1.342	1.977	1.315	2.009	1.287	2.040	1.260	2.073	1.232	2.105	1.205	2.139	1.177	2.172	1.149	2.206	1.121	2.241
90	1.395	1.937	1.369	1.966	1.344	1.995	1.318	2.025	1.292	2.055	1.266	2.085	1.240	2.116	1.213	2.148	1.187	2.179	1.160	2.211
95	1.418	1.929	1.394	1.956	1.370	1.984	1.345	2.012	1.321	2.040	1.296	2.068	1.271	2.097	1.247	2.126	1.222	2.156	1.197	2.186
100	1.439	1.923	1.416	1.948	1.393	1.974	1.371	2.000	1.347	2.026	1.324	2.053	1.301	2.080	1.277	2.108	1.253	2.135	1.229	2.164
150	1.579	1.892	1.564	1.908	1.550	1.924	1.535	1.940	1.519	1.956	1.504	1.972	1.489	1.989	1.474	2.006	1.458	2.023	1.443	2.040
200	1.654	1.885	1.643	1.896	1.632	1.908	1.621	1.919	1.610	1.931	1.599	1.943	1.588	1.955	1.576	1.967	1.565	1.979	1.554	1.991

Note: n = number of observations, k' = number of explanatory variables excluding the constant term.

Source: This table is an extension of the original Durbin-Watson table and is reproduced from N. E. Savin and K. J. White, "The Durbin-Watson Test for Serial Correlation with Extreme Small Samples or Many Regressors," *Econometrica*, vol. 45, November 1977, pp. 1989–96 and as corrected by R. W. Farebrother, *Econometrica*, vol. 48, September 1980, p. 1554. Reprinted by permission of the Econometric Society.

Example E.1.

If $n = 40$ and $k' = 4$, $d_L = 1.285$ and $d_U = 1.721$. If a computed d value is less than 1.285, there is evidence of positive first-order serial correlation; if it is greater than 1.721, there is no evidence of positive first-order serial correlation; but if d lies between the lower and the upper limit, there is inconclusive evidence regarding the presence or absence of positive first-order serial correlation.

TABLE E-5b DURBIN-WATSON d STATISTIC: SIGNIFICANCE POINTS OF d_L AND d_U AT 0.01 LEVEL OF SIGNIFICANCE

	k′ = 1		k′ = 2		k′ = 3		k′ = 4		k′ = 5		k′ = 6		k′ = 7		k′ = 8		k′ = 9		k′ = 10	
n	d_L	d_U	d_L	d_U	d_L	d_U	d_L	d_U	d_L	d_U	d_L	d_U	d_L	d_U	d_L	d_U	d_L	d_U	d_L	d_U
6	0.390	1.142	—	—	—	—	—	—	—	—	—	—	—	—	—	—	—	—	—	—
7	0.435	1.036	0.294	1.676	—	—	—	—	—	—	—	—	—	—	—	—	—	—	—	—
8	0.497	1.003	0.345	1.489	0.229	2.102	—	—	—	—	—	—	—	—	—	—	—	—	—	—
9	0.554	0.998	0.408	1.389	0.279	1.875	0.183	2.433	—	—	—	—	—	—	—	—	—	—	—	—
10	0.604	1.001	0.466	1.333	0.340	1.733	0.230	2.193	0.150	2.690	—	—	—	—	—	—	—	—	—	—
11	0.653	1.010	0.519	1.297	0.396	1.640	0.286	2.030	0.193	2.453	0.124	2.892	—	—	—	—	—	—	—	—
12	0.697	1.023	0.569	1.274	0.449	1.575	0.339	1.913	0.244	2.280	0.164	2.665	0.105	3.053	—	—	—	—	—	—
13	0.738	1.038	0.616	1.261	0.499	1.526	0.391	1.826	0.294	2.150	0.211	2.490	0.140	2.838	0.090	3.182	—	—	—	—
14	0.776	1.054	0.660	1.254	0.547	1.490	0.441	1.757	0.343	2.049	0.257	2.354	0.183	2.667	0.122	2.981	0.078	3.287	—	—
15	0.811	1.070	0.700	1.252	0.591	1.464	0.488	1.704	0.391	1.967	0.303	2.244	0.226	2.530	0.161	2.817	0.107	3.101	0.068	3.374
16	0.844	1.086	0.737	1.252	0.633	1.446	0.532	1.663	0.437	1.900	0.349	2.153	0.269	2.416	0.200	2.681	0.142	2.944	0.094	3.201
17	0.874	1.102	0.772	1.255	0.672	1.432	0.574	1.630	0.480	1.847	0.393	2.078	0.313	2.319	0.241	2.566	0.179	2.811	0.127	3.053
18	0.902	1.118	0.805	1.259	0.708	1.422	0.613	1.604	0.522	1.803	0.435	2.015	0.355	2.238	0.282	2.467	0.216	2.697	0.160	2.925
19	0.928	1.132	0.835	1.265	0.742	1.415	0.650	1.584	0.561	1.767	0.476	1.963	0.396	2.169	0.322	2.381	0.255	2.597	0.196	2.813
20	0.952	1.147	0.863	1.271	0.773	1.411	0.685	1.567	0.598	1.737	0.515	1.918	0.436	2.110	0.362	2.308	0.294	2.510	0.232	2.714
21	0.975	1.161	0.890	1.277	0.803	1.408	0.718	1.554	0.633	1.712	0.552	1.881	0.474	2.059	0.400	2.244	0.331	2.434	0.268	2.625
22	0.997	1.174	0.914	1.284	0.831	1.407	0.748	1.543	0.667	1.691	0.587	1.849	0.510	2.015	0.437	2.188	0.368	2.367	0.304	2.548
23	1.018	1.187	0.938	1.291	0.858	1.407	0.777	1.534	0.698	1.673	0.620	1.821	0.545	1.977	0.473	2.140	0.404	2.308	0.340	2.479
24	1.037	1.199	0.960	1.298	0.882	1.407	0.805	1.528	0.728	1.658	0.652	1.797	0.578	1.944	0.507	2.097	0.439	2.255	0.375	2.417
25	1.055	1.211	0.981	1.305	0.906	1.409	0.831	1.523	0.756	1.645	0.682	1.776	0.610	1.915	0.540	2.059	0.473	2.209	0.409	2.362
26	1.072	1.222	1.001	1.312	0.928	1.411	0.855	1.518	0.783	1.635	0.711	1.759	0.640	1.889	0.572	2.026	0.505	2.168	0.441	2.313
27	1.089	1.233	1.019	1.319	0.949	1.413	0.878	1.515	0.808	1.626	0.738	1.743	0.669	1.867	0.602	1.997	0.536	2.131	0.473	2.269
28	1.104	1.244	1.037	1.325	0.969	1.415	0.900	1.513	0.832	1.618	0.764	1.729	0.696	1.847	0.630	1.970	0.566	2.098	0.504	2.229
29	1.119	1.254	1.054	1.332	0.988	1.418	0.921	1.512	0.855	1.611	0.788	1.718	0.723	1.830	0.658	1.947	0.595	2.068	0.533	2.193
30	1.133	1.263	1.070	1.339	1.006	1.421	0.941	1.511	0.877	1.606	0.812	1.707	0.748	1.814	0.684	1.925	0.622	2.041	0.562	2.160
31	1.147	1.273	1.085	1.345	1.023	1.425	0.960	1.510	0.897	1.601	0.834	1.698	0.772	1.800	0.710	1.906	0.649	2.017	0.589	2.131
32	1.160	1.282	1.100	1.352	1.040	1.428	0.979	1.510	0.917	1.597	0.856	1.690	0.794	1.788	0.734	1.889	0.674	1.995	0.615	2.104
33	1.172	1.291	1.114	1.358	1.055	1.432	0.996	1.510	0.936	1.594	0.876	1.683	0.816	1.776	0.757	1.874	0.698	1.975	0.641	2.080
34	1.184	1.299	1.128	1.364	1.070	1.435	1.012	1.511	0.954	1.591	0.896	1.677	0.837	1.766	0.779	1.860	0.722	1.957	0.665	2.057
35	1.195	1.307	1.140	1.370	1.085	1.439	1.028	1.512	0.971	1.589	0.914	1.671	0.857	1.757	0.800	1.847	0.744	1.940	0.689	2.037
36	1.206	1.315	1.153	1.376	1.098	1.442	1.043	1.513	0.988	1.588	0.932	1.666	0.877	1.749	0.821	1.836	0.766	1.925	0.711	2.018
37	1.217	1.323	1.165	1.382	1.112	1.446	1.058	1.514	1.004	1.586	0.950	1.662	0.895	1.742	0.841	1.825	0.787	1.911	0.733	2.001
38	1.227	1.330	1.176	1.388	1.124	1.449	1.072	1.515	1.019	1.585	0.966	1.658	0.913	1.735	0.860	1.816	0.807	1.899	0.754	1.985
39	1.237	1.337	1.187	1.393	1.137	1.453	1.085	1.517	1.034	1.584	0.982	1.655	0.930	1.729	0.878	1.807	0.826	1.887	0.774	1.970
40	1.246	1.344	1.198	1.398	1.148	1.457	1.098	1.518	1.048	1.584	0.997	1.652	0.946	1.724	0.895	1.799	0.844	1.876	0.749	1.956
45	1.288	1.376	1.245	1.423	1.201	1.474	1.156	1.528	1.111	1.584	1.065	1.643	1.019	1.704	0.974	1.768	0.927	1.834	0.881	1.902
50	1.324	1.403	1.285	1.446	1.245	1.491	1.205	1.538	1.164	1.587	1.123	1.639	1.081	1.692	1.039	1.748	0.997	1.805	0.955	1.864
55	1.356	1.427	1.320	1.466	1.284	1.506	1.247	1.548	1.209	1.592	1.172	1.638	1.134	1.685	1.095	1.734	1.057	1.785	1.018	1.837
60	1.383	1.449	1.350	1.484	1.317	1.520	1.283	1.558	1.249	1.598	1.214	1.639	1.179	1.682	1.144	1.726	1.108	1.771	1.072	1.817
65	1.407	1.468	1.377	1.500	1.346	1.534	1.315	1.568	1.283	1.604	1.251	1.642	1.218	1.680	1.186	1.720	1.153	1.761	1.120	1.802
70	1.429	1.485	1.400	1.515	1.372	1.546	1.343	1.578	1.313	1.611	1.283	1.645	1.253	1.680	1.223	1.716	1.192	1.754	1.162	1.792
75	1.448	1.501	1.422	1.529	1.395	1.557	1.368	1.587	1.340	1.617	1.313	1.649	1.284	1.682	1.256	1.714	1.227	1.748	1.199	1.783
80	1.466	1.515	1.441	1.541	1.416	1.568	1.390	1.595	1.364	1.624	1.338	1.653	1.312	1.683	1.285	1.714	1.259	1.745	1.232	1.777
85	1.482	1.528	1.458	1.553	1.435	1.578	1.411	1.603	1.386	1.630	1.362	1.657	1.337	1.685	1.312	1.714	1.287	1.743	1.262	1.773
90	1.496	1.540	1.474	1.563	1.452	1.587	1.429	1.611	1.406	1.636	1.383	1.661	1.360	1.687	1.336	1.714	1.312	1.741	1.288	1.769
95	1.510	1.552	1.489	1.573	1.468	1.596	1.446	1.618	1.425	1.642	1.403	1.666	1.381	1.690	1.358	1.715	1.336	1.741	1.313	1.767
100	1.522	1.562	1.503	1.583	1.482	1.604	1.462	1.625	1.441	1.647	1.421	1.670	1.400	1.693	1.378	1.717	1.357	1.741	1.335	1.765
150	1.611	1.637	1.598	1.651	1.584	1.665	1.571	1.679	1.557	1.693	1.543	1.708	1.530	1.722	1.515	1.737	1.501	1.752	1.486	1.767
200	1.664	1.684	1.653	1.693	1.643	1.704	1.633	1.715	1.623	1.725	1.613	1.735	1.603	1.746	1.592	1.757	1.582	1.768	1.571	1.779

n	$k' = 11$		$k' = 12$		$k' = 13$		$k' = 14$		$k' = 15$		$k' = 16$		$k' = 17$		$k' = 18$		$k' = 19$		$k' = 20$	
	d_L	d_U	d_L	d_U	d_L	d_U	d_L	d_U	d_L	d_U	d_L	d_U	d_L	d_U	d_L	d_U	d_L	d_U	d_L	d_U
16	0.060	3.446	—	—	—	—	—	—	—	—	—	—	—	—	—	—	—	—	—	—
17	0.084	3.286	0.053	3.506	—	—	—	—	—	—	—	—	—	—	—	—	—	—	—	—
18	0.113	3.146	0.075	3.358	0.047	3.357	—	—	—	—	—	—	—	—	—	—	—	—	—	—
19	0.145	3.023	0.102	3.227	0.067	3.420	0.043	3.601	—	—	—	—	—	—	—	—	—	—	—	—
20	0.178	2.914	0.131	3.109	0.092	3.297	0.061	3.474	0.038	3.639	—	—	—	—	—	—	—	—	—	—
21	0.212	2.817	0.162	3.004	0.119	3.185	0.084	3.358	0.055	3.521	0.035	3.671	—	—	—	—	—	—	—	—
22	0.246	2.729	0.194	2.909	0.148	3.084	0.109	3.252	0.077	3.412	0.050	3.562	0.032	3.700	—	—	—	—	—	—
23	0.281	2.651	0.227	2.822	0.178	2.991	0.136	3.155	0.100	3.311	0.070	3.459	0.046	3.597	0.029	3.725	—	—	—	—
24	0.315	2.580	0.260	2.744	0.209	2.906	0.165	3.065	0.125	3.218	0.092	3.363	0.065	3.501	0.043	3.629	0.027	3.747	—	—
25	0.348	2.517	0.292	2.674	0.240	2.829	0.194	2.982	0.152	3.131	0.116	3.274	0.085	3.410	0.060	3.538	0.039	3.657	0.025	3.766
26	0.381	2.460	0.324	2.610	0.272	2.758	0.224	2.906	0.180	3.050	0.141	3.191	0.107	3.325	0.079	3.452	0.055	3.572	0.036	3.682
27	0.413	2.409	0.356	2.552	0.303	2.694	0.253	2.836	0.208	2.976	0.167	3.113	0.131	3.245	0.100	3.371	0.073	3.490	0.051	3.602
28	0.444	2.363	0.387	2.499	0.333	2.635	0.283	2.772	0.237	2.907	0.194	3.040	0.156	3.169	0.122	3.294	0.093	3.412	0.068	3.524
29	0.474	2.321	0.417	2.451	0.363	2.582	0.313	2.713	0.266	2.843	0.222	2.972	0.182	3.098	0.146	3.220	0.114	3.338	0.087	3.450
30	0.503	2.283	0.447	2.407	0.393	2.533	0.342	2.659	0.294	2.785	0.249	2.909	0.208	3.032	0.171	3.152	0.137	3.267	0.107	3.379
31	0.531	2.248	0.475	2.367	0.422	2.487	0.371	2.609	0.322	2.730	0.277	2.851	0.234	2.970	0.196	3.087	0.160	3.201	0.128	3.311
32	0.558	2.216	0.503	2.330	0.450	2.446	0.399	2.563	0.350	2.680	0.304	2.797	0.261	2.912	0.221	3.026	0.184	3.137	0.151	3.246
33	0.585	2.187	0.530	2.296	0.477	2.408	0.426	2.520	0.377	2.633	0.331	2.746	0.287	2.858	0.246	2.969	0.209	3.078	0.174	3.184
34	0.610	2.160	0.556	2.266	0.503	2.373	0.452	2.481	0.404	2.590	0.357	2.699	0.313	2.808	0.272	2.915	0.233	3.022	0.197	3.126
35	0.634	2.136	0.581	2.237	0.529	2.340	0.478	2.444	0.430	2.550	0.383	2.655	0.339	2.761	0.297	2.865	0.257	2.969	0.221	3.071
36	0.658	2.113	0.605	2.210	0.554	2.310	0.504	2.410	0.455	2.512	0.409	2.614	0.364	2.717	0.322	2.818	0.282	2.919	0.244	3.019
37	0.680	2.092	0.628	2.186	0.578	2.282	0.528	2.379	0.480	2.477	0.434	2.576	0.389	2.675	0.347	2.774	0.306	2.872	0.268	2.969
38	0.702	2.073	0.651	2.164	0.601	2.256	0.552	2.350	0.504	2.445	0.458	2.540	0.414	2.637	0.371	2.733	0.330	2.828	0.291	2.923
39	0.723	2.055	0.673	2.143	0.623	2.232	0.575	2.323	0.528	2.414	0.482	2.507	0.438	2.600	0.395	2.694	0.354	2.787	0.315	2.879
40	0.744	2.039	0.694	2.123	0.645	2.210	0.597	2.297	0.551	2.386	0.505	2.476	0.461	2.566	0.418	2.657	0.377	2.748	0.338	2.838
45	0.835	1.972	0.790	2.044	0.744	2.118	0.700	2.193	0.655	2.269	0.612	2.346	0.570	2.424	0.528	2.503	0.488	2.582	0.448	2.661
50	0.913	1.925	0.871	1.987	0.829	2.051	0.787	2.116	0.746	2.182	0.705	2.250	0.665	2.318	0.625	2.387	0.586	2.456	0.548	2.526
55	0.979	1.891	0.940	1.945	0.902	2.002	0.863	2.059	0.825	2.117	0.786	2.176	0.748	2.237	0.711	2.298	0.674	2.359	0.637	2.421
60	1.037	1.865	1.001	1.914	0.965	1.964	0.929	2.015	0.893	2.067	0.857	2.120	0.822	2.173	0.786	2.227	0.751	2.283	0.716	2.338
65	1.087	1.845	1.053	1.889	1.020	1.934	0.986	1.980	0.953	2.027	0.919	2.075	0.886	2.123	0.852	2.172	0.819	2.221	0.786	2.272
70	1.131	1.831	1.099	1.870	1.068	1.911	1.037	1.953	1.005	1.995	0.974	2.038	0.943	2.082	0.911	2.127	0.880	2.172	0.849	2.217
75	1.170	1.819	1.141	1.856	1.111	1.893	1.082	1.931	1.052	1.970	1.023	2.009	0.993	2.049	0.964	2.090	0.934	2.131	0.905	2.172
80	1.205	1.810	1.177	1.844	1.150	1.878	1.122	1.913	1.094	1.949	1.066	1.984	1.039	2.022	1.011	2.059	0.983	2.097	0.955	2.135
85	1.236	1.803	1.210	1.834	1.184	1.866	1.158	1.898	1.132	1.931	1.106	1.965	1.080	1.999	1.053	2.033	1.027	2.068	1.000	2.104
90	1.264	1.798	1.240	1.827	1.215	1.856	1.191	1.886	1.166	1.917	1.141	1.948	1.116	1.979	1.091	2.012	1.066	2.044	1.041	2.077
95	1.290	1.793	1.267	1.821	1.244	1.848	1.221	1.876	1.197	1.905	1.174	1.934	1.150	1.963	1.126	1.993	1.102	2.023	1.079	2.054
100	1.314	1.790	1.292	1.816	1.270	1.841	1.248	1.868	1.225	1.895	1.203	1.922	1.181	1.949	1.158	1.977	1.136	2.006	1.113	2.034
150	1.473	1.783	1.458	1.799	1.444	1.814	1.429	1.830	1.414	1.847	1.400	1.863	1.385	1.880	1.370	1.897	1.355	1.913	1.340	1.931
200	1.561	1.791	1.550	1.801	1.539	1.813	1.528	1.824	1.518	1.836	1.507	1.847	1.495	1.860	1.484	1.871	1.474	1.883	1.462	1.896

Note: n = number of observations, k' = number of explanatory variables excluding the constant term.
Source: Savin and White, op. cit., by permission of Econometric Society.

TABLE E-6a   CRITICAL VALUES OF RUNS IN THE RUNS TEST

N_1	\(N_2\) 2	3	4	5	6	7	8	9	10	11	12	13	14	15	16	17	18	19	20
2											2	2	2	2	2	2	2	2	2
3				2	2	2	2	2	2	2	2	2	2	3	3	3	3	3	3
4			2	2	2	3	3	3	3	3	3	3	3	3	4	4	4	4	4
5			2	2	3	3	3	3	3	4	4	4	4	4	4	4	5	5	5
6		2	2	3	3	3	3	4	4	4	4	5	5	5	5	5	5	6	6
7		2	2	3	3	3	4	4	5	5	5	5	5	5	6	6	6	6	6
8		2	3	3	3	4	4	5	5	5	6	6	6	6	6	7	7	7	7
9		2	3	3	4	4	5	5	5	6	6	6	7	7	7	7	8	8	8
10		2	3	3	4	5	5	5	6	6	7	7	7	7	8	8	8	8	9
11		2	3	4	4	5	5	6	6	7	7	7	8	8	8	9	9	9	9
12	2	2	3	4	4	5	6	6	7	7	7	8	8	8	9	9	9	10	10
13	2	2	3	4	5	5	6	6	7	7	8	8	9	9	9	10	10	10	10
14	2	2	3	4	5	5	6	7	7	8	8	9	9	9	10	10	10	11	11
15	2	3	3	4	5	6	6	7	7	8	8	9	9	10	10	11	11	11	12
16	2	3	4	4	5	6	6	7	8	8	9	9	10	10	11	11	11	12	12
17	2	3	4	4	5	6	7	7	8	9	9	10	10	11	11	11	12	12	13
18	2	3	4	5	5	6	7	8	8	9	9	10	10	11	11	12	12	13	13
19	2	3	4	5	6	6	7	8	8	9	10	10	11	11	12	12	13	13	13
20	2	3	4	5	6	6	7	8	9	9	10	10	11	12	12	13	13	13	14

Note: Tables E-6a and E-6b give the critical values of runs n for various values of N_1 (+ symbol) and N_2 (− symbol). For the one-sample runs test, any value of n that is equal to or smaller than that shown in Table E-6a or equal to or larger than that shown in Table E-6b is significant at the 0.05 level.

Source: Sidney Siegel, *Nonparametric Statistics for the Behavioral Sciences,* McGraw-Hill, New York, 1956, Table F, pp. 252–253. The tables have been adapted by Siegel from the original source: Frieda S. Swed and C. Eisenhart, "Tables for Testing Randomness of Grouping in a Sequence of Alternatives," *Annals of Mathematical Statistics,* vol. 14, 1943. Used by permission of McGraw-Hill Book Company and *Annals of Mathematical Statistics.*

TABLE E-6*b* CRITICAL VALUES OF RUNS IN THE RUNS TEST

	N_2																		
N_1	2	3	4	5	6	7	8	9	10	11	12	13	14	15	16	17	18	19	20
2																			
3																			
4				9	9														
5			9	10	10	11	11												
6			9	10	11	12	12	13	13	13	13								
7				11	12	13	13	14	14	14	14	15	15	15					
8				11	12	13	14	14	15	15	16	16	16	16	17	17	17	17	17
9					13	14	14	15	16	16	16	17	17	18	18	18	18	18	18
10					13	14	15	16	16	17	17	18	18	18	19	19	19	20	20
11					13	14	15	16	17	17	18	19	19	19	20	20	20	21	21
12					13	14	16	16	17	18	19	19	20	20	21	21	21	22	22
13						15	16	17	18	19	19	20	20	21	21	22	22	23	23
14						15	16	17	18	19	20	20	21	22	22	23	23	23	24
15						15	16	18	18	19	20	21	22	22	23	23	24	24	25
16							17	18	19	20	21	21	22	23	23	24	25	25	25
17							17	18	19	20	21	22	23	23	24	25	25	26	26
18							17	18	19	20	21	22	23	24	25	25	26	26	27
19							17	18	20	21	22	23	23	24	25	26	26	27	27
20							17	18	20	21	22	23	24	25	25	26	27	27	28

Example E.2.

In a sequence of 30 observations consisting of 20 + signs ($=N_1$) and 10 − signs ($=N_2$), the critical values of runs at the 0.05 level of significance are 9 and 20, as shown by Tables E-6*a* and E-6*b*, respectively. Therefore, if in an application it is found that the number of runs is equal to or less than 9 or equal to or greater than 20, we can reject (at the 0.05 level of significance) the hypothesis that the observed sequence is random.

APPENDIX F

COMPUTER OUTPUT OF EVIEWS, MINITAB, EXCEL, AND STATA

In this appendix we show the computer output of EViews, MINITAB, Excel, and STATA, which are some of the popularly used statistical packages for regression and related statistical routines. We use the data given in Table 1-1 to illustrate the output of these packages. Recall that Table 1-1 gives data on the civilian labor force participation rate (CLFPR), the civilian unemployment rate (CUNR), and real average hourly earnings in 1982 dollars (AHE82) for the U.S. economy for the period 1980 to 2007.

Although in many respects the basic regression output is similar in all these packages, there are differences in how they present their results. Some packages give results to several digits, whereas some others approximate them to four or five digits. Some packages give analysis of variance (ANOVA) tables directly, whereas for some other packages they need to be derived. There are also differences in some of the summary statistics presented by the various packages. It is beyond the scope of this appendix to enumerate all the differences in these statistical packages. You can consult the Web sites of these packages for further information.

EVIEWS

Using Version 6 of EViews, we regressed CLFPR on CUNR and AHE82 and obtained the results shown in Figure F-1.

This is the standard format in which EViews results are presented. The first part of this figure gives the regression coefficients, their estimated standard errors, the t values under the null hypothesis that the corresponding population values of these coefficients are zero, and the p values of these t values. This is followed by R^2 and adjusted R^2. The other summary output in the first part relates to the standard error of the regression, the residual sum of squares (RSS), and the F value to test the hypothesis that the (true) values of all the

Dependent Variable: CLFPR
Method: Least Squares
Date: 04/08/09   Time: 18:08
Sample: 1980–2007
Included observations: 28

Variable	Coefficient	Std. Error	t-Statistic	Prob.
C	81.22673	3.395574	23.92136	0.0000
CUNR	−0.638362	0.071509	−8.927018	0.0000
AHE82	−1.444883	0.413692	−3.492654	0.0018

R-squared	0.766322	Mean dependent var	65.92143
Adjusted R-squared	0.747628	S.D. dependent var	1.050699
S.E. of regression	0.527836	Akaike info criterion	1.660893
Sum squared resid	6.965260	Schwarz criterion	1.803629
Log likelihood	−20.25250	Hannan-Quinn criter.	1.704529
F-statistic	40.99252	Durbin-Watson stat	0.784562
Prob(F-statistic)	0.000000		

Obs	Actual	Fitted	Residual	Residual Plot
1980	63.8000	65.1353	−1.33530	
1981	63.9000	64.9799	−1.07987	
1982	64.0000	63.6646	0.33540	
1983	64.0000	63.5936	0.40642	
1984	64.4000	64.9341	−0.53414	
1985	64.8000	65.1883	−0.38826	
1986	65.3000	65.2425	0.05752	
1987	65.6000	65.8928	−0.29285	
1988	65.9000	66.4168	−0.51676	
1989	66.5000	66.6492	−0.14919	
1990	66.5000	66.5829	−0.08290	
1991	66.2000	65.9240	0.27597	
1992	66.4000	65.5302	0.86985	
1993	66.3000	65.9312	0.36877	
1994	66.6000	66.4347	0.16530	
1995	66.6000	66.7599	−0.15990	
1996	66.8000	66.8454	−0.04543	
1997	67.1000	66.9864	0.11359	
1998	67.1000	66.9540	0.14602	
1999	67.1000	66.9781	0.12188	
2000	67.1000	67.0576	0.04237	
2001	66.8000	66.4892	0.31083	
2002	66.6000	65.6040	0.99605	
2003	66.2000	65.4293	0.77068	
2004	66.0000	65.8063	0.19370	
2005	66.0000	66.1471	−0.14713	
2006	66.2000	66.3844	−0.18443	
2007	66.0000	66.2582	−0.25820	

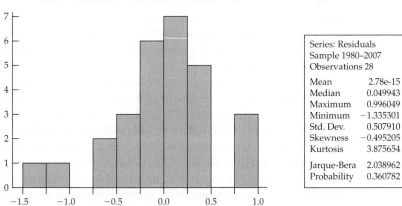

Series: Residuals
Sample 1980–2007
Observations 28

Mean	2.78e-15
Median	0.049943
Maximum	0.996049
Minimum	−1.335301
Std. Dev.	0.507910
Skewness	−0.495205
Kurtosis	3.875654
Jarque-Bera	2.038962
Probability	0.360782

FIGURE F-1   EViews output of civilian labor force participation regression

slope coefficients are simultaneously equal to zero. Akaike info(rmation) and Schwartz criteria are often used to choose between competing models. The lower the value of these criteria, the better the model is. The method of maximum likelihood (ML) is an alternative to the method of least squares. Just as in OLS we find those estimators that minimize the error sum of squares, in ML we try to find those estimators that maximize the possibility of observing the sample at hand. Under the normality assumption of the error term, OLS and ML give identical estimates of the regression coefficients. The Durbin-Watson stat(istic) is used to find out if there is first-order serial correlation in the error terms.

The second part of the EViews output gives the actual and fitted values of the dependent variable and the difference between the two, which represent the residuals. These residuals are plotted alongside this output with a vertical line denoting zero. Points to the right of the vertical line are positive residuals and those to the left represent negative residuals.

The third part of the output gives the histogram of the residuals along with their summary statistics. It gives the Jarque-Bera (JB) statistic to test for the normality of the error terms and also gives the probability of obtaining the stated statistics. The higher the probability of obtaining the observed JB statistic, the greater is the evidence in favor of the null hypothesis that the error terms are normally distributed.

Note that EViews does not give directly the analysis-of-variance (ANOVA) table, but it can be constructed easily from the data on the residual sum of squares, the total sum of squares (which will have to be derived from the standard deviation of the dependent variable), and their associated degrees of freedom. The F value given from this exercise should be equal to the F value reported in the first part of the table.

MINITAB

Using Version 14 of MINITAB, and using the same data, we obtained the regression results shown in Figure F-2.

MINITAB first reports the estimated multiple regression. This is followed by a list of predictor (i.e., explanatory) variables, the estimated regression coefficients, their standard errors, the T $(= t)$ values, and the p values. In this output S represents the standard error of the estimate, and R^2 and adjusted R^2 values are given in percent form.

This is followed by the usual ANOVA table. One characteristic feature of the ANOVA table is that it breaks down the regression, or explained, sum of squares among predictors. Thus of the total regression, sum of squares of 22.855, the share of CUNR is 19.446 and that of AHE82 is 3.408, suggesting that relatively, CUNR has more impact on CLFPR than AHE82.

A unique feature of the MINITAB regression output is that it reports "unusual" observations; that is, observations that are somehow different from the rest of the observations in the sample. We have a hint of this in the residual graph given in the EViews output, for it shows that the observations 1, 2, and 23

Regression Analysis: CLFPR versus CUNR, AHE82

The regression equation is
CLFPR = 81.3 − 0.639 CUNR − 1.45 AHE82

Predictor	Coef	SE Coef	T	P
Constant	81.286	3.404	23.88	0.000
CUNR	−0.63877	0.07146	−8.94	0.000
AHE82	−1.4521	0.4148	−3.50	0.002

S = 0.527351   R-Sq = 76.7%   R-Sq(adj) = 74.8%

Analysis of Variance

Source	DF	SS	MS	F	P
Regression	2	22.855	11.427	41.09	0.000
Residual Error	25	6.952	0.278		
Total	27	29.807			

Source	DF	Seq SS
CUNR	1	19.446
AHE82	1	3.408

Unusual Observations

Obs	CUNR	CLFPR	Fit	SE Fit	Residual	St Resid
1	7.10	63.8000	65.1342	0.1346	−1.3342	−2.62R
2	7.60	63.9000	64.9745	0.1461	−1.0745	−2.12R
23	5.80	66.6000	65.6016	0.1727	0.9984	2.00R

R denotes an observation with a large standardized residual.

Durbin-Watson statistic = 0.786311

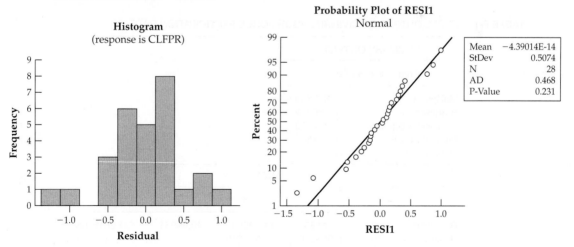

Mean	−4.39014E-14
StDev	0.5074
N	28
AD	0.468
P-Value	0.231

FIGURE F-2   MINITAB output of civilian labor force participation rate

are substantially away from the zero line shown there. MINITAB also produces a residual graph similar to the EViews residual graph. The St Resid in this output is the standardized residuals; that is, residuals divided by S, the standard error of the estimate.

Like EViews, MINITAB also reports the Durbin-Watson statistic and gives the histogram of residuals. The histogram is a visual picture. If its shape resembles the normal distribution, the residuals are perhaps normally distributed. The normal probability plot accomplishes the same purpose. If the estimated residuals lie approximately on a straight line, we can say that they are normally distributed. The Anderson-Darling (AD) statistic, an adjunct of the normal probability plot, tests the hypothesis that the variable under consideration (here residuals) is normally distributed. If the p value of the calculated AD statistic is reasonably high, say in excess of 0.10, we can conclude that the variable is normally distributed. In our example the AD statistic has a value of 0.468 with a p value of about 0.231 or 23 percent. So we can conclude that the residuals obtained from the regression model are normally distributed.

EXCEL

Using Microsoft Excel 2007 we obtained the regression output shown in Table F-1.

TABLE F-1 EXCEL OUTPUT OF CIVILIAN LABOR FORCE PARTICIPATION RATE

SUMMARY OUTPUT

Regression Statistics

Multiple R	0.875398
R Square	0.766322
Adjusted R Square	0.747628
Standard Error	0.527836
Observations	28

ANOVA

	df	SS	MS	F	Significance F
Regression	2	22.84188	11.42094	40.99251	1.281E-08
Residual	25	6.965270	0.278610		
Total	27	29.80714			

	Coefficients	Standard Err	t Stat	P-value	Lower 95%	Upper 95%
Intercept	81.22673	3.395574	23.92136	9.543E-19	74.23342	88.22005
CUNR	−0.638362	0.071509	−8.927018	3.008E-09	−0.785637	−0.49109
AHE82	−1.444883	0.413692	−3.492654	0.001798	−2.2969	−0.592868

Excel first presents summary statistics, such as R^2, multiple R, which is the (positive) square root of R, adjusted R^2, and the standard error of the estimate. Then it presents the ANOVA table. After that it presents the estimated coefficients, their standard errors, the t values of the estimated coefficients and their p values. It also gives the actual and estimated values of the dependent variable and the residual graph as well as the normal probability plot.

A unique feature of Excel is that it gives the 95% (or any specified percent) confidence interval for the true values of the estimated coefficients. Thus, the estimated value of the coefficient of CUNR is −0.638362 and the confidence interval for the true value of the CUNR coefficient is (−0.785637 to −0.49109). This information is very valuable for hypothesis testing.

STATA

Using STATA 8 version, we obtained the regression results shown in Table F-2. STATA first presents the analysis of variance table along with the summary statistics such as R^2, adjusted R^2, and the root mean-squared-error (MSE), which is just the standard error of the regression.

TABLE F-2   STATA OUTPUT OF CIVILIAN LABOR FORCE PARTICIPATION RATE

Statistics/Data Analysis
Project: Data of Table 1.1

regress CLFPR CUNR AHE82

Source	SS	df	MS		
Model	22.8546532	2	11.4273266	Number of obs =	28
Residual	6.95246119	25	.278098448	F(2, 25) = 41.09	
				Prob > F = 0.0000	
Total	29.8071144	27	1.1039672	R-squared = 0.7668	
				Adj R-squared = 0.7481	
				Root MSE = .52735	

CLFPR	Coef.	Std. Err.	t	P > |t|	[95% Conf. Interval]	
CUNR	−.6387723	.0714642	−8.94	0.000	−.7859556	−.491589
AHE82	−1.452054	.4147668	−3.50	0.002	−2.306282	−.5978256
_cons	81.28589	3.404245	23.88	0.000	74.27472	88.29706

STATA then gives the values of the estimated coefficients, their standard errors, their t values, the p values of the t statistics, and the 95% confidence interval for each of the regression coefficients, which is similar to the Excel output.

CONCLUDING COMMENTS

We have given just the basic output of these packages for our example. But it may be noted that packages such as EViews and STATA are very comprehensive and contain many of the econometric techniques discussed in this text. Once you know how to access these packages, running various subroutines is a matter of practice. If you wish to pursue econometrics further, you may want to buy one or more of these packages.

REFERENCES

www.eviews.com
www.stata.com
www.minitab.com
www.microsoft.com/excel

R. Carter Hill, William E. Griffiths, George G. Judge, *Using Excel for Undergraduate Econometrics*, John Wiley, New York, 2001.

SELECTED BIBLIOGRAPHY

INTRODUCTORY

Frank, C. R., Jr.: *Statistics and Econometrics,* Holt, Rinehart and Winston, New York, 1971.

Hu, Teh-Wei: *Econometrics: An Introductory Analysis,* University Park Press, Baltimore, 1973.

Katz, David A.: *Econometric Theory and Applications,* Prentice-Hall, Englewood Cliffs, NJ, 1982.

Klein, Lawrence R.: *An Introduction to Econometrics,* Prentice-Hall, Englewood Cliffs, NJ, 1962.

Koop, Gary: *Analysis of Economic Data*, Wiley, U.K., 2000.

Walters, A. A.: *An Introduction to Econometrics,* Macmillan, London, 1968.

INTERMEDIATE

Aigner, D. J.: *Basic Econometrics,* Prentice-Hall, Englewood Cliffs, NJ, 1971.

Dhrymes, Phoebus J.: *Introductory Econometrics,* Springer-Verlag, New York, 1978.

Dielman, Terry E.: *Applied Regression Analysis for Business and Economics,* PWS-Kent Publishing Company, Boston, 1991.

Draper, N. R. and H. Smith: *Applied Regression Analysis,* 2nd ed., John Wiley, New York, 1981.

Dutta, M.: *Econometric Methods,* South-Western, Cincinnati, 1975.

Goldberger, A. S.: *Topics in Regression Analysis,* Macmillan, New York, 1968.

Gujarati, Damodar N. and Dawn C. Porter: *Basic Econometrics,* 5th ed., McGraw-Hill, New York, 2009.

Huang, D. S.: *Regression and Econometric Methods,* John Wiley, New York, 1970.

Judge, George G., Carter R. Hill, William E. Griffiths, Helmut Lütkepohl, and Tsoung-Chao Lee: *Introduction to the Theory and Practice of Econometrics,* John Wiley, 1982.

Kelejian, H. A. and W. E. Oates: *Introduction to Econometrics: Principles and Applications,* 2nd ed., Harper & Row, New York, 1981.

Koutsoyiannis, A.: *Theory of Econometrics,* Harper & Row, New York, 1973.

Mark, Stewart B. and Kenneth F. Wallis: *Introductory Econometrics,* 2nd ed., John Wiley, New York, 1981. A Halsted Press Book.

Murphy, James L.: *Introductory Econometrics,* Richard D. Irwin, Homewood, IL, 1973.

Netter, J. and W. Wasserman: *Applied Linear Statistical Models,* Richard D. Irwin, Homewood, IL, 1974.

Pindyck, R. S. and D. L. Rubinfeld: *Econometric Models and Econometric Forecasts,* 4th ed., McGraw-Hill, New York, 1998.

Sprent, Peter: *Models in Regression and Related Topics,* Methuen, London, 1969.

Stock, James H. and Mark W. Watson: *Introduction to Econometrics*, Addison-Wesley, Boston, 2003.

Tintner, Gerhard: *Econometrics,* John Wiley (science ed.), New York, 1965.

Valavanis, Stefan: *Econometrics: An Introduction to Maximum-Likelihood Methods,* McGraw-Hill, New York, 1959.

Wonnacott, R. J. and T. H. Wonnacott: *Econometrics,* 2nd ed., John Wiley, New York, 1979.

Wooldridge, Jeffrey M.: *Introductory Econometrics*, 2nd ed., Thomson Learning, 2003.

ADVANCED

Chow, Gregory C.: *Econometric Methods,* McGraw-Hill, New York, 1983.

Christ, C. F.: *Econometric Models and Methods,* John Wiley, New York, 1966.

Davidson, Russell and James G. MacKinnon: *Econometric Theory and Methods*, Oxford University Press, New York, 2004.

Dhrymes, P. J.: *Econometrics: Statistical Foundations and Applications,* Harper & Row, New York, 1970.

Fomby, Thomas B., Carter R. Hill, and Stanley R. Johnson: *Advanced Econometric Methods,* Springer-Verlag, New York, 1984.

Gallant, Ronald A.: *An Introduction to Econometric Theory,* Princeton University Press, Princeton, NJ, 1997.

Goldberger, A. S.: *Econometric Theory,* John Wiley, New York, 1964.

Goldberger, A. S.: *A Course in Econometrics,* Harvard University Press, Cambridge, MA, 1991.

Greene, William H.: *Econometric Analysis,* Macmillan, New York, 1990.

Harvey, A. C.: *The Econometric Analysis of Time Series,* 2nd ed., MIT, Cambridge, MA, 1990.

Johnston, J.: *Econometric Methods,* 3rd ed., McGraw-Hill, New York, 1984.

Judge, George G., Carter R. Hill, William E. Griffiths, Helmut Lütkepohl, and Tsoung-Chao Lee: *Theory and Practice of Econometrics,* John Wiley, New York, 1980.

Klein, Lawrence R.: *A Textbook of Econometrics,* 2nd ed., Prentice-Hall, Englewood Cliffs, NJ, 1974.

Kmenta, Jan: *Elements of Econometrics,* 2nd ed., Macmillan, New York, 1986.

Madansky, A.: *Foundations of Econometrics,* North-Holland Publishing Company, Amsterdam, 1976.

Maddala, G. S.: *Econometrics,* McGraw-Hill, New York, 1977.

Malinvaud, E.: *Statistical Methods of Econometrics,* 2nd ed., North-Holland Publishing Company, Amsterdam, 1976.

Peracchi, Franco: *Econometrics,* John Wiley, New York, 2001.

Theil, Henry: *Principles of Econometrics,* John Wiley, New York, 1971.

SPECIALIZED

Belsley, David A., Edwin Kuh, and Roy E. Welsh: *Regression Diagnostics: Identifying Influential Data and Sources of Collinearity,* John Wiley, New York, 1980.

Dhrymes, P. J.: *Distributed Lags: Problems of Estimation and Formulation,* Holden-Day, San Francisco, 1971.

Goldfeld, S. M. and R. E. Quandt: *Nonlinear Methods of Econometrics,* North-Holland Publishing Company, Amsterdam, 1972.

Graybill, F. A.: *An Introduction to Linear Statistical Models,* vol. 1, McGraw-Hill, New York, 1961.

Rao, C. R.: *Linear Statistical Inference and Its Applications,* 2nd ed., John Wiley, New York, 1975.

Zellner, A.: *An Introduction to Bayesian Inference in Econometrics,* John Wiley, New York, 1971.

APPLIED

Berndt, Ernst R.: *The Practice of Econometrics: Classic and Contemporary,* Addison-Wesley, 1991.

Bridge, J. I.: *Applied Econometrics,* North-Holland Publishing Company, Amsterdam, 1971.

Brooks, Chris: *Introductory Econometrics for Finance,* Cambridge University Press, New York, 2002.

Cramer, J. S.: *Empirical Econometrics,* North-Holland Publishing Company, Amsterdam, 1969.

Desai, Meghnad: *Applied Econometrics,* McGraw-Hill, New York, 1976.

Kennedy, Peter: *A Guide to Econometrics,* 3rd ed., MIT Press, Cambridge, MA, 1992.

Leser, C. E. V.: *Econometric Techniques and Problems,* 2nd ed., Hafner Publishing Company, 1974.

Rao, Potluri and Roger LeRoy Miller: *Applied Econometrics,* Wadsworth, Belmont, CA, 1971.

Note: For a list of the seminal articles on the various topics discussed in this book, please refer to the extensive bibliography given at the end of the chapters in Fomby et al., cited previously.

NAME INDEX

SUBJECT INDEX

Page numbers followed by n refer to notes.